Bệ T

Essays and Data on
American
Ethnic Groups

Edited by
Thomas Sowell

with the assistance
of Lynn D. Collins

075411

CONTENTS

Tables and Figures, Part I

vii

PART II. STATISTICS

xi

WEST INDIANS

PREFACE

This volume is one of the products of a study of American ethnic groups that was conducted at The Urban Institute from 1972 to 1975 under the direction of Thomas Sowell. Of the dozen or so groups that were examined, six were selected for special emphasis here: those with black, Chinese, Japanese, Irish, Italian, or Jewish background. While the social and economic evolution of each of these groups is unique, they also hold some characteristics in common: they are all minorities, they share many aspects of the immigrant experience, although only blacks suffered the burden of slavery; and all have faced exceptional barriers and experienced frustration in achieving economic and social mobility.

One of the chief structural concepts implicit in this study is that the evolution of minority immigrant groups proceeds in parallel continua, in the course of which each group experiences similar developments, although not necessarily at the same time, with the same intensity, or in exactly the same way. For immigrant groups that have not been exposed to such a severe disability as slavery, data assembled over the decades fairly readily reveal the echoing of certain developments (especially higher levels of achievement) from one group to another, including West Indian blacks and the sizable number of American blacks who held the status of "free persons of color" long before the Civil War.

After reviewing carefully the powerful evidence presented by the authors on the course of economic progress made by each ethnic group, a thoughtful reader might reflect on several implications of the technical analysis. First, one might feel dismay at the tragic heritage of slavery, at the depth of deprivation imposed upon millions of black persons over several generations, a deprivation unique to this minority group. Second, one might feel satisfaction with a social and economic system in which castes do not prevail, in which each minority group can overcome severe initial conditions of deprivation, and, over time, shed the handicaps of minority status. Third, one might feel both impatience and optimism. One might wish that substantial progress could be measured in years rather than generations; the rate of progress for American blacks seems painfully slow compared to other minority groups. The "regimented dependence" of slavery was maintained too long by denial of equal opportunity to vote, to be educated, to demonstrate ability. In the last 15 years, however, the federal government has become a strong advocate of equal opportunity for all, and has put in place strictures which would promote that objective. We can be optimistic about rapid progress when equality has been fully realized.

William Gorham
President
The Urban Institute

June 1978

Introduction

This compendium of analysis and statistics on American ethnic groups is both an introduction to the subject and an exploration of the frontiers of knowledge in this field. Much of what appears in these pages is new information, new analysis, and new concepts. Students and scholars may learn from it, even though it is intended for the general public. The concept behind this book is that of an almanac or a one-volume encyclopedia on American ethnic groups — a work for either general reading or for looking up specific facts. Part One presents historical, economic, sociological, and psychological analyses of various aspects of ethnic life in the United States. Part Two presents statistical data on various ethnic groups. The purpose of this book is to make existing knowledge more accessible as well as to disseminate new knowledge growing out of its own research.

The essays in the first Part analyze the historical development of various American ethnic groups — European immigrants, Oriental immigrants, and black Americans — and consider some special topics such as I.Q., discrimination, and various factors accounting for intergroup differences in socioeconomic status. Most of these essays are written for a broad, general audience, but two are technical papers primarily for specialists. The choice of which groups to cover has been dictated largely by the available literature and by the available scholars, both of which reflect to some extent the demographic or historic prominence of the respective groups. However, there are groups of substantial importance from either or both of these points of view who are *not* covered simply because it proved impossible to identify sufficient factual material or to enlist the scholarly resources necessary to produce the kind and quality of material we could be proud to present.[1]

Part Two presents detailed statistical tables on the incomes, occupations, education, and fertility rates of American ethnic groups—arranged in such a way as to facilitate the search for causation. For example, if one thinks one ethnic group has higher income than another because of more education, these tables show at a glance how much income is earned by individuals in various ethnic groups with the *same* education, age, sex, or occupation. For some ethnic groups, most of the income differences are associated with differences in the average ages of the particular ethnic groups—some of whom differ by a decade or even *two* decades in median age. For other ethnic groups, the income differences may be associated with educational differences. For still others, even individuals in the same age brackets with the same number of years of schooling differ significantly in their incomes, suggesting deeper forces at work. Much of the statistical data is our own compilation from the Public Use Sample of the 1970 census, supplemented by data from other government or private sources.

The output of this project also includes a Bibliographic Index of American ethnic groups. It is available from ERIC Processing and Reference Facility, 4833 Rugby Avenue, Suite 303, Bethesda, Maryland 20014 (Document No. ED 129708).

Although the conception of this project was the work of one man, its execution depended crucially on the dedication, insights, and initiative of numerous men and women, including outside scholars, administrators, and technicians, as well as members of the project staff immediately responsible for its production. A deep debt of gratitude is owed to many individuals, too numerous to name, who poured their time, their intelligence, and sometimes their courage, into an effort whose outcome could not have been what it is without them. Foremost among these is Dr. Lynn D. Collins who, as coordinator of the project, assumed many of the burdens of day-to-day management, as well as being responsible for the intellectual task of turning general concepts into technical specifications for our statistical work, and sometimes recasting the concepts themselves to better get at the intellectual and social issues we were trying to analyze. Miss Janella Moore also deserves not only my gratitude but the gratitude of all who benefit from the I.Q. data we collected, for she spent many lonely months in faraway places exploring school records, as well as taking on the maddening task of coordinating the field work in many cities at one time while coping with a variety of regulations, records systems, and egos, not to mention a project director who was too harried to always understand her problems. Finally, none of this would have been possible without the generous financial support of the U.S. Office of Economic Opportunity, the Rockefeller Foundation, and the Ford Foundation. In short, *American Ethnic Groups* is the product of far more people than are listed in the table of contents, and they are due far more gratitude than I can adequately express.

THOMAS SOWELL

NOTE

1. The omission of a history of native American Indians is perhaps the most obvious example, and is due entirely to resource limitations. To present the complex mosaic of this unique group would require a study of many different tribes, with different languages, customs, religions, and with widely varying geographic distributions and sharp contrasts in their respective degrees of urbanization. Native American Indians were not covered in the historical section — though their socioeconomic statistics are presented in Part II — because we could not do so adequately within our own constraints, and to do so inadequately would be to add to misconcep tions which it is the purpose of this work to dispel.

Part One
Essays
On American
Ethnic Groups

Three
Black
Histories

THOMAS SOWELL

The history of black people in the United States is really the history of three distinct groups, with contrasting patterns of social evolution, urbanization, occupational distribution, dependency, crime rates, and even different fertility rates. The first of these groups to have an independent history in the American economy and society was the antebellum "free persons of color," who in the 1830s constituted 14 percent of the American Negro population.[1] They are more than an historical curiosity, for they and their descendants played a major role in the later history of black Americans, as well as providing some revealing contrasts in social patterns. The largest component of the American Negro population, of course, has consisted of those blacks emancipated by the Civil War and their descendants. Their pattern has been the dominant pattern of black life in the United States, but it has not been the exclusive pattern. The third group of Negroes in America consists of black immigrants, principally from other parts of the Western Hemisphere, and especially from the British West Indies. Here again there are contrasting lifestyles and contrasting economic and social positions.

The purpose of studying the black population of the United States as three separate groups is not merely historical clarification. Basic beliefs about the causes of various social phenomena involving Negroes may be tested by seeing whether similar social phenomena accompanied other black people from different cultures and at different periods of history. In short, an examination of the three black histories provides one way of separating the effect of being black in America from the effect of coming from a particular cultural background and confronting a particular set of historical factors in the United States.

I. "FREE PERSONS OF COLOR"

Slavery and freedom are among the sharpest contrasts in human existence, and yet even this dichotomy in concept was a continuum in practice. Between the legally free, socially developed, and economically self-sufficient Negro—who appeared as early as the seventeenth century—and the chattel slave who worked in the field under guard and driven by overseers with whips, there stretched a significant intermediate group of quasi-free Negroes. Some lacked only the legal technicality of freedom, being owned by relatives (black or white) who allowed them to live as they pleased, but who had not gone through the increasingly difficult and uncertain process of achieving legally recognized manumission. Most of the slaves owned by other Negroes were in this category.[2] Some slaves owned by whites were also free in all but name.[3] Other quasi-free Negroes in antebellum America were slaves who "hired their own time" to various employers, lived away from the slave owners, and simply paid those owners a share of their earnings, without being in direct contact with them or their agents for weeks or even months at a time.[4] These slaves, many of whose day-to-day lives were virtually those of ordinary employees, were concentrated in urban areas[5] and included a disproportionate representation of skilled workers.[6] Even on the classic plantation, however, there were a few quasi-free slaves, sometimes in charge of other slaves.[7] Between this class of quasi-free Negroes and the wholly abject field hand, there was still another intermediate group, the house servants, who had varying degrees of exemption from the most oppressive features of slavery, largely as a result of their personal relationships with various members of the slave owning household.[8]

Although the free and the quasi-free were a distinct minority among American Negroes throughout the antebellum period, they were not a negligible minority. The legally free Negroes averaged between 10 and 14 percent of the black population from 1800 to 1860,[9] and they appeared almost as far back as slavery itself. Surrounding this core of free blacks was a penumbra of quasi-free blacks whose numbers are as difficult to estimate as their boundaries are to define. They are important as a supplementary source of the more acculturated, educated (or education-minded) Negro middle class or leadership group in the later post-Civil War period. Like the "free persons of color," they included a disproportionate number of mulattoes,[10] sometimes because the source of their privileges was their biological descent from the slave owning family,[11] and sometimes simply because whites found mulattoes more acceptable in the better jobs.[12]

The origins of the "free persons of color" were varied. In the earliest days of African bondage in colonial America—in the first half of the seventeenth century—black bondsmen progressed through the same stages as white indentured servants, emerging as free men after a fixed number of years.[13] The status of chattel slave for life, with perpetual slavery for all descendants, was one which developed in the latter half of the seventeenth century.[14] In short, freedom was achieved automatically for the earliest Africans brought to the United States, and their offspring were free from birth. For later generations of slaves, freedom was achieved only through deliberate and special acts, such as (1) the voluntary manumission of slaves by slave owners, (2) self-purchase by slaves in a position to accumulate money, (3) the purchase of slaves by already free relatives or by philanthropic whites, (4) escapes, (5) freedom conferred by special legislative act as a reward for unusual service to the community, usually in time of danger, and finally (6) by general emancipation, first in the northern states in the late eighteenth and early nineteenth centuries, and then from Lincoln's Emancipation Proclamation in 1863. The immigration of foreign Negroes to the United States was negligible.[15] Mulattoes born to white women were free from birth, since the condition of the mother determined whether a child was slave or free, in the United States[16] as in ancient Rome.[17]

1. POPULATION GROWTH AND DISTRIBUTION

The population of "free persons of color" grew both from natural increase and from the addition of freedmen. Twenty black indentured servants were landed at Jamestown in 1619, providing the basis for the first "free persons of color." By 1790, there were about 60,000 such persons. By 1830 their numbers had grown to about 320,000 and in 1860 there were approximately 488,000 "free persons of color."[18] The free Negro population grew at a much more rapid rate than the slave population through about 1810, but after about 1840 the growth of the free Negro population fell to a slower rate than the growth of the slave population.[19] There were increasing legal obstacles to achieving manumission throughout the South after about 1830,[20] and the supply of freedmen fell sharply as a result,[21] reducing the growth of the free Negro population to that due largely to natural increase. In the earlier period, prior to the ending of the international slave trade in 1808, both the slave and the free Negro populations grew through additions from outside as well as through natural increase, while toward the end of the antebellum period, both groups grew at rates representing essentially their increase through the difference between births and deaths.

One reason for the greater fertility of the slave population may have been the unbalanced sex ratios among free Negroes. There were more females than males[22]—a condition common among "free colored" populations throughout the Western Hemisphere.[23] A major reason for manumission was that the slave owner had fathered a child by a slave woman and then freed the mother and her offspring. This was common in slaveholding societies of the Western Hemisphere,[24] though there were wide differences in the openness with which this was acknowledged.[25] Sometimes sexual relations without children also led to the same result. It is by no means apparent that most slave women who bore slaveowners' children were freed, but of those Negroes freed, a substantial proportion were freed for this reason. Therefore a chronic surplus of women existed among the "free persons of color," and this sex imbalance contributed to a lower rate of fertility thereafter.

Among the American Negro population in the pre-Civil War period, the free differed from the slave not only in fertility rate and in racial mixture—37 percent of the free were mulattoes, compared to only 8 percent of the slaves[26]— but also in their geographic distribution. Slaves were always concentrated in the South, and with the spread of emancipation in the northern states after the American revolution, all slaves were in the southern and border states. Within the South, the development of a cotton economy in the wake of the invention of the cotton gin in 1792 moved the slave population increasingly toward the Deep South, particularly into the so-called "black belt" stretching across Georgia, Alabama, Mississippi, Louisiana, and Arkansas. In the decades following the first census of 1790, the geographic center of the black population of the United States moved southwestward at an average rate of 49 miles per decade for a period of 90 years.[27] By contrast, the *free* Negro population was relatively evenly split between North and South;[28] within the South less than 10 percent of them were in the census divisions incorporating the "black belt"—and the proportions in these divisions were *declining.*[29]

The slave population was overwhelmingly rural, while among the "free persons of color" a much higher percentage (but still not quite a majority) were urbanized—indeed, more urbanized than the white population.[30] As the slave population moved increasingly to the rural areas of the Deep South, the free Negro population moved increasingly toward the urban, northern, and border states. Within the South, the "free persons of color" gravitated toward the more liberal regions, which were largely the regions where slavery—and particularly plantation slavery—was less prevalent,[31] usually due to economic conditions unsuitable to "the peculiar institution."[32] One consequence of this was that families descended from the "free persons of color" were urbanized generations before families descended from other Negroes.

Much of the later cultural contrast between the established Negro elite and underprepared black migrants to the cities had its origin in this difference between their respective ancestors. Many of the outstanding Negroes of the post-Civil War period and early twentieth century were descendants of the "free persons of color." Whites who pointed to those individual successes and asked, "Why can't the *others* do it?" were usually unaware that the other blacks were at an entirely different point in their social evolution. Looked at another way, the urban Negro population contained a much higher percentage of "free persons of color" than did the black population at large. Even though Negroes as a group were overwhelmingly rural, "there were 79% more free Negroes in the cities of America in 1860 than would be expected" from a random distribution of "free persons of color."[33]

The importance of this urban vanguard is demonstrated by their development in Washington, D.C. By 1830, half the Negroes in the District of Columbia were free, and by 1860, 78 percent of them were free.[34] As far back as 1800, there was a free black community of 500 persons in Washington.[35] In 1807, they built the city's first school for black children, and for decades their children went to a variety of private schools before being admitted to the public schools in 1862.[36] In 1870, the first public high school for Negroes in the United States was established in Washington as a result of the efforts of leading figures who came from a background as antebellum "free persons of color."[37] A small group of families from this background shaped the school in its formative years and continued to play a prominent, if not predominant, role in its development *on into the middle of the twentieth century.* By all indices this was a high-performance school: (1) over an 85 year period (1870-1955), more than three-quarters of its students went on to college,[38] (2) the average I.Q. of its students was above the national average,[39] (3) its alumni included the first black general, the first black cabinet member, the first black federal judge, the discoverer of blood plasma, and the first black Senator since Reconstruction,[40] as well as more holders of doctoral degrees than the alumni of any other black high school.[41] As far back as 1899, this school scored higher than any white high schools in Washington in city-wide tests.[42] Clearly the cultural head start of the "free persons of color" in Washington had a lasting impact on this school, and on successive generations of students, most of whom were descended from the general run of the black population, and simply benefited from what had been set up long before.

For a particular institution, it is possible to trace the continuing influence of specific families who go back to the antebellum "free persons of color." For larger social units, more indirect estimates are necessary. For example, a study of Negro professionals conducted in Washington, D.C., in 1950 showed that in 59.2 percent of the cases their paternal grandfathers were either professionals or owners of businesses or farms.[43] The Negro professionals of 1950, whose median age was about forty,[44] would have been born around 1910. Allowing the usual 30 years between generations, their grandfathers would have been born before the Civil War—and the statistical probability of a slave's becoming a professional, businessman, or farm owner was virtually nil. It therefore seems a reasonable estimate that over half of the black professionals in Washington in 1950 were descended from the antebellum "free persons of color," who constituted only about one-seventh of the black population of the United States. Another study, of 507 black holders of doctoral degrees, found their family backgrounds to include from three to eight literate generations, in all but two cases.[45] Again, this reaches back before the Civil War—and virtually no slaves were literate. Other scattered studies have turned up similar patterns.[46] The latter-day academic and career successes include not only descendants of the free Negro population but also others who later became part of their institutional or cultural orbit via the schools, churches, or other social processes.

The Negroes involved in the founding of the NAACP were descendants of the "free persons of color."[47] E. Franklin Frazier estimated that the descendants of free Negroes retained their leadership of blacks until World War I.[48] Moreover, the dissolution of the "free persons of color" and their descendants as a self-conscious class within the black community[49] did not extinguish the advantages which their family background gave them, as indicated by their continued overrepresentation among black scholars and professionals in the middle of the twentieth century.

There have been some efforts to represent the continuing prominence of free Negroes and their descendants among the black population as a predominance of mulattoes, as such.[50] However, the classic study of mulattoes employs such an elastic definition of "mulatto"[51] as to include Mary McLeod Bethune, Carter G. Woodson, and Kelly Miller[52]—all as dark as (or darker than) the general run of the American Negro population,[53] only about 22 percent of whom are of unmixed African ancestry.[54] The predominance of mulattoes, loosely defined, among Negro leaders parallels their predominance, similarly defined, in the general American Negro population. More strictly defined, mulattoes have still been overrepresented to some extent among the Negro middle class, as they were among the "free persons of color," but in nothing like the proportions[55] derived from the more elastic definition of the term.

2. *ECONOMIC AND SOCIAL EVOLUTION*

The "free persons of color" were not always an elite, except by comparison with slaves, and even here questions have been raised as to whether their purely economic condition was always better than that of their fellow blacks in bondage.[56] Most freed Negroes in the antebellum South were voluntarily freed by slave owners,[57] and in many cases this act of benevolence or conscience was accompanied by some financial provision for the individual to get a start in life.[58] A small minority of the free black families began their independent lives with a certain prosperity. Most, however, were the poorest of the working class. Slowly, over the decades, there was an increase in their occupational status, education, property ownership, and other indices of social advancement. Even so, on the eve of the Civil War, most were still working-class people,[59] though prosperous and even wealthy Negroes now existed in large absolute numbers.[60]

The wealthiest and most socially exclusive elite among the "free persons of color" existed in New Orleans[61] and in Charleston, South Carolina[62]—both urban centers in areas acquired by the United States from Latin countries.[63] In the Latin countries of the Western Hemisphere, the "free colored" population had far wider social and economic scope than in the United States,[64] and in several countries they dominated skilled occupations.[65] The rights of "free persons of color" were guaranteed in the treaties transferring the territories to the United States,[66] so Negroes in these states—and particularly in the urban centers of these states—had rights and status denied to similar individuals throughout most of the United States.[67]

In many ways, the development of the "free persons of color" in New Orleans and Charleston followed the pattern of Latin countries, more so than that of the rest of the United States.[68] In 1860, only one-tenth of the "free colored" population of New Orleans were common laborers, and there were a number of crafts in which they had a near monopoly,[69] as well as numerous small businesses that they ran.[70] The *gens de couleur* in Louisiana were armed and fought to defend New Orleans against the British in 1814,[71] carrying on a tradition of Negro military activity going back to the days of French rule.[72] This was in keeping with the military tradition of "free persons of color" in Latin America,[73] but not in the United States.[74] One of the reasons why the "free colored" populations in various Latin countries could be armed by the white rulers was that an elaborate multicolored caste system existed in such countries, in which the free mulattoes occupied a recognized position distinctly superior to the black masses,[75] though subordinate to whites, as part of a divide-and-rule strategy. The carry-over of this tradition was very strong in New Orleans and Charleston, where explicit color barriers were created by the "free persons of color" themselves against darker Negroes,[76] and where *commercial* slave owning by free Negroes was more prevalent than in other parts of the United States.[77]

In the United States as a whole, the stark dichotomy between black and white—with mulattoes being black for all legal and social purposes—precluded intermediate castes, and such color distinctions and barriers as formed among Negroes were only informal, implicit, and relatively weak compared to the intraracial divisions elsewhere in the Western Hemisphere.[78]

The legal and social fortunes of the "free persons of color" in the United States waxed and waned largely according to circumstances beyond their control. The special legal and traditional position of "free persons of color" in territories acquired from France and Spain afforded some protection from the full severity of southern "black codes" governing free Negroes as well as slaves. In the North, racial discrimination and segregation were in general directly proportional to the concentration of the black population.[79] In most northern cities, however, the antebellum free Negroes encountered the full range of racial segregation and discrimination in housing, employment, and public facilities.[80] In both North and South the severity of the laws and the extent to which they were enforced varied substantially over time, as well as from place to place.

The freest time period for the "free persons of color" was the early seventeenth century, before the limited bondage of Africans as indentured servants evolved into chattel slavery in perpetuity. In this era the black population was very thinly scattered among the white,[81] and became rapidly acculturated,[82] as well as racially mixed in many cases. Ever growing importations of Africans in bondage,[83] and their concentration on plantations,[84] produced a much less assimilated Negro population, and one which grew to be one-fourth of the total American population by 1800.[85] Parallel with these developments came the development of "black codes" designed to control the Negro population, both slave and free. Rights formerly enjoyed by "free persons of color" were taken away one by one, and increasingly restrictive legislation governed where they could live, work, or use public facilities,[86] progressively narrowed their access to normal political or legal processes,[87] and even restricted what goods they could buy.[88] These developments proceeded unevenly across the country and at different periods, but the general direction was clear, despite some reversals. The most severely restrictive period in the South was from about 1830 to 1860, the tension-filled decades preceding the outbreak of the Civil War.

"Free persons of color" were an incidental by-product of slavery, and their legal and social conditions were dominated by the changing requirements of slavery as a system. Once slavery became a massive commercial system, security and subordination became major problems. Slave rebellions, such as the bloody and successful uprising in Santo Domingo in 1793, spread panic and repression through the slave states of the United States.[89] The "free persons of color" were a constant menace to slavery *by their very existence*, independent of their words or deeds.[90] The mind conditioning of slaves was an indispensable supplement to brute force. The slaves' acceptance of slavery as inevitable for black people was undermined by the existence of free Negroes, and their awe of whites was undermined by any signs of independence, achievement, or pride by free Negroes. In economic terms, the "free persons of color" raised the cost of maintaining slavery as a system. Accordingly, the repression of the "free persons of color" was most severe in those parts of the South with the greatest concentration of slaves under the most severe day-to-day conditions—i.e., where there existed the strongest reasons for resistance, rebellion, or escape.

In the Deep South, all freed Negroes were legally required to leave the state,[91] under pain of reenslavement; other freed Negroes were forbidden to enter[92] (including black sailors on ships in port);[93] and intolerable conditions were created for those Negroes already free when these laws were passed. The most severe laws were passed in states with the largest plantation slave populations,[94] and the period of greatest severity of such laws throughout the South was the period following the Nat Turner rebellion[95] and the rise of militant abolitionist activity[96]—that is, the period between 1830 and the outbreak of the Civil War in 1861. During that same period there was an increasing migration of "free persons of color" away from the centers of slaveholding, toward urban communities,[97] toward the less repressive Piedmont and tidewater regions,[98] toward the seat of the national government in Washington,[99] and toward the North.[100]

Education was a particularly sensitive issue from the point of view of whites who were trying to maintain slavery with the least costs and dangers to themselves. After the Gabriel plot of 1800, a southern judge said, "The increase in knowledge is the principal agent in evolving the spirit we have to fear."[101] Later and larger insurrections were led by Denmark Vesey and by Nat Turner—both educated Negroes[102]—and the reaction to these rebellions included laws forbidding the education of slaves[103] and some-times free Negroes as well.[104] The urban centers enforced the laws less stringently[105]—in New Orleans and Charleston they were scarcely enforced at all[106]—as was the case also in the largely plantation-free regions of the Piedmont and tidewater. Among the southern states, North Carolina, Tennessee, and Kentucky (all states with few plantation slaves) never completely outlawed the education of Negroes,[107] nor did Maryland or Washington, D.C.,[108] among the border states (also areas where slave plantations were a minor or negligible factor). As with other repressive laws and practices applied to the "free persons of color," enforcement varied enormously,[109] and usually in a pattern related to the proximity of plantation slavery and the recency of insurrectionary panics. As the free Negro population began migrating into northern urban centers, the growth of the black population in their midst created adverse public opinion in the North as well, which was reflected in discriminatory laws and practices, and even in mob violence against black schools.[110]

The restrictions or outright prohibitions on educating Negroes make it difficult to tell how many children of free Negroes were attending schools, many of which were clandestine.[111] It is significant that in some areas where very few Negroes were officially reported as attending school, the illiteracy rate among "free persons of color" was virtually nil.[112] In 15 out of 16 cities with large free Negro populations in 1850, all but one had more literate than illiterate "free persons of color."[113] These included Deep South cities like Mobile, Savannah, and New Orleans. In Savannah, *no* Negroes were reported as attending school anywhere in the county, and yet the number of illiterate free Negroes in the county was less than one-third the free Negro population of Savannah alone.[114] Similar statistical anomalies appear in the data for other southern cities where the education of free Negroes was under legal restriction or prohibition. For example, in Charleston, where the illiteracy rate among free Negro adults was less than 2 percent, only 68 free Negro children were officially reported as attending school, in a community of 3,441 "free persons of color."[115] In a similar sized northern community —Cincinnati—there were several times more Negro children reported as attending school, even though the illiteracy rate among Cincinnati Negroes was several times higher than among those in Savannah.[116] A contemporary observer in Savannah noted that even slaves there were learning to read,[117] and it is known that there were schools for black children there,[118] just as in other parts of the South where such schools existed "in defiance of public opinion or in violation of the law." [119]

While it is clear that most "free persons of color" in the major urban centers (North and South) were literate by 1850,[120] there are no comparable national figures for rural Negroes or for the much larger enslaved black population. In largely rural North Carolina, 43 percent of adult "free persons of color" were literate in 1850,[121] but North Carolina was in many ways among the most liberal of the southern states; [122] and in neighboring Virginia—with tougher laws—the literacy rate was estimated at only about 17 percent.[123] However, other data from 1860 indicate that the range of literacy among the "free colored" in the 15 slave states was from 26.4 percent in Delaware to 71.9 percent in Louisiana, with the median being 59 percent in Missouri.[124] For the country as a whole, approximately 59 percent of the total free Negro population was literate in 1850.[125] By contrast, the much larger enslaved black population of four million was overwhelmingly illiterate.[126] Carter G. Woodson estimated that in 1860 only about 10 percent of the total Negro population—slave and free together—had "the rudiments of education." [127] This estimate accords with data on the post-emancipation literacy rate among Negroes. In the 15 former slave states where the bulk of the total Negro population lived as of 1870, the median state literacy rate among Negroes was 11.2 percent (Arkansas and Tennessee).[128] The stark contrast in literacy between the "free persons of color" and the bulk of the black population was only one index of the wide difference in acculturation between them at the time of the Emancipation Proclamation. Even the difference in the number of generations since freedom does not fully measure the cultural differences between families in these two streams of black history, for only those already in relatively privileged positions under slavery had a substantial possibility of achieving individual freedom, whether by self-purchase, escape, or gaining the slave owner's favor. In short, the head start of the "free persons of color" began even before they became free.[129]

Unlike some European minorities, or later generations of Negroes, the "free persons of color" were seldom recipients of public charity. They "cared for their own poor" [130] through numerous mutual aid organizations which sprang up in communities of free Negroes from the earliest times. The first recorded mutual aid society among free Negroes was formed in Philadelphia in

1787; [131] by 1813 there were 11 such organizations in the same city, and by 1838 there were a hundred mutual aid organizations among the free Negroes of Philadelphia. [132] In Baltimore, there was a mutual aid society in 1821, and by 1835 there were 30 such organizations among the free Negroes. [133] These numerous and widespread mutual aid organizations provided the basis for the later Negro-owned insurance companies, which were to become the most prominent of successful black businesses. [134]

The schools to which the free Negroes sent their children were likewise largely private schools, because the public schools were closed to them in most northern cities as well as in the South. [135] Some of the private schools were supported or aided by white religious groups—notably the Quakers [136] and the Catholics [137]— but most were supported by the black community. [138] Although the schools which most "free colored" children attended were at the elementary level, and of highly variable quality at that, [139] the cities which were the strongholds of the "free persons of color" before the Civil War produced the leading black academic high schools of the middle of the twentieth century, as measured by doctoral degrees earned by their alumni. The largest number of black doctorates in 1957-62 came from the alumni of high schools in Washington, New Orleans, and Baltimore [140]—which had contained some of the largest communities of "free persons of color" in the mid-nineteenth century. [141] In the case of the high school in Washington, the continuing influence of specific "free colored" families has been traced already. [142] In short, in education as in other social areas, it was not so much the immediate tangible progress of the "free persons of color" which was important as the longer run consequences of their early efforts and experience.

The economic conditions of the antebellum free Negroes reflected a similar pattern of difficult beginnings, modest progress, and substantial longer run gains and impact. In the states outside the South, the largest occupational category among free Negroes was domestic service, [143] while in the South itself a more varied—and on the whole somewhat higher—occupational level existed. In New Orleans in 1860, only one-tenth of the *gens de couleur* were classified as common laborers, and they were dominant in a number of skilled occupations and small businesses. [144] Similarly, in Charleston, only a fraction of the free Negroes were domestic servants or unskilled laborers—fewer than the whites of that city in both categories—and were far better represented among the skilled crafts and trades taken as a whole (tailors, carpenters, and masons)[145] which had far more "free persons of color." Partly this was due to the large slave predominance in domestic service. However, it is noteworthy that slaves in Charleston outnumbered free blacks and whites in such occupations as coopers, carpenters, masons, and bricklayers.[146] While New Orleans and Charleston were unique in the degree of advancement of free Negroes in the United States, skilled black workers were common in Georgia,[147] North Carolina,[148] Virginia,[149] and indeed throughout the South, where skilled Negro workers were more common than in the North.[150] For the South as a whole, skilled workers among the slave population formed a very large proportion of southern skilled workers—perhaps a majority[151]—even though most slaves were not skilled workers, but rather worked in the cotton fields.[152] Still, the large supply of skilled slaves indicates one source of the antebellum "free persons of color" and of the working class skills which were common among them. The difficulties of southern white workers in competing with free Negroes were a source of complaint throughout the South,[153] leading to both legal restrictions[154] and sporadic violence.[155]

One reason for the difference in the proportions of free Negroes in skilled occupations in the North and South was the nature of the competition in the two regions. The relative inefficiency of southerners compared to northerners was a common observation of travelers through the antebellum South[156]—and this applied to labor, management, or farmers. The quality of work done by slave artisans or by free Negro artisans was often held to be questionable,[157] though it was good enough to displace poor whites from various trades. In the North, the competition of the immigrants, particularly in the last two or three decades before the Civil War, was often economically disastrous to the "free persons of color" in that part of the country. There were substantial retrogressions of free Negroes in many occupations after the arrival of the Irish in the 1840s.[158]

The competition between the Irish and the Negroes was long and frequently bitter, producing great animosity and often violent conflict,[159] and though the large influx of Irish immigrants created serious economic setbacks for the black Americans, the results were not always one-sided. For example, in Boston in 1860, free Negroes had slightly higher occupational status than Irish-Americans.[160] In New Orleans, the influx of the Irish in the 1840s and 1850s failed to displace the "free persons of color" from skilled occupations, though they did replace them in some unskilled jobs.[161] New York hotels in the 1850s paid Negro waiters higher wages than Irish waiters.[162] In the explicitly discriminatory advertisements of the mid-nineteenth century, the phrase "any color or country except Irish" was not uncommon, and some advertisements were even more direct: "A colored man preferred. No Irish need apply." [163]

The competition of immigrant workmen led to absolute reductions in economic well-being among the "free persons of color" in some northern communities,[164] while in the South the ever more severe legal restrictions in the 1830-60 period[165] did not stop their economic advance. In various parts of the South the "free persons of color" lost the right to vote,[166] to bear arms,[167] to assemble peaceably,[168] to move freely,[169] to educate themselves,[170] to testify against whites,[171] or to engage in various occupations and businesses.[172] In addition, the burden of proof was always on them to establish their free status by having the necessary documents on their persons at all times, and many were re-enslaved through various processes,[173] including kidnapping.[174] Both the racial etiquette expected of Negroes in dealing with whites and penalties for law violations were the same for free Negroes as for slaves.[175] Toward the end of the antebellum period, the distinction between slave and free Negroes was narrowed almost to a technicality in some parts of the South.[176] Yet the *economic* advance of the "free persons of color" continued. Property ownership among free Negroes in Virginia doubled between 1830 and 1860.[177] Similar or larger increases occurred in other southern states.[178] In New Orleans, the property ownership of "free persons of color" increased from approximately $2.5 million in 1836 to between $13 million and $15 million in 1860.[179] The proportion of Negroes owning real estate increased several-fold between 1849 and 1865.[180] For the country as a whole, the free Negroes accumulated an estimated $50 million in real and personal wealth before the Civil War.[181]

The one right which was *not* rescinded during the repressive period of 1830-60 was *property* rights.[182] The continued economic progress of the free blacks suggests the economic effectiveness of that one right in isolation.

3. *FAMILY AND CLASS*

The family life of the antebellum "free persons of color" was characterized by stable, two-parent households, often with a strong sense of tradition across the generations. Data from a dozen cities (North and South) for the period 1855-80 show 70-90 percent of the black families were male-headed, 85 percent being the median.[183] Despite a large literature which has repeated, without evidence, the theory that slavery was responsible for broken or matriarchal homes among American Negroes,[184] it was precisely among freed slaves that the highest incidence of two-parent families was found in mid-nineteenth century Philadelphia,[185] and it is only in a much later era that the incidence of broken homes in urban ghettoes reached unusually large proportions. The economic, rather than historical, basis for the high incidence of broken homes and the female-headed families among ghetto blacks is indicated by (1) the similarly high rates of broken homes among other, nonenslaved but similarly impoverished ethnic groups, such as the Irish in an earlier era,[186] and Puerto Ricans and Mexican-Americans today,[187] (2) similarly high rates of broken homes among the poorest class of free Negroes before the Civil War,[188] and (3) the systematically inverse relationship between broken homes and economic well-being among the various classes of "free persons of color." [189]

Class distinctions among the "free persons of color" turned more upon such "moral" or social attributes as family stability and decorum rather than income or occupation.[190] Except in the exceptional cases of New Orleans and Charleston, there was no substantial Negro middle class in terms of material prosperity, though there were numerous affluent individuals.[191] Still, within the free Negro community there was considerable concentration of wealth. Ten percent of the black population in antebellum Philadelphia held 70 percent of the wealth held by all "free persons of color." [192] Similar inequalities were common within the black communities in the South.[193] This is consistent with mid-twentieth century data, which show the distribution of income to be slightly more unequal among blacks than among whites.[194] In fact there are any number of indices of a higher concentration of achievements among a small proportion of the American Negro population. For example, the alumni of 5.2 percent of the black high schools received 20.8 percent of all doctoral degrees awarded to Negroes in the United States during the period 1957-62.[195] Of 4.3 million black families in the United States in 1966, a mere 5.2 *thousand* produced *all* the black physicians, dentists, lawyers, and academic doctorates in the country.[196] How much of this is a measure of the continuing concentration of achievement in the descendants of the "free persons of color" is largely a matter of conjecture. In those cases where it has been possible to trace ancestry, their continued prominence has been striking.

II. EMANCIPATED SLAVES AND THEIR DESCENDANTS

Slavery is the dominant fact in the history of black Americans—not only because it spanned more than half of that history, but because of its continuing influence on their geographic distribution, cultural legacy, and economic and social opportunities in a country whose racial attitudes were formed during the era of slavery. The institution of slavery goes back thousands of years, but slavery as it existed in the United States was very different from slavery in ancient Greece and Rome,[197] or even in contemporary societies of the Western Hemisphere.[198] The later history of American race relations reflects some of those differences.

One of the peculiarities of the United States is that it was not only the first major democratic nation, and for many years the only major democratic nation, but that it has always been regarded by itself and by much of the rest of the world as the leading democratic nation. Slavery in this context raised questions and required rationalization going beyond anything conceived of in other slaveholding countries. For thousands of years slavery was simply accepted by many kinds of societies—even by the leading moralists of those societies [199]—but throughout its history in the United States, slavery was the subject of bitter controversy, legal and political conflict, and ultimately civil war. Nowhere else in the Western Hemisphere was either the existence of slavery or its abolition accompanied by so much turmoil.[200]

The defenders of slavery in the United States faced unparalleled pressures and responded with unparalleled racism, with unparalleled repression of the free Negro population, and eventually with unparalleled intolerance and repression of ideas and individuals considered unfriendly toward slavery.[201] The extremes to which all these reactions were carried varied directly with the regional prevalence of plantation slavery. The "black belt" and other plantation-dominated areas of the South saw these tendencies carried to their most extreme—and continued longest in history, for many generations after the Civil War. Milder or more liberal racial views centered historically in those parts of the country whose climatic or geological characteristics made mass cotton plantation slavery economically untenable—the North, the Piedmont region [202] of North Carolina, Kentucky, Tennessee, and western Virginia, and the tidewater region [203] of Maryland, Virginia, and the District of Columbia. Southern antislavery thought, and later southern liberalism, were centered in the Piedmont and tidewater regions.[204] Later resistance to desegregation was also weakest in these areas and strongest in the "black belt." Similar patterns are found in data on lynching,[205] peonage,[206] education expenditures,[207] and other indices of race relations. As a noted southern historian observed: "We do not live in the past, but the past in us."[208]

American slavery has always been so enveloped in controversy —both during its existence [209] and even a century after its abolition [210]—that the facts about it have often been obscured. Recent empirical research has uncovered much data, which has forced major revisions of traditional interpretations.[211] The human implications of slavery and other aspects not susceptible of scientific determination may never be definitively assessed.

Although the United States did not import as many African slaves as Brazil, Haiti, Jamaica, or Cuba,[212] the United States was by 1825 the leading holder of slaves.[213] It held 36 percent of all the slaves in the Western Hemisphere, compared to 31 percent for Brazil,[214] which imported six times as many slaves over the years.[215] The American slave population was unique in the Western Hemisphere in being able, almost from the outset, to reproduce itself and to grow by natural increase.[216] In most of Latin America, the death rate was so high and the birth rate so low that slave populations could be maintained only by continuous imports from Africa.[217] By contrast, most United States slaves were American-born Negroes as early as 1680; and by 1860 only 1 percent were imported.[218] The reasons for the difference include fewer, less virulent diseases in the United States than in the tropics, and a more even balance of the sexes, but also less harsh treatment. One of the few things on which historians on various sides of the controversies surrounding slavery are agreed is that the treatment of slaves was more overworking and brutal in most of Latin America than in the United States.[219] It was not greater humanitarianism which led to easier race relations among the populations of Latin countries, but those countries' greater need for "free colored" artisans and Negro workers generally, since *white* working class people did not immigrate to Latin

America in nearly the numbers that immigrated to the United States. Few, if any, regions of Latin America could have afforded to drive out the "free colored" population, as was done in the Deep South in the decades preceding the Civil War.

The fact that the slave population of the United States consisted predominantly of American-born Negroes had cultural implications as well. African cultural survivals were (and are) far more common among the black populations of other Western Hemisphere nations than among American Negroes.[220] Controversy has raged over the degree to which African culture has survived in the New World, but with regard to American Negroes the controversy has been over whether there are *any* significant African cultural survivals.[221]

1. *THE LEGACY OF SLAVERY*

Viewed purely as an economic system, slavery had its peculiar advantages and weaknesses. Its most obvious economic disadvantage was that the occupations of slaves were limited to those in which escape possibilities were minimized. Occupations requiring wide dispersion, travel, education, or possession of arms created obvious possibilities of escape. Work requiring trust, individual initiative, or creativity presented difficulties for a slave economy beyond what existed in a free economy in which such qualities were more readily brought forth by a wider variety of rewards. This meant that slavery could not achieve the maximum productivity possible with a mixture of men of given individual capabilities, nor develop the maximum capabilities for a mixture of men of given potentialities. The need to retain them as slaves limited their development as men or as workers. An obvious example was the taboo against allowing slaves to learn to read and write. Only about 1 or 2 percent of the slaves were literate.[222] Some handpicked slaves were used in almost every conceivable occupation,[223] but these typically involved not only unusual slaves and slave owners, but also required major modification of the classic plantation slave pattern of constraints and rewards.

Classic plantation slavery had as its chief economic advantage a high degree of control of the work pace and work pattern of many men performing routine tasks. It was the mass production principle applied in agriculture. Some crops—notably cotton—lent themselves to this approach, while others requiring more versatility and individual attention did not. Depending upon which crops suited local soil and weather conditions, some parts of the South were dominated by plantation slavery while other parts had virtually no plantations or slaves. In the North, slavery existed until the early nineteenth century, but was never on a scale to be economically significant. Special kinds of work were adaptable to slave labor only when slavery itself was modified in the direction of an employer-employee relationship. For example, in the urban communities of the South, approximately 31 percent of the slaves were hired workers [224] whose owners simply collected a portion of the wages they received from their employers.[225] These slaves not only drew salaries and bonuses, but typically arranged their own living conditions and daily lives.[226] This was an even more common pattern in Latin America,[227] where white workers were more scarce than in the United States. In short, the weaknesses of slavery as an economic mechanism for accomplishing certain kinds of work was demonstrated by the extent to which it had to be modified to an approximation of *other* economic systems in order to get such work done.

Although slavery restricted the development of Negroes in educational terms, it facilitated the development of manual skills in the black population. Unlike a conventional employer, who loses a certain proportion of the workers he trains, a slave owner was assured of receiving the economic benefits created by the skills of his slaves—either directly in work, or indirectly in higher prices for the sale or hiring out of such slaves. A larger number of skilled black artisans existed under slavery than after the era of freedom.[228] As freed workers, blacks faced racial discrimination by employers and, later, by labor unions. Moreover, in the later period, there was no one with both the resources and the incentive to invest in their training.

The efficiency of slavery as an economic system has been a subject of controversy among economists (and others) for two hundred years.[229] Empirical research in recent years has firmly established that slavery was quite profitable for slave owners.[230] Its efficiency from the point of view of the contemporary slave-holding society as a whole, or its effect on the long run economic development of the South, remain unsettled questions. Many of the costs created by slavery as a system were borne by southern society as a whole, rather than by that 5 percent of white southerners who actually owned slaves. These costs included not only government apparatus directly involved in the control of slaves (patrols to check passes, recapture escapees, etc.) but also restrictions increasingly imposed on the white population,[231] including the censoring of the mails to intercept abolitionist literature [232] and the destruction of academic freedom at southern colleges and universities in order to stamp out antislavery ideas and individuals.[233] The long run costs of extreme regionalism,[234] racial and ideological intolerance, and the lasting handicaps of southern education must also be counted among the costs of slavery borne by southern society, both in the antebellum period and in succeeding generations. While specific dollar estimates of these costs are not possible, it is notable that the South has long been the poorest region of the United States, and within the South, the poorest parts—for whites as well as blacks—have been those in which slavery was once heavily concentrated, such as Alabama and Mississippi. Conversely, the most economically and culturally flourishing parts of the South were (and are) typically in areas where slavery was less prevalent and/or existed in milder, modified forms.[235]

In narrowly material terms, black slaves in the United States had a level of food consumption, clothing, health care, and life expectancy not very different from that of the contemporary working poor. The average slave consumed slightly more calories than the average free American, somewhat less meat, considerably less milk, and more potatoes and grain.[236] Nutritionally, the slave's diet exceeded today's recommended allowances of protein, iron, calcium, and the main vitamins.[237] The life expectancy of slaves in 1850 was four years less than the life expectancy of the white population of the United States at that time, but exceeded the life expectancy of the contemporary populations of some countries in Europe.[238] Infant mortality was higher than for the United States as a whole, but not very different from that of southern whites.[239]

There were hard economic reasons why the preservation of the lives of slaves was in the self-interest of American slave owners. The United States, together with England, outlawed the international slave trade in 1808, causing a precipitous drop in the number of slaves imported into this country,[240] to a negligible number smuggled in thereafter. Unlike some other Western Hemisphere nations which continued to import Africans in large numbers, the United States slaveholders could no longer replace their slaves from abroad in the event of death, disease, or disability. Supply and demand in the United States were different from supply and demand in Latin America. It became common in the South for slave owners to hire Irish immigrants to do *dangerous* work[241] while using slaves for work that was simply hard, dirty, or degrading. As one slave owner explained: "The niggers are worth too much to be risked here; if the Paddies are knocked overboard, or get their backs broke, nobody loses anything."[242]

The slave family has long been the subject of speculation and impressionistic discussion, but recent empirical research has undermined or reversed much of what was previously believed. By all indications, slave families were "stable, nuclear families."[243] These were two-parent families, in which the father was clearly the head.[244] While slave marriages had no legal standing as far as the government was concerned,[245] the slaves' lives were controlled and determined by the slave owners' rules, and those rules typically promoted family units and discouraged either divorce or extramarital relations.[246] The average age at which slave women had their first child was in their early twenties[247]—i.e., long after they were biologically capable of having children. All this was in the slave owner's self-interest, for family ties reduced the probability of a slave's escaping, as well as avoiding the turmoil that would result from men fighting over women in a wholly unstructured situation. Overseers were often on notice that relations with slave women would cost them their jobs—because of its effect on discipline and morale. The extent to which overseers, slave owners, and other whites had sex relations with slave women is roughly indicated by the number of mulatto children born to such women. The proportion of mulatto children born to slave women was many times higher in the cities than on plantations. An estimated 1 to 2 percent of the children born to plantation slave women were fathered by white men[248] whereas in the southern cities this proportion approached 50 percent.[249] Since only about 6 percent of all slaves were in the cities, while 60 percent were on cotton plantations alone,[250] the bulk of American Negroes in the antebellum period came from a tradition of stable, two-parent families, with miscegenation a rarity. These families were seldom separated, even in the massive regional movements of slaves from the upper South to the Deep South and Southwest, for 84 percent of the slaves involved in that movement migrated with their respective slave owners rather than being sold in the market.[251]

The high incidence of broken homes and female-headed families among American Negroes in twentieth century ghettoes was not a continuation of a tradition from the era of slavery, but was instead the development of a new pattern—a pattern also common among European immigrant groups during their difficult adjustment periods in urban ghettoes.[252]

2. *FROM EMANCIPATION TO JIM CROW*

A combination of factors made emancipation in the United States unique: (1) there was no preparation for it; (2) the overwhelming bulk of the black population was freed at one time; and (3) the southern economy and society into which they were released was thoroughly devastated and disorganized by the bloodiest war ever fought in the Western Hemisphere and one of the bloodiest wars anywhere in history. Both the black and white populations of the South escaped starvation only through massive aid from the federal government.[253]

In various other slave societies of the Western Hemisphere, the black population achieved freedom in phases, either as individuals[254] or as a group whose prospective emancipation was planned years in advance.[255] Even before emancipation was imminent, most Latin countries had a much larger proportion of "free persons of color" than did the United States,[256] and in some countries, the majority of the black population had already achieved freedom as individuals before slavery itself was abolished.[257] In the United States, freedom came with literally overnight suddenness; many slaves first learned of it when some federal official came onto the plantation with the news. Slaves were in many cases literally called in from the cotton fields to be told for the first time that they were free.[258] Thousands of ex-slaves wandered from place to place for months,[259] partly in reaction to their former confinement, some seeking lost relatives, and others simply trying to find a niche in life. The situation was saved from total chaos by the movement into the South of many northern white missionaries and teachers to help the freedmen. The schools (including colleges) established by the American Missionary Association during this era were a permanent foundation for the development of black education in the United States.[260]

Some of the "free persons of color" assumed leadership of the newly freed slaves, but the numerical disproportion between the two groups reduced the effectiveness of this leadership, as did the cultural gulf between them and their very different patterns of geographical distribution. Only in the northern cities were the

existing Negro communities able to absorb and assimilate in-
coming freedmen—and this remained true only as long as the
newcomers' numbers remained small. By the turn of the century,
many northern black communities were inundated by migrants
from the South, and the previous pattern of absorption gave way
to chaos and bitter antagonism among blacks,[261] as well as between blacks and whites.[262]

The federal government's military occupation of the South
after the Civil War brought a revolution in race relations. The
Reconstruction era saw a marked rise in the political position of
Negroes—as voters, as office holders, and as citizens freed from
the severe restrictions placed on "free persons of color" in the
period preceding the Civil War. Negroes served as officials of
local communities, as members of state legislatures and as southern representatives in both houses of the United States Congress.
Civil rights legislation and constitutional amendments buttressed
these advances. Economically, the picture was by no means as
favorable, and in some important ways there was marked retrogression in the decades following the Civil War. For the mass of
Negroes who were in agriculture, peonage became common.[263]
For that substantial minority of blacks with skills, there was a
steady decline in opportunities to practice those skills and, with
the passing of the years, a decline in the number of persons
possessing such skills. In the war-ravaged South, grim economic
conditions led whites to enter occupations once regarded as "Negroes' work," and to hold onto them long enough for the same
jobs to become known as "white men's work" exclusively. In some
industries in which black workers were initially dominant in the
South—notably construction and the railroads [264]—their numbers
were first eroded and then almost totally eliminated.[265]

When the political balance shifted—particularly after the
Compromise of 1877—political and social retrogression were
added to the economic difficulties of southern Negroes, who still
constituted the overwhelming bulk of the black population. However, the political position and civil rights of southern Negroes
did not immediately and precipitously decline. Over the years, in
an uneven, uncertain, and zigzag pattern the political position
and civil rights of the black population deteriorated. As late as
the 1890s, however, Negroes were still voting in substantial numbers in the South, and Negro officeholders had not wholly disappeared.[266] Moreover, the pervasive system of discriminatory
segregation known as "Jim Crow" took hold across the South only

at the turn of the twentieth century,[267] though its proponents later represented it as part of the "southern way of life" from time immemorial. While the Jim Crow system was being installed, it was the subject of widespread criticism and ridicule by segments of white southern opinion,[268] though once completed it became so sacrosanct that only a handful of hardy individuals dared question it. Along with a thorough segregation of public facilities, Jim Crow meant the reduction or elimination of black voting, either through restrictive legal devices or through extralegal intimidation and terror.

The United States Supreme Court's "separate but equal" doctrine in the 1896 case of *Plessy v. Ferguson* provided legal sanction for the early beginnings of Jim Crow. The "equal" part of the "separate but equal" doctrine was seldom taken seriously in the South: per capita expenditure on the education of black children was often only a fraction of the amount spent for white people.[269] Similar patterns were followed with regard to public accommodations in general.[270] Along with the economic and legal repression of blacks came an era of mass violence and terror unequalled before or since. In the 1890s the lynching of Negroes reached a peak of 161 per year.[271] The southern debt peonage system also typically involved intimidation by agents of private employers and/or by local law enforcement officers.[272]

Ideologically, the turn of the century was the high tide of racism in America. The doctrine of Manifest Destiny was exemplified in the Spanish-American War and the creation of the first overseas American empire. Social Darwinism was at its peak among intellectuals,[273] and biological theories of racial differences reached new heights of scientific respectability.[274] Leading historians began to glorify the antebellum South and to rationalize the existence of slavery there.[275] The rising new fields of sociology, psychology, and economics were, in America, firmly in the hands of men committed to racist theories.[276] These doctrines permeated the popular press as well.

3. *LEADERSHIP*

The changing fortunes of black Americans brought changing patterns of Negro leadership. In the late antebellum period and in the post-Civil War era, the undisputed leader of American Negroes was Frederick Douglass. An educated urban slave who had escaped to the North, Douglass became a leading antislavery speaker and writer. His bitter eloquence was directed first at achieving freedom, and then civil and legal equality for black Americans, though he was also active in promoting economic development among the Negro population. The rise of Jim Crow in the South represented the negation of Douglass' ideals and of the early successes of those who had shared similar hopes. With the death of Frederick Douglass, there arose another black leader geared to the grim new sociopolitical realities—Booker T. Washington. Although Washington expressed reverence for Frederick Douglass,[277] his own approach and style were entirely different.

To Booker T. Washington the first order of business was not the struggle in the political arena, where the southern Negro's northern liberal allies had long since disappeared, but rather the struggle for economic self-advancement. Washington was an educator, and the kind of education he espoused was focused on regaining the industrial skills in which blacks had once been prominent, or even dominant. Along with skills, as such, Washington sought to inculcate an *attitude* favorable to work, discipline, practicality, and pride in tangible achievements. He did not renounce political or civil rights, but shifted the emphasis sharply away from such things, which appeared unattainable in the existing climate of opinion. In his celebrated Atlanta Exposition speech in 1895, Booker T. Washington urged southern Negroes to try to work out their destiny in the South ("cast down your buckets where you are") and appealed to the more moderate elements among southern whites to realize that black and white economic cooperation was essential to both, however much they remained apart socially. He said, "In all things that are purely social we can be as separate as the fingers, yet one as the hand in all things essential to mutual progress."[278] The enthusiasm with which Washington's speech was greeted among moderates of both races, across the country, catapulted him into national prominence, and made him a Negro "leader" in a sociopolitical sense, rather than just as an educator. His autobiography, *Up From Slavery*, found a ready market, as did his lectures and other writings.

Despite Booker T. Washington's public image as a plain and simple man, recent scholarship (including the publication of his papers) shows him to have been a wily and complex manipulator[279]—though always in the interest of black people, as he saw that interest. While controlling the minutest details at Tuskegee

Institute, which he founded,[280] Washington also maintained a farflung network of loyal supporters in politics and in the Negro press,[281] and used his influence to determine who would and would not receive financial support from major philanthropic organizations, and who would and would not receive appointed political offices—including in some cases white candidates for federal appointments in the South.[282] Although publicly disinterested in political and civil rights activism, Washington secretly financed many efforts in both directions—including federal court cases challenging Jim Crow laws and practices.[283] His was essentially a pragmatic, and in many ways defensive, leadership during a period of peril and severe constraints.[284]

While Booker T. Washington was rising to national prominence as "the" Negro leader, particularly in the eyes of whites, a very different kind of leader was developing in the person of W. E. B. DuBois. A descendant of free mulattoes, DuBois grew up among educated whites in Massachusetts [285] and ultimately became the first Negro to receive a Ph.D. from Harvard.[286] He too began as an educator, but as a scholar rather than as an administrator. His sociological research produced a series of landmark books, articles, and monographs on the life and history of the American Negro. His intellectual preeminence among black scholars was to remain unchallenged for decades, and his early work continues to be cited today.

Politically, DuBois went through a long metamorphosis which began with his letter of congratulation to Booker T. Washington on his Atlanta Exposition speech in 1895 and ended with DuBois joining the Communist Party in the 1950s. DuBois' early hopes for the advancement of the race were centered on the intellectual development of the "talented tenth." The education he emphasized was broad, liberal education in contrast to the vocationalism of Booker T. Washington. The social and political philosophy of DuBois centered on open demands for civil and political rights, and open denunciations of discrimination and attacks on the sociopolitical system of which discrimination was a part. In 1911, DuBois became one of the founders of the NAACP, and for many years edited its official magazine, *The Crisis*. DuBois became the foremost critic of Booker T. Washington,[287] and Washington in turn spent much effort undermining DuBois' position.[288] The differences between the two men on educational policy were relatively small differences of emphasis, for both openly recognized the need for more job skills and work discipline, as well as the need for an intellectual leadership cadre.[289] Even politically, the differences between them were tactical and stylistic rather than fundamental, for DuBois was still relatively moderate during the period when he was contesting the leadership of Booker T. Washington. Much of the bitterness of their antagonism may reflect personality clashes based in part on different social backgrounds —Washington "up from slavery" and intimately in touch with grass roots Negroes, DuBois an aristocratic, highly educated man whose frame of reference was the international intellectual community.

The era of one dominant black leader (Douglass) or of two contending leaders (Washington vs. DuBois) gave way, by the 1930s, to an era of multiple leaders and of organizational leadership, notably by the NAACP. Individual prominent Negroes continued to be significant, sometimes as models or pioneers whose personal popularity in the larger society had a favorable effect on the prospects of other members of the race. Joe Louis is perhaps the prime example of such a model, though Jackie Robinson's later pioneering in baseball had a similar effect, and numerous others pioneered in government (Ralph Bunche), music (Marian Anderson), the universities (Allison Davis), and in other aspects of American life.

Black "leadership" increasingly included prominence and influence beyond the political realm. Sociopolitical leadership continued to be important, however, and with the rise of the mass media and the growth of a militant civil rights movement in the 1960s, charismatic leadership became especially prominent—at least for a few years. Martin Luther King, Malcolm X, Stokely Carmichael, and others achieved national fame overnight. By the 1970s, however, charismatic leadership was no longer so important, and more prosaic and pragmatic programs were being adopted, even by groups and organizations that had once been more flamboyant.

4. THE GREAT MIGRATIONS

One of the reactions of southern Negroes to the growth of Jim Crow and violence in the South was an exodus from the region. This typically involved not only a regional shift of residence but also a more fundamental adjustment to new urban conditions for a people with a long agricultural history in the rural South. The northern black communities to which the southern Negroes moved were often culturally quite different from the world of southern blacks, and migrants were not universally welcomed.

By the late nineteenth century, northern black communities in such cities as New York, Philadelphia, and Chicago had achieved some modest economic advancement after many years of hard struggle against external obstacles and after cultural transformations which adapted the Negro to urban life. In New York, for example, by the 1890s there were few unskilled laborers in the black community, and most Negroes held modest but respectable jobs as barbers, waiters, caterers, and skilled craftsmen, which made them "better off than the mass of recent white immigrants."[290] Politically they had advanced sufficiently to hold a few municipal jobs.[291] The striking improvement of their living conditions was noted in Jacob Riis' 1890 classic, *How the Other Half Lives*.[292] In Philadelphia, Negroes were among the leading caterers of the city, serving a predominantly white clientele,[293] and there was a significant Negro business class, as well as a substantial representation in lower middle-class and upper working-class occupations.[294] One measure of the growing respectability of the black community was that legal restrictions on Negroes' use of public facilities were removed—not by judicial or federal decree, or even by the political power of the black community (which was too small to have any political power), but by white officials elected by white voters. In Chicago as well, there were also successful black businesses serving a predominantly white clientele,[295] and a much freer racial atmosphere than in later years. One indication of this was the racial housing pattern. In 1910, more than two-thirds of the black population of Chicago lived in neighborhoods where a majority of the other residents were white.[296] Throughout the North during the late nineteenth and early twentieth centuries, stable two-parent black families were overwhelmingly the rule,[297] as indeed they were in the South as well. The "broken home" and other ghetto patterns developed later.

The mass migrations of unskilled, undereducated Negroes from the South marked a major transformation of black urban communities. Although the migration of the Negroes from the South to the North was a longstanding pattern, extending back well before the Civil War, the numbers had previously been well within the range of absorption of existing black communities. But with the imposition of severe Jim Crow laws and the rise of lynchings and other mob violence in the South, the exodus of blacks to the North reached new highs. The percentage of New

York Negroes born outside the state rose to more than half for the first time in 1900.[298] By 1910, more than three-quarters of the Negroes in Manhattan were born outside the state.[299] The growing size and falling social level of the black community was reflected in a reversal of the trend to better race relations which had been noted in the 1890s.[300] Segregation became more common, along with other evidences of growing racial antagonism.[301] Similar retrogressions followed similar influxes from the South to other black communities around the country.[302] The older black residents often bitterly blamed the new migrants for the retrogression which all Negroes suffered.[303]

As unprecedented as the turn-of-the-century migration was, it was but a small foretaste of the massive migrations to follow. The record-breaking migration of the 1900-10 decade was nearly tripled in the 1910-20 decade, and that in turn was almost doubled again in the 1920-30 decade.[304] The economic boom brought on by World War I created many jobs in the North at a time when immigration from Europe was cut off by the war. At the same time, rising cotton prices enabled many southern black sharecroppers to escape peonage by finally paying off their debts to the company store and leaving. The rise of many northern ghettoes dates from this period, when housing restrictions hardened into rigid de facto segregation. In Chicago, where integrated neighborhoods had been common a few years earlier, attempts by Negroes to move into white neighborhoods were now met by bombings and mob violence.[305] Similar patterns appeared in other northern cities.[306] The Ku Klux Klan received a revival of membership, with many *northern* branches opening up. Race riots broke out in many cities.[307] There had always been black neighborhoods and some housing restrictions, but the age of the modern ghetto began in this period. The political repercussions affected the federal government where, under Woodrow Wilson's administration, segregation was introduced into the federal agencies, where it had not existed previously. The Civil Service Commission now required a photograph from job applicants, and allowed the employing agency to choose among the top three on the qualified list, not necessarily the highest scorer.[308] The number of blacks in well-paying federal jobs declined sharply over the next two decades.[309] At the municipal level, however, blacks increased their share of government jobs in those areas where large numbers of black voters were concentrated.[310]

Like other working class people, Negroes were especially hard hit by the Great Depression of the 1930s and were later especially benefited by the economic boom which accompanied World War II. World War II had another major impact on American Negroes. Nazi racism and its consequences discredited racism around the globe, and led to a new questioning of American racial practices, both by Americans and by world opinion. By the end of the war, American universities and other institutions began removing their restrictions against the Jews; California's long-standing racist restrictions on Orientals were rejected by the voters; for blacks, a long series of executive orders, court decrees, and civil rights legislation began to erode institutionalized segregation and discrimination. A landmark in this trend was the Supreme Court decision of May 1954, declaring that segregated facilities were inherently unequal and therefore unconstitutional.

The Supreme Court decision of 1954 ushered in an era of attempts at racial "integration" across the institutional and social spectrum of American life. Lawsuits, court orders, political pressures, economic boycotts, demonstrations, and extralegal sit-ins were all used by those promoting "integration." Political delays and evasions, violence, and "token" compliance were employed by those resisting, and when these failed, the resisters withdrew their children from public schools and/or withdrew their families from the cities to all-white suburbs. A decade after the 1954 decision and just over a hundred years after emancipation, the Civil Rights Act of 1964 was passed to use federal government power to destroy the remaining institutional barriers to the legal and political equality of American Negroes.

While greater legal and political rights brought an end to the most galling of the Jim Crow laws and practices in the South, the benefits had little immediate effect on the day-to-day life of the black populations that were now increasingly concentrated in northern urban ghettoes. These ghettoes became the scenes of annual summer riots during the early to mid-1960s. A rising tide of militant and occasionally revolutionary feeling among Negroes resulted in a repudiation of the integrationist goals of the civil rights movements and a substitution of separatist goals and a search for new "black identity." These trends in turn provoked a new resistance characterized as "white backlash." As the decade of the 1970s began, the more extreme black militant revolutionary movements were either losing adherents or moderating their positions or both.

5. ECONOMIC ADVANCEMENT

Emancipation found the overwhelming bulk of the black population working in agriculture in the South,[311] and this remained the dominant pattern on into the twentieth century. The small portion of American Negroes living in the North were largely nonagricultural [312]—chiefly servants and industrial workers, and few of the latter were skilled. A very tiny proportion of the black population were in the professions. Lack of education was the rule rather than the exception in the black labor force throughout the nineteenth century and into the early years of the twentieth century. Only 43 percent of the black population was literate in 1890,[313] and less than 2,000 Negroes received college degrees in the entire nineteenth century.[314] Moreover, the manual skills which blacks possessed in the 1860s eroded through disuse as job discrimination barriers went up.[315]

Despite many handicaps, economic advancement took place among blacks, even if slowly. By 1913—fifty years after emancipation—one-fourth of the black population of the South were homeowners rather than renters.[316] The literacy rate continued to rise, as did the number of black college graduates and the level of black income.

The twentieth century saw a massive shift from agricultural to nonagricultural occupations—largely as a result of black migration from the South to the North, but also as a result of urbanization within the South. A parallel shift was occurring simultaneously among whites but was not as pronounced. The Great Depression of the 1930s hit the Negro population especially hard. Unemployment rates among blacks rose even more sharply than among the general population, and incomes fell at a faster rate.[317] However, the prosperity accompanying World War II benefited Negroes more than the general population.[318] Over the years, the relative income of black and white Americans remained roughly in proportion—the black income being just over half of white income—as both rose over time. But the massive social changes of the 1960s saw an accelerated economic advancement of the black population.

Black income as a percentage of white income rose during the decade of the 1960s,[319] along with increases in occupational status [320] and education [321] and a decline in the unemployment rate among Negroes, absolutely and relative to the white unemployment rate.[322] Black family income doubled between 1960 and

1970, while white income rose by only about one-third.[323] The number of black families making $10,000 a year or more (in constant dollars to eliminate inflation) increased from 13 percent of all black families in 1961 to 30 percent of all black families in 1971.[324] At the same time, however, those black families at the lower end of the income distribution experienced greater difficulty in getting out of poverty than whites in the same brackets, and the numbers and proportions of blacks on welfare increased.[325] Social commentators noted that a more fortunate portion of the black population was increasing in prosperity very rapidly, while the least fortunate portion—the poorest, least educated, less skilled, less experienced in urban life—were not sharing in the general advance, and might even be retrogressing.[326]

For the black population as a whole, a more detailed breakdown of the statistical data shows that the economic advances of the 1960s were somewhat greater than indicated by raw totals and averages. *Younger* black families and individuals rose more sharply in income and occupation than their elders,[327] whose career patterns had formed before the recent social changes. Moreover, American Negroes are still more heavily concentrated in the South—a low-income region—than is the general population, so gross black-white income differences reflect substantial regional income differences as well as intergroup differences as such. Outside the South, younger black families with both husband and wife working earned virtually the same incomes in 1970 as young white families of the same description.[328] Paradoxically, blacks as a whole fell further behind whites in absolute dollar amounts while gaining relatively. The key to the paradox is inflation: even a narrowing gap in real terms can be a widening gap in dollar terms as inflation causes each dollar to represent less and less real wealth.

6. SOCIAL PATHOLOGY

The incidence of poverty, crime, disease, broken homes, and substandard educational performance has been perennially higher among American Negroes than among the United States population at large.[329] In all these characteristics, the black population follows a well-established pattern among American minority groups, beginning with the European immigrant groups of the nineteenth century.[330] Yet, even after the end of slavery, the black population has been unique in the degree of residential segregation [331] and other forms of sociocultural isolation which have been easily imposed via obvious skin color differences.

With poverty has gone a higher incidence of dependence on public and private charity, even though most Negroes are not on welfare and most people on welfare are not Negroes.[332] Rates of crime and violence have been so high in the black population as to produce more black murder victims in the United States (principally murdered by other blacks) than white murder victims (principally murdered by other whites) *in absolute numbers*,[333] despite the fact that the blacks are only about 10 percent of the American population. The incidence of traditional poverty-health hazards—malnutrition, infant mortality, tuberculosis—has long been high among Negroes, as it was among European immigrants in the nineteenth century. Black families show higher—and growing—rates of broken homes than in the general population, though closely followed in this respect by other low-income minorities, such as Mexican-Americans and Puerto Ricans.[334]

A special interest has long centered on substandard educational performance by American Negroes—with some observers insisting that such performance stems from innately inferior intellectual potential.[335] The average I.Q. of American Negroes has generally been around 85,[336] compared to a national average of 100, but this too is not unique. Numerous European immigrant groups had similar or lower I.Q.'s as recently as the 1920s.[337] Similar I.Q.'s have also been found among such socioculturally isolated groups as white mountaineers in the United States [338] and inhabitants of the Hebrides Islands off Scotland.[339] Moreover, the internal I.Q. patterns of American Negroes suggest strong environmental influences. Northern Negroes have consistently scored higher on I.Q. tests than have southern Negroes,[340] and while there have been theories that "selective migration" led the genetically more able blacks to move north,[341] further investigation has indicated that the better quality of northern schools caused the *same individuals* to have higher I.Q.'s after moving north.[342] In addition, high I.Q. Negroes are predominantly female, in contrast to the national sex pattern among high I.Q. persons, [343] and numerous studies have shown females in general to be less affected by environment than are males.[344]

The degree and kind of social pathology among black Americans has changed considerably over time. Malnutrition was apparently not a major problem among slaves,[345] but after emancipation it was one of many causes of a *rising* mortality rate among

Negroes in the last quarter of the nineteenth century.[346] In black urban communities in the nineteenth century, the death rate was so high, both absolutely and relative to the birth rate, that contemporary social commentators questioned whether Negroes could physically survive in northern cities.[347] In the twentieth century, the situation has been so reversed that black urban population growth has been striking.[348]

It is difficult to trace social pathology among Negroes prior to the Civil War. Crime was not unknown among slaves, however, and in fact one regional study showed 198 murders of whites by slaves in an 84 year period, including mostly murders of slave owners and overseers; rape was far less common than murder, despite traditional beliefs.[349] It is difficult to determine the incidence of dependency or of crime among the "free persons of color," for highly conflicting reports exist, and it is clear that there was strong emotional antagonism to this group on grounds that their *very existence* threatend slavery, independent of their conduct.[350] One study of the history of "free persons of color" in Georgia found no convictions for a capital offense among them.[351]

Paradoxically, suicide rates have long been lower among Negroes than among the general American population. In recent years, however, as the socioeconomic position of black Americans has risen toward that of whites, so too has their suicide rate.[352]

III. WEST INDIAN IMMIGRANTS

Only about one percent of the American Negro population consists of West Indians, and these are concentrated in and around New York City. However, West Indians have long been greatly overrepresented among prominent Negroes in the United States[353] —from Marcus Garvey, James Weldon Johnson, and Claude McKay in an earlier era to Stokely Carmichael, Shirley Chisholm, Malcolm X, Kenneth Clark, James Farmer, Roy Innes, W. Arthur Lewis, Harry Belafonte, Sidney Poitier, and Godfrey Cambridge in more recent times. West Indian Negroes in the United States have long had higher incomes, more education, higher occupational status, and proportionately far more business ownership than American Negroes.[354] Both their fertility rates and their crime rates have been lower than those of native blacks—or native whites.[355] Such differences continue to persist, as shown

by data compiled from the 1970 Census (table 1). The low proportion of "laborers" among West Indians confirms the long-
standing impression that they had a "distinct aversion" to manual
labor.[356]

Table 1

	American Negroes	West Indians	National Average
Median Family Income, 1969	$5,888	$8,971	$9,494
Median Years of Education	10.0	10.7	10.9
Percent in Learned Professions	0.5	1.9	3.0
Percent in Other Professions	7.1	13.3	11.0
Percent Laborers	8.9	2.6	4.3
Mean Number of Children per Woman	2.4	1.8	2.1

SOURCE: Public Use Sample, 1970 Census.

Despite the rhetoric of "black solidarity," West Indian Negroes
and American Negroes have remained quite distinct social groups.
A study of marriage patterns among West Indian women attending American Negro colleges in the 1930s showed that 98 percent
of them married West Indian men.[357] A more recent study (1972)
of Barbadians in New York City showed that 87 percent of them
married other Barbadians.[358] A survey of a middle-class black
community in 1962 found that 98 percent of the West Indians
living there had almost all their friendships either with other
West Indians or with a few whites. Similarly, American Negroes
in the same community had 93 percent of their friendships either
with other American Negroes or with whites.[359] In short, West
Indians are not only different by the usual socioeconomic indicators, but are perceived and perceive themselves as socially distinct from black Americans.

West Indians in the United States are significant not only
because of their overrepresentation among prominent or successful blacks, but also because their very different background makes
them a test case of the explanatory importance of color, as such,
in analyzing socioeconomic progress in the American economy
and society, as compared to the importance of the cultural traditions of the American Negro. Their history also provides a test
of beliefs about the particular aspects of slavery which constitute
the most crippling continuing handicaps as far as socioeconomic
advancement is concerned. Moreover, since West Indian immigrants to the United States—unlike the "free persons of color"—
are seldom mulattoes, biological influences may also be gauged.

Gross statistical comparisons do not tell the whole story, though they give some general indication of the magnitudes of the differences between these two black groups in the United States. West Indian families earn substantially higher incomes than native black families, and only slightly less than the national average. However, a substantial part (though no longer a majority) of the native black population of the United States still live and work in the South, a lower income region, while West Indians are concentrated in and around New York City.[360] There are substantial differences in income (and other social indicators) between southern blacks and blacks in other parts of the country. For example, data compiled from the 1970 census (Public Use Sample) showed that southern blacks' median family income in 1969 was $4,760 compared to $7,321 for black families living outside the South. The number of children per woman was 2.7 for southern blacks and 2.2 for black women elsewhere. On these and other indicators, southern blacks differ from other blacks as much as native blacks as a group differ from West Indians—and these differences arc greater than the differences between all blacks in the United States and the United States population as a whole. Color alone, or racism alone, is clearly not a sufficient explanation of income disparities within the black population or between the black and white populations.

While differences in geographic distribution account for some of the differences between the income, occupational status, and so forth of native blacks and West Indians, there are still large differences between the two groups, even in the New York City metropolitan area:

Table 2

	American Negroes	West Indians
Median Family Income, 1969	$6,881	$8,830
Median Years of Education	10.5	10.5
Percent in Learned Professions	0.4	1.0
Percent in Other Professions	8.2	14.4
Percent Laborers	5.2	2.0
Mean Number of Children per Woman	2.2	1.7

SOURCE: Public Use Sample, 1970 Census, for the New York City Standard Metropolitan Statistical Area.

Even educational disparities do not account for the West Indians' higher socioeconomic status, for in the New York metro-

politan area they have no educational advantage, in terms of years
in school,[361] over native blacks (table 2). Moreover, the census
data show significant income differences between the two groups,
even when comparing individuals with four years of college or
with two or more years of postgraduate training (table 3). However, these differences shrink considerably when education and
regional distribution are both held constant. A northern black
with four years of college makes only a few hundred dollars per
year less than a West Indian with four years of college, though
the difference is a little larger among those with postgraduate
training.

Table 3

	American Negroes			West Indians
	Total	North	South	
Personal Income after 4 Years of College (1969)	$6,573	$7,330	$5,887	$7,662
Personal Income after 2 or More Postgraduate Years (1969)	$10,565	$12,202	$9,536	$13,409

SOURCE: Public Use Sample, 1970 Census.

Some people have attributed the West Indians' success either to
superior education under the British system or to different treatment by white American employers. One way to test these theories
would be to isolate *second generation* West Indians—those blacks
born in the United States of West Indian-born parents, and therefore likely to have been educated in the United States and un-
likely to have an accent that would enable a white employer to
distinguish them from native blacks.[362] A compilation of 1970
census data for second-generation West Indians in the New York
City area showed them to *exceed* the socioeconomic status of
other West Indians, as well as that of native blacks—and of the
United States population as a whole—in family income ($10,900),
education (11.5 years), and proportion in the professions (18.3
percent).

The explanation of biological differences (white ancestry),
such as some have invoked to explain the greater achievement of
mulattoes,[363] cannot apply here, for West Indians have a higher
proportion of African ancestry than do American Negroes.[364]
Neither discrimination nor genetics offers any obvious explanation for the very different income and occupational achievement

between these two subgroups of the black population in the United States. "Selective migration" has sometimes been offered as an explanation—assuming that the more able people migrate to the United States from the West Indies. However, this explanation also does not withstand scrutiny very well. The magnitude of the outmigration from the West Indies to various parts of the world is so great that "selective" is hardly an appropriate description. Moreover, the small, higher-income, better-educated elite of the West Indies is disproportionately either white or mulatto [365] —and these groups typically do *not* migrate.

Any attempt to assess the factors behind the success of West Indian immigrants can be made only after a survey of the history of this black subgroup, both in the West Indies and in the United States.

1. SLAVERY IN THE WEST INDIES

Slavery was as dominant a factor in black history in the British West Indies as in the United States. By all indications, the treatment and conditions of slaves were harsher in the West Indies than in the United States.[366] Infant mortality was much higher among West Indian slaves than among slaves in the United States.[367] The concubinage of slave women was the prevalent pattern in the islands,[368] where bachelor overseers [369] and absentee owners [370] were the rule. The severe "black codes" of the American Deep South were copied from the laws of the West Indies.[371] The slave population of the West Indies never reproduced itself, and constant imports from Africa were necessary to maintain their numbers.

In addition to importing slaves for its own use, the West Indies served as a transition area for slaves to be shipped to the United States. It was a "seasoning" place for slaves—meaning not only a breaking-in place, but a place where newly arrived Africans acquired biological resistance to Europeans' diseases. The mortality rate among Africans was high from what are normally mild diseases in a population with resistance to them. However, the survivors who were shipped to the United States were not nearly as vulnerable to those diseases.

The racial composition of the West Indian population has long been very different from the racial composition of the United States population, or even the population of the South. Instead of a minority of blacks surrounded by a larger white society, the West Indies has long been a place with an overwhelmingly black

population, with a small group of whites, and with a small group
of mulattoes. This simple demographic fact had important implications for the development of black West Indians, both during
the era of slavery (ending in 1836) and afterwards:

1. Slave escapes and slave rebellions were both more feasible
    in the West Indies than in the United States, where the
    numerical superiority of the surrounding white population
    made the prospects far more grim. Moreover, the tropical
    jungles of the West Indies afforded an opportunity for
    escape to an area that could sustain life and was almost
    wholly free of whites. Slave uprisings were both more fre-
    quent and more successful in the West Indies[372]—i.e.,
    blacks were not psychologically crushed by a sense of the
    futility of resistance to whites.
2. The West Indian plantation could not draw upon a larger
    white society for its economic needs, and in fact members
    of the enslaved black population grew their own food indi-
    vidually, and sold the surplus in the market off the planta-
    tion. Unlike slaves in the United States, who were typically
    either issued rations or were fed from communal kitchens,
    slaves in the West Indies were assigned individual plots of
    land in which each family grew its own food.[373] In short,
    even during the era of slavery, black West Indians had
    generations of experience in individual reward for indi-
    vidual effort, in at least part of their lives, as well as experi-
    ence in marketing their surplus, and in managing their
    own food needs and monetary returns.
3. The virtual absence of a white working class meant that
    "free persons of color," and later the whole free black popu-
    lation, could not be restricted to the most menial occupa-
    tions, as in the United States, or the more skilled and more
    responsible positions would have gone unfilled. In short,
    black West Indians faced a wider occupational range than
    American Negroes, though in both societies the top posi-
    tions were reserved for whites.

The racial attitudes of whites were very similar in the West
Indies and in the United States. Slavery was as foreign to British
tradition as to that of the United States, and was under severe
and continuous attack from British intellectuals; and the white
West Indians responded with a fierce racism and regionalism,

very much like that of the South—and more severe than that in Latin America. As in the United States, slavery was ended by a decision of the national government—i.e., in London—over local opposition. However, the relative power of the central government and the local population was too obviously out of proportion for a civil war to develop. The West Indies were therefore spared the physical devastation and disorganization which characterized the South after the Civil War. But while the emancipated West Indians entered a society and economy which were physically intact, there was a long transitional period of reorganization and of disastrous decline in the market for the islands' principal crop —sugar.[374] Peonage virtually re-enslaved the black population of the West Indies,[375] as in the southern United States. Moreover, the islands lacked the economic resources and economic development of the United States, so poverty, ignorance, and disease were at least as common among the black population of the West Indies as of the United States, or even the American South. Massive out-migration was one response. The United States was but one of many destinations.

2. *WEST INDIAN IMMIGRANTS IN THE UNITED STATES*

The history of black immigration from the West Indies to the United States extends back into the nineteenth century, even before the end of slavery in the United States. However, the early immigration was very small. Significant numbers of black West Indians began arriving in the United States around the turn of the century—largely concentrated in and around New York City, then as today. In the 1920s approximately one-fourth of the black population of Harlem was West Indian.[376] Cultural differences and intergroup hostility between native blacks and West Indians extended from the man in the street[377] to their respective intellectuals.[378] West Indians were far more successful in business than were native blacks.[379] The whole West Indian experience followed a pattern reminiscent of European immigrants rather than the pattern of their native black contemporaries. West Indians typically arrived in the United States in poverty, took whatever jobs they could find, saved, started small businesses, educated their children at considerable sacrifice, and moved up the occupational ladder at a faster rate than their native black counterparts.

West Indian "identity" has long been a subject of social comment, criticism, and bitter satire. West Indians have long been Anglophiles.[380] The only major efforts to ameliorate the lot of the slaves in the West Indies came from British humanitarians and the British government. It was the British navy which stopped the international slave trade in 1808, and the British government which ended slavery in the West Indies twenty-eight years later. In the long struggle for political rights and advancement of blacks in the West Indies, the British government was a valuable ally against local whites. Black West Indians' loyalty to Britain extended beyond the political sphere to such cultural features as British clothing (in a climate wholly unsuitable for it), cricket, and the religion of the Anglican Church. In the United States, West Indian immigrants were reluctant to sever their ties with Britain by becoming American citizens.[381] Aside from sentimental attachments, the British Embassy was a place to turn for help in racial discrimination cases in the United States.[382]

IV. SUMMARY AND CONCLUSIONS

The history of black people in the United States is the history of subgroups at very different stages of social evolution. For example, in the nineteenth century, the "free persons of color" had literacy rates more than ten times higher than those of blacks in bondage—and, in fact, literacy rates higher than those of the American Negro population for decades after emancipation. In urbanization the "free persons of color" were about 80 years ahead of the rest of the black population, and their migration to the North presaged a similar movement of the Negro population as a whole, which would take about a century to achieve a similar regional distribution. Empirical evidence indicates that the descendants of the "free persons of color" were disproportionately overrepresented among successful Negroes well into the twentieth century. Moreover, the institutions and traditions of the "free persons of color" had a continuing impact on the success of other blacks who came within their orbit.

Another Negro subgroup, the West Indian immigrants and their descendants, also has a socioeconomic pattern quite different from that of the bulk of the black American population—in particular, a high incidence of "success" (income, education, occupation, etc.), and lower incidences of social pathology (crime rates, unemployment, divorce, etc.). Their success pattern contradicts earlier "explanations" of the success of the Negro middle class as a mulatto—i.e., biological—phenomenon, since West Indians are somewhat more African than American Negroes in both genetic and cultural terms. The West Indian success pattern likewise undermines the explanatory power of current white discrimination as a cause of current black poverty. Moreover, even in weighing the heavy burden of history in general and slavery in particular, it is necessary to separate questions of morality from questions of causation. The history of black West Indians in the United States suggests that what was most morally reprehensible about slavery—brutality, overwork, sexual exploitation —may have been less causally important, as factors in later group development, than such features as regimented dependence (as contrasted with economic incentives and market experience).

The history of black Americans has been a history of a rise from a position lower than that of any other minority in America. That rise was so painfully slow as to be almost imperceptible at various times, but over the decades the socioeconomic rise of black Americans has been consistent and has finally accelerated to a level approaching that of others with far more initial advantages.

NOTES

1. Bureau of the Census, *Negro Population: 1790-1915* (Government Printing Office, 1918), p. 53.

2. Kenneth M. Stampp, *The Peculiar Institution* (Vintage Books, 1956), p. 194.

3. Ira Berlin, *Slaves without Masters* (Pantheon, 1974), pp. 31-33, 143-44, 148-49, 263; John Hope Franklin, "Slaves Virtually Free in Ante-Bellum North Carolina," *Journal of Negro History*, July 1943, pp. 284-310; Booker T. Washington, *The Story of the Negro* (Negro Universities Press, 1969), vol. 1, pp. 206-7. For a detailed study of a quasi-free slave, see John Hebron, "Simon Gray, Riverman: A Slave Who Was Almost Free," *Mississippi Valley Historical Review*, December 1962, pp. 472-84.

4. Clement Eaton, "Slave-Hiring in the Upper South: A Step toward Freedom," *Mississippi Valley Historical Review*, March 1960, pp. 671-72; Richard C. Wade, *Slavery in the Cities* (Oxford University Press, 1967), p. 48; Stampp, *The Peculiar Institution*, pp. 68, 72; Ulrich B. Phillips, *Life and Labor in the Old South* (Little, Brown and Co., 1963), p. 181.

5. Ulrich B. Phillips, *American Negro Slavery* (Louisiana State University Press, 1969), p. 414; Wade, *Slavery in the Cities*, pp. 38, 49-50.

6. Stampp, *The Peculiar Institution*, p. 72.

7. Robert W. Fogel and Stanley L. Engerman, *Time on the Cross* (Little, Brown and Co., 1974), pp. 211-15; Berlin, *Slaves without Masters*, pp. 150-51.

8. E. Horace Fitchett, "The Origin and Growth of the Free Negro Popu-

lation of Charleston, South Carolina," *Journal of Negro History,* October 1941, p. 427; Stampp, *The Peculiar Institution,* pp. 151, 323-24, 325-26, 333.

9. Bureau of the Census, *Negro Population: 1790-1915,* p. 53.

10. E. Franklin Frazier, *The Negro in the United States* (The Macmillan Co., 1971), pp. 54-56; Berlin, *Slaves without Masters,* p. 151.

11. Gunnar Myrdal, *An American Dilemma* (McGraw-Hill, 1964), vol. 2, pp. 696-97; Frazier, *The Negro in the United States,* p. 68; Berlin, *Slaves without Masters,* p. 151.

12. Stampp, *The Peculiar Institution,* p. 196; Myrdal, *An American Dilemma,* vol. 2, pp. 696-97.

13. Maldwyn Allen Jones, *American Immigration* (University of Chicago Press, 1970), pp. 13, 32.

14. John H. Russell, *The Free Negro in Virginia, 1619-1865* (Dover Publications, Inc., 1969), pp. 16-33; Frazier, *The Negro in the United States,* pp. 22-28.

15. Bureau of the Census, *Negro Population: 1790-1915,* pp. 54-61.

16. Russell, *The Free Negro in Virginia,* p. 37; Stanley Elkins, *Slavery* (University of Chicago Press, 1969), p. 55; Stampp, *The Peculiar Institution,* p. 193.

17. William L. Westerman, *The Slave Systems of Greek and Roman Antiquity* (The American Philosophical Society, 1955), p. 105.

18. Bureau of the Census, *Negro Population: 1790-1915,* p. 53.

19. *Loc. cit.*

20. Berlin, *Slaves without Masters,* pp. 138-41.

21. Frazier, *The Negro in the United States,* p. 62.

22. Wilbur Zelinsky, "The Population Geography of the Free Negro in Ante-Bellum America," *Population Studies,* March 1950, p. 388; Bureau of the Census, *Negro Population: 1790-1915,* pp. 54-55. See also Berlin, *Slaves without Masters,* pp. 151-52; Theodore Hershberg, "Free Blacks in Antebellum Philadelphia: A Study of Ex-Slaves, Freeborn, and Socioeconomic Decline," *Journal of Social History,* Winter 1971-72, p. 190; David Y. Thomas, "The Free Negro in Florida before 1865," *South Atlantic Quarterly,* October 1911, p. 338. More females than males on slave plantations also led to low fertility. Fogel and Engerman, *Time on the Cross,* p. 83.

23. David W. Cohen and Jack P. Greene, eds., *Neither Slave nor Free* (Johns Hopkins University Press, 1972), p. 7; Frederick P. Bowser, "Colonial Spanish America," ibid., p. 31; H. Hoetink, "Surinam and Curaçao," ibid., p. 62; Jerome S. Handler and Arnold A. Sio, "Barbados," ibid., pp. 221, 229; Franklin W. Knight, "Cuba," ibid., p. 286; Herbert S. Klein, "Nineteenth-Century Brazil," ibid., pp. 317-18. A similar sex imbalance in other Western Hemisphere countries did not prevent those countries from having a higher rate of increase in their free Negro populations than in their slave and/or white populations (Cf. Herbert S. Klein, "The Colored Freedman in Brazilian Slave Society," *Journal of Social History,* Fall 1969, pp. 34, 37; Bowser, "Colonial Spanish America," in Cohen and Greene, eds., *Neither Slave nor Free,* pp. 36, 38; A. J. R. Russell-Wood, "Colonial Brazil," ibid., pp. 97, 98, 132; Leo Elisabeth, "The French Antilles," ibid., p. 150; Gwendolyn Midlo Hall, "Saint Domingue," ibid., p. 188; Douglas Hall, "Jamaica," ibid., p. 194; Handler and Sio, "Barbados,"

ibid., pp. 222, 223). However, it is difficult to separate the increase of the free Negro population due to manumission from that due to natural increase (Handler and Sio, "Barbados," p. 222; Knight, "Cuba," p. 285), and in most other Western Hemisphere slave societies, manumission was more widespread than in the United States. In the largest of the Western Hemisphere free colored societies, that of Brazil, the free colored "was the fastest growing class" but their *natural increase* was not as rapid as that of the whites (Klein, "The Colored Freedman in Brazilian Slave Society," p. 37).

24. Bowser, "Colonial Spanish America," p. 29; Hall, "Saint Domingue," p. 185; Laura Foner, "The Free People of Color in Louisiana and St. Domingue," *Journal of Social History*, Summer 1970, pp. 408, 410, 412; Klein, "The Colored Freedman in Brazilian Slave Society," p. 40; Phillips, *American Negro Slavery*, p. 62.

25. Berlin, *Slaves without Masters*, pp. 109-10, Foner, "The Free People of Color in Louisiana and St. Domingue," pp. 409, 411, 412, 413, 414-15. Cf. Bowser, "Colonial Spanish America," p. 29; Hall, "Jamaica," p. 209; Klein, "The Colored Freedman in Brazilian Slave Society," pp. 40, 41.

26. E. Franklin Frazier, *Black Bourgeoisie* (The Free Press, 1962), pp. 18-19.

27. Bureau of the Census, *Negro Population: 1790-1915*, p. 41.

28. Ibid., p. 55.

29. Loc. cit. While the number of slaves in Mississippi more than doubled between 1840 and 1860, the number of "free persons of color" was nearly halved in the same period. In Arkansas, the number of slaves increased fivefold between 1840 and 1860, while the number of free Negroes fell by more than two-thirds. Ibid., p. 57.

30. Zelinsky, "The Population Geography of the Free Negro in Ante-Bellum America," p. 387.

31. Frazier, *Black Bourgeoisie*, p. 19; E. Franklin Frazier, *The Negro Family in the United States* (University of Chicago Press, 1969), p. 144; Carter G. Woodson, *A Century of Negro Migration* (AMS Press, 1970), chap. 2; Berlin, *Slaves without Masters*, pp. 126-37, 175-79.

32. Thomas Sowell, *Race and Economics* (David McKay, 1975), pp. 21-23; Ulrich Bonnell Phillips, *The Slave Economy of the Old South* (Louisiana State University Press), pp. 22, 108, 153-54; Woodson, *A Century of Negro Migration*, pp. 31-33.

33. Zelinsky, "The Population Geography of the Free Negro in Ante-Bellum America," p. 387.

34. Constance M. Green, *The Secret City* (Princeton University Press, 1970), p. 33.

35. *Loc. cit.*

36. Ibid., p. 17.

37. Thomas Sowell, "Black Excellence: The Case of Dunbar High School," *The Public Interest*, Spring 1974, pp. 5-7, 10-11, 12.

38. Mary Gibson Hundley, *The Dunbar Story*.

39. Sowell, "Black Excellence," p. 8.

40. Ibid., p. 4.

41. Horace Mann Bond, "The Negro Scholar and Professional in America" in J. P. Davis, ed., *The American Negro Reference Book* (Prentice-Hall, 1970), p. 562.

42. Sowell, "Black Excellence," p. 3.
43. G. Franklin Edwards, *The Negro Professional Class* (The Free Press, 1959), p. 71.
44. Ibid., p. 78.
45. Kent G. Mommsen, "Career Patterns of Black American Doctorates," Ph.D. thesis, Florida State University, 1970, p. 13.
46. Berlin, *Slaves without Masters*, pp. 385, 390.
47. A telling sketch of the group can be found in Elliot M. Rudwick, *W.E.B. DuBois: Propagandist of the Negro Protest* (Atheneum, 1969), p. 118.
48. G. Franklin Edwards, ed., *E. Franklin Frazier on Race Relations* (University of Chicago Press, 1968), pp. 24-25.
49. Frazier, *Black Bourgeoisie*, pp. 98-100.
50. Edward Byron Reuter, *The Mulatto in the United States* (Richard G. Badger, 1918), chaps. 8-11.
51. Ibid., pp. 11, 244n.
52. Ibid., pp. 194, 266, 270.
53. See photographs of Bethune, Miller, and Woodson in Carter G. Woodson and Charles H. Wesley, *The Negro in Our History*, 11th ed. (The Associated Publishers), pp. 432, 543, 545, 625, 725.
54. Myrdal, *An American Dilemma*, vol. 1, pp. 132-33.
55. Reuter, *The Mulatto in the United States*, chaps. 8-11, passim, especially pp. 213, 243-44, 291-92, 314.
56. Berlin, *Slaves without Masters*, pp. 223-28.
57. Frazier, *The Negro in the United States*, p. 60; Phillips, *American Negro Slavery*, p. 436.
58. Phillips, *Life and Labor in the Old South*, p. 205; Edwards, ed., *E. Franklin Frazier on Race Relations*, p. 92; James H. Brewer, "Negro Property Owners in Seventeenth Century Virginia," *William and Mary Quarterly*, October 1955, pp. 579-80; Berlin, *Slaves without Masters*, p. 222.
59. Berlin, *Slaves without Masters*, pp. 217-18; Eugene D. Genovese, "The Slave States of North America" in Cohen and Greene, eds., *Neither Slave nor Free*, p. 267.
60. Sowell, *Race and Economics*, pp. 39-40.
61. Foner, "The Free People of Color in Louisiana and St. Domingue," p. 407; Frazier, *Black Bourgeoisie*, p. 33; James E. Winston, "The Free Negro in New Orleans, 1803-1860," *Louisiana Historical Quarterly*, October 1938, pp. 1080-82, 1084-85; Sowell, *Race and Economics*, pp. 40-41.
62. E. Horace Fitchett, "The Origin and Growth of the Free Negro Population of Charleston, South Carolina," *Journal of Negro History*, October 1941, pp. 421-37; C. W. Birnie, "Education of the Negro in Charleston, South Carolina, prior to the Civil War," *Journal of Negro Education*, January 1927, pp. 13-21; Frazier, *The Negro in the United States*, pp. 76-79; Genovese, "The Slave States of North America," pp. 267, 271.
63. Genovese, "The Slave States of North America," p. 270.
64. Sowell, *Race and Economics*, pp. 28, 31.
65. Klein, "The Colored Freedman in Brazilian Society," pp. 45-47; Bowser, "Colonial Spanish America," p. 50; Russell-Wood, "Colonial Brazil," pp. 88, 129; Herbert S. Klein, "Nineteenth Century Brazil," pp. 325, 328.

66. Berlin, *Slaves without Masters*, pp. 118-19; Alice Dunbar-Nelson, "People of Color in Louisiana, Part I," *Journal of Negro History*, October 1916, p. 366n; Carter G. Woodson, *The Education of the Negro prior to 1861* (The Associated Publishers, Inc., 1919), p. 166. See also James E. Winston, "The Free Negro in New Orleans, 1803-1860," *Louisiana Historical Quarterly*, October 1938, p. 1076; Thomas, "The Free Negro in Florida Before 1865," p. 342.

67. Foner, "The Free People of Color in Louisiana and St. Domingue," pp. 407-8, 413-14, 416-17, 425; Winston. "The Free Negro in New Orleans, 1803-1860," p. 1085; Frazier, *Black Bourgeoisie*, p. 33; Berlin, *Slaves without Masters*, p. 131.

68. Berlin, *Slaves without Masters*, p. 214; Genovese, "The Slave States of North America," pp. 269n, 271n.

69. Foner, "The Free People of Color in Louisiana and St. Domingue," pp. 407, 425.

70. Ibid., p. 416.

71. Winston, "The Free Negro in New Orleans, 1803-1860," p. 1079.

72. Dunbar-Nelson, "People of Color in Louisiana, Part I," pp. 371-74; Dunbar-Nelson, "People of Color in Louisiana, Part II," *Journal of Negro History*, January 1917, pp. 58-59; Foner, "The Free People of Color in Louisiana and St. Domingue," pp. 415-16.

73. Russell-Wood, "Colonial Brazil," pp. 118, 121; Elisabeth, "The French Antilles," p. 136; Hall, "Saint Domingue," pp. 173, 174; Hall, "Jamaica," p. 206; Handler and Sio, "Barbados," p. 234n; Klein, "The Colored Freedman in Brazilian Slave Society," pp. 32-33.

74. Berlin, *Slaves without Masters*, p. 19; Foner, "The Free People of Color in Louisiana and St. Domingue," p. 421; John Hope Franklin, *From Slavery to Freedom* (New York: Vintage Books, 1969), p. 220.

75. Cohen and Greene, eds., *Neither Slave nor Free*, pp. 7, 12; Bowser, "Colonial Spanish America," p. 55; Hoetink, "Surinam and Curaçao," pp. 63, 68; Russell-Wood, "Colonial Brazil," pp. 84-85, 117; Hall, "Jamaica," pp. 195-96; Knight, "Cuba," p. 283.

76. Berlin, *Slaves without Masters*, p. 214; Frazier, *Black Bourgeoisie*, p. 117; Frazier, *The Negro in the United States*, pp. 70n, 77; Fitchett, "The Origin and Growth of the Free Negro Population in Charleston, South Carolina," p. 434.

77. Frazier, *Black Bourgeoisie*, p. 33; Genovese, "The Slave States in North America," p. 269.

78. Compare the situation described in Berlin, *Slaves without Masters*, p. 214, with that described in Cohen and Greene, "Introduction," *Neither Slave nor Free*, pp. 11-16.

79. Sowell, *Race and Economics*, p. 39; Franklin, *From Slavery to Freedom*, p. 234; Woodson, *A Century of Negro Migration*, chap. 3.

80. Leon Litwack, *North of Slavery* (University of Chicago Press, 1961); Woodson, *A Century of Negro Migration*, chap. 3.

81. Berlin, *Slaves without Masters*, pp. 4-5.

82. Ibid., p. 10.

83. Fogel and Engerman, *Time on the Cross*, p. 25.

84. Frazier, *The Negro in the United States*, pp. 48-49.

85. Bureau of the Census, *Historical Statistics of the United States* (Government Printing Office, 1960), p. 9.

86. Berlin, *Slaves without Masters*, pp. 92-187; Phillips, *American Negro Slavery*, pp. 448-49; Stampp, *The Peculiar Institution*, pp. 215-16.

87. G. James Fleming, "The Negro in American Politics: The Past," in J. P. Davis, ed., *The American Negro Reference Book*, pp. 416-18; John Hope Franklin, *The Free Negro in North Carolina* (W. W. Norton Co., 1971), chap. 3; John H. Russell, *The Free Negro in Virginia, 1619-1865* (Dover Publications, 1969), chap. 4.

88. Franklin, *The Free Negro in North Carolina*, p. 81.

89. Berlin, *Slaves without Masters*, pp. 95-96; Franklin, *The Free Negro in North Carolina*, p. 60; Russell, *The Free Negro in Virginia, 1619-1865*, p. 167; Phillips, *American Negro Slavery*, p. 133; Woodson, *The Education of the Negro prior to 1861*, pp. 155-58.

90. Phillips, *American Negro Slavery*, p. 453; Berlin, *Slaves without Masters*, pp. 316, 348; Genovese, "The Slave States of North America," pp. 264, 273, 276 (see also p. 184).

91. Stampp, *The Peculiar Institution*, p. 232; Berlin, *Slaves without Masters*, p. 138.

92. Frazier, *The Negro in the United States*, p. 61; Stampp, *The Peculiar Institution*, p. 216.

93. Franklin, *From Slavery to Freedom*, p. 218; Berlin, *Slaves without Masters*, pp. 215-16.

94. Sowell, *Race and Economics*, p. 22.

95. Phillips, *American Negro Slavery*, p. 497.

96. Clement Eaton, *The Freedom of Thought Struggle in the Old South* (Harper and Row, 1964), p. 126.

97. Frazier, *The Negro in the United States*, pp. 66-67.

98. Ibid., p. 63.

99. Ibid., p. 65.

100. Ibid., p. 66.

101. Woodson, *The Education of the Negro prior to 1861*, p. 157.

102. Ibid., pp. 157, 162.

103. Ibid., p. 161.

104. Genovese, "The Slave States of North America," p. 263; Berlin, *Slaves without Masters*, pp. 305-6.

105. Wade, *Slavery in the Cities*, p. 177.

106. Frazier, *The Negro in the United States*, p. 73. See also Wade, *Slavery in the Cities*, pp. 175-77; Woodson, *The Education of the Negro prior to 1861*, pp. 128-29.

107. Woodson, *The Education of the Negro prior to 1861*, pp. 167-68, 169.

108. Ibid., pp. 130-38, 169.

109. Ibid., p. 205.

110. Ibid., pp. 171-76, 243.

111. Berlin, *Slaves without Masters*, pp. 305-6; Sowell, *Race and Economics*, p. 39.

112. Frazier, *The Negro in the United States*, p. 73.

113. Ibid., p. 74.

114. *Loc. cit.*

115. Ibid.
116. Ibid.
117. Woodson, *The Education of the Negro prior to 1861*, p. 206.
118. One of which had operated for thirty years was later accidentally discovered by the Union Army during Sherman's march through Georgia. Ibid., p. 217.
119. Ibid., p. 215.
120. Frazier, *The Negro in the United States*, p. 74.
121. Franklin, *The Free Negro in North Carolina*, p. 169.
122. Frederick Law Olmsted, *A Journey in the Seaboard Slave States* (New American Library, 1969), p. 367; Washington, *The Story of the Negro*, vol. 1, p. 201.
123. Russell, *The Free Negro in Virginia*, p. 145.
124. Bond, "The Negro Scholar and Professional in America," p. 551.
125. Computed from *The Seventh Census of the United States: 1850* (Robert Armstrong, public printer, 1853), pp. xliii, lxi.
126. Washington, *The Story of the Negro*, vol. 2, p. 114.
127. Woodson, *The Education of the Negro prior to 1861*, p. 228.
128. Bond, "The Negro Scholar and Professional in America."
129. Berlin, *Slaves without Masters*, p. 45; Bond, "The Negro Scholar and Professional in America," p. 559.
130. Benjamin Brawley, *Social History of the American Negro* (Collier, Macmillan, 1970), p. 243. See also Litwack, *North of Slavery*, pp. 17-18.
131. Frazier, *The Negro in the United States*, p. 368.
132. Ibid., p. 369.
133. Ibid., p. 370.
134. Frazier, *Black Bourgeoisie*, pp. 41, 52.
135. Woodson, *The Education of the Negro prior to 1861*, chap. 13.
136. Ibid., pp. 4, 11, 43-48, 100, 111-12, 183, 243.
137. Ibid., pp. 11, 108, 138, 183; Joseph Butsch, "Catholics and the Negro," *Journal of Negro History*, October 1917, p. 404.
138. Genovese, "Slave States of North America," p. 263; Berlin, *Slaves without Masters*, p. 306.
139. Woodson, *The Education of the Negro prior to 1861*, chap. 6.
140. Bond, "The Negro Scholar and Professional in America," p. 562.
141. Frazier, *The Negro in the United States*, p. 74.
142. Sowell, "Black Excellence," pp. 6-7, 10, 11, 12.
143. Lorenzo J. Greene and Carter G. Woodson, *The Negro Wage Earner* (A.M.S. Press, 1970), pp. 3, 4. See also Hershberg, "Free Blacks in Antebellum Philadelphia," pp. 191, 198-99; Frazier, *The Negro Family in the United States*, p. 149; Ray Marshall, *The Negro Worker* (Random House, 1967), p. 9; Robert Ernst, "The Economic Status of New York City Negroes, 1850-1863," in August Meier and Elliott Rudwick, eds., *The Making of Black America* (Atheneum, 1969), vol. 1, p. 254.
144. Foner, "The Free People of Color in Louisiana and St. Domingue," pp. 407, 425, 427; James E. Winston, "Free Negro in New Orleans, 1803-1860," *Louisiana Historical Quarterly*, October 1938, p. 1084; Phillips, *American Negro Slavery*, p. 439.
145. Phillips, *American Negro Slavery*, p. 403.
146. *Loc. cit.*

147. Ralph B. Flanders, "The Free Negro in Ante-Bellum Georgia," *North Carolina Historical Review*, July 1932, pp. 266-67.

148. Franklin, *The Free Negro in North Carolina*, pp. 139-43.

149. Russell, *The Free Negro in Virginia, 1619-1865*, pp. 147, 151.

150. Greene and Woodson, *The Negro Wage Earner*, pp. 4, 7; Phillips, *American Negro Slavery*, pp. 440-41; Frazier, *The Negro in the United States*, p. 70; Reynolds Farley, "The Urbanization of Negroes in the United States," *Journal of Social History*, Spring 1968, p. 246.

151. Marshall, *The Negro Worker*, p. 8.

152. Greene and Woodson, *The Negro Wage Earner*, p. 8.

153. Ibid., pp. 15-17; Russell, *The Free Negro in Virginia, 1619-1865*, p. 147; Franklin, *The Free Negro in North Carolina*, pp. 136-39; Genovese, "Slave States of North America," p. 264.

154. Franklin, *The Free Negro in North Carolina*, p. 136; Greene and Woodson, *The Negro Wage Earner*, p. 16; Franklin, *From Slavery to Freedom*, p. 22.

155. Frazier, *The Negro in the United States*, p. 71.

156. Cf. Frederick Law Olmsted, *The Cotton Kingdom* (Modern Library, 1969), pp. 29, 38, 43, 44, 126, 152, 158, 168, 177, 186, 212, 214, 220, 232, 258-59, 294, 307, 317-18, 330, 374, 423, 425, 427.

157. Greene and Woodson, *The Negro Wage Earner*, p. 17.

158. Hershberg, "Free Blacks in Antebellum Philadelphia," pp. 191-92; Reynolds Farley, "The Urbanization of Negroes in the United States," *Journal of Social History*, Spring 1968, p. 248; Genovese, "Slave States of North America," pp. 264, 266.

159. Woodson and Wesley, *The Negro in Our History*, p. 329; Green, *The Secret City*, pp. 49, 93, 128, 134; Greene and Woodson, *The Negro Wage Earner*, p. 23; Frazier, *Black Bourgeoisie*, p. 13; Carl Wittke, *The Irish in America* (Russell and Russell, 1970), pp. 125-32, 168-69; St. Clair Drake and Horace B. Cayton, *Black Metropolis*, vol. 1, pp. 44, 62, 66, 110n; Gilbert Osofsky, *Harlem: The Making of a Ghetto* (Harper and Row, 1968), pp. 45-46, 48, Litwack, *North of Slavery*, pp. 162, 166; Williston H. Lofton, "Northern Labor and the Negro During the Civil War," *Journal of Negro History*, July 1949, pp. 256-61, 262, 268-70.

160. Stephan Thernstrom, *The Other Bostonians* (Harvard University Press, 1974), p. 186.

161. Foner, "The Free People of Color in Louisiana and St. Domingue," p. 427.

162. Ernst, "The Economic Status of New York City Negroes, 1850-1863," pp. 257-58.

163. Ibid., p. 255; Litwack, *North of Slavery*, p. 163.

164. Herbert G. Gutman, "Le phénomène invisible: la composition de la famille et du foyers noirs après La Guerre de Secession," *Annales-Economies, Sociétés, Civilisation*, Juillet-Octobre 1972, p. 1215; Woodson, *The Education of the Negro prior to 1861*, p. 388; Hershberg, "Free Blacks in Antebellum Philadelphia," pp. 191-92; Farley, "The Urbanization of Negroes in the United States," p. 248.

165. Franklin, *From Slavery to Freedom*, pp. 217-21; Clement Eaton, *The Growth of Southern Civilization* (Harper and Row, 1961), pp. 93-94.

166. John Hope Franklin, "A Brief History of the Negro in the United States," in J. P. Davis, ed., *The American Negro Reference Book*, p. 34; Berlin, *Slaves without Masters*, pp. 190-91.

167. Franklin, *From Slavery to Freedom*, p. 218.

168. *Loc. cit.*

169. *Loc. cit.;* Berlin, *Slaves without Masters*, p. 319.

170. Woodson, *The Education of the Negro prior to 1861*, chap. 7.

171. Franklin, *From Slavery to Freedom*, p. 220.

172. Ibid., p. 219-20.

173. Ibid., p. 218.

174. *Loc. cit.*

175. Berlin, *Slaves without Masters*, pp. 317-18, 320, 334.

176. *Loc. cit.*

177. Frazier, *The Negro in the United States*, p. 70.

178. Berlin, *Slaves without Masters*, pp. 244-45.

179. *Loc. cit.*

180. Ibid.

181. Frazier, *Black Bourgeoisie*, p. 35.

182. Franklin, *From Slavery to Freedom*, p. 221; James H. Brewer, "Negro Property Owners in Seventeenth Century Virginia," *William and Mary Quarterly*, October 1955, p. 576; C. S. Sydnor, "The Free Negro in Mississippi Before the Civil War," *American Historical Review*, July 1927, p. 773; Foner, "The Free People of Color in Louisiana and St. Domingue," pp. 416-17, 428; Franklin, *The Free Negro in North Carolina*, pp. 150, 152, 224; Russell, *The Free Negro in Virginia*, pp. 88-89, 90, 163; J. Merton England, "The Free Negro in Ante-Bellum Tennessee," *Journal of Southern History*, February 1943, p. 51.

183. Gutman, "Le phénomène invisible," p. 1207. The supposedly "classic" grandmother-headed family was found empirically in only 6 percent of black families. Ibid., pp. 12, 13.

184. See, for example, Myrdal, *An American Dilemma*, pp. 930-31; Frazier, *The Negro Family in the United States*, chap. 2; [D. P. Moynihan,] *The Negro Family* (U.S. Department of Labor, 1965), pp. 15-17; W. E. B. DuBois, *The Negro American Family* (New American Library, 1969), pp. 21, 37, 41, 49. But compare Fogel and Engerman, *Time on the Cross*, pp. 84-85.

185. Hershberg, "Free Blacks in Antebellum Philadelphia," p. 194.

186. Edward C. Banfield, *The Unheavenly City* (Little, Brown and Co., 1970), p. 72.

187. Sowell, *Race and Economics*, p. 111.

188. Hershberg, "Free Blacks in Antebellum Philadelphia," p. 190.

189. *Loc. cit.*

190. Frazier, *The Negro in the United States*, p. 281.

191. Genovese, "Slave States of North America," pp. 267, 271n.

192. Hershberg, "Free Blacks in Antebellum Philadelphia," p. 187.

193. Berlin, *Slaves without Masters*, pp. 245-46.

194. Bureau of the Census, "Negro Population: March 1966," *Current Population Reports*, Series P-20, no. 168 (Government Printing Office), p. 5.

195. Bond, "The Negro Scholar and Professional in America," p. 562; Mommsen, "Career Patterns of Black American Doctorates," pp. 13-14.

196. Horace Mann Bond, *A Study of Factors Involved in the Identification and Encouragement of Unusual Academic Talent among Underprivileged Populations* (U.S. Department of Health, Education, and Welfare, January 1967, p. 147. [Contract No. SAE 8028, Project No. 5-0859]

197. See Westerman, *Slave Systems of Greek and Roman Antiquity.*

198. See Herbert S. Klein, *Slavery in the Americas* (University of Chicago Press, 1967); Elkins, *Slavery.*

199. Fogel and Engerman, *Time on the Cross*, pp. 29-30.

200. Frank Tannenbaum, *Slave and Citizen* (Alfred A. Knopf, 1947), p. 106.

201. Eaton, *The Freedom of Thought Struggle in the Old South.*

202. Ibid., p. 33; Phillips, *Life and Labor in the Old South*, pp. 9, 10, 11. See also Woodson, *A Century of Negro Migration*, pp. 31-33, for a discussion of the Appalachian region.

203. Eaton, *The Freedom of Thought Struggle in the Old South*, p. 46.

204. Ibid., pp. 166, 178, 180, 182-83, 190.

205. Franklin, *From Slavery to Freedom*, p. 439.

206. Frazier, *The Negro in the United States*, p. 155.

207. Ibid., p. 427.

208. Phillips, *The Slave Economy of the Old South*, p. 269.

209. Franklin, *From Slavery to Freedom*, chap. 15.

210. David Brion Davis, "Slavery and the Post-World War II Historians," *Daedalus* (Spring 1974), pp. 1-16.

211. The prime example being Fogel and Engerman, *Time on the Cross.*

212. Ibid., p. 18.

213. Ibid., p. 28.

214. *Loc. cit.*

215. Ibid., p. 18.

216. Ibid., pp. 21-22.

217. Ibid., p. 25.

218. Ibid., pp. 23-24. Even among imported slaves, many came from the West Indies rather than directly from Africa.

219. Elkins, *Slavery*, pp. 51n, 78; Phillips, *American Negro Slavery*, p. 52; Lewis C. Gray, *History of Agriculture in the Southern United States*, vol. 2, p. 519.

220. Frazier, *The Negro in the United States*, pp. 4-7.

221. Ibid., pp. 10, 19-21.

222. Woodson, *The Education of the Negro prior to 1861*, pp. 227-28.

223. See, for example, Hebron, "Simon Gray, Riverman," pp. 474-84.

224. Fogel and Engerman, *Time on the Cross*, p. 56.

225. Sowell, *Race and Economics*, pp. 12-13.

226. Wade, *Slavery in the Cities*, chap. 6.

227. Sowell, *Race and Economics*, pp. 26-28.

228. Fogel and Engerman, *Time on the Cross*, p. 261.

229. Thomas Sowell, *Classical Economics Reconsidered* (Princeton University Press, 1974), pp. 11, 12-14; Harold B. Woodman, "The Profitability of Slavery: A Historical Perennial," *Journal of Southern History*, August 1963, pp. 303-325.

230. Alfred H. Conrad and John R. Meyer, "The Economics of Slavery in the Antebellum South," *Journal of Political Economy*, April 1958, pp.

95-130; Fogel and Engerman, *Time on the Cross*, pp. 59-106, 174, 184-90.

231. Eaton, *The Freedom of Thought Struggle in the Old South*.

232. Ibid., pp. 127, 212.

233. Ibid., pp. 220, 222, 228-29.

234. William H. Nicholls, *Southern Tradition and Regional Progress* (University of North Carolina Press, 1960); Phillips, *The Slave Economy of the Old South*, p. 290.

235. As one index of this, the highest ranked universities in the South are in environments of this sort: Duke, University of North Carolina, University of Virginia, Tulane, and Vanderbilt. The first two are in a state in which plantation slavery was not the dominant pattern. The University of Virginia is in the southwestern part of its state, while slavery was concentrated in the northeastern part of the state. Tulane is located in New Orleans—easily the most liberal antebellum southern city, and very different from northern Louisiana, which is part of the black belt. Vanderbilt is located in a state that had fewer slaves than most and was a center of antislavery activity. By contrast, no such institutions arose in the vast "black belt" stretching across several states of the Deep South.

236. Fogel and Engerman, *Time on the Cross*, p. 112.

237. Ibid., pp. 114, 115.

238. Ibid., p. 125.

239. Ibid., p. 124.

240. Ibid., p. 25.

241. Olmsted, *The Cotton Kingdom*, p. 215; Phillips, *American Negro Slavery*, pp. 301-2; Phillips, *Life and Labor in the Old South*, p. 186; Phillips, *The Slave Economy of the Old South*, pp. 130-31; Gray, *History of Agriculture in the Southern United States*, vol. 2, p. 520; J. C. Furnas, *The Americans* (G. P. Putnam and Sons, 1969), p. 394.

242. Olmsted, *The Cotton Kingdom*, p. 215.

243. Fogel and Engerman, *Time on the Cross*, p. 139.

244. Ibid., pp. 141-42.

245. Stampp, *The Peculiar Institution*, p. 198.

246. Fogel and Engerman, *Time on the Cross*, p. 128.

247. Ibid., p. 137.

248. Ibid., p. 133.

249. Wade, *Slavery in the Cities*, p. 124.

250. Fogel and Engerman, *Time on the Cross*, pp. 38, 95.

251. Ibid., p. 48.

252. Banfield, *The Unheavenly City*, p. 72.

253. Franklin, *From Slavery to Freedom*, pp. 306-7.

254. Cohen and Greene, eds., *Neither Slave nor Free*, p. 8; Bowser, "Colonial Spanish America," pp. 23-24, 25-26.

255. Philip Curtin, *Two Jamaicas* (Atheneum, 1970), p. 61.

256. Cohen and Greene, eds., *Neither Slave nor Free*, pp. 3-5.

257. Sowell, *Race and Economics*, pp. 27-28.

258. Frazier, *The Negro in the United States*, pp. 109-111.

259. Greene and Woodson, *The Negro Wage Earner*, p. 24.

260. Loretta Funke, "The Negro in Education," *Journal of Negro History*, January 1920, p. 5; Virgil A. Clift, "Educating the American Negro," in Davis, ed., *The American Negro Reference Book*, p. 367.

261. Gilbert Osofsky, *Harlem: The Making of the Ghetto* (Harper and Row, 1966), pp. 43-44; Allan H. Spear, *Black Chicago* (University of Chicago Press, 1967), pp. 168-69; Frazier, *The Negro in the United States*, p. 270.

262. Osofsky, *Harlem: The Making of a Ghetto*, pp. 40-41, 45-52, 105-110.

263. Frazier, *The Negro in the United States*, chap. 10; Franklin, *From Slavery to Freedom*, pp. 310-11.

264. Marshall, *The Negro Worker*, p. 10; Greene and Woodson, *The Negro Wage Earner*, p. 13; Sterling D. Spero and Abram L. Harris, *The Black Worker* (Atheneum, 1972), chap. 13.

265. Greene and Woodson, *The Negro Wage Earner*, pp. 33, 34, 316.

266. C. Vann Woodward, *The Strange Career of Jim Crow*, 2d ed. (Oxford University Press, 1966), pp. 53-59.

267. Ibid., pp. 33, 53-59.

268. Ibid., pp. 67-69.

269. Frazier, *The Negro in the United States*, pp. 425-27.

270. Myrdal, *An American Dilemma*, pp. 334-37.

271. Constance Baker Motley, "The Legal Status of the Negro in the United States," in Davis, ed., *American Negro Reference Book*, p. 516.

272. Myrdal, *An American Dilemma*, p. 229.

273. Richard Hofstadter, *Social Darwinism in American Thought* (Beacon Press, 1955), chaps. 8, 9.

274. Leon Kamin, *The Science and Politics of I.Q.* (Lawrence Erlbaum Associates, 1974).

275. Michael R. Winston, "Through the Back Door: Academic Racism and the Negro Scholar in Historical Perspective," *Daedalus*, Summer 1971, pp. 684-85; C. Vann Woodward, "Introduction," in Phillips, *Life and Labor in the Old South*, pp. iii-vi; Sterling A. Brown, "Unhistoric History," *Journal of Negro History*, April 1930, pp. 134-51.

276. Winston, "Through the Back Door," pp. 684-87, 688.

277. Booker T. Washington, *The Future of the American Negro*, p. 180.

278. Louis R. Harlan, *Booker T. Washington* (Oxford University Press, 1972), p. 212.

279. Louis R. Harlan, "The Secret Life of Booker T. Washington," *Journal of Southern History*, August 1971, pp. 396-98, 399, 400, 401, 402.

280. Harlan, *Booker T. Washington*, pp. 272-75.

281. Ibid., chaps. 13, 15.

282. Ibid., pp. 320-21.

283. August Meier, "Toward a Reinterpretation of Booker T. Washington," in Meier and Rudwick, eds., *The Making of Black America*, vol. 2, pp. 126-27, 130; Harlan, "The Secret Life of Booker T. Washington," pp. 396-98, 399, 400, 401, 402.

284. Harlan, *Booker T. Washington*, chap. 15.

285. Elliott M. Rudwick, *W. E. B. DuBois* (Atheneum, 1969), pp. 15-17.

286. Rayford W. Logan, ed., *W. E. B. DuBois* (Hill and Wang, 1971), p. xix.

287. Harlan, *Booker T. Washington*, p. 266.

288. Ibid., p. 303; Louis R. Harlan, "Booker T. Washington in Biographical Perspective," *American Historical Review*, October 1970, p. 1586;

Harlan, "The Secret Life of Booker T. Washington," pp. 407-9.

289. Thomas Sowell, "The Plight of Black Students in the United States," *Daedalus*, Spring 1974, p. 189.

290. Oscar Handlin, *The Newcomers* (Anchor Books, 1962), p. 47.

291. *Loc. cit.*

292. Jacob Riis, *How the Other Half Lives* (Harvard University Press, 1970), p. 99.

293. Frazier, *The Negro in the United States*, p. 71.

294. W. E. B. DuBois, *The Philadelphia Negro* (Schocken Books, 1967), pp. 33-36, 119-21.

295. Frazier, *The Negro in the United States*, p. 405.

296. St. Clair Drake and Horace B. Cayton, *Black Metropolis*, vol. 1, p. 176n. See also Spear, *Black Chicago*, chap. 1.

297. Gutman, "Le phénomène invisible," pp. 1197-1218.

298. Osofsky, *Harlem: The Making of a Ghetto*, p. 8.

299. Ibid., p. 18.

300. Ibid., pp. 36-37.

301. Ibid., pp. 40-42.

302. Frazier, *The Negro in the United States*, pp. 253-56, passim; Drake and Cayton, *Black Metropolis*, vol. 1, pp. 66-67, 73-75, 176-77.

303. Osofsky, *Harlem: The Making of a Ghetto*, p. 44; Ivan H. Light, *Ethnic Enterprise in America* (University of California Press, 1972), figure 1 (after p. 100).

304. Farley, "The Urbanization of Negroes in the United States," p. 251.

305. Drake and Cayton, *Black Metropolis*, vol. 1, p. 64.

306. Brawley, *Social History of the American Negro*, pp. 347-49.

307. Franklin, *From Slavery to Freedom*, pp. 474-75.

308. Myrdal, *An American Dilemma*, p. 327.

309. *Loc. cit.*

310. Sowell, *Race and Economics*, p. 183.

311. Ibid., p. 50.

312. *Loc. cit.*

313. John K. Folger and Charles B. Nam, *Education of the American Population*, U.S. Bureau of the Census (Government Printing Office, 1967), p. 114.

314. C. S. Johnson, *The Negro College Graduate* (University of North Carolina Press, 1938), p. 8.

315. Greene and Woodson, *The Negro Wage Earner*, chaps. 1 and 2.

316. Brawley, *Social History of the American Negro*, p. 342.

317. Myrdal, *An American Dilemma*, vol. 2, p. 754.

318. Thernstrom, *The Other Bostonians*, p. 198.

319. Ben J. Wattenberg, *The Real America* (Doubleday and Co., 1974), p. 125.

320. Ibid., p. 132.

321. Ibid., p. 133.

322. Ibid., pp. 129-31.

323. Ibid., p. 125.

324. Ibid., p. 126.

325. Ibid., p. 138.

326. Daniel Patrick Moynihan, "The Schism in Black America," *The Public Interest*, Spring 1972, pp. 3-24.

327. Wattenberg, *The Real America*, p. 128.

328. *Loc. cit.*

329. Frazier, *The Negro in the United States*, chaps. 22-26; U.S. Department of Labor, *The Negro Family: The Case for National Action* ("Moynihan Report"), March 1965.

330. Sowell, *Race and Economics*, pp. 61-63.

331. "Demographic Aspects of the Black Community," *Milbank Memorial Fund Quarterly*, vol. 48, no. 2 (April 1970), part 2, p. 89; Thernstrom, *The Other Bostonians*, pp. 208-210.

332. Wattenberg, *The Real America*, p. 138.

333. Ibid., p. 142.

334. Sowell, *Race and Economics*, p. 129.

335. Arthur R. Jensen, "How Much Can We Boost IQ and Scholastic Achievement?" *Harvard Educational Review*, Winter 1969, pp. 1-123; Richard Herrnstein, "IQ," *The Atlantic*, September 1971, pp. 43-64.

336. Audrey M. Shuey, *The Testing of Negro Intelligence* (Social Science Press, 1966), pp. 493-99, passim.

337. Rudolf Pintner, *Intelligence Testing* (Henry Holt and Co., 1923), pp. 352-53, 354.

338. Mandel Sherman and Cora B. Key, "The Intelligence of Isolated Mountain Children," *Child Development*, vol. 8, no. 4 (1932), p. 283; Lester R. Wheeler, "A Comparative Study of the Intelligence of East Tennessee Mountain Children," *Journal of Educational Psychology*, vol. 33, no. 5 (May 1942), pp. 322, 328.

339. Philip E. Vernon, *Intelligence and Cultural Environment* (Methuen and Co., 1970), p. 155.

340. Shuey, *The Testing of Negro Intelligence*, pp. 489-90.

341. Ibid., chap. 10.

342. John C. Loehlin, Gardner Lindzey, and J. N. Spuhler, *Race Differences in Intelligence* (W. H. Freeman and Co., 1975), pp. 154-55.

343. Thomas Sowell, *Black Education: Myths and Tragedies* (David McKay Co., 1972), pp. 286-87.

344. See Arthur R. Jensen, "The Race X Sex X Ability Interaction," in Robert Cancro, ed., *Intelligence: Genetic and Environmental Factors* (Grune and Stratton, Inc., 1971), pp. 116-18.

345. Fogel and Engerman, *Time on the Cross*, pp. 109-115.

346. Frazier, *The Negro in the United States*, p. 168.

347. Ibid., p. 567.

348. Farley, "The Urbanization of the Negro in the United States," pp. 241-58.

349. Philips, *American Negro Slavery*, pp. 457-59.

350. Ibid., p. 453; Genovese, "The Slave States of North America," pp. 273, 276. Some of the same considerations applied in Latin America. Hall, "Saint Domingue," p. 184.

351. Ralph B. Flanders, "The Free Negro in Antebellum Georgia," *North Carolina Historical Review*, July 1932, p. 265.

352. U.S. Bureau of the Census, *Statistical Abstract of the United States: 1976* (Government Printing Office, 1976), p. 158.

353. Ira De A. Reid, *The Negro Immigrant* (Columbia University Press, 1939), pp. 121, 220, 221n.

354. David Lowenthal, "Race and Color in the West Indies," *Daedalus*, Spring 1967, p. 611; Reid, *The Negro Immigrant*, pp. 226-27; Light, *Ethnic Enterprise in America*, pp. 33-35; Nathan Glazer and Daniel Patrick Moynihan, *Beyond the Melting Pot* (MIT Press, 1963), p. 35.

355. Reid, *The Negro Immigrant*, pp. 138-40, 141-42.

356. Ibid., p. 229.

357. Johnson, *The Negro College Graduate*, pp. 71, 73.

358. E. S. Maynard, "Endogamy among Barbadian Immigrants to New York City," Ph.D. thesis, New York University, 1972, pp. 57, 95.

359. John J. Spurling, "Social Relationships between the American Negro and West Indian Negroes in a Long Island Community," Ph.D. thesis, New York University, 1962, p. 44.

360. Most foreign-born Negroes in the United States live in and around New York City, and seventy-three percent of foreign-born Negroes are from the West Indies. Reid, *The Negro Immigrant*, pp. 44, 85.

361. The attitudes and performances of West Indians in school are a different matter. These have long been observed to be better than the attitudes and performances of American Negroes. Ira Reid, *The Negro Immigrant*, pp. 222-23, 226-27.

362. "The second generation of Negro Immigrants . . . have lost most of the social characteristics of their parents. . . ." Reid, *The Negro Immigrant*, p. 144.

363. For example, Reuter, *The Mulatto in the United States*.

364. Lowenthal, "Race and Color in the West Indies," p. 600; Reid, *The Negro Immigrant*, p. 228.

365. Lowenthal, "Race and Color in the West Indies," p. 592.

366. Ibid., p. 587.

367. Compare Phillips, *American Negro Slavery*, p. 62; Fogel and Engerman, *Time on the Cross*, pp. 29, 123.

368. Phillip Curtin, *Two Jamaicas*, p. 18; Douglas Hall, "Jamaica," in D. W. Cohen and J. P. Greene, eds., *Neither Slave nor Free*, pp. 208-9; Eric Williams, *The Negro in the Caribbean* (Negro Universities Press, 1971), p. 57.

369. Hall, "Jamaica," pp. 208-9.

370. Curtin, *Two Jamaicas*, pp. 14, 15.

371. Ibid., p. 464.

372. Franklin, *From Slavery to Freedom*, p. 67; Curtin, *Two Jamaicas*, pp. 10, 81-98.

373. Curtin, *Two Jamaicas*, p. 19.

374. Ibid., pp. 107-9.

375. Ibid., p. 127.

376. Osofsky, *Harlem: The Making of a Ghetto*, p. 131.

377. Ibid., pp. 134-35; Reid, *The Negro Immigrant*, pp. 25-26, 109, 114-15, 150-51, 152, 159, 168-69, 194, 223.

378. Osofsky, *Harlem: The Making of a Ghetto*, pp. 134-35; Harold Cruse, *The Crisis of the Negro Intellectual* (William Morrow, 1967), pp. 44-47.

379. Light, *Ethnic Enterprise in America*, pp. 33-35; Glazer and Moynihan, *Beyond the Melting Pot*, p. 35; Osofsky, *Harlem: The Making of a Ghetto*, p. 133; Claude McKay, *Harlem: Negro Metropolis* (Harcourt, Brace, Jovanovich, Inc., 1968), p. 93.

380. Curtin, *Two Jamaicas*, p. 46.

381. Reid, *The Negro Immigrant*, pp. 160-64.

382. Ibid., pp. 109-110.

Chinese Americans and Japanese Americans

Neither their numbers nor their nationwide significance would warrant a discussion of Chinese and Japanese in any but the most exhaustive review of American minorities. Their importance lies rather in their characteristics, which in a number of ways challenge generalizations based on more numerous nationalities. As Asian immigrants to a population predominantly of European origin, they were set apart by their religious beliefs, cultural attributes, and social organizations—as well as their race, under which all other attributes were often subsumed. These manifold differences tested America's open immigration policy and eventually broke it asunder. Not only were the Chinese the first immigrant group to be specifically excluded, but from this precedent there developed the criterion that all aspirant immigrants should be judged mainly by their place of origin.[1]

The gross discrimination, the collective frustrations, to which Chinese and Japanese have been subjected ordinarily result in a pattern of poor education, low income, high crime rate, and unstable family life, with each of these reinforcing all the other components of a self-sustaining slum. Efforts to assist members of such "problem minorities" in achieving parity with the general population have seldom been altogether successful. However, these two minorities, as we shall note in some detail, themselves

65

broke through the barriers of prejudice and, by such key indices as education and income, surpassed the average levels of native-born whites. This anomalous record, like the earlier one of Jews, challenges the premises from which the etiologies of poverty, crime, illegitimacy, and other social ills are typically deduced. That discrimination is evil in itself is beyond question by the norms of American democracy; the question is whether even the most debilitating discrimination need incapacitate a people if it is not reinforced by other pressures. In the large field of ethnic and race relations, hardly any theory or social policy would remain unchanged if one applied the new insights that the extraordinary success of Japanese and Chinese immigrants suggests.

I. IMMIGRATION FROM CHINA AND JAPAN

A scant century and a half ago, when contact between China or Japan and the West was close to nil, the ignorance of each other was almost total on both sides. The Chinese were forbidden to teach their language to a foreigner or to send books abroad. Japan was even more isolated, cut off for centuries from all touch with the rest of the world, apart from the so-called "Dutch learning" trickling through the port of Nagasaki. The first edition of the *Encyclopaedia Britannica* (1768) summed up the available knowledge about Japan in a single short sentence, giving its latitude and longitude.

With the push of Western powers to open up the two countries to trade, their self-imposed isolation was reluctantly relinquished. In 1842, after a war that the British won with disconcerting ease, the Emperor's representatives signed the first of the treaties through which the ensuing century of China's humiliation was given apparent legality. Only three years later the Chinese agreed that the troublesome foreigners should administer their own courts of justice and, in another move to keep them at arm's length, leased in perpetuity land on which the British at Shanghai could build their own homes and offices. Paradoxically, two reasons for the greatest resentment later on, extraterritoriality and foreign settlements, were arranged by Chinese officials so harassed that they welcomed the lessening of their responsibilities.

Incursions by other great powers following Britain's initiative led to comparable trade concessions and slices of territory. Thus, during the major Chinese emigration to the United States, up to the establishment of the Republic in 1912 and partly also beyond, the country was in shambles, with a pitiful regime able to continue in its faltering steps mainly because the several imperialist powers found its weakness to their advantage and at the same time prevented each other from making the whole country a colony. In the so-called Taiping Rebellion, Chinese patriots attempted for more than a decade to overthrow the alien Manchu Dynasty and, in a strange combination of forward-looking reaction, to lay a basis for modernizing the country by restoring the Ming emperor to the throne. Ultimately they failed, and the civil war weakened China still more.

The opening up of Japan began in much the same fashion. In 1854, when Commodore Perry of the United States Navy sailed up Suruga Bay for the second time and refused to leave until Japan ended the self-seclusion it had imposed two centuries before, this was a milder imitation of Britain's forcible acts against China. During one decade the harried Tokugawa officials signed no less than forty-four treaties with foreign powers giving them access to other ports, fixing tariff rates, and establishing extraterritorial rights for foreigners. The parallel with China needs no emphasis; the difference is that the counterpart to the Taiping Rebellion succeeded in Japan. The Meiji Restoration in 1868 also combined a revival of ancient prerogatives (in Japan's case, the Tokugawa clan was ousted and the Emperor was restored to full power) with ardent progressivism, a virulent xenophobia with an efficient determination to incorporate all the elements of Western culture that made Japan's enemies strong. The divergent paths of the two countries reached a climax in the Chinese-Japanese war of 1894-95. After her victory, Japan annexed Formosa and other territories, and China was able to pay the indemnity of $200 million only by borrowing from all the other imperialist powers, who thus obtained a firmer grasp on her economy.

The first effect of this contrast on migrants from China and Japan was the different views that the American public had of the two countries, and thus to some degree of those who had come from them. Within the bounds of general disinterest and misinformation, American images of China vacillated between two incompatible extremes, timeless stability and almost unlimited chaos, sage wisdom and superstitious ignorance, great strength and contemptible weakness, philosophic calm and explosive violence.[2] The cycle of opinion concerning Japan was in part the same, if only because in Western minds the two countries were not sharply differentiated. More consistently, however, it was an alternation between admiration for Japan's stupendous achievement—the most rapid and efficient industrialization in world history—and fear of what this meant for American interests.

The nature of the two states influenced also the types of persons who emigrated from China and from Japan. According to the religious beliefs that prevailed in both cultures, only constant care by the living could keep the spirits of the dead content, and to forsake one's native village incurred the greatest of Confucian sins, a lack of filial piety. Chinese emigrants were perceived as "outcasts and vagabonds" and therefore included "a great many refugees and criminals."[3] In both countries, moreover, religion was at first reinforced by government policy. The prohibition of emigration from Tokugawa Japan was so strictly enforced that shipbuilders were forbidden to construct any boats except those suitable only for coastal traffic. But Emperor Meiji proclaimed that "knowledge shall be sought throughout the world, so that the foundations of the Empire may be strengthened." The emigration that the new regime encouraged took place largely under state auspices. The first to leave, 148 contract laborers who went to Hawaii in the year "Meiji One," or 1868, were treated so shabbily by their employers that an agent dispatched from Tokyo to investigate arranged to have the most dissatisfied return home at Hawaii's expense.[4]

In China, in contrast, persons who attempted to emigrate and minor officials who connived at their act were officially subject to death by beheading. Like most of the country's other laws, this one was not enforced except in the sense of enveloping emigration in crime and corruption. In Cuba in 1876, a joint commission with Chinese, British, and French members made perhaps the most thorough of many investigations of how coolies were recruited and how they were treated in passage and on arrival. Of the total of 40,413 Chinese coolies shipped to Cuba, 80 percent had been decoyed or kidnapped, 10 percent had died in passage. On their arrival in Havana, the survivors were taken to "man-markets," where they were "stripped and their bodies examined in the manner practiced when oxen or horses are being bought." Sold to the highest bidder, most went to sugar plantations, the rest to tobacco and coffee estates or other menial tasks.[5]

In the decades following the American Civil War, some of the most principled opponents of Negro slavery were also the least willing to admit another slave population to the United States. "Eastern Congressmen were often more unyielding in their hostility than colleagues from California, who settled for such terms as 'quasi-voluntary servitude' and 'quasi-slavery,' . . . [as contrasted with] a 'modern slave trade system' pure and simple." In 1874, President Grant expressed a widespread sentiment when he stated: "The great proportion of the Chinese immigrants who come to our shores do not come voluntarily, to make their homes with us and their labor productive of general prosperity, but come under contracts with headmen who own them almost absolutely." [6] Much of the fear and hostility expressed by proponents of exclusion, one should recall, derived from an at least partially correct estimation of the conditions of Chinese emigration. Not all the malevolence was based on prejudice—literally, judgment before the facts are known—but on increasingly solid evidence concerning *some* migrants, whose characteristics were too often generalized to the whole population, or to the whole race, including Japanese.

1. *GOVERNMENT CONTROL OF MIGRATION*

The first law concerning the movement of Chinese into the United States was the treaty of 1868, negotiated by Anson Burlingame, America's first Minister to China. Its preamble reads:

> The United States of America and the Emperor of China cordially recognize the inherent and inalienable right of man to change his home and allegiance and also the mutual advantage of the free migration and emigration of their citizens and subjects, respectively, from one country to the other for the purpose of curiosity, of trade, or as permanent residents. [7]

The treaty was arranged in order to facilitate American residence and trade in China. Its reciprocity, at the time a seemingly empty courtesy, became the exclusionists' main target over the next several decades.

Hostility to Chinese immigration existed throughout the United States, but the antagonism developed first in California, was strongest there, and in large measure spread from that state to the rest of the country. [8] Gold was discovered at Coloma, California, on January 24, 1848. One week later Mexico signed the treaty ending its war with the United States and, in return for $15 million, ceded to its victorious northern neighbor a considerable territory, including California. The frantic gold rush, thus, coincided with an ardent postwar patriotism, so the effort of law-abiding citizens to hold their own against the riffraff attracted to easy riches, a problem throughout the frontier, was typically expressed in nationalist terms. As San Francisco's main news-paper, the *Daily Alta California* (March 5, 1852), put it: "To those who permanently settled here, and who have families, the moral worth of foreign arrivals commands more than a passing thought. The prosperity of our State, the peace and comfort of our citizens, and the happiness of society generally, are in a great measure affected by those who come from foreign climes to seek their fortunes in this country." In line with this sentiment, a special tax was imposed on foreign miners; though directed mainly at Spanish Americans and French, it was collected espe-cially from Chinese, the quintessential foreigners who, almost accidentally, became the main target of California's first anti-alien legislation.[9] The hostility that developed thereafter was based in considerable part on ignorance, which was maintained and reinforced in part by the extreme clannishness of the Chinese.

Governor John Bigler of California, campaigning for reelection in 1852, proposed that the influx of coolies be checked. The issue, thus drawn between free and indentured labor only a few years after the Chinese first appeared in California,[10] was sharpened by a number of fortuitous events. The *Daily Alta California*, until then warmly pro-Chinese, got a new editor and reversed its stand. The number of aliens in the state increased greatly, reaching by 1870 some 210,000 out of a population of 560,000. About a quar-ter of the foreign-born were Irish, who competed with the Chinese as unskilled laborers and, presumably for that reason, were espe-cially hostile to them.[11]

Anti-Oriental bills were introduced in the California legislature over the next several decades, but the crucial decisions were made in Washington. The 1868 treaty, already quoted, provided that Chinese subjects resident in the United States "shall enjoy the same privileges, immunities, and exemptions in respect to travel or residence as . . . citizens or subjects of the most favored nation." From the beginning, however, this status was inter-preted as excluding the right of naturalization. Even before 1870, when Congress passed a law to that effect, foreign-born Chinese were usually barred from citizenship. Also in 1870, China agreed in an amended treaty that the United States "may regulate, limit, or suspend," but "may not absolutely prohibit," the immigration of Chinese laborers. In line with these provisions, the Chinese Exclusion Act of 1882 suspended immigration of Chinese laborers for ten years. That the bar had to be renewed each decade meant that anti-Asian agitation was given a recurrent focus, an issue around which to rally those striving for full and permanent exclusion. This goal was finally achieved in the Immigration Act of 1924, under which aliens ineligible for naturalization were not permitted to immigrate.[12]

Exclusion had been extended from Chinese to other Asians mainly by a series of partly inconsistent court decisions. In 1906, when the notorious political machine ruling San Francisco decided to segregate all Oriental children into a single inadequate school, this parochial affair developed into an international incident. President Theodore Roosevelt, who received an official complaint from Tokyo, dared not ignore it: after its amazing victories over China and Russia, Japan was a power that other nations respected. After an investigation on the spot by a member of his cabinet[13] and almost two years of negotiations, Roosevelt signed the famous Gentlemen's Agreement, under which the Japanese government itself undertook to restrict emigration to the United States to nonlaborers or members of prior residents' families. In substance the difference from the Oriental Exclusion Act of 1882 was slight, but face was saved on both sides—at least until the Act of 1924.

Proscribing citizenship barred a class of permanent residents from their only legitimate route to political power. Moreover, citizenship is often a prerequisite to certain upper-class economic activities, and by a series of laws in Western states those ineligible for naturalization were denied legal access also to several middle-rank occupations. The right to vote entails much more than making a choice on election day.

2. *IMMIGRATION STATISTICS*

In the modern period, characterized by swollen populations and efficient mass transportation, a migration must be measured in the millions to be numerically significant. Despite the large and rapidly growing populations of China and Japan, emigration from these countries has been relatively modest. From 1820, when American immigration records started, to 1924, when the national-quota system was enacted, of the total of 36 million listed as entering the United States, only 1 percent were Chinese and .8 percent were Japanese. Moreover, these data on gross immigration overstate by a considerable margin the number who remained. It is difficult in retrospect to construe these figures as "The Oriental Invasion," the title of an article by a leading sociologist,[14] or *The Japanese Invasion*, a book introduced by Robert Park, probably the foremost American sociologist of that period.[15] The language was stronger in the brochures of nativist organizations, but a spirit of exaggeration was to be found also in official publications and scholarly works.[16]

Immigration statistics, in general not a highly reliable source, were especially deficient with respect to the Chinese, for two reasons. The count of those departing was even less accurate than that of arrivals, and in many years more Chinese left the United States than came to it. And especially after the Exclusion Act was passed in 1882, a large but indeterminate number entered illegally. The issue was raised time and again in Congress, which took testimony on the many means used to evade the law,[17] but with little result.

Many persons of Asian stock presently resident in the United States live in Hawaii, and from the time of its annexation as an American territory in 1898 to its admission as a state in 1959, confusion concerning its status in national statistics was a constant source of error. Local accounts about the Islands estimated the proportions of Japanese, say, who remained there as against those who departed "either to the mainland or back to Japan," and many works focused on the West Coast, on the other hand, counted in-migrants from Hawaii as new immigrants; thus many persons were counted twice.[18]

Whatever their number, most immigrants from Asia were young men. For example, according to the censuses of 1880 and 1890, which enumerated more than 100,000 Chinese males on the mainland, Chinese females numbered only about 4,000. Sex ratios almost as skewed as this were characteristic also of the Japanese during the first decades of their immigration, and of both groups also in Hawaii. Until the laws were declared unconstitutional most western states prohibited interracial marriages, so for a very considerable period a normal family life was all but impossible for many of the Asians living there. Hawaii, on the contrary, became famous as an interethnic melting pot in the literal sense. The Japanese there, however, "married within their own group in higher proportion than any other of the peoples of Hawaii," for when the interest of the family is decisive, as was typically the case, "marriage with persons of another race or people never takes place." [19] The Hawaiian Chinese, on the contrary, often mated with women of other races, especially native Hawaiians,[20] and how one designates the offspring from such marriages has remained a puzzle until the present time.[21]

In sum, no set of official statistics concerning the Chinese and Japanese in the United States can be accepted at face value. The attempts to correct these data that various authors have made,[22] however much an improvement, also reflect to some degree the irremediable gaps in the sources. With no firmly established population figures, the debate over Asian immigration was conducted in large part on the basis of rumored or fabricated "hordes" versus overmodest estimates by partisans on the other side.

II. SOCIAL MOBILITY

Most Chinese and, several decades later, most Japanese began in Hawaii or on the mainland as poorly paid unskilled laborers. The most important employers in Hawaii were the sugar plantations, which developed so rapidly that they soon dominated the whole economy. As early as 1865, a Dr. William Hillebrand was sent to China as royal commissioner of immigration; he chartered two vessels and transported some 500 workers on five-year contracts. These contracts were expansible, however, for under Hawaiian law any district or police magistrate could sentence a laborer who willfully shirked his work to serve double the time lost from his contract. Later, when a fine or imprisonment was substituted for such an extension, the contracts became all but unenforceable, for the fieldhands generally had nothing to forfeit but their freedom. The percentage of Chinese in Hawaii's population rose from 0.5 in 1853 to a high of 22.3 in 1884, and this rapid increase excited much opposition. The further immigration of Chinese became a prominent political issue: planters pleaded their case in economic terms, while opponents charged that the too-numerous Chinese were a danger to health and civil order. The dispute was resolved during the 1880s by substituting Japanese for Chinese.[23]

The same cycle was then repeated: initially welcomed as industrious workers, the Japanese were admitted in ever larger numbers until they too were seen as a political threat. Indeed, the Hawaiian Republic that was established in 1894, with citi-

zenship limited to Caucasians and native Hawaiians, was not
viable under those conditions. According to the 1896 census,
there were 3,086 Americans plus perhaps twice as many Europeans compared to 24,407 Japanese and 21,616 Chinese.[24] In
1898, under the new administration, America's prohibition of
contract labor was extended to the territory of Hawaii, but this
formal regulation seemingly had little effect on actual working
conditions. As one official report noted, "It is perhaps inevitable
that for a time the technical rights of laborers under American
law will be disregarded. . . . It must be remembered that our legal
codes were made for a country where social conditions prevail
quite different from those in Hawaii."[25] Two reports in the same
series suggest how the training that Asians received on the plantations prepared them for later jobs as skilled workers. The two
passages, though written several years apart, might be successive
paragraphs of a single commentary:

> A [white] carpenter wants a board and tells a Japanese to get it;
> then he finds it convenient to have the man saw it, hold it in place,
> nail it; and so unconsciously he gradually begins . . . to associate
> an idea of degradation with the manual parts of his craft, and he
> becomes morally and physically unfit to ply his trade under the
> conditions surrounding him.[26]

.   .   .   .

> Wherever a Japanese is given a position as assistant to a skilled
> worker or in a mechanical position, he becomes a marvel of indus-
> try, disregarding hours, working early and late, and displaying a
> peculiarly farsighted willingness to be imposed upon and do the
> work which properly belongs to the workman he is assisting.[27]

During the first decades of this century, both Chinese and
Japanese were able to move off the plantations, which eventually
had to substitute more and more machinery to replace field labor.
Alternative means of earning a living were generally a step up,
though usually still a small one. The crucial prerequisite to becoming either an independent craftsman or a small businessman
was the accumulation of a modest capital; one might wonder
how this could have been amassed out of the meager wages paid
to fieldhands. A budget of a Japanese worker in a Hawaiian sugar
plantation, reconstructed from data out of the early years of this
century, is given in table 1. The continuing link to Japan is
indicated by charges for stationery, lamp oil, and a portion of the
contributions and gifts. Out of the monthly wage of $18.00 the
companies withheld originally 25 percent, or at this time $3.40,
as a deposit against possible future charges (this practice was

Table 1

TYPICAL MONTHLY BUDGET OF A SINGLE MALE
JAPANESE FIELD WORKER IN THE SUGAR PLANTATIONS,
HAWAII, CIRCA 1909-16

Monthly wage			$18.00
Withheld by employer against contingencies			−3.40
Food		$ 7.00	
Clothing			
Work clothes	$0.75		
Rainwear	.50		
Oil for raincoat	.15		
Footwear	.60		
Cap	.08		
Laundry	.75		
		2.83	
Personal			
Cigarettes	$1.00		
Stationery	.30		
Baths	.25		
Lamp oil	.15		
Barber	.05	1.75	
Miscellaneous			
Contributions and gifts	$0.50		
Entertainment	.25		
Unknown	.17	0.92	
Total expenditures		$12.50	
Savings		2.10	
Net monthly wage		$14.60	$14.60

SOURCE: Ernest K. Wakukawa, *A History of the Japanese People in Hawaii*
(Honolulu: Toyo Shoin, 1938), p. 177, as amended in *The Hawaii
Hochi,* Honolulu, June 15, 1968.

abolished soon after the time of this schedule). Yet a frugal man
could save $2.10 of the net monthly wage of $14.60. Whether
in Hawaii or on the mainland, among Japanese or Chinese, the
same abstemious regimen was typical.

On the mainland the initial jobs of Oriental immigrants were
more diverse. Many Chinese were engaged in mining, either as
especially prodigious independent prospectors or as helpers in
the larger enterprises. They, and later the Japanese, were employed as field laborers or in plants that processed agricultural
products. It was Chinese who built the Central Pacific Railroad.
E. B. Crocker, the director of the company, at first doubted

whether these short, slight men could do the heavy work required; he was persuaded to try out a batch only because the white workers kept deserting to seek their fortune in the gold fields. The experiment was a glowing success, and every Chinatown was searched for men who could be tempted by steady work at forty dollars a month. A San Francisco firm contracted to bring in as many more as might be required from China. Opposition to "Crocker's Pets" grew with their numbers, particularly among the Irish laborers struggling to complete the rival Union Pacific line.[28]

The same capacity for hard work that recommended Asians to the employers of unskilled laborers enabled them to rise from this lowest level to one where their industry and perseverance were reinterpreted as unfair competition. Legal impediments in great variety were contrived to block the advance of Asians to middle occupational ranks. In Hawaii a 1903 law stipulated that only citizens or persons eligible to become citizens (that is, not Asians) were to be employed as mechanics or laborers on "any work carried on by this Territory, or by any political subdivision thereof, whether the work is done by contract or otherwise." In the western states, similarly, the noncitizenship of foreign-born Chinese and Japanese was used to bar them not only from professions and such licensed occupations as realtors and beauticians but, more fundamentally, from mining, fishing in coastal waters, and the ownership of agricultural land. Great ingenuity was expended in finding harassments applicable to other occupations. San Francisco, for instance, imposed a special tax on laundrymen who delivered their goods with a pole rather than by horse and wagon.[29]

The reactions of the Chinese and the Japanese to this pattern of discrimination differed. In general, the Chinese retreated, the Japanese persevered; and this contrast affected much in the way of life of the two ethnic groups.

The retreat of the Chinese was by three routes: migratory, residential, and occupational. The sojourners who had come with the intention of returning home in any case departed in greater numbers than those arriving. However inadequate, the population statistics reflect a decline in numbers and a gradual rise in the median age of those remaining.[30] Second, the vast majority of the Chinese in the United States established Chinatowns in the larger cities. Most fundamentally, the Chinese withdrew from economic competition. Only in the Deep South did they act as middlemen,[31] a typical role of the Chinese minorities elsewhere in the world that often arouses hostility from both of the other sectors. The usual business in the Chinatowns was devoted to one of two functions, either serving the Chinese community itself or offering exotic foods and commodities to visiting tourists. Those who settled in cities with too few Chinese to congregate into a special quarter also had a narrow range of specialties. They carried over the "women's work" that they had done in mining camps: cooking was transformed into Chinese restaurants, washing into Chinese laundries, and both into personal service with private families. By 1909, when the Immigration Commission of the U.S. Senate conducted its massive investigation of immigrant peoples, the threat from the Chinese had so much dissipated that it was not thought worthwhile to include them. "Such data as were obtained were secured incidentally to the investigation of other races." [32]

Few generalizations are valid concerning the whole shifting labor force of Japanese. Typically they were paid less than other workers, except sometimes Chinese or Mexicans. Often they were hired in gangs through an agent, who for an additional fee also supplied the workers with Japanese food on the job. According to the Immigration Commission's detailed investigation, during the summer of 1909 about 40 percent were working as farm laborers, with piecework earnings about twice as high as other nationalities. Once their competitors had been eliminated from particular areas, however, Japanese field hands became "less accommodating and [did] less work in a day; . . . by strikes and threats of strike and boycott they raised wages." [33] Among non-agricultural employers of Japanese, the most important were the railroads; others included canneries, lumber mills, mines, and smelters.

No matter what their first jobs, most Japanese wanted to acquire a plot of land, and many accomplished this goal piecemeal through a succession of different types of tenure. By 1909, according to the Immigration Commission's estimate, throughout the West some 6,000 Japanese were farming a total area of more than 210,000 acres. The success of these farms derived in part from an unusual degree of specialization, but more fundamentally from the hard work and extraordinary efficiency of their owners or tenants.[34] To block this advance, California enacted the first anti-Japanese land law in 1913. Even though President Wilson sent his Secretary of State to Sacramento to argue against it, the bill passed by 35 to 2 in the Senate and 72 to 3 in the House. Under its terms, persons ineligible for citizenship could not own agricultural land or lease it for more than three years. In a decision on the law's constitutionality, the U.S. Supreme Court held that, in the absence of a treaty stipulating aliens' rights, each state had the power to set its own legal structure. Over the following years California's initiative was followed by ten other western states.[35] How much of an impediment these laws were to Japanese agriculturists is a matter of dispute. Their provisions were often evaded by various quasi-legal means: land was bought in the name of native-born minor sons; partnerships were formed with whites who could front for both members. Though the legal impediments were sufficient to aggravate the already great difficulties in reclaiming land from the desert, by 1940 Japanese controlled a sizable share of agricultural production and distribution, particularly in Los Angeles.[36]

In two crucial respects, thus, the Japanese were more vulnerable than the Chinese: they lived in small, often rural communities scattered widely throughout the West, and they remained in constant and growing competition with white farmers, whose organizations amassed great political power during the interwar years. By December 7, 1941, when Japanese planes attacked Pearl Harbor, Japanese Americans had few influential friends and many strong enemies.

1. COMMUNITY ORGANIZATIONS

The effects of residential and economic isolation were reinforced by the array of separate community organizations to which both Chinese and Japanese belonged. These were of several types, some distinct to one of the groups and some set up by both. Among the Chinese the putative extended kin indicated by the clan name[37] can be important in establishing links, especially in Chinatowns abroad. In all of China, apart from those sinicized from Manchu or other foreign languages, there are only 400 or 500 clan names, of which a mere fraction are represented among Chinese-Americans.

Virtually, all of the pre-1945 immigrants from China came from one province—Kwantung—and within that province most came from the single district of Toishan. The Toishanese dialect, radically different from Mandarin, therefore became the dominant Chinese speech in America.[38] Similarly, most of the Japanese immigrants to the United States came from six prefectures out of the total of forty-seven, the six that had constituted the most developed area of pre-Meiji Japan. Most of the migrants to Hawaii came from three of the same six prefectures or—a difference that the Japanese themselves made much of—from Okinawa.[39] In general, thus, both the Chinese and the Japanese constituted more homogeneous groups, sharing more traits and values than was typical of immigrants originating over a wider range of their native countries.

In the United States those originating in each district of China, or each prefecture of Japan, established associations that in principle included all their compatriots.[40] The largest of the Chinese brotherhoods, thus, comprised all those who hailed from Toishan. Then all of these local-based units joined together into federations, of which the most famous was the "Six Companies" in San Francisco, now known officially as the Chinese Consolidated Benevolent Association.[41] Its president, popularly termed "the mayor of Chinatown," often speaks for the whole community in dealings with non-Chinese institutions. The parallel federations of prefectural *kai* were called the Japanese Associations of America, of which there were four on the mainland (in Los Angeles, San Francisco, Portland, and Seattle) and two in Hawaii (with memberships originating in Japan proper and Okinawa). These associations acted as quasi-official representatives of the Japanese government, which gave them the right to endorse, for a fee that they kept, the legal documents that virtually all their members needed from time to time.[42] After the Immigration Act of 1924 was passed and this function lapsed, the Japanese Associations began to decline.

The functions of these federations, in part social or political, were largely economic in one sense or another. Those just arriving from China or Japan were helped to establish themselves. This meant (as also with other nationalities) that persons from a particular locality tended to congregate in the same place in the United States and often in the same occupation. Neither those seeking employment nor the indigent typically sought assistance outside the ethnic community. For example, the amount of relief funds distributed during the depression of the 1930s to Negroes or whites contrasted greatly with those to Chinese or especially Japanese (table 2). During the initial evacuation of Japanese from the West Coast, a federal agency started a temporary relief program for the families that had been forcefully evicted from their homes. Even under these extreme conditions, they had little

Table 2

PERSONS RECEIVING FEDERAL EMERGENCY
UNEMPLOYMENT RELIEF AS A PERCENTAGE OF
RESIDENT SUBPOPULATIONS, BY ETHNIC GROUP IN
SELECTED CITIES, UNITED STATES, 1933

| City | ETHNIC GROUP | | | |
	Negro	White	Chinese Americans	Japanese Americans
Chicago	38.4	10.1	4.3[a]	[b]
Los Angeles	33.3[a]	8.8[a]	3.6[a]	0.3[a]
New York	23.9	9.2	1.2[a]	0.1[a]
Philadelphia	34.4	8.2	1.8[a]	[b]
San Francisco	21.9[a]	11.0[a]	13.3[a]	0.0[a]

a. Estimates.
b. Total resident population less than 1,000.
SOURCE: Federal Emergency Relief Administration, *Unemployment Relief Census, October 1933*, Report No. 1: United States Summary (U.S. Government Printing Office, 1943), Table 9-A, p. 78; cited in Ivan Light, *Ethnic Enterprise in America*, p. 88.

to do until a few Japanese, virtually none of whom had ever had any prior contact with a welfare organization, were referred to them for assistance or advice. "A humorous touch[!] was added to [such] situations when the social worker groped for elementary synonyms for 'social security benefits,' 'eligibility,' 'regulations,' 'resources,' and other stock-in-trade terms."[43]

The help that the associations gave Japanese agriculture was a crucial element in their getting established and surviving.

> The early Japanese farm organizations . . . aided their members in finding ranches, served to limit the competition for land by fixing a maximum rental that a Japanese should pay, assisted in marketing the crops and obtaining supplies, interested themselves where disputes arose between a landlord and a tenant, and disseminated scientific knowledge of agriculture and horticulture through publications of their own.[44]

Perhaps the most important type of assistance was through a rotating credit association, called *hui* in Chinese and *tanomoshi, ko,* or *mujin* in Japanese. Like Negroes, Orientals got few loans from regular banks; but unlike Negroes, they used traditional institutions to amass the capital needed to establish small businesses.[45] One system has worked more or less like a building-and-loan association: subscribers paid in regularly, received interest for their deposits, and were eligible for interest-bearing loans when they needed them. Another system can be exemplified with the following minor example, organized by several Japanese women who wanted wrist watches. With several friends and acquaintances, they established a *tanomoshi* of ten members, each of whom contributed five dollars a month to the common fund. In successive months, thus, the members could each buy a fifty-dollar watch without having to seek credit outside the community.[46] The, cooperation is built on absolute trust (the Japanese word derives from *tanomu*, meaning "dependable"); nothing binds a person to pay his share except honor, but to default is rare.

2. INTERNMENT

Up to World War II, whatever differences there were between the Chinese and the Japanese in the United States, one could reasonably hold that their similarities were greater, similarities derivative from both the common elements of the two cultures and the parallel discriminations under American law. During the war, however, Chinese Americans benefited somewhat from the good will toward America's ally (the Oriental Exclusion Act, as we have noted, was repealed), but Japanese Americans were stereotyped as potential or actual enemies of the United States.

Across a large part of the western United States, all persons of any degree of Japanese descent —a total of more than 110,000 citizens and aliens, men and women, grandmothers and babes in arms, simple gardeners and professionals—were transferred en masse to "relocation camps," where they were kept behind barbed wire and guarded by armed soldiers. No charge of disloyalty was brought against any person; the basis for the evacuation of a whole subnation was a loosely specified "military necessity." Indeed, in time of war extraordinary precautions are appropriate, but the FBI and naval intelligence officers had already rounded up everyone who, by the widest interpretation of national security, could be regarded as the slightest threat. These persons had been screened on the basis of specific evidence applied to particular persons, and those who might have constituted any danger were out of circulation long before the mass internment was conceived.

The unprecedented act of setting up concentration camps in the United States was accomplished seriatim. Japanese Americans were first instructed to leave the coastal area and, on their own, to find new homes elsewhere. Depending on assurances from both military and civilian authorities, some three or four thousand of them moved to inland California counties. When these counties were subsequently included in the proscribed zone, this meant a second forced move. Less than a month later, officials decided to intern all Japanese Americans for the duration of the war. While permanent camps were being constructed, temporary "assembly centers" were hurriedly established at such sites as fairgrounds or racetracks, and from March to November of 1942 all Japanese Americans were congregated in these quarters. Over the same period, some were moved to one of the ten camps scattered through the Rocky Mountain area.

In their function and mode of operation, the places of sequestration were prison camps. But everything in them was overlaid with a thick patina of official euphemism, beginning with "relocation centers," or "projects," for camps. Inmates were called "colonists" or "residents." The wages they were paid—according to the level of skill, twelve, sixteen, or nineteen dollars per month for forty-eight-hour weeks—were called "cash advances." The official reason for the evacuation, military necessity, was gradually displaced by a professed intention of shielding the Japanese from the wrath of the populace, a rationalization repeated often enough to convince even some of the prisoners themselves of "the soundness of 'protective custody.'"[47] Under Milton S. Eisenhower, the first director of the War Relocation Authority (the agency instituted to run the camps), the policy was to hold all Japanese in the camps as long as the war continued; and initially such long-term activities as "Work Corps" and "Producers' Cooperatives" were established. Eisenhower resigned after only two months and was replaced as director by Dillon S. Myer, who tried on the contrary to resettle evacuees outside the camps as quickly as possible. Well before November 1942, when the last Japanese in the West was incarcerated, outward movements of certain designated categories began: students allowed to attend colleges in the Middle West or East, field workers granted extended furloughs for agricultural labor, young men permitted —after a change in military policy—to volunteer from the camps for service in the armed forces.[48]

In the words of one of the country's foremost constitutional lawyers, the incarceration of Japanese Americans in concentration camps during the war was "the most drastic invasion of the rights of citizens of the United States by their own government that has thus far occurred in the history of our nation."[49] No evidence was ever offered to suggest that any inmate was guilty of anything. Part of the history of the internment was the failure of the nation's judicial system to provide equal protection under law. The most important cases were three that reached the Supreme Court to test the legality, respectively, of the curfew that had been imposed prior to the mass evacuation, the evacuation itself, and the detention in camps.[50] In fact, all three cases pertained to the same issues, which the Court chose quite arbitrarily to consider seriatim.[51] On the same day, December 18, 1944, the Court decided both that Fred Korematsu's constitutional rights had not been abrogated, since he had not been "excluded from the Military Area because of hostility to him or his race," and that Mitsuye Endo's detention, in the words of Justice Murphy's opinion concurring with a unanimous decision, exemplified the "racism inherent in the entire evacuation program." This kind of discrimination, he continued, "bears no reasonable relation to military necessity and is utterly foreign to the ideals and traditions of the American people." During the two and a half years that the case took to reach this conclusion, however, the camps had been built and peopled.

In a shamefaced review of the policy after the war was over, blame was assigned to various groups or factors. A number of conservative or reactionary organizations, such as the American Legion and the Native Sons of the Golden West, had long agitated against Asians, and their denunciations of Japanese Americans grew far more fervent after Pearl Harbor. One can say that they set the mood, but they had no power to carry out what they advocated. President Roosevelt signed the executive order authorizing the evacuation; his attorney general, Francis Biddle, implemented that order with the assistance of such relatively minor figures as Tom Clark, acting as liaison between the federal government and the army. In California, the mainland state with the largest number of Japanese Americans, the attorney general was Earl Warren (later to become chief justice of the Supreme Court). Called to testify before a committee of the U.S. House of Representatives considering the evacuation, Warren came armed with maps to demonstrate that the Japanese Americans (like the less affluent of whatever ethnic stock) lived close to airports, railroads, transmission lines, and other likely sabotage targets. True, there had not been a single act of sabotage in the more than six weeks since the war had started, but the attorney general used this very absence of evidence as proof of collective guilt:

Many of our people in other parts of the country are of the opinion that because we have had no sabotage and no fifth-column activities in this State since the beginning of the war, that means that none have been planned for us. But I take the view that that is the most ominous sign in our whole situation. It convinces me more than perhaps any other factor that the sabotage that we are to get, the fifth-column activities that we are to get, are timed just like Pearl Harbor was timed. . . . If there were sporadic sabotage at this time or if there had been for the last two months, the people of California or the Federal authorities would be on the alert to such an extent that they could not possibly have any real fifth-column activities when M-day comes.[52]

Most of the Japanese Americans put in camps incurred considerable losses by the forced sale of their property or its destruction during their absence. Under the compensation program set up after the Supreme Court's condemnation of the internment, payments totaling about $38 million were made to approximately 26,500 claimants.[53] At the time of the evacuation, the Federal Reserve Bank estimated the property losses incurred by Japanese Americans at $400 million. Thus, the payments averaged 10 cents per dollar lost and claimed, less 10 percent for attorneys' fees—and less also a considerable deduction for the inflation during the interim (the last payment was made in 1965), for which no adjustment was made. Grudging justice was often so delayed that the plaintiffs had died before their heirs received amounts barely sufficient to pay the legal costs.

3. UPWARD MOBILITY SINCE 1945

One might have anticipated that the camp inmates would succumb to bitterness and apathy. Instead most lived out the Japanese proverb, "Six times down, seven times up!"

The Japanese American community disintegrated during the war, and much of it was never revived. The effect of this dissolution on the younger people was ambivalent: the kin links and community organizations, indispensable means to advancement in the earlier period, could easily have become constrictive after broader opportunities became independently available. Once the prodigious effort needed to overcome the economic and psychological consequences of the camp experience was successfully exerted, young men and women were not impeded by family pressure, for example, to take over their father's store or to continue in his skilled trade. The occupational traps of young, second-generation Japanese working at Los Angeles vegetable stands, the often unreasonable control that patriarchs of the first generation exerted on their families, the restrictive life in a Little Tokyo—all these elements of the prewar existence were reduced in importance or eliminated, together with much of the agricultural economy, the Japanese Associations, the consular authority, and a good deal of the informal community solidarity.

This extraordinary thesis, that some Japanese Americans were liberated (as well as damaged) by the partial destruction of their community, can seemingly be validated by two comparisons. The Japanese in Hawaii, who were not put in camps, advanced greatly during the postwar years, but their upward mobility seems to have been less than that of the mainland Japanese.[54] And while the high proportion of both Japanese and Chinese who moved up to become professionals reflects the extraordinary skill and energy of the two ethnic groups, the continuing high proportion of Chinese (but not Japanese) in service occupations reflects, one can surmise, a continuing pressure to remain in the traditional setting, living in a Chinatown and working, say, in a Chinese restaurant.[55]

Whatever validity there may be to this paradoxical hypothesis, it is certainly the case that by most indices of economic and social well-being Japanese and Chinese rank higher than any other ethnic group identifiable from census statistics (table 3). According to data on religion collected in private polls, Jews and some categories of Protestants or Catholics sometimes have shown a faster rise or a higher status, but the number of Asians included in these typically quite small samples is so tiny that the comparisons are hardly meaningful. The contrast between Asians and other racial minorities is especially strong. The key factor in table 3 is the significantly higher level of education, which helped bring about markedly lower rates of unemployment, a higher proportion in the upper occupations, significantly greater incomes, and a better style of life as indicated by housing. Whether Japanese or Chinese ranked higher along such dimensions depends on which of these criteria one uses; but by most indices Japanese showed a slightly better position, as in education, or a much better one, as in income. An even larger proportion of Chinese than Japanese were in the top occupational grouping, but their average was brought down, as we have noted, by the relatively large percentage of service workers.

Nor is the contrast with other racial minorities the most striking one. We can assume that in general the most favored group-

Table 3

VARIOUS DEMOGRAPHIC, SOCIAL, AND
ECONOMIC INDICATORS OF ETHNIC GROUPS, UNITED STATES, 1970

Indicator	Total Population	Japanese Americans	Chinese Americans	Filipinos	Spanish Origin[a]	Negroes	American Indians
Population (thousands)	203,210	588	432	337	9,073	22,550	764
Sex ratio	94.8	85.7	110.7	119.3	96.4	90.8	96.7
Median age	28.1	32.3	26.8	26.2	21.1	22.3	20.4
Persons per average family	3.57	3.67	4.01	4.23	4.26	4.15	4.46
Median school years completed by persons aged 25 and over	12.2	12.5	12.4	12.2	9.1	9.8	9.8
Percent males age 16 and over in the labor force	76.6	79.3	73.2	79.0	78.2	69.8	63.4
Percent unemployed males in civilian labor force	3.9	2.0	3.0	4.7	5.5	6.3	11.6
Percent employed males age 16 and over by major occupational groups:							
Professional and technical workers	14.0	21.5	28.7	18.1	7.5	5.9	11.4
Nonfarm managers and administrators	10.9	11.7	11.4	3.1	5.4	3.0	5.8
Sales workers	5.6	6.0	4.4	2.1	4.0	2.1	3.2
Clerical workers	7.6	9.0	9.6	9.2	7.5	8.1	7.3
Craftsmen and foremen	21.3	19.7	7.3	13.1	20.4	15.3	23.1
Operators, including transportation	19.8	10.3	10.6	14.3	26.9	29.6	25.6
Nonfarm laborers	7.0	9.9	3.2	8.2	10.4	15.8	10.8
Farmers and farm managers	2.7	3.1	0.3	0.7	0.8	0.9	0.2

Farm laborers and foremen	1.7	2.1	0.2	11.0	5.2	3.5	1.8
Service workers, except private household	8.1	6.3	24.0	19.9	11.8	15.6	10.6
Private household workers	0.1	0.2	0.4	0.3	0.1	0.4	0.2
Median 1969 income (dollars)							
Males, 16 years and over	6,444[b]	7,574	5,223	5,019	5,217	4,158	3,509
Females, 16 years and over	2,328[b]	3,236	2,686	3,513	2,313	2,041	1,697
All families	9,596	12,515	10,610	9,318	7,328	6,063	5,832
Families with female head	4,962	6,467	6,627	4,708	3,654	3,398	3,198
Households in owner-occupied units (percent)	62.9	56.1	43.8	39.7	43.7	42.1	45.0
Median value of owner-occupied unit (dollars)	17,000	27,900	29,300	21,700	3,700	13,200	9,600
Median rent paid (dollars)	89	113	100	96	83	80	74

a. "Persons of Spanish Origin," a category used for the first time in 1970. This constitutes mainly those commonly identified as Mexican Americans, Puerto Ricans, and Cubans. Of the persons so classified, 93.3 percent were white, 5.0 percent Negro, 0.3 percent Indian, and 1.4 percent of other races. The supplementary classification also used by the Census Bureau, "Persons of Spanish Surname," is useful mainly in the Southwest.

b. Persons 14 years and over.

SOURCES: U.S. Bureau of the Census, *Census of Population, 1970.* Detailed Characteristics, PC(1)-D1, "United States Summary," 1973; General Housing Characteristics, HC(1)-A1, "United States Summary," 1971. Subject Reports, Final Reports PC(2)-1G, "Japanese, Chinese, and Filipinos in the United States," 1973; PC(2)-1C, "Persons of Spanish Origin," 1973; PC(2)-1B, "Negro Population," 1973.

ing identifiable from census data is native-born whites of native parents, who are used as the standard of comparison in table 4.

Table 4

INDEX NUMBERS FOR DEMOGRAPHIC, SOCIAL, AND ECONOMIC INDICATORS (NATIVE WHITES OF NATIVE PARENTS = 100), JAPANESE AMERICANS AND CHINESE AMERICANS, UNITED STATES, 1970

Indicator	Japanese Americans	Chinese Americans
Population	0.4	0.3
Sex ratio	88.8	114.7
Median age	130.2	108.1
Median school years completed by persons aged 25 and over	102.5	101.6
Males aged 16 and over in the labor force (percent)	101.6	93.7
Unemployed males in civilian labor force (percent)	52.6	78.9
Employed males aged 16 and over by major occupational groups (percent)		
Professional and technical workers	146.3	195.2
Nonfarm managers and administrators	100.9	98.3
Sales workers	82.2	60.3
Clerical workers	120.0	128.0
Craftsmen and foremen	90.0	33.3
Operatives, including transportation	53.6	55.2
Nonfarm laborers	167.8	54.2
Farmers and farm managers	93.9	9.1
Farm laborers and foremen	131.3	12.5
Service workers, except private household	90.0	342.9
Private household workers	a	a
Median family income in 1969	128.2	108.7

a. Less than 0.1 percent of native white males of native parents were in this category.
SOURCES: U.S. Bureau of the Census, *Census of Population, 1970.* Subject Reports, Final Reports PC(2)-1A, "National Origin and Language," 1973; PC(2)-1G, "Japanese, Chinese, and Filipinos in the United States," 1973. (U.S. Government Printing Office.)

This category includes, it is true, most of the population of Appalachia, but also almost all the groupings congregated at the top, from Boston Brahmins to Los Angeles Jews. In 1970, both Oriental minorities, two groups subjected to harsh color prejudice, had higher levels of education and income, and their occupational distribution was especially distinctive. Proportionately almost twice as many Chinese, and almost one and a half times as many Japanese, were classified as professional or upper level technical workers as members of this most favored grouping. The anomaly demands an explanation.

As we have noted, the first steps up were taken as a consequence of unrelenting hard work and abstemious habits of consumption. Yet, as we have also seen, not even the most abstinent man could ordinarily save enough by himself to furnish even the meager capital needed for a small business or an artisan's shop. The principal clue to these initial advances was that, for both Chinese and Japanese, the self-discipline of individuals was supplemented by various types of their own organizations designed to further their joint efforts. While this cooperation may have been reinforced by the factitious unity resulting from the surrounding hostility, it derived basically from old-country institutions. As younger men were able to seek more profitable and pleasant work, moreover, many of them avoided the jobs that had become stereotyped "Chinese" or "Japanese." That Chinese laundries are disappearing, for instance, is due only partly to the increasing competition from mechanized enterprises; more fundamentally, the older Chinese working as laundrymen are not being replaced as they die off.[56]

III. SOCIAL PATHOLOGY

Extraordinary as have been the positive achievements of Chinese and Japanese, the lack of a countervailing negative record is in a sense even more surprising. Of course, statistics on various types of social pathology are notoriously poor, and many of the series do not include separate totals for the two Asian groups. But of all types of crime, delinquency, dependency, or social disorganization about which we have usable statistics, the recorded incidence is typically lower for Chinese and Japanese than for any other ethnic group in the American population, including again native whites of native parents. The meaning of these statistics, however, is not always the same with respect to the two communities. The extremely low rate of Japanese crime reflects reality, but the comparable rate for Chinese is at least partly spurious, a consequence merely of the fact that criminal acts in a Chinatown generally do not get into the general statistics.

Several elements of Chinese and Chinese American cultures coalesced to produce an environment especially prone to law breaking. So-called secret societies, a traditional form of organization since the first century B.C., were always an incipient threat to the Chinese state, quiescent for long periods but then the center of revolutionary-criminal behavior.[57] During the almost three centuries of the Ch'ing Dynasty, with the alien Manchus controlling the central regime, the illegal or quasi-legal organization of local affairs proliferated both in China and abroad. In the United States their antigovernment spirit was transferred to the tong, an institution specific to Chinese American communities (the word comes from the Cantonese pronunciation of *t'ang*, "brotherhood"). Just as the prohibition of emigration was circumvented in China by criminal bands, so indentured immigrants, forbidden by American law, were brought in by extralegal methods. No more loyalty was felt to the Manchu Empress at one end than to Washington or Sacramento at the other. Behind a facade of benevolent precepts, the Chinese companies and tongs of California began as early as the 1850s to supervise and oppress their countrymen. Later, open force was substituted for more subtle pressures, and spheres of influence were defined in open battles.[58] Rival tongs had on their payrolls full-time gangsters who used knives, hatchets, guns, and in at least one instance machine guns in their internecine wars.

> Tongs are synonymous with racketeering, white slave traffic, narcotics, gambling, murders by "hatchetmen," blackmailing, extortion, intimidation, threats, and destruction of property. . . . Their persistence testifies to the continuance of many of the older practices.[59]

Police found it hard to protect the gangs' victims, for Chinese were reluctant to appear as witnesses. "To do so meant death; this is still true today."[60] "Possibly the American courts thought justice was being meted out, but among the Chinese it was known that in reality the interpreter was judge and jury. And . . . the interpreters were under the influence of the larger family guilds" or, later, of the tongs themselves.[61]

The same family cohesion that gave illegal organizations their structure also helped furnish them with their victims. In their native setting, Chinese have been embedded in nuclear and extended family, "house" and clan. Cut off from these normal surroundings, the immigrants sought substitutes, sometimes illegal ones. Most obviously, so long as the sex ratio was badly skewed, many of the Chinese women became prostitutes rather than wives.[62] Similarly, the relatively high rate of drug addiction among Chinese, though also a transfer of a Chinese culture trait, has been especially marked among unsuccessful sojourners, lonely men who know they will spend the rest of their lives in barren rooms, doing menial work in laundries and restaurants.[63]

With the ambiguous evidence, the present status of tongs (or, as they are now euphemistically termed, merchants or district associations) is a matter of dispute. According to Sung, for example, the activities of the remaining organizations are "apt to be for social, cultural, or recreational purposes," with the functions even of the Chinese Benevolent Association "reduced to the ceremonial."[64] Lee, on the contrary, noted a decline after the tong wars of the 1920s but then "a revival following the arrival of young male adults after World War II."[65] Some of the factors influencing the trend have been more or less fortuitous. The Chinese who moved away from Chinatowns, of whom there have been more in recent decades, were usually able to escape the gangsters' domination. And with the increased average age among the sojourners and the balancing of the sex ratio among young Chinese, organized prostitution declined from a lack of sufficient custom. It would seem that organized crime has shifted mainly to the importation of narcotics, though the evidence is not firm.[66]

The most visible disruption in the Chinese communities is the renewal of rampant gangsterism and open warfare among the rival organizations. One important factor has been the immigration of relatively large numbers of so-called Hong Kong Chinese (usually, in fact, persons from other parts of mainland China who merely left through the port of Hong Kong). They receive little help from the cities where they settle, since the pattern has been that Chinatowns always care for their own. In these cases, however, the differences among the Chinese are too great. Most of the newcomers speak a different dialect and know very little or no English; the young males usually have little skill in any occupation; some are ardent propagandists for Maoism, in contrast to the still strong support for the Kuomintang among the older generation. Many of the Hong Kong Chinese feel, thus, that they are the objects of discrimination by both whites and resident Chinese, and they have reacted with bitterness and sometimes extraordinary violence.

The recorded rates of crime and delinquency are generally slightly lower for Japanese than for Chinese, and in the Japanese case there is no reason to suppose that the statistics distort reality. The control of Japanese communities has never been exercised by gangsters; on the contrary, community norms have generally been strong enough to offset factors "causing" crime among members of other groups. In Seattle, for example, where Japanese used to live in a high-delinquency slum, of the 710 boys sent to a special school for delinquents over the period 1919-30, only three were Japanese—and those three lived in a portion of the neighborhood isolated from other Japanese.[67] The English section of the Japanese-language Los Angeles paper used to publish a "police blotter" listing such offenders as a licentious minister and an abortionist. Moral offenders who did not respond to the sanction of public denunciation were sometimes helped to return to Japan.[68]

It is often assumed that the characteristics of the two Oriental minorities derive mainly or entirely from their family life—in particular, that their low rates of delinquency are due to the effective control by Japanese or Chinese parents. Since in almost every culture the family is the principal socializing agency, to ascribe to it an important influence on the behavior of the young is both plausible and certainly partly valid. But according to the theory developed when immigration to the United States was at its high point, the typical conflict between parents and their children is likely to be especially disruptive when it is reinforced by one between foreign-born immigrants and their native-born offspring. The open structure of American society permits the second generation to rise above their parents' social class, and in anticipation of this possibility the teenager already feels superior to those over him. He speaks better English than his father and in other respects has a fuller, more natural acquaintance with American culture. Thus, the thesis goes, as the growing child or young man comes to view his father with contempt or shame, he generalizes this perception into a rejection of all authority. And a number of early studies based on data about several different nationalities did show delinquency rates higher in the second generation than in either the first or the third.

Not only should the theory hold for Asian youth, but their particular circumstances aggravated the usual tensions. From puberty on, the typical Chinese or Japanese youth was subjected to a straiter discipline than the usual American child ever knows.

The distance between the Asian and the American cultures, and thus between the two generations in Asian-American families, was also far greater than the average. And the immigrant generation, ineligible for citizenship and in other respects relegated to a low level of American society, were markedly subject to their own children's denigration. There is a good deal of evidence that intergenerational conflict was as sharp in Oriental American families as one would anticipate. For example, according to Dorothy Thomas's compilation of life histories, "Dad was strict to the point of tyranny"; "This revolt process then went down to my next sister and so on down the line."[69] The most common source of irritation was that parents wanted to arrange their children's marriages, as in China or Japan, while the young people wanted to date, choose their partners, and finally marry for love.[70] More generally, the deference due to older persons under Confucian norms is so excessive by American standards that the second generation were bound to feel put upon.

The thesis that the low incidence of social pathology is due to effective child rearing in Asian American families, in short, is inadequate. The explanation would seem to be rather that the parents' responsibility for rearing their offspring is to some degree borne by the whole ethnic community. A dramatic example is the reaction of the Japanese Americans of Sacramento to a few delinquents who had been arrested for shoplifting. The local chapter of the Japanese American Citizens League (the post-1945 successor of the prewar Japanese Associations) organized a Japanese Family Guidance Council. At public meetings that the Council sponsored, probation officers, psychiatrists, and other "experts" addressed virtually the whole of the Japanese American community. The pressure was only partly on teenagers; the Council's principal effort was to arrange for whatever services might seem appropriate when parents were unable (or unwilling) to control their own children. In the view of the Council's officers, negative publicity was itself salutary, for it brought parents back to a sense of their responsibility not only to their family but to the community.[71]

IV. THE FUTURE

In the 1920s, when immigration to the United States was an important political issue, the newcomers' differences from the natives were often exaggerated or, perhaps more often, were minimized. The latter ideology was symbolized in the metaphor of "the melting pot": once permitted to enter, immigrants would lose all ties to their homeland and disappear without a trace into the Anglo-American population. A generation later, when the sons, and especially the grandsons, of immigrants had acquired more self-confidence, the symbol changed to "cultural pluralism" or, still more assertively, "a nation of nations": no one need give up his ethnic identity and loyalty in order to acquire the full rights of American citizenship. It is useful to recall this sequence as a comment on the usual assumption that assimilation is a linear process, from a minimum to a maximum absorption of minorities into the receiving society. As Marcus Lee Hansen pointed out, the procession of nationalities coming to the United States was followed two generations later by a succession of amateur historical societies, folklore associations, and other organized efforts to keep alive specific elements of various overseas cultures. It is an "almost universal phenomenon that what the son wishes to forget the grandson wishes to remember." [72]

In spite of their manifest differences from European nationalities, it would seem that Hansen's thesis applies also to the two Asian ethnic groups. The main overall effect of the assimilation of some Japanese and Chinese, the adherence of others to their traditions, and what might be termed the reverse assimilation of still others, has been to break up the two populations into smaller, very often somewhat hostile subgroups. And the seeming unity of the earlier period, one should recall, was based more on stereotypes than on actuality. Antagonisms were strong among those originating in different localities of China or Japan; between those resident in Hawaii and on the mainland; among the Issei, Nisei, and Sansei (Japanese for first, second, and third generations) or the Chinese equivalents; and so on. These divisions have remained, and as others have arisen—such as the immeasurable gap between sophisticated professionals and the service workers —both populations have become increasingly heterogeneous. Age differences give some indication of the probable trend, but not always a precise one.

Let us begin with tradition, which sometimes shows an amazing longevity. In a Buddhist temple in Marysville, California, the central altar figure of Pei-ch'i was, in the early 1960s, still protecting the settlement against the Yuba River. [73] One could easily draw up a list of such vestiges, but many of them would turn out rather to be partial revivals. Still in the 1920s, few Chinese in California observed American holidays and Sundays, celebrating only the festivals of their native culture. Around the time of World War II (when China was being praised as an ally), the younger generation, who had branded such transfers as medieval superstitions, began to accept and enjoy them as much as their parents and grandparents. "More, they are becoming decidedly conscious of the color and symbols of these old-China festivals and on occasions are even inviting their American [!] friends to join them in their celebration." [74] Very few of these "Chinese" or "Japanese" traits, however, survived the sea voyage without undergoing modifications. As early as the 1880s, a San Francisco festival commemorating the birthday of Goon Yum ("Queenly Sound"), the goddess of mercy, ended by offering her meats dripping in fat—an oblation that those newly arrived from China found strange for a vegetarian Buddhist goddess. [75] When a Buddhist priest, the fourteenth generation that succeeded to the hereditary position, moved from a temple in rural Japan to one in suburban Honolulu, he found that the temple building and its surrounding property were not owned by the priest, as according to tradition, but by an abstract entity called "the Mission," whose members, following the congregational principle of American Protestantism, also controlled many of his activities. [76]

How complex a process assimilation can be is illustrated from the replies given to the same questions (some of which are reproduced in table 5) by samples of Japanese and Hawaiians of Japanese origin. In both countries without a significant difference, a good majority believed that children should be reared to respect discipline (question 1); but when this abstract desideratum was contrasted with teaching respect for the truth, many more Americans chose the latter (question 2). As one would expect, American respondents considered old-country ceremonies less important than did Japanese (question 3), and women ranked themselves higher in the United States (question 4). On the most basic differentiation between "traditional" and "modernist" points of view, man's attitude toward nature, Japanese ranked surprisingly low and Americans much higher (question 5). But many more Americans than Japanese expressed both a belief in religion and a higher regard for religious institutions (questions 6 and 7). As might have been anticipated, more American respondents reacted positively to the concept of "democracy" (question 8), but they also expressed more faith in leaders defined as "good" and held

Table 5

COMPARATIVE REPLIES BY SAMPLE POPULATIONS IN JAPAN (1968)
AND AMONG HAWAIIAN JAPANESE (1970)

Question (abbreviated)	Reply	Percent giving designated reply	
		Japan	Hawaii
1. In raising children of elementary school age, is it more important to stress the value of freedom or the value of discipline?	Discipline	68	70
2. If a child heard a rumor that his teacher had misbehaved, and if the parent knows this to be true, should he so inform the child or deny it?	Tell the truth	52	76
3. Weddings and funerals should involve a lot of people, even if they are costly and complicated. Do you agree or not?	Should be according to one's means	47	70
4. If you could be born again, would you rather be a man or a woman? Male respondents	Man	89	92
Female respondents	Woman	48	73
5. In order to be happy, should man follow nature, make use of nature, or conquer nature?	Make use of nature	40	68
6. Do you have any personal religious faith?	Yes	31	71
7. There are many sects all with their own different positions, but really their teachings all amount to the same thing. Would you agree or not?	Agree	66[a]	81
8. What do you think about "democracy"?	Good	38	74

9. If we get good political leaders, the best way to improve the country is for the people to leave everything to them. Do you agree or not?	Agree	51	70
10. It cannot be helped if public interest is sometimes sacrificed to individual rights, or individual rights to public interest. Which do you agree with?	Public interest is more important	57	70

a. From a 1958 survey.

SOURCE: Tatsuzo Suzuki, Chikio Hayashi, Sigeki Nisihira, Hirojiro Aoyama, Kikuo Nomoto, Yasumasa Kuroda, and Alice K. Kuroda, "A Study of Japanese-Americans in Honolulu, Hawaii," *Annals of the Institute of Statistical Mathematics*, 1972, Supplement 7, pp. 1-60, table 17.

more often that public interests override private ones (questions 9 and 10).

From the same survey, one can see interesting differences among three generations of Japanese Americans in Hawaii or—more or less the same thing—among those with three levels of education. The question was asked, "If you were not a Japanese, which of the following nationalities would you like to be (choose as many as you like): Chinese, Korean, Filipino, native Hawaiian, Portuguese, local haole [i.e., white Hawaiian], Arab, Jewish, Russian, German, French, and English?" The five nationalities chosen most often are listed in order in table 6. The Issei said they would rather be white, certainly not Chinese (for them the Chinese-Japanese war was a vivid memory). The self-assertion of the Sansei, on the other hand, was expressed in a reduced proportion choosing haole and an increased proportion choosing every other alternative.

Such data contradict the conventional view of Hawaii, whose sociologists have held to the myth of the melting pot far longer than those on the mainland. The principal prop of this stance has been the remarkably high rate of interracial marriages already noted, which, projected into the future, would result in the creation of a new racial type, sometimes termed "cosmopolitan." In cultural rather than biological terms, however, there has been a greater persistence of ethnic boundaries; many Chinese, for example, are part Polynesian, white, or whatever but feel themselves nevertheless to be members of the Chinese community. "When asked if their social activities were usually with other Chinese families, 100 percent of the immigrant and 72.7 percent of the local mothers replied in the affirmative." [77] And the two largest subgroups, Japanese and whites, have remained distinct also biologically, with only their edges blurred by occasional interracial breeding.

One should note, moreover, that the contra-assimilative trend has become a new fashion; the melting pot hardly serves any longer even as a target. Under the Ethnic Heritage Studies Act, the federal government distributes a few million dollars annually for the many imitations of black studies. In the summer of 1973, some 300 persons either involved in Asian-American programs or interested in starting one convened in San Jose to evaluate the progress to date. Most colleges with any Asian students had been under pressure to follow the crowd, and many had at least a course or two at an introductory level. As measured by either

Table 6

PERCENTAGE DISTRIBUTION[a] OF ALTERNATIVE
NATIONAL IDENTITIES CHOSEN BY A SAMPLE OF JAPANESE
HAWAIIANS, BY GENERATION AND EDUCATION, 1970

Alternative Nationality	Total	Generation			Education		
		Issei	Nisei	Sansei	Primary and Junior High	High School	College
Local White	36	50	37	31	43	32	36
Chinese	29	8	26	35	21	27	35
Native Hawaiian	26	17	24	31	16	29	28
English	21	8	15	30	8	18	30
French	19	17	13	29	7	15	30

a. Totals may add up to more than 100 because persons were asked to select several nationalities if they so chose.
SOURCE: Tatsuzo Suzuki *et al.*, "A Study of Japanese-Americans in Honolulu," table 19.

enrollment or budget, the largest programs were at Berkeley, UCLA, the University of Hawaii, San Francisco State University, and the City College of New York.[78]

In other words, the acculturation of Asian Americans means, among other things, that one or two decades later they try to imitate some of the sillier extravagances of other Americans. For the concept of assimilation implies that Japanese Americans and Chinese Americans are approaching the national averages in political immaturity, crime and delinquency, desertion and divorce, and other deficiencies, as well as in the qualities by which they have excelled in the past. Having partly broken out of the patterns that shaped them to their anomalous virtues, both groups will become more differentiated and thus, to some degree and in some respects, less worthy of emulation. As the distinguished Nisei journalist Bill Hosokawa put it:

> Japanese Americans, like others [including Chinese Americans], are individuals, each with his own idiosyncrasies. And it is a mistake to try to lump all the various individuals into two molds labeled Nisei and Sansei and say with assurance, "This is how they think." . . . Certainly it's not valid to say the American people think this way or that way about the war in Vietnam, President Nixon's economic policies, or the recognition of Red China. Why should it be any more valid to report a consensus about almost any subject among Japanese Americans? [79]

Let us hope, however, that these ethnic groups are not to be completely melted into the national pot, but that they will rather continue to train their members in the courage, perseverance, and dignified self-esteem that have marked these peoples' histories in the United States.

NOTES

1. This is the principal theme of Milton R. Konvitz, *The Alien and the Asiatic in American Law* (Cornell University Press, 1946).

2. Harold R. Isaacs, *Images of Asia: American Views of China and India* (Capricorn Books, 1962), p. 64; Stuart C. Miller, *The Unwelcome Immigrant: The American Image of the Chinese, 1785-1882* (University of California Press, 1969), passim.

3. Victor Purcell, *The Chinese in Southeast Asia* (Oxford University Press, 1951), p. 33.

4. Hilary Conroy, *The Japanese Frontier in Hawaii, 1868-1898* (University of California Press, 1953), pp. 15-40.

5. Persia C. Campbell, *Chinese Coolie Emigration to Countries within the British Empire* (P. S. King, 1923), pp. 135 ff.

6. Miller, *The Unwelcome Immigrant*, p. 153.

7. Betty Lee Sung, *Mountain of Gold: The Story of the Chinese in America* (Macmillan Co., 1967), p. 47.

8. This is the view expounded even in Miller, *The Unwelcome Immigrant*, which documents the considerable anti-Chinese sentiment outside of California.

9. Mary Coolidge, *Chinese Immigration* (Henry Holt, 1909), chap. 4.

10. Gunther Barth, *Bitter Strength: A History of the Chinese in the United States, 1850-1870* (Harvard University Press, 1964), pp. 130, 145-48; Isabella Black, "American Labour and Chinese Immigration," *Past and Present*, July 1963, pp. 59-76; Rodman W. Paul, "The Origin of the Chinese Issue in California," in Leonard Dinnerstein and Frederic C. Jaher, eds., *The Aliens: A History of Ethnic Minorities in America* (Appleton-Century-Crofts, 1970), pp. 161-72; Stanford M. Lyman, *Chinese Americans* (Random House, 1974), chap. 4. Mary Coolidge (*Chinese Immigration*, chap. 3) had termed the existence of coolie labor a "fiction," a "myth," a "superstition"; and her massive scholarship has been the basis of much subsequent argumentation in a similar vein. One example that she cited to buttress her thesis suggests its weakness: The Central Pacific Railroad sent an agent to China who hired several thousand laborers against promissory notes that would be repaid by a charge against their wages. One can term this practice indentured service, coolie labor, or quasi-slavery; it was not a fiction.

11. Coolidge, *Chinese Immigration*, chap. 4; Paul, "The Origin of the Chinese Issue"; Miller, *The Unwelcome Immigrant*, p. 201.

12. The law was repealed in 1943, mainly as a gesture toward America's wartime ally. Like the earlier pressure groups that had engineered the passage of xenophobic laws, the Citizens Committee to Repeal Chinese Exclusion was tiny. Its decisive role was based on the premise that "the United States was full of uninformed good will, and that informing the people was the surest way of securing their support for repeal. This assumption proved to be correct beyond the Committee's brightest dreams." See Fred W. Riggs, *Pressures on Congress: A Study of the Repeal of Chinese Exclusion* (King's Crown Press, 1950), p. 57 and passim.

13. V. H. Metcalf, "Japanese in the City of San Francisco, Cal.," U.S. Senate, 59th Congress, 2d session, Document 147 (Government Printing Office, 1906).

14. R. D. McKenzie, "The Oriental Invasion," *Journal of Applied Sociology*, 1925, pp. 120-30.

15. Jesse F. Steiner, *The Japanese Invasion: A Study in the Psychology of Interracial Contacts* (McClurg, 1917).

16. The count of a frontier population was not very accurate. The total recorded in the California state census of 1852, for instance, was 264,435, but when the superintendent of the federal census recalculated the same returns, he came up with 255,122. Compared with other sectors of the state's population, the Chinese were undoubtedly less likely to understand instructions and more fearful of any contact with authority; both factors would have resulted in their greater underenumeration. On the basis of admittedly incomplete returns, the census gave their number in 1852 as 25,000; another local authority thought that 17,000 was more probable,

and S. E. Woodworth, the legal representative of the Chinese community, gave their population as 11,787. One must assume that, just as many later figures from anti-Chinese sources were magnified, Mr. Woodworth's very low estimate may well have represented a partisan effort to minimize the Chinese threat. In any case, as early as 1852, when the anti-Chinese movement was just beginning, responsible approximations of their number in California ranged from under 12,000 to over 25,000 (Paul, "The Origin of the Chinese Issue").

17. Chinese going home would change places with seamen who deserted their ships. Others would claim to have been born in the United States, with the right to enter as citizens. When anyone who had established a legal residence died, his certificate was sold. "It is no exaggeration to say that the Exclusion Act actually helped thousands of Chinese, Americans, and Europeans to make millions of dollars by taking up smuggling as a regular and profitable business." In later decades there was also a sizable illegal movement of Japanese through Canada and Mexico. As one indication, of the 12,000 Japanese passports issued for Mexico over the period 1892-1924, about three-quarters were to persons departing in 1906-07, undoubtedly in response to America's bar to Japanese laborers then pending. See S. W. Kung, *Chinese in American Life: Some Aspects of Their History, Status, Problems, and Contributions* (University of Washington Press, 1962), pp. 91-92; Yamato Ichihashi, *Japanese in the United States: A Critical Study of the Problems of the Japanese Immigrants and Their Children* (Stanford University Press, 1932), pp. 8-9.

18. One instance of this recurrent confusion is worth recounting in detail. When the 1920 census reported that there were 81,338 foreign-born Japanese in the United States, many questioned the accuracy of the datum: ten years earlier the census count had been 67,655, and during the decade the net immigration amounted to 67,109. Allowing for the probable slight excess (because of the subnation's age structure) of mortality over fertility, the 1920 figure therefore represented an underenumeration of some 45,-000, or about 55 percent. The racist press made much of the supposed error, and two professors who authored responsible works on Oriental Americans cited the data without comment: R. D. McKenzie, *Oriental Exclusion: The Effect of American Immigration Laws, Regulations, and Judicial Decisions upon the Chinese and Japanese on the American Pacific Coast* (University of Chicago Press, 1928); Eliot G. Mears, *Resident Orientals on the American Pacific Coast: Their Legal and Economic Status* (University of Chicago Press, 1928). The discrepancy, however, was only in how two federal agencies defined "the United States." By the usage of the Bureau of the Census, Hawaii was excluded, but the Commissioner General of Immigration included territories—in both cases with no special warning to those using the tables. When the figures were assigned to the proper populations and estimates made of the probable changes during the decade, the count in 1920 proved to be not significantly lower than an extrapolation from 1910, but slightly higher. See Romanzo C. Adams, "Japanese Migration Statistics," *Sociology and Social Research*, 1929, pp. 436-45.

19. Romanzo C. Adams, *Interracial Marriage in Hawaii: A Study of the*

Mutually Conditioned Processes of Acculturation and Amalgamation (Macmillan Co., 1937), pp. 160-71.

20. Cf. Newton E. Morton, Chin S. Chung, and Ming-pi Mi, *Genetics of Interracial Crosses in Hawaii* (S. Karger, 1967).

21. In 1970, thus, the federal census listed 52,375 Chinese in the Islands, as contrasted with only 33,750 according to a 1971 survey by the Hawaii Health Department, which, like state agencies generally, is more apt to designate persons with some Polynesian forebears as "Part Hawaiians." Cf. William Petersen, "The Classification of Subnations in Hawaii: An Essay in the Sociology of Knowledge," *American Sociological Review*, 1969, pp. 863-77.

22. For example, Kung, *Chinese in American Life*, pp. 94-103; William Petersen, *Japanese Americans: Oppression and Success* (Random House, 1971), pp. 14-19.

23. Chen Ta, *Chinese Migrations, with Special Reference to Labor Conditions*, U.S. Bureau of Labor Statistics, Bulletin 340 (Government Printing Office, 1923).

24. Robert C. Schmitt, *Demographic Statistics of Hawaii: 1778-1965* (University of Hawaii Press, 1968), tables 16-17.

25. U.S. Bureau of Labor Statistics, *Report of the Commissioner of Labor on Hawaii, 1905* (Government Printing Office, 1906), p. 142.

26. U.S. Bureau of Labor Statistics, *Report of the Commissioner of Labor on Hawaii, 1902* (Government Printing Office, 1903), p. 103.

27. U.S. Bureau of Labor Statistics, *Report of the Commissioner of Labor on Hawaii, 1905*, p. 31.

28. Oscar Lewis, *The Big Four: The Story of Huntington, Stanford, Hopkins, and Crocker, and of the Building of the Central Pacific* (Alfred A. Knopf, 1969), pp. 70-71.

29. Lyman, *Chinese Americans*, p. 23.

30. U.S. Senate Immigration Commission, *Report* (Government Printing Office, 1911), vol. 1, table 20.

31. James W. Loewen, *The Mississippi Chinese: Between Black and White* (Harvard University Press, 1971).

32. Senate Immigration Commission, *Report*, vol. 1, p. 654.

33. Ibid., vol. 23, pp. 61-75.

34. Ibid., pp. 75-89.

35. Dudley O. McGovney, "The Anti-Japanese Laws of California and Ten Other States," *California Law Review*, 1947, pp. 7-60.

36. Masakuzu Iwata, "The Japanese Immigrants in California Agriculture," *Agricultural History*, 1962, pp. 25-37.

37. The typical Chinese name (take Chiang Kai-shek as an example) has three parts. Of these, the first (in this case, Chiang) designates the *pen chia* or "clan," or all those descended in the male line from a single putative ancestor. The second (or Kai) denotes the generation; thus, all brothers have the same second name. The third one (or Shek) is the personal name.

38. More precisely, up to World War II American Chinese used three dialects: Seyap (or "four places," referring to the district of Toishan and its immediate vicinity), Sanyap (or "three places," referring to three dis-

tricts close to the city of Canton), and Hakka, the speech of a distinct ethnic group (sometimes called "Chinese Gypsies") that had some centuries earlier moved into Kwantung from the north.

39. Irene B. Taeuber, *The Population of Japan* (Princeton University Press, 1958), p. 199.

40. Ivan H. Light, *Ethnic Enterprise in America: Business and Welfare among Chinese, Japanese, and Blacks* (University of California Press, 1972), chaps. 4-5; Lyman, *Chinese Americans*, chap. 2.

41. William Hoy, *The Chinese Six Companies: A Short, General Historical Resumé of Its Origin, Function, and Importance in the Life of the California Chinese* (Chinese Consolidated Benevolent Association, 1942); Barth, *Bitter Strength*, chap. 4.

42. Michinari Fujita, "The Japanese Associations in America," *Sociology and Social Research*, 1929, pp. 211-28.

43. George D. Nickel, "Evacuation, American Style," *Survey Midmonthly*, 1940, pp. 99-103.

44. Iwata, "The Japanese Immigrants"; cf. Senate Immigration Commission, *Report*, vol. 23, pp. 131-34.

45. Light, *Ethnic Enterprise in America*, chaps. 4-5; Lyman, *Chinese Americans*, chap. 2. Light makes a point of distinguishing between Negroes native to the mainland, among whom such traditional institutions had disappeared, and those who immigrated from the West Indies, where they were still viable.

46. Ruth N. Masuda, "The Japanese 'Tanomoshi,'" *Social Process in Hawaii*, 1937, pp. 16-19.

47. Daisuke Kitagawa, *Issei and Nisei: The Internment Years* (Seabury Press, 1967), p. 81.

48. A total of about 33,000 Japanese-Americans, about half each from Hawaii and the mainland, fought in World War II—in the Pacific theater generally as interpreters or in combat intelligence and in Europe as members of one of two segregated units, the 100th Infantry Battalion and the 442nd Regimental Combat Team. By the end of the war, the latter unit had won seven Presidential citations and 18,143 individual decorations at a cost of 9,486 casualties. No other unit in any branch of the armed forces established a comparable record. For details, see Allan R. Bosworth, *America's Concentration Camps* (Norton, 1967), pp. 13-20.

49. Edward S. Corwin, *Total War and the Constitution* (Alfred A. Knopf, 1947), p. 91. See also Michi Weglyn, *Years of Infamy: The Untold Story of America's Concentration Camps* (William Morrow, 1976).

50. Hirabayashi v. United States, 320 U.S. 81 (1943); Korematsu v. United States, 323 U.S. 214 (1944); Ex parte Endo, 323 U.S. 283 (1944).

51. Jacobus tenBroek, Edward N. Barnhart, and Floyd W. Matson, *Prejudice, War and the Constitution* (University of California Press, 1968), chap. 5.

52. U.S. House of Representatives, Select Committee Investigating National Defense Migration [The Tolan Committee], *Hearings*, 77th Congress, 2d session (Government Printing Office, 1942), pp. 11,011-11,012. Much of Earl Warren's testimony constituted, as it were, a first draft of the Western Defense Command's *Final Report*. In his *post factum* arguments

defending the evacuation and internment, Colonel Karl R. Bendetsen borrowed whole paragraphs from the pre-evacuation testimony of California's attorney general; see the two in parallel columns in Morton Grodzins, *Americans Betrayed: Politics and the Japanese Evacuation* (University of Chicago Press, 1949), pp. 287-88.

53. For details, see Walter F. Banse, ed., *Adjudications of the Attorney General of the United States*, vol. I: *Precedent Decisions under the Japanese-American Evacuation Claims Act, 1950-1958* (Government Printing Office, 1956).

54. Petersen, *Japanese Americans*, pp. 122-26.

55. See also Monica Boyd, "The Chinese in New York, California, and Hawaii: A Study of Socio-economic Differentials," *Phylon* (1971), pp. 198-206.

56. D. Y. Yuan, "Division of Labor between Native-born and Foreign-born Chinese in the United States: A Study of Their Traditional Employment," *Phylon*, 1969, pp. 160-69.

57. Wolfram Eberhard, *A History of China* (University of California Press, 1960), p. 95.

58. Barth, *Bitter Strength*, chap. 4.

59. Rose Hum Lee, *The Chinese in the United States of America* (Hong Kong University Press, 1960), p. 161.

60. Ibid., p. 164.

61. Eng-ying Gong and Bruce Grant, *Tong War!* (Nicholas L. Brown, 1930), pp. 26-27.

62. Stanford M. Lyman, "Marriage and the Family among Chinese Immigrants to America, 1850-1960," *Phylon*, 1968, pp. 321-30; Norman S. Hayner and Charles N. Reynolds, "Chinese Family Life in America," *American Sociological Review*, 1937, pp. 630-37.

63. John C. Ball and M. P. Lau, "The Chinese Narcotic Addict in the United States," *Social Forces*, 1966, pp. 68-72. See also Richard P. Wang, "A Study of Alcoholism in Chinatown," *International Journal of Social Psychiatry*, 1968, pp. 260-67.

64. Sung, *Mountain of Gold*, pp. 138-39.

65. Rose Hum Lee, *The Chinese in the United States*, pp. 166-67.

66. Lyman, *Chinese Americans*, pp. 43-44.

67. Norman S. Hayner, "Delinquency Areas in the Puget Sound Region," *American Journal of Sociology*, 1934, pp. 314-28.

68. John Modell, "The Japanese of Los Angeles: A Study in Growth and Accommodation," Ph.D. dissertation, Columbia University, 1969.

69. Dorothy Swaine Thomas, *The Salvage* (University of California Press, 1952), pp. 153, 323.

70. Ibid., pp. 259-60; Stanley L. M. Fong, "Identity Conflicts of Chinese Adolescents in San Francisco" in Eugene B. Brody, ed., *Minority Group Adolescents in the United States* (Williams and Wilkins, 1968), pp. 111-32.

71. Cf. Petersen, *Japanese Americans*, pp. 139-43.

72. Marcus Lee Hansen, *The Problem of the Third-Generation Immigrant* (Augustana Historical Society, 1938), reprinted in *Commentary*, November 1952, pp. 492-500.

73. Wolfram Eberhard, "Economic Activities of a Chinese Temple in California," *Journal of the American Oriental Society*, 1962, pp. 362-71.

74. William Hoy, "Native Festivals of the California Chinese," *Western Folklore*, 1948, pp. 240-50.

75. L. A. Littleton, "Chinese Mythology in San Francisco," *Overland Monthly*, June 1883, pp. 612-17.

76. Hidefumi Akahoshi, "Hongwanji in Rural Japan and Cosmopolitan Hawaii," *Social Process*, 1963, pp. 80-82.

77. Nancy F. Young, "Changes in Values and Strategies among Chinese in Hawaii," *Sociology and Social Research*, 1972, pp. 228-41. For similar attitudes and behavior patterns among Japanese in Hawaii, see Elizabeth Wittermans, *Interethnic Relations in a Plural Society* (Groningen, Netherlands: Wolters, 1964).

78. *New York Times*, 26 July 1973. In part because of the market that such courses offer, the bibliography on Japanese and Chinese Americans has grown rapidly. The Asian American Studies Center at UCLA and the Asian American Students Association at Yale have jointly sponsored a new periodical, *Amerasia Journal*, of which the first issue appeared in 1971. Like counterparts focused on other ethnic groups, such courses and publications are often antischolarly in their basic premise—that to understand the history and condition of Chinese or Japanese one must be Chinese or Japanese. Thus, as one example, a graduate student named Ben Tong commented on a piece by Kenneth Abbott in a style that might have been copied verbatim from black or Chicano models: "And out of the ivory towers of Smith College rides yet another great white social worker to tell Chinese-Americans who they are supposed to be. So, Doctah Abbott, you say I no hip savvy right way to look at Chinese-American experience, eh? You, with 'knowledge' wrung from the sterile pot of verifiable propositions and empirically replicable data. . . ." (*Amerasia Journal*, February 1972, p. 74). Such effusions blend naturally with New Left manifestos (cf. Stanford M. Lyman, *The Asian in the West* (Desert Research Center, University of Nevada, 1970), pp. 99-118). In vol. 1, no. 1 of *Aion* (published by Asian American Publications), there is an interview with Alex Hing, "minister of information" of the Red Guard "party." "We believe," he said, "that the Black Panther Party is the vanguard of the socialist revolution in the United States . . . and that it's up to us to support the vanguard and to move . . . our people towards liberation."

79. *Pacific Citizen*, 17 December 1971.

European Immigrant Groups

ALICE KESSLER-HARRIS
AND
VIRGINIA YANS-McLAUGHLIN

This chapter explores the economic and social mobility of European immigrants and their descendants in the nineteenth and twentieth centuries. Its focus is on the Irish, the Italians, and the Jews—three major groups illustrating differences in social mobility patterns. The chapter analyzes those patterns, focusing on a series of possible explanations for differential group achievement, including economic status upon entering the United States, education, religion, political power, community institutions, family patterns, and discrimination. Present data permit limited but informed evaluations of these variables.[1]

In the one hundred years from 1820 to 1920, about 33 million immigrants entered the United States (see table 1). Until 1880, upwards of 85 percent of those who came to America were the so-called "old immigrants"—those from northern and western European cultures including Britain, Germany, Scandinavia, Ireland, and Canada. By the 1890s, "new immigrants" from southern and eastern Europe had altered the balance. More than 50 percent of these came from Italy, Russia, and the Austro-Hungarian empire.[2] Altogether between 1820 and 1950 about 4.5

Table 1

DECENNIAL IMMIGRATION TO THE UNITED STATES, 1820-1919

	1820-29	1830-39	1840-49	1850-59	1860-69	1870-79	1880-89	1890-99	1900-09	1910-19
Total in Millions	0.1	0.5	1.4	2.7	2.1	2.7	5.2	3.7	8.2	6.3
Percent of Total from:										
Ireland	40.2	31.7	46.0	36.9	24.4	15.4	12.8	11.0	4.2	2.6
Germany[a]	4.5	23.2	27.0	34.8	35.2	27.4	27.5	15.7	4.0	2.7
United Kingdom	19.5	13.8	15.3	13.5	14.9	21.1	15.5	8.9	5.7	5.8
Scandinavia	0.2	0.4	0.9	0.9	5.5	7.6	12.7	10.5	5.9	3.8
Canada[b]	1.8	2.2	2.4	2.2	4.9	11.8	9.4	0.1	1.5	11.2
Russia[a]					0.2	1.3	3.5	12.2	18.3	17.4
Austria-Hungry[a]					0.2	2.2	6.0	14.5	24.4	18.2
Italy					0.5	1.7	5.1	16.3	23.5	19.4

a. Continental European boundaries prior to the 1919 peace settlement.
b. British America to 1867; Canada includes Newfoundland: Canadian immigration was not recorded between 1885 and 1893.

SOURCE: Niles Carpenter, "Immigrants and Their Children," U.S. Bureau of the Census, Monograph, No. 7 (1927), pp. 324-25.

million Irish, 5 million Italians, and 3 million Russians, most of them Jews, have entered the United States.[3]

Immigrants came for different reasons. The vast majority left agricultural areas to labor in an industrial economy. Except for a minority of political and religious refugees, most were seeking relief from economic pressures. Enclosures, famine, overpopulation, land fractionalization, and crop failures all contributed to the great migration. The Irish potato famine of the late 1840s which forced one and a half million people to flee their native soil in a ten-year period was the most dramatic example of what historians have called "push" factors. Political upheavals across western Europe in 1848 swept many refugees to an American haven. The arrival of the steamship in the 1850s facilitated immigration by reducing passage time from months to ten days. By the late nineteenth century, southern and eastern Europeans seeking temporary seasonal employment in America or more permanent religious asylum, found inexpensive transportation provided by steamship companies in ports readily accessible to them.

Like their predecessors, immigrants who came to America in the late nineteenth and early twentieth centuries had a variety of motivations. Religious persecution in eastern Europe touched off the Jewish migration. Poles, Italians, Slavs, Greeks, Serbo-Croats, all suffering from less immediate pressures, were often drawn to America by news of economic opportunities. Many Italians, like some eastern Europeans, saw America as a temporary haven where they hoped to accumulate large sums of money and return home with their savings to buy land. They focused their mobility aspirations on the Old World, not the New, and the proportion who returned home was higher than that of any other group. Others, such as the Irish and Jews, viewed their immigration as permanent. Religious persecution and economic discrimination in eastern Europe influenced the Jewish attitude. Jews were often denied access to professional occupations, were forced to live in restricted geographical areas, and could not own property. Famine and overpopulation at home discouraged the return of Irish immigrants. Unlike the Italians, the Jews and Irish who were unable to return home focused their aspirations on America.

Immigrants who came in the mid-nineteenth century confronted a different world from those who arrived later. Those who came in the 1840s found a largely agrarian nation only beginning to construct its railroads and canals. These conditions influenced the fate of the Irish. Lacking both the capital and the know-how to farm in America and unable to compete successfully with skilled British immigrants who filled the demand for artisans, the Irish became unskilled laborers.

In contrast, when Italians and Jews entered the United States in the great wave of immigration fifty years later, they faced an already industrial nation. In addition to jobs in transportation, construction, metal, and other heavy industries, Jews and Italians had the additional option of moving into office jobs and the professions. These opportunities had not been readily available to the first-generation Irish. Italians and Jews without skills or language facility still had the limited security of heavy demand for unskilled labor. Changes in technology and the division of labor altered the kinds of jobs available, and the achievements of the Irish, Jews, and Italians must be measured against these changes.

Despite the complexities of this changing background, the comparative social mobility of immigrant groups, based on education, income, and occupation, is broadly discernible.[4] All immigrants had difficulty "making it" in the first generation. But, as the following material reveals, the Jews most rapidly achieved financial security and occupational success. Italian immigrants advanced less rapidly up the occupational ladder and, as a group, have not achieved the economic security of the Jews. The nineteenth century Irish advanced more slowly than either Italians or Jews, but their achievement must be measured against the different economic circumstances they faced, which involved fewer opportunities for poor and unskilled groups to advance. By 1960, Jews were the nation's highest achievers, as measured by education, income, and occupation. Italians outstripped the Irish and rated ahead of the native white norm. Old immigrants, such as the Irish, ranked below the native white norm.[5]

I. OCCUPATIONAL MOBILITY

1. THE IMMIGRANT GENERATION

Analysis of occupational achievement provides one measure of comparative mobility. The mid-nineteenth-century Irish immigrants were overwhelmingly unskilled laborers. National reports and local studies indicate that at least 50 percent, and probably closer to two-thirds, of the urban Irish were day laborers working in such occupations as outdoor labor on canals and railways, as domestics, bartenders, teamsters, draymen, and carters. The Irish were also heavily represented in quarrying and mining. Skilled workers, who comprised 25 to 30 percent of the total number of male Irish immigrants, most often worked in the expanding textile industry. Irish women frequently worked as domestic servants or as mill hands before marriage. Very few Irish immigrants attained professional or even white-collar status. In late nineteenth-century Boston, a major Irish settlement, less than 1 percent of working Irish males achieved professional status. Over the nation in the 1880s, they had the lowest representation in the professions of all foreign-born groups.[6] Many Irish white-collar workers, approximately 10 percent of the total Irish immigrants, were small shopkeepers, most of whom catered to the immigrant community.

Compared to Irish immigrants, Germans who entered in the same period were a labor aristocracy. They dominated such trades as shoemaking, tailoring, and butchering. In 1850, almost half of Philadelphia's Germans were skilled and only 14 percent were day laborers. By 1880, the percentage of day laborers among the Germans had fallen while the Irish still remained heavily concentrated in that field.[7] While we do not know if opportunities were as great in other cities, in nineteenth century Poughkeepsie, New York, first-generation Germans greatly outstripped the Irish as self-employed persons and shop owners who catered to the general population.[8]

Some of the large German population who entered the United States in the mid-nineteenth century were Jews whose progress can be distinguished from that of Germans at large. Of 10,000 Jewish families entering the United States between 1850 and 1880, more than three-quarters experienced a spectacular rise in status. These achievers began as peddlers, small shopkeepers and skilled craftsmen. By 1880, only one of eight was a manual worker and some of these workers were highly skilled. Half were in business. Twenty percent were clerks, accountants, or other white-collar workers. Ten percent were salespeople and 7 percent were bankers or professionals. Their prosperity becomes apparent when one notes that fully 40 percent of the German-Jewish families had at least one servant; only one of every one hundred family heads was still a peddler; and one of every two hundred was an unskilled laborer or a domestic.[9]

Earlier successes were repeated more slowly when the mass migration of east European Jews began in the 1880s. A large proportion (67.1 percent) of those who entered the United States between 1899 and 1910 reported that they held skilled jobs in 1910. About one-third of all gainfully employed Jews worked in the garment industry as capmakers, tailors, dressmakers, and furriers. Carpenters, shoemakers, painters, and butchers were also well represented. A comparatively low 13.8 percent were unskilled, and only 1.3 percent were professionals.[10] Members of this early group of migrants frequently moved into low white-collar jobs by the end of their careers. Many became small businessmen, though some of these were street peddlers. In early twentieth-century Boston a staggering 45 percent were "in business for profit."[11] In the early stages of their immigration, Jews were already climbing into the middle class.

Italians, most of whom were once laborers in agricultural southern Italy, began at a lower place on the socioeconomic scale and advanced more slowly than Jews. Like the Irish in the 1840s, high proportions of southern Italians worked as day laborers. More than three-quarters of southern Italians who entered the United States between 1899 and 1910 reported that they had been employed as day laborers, compared to less than an eighth of the Jewish immigrants. Construction, general outdoor labor, railroad work, and mining occupied most of them. Only 14.6 percent reported themselves as skilled workers. More northern Italians arrived with skills (20.4 percent), and proportionately fewer were unskilled (66.5 percent).[12] In New York City, a major Italian settlement, the most popular occupations among skilled Italians until the 1930s were tailors, barbers, shoemakers, and carpenters, a rank ordering reflecting the Italian American national pattern. Although precise figures do not exist, many craftsmen worked alone as hucksters and peddlers. Less than one-half of 1 percent of the immigrant group were professionals. However, the proportion of New York Italians who were laborers declined from 50 percent in 1916 to 31.4 percent by 1931 as they slowly entered skilled jobs.[13]

By the 1920s and 1930s, first-generation Italians expanded their job options beyond what had become "Italian occupations" to include such city and federal jobs as street, park, and playground maintenance, postal service, and police service. But the overwhelming majority remained unskilled or semiskilled throughout their lifetimes.[14] Upwardly mobile Italians most often distinguished themselves by acquiring skills in the construction and consumer trades or by becoming small proprietors.[15] By retirement, few had achieved managerial, white-collar, or professional status. Italian-speaking colonies guaranteed a clientele to those entering medicine and law. But these most favored professions insured only limited success within Italian enclaves, and in most instances northern Italians, who had educational and class advantages when they entered the country, formed the vanguard. Outstanding business successes outside the immigrant community occurred chiefly in California, where immigrants capitalized on past experience as vintners and farmers.[16] Even here, the enormously profitable banking enterprise of the Giannini family proved extremely unusual. Chicago gangland figures like "Diamond Jim" Colosimo, John Torrio, and Al Capone daringly manipulated illegal enterprises to achieve their power and wealth.[17]

2. LATER GENERATIONS

Differences in group achievement continued to mark second-generation career patterns, but the children of immigrants usually outstripped their parents. The Irish ascent up the ladder of mobility, which had been slow in the first generation, achieved momentum in the second. Among the Boston Irish, who had reached maturity in the 1890s, only 36 percent of the second generation ended their careers in unskilled and semiskilled jobs, whereas 90 percent of their fathers had ended their careers still manual workers.[18]

Second-generation Italians concentrated in service, labor, and operative categories. They began entering the professions, but in lesser numbers than the earlier arriving Irish, and considerably less than the largely Jewish Russians.[19] New York Italians illustrate the improvement. Only 10.6 percent of the second-generation group were laborers in 1931, compared to 31.4 percent of the immigrant Italians. But the intergenerational improvement was not consistent. In Boston in 1950, 69 percent of Italian immigrant sons were still in blue-collar jobs.[20] Boston and New York may not be representative. If the second-generation Irish superseded New York and Boston Italians in occupational achievement, Italians outranked them nationally in overall achievement. In the 1960s a combined index of income, education, and occupation placed the Italians above the Irish.[21]

Jewish mobility is legendary and supported by abundant statistical data. Seventy-five percent of the sons of Jewish immigrants had moved up to middle-class status by 1950,[22] an almost exact reversal of the proportions among Italians. As early as 1900, 15,000 native-born sons of Jewish immigrant fathers, among whom only 5 percent were tailors, revealed that 20 percent of their fathers had plied the needle to make a living. Two percent of the fathers, but 10 percent of the sons were office clerks. A 1937 survey confirmed the pattern. Among all gainfully employed Jews, 6.6 percent of the foreign-born and 19.1 percent of the native-born were in the professions.[23] Among second-generation fathers and their suburban-dwelling third-generation sons in 1956, fully 46.5 percent of the sons were now professionals, compared to 11.9 percent of the fathers. While 21.4 percent of the fathers were still employed in factories or as peddlers, only 7.1 percent of the sons were so employed.[24] By 1953, 66 percent of New York City Jews were in nonmanual occupations, a figure that almost exactly reverses that of 1900, when about 67.6 percent of employed Jews were in manual occupations.[25]

Property acquisition, the ownership of a home or business place, provides another index of comparative mobility among minorities. Thousands of immigrants, even the unskilled, invested in family homes. Italians and Jews were prone to invest in commercial properties; the Irish were less enterprising. Unlike today's suburban property owners, small investors paid mortgages by taking in boarders, renting one story of their homes, creating apartments to rent, or sharing home costs with relatives. This kind of mobility choice was made possible because the whole family could contribute to and benefit from it. Wives contributed their household skills by cooking and caring for boarders. When choices had to be made, such groups as Italians, Irish, and Poles would sacrifice the educational interests of their young, withdrawing them from school, sending them to work, and absorbing their earnings. Such decisions increased present earnings at the expense of future skills.[26] Jews do not seem to have made similar compromises.

Failure to acquire property was not always a sign that the group was progressing slowly. For example, movement to the suburbs, widely considered a sign of upward mobility, was sometimes resisted by first-generation Italians, who preferred not to dissociate from their family groups and old neighborhoods. Instead of fleeing to the suburbs, Italians in some cities preferred to refurbish old neighborhoods.[27] Working wives and overcrowded homes, often considered to be characteristics of low status, were for many immigrants a sign of upward mobility. Wives' wages were often saved to purchase homes and Jewish women often worked in shops their families were prosperous enough to own.[28] All immigrant groups took in boarders, and the overcrowded conditions that resulted were endured with longer term interests in mind. If such conditions are interpreted by modern scholars as symptoms of poverty, immigrants and their children did not perceive their situation in that way.

Recent income and education figures for persons who identify themselves as Irish or Italian—that is, persons of either Italian or Irish birth and ancestry—indicate similar achievement levels for both groups. The median family income in 1969 for Italians was $8,808; for the Irish, $8,127. Assuming that the majority who reported themselves as Russians were also Jewish, the Jews had an astounding success here: their median family income was $11,554.[29] Italians and Irish achieved similar educational levels. The median school years completed by Italians and Irish aged 25-34 were 12.5 and 12.6 respectively; for Italians and Irish 35 years old and over, the figures are 10.3 and 12.0. The median number of school years completed by second-generation Italian-Americans was 10.9, compared to 11.5 for the Irish and 12.4 for the Jews.[30] Once again, the Jewish comparison reveals extraordinary achievement. The median number of school years for Russians, aged 25 to 34 years, was 16 or more; for Russians aged 35 and over, the median was 12.4.[31] The Irish and Italians have achieved levels of income and education similar to each other. We cannot conclude from this that their mobility rates are comparable, for the Irish arrived in the United States fifty years before the Italians.

These data elucidate the various styles of mobility represented by three groups. The Jews moved rapidly into white-collar, professional, and entrepreneurial occupations, using education as their channel. Italians tended to remain blue-collar workers but achieved financial security through the skilled trades and property ownership. By the twentieth century, the Irish had achieved about the same level of socioeconomic status as the Italians.

II. FACTORS IN INTERGROUP MOBILITY

Many factors contributed to intergroup differences in socioeconomic advancement. Material wealth and occupational skills on arrival, education, cultural values, community institutions, political power, family stability, and the effects of discrimination influenced group mobility in different ways. Although no single factor provides a satisfactory explanation, their interplay offers clues to differential mobility.

1. ADVANTAGES AND DISADVANTAGES UPON ARRIVAL

A glance at crude indices of material well-being reveals that the amount of capital a group had on arrival did not determine the relative speed of social mobility. The Jews who arrived in 1900 had less money on arrival than most other immigrants— an average of nine dollars per person as opposed to an average of fifteen dollars per person for all immigrants who arrived that year.[32] They continued to enter the United States with substantially less money than their fellow immigrants. While one-seventh of the Irish and only one-thirteenth of the Italians who arrived in 1910 had less than fifty dollars, almost half of all Jews had less than that sum.[33] These figures suggest that Jewish social mobility did not rest on funds accumulated in the Old World.

Jews did come equipped with skills appropriate to urban America. A glance at table 2 reveals that the proportion of skilled Jews who arrived in the United States between 1899 and 1910 was higher than that of any other arriving immigrant group. Southern Italians, on the other hand, had a far smaller proportion of skilled laborers. This important distinction contributed to their slower ascent up the occupational ladder. The greater proportion of skilled workers among northern Italians explains their vanguard position among Italian achievers.

Skills, as the experience of nineteenth-century Germans and Irish indicates, did not always guarantee future position. The skills brought to America by German, English, and Scottish workers gave them greater access to jobs and opportunities than their unskilled Irish contemporaries. By the 1880s, however, their initial advantage had lost its importance. For example, the sons of Philadelphia Germans working in declining consumer crafts like shoemaking, textiles, and woodworking abandoned their fathers' crafts for such developing industries as printing, the

OCCUPATIONS OF EUROPEAN IMMIGRANTS[a] REPORTING EMPLOYMENT, 1899-1910[b]

Immigrant Type	Number Reporting Employment	Percent			
		Professional Occupations	Skilled Occupations	Laborers, incl. Farm Laborers	Miscellaneous
Jewish	590,267	1.3	67.1	13.7	18.0
Bohemian and Moravian	60,489	1.3	40.8	28.5	29.4
Bulgarian, Servian, and Montenegrin	90,901	.1	3.3	92.0	4.6
Croatian and Slovenian	298,324	.1	5.0	86.4	8.5
English	249,998	9.0	48.7	14.1	28.1
Finnish	123,008	.3	6.0	67.2	26.5
French	70,038	9.3	34.5	26.0	30.2
German	458,293	3.5	30.0	37.7	28.8
Greek	197,718	.3	7.7	86.2	5.8
Irish	376,268	1.3	12.6	35.3	59.9
Italian (North)	296,622	1.1	20.4	66.5	12.0
Italian (South)	1,471,659	.4	14.6	77.9	7.9
Lithuanian	141,540	.1	6.7	76.1	17.2
Magyar	259,276	.5	8.6	77.5	13.4
Polish	748,430	.2	6.3	75.3	18.1
Roumanian	75,531	.2	2.7	93.8	3.3
Russian	69,986	1.4	9.1	82.7	6.8
Ruthenian	128,460	.1	2.0	80.6	17.4
Scandinavian	475,094	1.2	20.5	43.8	34.5
Scotch	89,208	5.7	57.9	12.1	24.3
Slovak	290,247	.1	4.4	80.0	15.5
TOTAL[c]	7,048,953	1.4	20.2	79.3	19.1

a. All races with an immigration below 50,000 are omitted.
b. From *Statistical Review of Immigration*, p. 53.
c. Total includes all races.
SOURCE: Samuel Joseph, *Jewish Immigration to the United States from 1881 to 1910*, vol. 59, Columbia University Studies in History, Economics and Law (Columbia University Press, 1914), **p. 190.**

metal trades, and construction. There they met the sons of unskilled Irish immigrants, who had entered the same industries.[34]
In contrast, Jews, whose relative skills as tailors matched the
needs of New York's expanding garment industry, managed to
put their advantage to excellent use.

Along with technical knowledge, immigrants carried to America traditional values, styles of socialization, and a world view
that had evolved to meet the needs of their Old World lives. Those,
like the southern Italians and the Irish, who came from agrarian
settings, had to learn to adjust to a competitive urban environment. A few Irish immigrants had acquired industrial experience
in England before emigrating to America. Most had not.[35] Later
arriving Irish men and women, though not highly skilled in industry, often had other training as office clerks, shopkeepers, and
entrepreneurs that prepared them to move into metropolitan
areas. In contrast, southern Italians, who came from agrarian
backgrounds with low proportions of skilled workers, did not
have equivalent training as clerical workers. Yet striking numbers of them moved from the ranks of unskilled labor to become merchants and tradesmen.[36] Their advance is more impressive when compared with the urban background from which
Jews more typically came. Speaking now only of the Russian
Jews, nearly 31 percent were engaged in trade in Russia, and
almost 40 percent were in manufacturing. Of this group, 17 percent already worked in the apparel trade.[37]

The previous urban experience of many Jews and northern
Italians facilitated their adjustment to the American cities in
which they settled. Unlike southern Italian and Irish peasants,
many Russian Jews had worked in factories, had organized into
trade unions, and had read and published their own newspapers.
They brought these experiences with them to the United States,
and built out of them an urban movement effective enough to
protect many workers. By 1890, enough Jews had joined unions
to create the United Hebrew Trades, an umbrella organization.
Urbanized northern Italians proved themselves as community
leaders and organizers; "village-minded" southern Italians were
initially less able community organizers and less inclined to join
unions.[38] Dominated by the *padrone*, and often concerned more
about going home than improving conditions in the United
States, southern Italians did not so quickly come to an awareness
of the need for collective action. The Old World urban experience

of the Jews seems to have given them an enormous advantage over the Italians.

2. EDUCATION

Education is often considered critical to rapid social mobility. If literacy rates are any guide, few distinctions can be made in the education of southern and eastern European groups. The average rate of illiteracy for all immigrants hovered around 26 percent between 1899 and 1910. Twenty-six percent of all Jews over 14 entering in those years could not read or write.[39] There is no evidence indicating that language barriers inhibited upward mobility. Italians and Jews, who had to learn English, met or superseded the mobility rates of the Irish, who had the benefit of already speaking English on arrival in the U.S.[40]

Immigrant cultures varied in the emphasis they placed on their children's education, and some groups got an extra push up the occupational ladder as a result. The Irish, who isolated their children in parochial schools in order to perpetuate their religious identities, may have succeeded in perpetuating class and economic differences too.[41] Italians, in need of the income children could contribute, and anxious to preserve their primary allegiance to the family, discouraged children from attending school as they grew older. Italian students have had high truancy and dropout rates from high school and equally high rates of problem behavior, such as lateness and cut classes in school.[42] Jews and Italians, in this regard, appear in sharp contrast to each other. In 1914, Italians had the lowest percentage of children in school, and Jews the highest, of any immigrant group. Children of Jewish immigrants went to college and even beyond in astoundingly high numbers. In 1908, when Jews were only 2 percent of the population, they were 8.5 percent of the students in seventy-seven institutions of higher education all over the country. They were 18 percent of all pharmacy students and 13 percent of law students.[43] The correlation between education and achievement is particularly clear for the Jews.

Explanations for differences in educational attainment appear to lie directly in old country cultural values. The Italian peasant, suspicious of modern ideas and fearful of the extent to which Americanization would disrupt the integrity of the family, withdrew his children from school as soon as possible. Economic need conspired with culture in this respect, for the earnings of children were often essential to family well-being. Jews, whose landless status and religious training had taught them to respect learning, hungered for education. In the *shtetl* (small town or village), the learned man was the single most respected member of the community, and the entire population contributed to the support of its students. Mothers encouraged their sons to become scholars and their daughters to marry even poverty-stricken learned men. Though learning was conceived of only in the context of religious laws, respect was easily transferred to more secular areas in America.[44]

Religious tradition and community approval encouraged the Jew in America to invest in education and correspondingly to increase his upward mobility. No other group had this advantage. The authoritarian and hierarchical structure of the Catholic Church discouraged questions in the interest of dogma and de-emphasized learning in order to encourage faith. Neither Irish nor Italian Catholics expected families to sacrifice to educate their young. Jews came to America with a tradition of such sacrifice. Swedes, Germans, and other northern European Protestants, who were more open to American secular education, nevertheless lacked the extraordinary community support so prominent among Jews. By 1953, the results were evident in their educational status. While one in every 20 Americans had completed college, one in every 6 Jews had done so.[45]

3. *LIVING CONDITIONS*

The effects of other cultural barriers, such as housing and clothing are difficult to gauge; we have no way of knowing how they affected mobility. We do know that all immigrants lived in filthy and overcrowded housing when they first arrived. By all accounts, the mid-nineteenth century Irish were subjected to far worse conditions than later arrivals. Comparing New York tenement conditions of the Jews and Italians in 1900 with those of the Irish and Germans in the 1860s, one observer concluded "the visitor of 1900 could go about dry-shod, at least, in tenement yards and courts where 35 years before the accumulation of what should have gone off in sewers and drains made access almost impossible."[46] Though Jews and Italians lived five and ten to a room in roach-infested, dilapidated, and dark buildings, their conditions do not seem to have been as horrendous as those of the Irish.[47] The latter, of course, were also the slowest achievers;

this seems to imply some relationship between living circumstances and social mobility, but the evidence is insufficient to support a causal connection. No European group was as distinctive as Jews in terms of clothing on first arrival. Pious males distinguished by beards and earlocks (*peias*) were accompanied by wives in wigs and headscarves. But men quickly cut their hair, and women abandoned their scarves. "Greenhorn" was a term of opprobrium that most immigrants tried to shed as quickly as possible.

4. *COMMUNITY COHESION*

Every European group that has been successful has come from a cohesive community, one characterized by concerned participation in religious institutions, charitable enterprises, and self-help groups. This kind of community involvement is difficult to quantify, but we will delineate broad trends. Jewish community life, particularly noted for strong religious, charitable, and mutual aid organizations, provides the clearest instance of the connection between group cohesion and socioeconomic success. In contrast, groups such as the southern Italians, less involved in community life, have been less successful than Jews. These generalizations need to be qualified by evaluations of specific styles of cohesion, some of which are more clearly connected to social mobility than others.

Churches and synagogues played an active role within ethnic communities, but this could have hindered group success. The experience of forming their own national churches was an early introduction to urban associational patterns for many groups, including Poles, Italians, and Scandinavians. But in enabling immigrants to avoid the challenges of language and other associations, the church or synagogue discouraged familiarity with American life. The Hasidic Jews, who have not achieved the economic success of their less orthodox coreligionists, provide a clear example of this.[48] Their case implies that religious institutions that encompass their members' lives to the exclusion of outside social participation seem to hinder group mobility.

Exclusive participation in church-related educational institutions may have had the same negative effect upon social mobility. The Irish and the Jews had opposite experiences. The Irish, who had a consistently firm commitment to the Catholic Church, were slow to achieve upward mobility.[49] Some have speculated that the church's emphasis on other-worldliness contradicted the spirit of competitiveness essential to success in a capitalist society. Irish children who attended parochial schools were isolated from public school efforts to socialize working-class children with the success ethic.[50] Like the Irish, the Jews had strong religious commitments, but they experienced a different mobility pattern. Jews retain high rates of financial support to the synagogue even after their attendance at formal services falls off. Although they send their children to religious schools in enormous numbers, these, unlike the parochial schools of the Irish, almost always supplement the public schools that Jewish children attend. Public education may account for the outstanding achievement of Jewish children. The mobility rate of religiously indifferent Italians was higher than that of the Irish, but did not match the Jewish rate. Anticlericalism and disaffection with the Irish-dominated church hierarchy contributed to Italian reluctance to send their children to parochial schools. The evidence seems to indicate that religious commitment by itself does not hinder social mobility, but withdrawal from secular educational institutions may be a disadvantage.

Insofar as the Catholic Church retarded collective action, it may have negatively influenced social mobility. In the late nineteenth century the church opposed both socialist organizations and trade unions. The Knights of Labor, for example, an idealistic organization of both workers and producers, foundered on Catholic Church opposition to secret organizations. The 1891 papal encyclical, *Rerum Novarum*, explicilty opposed socialism, and clerics used their pulpits to influence their congregations. Jews, unconstrained by religious institutional sanctions against socialism, engaged in active trade union organization, which may help to account for their relatively higher wages.[51]

Strong charitable and self-help organizations, good indications of cohesion within ethnic groups, provided many immigrants with security. All groups had mutual aid societies that provided life insurance, sickness benefits, and funeral costs. The unusual strength of Jewish charitable agencies gave this group a head start. Jews brought to the urban ghetto a strong tradition of charity justified by talmudic law and supported by generations of *shtetl* life.[52] They also benefited from a prosperous German-Jewish community who, though threatened by loss of social position, were willing to share their wealth and accept responsibility for their coreligionists.[53] The United Hebrew Charities, a German-Jewish agency, proudly pointed out in 1900 that it had taken care of virtually every poverty-stricken Jew. These strong feelings of group responsibility among Jews seem to be directly correlated with their rapid social mobility. Neither the Irish nor the Italians benefited from significant charity efforts from their own compatriots.

5. POLITICS

Sometimes group cohesion is reflected in political activity such as bloc voting, ward politics, and appeals to ethnic loyalty. Irish political acumen, as evidenced in the big city political machines of New York, Chicago, and Boston, was not translated into mobility for the ethnic group. Neither Italian nor Jewish group identity crystallized itself into formal political power, or into nationalist movements.

Among Jews, reluctance to make political capital out of their ethnic identity derived partly from a fear of anti-Semitic outbursts. In running for elective office, the new eastern European Jewish immigrants faced the problem of contending with the German Jews, who, though comfortably represented in positions of some prestige and power, were Republicans who never identified themselves as Jews or appealed to Jewish voters. To some extent, the more recent immigrants also followed this pattern. They ran for office as Democrats or Republicans, finally achieving representation beyond their proportions. The *American Jewish Year Book*, for example, counted fifty Jewish members of Congress between 1900 and 1929.[54] Like former Italian peasants, Jews lacked political influence in Europe where their communities had been run largely by rabbinical leaders. Partisan politics were not familiar to Jews, and, though they became citizens rapidly, they often spent their political energy on radical causes and labor organizations, acquiescing to Irish machine governments.

Irish group consciousness, already nationalistic, was reinforced by the nativistic antebellum Know-Nothing Party as well as by economic discrimination. Unlike the Jews, who tried not to become visible, the Irish asserted their identity proudly in many ways, such as the abortive Fenian movement and in Irish brigades in America's Civil War; aggressively in the draft riots that spread through New York in 1863; and rambunctiously in the firehouse brawls. Observance of St. Patrick's Day, the longest lasting popular legacy, originated in the 1840s.[55] With a centuries-old tradition of political action, derived from their struggle with Britain, the Irish had learned lessons that were to serve them well in gaining a foothold in the New World. Taking advantage of the opportunities presented by rapidly expanding American cities, they became politically powerful by the 1870s, building effectively the political machinery that was to provide urban control for decades.[56]

Italian *campanilismo*—loyalty to the town or province of origin —inhibited national consciousness and overall group cohesion. Compared to Irish peasants who were swept into anti-British fervor, Italian peasants remained relatively indifferent to nationalist movements in Italy. With no comparable political experience in the old country, they were slow to obtain citizenship in the new, and equally slow to challenge the entrenched power of the Irish. Yet they occupied municipal and state offices in some areas, and eventually exercised power through bloc voting, winning decisive victories in major cities in the 1920s. By then, however, control of powerful criminal syndicates throughout the United States vitiated much of the pressure for political power.[57] Some ambitious Italians used crime as their avenue to social mobility instead.

Political power does not seem to have enhanced the socioeconomic position of any group. The Boston Irish, who had political control of that city from the 1880s on, were twice as likely as any other group, native or foreign, to be low-level manual workers in the 1890s.[58] The Germans, who entered in the same period, outranked the Irish in the first and second generations by every available measure of socioeconomic success. Chicago's Italians, who managed to use politics successfully to avoid city and state ordinances, to provide patronage, to establish political connections for businessmen, or to build neighborhood facilities, do not seem to have fared better as a result.[59] Jews, on the other hand, with neither successful political organization nor organized ethnic appeal, achieved considerably more mobility than either of the other two groups.

6. *INTERMARRIAGE*

One of the clearest indications of long-term group cohesion is the rate of intermarriage. That endogamous marriages typify first-generation populations is not surprising. But strong preferences for in-group spouses remain pronounced in some groups into the second and third generations. First- and second-generation Jews and Italians, whether they lived in urban or rural locations, most consistently validated parental culture by expressing a preference for their own kind. In 1920, only 3.4 percent of marriages involving one New York Jew from eastern Europe involved a partner who was non-Jewish. Among southern Italians, 3.51 percent married outside their group. Northern Italians, Irish, Slovaks, Czechs, and Poles, on the other hand, had intermarriage rates of between 30 and 50 percent. Those who have a tendency to marry outside often marry, nevertheless, within their own religions, suggesting that individuals attempt to retain broad aspects of their culture. A study of 1,040 Russian-Polish men revealed that of the women they married, 756 were Russian-Polish, 194 Austrian-Polish, and 33 Slovak.[60] The Irish have retained consistently higher intermarriage rates than either Italians or Jews. Intermarriage rates imply once again some relationship between group cohesion and socioeconomic success. Jews and Italians, more successful than the Irish, also have lower intermarriage rates.

7. *THE FAMILY*

Conflicting evidence makes the relationship between family characteristics and social mobility difficult to assess. The Irish, and later the Jews, typically came to America in family groups. Most "new" immigrants—Italians, Poles, Greeks, and Slavs— sent males ahead; wives and children followed after months, or even years, of separation. Despite the potentially disorganizing effects of these immigration patterns, peasant families proved surprisingly resilient; temporary family dissolutions, for example, did not unduly handicap southern Italians. Nineteenth century Irishmen, who had the apparent advantage of family, rather than individual, migration experience, did not perform remarkably better than first-generation Italians, nor approach the Jews in achievement. Like all immigrant groups, Jews, Irish, and Italians sent money home to needy relatives and provided transportation costs for families left abroad. While Italian males crossed back and forth over the ocean, permanently settled Jews were investing family funds in American business enterprises and sending their young to American schools.[61] The unskilled Irish, handicapped by low incomes, did not have such options. Differences in first-generation Jewish and Italian performance can be partially attributed to the Jewish "head start" in investing in the family's economic potential.

Data concerning broken families among first-generation immigrants imply that family stability played a positive role in group achievement. First-generation Italians and Jews, more successful than first-generation Irish, experienced a lower incidence of female-headed households, a characteristic often considered an index of family weakness. Among New York City immigrants, for example, 93.2 percent of Jewish families and 92.9 percent of Italian families in 1905 had husbands and/or fathers present. In Buffalo, New York, in the same year, 96 percent of Italian families had husbands and/or fathers present.[62] The Irish had a much larger percentage of female-headed households. In nineteenth-century Buffalo, 13 percent of Irish immigrant households were headed by females. The city's more prosperous Germans had 6 percent, and the native-born, 10 percent.[63] These and data from other cities show that Irish families were indeed the victims of poverty, a condition that probably impeded the progress of fatherless children in them. But a high incidence of female-headed households does not prove a lack of family resilience or failure to adapt successfully to the harsh conditions of immigrant life. Supplementary evidence suggests other interpretations.

The Italian and Jewish advantage resulted partly from different immigration styles. Although the famine Irish often emigrated together as family groups, Irish females, unlike Italian women, were not discouraged from emigrating alone. The high incidence of female-headed households among New York City's Irish resulted from an oversupply of Irish-born women, as well as from the hesitancy of recently arrived Irish women to marry outside their ethnic and religious group.[64] Longer residence in the United States and a more balanced sex ratio eventually resulted in a lower proportion of female-headed households. Because fewer of them emigrated alone, Italian women were simply scarcer than first-generation Irish women and consequently in greater demand. This meant that if an Italian woman found herself heading a household, she was less likely to remain alone for long. These conditions were especially applicable in early days of Italian immigration, when the bulk of the Italian immigrant population was male. The Jews more consistently maintained a more balanced sex ratio than any other group.[65] This fact contributed to their easier adjustment.

The absence of fathers from households and the incidence of female employment had different implications for nineteenth and early twentieth century families than they do today. Neither necessarily indicated weakening traditional attitudes or declining patriarchal controls. In some cases, a father's employment away from home represented a continuation of past experiences. Irish and Italian peasant families living in areas characterized by seasonal unemployment learned to adjust to a father's absence long before coming to America.[66] Far from indicating low male commitment, a father's absence illustrated his determination to fulfill family obligations. Immigrant women who worked did not necessarily challenge patriarchal domination or disrupt family stability. Irish and Italian women often adopted work patterns least disruptive of wifely and motherly roles. This explains the popularity of various kinds of domestic industry and the common practice of taking boarders into the family household as a way of supplementing family income.[67] The way in which such women interpreted their work experiences explains why their employment is not symptomatic of family disorganization. They saw their work as a contribution to family needs, not as a vehicle to female independence. Unlike urban black women, immigrant wives saw themselves as supplementing their husbands' wages only temporarily. In evaluating relationships between family stability and socioeconomic advance, these qualifications must be kept in mind.

Minority and lower-class groups experiencing long-term family instability after the initial migration and settlement crises are rarely high achievers, but the converse has not been proven. While family stability has aided and encouraged some ethnics in their pursuit of the American dream, it has restrained others. Jewish family traditions place high priority upon the career success of the young; Jewish occupational and educational achievements suggest a positive relationship between these family values and this group's outstanding success. But family strength appears to have discouraged Italian mobility aspirations because the highly individualized values consistent with American-style success conflicted with more familistic Italian ones.[68] For first-generation Italians, the family continued to be the central institution around which all community life revolved and the "retention of the [Old World] cultural basis . . . the source of . . . retarded [Italian] adjustment."[69]

Correlations between family cohesion and occupational success may weaken over time as the ethnic group makes its way up the occupational ladder. The changing role of the extended family between the first and later generations illustrates this point. In many immigrant groups, Jews and Italians among them, kin helped newcomers to find jobs and homes, and provided emotional support.[70] Reluctance to break away from kin and neighborhood ties may explain why first-generation Italians fared less well than first-generation Jews. Although Jewish family loyalties were strong, Jewish emphasis on career success permitted this group to adapt more readily to the geographic mobility frequently attending job improvement in industrial societies. Traditional Jewish culture did not set up such conflict of interests between family needs and individual achievement in the outside world.[71] By the second generation a different pattern emerged. Italians of all classes, for example, still maintained closer family ties than most ethnics, but middle-class Italians showed the same willingness to move away from ethnic neighborhoods as did other middle-class people. Apparently, once second-generation Italians achieved middle-class status, mobility aspirations superseded extended family traditions in importance.[72]

Other family patterns deserve mention. Family instability, as indicated by divorce rates, does not vary much among the three ethnic groups considered here. About 2 percent of the Jewish population in Providence, Rhode Island, in the 1950s were reportedly divorced or separated, and 12 percent married more than once.[73] Both figures were substantially below those reported for greater Providence, indicating possible long-term persistence of traditional group pressures against divorce. But the rates for Italians and Irish are equally low. Recent national figures indicate that 2.1 percent of Italian males and 2.8 percent of Italian females are divorced, compared to 2.9 percent of Irish males and 3.4 percent of Irish females.[74] If divorce rates are approximately equal for all three groups, family stability as measured by this index cannot explain differential group success.

Birth rates, certainly a potential influence upon group progress, suggest a clearer relationship. Native-born Jews, the most successful group, have consistently lower birth rates than Protestants or Catholics.[75] Of course, family size may reflect current differences in income and education and not be their cause.

The long-term effects of ethnic family traditions in explaining social mobility patterns are difficult to confirm, especially once they begin to play themselves out in differing class, temporal, and social contexts. Irish cultural traditions, for example, may have fostered extended periods of dependence of the young male on the family, while Italian youths were encouraged to make their own way in the world. In the case of the Irish, the labor of young men was needed on farms that could not support additional families. But Italian adolescents who came from families that did not require their labor were sent out into the world to earn their livings. These two groups brought with them to America very different sets of cultural attitudes which may account, in part, for the higher success rates of Italians.[76]

Complex data and varieties of ethnic experience make causal connections between family strength and socioeconomic advance difficult to verify with certainty. In the Jewish case, mutually supportive family and community institutions, along with familial respect for individual achievement, provided a stronger foundation for success seekers than the more familistically oriented Italian culture. Because the Irish, the lowest achievers, experienced comparatively more broken households, they provided the clearest instance of the retarding effects which family difficulties can have upon achievement.

8. *DISCRIMINATION IN HOUSING AND EMPLOYMENT*

If housing discrimination against ethnics retarded achievement, its effects were short-term and indirect. Most white ethnics have not been highly segregated from each other in distinct neighborhoods. In most American cities, neither "new" immigrants nor "old" found themselves trapped in ghettos in which more than half of the population was part of the same ethnic group.[77] Usually no single nationality dominated a particular urban area. Earlier arrivals, such as the Irish, clung tenaciously to their old neighborhoods and to low-rent housing. New immigrants generally gathered more closely; this is not surprising, since language differences and unfamiliarity with American culture encouraged clustering.[78] The degree of segregation from native-born urbanites had more to do with differences in the ethnic origins of a city's white population or the relative size of an ethnic group than with consistent discrimination on the part of the native-born against any one group.[79] Moreover, despite their language difficulties and religious differences, Italian and other new immigrant groups moved around American cities more often than English-speaking Irish and English people.[80] Many, it is true, often sought cheaper housing in other parts of the city, but by the 1920s and 1930s, some had earned enough to buy suburban homes. Ghettoization had no consistent relationship to occupational success. The successful English and the unsuccessful Irish were the least segregated groups in nineteenth- and twentieth-century Boston. Although both Russian Jews and southern Italians experienced high residential segregation, Jews were highly mobile, Italians less so.[81]

The Irish seem to have experienced more overt economic and legal discrimination than any other group, partly because they were the first large ethnic group entering the nation to present the triple threat of religious, class, and ethnic differences. The Know-Nothing political party attempted to win adherents in the 1850s by making anti-Irish policies part of its program. Anti-Irish riots in the Civil War era, deprivation of civil rights, and legalized discrimination solidified patterns of Irish exclusion.[82] While Jews were subject to some social and economic discrimination, especially in the 1920s and 1930s, they did not experience as many institutionalized and legally sanctioned barriers.

Prejudice played a part in limiting job options for all groups save the English. Some historians argue that labor market traditions, as well as overt employer prejudices explain why immigrants did not move more quickly out of manual occupations.[83] The *padrone* system of labor contracting remained in effect as late as the 1900s despite the passage in 1885 of the Foran Act, which explicitly forbade it. Italians, Austrians, Greeks, and eastern Europeans, many of whom spoke no English and did not originally plan to remain in the United States long enough to familiarize themselves with American hiring practices, had no choice but to rely on private labor contractors.[84] Jews who worked in the needle trades had no option but to accept the low wages offered by small entrepreneurs and sweatshop owners.[85] Newly arrived immigrants, who relied on friends and relatives to help them find work, filtered into the manual, low-skilled jobs in which their predecessors had established themselves. Unskilled immigrants without training, experience, language facilities, or education remained in blue-collar jobs. In this way, immigrant occupational patterns were reproduced. The assets immigrants brought with them seem to have had as much to do with explaining future success as the negative effects of job discrimination. Only in this way can the relative achievement of Jews be understood. They endured as much economic discrimination as any other group, yet they had the most outstanding career records.

III. SUMMARY

In the final analysis, there is no way of knowing how important ethnicity is in achieving social mobility. Other factors, such as religion and original class position on entering the United States, may be equally important. Among white ethnics, Jews achieved the highest rate of social mobility. This seems to be explained by such factors as group cohesion, strong families, urban values, education, and a background of occupational skills. Jews exhibit these traits in higher proportions than any other ethnic group. Italians do not have as much education or as high levels of skill. The Irish fall short on many counts. By the third generation, links between these traits and ethnic group affiliation weaken, and class factors seem to explain more than ethnicity.[86] This suggests that as America becomes further removed from its immigrant experience, we may have to search for new explanations for social mobility.

NOTES

1. Among the problems of presently available sources are: the absence of consistent data and of comparative studies; our inability to determine the representative nature of community studies; and the difficulties of using census data which often fail to distinguish religion and national origin. Definitive analysis awaits more studies like Stephan Thernstrom's *The Other Bostonians: Poverty and Progress in the American Metropolis, 1880-1970* (Harvard University Press, 1973). Though hampered by problems of data collection, this sophisticated description of Boston's ethnic groups manages to reach the level of significant hypothesis testing. It is distinguished from earlier sociological studies by its sensitivity to historical context, to changing occupational categories, to developing industrial structures, and to the varieties of urbanization. Other sociological studies include Richard Sennett, *Families Against the City* (Harvard University Press, 1970) and W. Lloyd Warner and Leo Srole, *The Social Systems of American Ethnic Groups* (Yale University Press, 1945). See Thernstrom's indictment of Warner and Srole's ahistorical approach in *Progress and Poverty: Social Mobility in a Nineteenth Century City* (Atheneum, 1970), pp. 225-40.

2. David Ward, *Cities and Immigrants: A Geography of Change in Nineteenth Century America* (Oxford University Press, 1971), pp. 53 ff.

3. See Oscar Handlin, ed., *Immigration as a Factor in American History* (Prentice-Hall, 1959), pp. 16.

4. Scholars have been forced to rely almost exclusively upon objective indicators of socioeconomic advance—occupation, income, and property ownership—simply because prestige and status rankings based upon interpersonal evaluations of previous generations are not available. Data concerning such class characteristics as life-style, consumption patterns, and organizational participation rarely exist in retrievable form. There is a real question, moreover, as to whether objective indices can measure social mobility. Apparent improvements in the socioeconomic position of immigrants should be tested against structural economic and occupational changes, the degree of urbanization, general increases in living standards, and changing expectations. Short of this, we may be describing as group improvement what is in reality a reflection of socioeconomic changes in society.

5. See Leonard Broom, Cora Ann Martin, and Betty Maynard, "Status Profiles of Racial and Ethnic Populations" (paper read at the meetings of the Pacific Sociological Association, March 1967) cited in Joseph Lopreato, *Italian Americans* (Random House, 1970), pp. 162 ff.

6. Thernstrom, *The Other Bostonians*, p. 131; E. P. Hutchinson, *Immigrants and Their Children, 1850-1950* (John Wiley, 1956), pp. 112 ff., 149; Bruce Laurie, Theodore Hershberg, and George Alter, "Immigrants and Industry, The Philadelphia Experience: 1850-1880" (unpublished paper), pp. 14 ff.; Clyde Griffen, "Making It in America: Ethnic Differences in Social Mobility in Mid-Nineteenth Century Cities: Poughkeepsie" (unpublished paper), pp. 4 ff.

7. Laurie et al., "Immigrants and Industry," pp. 14-15.

8. Griffen, "Making It in America," p. 8.

9. Nathaniel Weyl, *The Jew in American Politics* (Arlington House, 1969), pp. 62-63.

10. Samuel Joseph, *Jewish Immigration to the United States from 1881-1910,* Columbia University Studies in History, Economics and Public Law, vol. 59 (Columbia University Press, 1914), pp. 188-90; Nathan Goldberg, *Occupational Patterns of American Jewry* (Jewish Teachers' Seminary and People's University, 1947), pp. 15 ff.

11. Cited in Thernstrom, *The Other Bostonians*, p. 137. Nathan Glazer, "Social Characteristics of American Jews, 1654-1954," *American Jewish Yearbook,* vol. 56 (1955), p. 16, argues that most immigrants stayed garment workers; Goldberg, *Occupational Patterns of American Jewry*, p. 16, notes that in 1900, 24.5 percent of those in trade were peddlers, while 47.4 percent owned stores.

12. Joseph, *Jewish Immigration*, p. 190.

13. Federal Writers' Project, *The Italians of New York* (Random House, 1938), p. 62 (the New York figures are based upon selected samples); Hutchinson, *Immigrants and Their Children*, p. 178; Eliot Lord, *The Italian in America* (Young People's Missionary Movement, 1905), p. 65, contains figures for 1890.

14. Broom, Martin, and Maynard, "Status Profiles of Racial and Ethnic Populations," pp. 162 ff.; see also Stanley Lieberson, *Ethnic Patterns in American Cities* (The Free Press, 1963), pp. 174-75; Stephan Thernstrom, "Immigrants and Wasps: Occupational Mobility in Boston, 1890-1940," in

Thernstrom and Richard Sennett, eds., *Nineteenth Century Cities* (Yale University Press, 1969), pp. 155-57, confirms this trend for Boston.

15. Details on occupational trends are contained in Federal Writers' Project, *The Italians of New York,* p. 63; Humbert S. Nelli, *Italians in Chicago, 1880-1930* (Oxford University Press, 1970), p. 74; Hutchinson, *Immigrants and Their Children,* pp. 178-258.

16. Nelli, *Italians in Chicago,* p. 52; Andrew Rolle, *The American Italians: Their History and Culture* (Wadsworth Publishing Co., 1972), pp. 95-96; Rudolf Glanz, *Jew and Italian: Historic Group Relations and the New Immigration, 1881-1924* (Shulsinger Bros., 1971), pp. 146-47.

17. Nelli, *Italians in Chicago,* pp. 148 ff., discusses organized crime as a means of social mobility among Italians.

18. Thernstrom, *The Other Bostonians,* pp. 132 ff.; see also ibid., p. 141, and Hutchinson, *Immigrants and Their Children,* pp. 228 ff., 241.

19. Hutchinson, *Immigrants and Their Children,* pp. 224 ff., 258.

20. These figures are based on selected samples. New York figures are from Federal Writers' Project, *The Italians of New York,* p. 62; Boston figures are from Thernstrom, *The Other Bostonians,* p. 141.

21. Broom, Martin, and Maynard, "Status Profiles of Racial and Ethnic Populations," p. 164.

22. Thernstrom, *The Other Bostonians,* pp. 141-42. See also Glazer, "Social Characteristics of American Jews," p. 16.

23. Goldberg, *Occupational Patterns of American Jewry,* p. 52.

24. Judith Kramer and Seymour Leventman, *Children of the Gilded Ghetto: Conflict Resolutions of Three Generations of American Jews* (Yale University Press, 1961), p. 130.

25. Glazer, "Social Characteristics of American Jews," p. 26; Goldberg, *Occupational Patterns of American Jewry,* p. 15. The 1900 figure excludes those in "trade," many of whom were peddlers who drifted in and out of factories, so the real figure for manual laborers may be higher.

26. Thernstrom, *Poverty and Progress,* found that while Newburyport's Irish laborers and their sons failed to distinguish themselves in their careers, many bought homes. Poughkeepsie's first generation Irish also invested in property. See Clyde Griffen, "Workers Divided: The Effect of Craft and Ethnic Differences in Poughkeepsie, New York, 1850-1880," in Thernstrom and Sennett, eds., *Nineteenth Century Cities,* pp. 58 ff. Nelli, *Italians in Chicago,* pp. 34 ff., and Lord, *The Italian in America,* pp. 74 ff., each report that Italians looked upon homeownership as a prestigious achievement. On commercial investments in Philadelphia at the turn of the century see John F. Sutherland, "Housing the Poor in the City of Homes: Philadelphia at the Turn of the Century," in Allen F. Davis and Mark Haller, eds., *The Peoples of Philadelphia: A History of Ethnic Groups and Lower Class Life, 1790-1940* (Temple University Press, 1973), pp. 188 ff.

27. Nathan Glazer and Daniel P. Moynihan, *Beyond the Melting Pot* (M.I.T. Press, 1963), p. 187, observe this phenomenon in New York City.

28. See, for example, Barbara Klaczynska, "Why Women Work: A Comparison of Various Ethnic Groups—Philadelphia, 1910-1930," *Labor History,* vol. 17 (Winter, 1976), pp. 73-87.

29. *U.S. Census Bureau Current Population Reports,* "Characteristics of the Population by Ethnic Origin: Nov., 1969" (Government Printing Office,

1971), p. 22. The following figures based on *Current Population Reports* differ from Lopreato who presents figures on intergenerational mobility.

30. Ibid., 1960, p. 46.

31. Ibid., 1972, p. 23.

32. Weyl, *The Jew in American Politics*, p. 78.

33. Lieberson, *Ethnic Patterns in American Cities*, p. 72.

34. Laurie et al., "Immigrants and Industry," p. 21.

35. Oscar Handlin, *Boston's Immigrants* (Atheneum, 1968), p. 42.

36. U.S. Senate, 61st Cong., 2d sess., *Abstracts of the Report of the Immigration Commission*, Doc. no. 747, 1911, vol. I, pp. 325-26; Glanz, *Jew and Italian*, p. 32; less than 6 percent were merchants and tradesmen in Italy. More than 20 percent ended their careers in America in that role.

37. The figures are from the Russian Census of 1897, quoted in Goldberg, *Occupational Patterns of American Jewry*, p. 17; also see Glazer, "Social Characteristics of American Jews," p. 12; Rudolf Glanz, *Jew and Irish: Historic Group Relations and Immigration* (Alexander Kohut Foundation, 1966), p. 31; Joseph, *Jewish Immigration*, p. 190, indicates that about ten times more Jews than Poles were skilled.

38. Lopreato, *Italian Americans*, p. 96, citing Edwin Fenton, "Immigrants and Unions, a Case Study: Italians and American Labor, 1870-1920" (unpublished Ph.D. dissertation, Harvard University, 1957); see also Glanz, *Jew and Italian*, pp. 43, 56 ff. There is some disagreement among scholars concerning Italian inability to organize. Nelli, *Italians in Chicago*, p. 78 ff., reports considerable union activity.

39. Joseph, *Jewish Immigration*, p. 146. The high proportion of women among Jewish immigrants may distort this figure since the female illiteracy rate is about double that of males—36.8 percent for women and 19.7 percent for men.

40. Griffen, "Making It in America," p. 4; U.S. Census of Population, Special Report, 1960, Subject Reports: *Nativity and Parentage, Social and Economic Characteristics of Foreign Stock by Country of Origin* (Government Printing Office, 1965), pp. 42 ff.; Lord, *The Italian in America*, p. 66; Lieberson, *Ethnic Patterns in American Cities*, p. 16.

41. Edward M. Levine, *The Irish and Irish Politicians* (University of Notre Dame Press, 1966), p. 9.

42. Leonard Covello, *The Social Background of the Italo-American School Child* (Rowman and Littlefield, 1972), pp. 281, 285; Nelli, *Italians in Chicago*, pp. 23, 66; Federal Writers' Project, *The Italians of New York*, p. 53.

43. Weyl, *The Jew in American Politics*, p. 71; see Kramer and Leventman, *Children of the Gilded Ghetto*, p. 137, for educational levels of second- and third-generation immigrants. Of the third generation, 88.2 percent had some college or more.

44. Mark Zborowski and Elizabeth Herzog, *Life Is with People: the Culture of the Shtetl* (Schocken, 1952), p. 80.

45. Glazer, "Social Characteristics of American Jews," p. 28.

46. *Reports of the United States Industrial Commission*, vol. 15 (on immigrants, including testimony with review and digest] and *Special Reports on Education* (Government Printing Office, 1901), p. 488; see also Isaac Hourwich, *Immigration and Labor: The Economic Aspects of Euro-*

pean Immigration to the United States (B. W. Huebsch, 1922), p. 232, for a description of New York shanty Irish in the 1860s.

47. Maxwell Whiteman, "Philadelphia Jewish Neighborhoods" in Davis and Haller, eds., *The Peoples of Philadelphia*, pp. 243-44. Jews, in any event, moved out of the ghetto faster than other groups. See Glazer, "Social Characteristics of American Jews," p. 16; Sidney Goldstein and Calvin Goldschneider, *Jewish Americans: Three Generations in a Jewish Community* (Prentice-Hall, 1968), pp. 46 ff., has figures on movement out of the Providence, R.I., ghetto.

48. Solomon Poll, *The Hasidic Community of Williamsburg: A Study in the Sociology of Religion* (Schocken, 1969).

49. Carl Wittke, *We Who Built America* (Prentice-Hall, 1939), p. 153; Thernstrom, *Poverty and Progress*, p. 176, suggests that the church may have been a heavy drain on resources that could have been put to more worldly uses.

50. See Michael Katz, *The Irony of Early School Reform: Educational Innovation in Mid-19th Century Massachusetts* (Harvard University Press, 1968) for a general interpretation of the role of education; Barbara Solomon, *Ancestors and Immigrants* (John Wiley, 1956) contains much on Irish education.

51. Hourwich, *Immigration and Labor*, chap. 15.

52. Zborowski and Herzog, *Life Is with People*; Herman D. Stein, "Jewish Social Work in the United States, 1654-1954," *American Jewish Yearbook*, vol. 57 (1956), p. 11.

53. Zosa Szajkowski, "The Yahudi and the Immigrant: A Reappraisal," *American Jewish Historical Quarterly*, vol. 63 (Sept. 1973), pp. 13-44.

54. *American Jewish Yearbook*, vol. 31 (1929).

55. See Handlin, *Boston's Immigrants*, pp. 209, 155; for the class-based nature of riots, see David Montgomery, *Beyond Equality: Labor and the Radical Republicans, 1862-1872* (Alfred A. Knopf, 1967), chap. 3.

56. For the Irish, see Glanz, *Jew and Irish*, p. 83; and Levine, *The Irish and Irish Politicians*, p. 5.

57. Federal Writers' Project, *The Italians of New York*, p. 96; Rolle, *The American Italians*, p. 86; Wittke, *We Who Built America*, p. 443; Glanz, *Jew and Italian*, p. 76; Nelli, *Italians in Chicago*, pp. 120, 227.

58. Thernstrom, *The Other Bostonians*, p. 131.

59. Nelli, *Italians in Chicago*, pp. 88 ff.

60. The remainder married into other ethnic groups. The figures are from Julius Drachsler, "Intermarriage in New York City," *Studies in History, Economics and Public Law* (Longmans, Green and Agents, 1921), pp. 66-70; Philip Taylor, *The Distant Magnet* (Harper and Row, 1971), p. 271, is a good summary of studies on ethnic group intermarriage. For second- and third-generation Jews, see Erich Rosenthal, "Studies of Jewish Intermarriage in the United States," *American Jewish Yearbook*, vol. 71 (1970), pp. 101-121; Nelli, *Italians in Chicago*, p. 195, offers information on Chicago Italians; on the continuing importance of religious background in marriage see Ruby Jo Reeves Kennedy, "Single or Triple Melting Pot: Intermarriage in New Haven, 1870-1950," *American Journal of Sociology*, vol. 58 (July 1952), pp. 56-59. These studies show that inter-

marriage rates are inversely related to the size of an ethnic group in a particular area, but the generalizations made in the text hold true.

61. Glanz, *Jew and Italian*, pp. 14-15.

62. The New York figures are in Herbert Gutman, "Work, Culture, and Society in Industrializing America, 1815-1919," *American Historical Review*, vol. 78, no. 3 (June 1973), p. 588; Buffalo figures for 1905 are in Virginia Yans-McLaughlin, "Patterns of Work and Family Organization: Buffalo's Italians," *The Journal of Interdisciplinary History*, vol. 11, no. 2 (Autumn 1971), p. 304.

63. Laurence A. Glasco, "Ethnicity and Social Structure: Irish, Germans, and Native Born of Buffalo, New York, 1850-1860." Ph.D. dissertation, University of Buffalo, June 1973, p. 145.

64. Carol Groneman, "The 'Bloody Ould Sixth': A Social Analysis of a Mid-Nineteenth Century New York Working Class Community" (Ph.D. dissertation, University of Rochester, 1973) treats the Irish in New York's infamous Five Points section. Between 1899 and 1910, 47.9 percent of Irish immigrants were male and 52.1 percent were female. The Irish had a lower proportion of males than any other group. See Joseph, *Jewish Immigration*, p. 179, for comparisons. It is possible that the Irish figures were more balanced late in the nineteenth century than they were in the 1840s, the heaviest period of Irish immigration.

65. Joseph, *Jewish Immigration*, p. 179, gives percentages of male and female immigrants for 1899-1910 as follows: Irish—47.9 percent male and 52.1 percent female; Jews—56.6 percent male and 43.4 percent female; south Italians—78.6 percent male and 21.4 percent female.

66. Handlin, *Boston's Immigrants*, p. 71; Yans-McLaughlin, "Patterns of Work and Family Organization," p. 308.

67. On the Italians, see Yans-McLaughlin, "Patterns of Work and Family Organization"; Carol Groneman, "She Earns as a Child, She Pays as a Man: Women Workers in a Mid-Nineteenth Century New York City Community" (Unpublished paper delivered at the Conference on Immigrants in Industrial America, Eleutherian Mills Historical Society and the Balch Institute, Nov. 1973), pp. 8-9, contains information on Irish women.

68. See, for example, Herbert Gans, *The Urban Villagers: Group and Class in the Life of Italian-Americans* (Free Press, 1962), pp. 219 ff.; on the Jews, see Glazer and Moynihan, *Beyond the Melting Pot*, pp. 155 ff.

69. Covello, *Italo-American School Child*, p. 280.

70. John S. and Leatrice D. MacDonald, "Chain Migration, Ethnic Neighborhood Formation and Social Network," *Milbank Memorial Fund Quarterly*, vol. 42 (Jan. 1964), pp. 82-97.

71. Fred Strodtbeck, "Family Interaction, Values and Achievements" in David McClelland, et al., eds., *Talent and Society* (D. Van Nostrand, 1958), p. 151; Glazer and Moynihan, *Beyond the Melting Pot*, pp. 197-98, draw interesting contrasts between Italians and Jews.

72. See Lopreato, *Italian Americans*, p. 51, for a description of that group; there is evidence that Jewish kinship ties are also weakening. See Goldstein and Goldscheider, *Jewish Americans*, p. 52; Eugene Litwak, "Geographic Mobility and Extended Family Cohesion," *American Sociological Review*, vol. 25 (1960), pp. 385-94 and Litwak, "Occupational Mobility and Extended Family Cohesion," *ibid.*, pp. 9-21, criticize a com-

mon assumption that mobility and extended family cohesion are incompatible. Andrew M. Greeley, *Why Can't They Be Like Us?* (Institute for Human Relations Press, 1969), p. 52, notes that in a 1967 survey of Italians, Irish, Germans, Poles, French, English, Scandinavians, and Jews, Italians were most likely to visit and live in the same neighborhood as parents and siblings. Jews are more likely to visit parents weekly than Irish and German Catholics or any Protestant ethnic group.

73. Goldstein and Goldschneider, *Jewish Americans*, pp. 20, 24.

74. U.S. Bureau of the Census, *Current Population Reports*, "Characteristics of the Population by Ethnic Origin: March, 1972 and 1971" (Government Printing Office, 1973), p. 28.

75. Goldstein and Goldschneider, *Jewish Americans*, pp. 15-16, cites comparative figures for 1905 and 1955.

76. The material in this paragraph has been suggested by Thomas Sowell, *Race and Economics* (David McKay Co., 1975), pp. 87-90.

77. Nelli, *Italians in Chicago*, indicates that few Chicago streets had more than 50 percent Italians and their children; Howard P. Chudakoff, *Mobile Americans: Residential and Social Mobility in Omaha, 1880-1920* (Oxford University Press, 1972), pp. 65 ff., points to low ethnic concentrations for nineteenth and early twentieth century Omaha.

78. Chudakoff, *Mobile Americans*, indicates that this is true for Omaha in 1910 and 1920, and reports the same patterns in antebellum Boston as well as for Philadelphia in 1860 and 1930.

79. Lieberson, *Ethnic Patterns in American Cities*, p. 81.

80. Chudakoff, *Mobile Americans*, pp. 65 ff.; Nelli, *Italians in Chicago*, pp. 24, 207, 73.

81. Thernstrom, *The Other Bostonians*, p. 165.

82. For discrimination against the Irish, see Handlin, *Boston's Immigrants*, p. 215 and passim; on the Italians, see Nelli, *Italians in Chicago*, p. 130; on the Jews, see Oscar and Mary Handlin, "The Acquisition of Political and Social Rights by Jews in the United States," *American Jewish Yearbook*, vol. 54 (1955), pp. 43-98.

83. Thernstrom, *The Other Bostonians*, pp. 160 ff. Much of the following discussion is based upon Thernstrom's observations. A new study by economists Richard C. Edwards, Michael Reich, and David Gordon, *Labor Market Segmentation* (Lexington Books, 1975), explores the way in which early twentieth century employers deliberately manipulated ethnic groups for corporate advantage.

84. Nelli, *Italians in Chicago*, p. 56.

85. Glanz, *Jew and Italian*, p. 26.

86. This position is taken by Gans, *The Urban Villagers*, passim, who discusses second-generation Italians.

Ethnic Income Variations: Magnitudes and Explanations

ERIC HANUSHEK

Income variations among ethnic groups exist within a wider context of general income inequalities in the American economy, and among the various nations of the world. Indeed, similarly obvious and dramatic income disparities existed in ancient Rome. Interpreting interethnic differences in incomes is complicated by the fact that ethnic groups differ systematically in many ways other than ethnicity per se. This chapter attempts to sort out some of he factors affecting ethnic differences in the distribution of incomes.

As an illustration of persisting income differentials in the United States, table 1 shows the percent of aggregate income received by each fifth of all U.S. families (ranked by total income) for each decade since 1950. The top fifth of families, in terms of income, received over 40 percent of the total income while the bottom fifth received around 5 percent. And, this skewed distribution has remained virtually unchanged over the past two decades. Interestingly, such disparities exist even within sub-populations. Considering just families with a white head

Table 1

PERCENT OF AGGREGATE INCOME RECEIVED BY
EACH FIFTH OF U.S. FAMILIES: 1950, 1960, 1970

Income Rank	1950	1960	1970
Lowest Fifth	4.5	4.9	5.5
Second Fifth	12.0	12.0	12.0
Middle Fifth	17.4	17.6	17.4
Fourth Fifth	23.7	23.6	23.5
Highest Fifth	41.6	42.0	41.6

SOURCE: U.S. Bureau of the Census, *Statistical Abstract of the United States, 1973* (Government Printing Office, 1973), p. 330.

for 1970, the top fifth captured 41 percent of white income while the bottom fifth managed only 5.8 percent; for the black population, the corresponding figures were 44 percent and 4.5 percent.[1]

This aggregate income distribution can be collapsed to observe racial disparity in incomes. As table 2 shows, median family income of whites and nonwhites is nowhere near being equal. (While it would be desirable to analyze additional ethnic groups, this study will focus primarily upon black-white differences because of data availability. Where possible, "Spanish Americans"— defined as Mexican Americans and Puerto Ricans combined— will also be studied. However, it is not possible to go further in disaggregating ethnic groups.) Even though nonwhite income has improved relative to white income in recent years, nonwhite income remained less than two-thirds of white income. Moreover, such racial differences are found at points other than the median of the income distribution.

Interest in the racial and ethnic aspects of the distribution of income arises from several obvious factors. First, there are clear moral and legal interests that revolve around discriminatory treatment. Second, it is a type of comparison which we can more comfortably and more validly make than comparisons of individual incomes. At the individual level, personal characteristics such as innate ability, training, experience, attitudes, and personality along with luck and good fortune become overwhelmingly important.[2] But, for a racial or ethnic group as a whole these factors—often unmeasurable—either may be reasonably presumed to be similar across the group or the differences must be the subject of public policy consideration.

Nevertheless, the significance and interpretation of racial and ethnic differences in incomes depend importantly upon understanding the reasons behind observed differences. Most important among the potential underlying factors that have been considered has been education. The distribution of education has been labeled as both a significant cause of the current income dis-

Table 2

MEDIAN INCOME OF FAMILIES BY RACE OF HEAD, 1947 TO 1974

(Current Dollars)

Year	White	Negro and Other	Ratio Nonwhite to White
1947	$3,157	$1,614	.51
1948	3,310	1,768	.53
1949	3,232	1,650	.51
1950	3,445	1,869	.54
1951	3,859	2,032	.53
1952	4,114	2,338	.57
1953	4,392	2,461	.56
1954	4,339	2,410	.56
1955	4,605	2,549	.55
1956	4,993	2,628	.53
1957	5,166	2,764	.54
1958	5,300	2,711	.51
1959	5,643	2,917	.52
1960	5,835	3,233	.55
1961	5,981	3,191	.53
1962	6,237	3,330	.53
1963	6,548	3,465	.53
1964	6,858	3,839	.56
1965	7,251	3,994	.55
1966	7,792	4,674	.60
1967	8,274	5,141	.62
1968	8,937	5,590	.63
1969	9,794	6,191	.63
1970	10,236	6,516	.64
1971	10,672	6,714	.63
1972	11,549	7,106	.62
1973	12,595	7,596	.60
1974	13,356	8,265	.62

SOURCE: U.S. Bureau of the Census, "Money Income in 1974 of Families and Persons in the United States," *Current Population Reports*, Series P-60 (Government Printing Office, 1976).

tribution and a focal point for changing the distribution. Further, in looking at the racial distribution of income, many have pointed to the large racial differences in both quantity and quality of schooling. These differences are assumed to be an important cause for racial income discrepancies and are thought of as a natural and compelling place for governmental action, partially because a basic societal premise has been the right to free and equal educational opportunity.

Table 3 shows the degree of difference in schooling by age and race. The differences in median schooling are most dramatic for older members of the population, but they remain significant for even the 25- to- 29-year-old group. Blacks consistently receive less schooling.

As dramatic as these differences appear, the educational disparity portrayed is an understatement of reality. Data for 1965 from the "Coleman report" show the equally dramatic quality disparity in schooling.[3] As seen in table 4, twelfth-grade blacks in the rural South perform at the seventh-grade level of whites in the urban Northeast. Similar though not as large differences exist for other regions.

Table 3

YEARS OF SCHOOL COMPLETED BY RACE AND AGE,
1972 (PERSONS 25 YEARS AND OLDER)

| Race and Age | Percent of Population Completing | | | | | | | |
| | Elementary | | | High School | | College | | |
	0-4 yrs.	5-7 yrs.	8 yrs.	1-3 yrs.	4 yrs.	1-3 yrs.	4 or more yrs.	Median yrs.
All Races	4.6	8.3	11.9	17.0	35.2	10.9	12.0	12.2
25-29 yrs.	.8	2.7	3.1	13.6	43.8	17.0	19.0	12.7
30-34 yrs.	1.4	3.3	4.7	16.7	43.9	13.5	16.5	12.5
35-44 yrs.	2.5	5.4	6.9	18.5	41.5	11.5	13.8	12.4
45-54 yrs.	3.4	7.3	10.8	18.6	38.6	10.6	10.6	12.3
55 and over	9.0	14.3	21.2	16.4	23.6	7.6	7.9	11.6
Negro	12.8	17.0	9.6	24.0	24.9	6.5	5.1	10.3
25-29 yrs.	1.3	5.6	4.9	24.1	42.9	13.0	8.2	12.3
30-34 yrs.	1.6	6.4	6.3	29.4	40.5	8.4	7.4	12.2
35-44 yrs.	5.4	12.7	8.4	31.9	28.7	7.3	5.7	11.2
45-54 yrs.	10.5	20.0	12.1	26.2	21.2	5.9	4.1	9.9
55 and over	29.7	27.8	12.3	14.5	10.1	2.6	2.9	7.2

SOURCE: U.S. Bureau of the Census, *Statistical Abstract of the United States: 1973* (Government Printing Office, 1973), p. 116.

Table 4

ACHIEVEMENT DIFFERENTIALS BY RACE AND REGION:
AVERAGE GRADE LEVELS BEHIND THE AVERAGE
WHITE IN THE METROPOLITAN NORTHEAST,
VERBAL ABILITY

Race and Region	Grade Levels Behind		
	Grade 6	Grade 9	Grade 12
White, Nonmetropolitan			
South	.7	1.0	1.5
Southwest	.3	.4	.8
North	.2	.4	.9
White, Metropolitan			
Northeast	—	—	—
Midwest	.1	.0	.4
South	.5	.5	.9
Southwest	.5	.6	.7
West	.3	.3	.5
Negro, Nonmetropolitan			
South	2.5	3.9	5.2
Southwest	2.0	3.3	4.7
North	1.9	2.7	4.2
Negro, Metropolitan			
Northeast	1.6	2.4	3.3
Midwest	1.7	2.2	3.3
South	2.0	3.0	4.2
Southwest	1.9	2.9	4.3
West	1.9	2.6	3.9
Mexican American	2.0	2.3	3.5

SOURCE: James S. Coleman et al., *Equality of Educational Opportunity* (Government Printing Office, 1966), table 3.121.1.

This chapter analyzes the strength of these underlying relationships and their implications for earnings distributions. First, a systematic appraisal of the relationship between schooling and earnings is undertaken. This appraisal relies upon the data from the 1970 Census of Population. Second, the analysis considers other basic factors which influence incomes—namely, experience and labor market locations. Finally, the racial and ethnic disparity in incomes is analyzed to determine the relative importance of input differences (such as in tables 3 and 4) and of the discriminatory aspects of labor markets.

I. MODELS AND DATA

The objective of this analysis is to gain a better understanding of the process of income determination. Such understanding, in turn, allows consideration of alternative strategies for changing the current distribution of income. The determination of individual incomes clearly cannot be understood by simply looking at the average incomes obtained by a person of a given ethnic group or given schooling class. The process is too complicated for that, and the apparent influence of any single factor is masked by the correlations among groups of factors. For example, while we found that blacks on the average earned less than whites, we also found that blacks on the average have less schooling, that blacks tend to be more concentrated in the South, and so forth. For that reason we must go to more complicated models and more sophisticated analytical techniques than simple comparisons of average earnings.

The basic conceptual model for looking at income determination relied upon in this analysis is an offshoot of the human capital model. This model, developed over the past 15 years, views schooling and training as an investment.[4] Using the analogy of investing in physical capital, a person can increase his future earnings capacity by investing in himself. A corollary of this model is that earnings can be viewed as a function of the past history of human capital investments.[5]

There are, of course, many nuances to this basic model because there are many ways in which one can invest in himself. Investment can be made through formal schooling, on-the-job training, health care, or migration to a different region, to name a few. It is also possible to view the costs of such investments as coming from a variety of sources: tuition payments, direct cash outlays, or foregone earnings.

With varying allowance for some of these factors, this basic model relating earnings to schooling and other attributes has been estimated in a variety of situations. Relying chiefly upon cross-sectional data, these studies have produced estimates of the value of additional schooling and of other types of investments. These estimates, in turn, have been used: (1) to predict how additional schooling might affect the income distribution; and, (2) to say something about the relative value of schooling (and discrimination) across races and ethnic groups.

Without going into the details of either human capital models or the offshoots of such models, it is instructive to note that these models are really reduced form models. The reasons why investments in schooling and training raise the future incomes of individuals are not addressed directly, but an underlying presumption is that the returns to additional schooling or investment reflect both the demands for skills and training and the relative supplies of these attributes. As such, the advisability of further investment from the individual's perspective must be conditioned by both the current and future balance of these underlying factors.[6]

Calculating the effect on earnings of an increase in schooling for the entire country and projecting these results into the future assumes that the historical relationship between supply and demand for skilled labor will be maintained. Further, it implies that it is reasonable to think of a national labor market with a single wage for individuals of different schooling categories. Both of these presumptions are open to considerable question.

Studies of schooling-earnings relationships relying upon cross-sectional data for different samples and different periods of time have yielded significantly different results. These differences have been explained in part by differences in aggregate labor market conditions; i.e., with different demand conditions for skilled labor, one finds different reduced form relationships between schooling and earnings.[7]

Past research into earnings models also has shown large differences in earnings for macrogeographical regions of the country such as the South. While there has not been much investigation of smaller regions, there is, on the other hand, little reason to presume that the gross regional measurements of past studies adequately capture geographical, or labor market variations in earnings relationships.[8]

In recognition of the potential importance of labor market differences—both in describing earnings relationships and in formulating policies with respect to earnings, this analysis is designed to allow labor market interactions with schooling-earnings relationships. The analytical design in this chapter follows directly from that previously considered by the author.[9] Earnings data are analyzed within individual labor markets, or individual Standard Metropolitan Statistical Areas (SMSAs). By considering the relationship between earnings and various inputs to earnings for each SMSA separately, it is then possible to sort out the relative importance of input factors (such as schooling), of race and ethnic background, and of specific labor market conditions.

Observing earnings within individual labor markets allows testing of whether or not migration and trade between different geographical markets is sufficient to bring the markets into equilibrium with respect to payments to different types of labor; i.e., are the earnings of similar individuals in different regions the same? [10]

The empirical analysis here relies upon the 1970 census data from the Public Use Samples. These data provide a picture of the earnings in 1969, the occupations, and the backgrounds of individuals. Further, the county group data from the Public Use Samples allow identification of individuals by Standard Metropolitan Statistical Area (SMSA) provided there are at least 250,000 people in the SMSA.

The basic criteria for inclusion in the analysis were that: (1) the individual was a male between 16 and 65 years old; (2) the individual had worked full time (35 + hours) and full year (48-52 weeks); (3) his earnings from wages, self-employment, and farming were positive; and (4) he had a known U.S. state of birth. These criteria were applied generally to eliminate certain sources of earnings variations which were not central to this study and thereby to simplify the task of modeling earnings of individuals. The analysis was restricted to males, in part, because of the widely observed differences in male and female career progressions and, in part, because attempts to develop models of female earnings have not been too successful. The age restriction mirrors the accepted working life prescribed by child labor laws and Social Security regulations and represents an attempt to avoid peculiar working relationships, particularly for individuals over 65. The full-time, full-year work restriction was introduced to minimize problems of interactions between work activity and wage rates.[11] Earnings were required to be positive both because the models considered apply best to permanent income for which negative values do not make much sense and because negative values are difficult to handle analytically.[12] Finally, since attempts will be made to correct for differences in school quality, it was necessary to know the state of birth for the individual in order to estimate where the education was received.

Within each of the SMSAs identified in the Public Use Sample, several subsamples of observations were created. Individuals were divided by race (into white, black, and Spanish samples) and by years of schooling (into schooling less than or equal to 12 years and schooling greater than 12 years). A subsample was required to have at least 50 observations (meeting the criteria above) in order to be included in the analysis. Table 5 shows the number of regional subsamples created by race and schooling categories. This table also shows the geographical distribution of these SMSAs by the nine census regions of the country. Table 6 shows the corresponding number of observations in each of these samples. In total, there are over 175,000 observations for analysis.

The mean 1969 earnings for this sample are displayed in table 7.[13] It is clear from this table that there are large and systematic differences in earnings by race, region, and schooling categories. For example, within the urban Northeast, the average white with a high school education or less earns $1,900 more than a corresponding black even though they work the same amount; this is a full 27 percent more. Similar disparities are evident across regions and across schooling categories.

Corresponding to these income differences are a number of fundamental differences, as in amount of schooling. Table 8 shows the mean schooling levels by race and region for each of the samples. The "unadjusted" levels give the years of schooling completed in 1970. The "adjusted" values represent a crude attempt to allow for quality differences in the schooling received by each individual. These quality adjustments are based upon the 1965 nationwide testing done to calculate school quality for *Equality of Educational Opportunity* (the "Coleman report").[14] These school quality data, reproduced in table 4 of this chapter, compare the verbal achievement scores by race and region to the performance of whites in the urban Northeast. For each individual, based upon state of birth, years of school completed, and race, a quality-adjusted score was calculated; for schooling past grade 12, the twelfth-grade adjustment was used.[15] As table 8 vividly shows, the distribution of schooling, when quality adjusted, looks much more skewed than it does when not quality adjusted.

Using these data, for SMSAs, the relationship between earnings and human capital was estimated through regression analysis. Human capital, following the work of Mincer, was measured by schooling completed (or school quality), experience, and experience squared.[16] The quadratic experience term permits varying returns to length of experience—a situation which would exist if there was on-the-job training at the beginning of a work career. Individual estimates of such earnings functions were obtained for each race/schooling group (with over 50 observa-

Table 5

NUMBER OF SAMPLED SMSAs BY RACE, SCHOOLING CATEGORY, AND CENSUS REGION

Census Region[a]	White			Black			Spanish		
	S ≤ 12[b]	S > 12[b]	Total[c]	S ≤ 12[b]	S > 12[b]	Total[c]	S ≤ 12[b]	S > 12[b]	Total[c]
Northeast	7	7	7	2		2	1		1
Mid-Atlantic	21	21	21	7	2	7	1		1
E. North Central	25	25	25	10	3	11			
W. North Central	8	8	8	2	1	2			
S. Atlantic	18	18	18	18	2	18	1		3
E. South Central	9	9	9	7		7			
W. South Central	14	14	14	7	1	9	5	1	6
Mountain	5	5	5				4		4
Pacific	18	18	18	2	2	3	8	5	9
All Regions	125	125	125	55	11	59	20	6	24

a. Regional divisions follow census definitions: *Northeast*—Maine, New Hampshire, Vermont, Massachusetts, Rhode Island, Connecticut; *Mid-Atlantic*—New York, New Jersey, Pennsylvania; *E. North Central*—Ohio, Indiana, Illinois, Michigan, Wisconsin; *W. North Central*—Minnesota, Iowa, Missouri, North Dakota, South Dakota, Nebraska, Kansas; *S. Atlantic*—Delaware, Maryland, D.C., Virginia, W. Virginia, North Carolina, South Carolina, Georgia, Florida; *E. South Central*—Kentucky, Tennessee, Alabama, Mississippi; *W. South Central*—Arkansas, Louisiana, Oklahoma, Texas; *Mountain*—Montana, Idaho, Wyoming, Colorado, New Mexico, Arizona, Utah, Nevada; *Pacific*—Washington, Oregon, California, Alaska, Hawaii.

b. S = Years of schooling completed.

c. The "total" samples for an ethnic group may be larger than the numbers for the schooling subgroup because of the observational cutoff of 50 sample points; i.e., there may be less than 50 in either schooling group but more than 50 if the samples are combined.

Table 6

NUMBER OF OBSERVATIONS IN SAMPLED SMSAs BY RACE, SCHOOLING CATEGORY, AND CENSUS REGION[a]

Region	White			Black			Spanish		
	S ≤ 12[b]	S > 12[b]	Total[c]	S ≤ 12[b]	S > 12[b]	Total[c]	S ≤ 12[b]	S > 12[b]	Total[c]
Northeast	7,374	3,987	11,361	131		166			
Mid-Atlantic	26,290	12,678	38,968	2,895	394	3,398	99		114
E. North Central	23,105	11,579	34,684	2,727	427	3,324	131		170
W. North Central	7,060	3,687	10,747	407	65	492			
S. Atlantic	10,848	6,533	17,381	2,895	237	3,316	57		206
E. South Central	4,213	2,040	6,253	859		937			
W. South Central	7,026	4,812	11,838	1,171	76	1,471	966	59	1,195
Mountain	2,089	1,717	3,806				483		599
Pacific	12,754	11,364	24,118	827	346	1,223	1,727	575	2,446
Total	100,759	58,397	159,156	11,912	1,545	14,327	3,463	634	4,730

a. Number of observations based on full-time, full-year workers contained in the 1/100 sample; see sampling criteria in text.

b. S = Years of schooling completed.

c. The "total" samples for an ethnic group may be larger than the numbers for the schooling subgroup because of the observational cutoff of 50 sample points; i.e., there may be less than 50 in either school group but more than 50 if the samples are combined.

SOURCE: 1970 Census of Population (Public Use Sample).

Table 7

1969 SAMPLE MEAN EARNINGS BY RACE, SCHOOLING,[a] AND CENSUS REGION[b]

(Hundreds of dollars)

Region	White			Black			Spanish		
	S ≤ 12	S > 12	Total	S ≤ 12	S > 12	Total	S ≤ 12	S > 12	Total
Northeast	$ 90	$143	$108	$71	$	$61	$	$	$
Mid-Atlantic	93	148	111	68	96	72	76		66
E. North Central	99	140	113	74	97	78	84		71
W. North Central	94	130	106	65	86	68			
S. Atlantic	89	142	109	57	85	60	81	126	100
E. South Central	83	127	97	51	62	52			
W. South Central	89	129	105	53	67	55	61	105	69
Mountain	92	125	107	60			68	104	75
Pacific	100	135	117	73	91	78	85	112	92

a. S = Years of schooling completed.

b. Means calculated for full-time, full-year workers in SMSAs; see sampling criteria in text.

SOURCE: 1970 Census of Population (Public Use Sample).

Table 8

1970 MEAN SCHOOLING—ADJUSTED AND UNADJUSTED[a]

Census Region	White		Black		Spanish	
	Unadj.	Adj.[b]	Unadj.	Adj.[b]	Unadj.	Adj.[b]
Northeast	12.3	12.3	8.7	5.9		
Mid-Atlantic	12.2	12.2	10.6	7.4	9.0	6.2
E. North Central	12.2	11.8	10.5	7.3	7.9	5.6
W. North Central	12.2	11.9	10.5	7.4		
S. Atlantic	12.2	11.8	9.8	6.7	12.3	9.1
E. South Central	11.8	11.1	9.3	6.2		
W. South Central	12.3	11.7	9.8	6.5	9.5	6.8
Mountain	12.8	12.4			10.6	7.6
Pacific	13.0	12.6	11.2	7.7	11.3	8.2

a. Means calculated for full-time, full-year workers in SMSAs; see sampling criteria in text.

b. Schooling adjusted for estimated quality differences in elementary and secondary schools. Quality differences come from *Equality of Educational Opportunity*, p. 274; see table 4 above and footnote 15.

SOURCE: 1970 Census of Population (Public Use Sample).

tions) in each SMSA.[17] The results are discussed in the next section.

II. PRELIMINARY RESULTS

Estimation of the earnings models for the individual regions and race/schooling subsamples produces a large number of individual results. The discussion here will concentrate on some of the more important summary conclusions.

Table 9 summarizes the overall explanatory power of the basic regional estimation. The first column (R^2) shows the "average" proportion of variance explained within each of the subregions and groups. The next three columns relate to the national variance in earnings (or, more precisely, log earnings). The within region explained variance plus the between region explained variance yields the total explained variance (col. 4).[18] The within region explained variance tells how well the estimated SMSA models do at explaining the differences in individual earnings. The between region explained variance results from the stratification of the sample into different SMSAs; the size of this explained variance is related to the differences in mean earnings across SMSAs. For whites with a high school education or less, 11 percent of the variation in individual incomes is explained by differences in schooling and differences in labor force experience (i.e., the model estimated *within* each region); 3 percent of the variation in individual earnings is accounted for by geographical location (i.e., differences in mean earnings *between* SMSAs; this leaves 86 percent of the variation in earnings for this group unaccounted for by this analysis). As can be seen by the fourth column, this analysis accounts for between 15 and 30 percent of the variation in individual earnings. In other words, there remains a considerable amount in the income generation process that we do not understand, or that at least is not explained by this basic model.

Table 9 has another interesting aspect. The between region explained variance is a measure of how different the regions are in terms of earnings. For each racial group, the difference between regions is more important for those with a high school education or less than for those with more than a high school education. This is most pronounced for black and Spanish males. This is consistent with a hypothesis that the labor market for

Table 9

AGGREGATE EXPLANATORY POWER OF EARNINGS MODELS[a]

Group	R-Squared[b]	Individual Income Variance Explained			No. of SMSAs	No. of Observ.
		Within SMSAs	Between SMSAs	Total		
White						
S ≤ 12	.115	.112	.031	.143	125	100,759
S > 12	.239	.233	.026	.259	125	58,397
Total	.216	.210	.030	.240	125	159,156
Black						
S ≤ 12	.073	.067	.084	.151	55	11,912
S > 12	.147	.143	.027	.170	11	1,545
Total	.099	.091	.086	.177	59	14,327
Spanish						
S ≤ 12	.172	.153	.110	.263	20	3,463
S > 12	.276	.270	.023	.293	6	634
Total	.224	.205	.086	.291	24	4,730

a. The calculations of regional variance explained relate to national variance in income for the given racial/schooling sample. deviations in the dependent variable.

b. R-squared is defined as tne aggregate of explained sum of squares in eacn region divided by the aggregate of sum squared deviations in the dependent variable.

college-educated individuals is more national in character while
the labor market for less-educated individuals is more local.
Thus, the higher mobility of college-educated people tends to
equalize the individual labor markets to a greater extent than is
the case for less-educated and less-mobile individuals. This im-
mobility could arise either because of differences in information
or differences in the rewards to moving, relative to the costs of
moving. There is, however, more to the study of geographic or
labor market differences. As we shall see below, we are interested
in the shape of the earnings function as well as the level (as
given by the SMSA mean earnings for the race/schooling
groups).

When looking at earnings functions, most attention is naturally centered upon the returns to additional schooling. The government has traditionally taken an interest in the schooling of the
population, and schooling is seen as the most legitimate way for
the government to attempt changes in the income distribution.
The analysis here concentrates on the earnings function for
whites and blacks. Earnings of Spanish Americans (both Mexican American and Puerto Rican) are included with the other
analyses, but the sample sizes for this group are generally quite
small, and the estimates tend to be unreliable.

For comparisons of the estimated relationship between earnings and schooling, we will concentrate upon the value of an additional year of schooling. Specifically, we will look at the percentage increase in earnings that would be expected from one
more year of schooling or, alternatively, one more year of quality
equivalent schooling. This provides a summary measure of the
value of additional schooling and allows comparisons to be made
across race and schooling groups. At the same time, we shall
also be looking at the effect of individual labor market conditions
on the return to additional schooling.

Table 10 provides some insights into the effect of labor market
conditions on earnings of whites. Each of the SMSAs which were
sampled are placed in one of the nine census regions so that the
range of estimated schooling-earnings relationships can be
viewed. Clearly, even within the census regions, there is wide
disparity in the returns to schooling. The returns to schooling,
or percentage increase in earnings that is related to an additional year of schooling, differ within regions by at least 2.9 percent (for individuals with a high school or less education in the
Northeast) but go as high as almost 19 percent in the Pacific

Table 10

RANGE OF ESTIMATED PERCENTAGE INCREASES IN EARNINGS PER YEAR OF SCHOOLING BY REGION AND SCHOOLING CLASS: WHITES

Census Region	No. of SMSAs	S ≤ 12			S > 12		
		Min.	Max.	Range	Min.	Max.	Range
Northeast	7	2.7	5.6	2.9	8.0	11.0	3.0
Mid-Atlantic	21	2.3	9.3	7.0	.2	13.5	13.3
E. North Central	25	2.2	7.5	5.3	2.2	13.2	11.0
W. North Central	8	3.0	6.4	3.4	6.0	12.6	6.6
S. Atlantic	19	2.6	8.9	6.3	6.7	14.5	7.8
E. South Central	8	3.7	7.9	4.2	4.4	11.9	7.5
W. South Central	14	2.4	9.6	7.2	−.2	15.1	15.3
Mountain	5	−2.8	5.1	7.9	5.3	12.0	6.7
Pacific	19	−2.6	16.2	18.8	4.1	13.0	8.9

region. Some of this variance arises from the sampling distribution of the estimates, and there are even a few negative estimates for the effect of additional schooling.[19] Nonetheless, since the standard errors of these estimates tend to range between .5 and 1.5 for all but the smallest SMSAs, the effect of individual labor market conditions on the schooling-earnings relationship cannot be disregarded.

For black and Spanish individuals, the lesser number of SMSAs precludes meaningfully looking at the ranges of estimates within census regions. However, similar variance among SMSAs appears for these groups. With blacks, the estimated percentage increase in earnings arising from an additional year of schooling ranges from negative to 10.4 percent when schooling completed is 12 years or less and from 8.2 to 11.4 percent for more than 12 years of schooling. With the Spanish samples, the similar ranges are 3.0 to 8.8 percent for high school or less schooling and 7.4 to 17.4 percent for post-secondary schooling. (The problem of large sampling errors is more critical for the black and Spanish samples because more of the SMSAs tend to be close to the 50 observation cutoff and, thus, the estimated relationships are not as precise.)

Previously, we noted the importance of mean differences across SMSAs. Particularly for less educated minorities, a significant portion (8-11 percent) of the variance in individual earnings was explained by overall labor market differences. We now find that the shape of the earnings function also differs significantly by region.

In order to understand better the relationship between schooling, school quality, and earnings, we will shift to a discussion of the mean effect on earnings of increasing schooling. However, throughout these discussions the variance in earnings relationships across regions should not be forgotten. The range of predicted effects within a region-race-schooling group is often larger than the observed differences between racial groups or regions.

Table 11 presents the estimated mean relationship between schooling and earnings for different aggregations of individuals. The values given are the average estimated percentage effect on earnings of an increase of one year in schooling (or quality adjusted schooling) where each SMSA value is weighted by the number of observations in the SMSA. There are several striking features in this table.

Table 11

ESTIMATED PERCENTAGE INCREASE IN EARNINGS PER YEAR OF SCHOOLING

(Weighted Average of Individual SMSAs)

Sample	No. of SMSAs	Schooling	School Quality[a]
White			
S ≤ 12	125	4.44	4.55
S > 12	125	9.81	9.67
Total	125	7.55	
Black			
S ≤ 12	55	3.66	5.08
S > 12	11	9.02	8.73
Total	59	5.02	
Spanish			
S ≤ 12	20	5.22	7.12
S > 12	6	11.88	11.89
Total	24	6.82	
All Individuals			
S ≤ 12	125	5.24	
S > 12	125	10.11	
Total	125	7.96	

a. Results indicate average coefficients when model is estimated using adjusted schooling, defined in footnote 15, instead of actual schooling.

First, looking at the unadjusted schooling column, the difference in returns to schooling for the high school and less group and the more than high school group is dramatic. For each racial group, the percentage increase in earnings for the more educated group is at least double that of the less educated group; for both blacks and whites, each year of advanced schooling increases earnings by over 5 percent more than does a year of secondary schooling. The existence of a stable differential in the earnings of college educated individuals relative to others has been noted in the past.[20] The estimated difference here surprisingly seems even larger than those differencs given for past periods.

Second, the effect of quality-adjusting the quantity of schooling each individual receives is noteworthy.[21] The quality adjustment is, as explained above, quite crude; years of school are adjusted for estimated 1965 quality differences based upon region of birth. This adjustment is most appropriate for younger individuals with 12 years or less schooling than it is for older individuals and individuals with some college, because the errors in estimating region of education and quality of schooling actually received will be less for the former individuals. The explained variance (R^2) is virtually identical for the adjusted and unadjusted models. The quality adjustment has a very significant effect on the aggregate earnings relationship portrayed. In unadjusted terms, the percentage increase per year of schooling for whites appears generally above that for blacks. When the quality adjustment is introduced, this conclusion no longer holds for the lesser educated individuals. Per year of "constant quality" schooling, black earnings increase by 5.1 percent while white earnings increase by only 4.5 percent. In each of the educational subgroups and for both adjusted and unadjusted, the returns to an additional year of schooling are higher for Spanish than for either white or black.[22] The quality adjustment is considerably weaker for post-secondary education, and, as might be expected, the adjustment has less affect on the estimated post-secondary functions.[23]

The estimated returns to schooling can also be aggregated over the census regions to provide additional information about the geographical distribution of returns to schooling. Table 12 displays the weighted average of estimated percentage increases in earnings per year of schooling for each of the nine regions. For less educated whites ($S \leq 12$) the returns are highest in the Mid-Atlantic region and in the South (S. Atlantic, E. South Central, and W. South Central). Patterns within the other racial and schooling groups are, however, less discernible.

Table 12 also indicates that, in all but two of the fourteen instances where black-white regional comparisons are possible, the average white returns are higher than the average black returns. Thus, the finding for nationally aggregated returns to schooling holds for almost all regions of the country.

The picture is somewhat different when quality adjustments are made to the schooling data. Table 13 displays the unadjusted and adjusted estimates by region for the high-school-or-less samples. In the adjusted estimates the pattern of high returns to school in the South still holds for whites. However, a similar pattern is now clearly visible for blacks. Moreover, in six of the eight regional black-white comparisons, the black earnings increase is higher than whites for the adjusted coefficients. The interpretation of the adjusted schooling models should be re-empha-

Table 12

ESTIMATED PERCENTAGE INCREASE IN EARNINGS PER YEAR OF SCHOOLING

(Weighted Average of Individual SMSAs)

Census Region [a]	White			Black			Spanish		
	S ≤ 12	S > 12	Total	S ≤ 12	S > 12	Total	S ≤ 12	S > 12	Total
Northeast	4.0	9.9	8.0	−1.9		3.7			
Mid-Atlantic	4.8	10.4	8.3	4.0	9.4	5.5	5.6		7.3
E. North Central	4.2	8.9	6.8	3.5	10.6	4.9	3.0		5.7
W. North Central	4.7	10.1	7.2	4.0	4.2	5.1			
South Atlantic	4.9	10.3	7.8	3.7	9.0	5.2	−3.0		6.6
E. South Central	6.2	9.6	8.2	3.6		4.3			
W. South Central	4.8	9.6	7.6	3.6	5.3	4.2	6.4	17.4	8.0
Mountain	3.4	9.7	6.6				5.3		7.1
Pacific	3.1	9.8	7.1	3.9	8.4	5.1	5.0	11.3	6.2
Total	4.4	9.8	7.6	3.7	9.0	5.0	5.2	11.9	6.8

a. Regions follow Bureau of Census definitions.

Table 13

ESTIMATED PERCENTAGE INCREASE IN EARNINGS PER YEAR OF SCHOOLING—
SCHOOLING ≤ 12 YEARS

(Weighted Average of Individual SMSAs)

Census Region[a]	White		Black		Spanish	
	Sch.	Sch. Qual.	Sch.	Sch. Qual.	Sch.	Sch. Qual.
Northeast	4.0	4.0	−1.9	−3.8		
Mid-Atlantic	4.8	4.8	4.0	5.3	5.6	7.5
E. North Central	4.2	4.4	3.5	4.7	3.0	4.0
W. North Central	4.7	5.0	4.0	5.1		
South Atlantic	4.9	5.0	3.7	5.3	−3.0	−3.9
E. South Central	6.2	6.6	3.6	5.4	6.4	8.7
W. South Central	4.8	5.1	3.6	5.5	5.3	7.4
Mountain	3.4	3.6			5.2	7.1
Pacific	4.4	4.5	3.7	5.1		

a. Regions follow Bureau of Census definitions.

sized, however. These coefficients can no longer be interpreted as rates of return since the costs of achieving a "quality-adjusted" year of schooling are radically different across ethnic groups. Thus these comparisons relate more to the labor market valuation of "equal" inputs than to rewards for investment in human capital or to overall inequities in income distribution.

The regional estimates for the Spanish samples are based upon considerable fewer SMSAs and sampled individuals. Therefore, it is not possible to discuss confidently the regional pattern of these estimates.

III. SOME CONCLUSIONS

The process of income determination has received a fair amount of consideration in the last decade. And, yet, there remain significant amounts of uncertainty and controversy over the factors which determine income and over which potential government policies might be most appropriate to effect changes in the distribution of income.

This chapter presented some new evidence about income determination. In particular, data from the Public Use Sample of the 1970 Census of Population were used to investigate the relationship between earnings and some of the underlying factors affecting earnings. The study concentrates upon the earnings of males between the ages of 16 and 65. Earnings in 1970 are related to the individual's schooling and estimated labor force experience. Further, the analysis allows for differences in earnings functions by Standard Metropolitan Statistical Area (SMSA) —our attempt at capturing differences among local labor markets.

The findings of this analysis are:

1. There appear to be significant differences in earnings among individual labor markets.

2. Less educated—and less mobile—individuals appear more dependent upon local labor market conditions, and thus geographic location has a stronger overall earnings effect (i.e., mean difference) for this group than on earnings of more educated individuals; this is especially true for black and Spanish males.

3. There is also a significant variance in the shape of the earnings relationship across labor markets; the estimated percentage increase in earnings per year of schooling is widely differ-

ent among SMSAs, and these differences are larger than those between racial groups.

4. The returns for a year of post-secondary education are at least double those for a year of elementary or secondary education.

5. In terms of average increases in earnings per year of schooling, whites receive a higher return on schooling than blacks; this holds across regions and schooling categories.

6. When a crude quality adjustment is made for the schooling input into earnings, there are significant changes in the results; blacks at the elementary and secondary levels appear to receive higher returns per year of quality-equivalent schooling than comparable whites.

7. On a regional basis, the returns to elementary and secondary schooling appear highest in the Mid-Atlantic and Southern regions; there is no discernible pattern to the returns over macroregions for post-secondary education.

These findings leave the strong impression that we must better understand the workings of local labor markets. Local conditions appear to have a powerful impact upon earnings—perhaps more important than race, and at least equal to several years of schooling. The similarity of these findings for females, for less than full-time, full-year workers, and for other minorities needs confirmation, but this analysis dictates a change in our way of viewing the earnings process.

NOTES

1. U.S. Bureau of the Census, *Statistical Abstract of the United States: 1973* (Government Printing Office, 1973), p. 330.

2. There have been some analyses which have concentrated on individual differences and not group or class differences. Most notable is Christopher Jencks et al., *Inequality* (Basic Books, 1972).

3. The "Coleman report" is the massive governmental study of American primary and secondary education which was undertaken to assess the racial and ethnic differences in education. James S. Coleman et al., *Equality of Education Opportunity* (Government Printing Office, 1966).

4. There has been a large amount of research in this area. The foundations of the analysis are found in the works of T. W. Schultz (for example, "Investment in Human Capital," *American Economic Review*, March 1961) and of Gary S. Becker (for example, *Human Capital*. [National Bureau of Economic Research, 1964]). A survey of human capital research can be found in Jacob Mincer, "The Distribution of Labor Incomes: A Survey with Special Reference to the Human Capital Approach," *Journal of Economic Literature*, March 1970; see also his *Schooling, Experience, and Earnings* (National Bureau of Economic Research, 1974).

5. It is important to note that the human capital model does not depend upon the specific mechanism by which the earnings of the individual increase. Schooling may increase the productivity of the individual by adding skills which are valuable in work. On the other hand, schooling may simply identify, or "screen," more productive individuals. While the former model usually seems to be implied in the human capital literature, the model works perfectly well in the latter world. Discussions of the screening hypothesis can be found in Paul Taubman and Terrance Wales, *Higher Education and Earnings: College as an Investment and a Screening Device* (McGraw-Hill, 1974); Kenneth Arrow, "Higher Education as a Filter," *Journal of Public Economics* (July 1973); and Michael Spence, "Job Market Signaling," *Quarterly Journal of Economics* (August 1973). The main implication of the screening model is that private returns to schooling may diverge from social returns to schooling. When we are interested in the distribution of income, we are generally talking about the private returns to schooling, and thus it is not necessary to distinguish between these alternative explanations. One caveat is necessary, however. The different models of the role of education may have differing implications in the long run when dynamic matters are important.

6. Again, as long as schooling screens on the basis of productivity differences, it is still possible to talk about demands and supplies of underlying characteristics. Thus, the importance of the underlying structural characteristics holds even in a screening world.

7. See, for example, James Smith and Finis Welch, "Black-White Male Earnings and Employment: 1960-1970" R-1666-DOL (Santa Monica: The Rand Corporation, 1975).

8. Most earnings studies have included some regional measures. The only studies going into more detail have been F. Welch, "Measurement of the Quality of Schooling," *American Economic Review* (May 1966), which considers rural male earnings by state; and E. Hanushek, "Regional Differences in the Structure of Earnings," *Review of Economics and Statistics* (May 1973), which analyzes metropolitan area differences in earnings for young males.

9. E. Hanushek, "Regional Differences."

10. Economic theory predicts that either the movement of factors of production (e.g., migration of labor) or trade in finished goods will tend to bring about equality in the relative payments to factors of production. There is some evidence that the returns to capital are roughly equal; see M. Straszheim, "An Introduction and Overview of Regional Money Capital Markets," in J. F. Kain and J. R. Meyer (eds.), *Essays in Regional Economics* (Harvard University Press, 1971). This should, according to factor price equalization theorems, imply absolute equality of payments to other factors of prod16unction, in particular, different skill categories of labor.

11. This restriction will lead to an understatement of the returns to human capital investment because length of work along with the wage rate is one way of securing returns to capital investment. Nevertheless, because of the possibility of interactions with hourly earnings (see Mincer, *Schooling, Experience, and Earnings*) and because of the lack of data on other key factors such as part-time work by students, this factor was eliminated from the modeling efforts through sample design.

12. As will be discussed below, the actual models analyzed view the logarithm of income as a function of input factors. The logarithm of a negative number is not defined.

13. The entire analysis from this point on concentrates on earnings rather than income. Earnings depend upon current labor force activity and, therefore, are the subject of most theoretical analysis. Income other than earnings include: Social Security and government railroad retirement; dividends, interest, rental income, and royalties; public assistance and welfare payments; unemployment and workmen's compensation; government pensions and veterans' payments; and private pensions, annuities, alimony, etc. Earnings are by far the most important part of total income, representing 88 percent in 1971. The distribution of total income by source, of course, varies considerably by income level. See Bureau of Census, "Money Income in 1971 of Families and Persons in the United States," *Current Population Reports,* Series P-60, No. 85 (Government Printing Office, 1972), p. 25.

14. James S. Coleman et al., *Equality of Educational Opportunity* (Government Printing Office, 1966). Approximately 570,000 students spread among grades 1, 3, 6, 9, and 12 were given a battery of standardized achievement and ability tests.

15. Grade level differences for verbal ability tests (*Equality of Educational Opportunity,* table 3.121.1) were interpolated to give differences by race and region for each year of schooling from 1 to 12. Region of schooling was assumed to be region of birth. Since urban-rural distinctions for birthplace are unavailable, urban school quality differences were used throughout. All schooling above high school was adjusted using the twelfth-grade adjustment for the given race-region cell. Previous uses of this type of adjustment can be found in Randall Weiss, "The Effects of Education on the Earnings of Blacks and Whites," *Review of Economics and Statistics* (February 1970).

16. See Jacob Mincer, *Schooling, Experience, and Earnings.* Experience is estimated by age−schooling−6. This assumes all time outside of school was spent in the labor force. It would be preferable to include actual labor market experience instead of "potential" experience, as is done here. Unfortunately this information is not available in the census data. A discussion of the difference between actual and "potential" experience is contained in E. Hanushek and J. Quigley, "Explicit Tests of the Human Capital Model and Intertemporal Adjustments in Relative Wages," ISPS Working Paper No. 767 (Yale University, 1976).

17. The actual form of the models estimated was $\log Y = a_0 + a_1 E + a_2 E^2 + a_3 S$ where Y = total earnings; E = experience = age−schooling−6; S = years of school completed. The logarithmic form has commonly been used; see the explanation by Mincer, "The Distribution of Labor Incomes." In the logarithmic form, the estimated coefficients times 100 can be interpreted as (approximately) the percentage increase in earnings attributable to a one unit increase in the explanatory variable—e.g., one year more of schooling.

18. The individual variance explained is related to the R^2 shown in the table. The total individual earnings variance can be decomposed into within and between region variance. R^2 tells what percentage of the within

region variance is explained by the models so that within-region explained variance is R^2 times the proportion of total variance within regions. Thus, for example, in the total "white" line of table 9, 3 percent of the variance in individual earnings is between regions—leaving 97 percent within regions. The models explain 21.6 percent of the within region variance (R^2), or $21.6 \cdot .97 = 21.0$ percent of the total variance is within-region explained variance.

19. Since these estimates result from analysis of census sample information, they are subject to sampling errors. Some of these errors can be large enough to yield negative estimates; i.e., additional schooling is predicted to *lower* earnings. The estimation problems are most severe when there are fewer observations. Thus, the black and Spanish samples, which tend to have fewer observations per SMSA than the white samples, are more affected by estimation problems.

20. The constancy of earnings differentials have been noted in a number of places. See, for example Zvi Griliches, "Notes on the Role of Education in Production Functions and Growth Accounting," in W. Lee Hansen (ed.), *Education, Income, and Human Capital* (National Bureau of Economic Research, 1970), or Finis Welch, "Education in Production," *Journal of Political Economy* (January-February 1970). This constancy is perplexing given the large increase in educational attainments over time. Since education is becoming more abundant, the returns to education would be expected to fall, *ceteris paribus*. Recent work by Richard Freeman, "Overinvestment in College Training?" *Journal of Human Resources* (Summer 1975) suggests this constancy may be disappearing in the 1970s. However, these data suggest no fall in returns to college through 1969, and perhaps even an increase.

21. The interpretation of the "adjusted" return to schooling is quite different from the "unadjusted" return. In the unadjusted model, the coefficient on schooling (which has been the focus of attention throughout) can be interpreted as a rate of return on an investment in schooling if certain conditions are met. The most important condition is that the cost of the investment is simply the amount of earnings foregone by going to school rather than working. This rate of return can then be compared with rates of return on other investments such as capital.

In the adjusted model, such interpretations are no longer possible. "Quality years" of schooling no longer represent the costs of schooling. It may take twice as many chronological years to achieve a given number of quality years. Because adjusted years are so different from chronological years, the estimated returns in these two models should also not be compared with each other.

It is difficult within the sample to answer the question of "which measure is better." This choice would presumably best be made on an explained variance criterion, but the near identity of R^2's across the two alternative forms does not allow a reasonable choice.

22. For the total samples, the estimated white returns to schooling are higher than for Spanish. This primarily reflects the different weighting due to different school completion distributions. Because of the significant differences in the estimated earnings functions for the two schooling categories, the "total" models should not, on statistical grounds, be esti-

mated, and these results will not be emphasized here.

23. The adjustment of post-secondary schooling was based upon quality differences in the twelfth grade. This is a less reasonable adjustment because: (1) region of birth is likely to be a less reliable indicator of post-secondary school location than it was for primary and secondary, and (2) it assumes constant quality of post-secondary institutions. To the extent that it is a constant adjustment to the schooling values within a SMSA racial grouping, the estimated returns to schooling will be unchanged in the quality adjusted instance as compared to quality unadjusted.

Discrimination in the Academic Marketplace

RICHARD B. FREEMAN

Special features of the academic world make it possible to separate racial or ethnic discrimination from various other sources of group income differentials to a greater extent than in many other occupations. The elusive qualitative variables which make it difficult to separate differentials from discrimination are somewhat less elusive among academic personnel. For example, the quality of an academic individual's training is at least crudely indicated by (1) the level of his highest degree,[1] and by (2) the ranking of the institution granting the degree, as compiled from the respective academic disciplines themselves by the American Council on Education. A widely recognized indicator of performance on the job is also available in the number of publications, in a profession where much emphasis is placed on research "productivity" ("publish or perish").

The available data permit several important questions to be asked about the extent and trend over time of ethnic discrimination among college and university professors, deans, and other academic individuals. First, there can be a raw measure of gross annual income differentials between white academics and academics from black, Oriental, and other ethnic minority backgrounds. Second, there are measures of the extent to which the various groups differ in such major income-determining variables as degree level and quality, amount of publication, and experience —with "discrimination" being confined within the differences

that remain, after holding constant other sources of group income differences. Third, multiple regression analysis will permit
estimates of the ways in which the same variables differ in their
effect among ethnic groups—for example, how much of a black
academic's salary is affected by his publications compared to how
much a white academic's salary is affected by the same variable.
Finally, our data will permit comparisons of all these factors over
the past few decades, to determine what apparent effect there
has been from various programs aimed at securing minority
economic opportunity in society at large or in the academic
world in particular. These programs include various laws, regulations, and practices, evolving in the 1960s, designed to achieve
"equal opportunity," "nondiscrimination," "affirmative action,"
and so forth.

Most of the evidence in this paper comes from two data
sources: (1) the U.S. Census of Population, and (2) two faculty
surveys carried out by the American Council on Education
(ACE).[2] The census contains general data about faculty, which
has the advantage of coming from a large sample. The ACE surveys covered over 60,000 teaching faculty at 303 institutions in
1968-69 and over 42,000 faculty from 301 institutions in 1972-
73. Our analysis is based on a complete count of black faculty in
the surveys and a random sample of about 3,500 white faculty,
appropriately weighted to reflect national distributions, given the
ACE sample procedures (see, in particular, the ACE descriptions
of the survey, 1970, 1973). The 1968-69 and 1972-73 dates are
particularly valuable as "before" and "after" indicators of the
effect of "affirmative action" programs.

This chapter is divided into four sections. Section I analyzes
trends over time in the academic marketplace as regards the
representation and incomes of minority faculty members—with
particular emphasis on changes before and after the pressures for
minority faculty recruitment as a result of student demands and
governmental programs for "affirmative action." Sections II and
III focus on the changing economic position of black faculty.
The former uses multiple regression computations to compare
the earnings of black and white academicians with similar
"quality" as indicated by academic training and publications.
The latter examines the employment consequences of the increase in demand for black faculty—the movement of blacks
into primarily white institutions and possible changes in hiring
standards. Section IV turns to the position of Oriental faculty,

using the ACE survey data. The paper concludes with a brief summary of the implications of these findings.

I. MINORITY FACULTY IN A CHANGING ACADEMIC JOB MARKET

What was the economic status of black and other minority faculty in the years preceding the pressures for increased minority hiring in the late 1960s and early 1970s? How did "affirmative action" programs operate to alter university personnel policy? What features of the academic marketplace shaped the response to these programs?

The available Census of Population and related evidence regarding the status of nonwhite (largely black) faculty is summarized in table 1, which compares incomes of black (nonwhite) and total faculty, by sex, from 1950 to 1970. The table shows that the relative number of black male or female faculty changed little in the 1950-70 period preceding affirmative action pressures: in 1950, 2.6 percent of male and 5.1 percent of female faculty were black; in 1970, 2.5 percent male and 5.4 percent female. With regard to income, while the census data suffer from several problems—such as failure to control adequately for levels of education (notably, whether or not the individual has the Ph.D.) and refer to nonwhites in 1950 and 1960 but to blacks in 1970—they suggest some improvement, particularly for black female faculty, whose income relative to total female faculty rose from 83 percent to 91 percent in the 1960s. The gain for black male faculty is smaller but nevertheless probably indicative of real changes, as the shift in the average from nonwhite to blacks is likely to bias changes downward. With some increases in relative incomes but little or none in relative employment of black faculty, the general picture is of only slight advances in the market in the decades preceding initiation of significant equal employment pressures.

The employment of other minority faculty, as well as blacks and whites, is considered next in table 2. This table compares the number of blacks, whites, American Indians, Japanese Americans, Chinese Americans, Filipinos, and persons of Spanish origin working as faculty or administrators in higher education in 1960 and 1970, by sex. Columns 1-4 give the numbers employed in the two years; columns 5 and 6 show the percentage

Table 1

ECONOMIC STATUS OF NONWHITE (BLACK) FACULTY, 1950-70

	MALE		
	1950	1960	1970
1. Numbers of Faculty[a]			
black	2,490	3,518	8,851
total	96,030	138,889	354,671
ratio	.026	.025	.025
2. Incomes of Faculty[b]			
nonwhite (black)	$3,300[c]	$5,738[c]	$8,867
total	4,366	7,510	11,657
ratio	0.76	0.76	0.79
	FEMALE		
3. Numbers of Faculty[a]			
black	1,410	1,897	7,535
total	27,780	38,859	139,278
ratio	.051	.049	.054
4. Incomes of Faculty[b]			
nonwhite (black)	—	$4,154[c]	$5,637
total	—	5,013	6,220
ratio	—	.83	.91

a. Numbers in 1950 and 1960 include college presidents and deans.

b. Incomes for preceding years.

c. Refers to nonwhites in 1950 and 1960 and to blacks in 1970.

SOURCE: U.S. Census of Population 1970, *U.S. Summary,* table 205; U.S. Census of Population 1950, *Occupational Characteristics,* tables 3, 19, 21; U.S. Census of Population 1960, *Occupational Characteristics,* tables 25, 26; U.S. Census of Population 1970, *Occupational Characteristics,* tables 2, 16, 17.

of each group employed as faculty and administrators. The table shows that some minorities, notably Japanese and Chinese Americans, were well-represented among faculty in both 1960 and 1970, having proportions employed above those of the majority white population. Indeed a remarkable 3.5 percent (male) and 1.6 percent (female) of Chinese Americans were college and university professors or administrators in 1970. American Indians, Filipinos, and persons of Spanish origin, on the other hand, were, like blacks, relatively underrepresented as professors and administrators. Between 1960 and 1970, the number of faculty in all of the groups increased markedly due to the

Table 2

NUMBER OF FACULTY AND ACADEMIC ADMINISTRATORS, BY RACE, 1960-70

	Numbers of Faculty		Numbers of Administrators		Percent of Group Employed as Faculty and Administrators	
	1960	1970	1960 a	1970	1960	1970
Male, by Group b						
Black	3,286	8,851	281	1,295	0.10	0.24
American Indian	83	381	0	82	0.11	0.35
Japanese	492	1,764	21	53	0.43	1.20
Chinese	1,067	4,077	0	49	1.49	3.52
Filipino	—	113	—	68	—	0.22
Spanish origin c	—	6,032	—	226	—	0.32
White	127,853	337,689	5,221	28,275	0.32	0.82
Female, by Group						
Black	2,343	7,731	105	520	0.10	0.23
American Indian	0	235	0	19	0.00	0.32
Japanese	139	741	0	51	0.19	0.66
Chinese	199	1,081	0	13	0.73	1.57
Filipino	—	256	—	0	—	0.46
Spanish origin	—	2,722	—	0	—	0.25
White	35,564	131,370	1,547	8,280	0.19	0.53

a. College presidents and deans in 1960 used to indicate administrators.

b. Numbers for 1960 differ slightly from those in table 1 due to the different census volumes used.

c. Since "Spanish origin" does not reflect race, persons in this category may be white or black and are thus double-counted.

SOURCE: U.S. Census of Population 1970, *Occupational Characteristics*, table 2, pp. 13, 15; U.S. Census of Population 1960, *Characteristics of Professional Workers*, table 2, pp. 9, 10; *Nonwhite Population by Race*, pp. 101, 104, 108, 111.

boom in higher education. Relative to their proportion of the population, moreover, Japanese Americans and Indians made especially large gains, though the number of the latter is too small in absolute figures for changes to be meaningful.

Table 3 takes the analysis a step further, comparing minority shares of faculty to analogous shares of qualified specialists, namely doctorates. Because data on doctorates by ethnic origin are hard to come by, figures are given for both new Ph.D.'s and all Ph.D.'s. American citizens are reported separately so as to differentiate between Americans of Oriental descent and foreign students. The data on minority shares of all Ph.D.'s in the final column are my estimates, obtained as described in note c to table 3.

The table shows that the distribution of faculty by racial group is roughly similar to the distribution among Ph.D.'s, with Ori-

Table 3

MINORITY SHARES OF FACULTY, COLLEGE
GRADUATES, AND Ph.D.'s, 1970-73[a]

Group	Percent Faculty 1970	Percent New Ph.D.'s 1973	Percent New Ph.D.'s (U.S. Citizens) 1973	Percent All Ph.D. Scientists and Engineers 1973	Percent All Ph.D.'s[b] 1973
Black	3.3	2.9	2.7	0.8	1.8
American Indian	0.1	0.4	0.5	0.1	0.1
Japanese	0.5				
Chinese	1.0	} 7.2	} 1.2	} 4.9	} 3.3
Filipino	0.1				
Spanish Origin[c]	1.8	1.0	0.8	0.6	0.7
White	94.5	86.1	94.7	93.5	94.2

a. Columns do not necessarily sum to 100 percent due to omitted groups and rounding.

b. Estimated by obtaining the approximate number of all Ph.D's for each group by multiplying the number of science and engineering Ph.D.'s by the ratio of all new Ph.D. recipients in 1973 by the number of new Ph.D.'s in science and engineering fields and then dividing by the total. This method assumes that the ratio of all nonscience to science Ph.D.'s for each group is roughly equal to the ratio of new nonscience to science Ph.D.'s in 1973.

c. Persons of Spanish origin in column 1 may be white or black and are thus double counted. In columns 2-5 they are a separate group.

SOURCE: National Academy of Sciences, *Minority Groups among United States Doctorate Level Scientists, Engineers and Scholars,* 1973 (Washington, 1974), table 1, p. 8; table 3, p. 13; table 11, p. 30. U.S. Census of Population 1970, *Occupational Characteristics,* p. 13.

entals underrepresented relative to all new Ph.D.'s but somewhat overrepresented relative to the share of Ph.D.'s awarded those who are American citizens, and black Ph.D.'s modestly more likely to work as faculty than the average Ph.D. recipient, possibly because of concentration in education and other nonscience areas where most Ph.D.'s are academics. The problem of increasing minority employment as faculty is obviously closely intertwined with increasing the proportion of minority graduate students and doctorates.

All told, the data in tables 2 and 3 highlight the disparate experience of various minorities in the academic marketplace and higher education. Some groups, notably Japanese and Chinese Americans, are found in larger proportions on academic faculties than in the general population, while others who tend to have lower socioeconomic status in the nation as a whole—blacks, Filipinos, American Indians, and persons of Spanish origin—are underrepresented relative to their proportion in the general population, though not relative to their proportion of either new or old Ph.D.'s. Whatever the concatenation of forces producing these differences, the figures suggest that minority hiring pressures would be focused on, and if successful will alter, the economic position of faculty from these groups—which in fact appears to have occurred.

1. *EFFECT OF INCREASED DEMAND*

The way increases in demand affect the market for minorities that are relatively underrepresented in academia depends on supply conditions and the institutional features of the marketplace. Because of the lengthy training period for Ph.D.'s and the limited stock of black doctorates in the sixties and seventies, the supply of black faculty was relatively fixed or inelastic in the period under study, suggesting that increased demand would improve the income status of black faculty, possibly substantially, but would raise employment only moderately. Because of the importance of quality dimensions in academia, there are several distinct ways in which an improvement might be effected. Institutions could reduce hiring standards for the group in heavy demand, producing the type of quality deterioration which some have feared. If only standards were changed, one would find average incomes roughly the same but would find incomes adjusted for quality rising; the relative number of persons in the group attaining "good" academic jobs increasing; and sizable

quality differences (say, in terms of publications) within specified institutions. On the other hand, increases in demand could
show up largely in the willingness to pay a premium for persons
with strong qualifications for a job and, thus, in an increase in
income for the more qualified and in the slope of the curve link-
ing income to "qualifications." Under this adjustment mode,
persons with many publications or related accomplishments in
the group in great demand would receive a premium, their number would increase modestly in top jobs (given inelastic supply),
and there would be no substantial quality differences within
those institutions desiring members of the group. Third, there
could develop a "pure" premium for members of the group, much
like the traditional discrimination coefficient. Quality standards
and the reward for quality would be unchanged but every member
of the group would receive a given amount of extra income.
Which, if any, of these various adjustment modes operated in the
late sixties and early seventies is an empirical question which
the remainder of this study seeks to answer.

II. RELATIVE INCOMES OF BLACK FACULTY

This section contrasts the incomes of black and white faculty
with similar characteristics and scholarship productivity, defined
by numbers of publications in the 1969-73 period of intense equal
employment pressures, using the ACE data. We estimate the
effect of various human capital or productivity variables on
faculty incomes for blacks and whites, men and women, taken
separately and adjust incomes for differences in "quality" in the
hedonic price methodology.[3] There are two findings. First, in
both 1969 and 1973 black male faculty earned approximately
the same as comparable ("quality adjusted") white male faculty
while black female faculty earned more than comparable white
female faculty. Second, in 1973, but not in 1969, black male
scholars with numerous publications obtained a premium on the
order of $2,000-$3,000 over equally productive white scholars,
suggesting that the various pressures for minority faculty hiring
caused an especially large shift in demand for the more productive Ph.D.'s.

1. *FACULTY CHARACTERISTICS*

The economic position and academic characteristics of black
and white faculty in 1969 and 1973 are examined first in table 4.

The figures for blacks are obtained from a complete count of black respondents to the ACE questionnaire; the figures for whites, from a random sample of about 3,500 respondents. Both are weighted by the ACE stratification sample weights (see ACE, 1969, 1973). Comparisons of the characteristics of whites in the random sample with those of the entire population as reported in the ACE publications indicate that the 3,500 are a representative sample. Line 1 records the proportion of faculty who were black or white in 1969 and 1973; line 2 gives mean salaries; the following lines deal with academic training, age and experience, and academic productivity in terms of articles or books published; and finally, lines 6 and 7 show the distribution of workers by field of study and academic rank.

In 1969 just 1.8 percent of male and 3.9 percent of female faculty were black. When the market improved in the early 1970s, the proportions rose to 2.4 percent and 4.8 percent, respectively— large percentage gains for a four-year span but gains which still left a sizable gap between academic employment of the two groups. Underlying the increase in black employment was substantially greater numbers of job offers tendered to black as compared to white faculty, with 65 percent of the former, but just 34 percent of the latter reporting offers "within the past two years" in 1973.[4] It should also be noted, moreover, that evidence on employment of blacks in nonteaching administrative and staff jobs in specific institutions suggests even larger increases in black employment in these types of jobs, apparently because of the greater ease of finding qualified administrators (who are not required to be Ph.D.'s).[5]

The salaries in line 2 show that, without adjusting for differences in academic qualifications, white male faculty earned a moderate premium over blacks in 1969 and 1973—$877 (7 percent) in the former and $1,140 (also 7 percent) in the latter year—while black women faculty did modestly better than whites in the first year and modestly worse in the second. All of which suggests, all else being the same, rough stability in differentials during the period. Turning to academic qualifications, there appear to be sizable differences between blacks and whites in training and number of publications (lines 3, 5) but not in age or experience, measured by years since the highest degree was obtained (line 4). White academicians are more likely to hold doctorates than blacks and, correspondingly, less likely to have masters' degrees as their highest qualification. They also have a greater

Table 4

INCOME AND CHARACTERISTICS OF BLACK AND WHITE FACULTY, BY SEX, 1969-73

	Male				Female			
	1969		1973		1969		1973	
	Black	White	Black	White	Black	White	Black	White
1. Percentage of Total Faculty	1.8	96.6	2.4	95.1	3.9	94.7	4.8	93.6
2. Salary	$12,526	$13,403	$16,169	$17,309	$10,461	$10,202	$14,425	$14,589
3. Academic Training (Percent with Degrees)								
Ph.D.	23	40	20	37	12	17	7	17
Ed.D. and Other Professional Degrees	25	16	9	10	24	16	5	5
Master's	39	35	62	44	57	57	69	62
Less than Masters	12	9	9	8	7	10	19	11
4. Age	44	42	44	44	44	42	43	45
Years since Completed Highest Degree	10	12	12	13	10	9	10	11
5. Academic Productivity (Percent Published)								
1+ articles	47	58	46	61	28	36	24	42
5+ articles	15	27	16	38	6	8	3	11
1+ books	20	29	30	42	20	16	19	27

6.	Field							
	Social science	21	25	28	25	22	23	19
	Science	18	28	23	31	9	12	9
	Humanities	13	19	18	24	30	28	27
	Other	48	28	31	20	39	37	45
7.	Rank							
	Professor	21	24	23	31	8	5	10
	Associate professor	20	20	23	24	16	15	24
	Assistant professor	28	29	30	26	30	35	29
	Other	31	27	24	19	46	45	37

SOURCE: Calculated from ACE tapes for 1968-69, 1972-73 using ACE sampling weights.

number of publications, with 61 percent of white men and 42 percent of women faculty reporting one or more articles compared to 46 percent of black male and 24 percent of black female faculty. With respect to fields of specialization, the data in line 6 reveal different distributions of blacks and whites among academic specialties. White men, but not white women, are more likely than blacks to be scientists, while both white men and white women are found proportionately less frequently in the "other fields" than blacks. These differences, however, and others in the field distribution of teachers appear to be diminishing over time: in 1969 the summation of the absolute value of the difference in the distribution was 40 (men) and 32 (women); in 1973, 26 (men) and 16 (women). Finally, the evidence in line 7 on academic rank shows a moderate white advantage on both counts with no indication of diminution over time.

2. *QUALITY-ADJUSTED INCOMES*

To examine the income of black and white faculty with similar qualifications, it is necessary to estimate the effect of various faculty characteristics, such as numbers of publications, on income and to use these estimates to calculate quality-adjusted income. If $â_i$ is the effect of the ith income determining variable X_i and if blacks and whites differ in their level of X_i by say $X_i^w - X_i^b$, then $\sum â_i[X_i^w - X_i^b]$ of the black-white difference in income can be attributed to differences in quality. The remaining difference represents the quality-adjusted market differential.

Step one in this adjustment procedure is taken in table 5, which records the coefficients of income determination equations for black and white faculty, respectively. Since whites constitute 95 percent or more of the faculty, the white equations show the overall process of faculty income determination while the black equations pinpoint distinctive factors at work among black faculty. The dependent variable in the regressions is the log of academic salary; regressions with the dollar value of salary yielded similar patterns of results. There are five sets of independent variables: (1) those relating to academic training, degree held, and quality of graduate institution awarding the Ph.D. (as defined in the Roose-Anderson[6] study); (2) those relating to age and experience, measured as years since receipt of highest degree, with squared terms entered to pick up the downward curvature of income profile near retirement; (3) those relating to scholarly productivity in terms of articles and books published;

(4) those relating to hours spent at various academic tasks; and (5) finally, in equations 5-8, variables for institution of employment. The latter can be viewed as indicators of perceived quality on the hypothesis that high quality institutions attract better scholars, or simply as controls that focus on the incomes of persons in similar types of institutions. In the cases where the variables are dummy classifications, the coefficients compare the effect of having a specified characteristic to having the characteristic of the omitted group: persons with a B.A. or less (a very odd group for faculty) in the first set; those with no articles and books in the third set; and to those employed in lower quality public colleges—defined as having students with SAT scores below 500 —in the last set. In addition to the variables in the table, each calculation also includes the "basis of pay" (on a nine- or twelve-month basis), field dummies (social sciences, science, humanities, vs. other), and a constant. The coefficients of these variables are not recorded, being of little concern except as a control in this study.

There are two important findings reported in the table. The first relates to the differences and similarities in the income determination process for black and white male faculty. The estimated coefficients for age and experience, hours of work, and, to a lesser extent, for training, are roughly similar in columns 1 and 2. The age coefficient is somewhat higher for blacks than whites but is offset by a somewhat lower experience coefficient, indicating approximately similar life-cycle earnings profiles. The coefficient on Ph.D. and Master's degrees differ by .12 for white and .16 for blacks, a modest black advantage, while the other educational attainment coefficients, which reflect small and often disparate groups, differ unevenly. The coefficients on the hours of work activity, which measure the impact of an hour of work time spent per week in administration, teaching, and research, are virtually identical. By contrast, there are marked differences in the coefficients on articles published, with blacks apparently receiving *greater marginal* reward for articles than whites (the coefficients on books are mixed): a black with one to two articles, for example, earned 6 percent more relative to one with no publications than did a comparable white; while blacks with five to ten articles earned 23 percent more in relative terms. There are also some differences in the impact of institution of employment on income (columns 5 and 6) with blacks appearing to earn somewhat more than whites in medium quality

Table 5

COEFFICIENTS FOR FACULTY INCOME DETERMINATION EQUATIONS,
BY SEX AND RACE, 1973[a]

Explanatory Variables	Men		Women[b]	
	White (1)	Black (2)	White (3)	Black (4)
Training				
Ph.D.	.06 (.02)	.09 (.08)	.02 (.06)	.13 (.09)
Ed.D.	.12 (.04)	-.04 (.12)	.15 (.09)	.21 (.11)
other post-grad.	.06 (.03)	-.30 (.10)	-.10 (.10)	-.15 (.29)
master's	.05 (.02)	-.05 (.06)	-.22 (.04)	-.07 (.06)
high quality Ph.D.[c]	.02 (.02)	.05 (.06)	.05 (.05)	-.07 (.09)
Age and Experience				
age	.042 (.007)	.043 (.017)	-.032 (.012)	.044 (.017)
age squared	-.0004(.0001)	-.0004(.0002)	.0004(.001)	-.0004(.0002)
years since highest degree	.014 (.003)	.008 (.008)		-.004 (.008)
years squared	-.0001(.0001)	-.0001(.0002)	-.001 (.002)	.0002(.0002)
Scholarly Productivity				
Articles				
1-2	-.07 (.02)	.01 (.01)	-.02 (.04)	-.03 (.06)
3-4	-.01 (.02)	.04 (.06)	-.02 (.05)	-.03 (.09)
5-10	-.01 (.02)	.24 (.08)	-.06 (.07)	.22 (.17)
11-20	.10 (.03)	.15 (.12)	.06 (.09)	.24 (.18)
21+	.14 (.03)	.33 (.10)	.19 (.11)	.22 (.22)
Books				
1-2	.07 (.02)	-.06 (.05)	.08 (.04)	.03 (.06)
3-4	.06 (.02)	.11 (.09)	.16 (.08)	.04 (.10)
5+	-.08 (.03)	-.08 (.14)	.13 (.08)	-.11 (.14)

| | Men | | Women[b] | |
	White (5)	Black (6)	White (7)	Black (8)
Hours of Activity				
administrative	.008 (.007)	.006 (.002)	.012 (.002)	.006 (.002)
teaching	.003 (.001)	.001 (.002)	.009 (.002)	-.006 (.003)
preparing class	.002 (.001)	.003 (.003)	.005 (.002)	.001 (.002)
advising students	.005 (.001)	.005 (.003)	.007 (.003)	.006 (.004)
research				
R^2	.417	.356	.256	.473
SEE	.298	.351	.415	.226
Explanatory Variables				
Training				
Ph.D.	.04 (.02)	.09 (.08)	.04 (.06)	.26 (.08)
Ed.D.	.10 (.04)	-.03 (.12)	.14 (.09)	.31 (.11)
other	.05 (.03)	-.44 (.10)	-.05 (.10)	-.11 (.26)
master's	-.08 (.02)	-.07 (.07)	-.17 (.04)	-.00 (.06)
high quality Ph.D.[c]	.02 (.02)	.05 (.06)	.04 (.05)	-.01 (.08)
Age and Experience				
age	.039 (.007)	.049 (.017)	-.030 (.013)	.042 (.015)
age squared	-.0004 (.00008)	-.0005 (.0002)	.0004 (.0001)	-.0004 (.0002)
years since highest degree	.016 (.003)	.006 (.008)	.022 (.006)	.006 (.008)
years squared	-.0002 (.003)	-.0001 (.0003)	-.006 (.0002)	-.0001 (.002)
Scholarly Productivity				
Articles				
1-2	-.05 (.02)	.01 (.06)	-.04 (.04)	.02 (.05)
3-4	.01 (.02)	.08 (.06)	-.04 (.05)	.05 (.09)
5-10	.01 (.02)	.22 (.08)	-.07 (.06)	.22 (.15)
11-20	.11 (.03)	.15 (.12)	.08 (.08)	.24 (.16)
21+	.16 (.03)	.33 (.10)	.20 (.11)	.23 (.20)

(Table 5 cont'd)

	(5)		(6)		(7)		(8)	
Books								
1-2	.06	(.02)	−.04	(.05)	.09	(.04)	.01	(.06)
3-4	.07	(.02)	.10	(.09)	.15	(.08)	.10	(.10)
5+	.07	(.03)	−.07	(.14)	.11	(.08)	−.08	(.13)
Hours of Activity								
administrative	.008	(.0007)	.008	(.002)	.013	(.002)	.005	(.002)
teaching	.002	(.0001)	.002	(.002)	.007	(.002)	−.001	(.003)
preparing class	.002	(.0009)	.003	(.002)	.004	(.002)	−.000	(.002)
advising students	.002	(.002)	.002	(.003)	−.008	(.003)	−.001	(.004)
research	.005	(.001)	.006	(.003)	.006	(.003)	.003	(.004)
Institution of Employment[d]								
univ. high quality	−.00	(.025)	.04	(.090)	−.17	(.06)	−.01	(.23)
univ. medium quality	.05	(.024)	.26	(.105)	−.13	(.06)	.06	(.25)
univ. other	−.05	(.028)	.07	(.114)	−.24	(.06)	.16	(.25)
high quality college	.13	(.03)	.29	(.088)	−.11	(.05)	.08	(.22)
other college	−.08	(.03)	.09	(.11)	−.28	(.05)	.03	(.23)
2-yr. college	.12	(.02)	.22	(.10)	−.14	(.05)	.31	(.22)
Negro	−.08	(.08)	−.01	(.01)	−.07	(.15)	−.01	(.22)
R^2	.446		.413		.281		.601	
SEE	.291		.339		.409		.202	

a. The dependent variable is the log of income; numbers in parentheses are standard error; all regressions include variables for the basis (9 or 12 months) of pay and dummies for field (social sciences, science, humanities, other).

b. Regressions for women include additional variables for number of dependents and whether or not the woman is married.

c. Quality Ph.D. defined as having obtained a degree from an institution in the Roose-Anderson ranking.

d. High quality universities defined as having student SAT scores of 600 or more; medium quality—500-599; other—less than 500; good college (public and private) as having student SAT scores of 500 or higher; other colleges (Protestant, Roman Catholic, and private)—4-year.

universities, high quality colleges, and two year colleges, compared to the base group. Overall, however, the income determination process for black and white male faculty appears, except for the difference in the impact of articles published on salary, to be reasonably similar.

The second and very different finding relates to the marked difference in the income determination equations for white and black women. While, except for the excluded B.A. or less group, the training coefficients are quite similar, there are substantial differences in the coefficients for age and experience, scholarly productivity, and hours. As black female faculty age, they obtain similar gains in income to those of black or white men while, by contrast, white women *lose*: the age coefficient is negative in column 3, suggesting a distinct age/income profile for white women. With respect to articles, the figures show that among women as among men, blacks earn a sizable marginal premium compared to whites by publishing. In this case, however, white women with articles in the range from 1-10 do relatively poorly while black women earn more than those with 0 articles, though not by statistically significant amounts. On the other hand, white women appear to have a greater return to hours of research than black women. Finally, the institution coefficients also show a strikingly different pattern, with white women earning relatively more in low-quality public colleges (the omitted group) than blacks, who do particularly well in junior colleges and lower quality universities. In short, the evidence suggests distinct and quite different income determination processes for black and white women faculty, an issue which merits detailed considerations, but which lies outside the scope of this study.

The regressions in table 5 provide two sets of weights for evaluating the impact of academic quality on incomes—the white or overall market coefficients and the black coefficients. Because the white coefficients reflect the predominant pattern of income determination in the market, they are used as the chief quality weights for men, although estimates of quality-adjusted incomes are made with both black and white weights. Because of the "peculiar" pattern of female income determination, it is less clear which weights are best and the computations are done with the estimates for black and white women and with those for white men. Table 6 lists the major contributing factors, their contribution to black-white income differences $[\hat{a}_1(X_i^w - X_i^b)]$, and then the sum of the contributions. Subtracting the sum of the effects on income differences from the actual differential yields the "quality-adjusted" differential in the final line. Columns 1-5 present computations which use regressions 1-4 of table 5, in which the type of institution for which the persons worked was ignored, while columns 6-10 deal with regressions 5-8 that include institution of employment. If the institution data are regarded as additional information on individual quality, the latter set provides the correct market quality adjustments. If the data are not so regarded, the latter are to be interpreted as measuring the effect of quality differences on income within a particular type of institution.

The regression findings for men tell a reasonably straightforward story, with differences in black and white characteristics contributing about .07 points to the observed differential when institutional employment differences are omitted and .14 points in the complete adjustment. Compared to the actual income differential of .07, the adjustments entirely eliminate the black disadvantage in the former case and produce a nonnegligible, but still modest, premium of about 7-8 percent or $1,200 in the latter. Black male faculty, according to these computations earned roughly as much as, or more than, white male faculty with similar characteristics in the market as a whole and definitely earned more in similar types of academic institutions.

The situation among women is less clear because of the difference between the black and white female income determination equations and, in particular, the differential effect of institution of employment on incomes. In columns 3 and 4 the income equations accord a 8.2 percent (white female equation) and 2.9 percent (black female equation) income advantage to white women due to their superior characteristics, which yields a black quality-adjusted premium of 7.2 percent to 1.9 percent. In columns 8 and 9 the strikingly different effect of type of institution reverses the magnitude of the adjustments, yielding a 2.8 to 7.4 percent black premium. If the white male income weights are used as the best indicator of academic quality, both calculations suggest a significant black female advantage—from 5.2 to 8.9 percent. Although the size of the quality-adjusted salary difference between black and white women differs considerably depending on the precise equation used, all of the estimates show that black women faculty earn somewhat more than white women with nominally similar characteristics. The peculiar coefficients in female income determination equations which

Table 6

LOGARITHMIC DIFFERENCES BETWEEN WHITE AND BLACK FACULTY INCOMES IN 1973 DUE TO "QUALITY OF PERSONS AND INSTITUTIONS OF EMPLOYMENT"[a]

	Men		Women			Men		Women		
	White Equation (1)	Black Equation (2)	White Equation (3)	Black Equation (4)	White Male Equation (5)	White Equation (6)	Black Equation (7)	White Equation (8)	Black Equation (9)	White Male Equation (10)
Basis of Pay	-.012	-.022	.002	.001	.002	-.012	-.018	.001	.002	.000
Training	.031	.027	.012	.003	.007	.023	.022	.012	.011	.007
Scholarly Production	.031	.047	.007	.019	.009	.034	.050	.006	.019	.011
Age/Experience	.025	.014	.037	.019	.035	.019	.012	-.036	.040	.022
Hours Worked	.009	.014	.019	-.017	.002	.011	.017	.012	-.013	.000
Field	-.007	-.015	.004	-.003	.007	-.007	-.014	.003	-.006	.006
Type of Institution	—	—	—	—	—	.069	.082	-.028	.019	.053
Marital Status/Dependents	—	—	.001	.007	—	—	—	-.001	.012	—
Total Impact	.077	.065	.082	.029	.062	.137	.151	.038	.084	.099
Actual Differential	.071	.071	.010	.010	.010	.071	.071	.010	.010	.010
Quality-Adjusted Differential	-.006	.006	-.072	-.019	-.052	-.066	-.080	-.028	-.074	-.089

a. Calculated by estimates of equation 1-8 of table 5 for whites and blacks, separately, following the procedure described in the text.

turned up in the estimates—due to discrimination, to women leaving the market for years to raise children, and so forth—raise important issues beyond our purview.

Comparable estimates for 1969 (not given here) reveal a similar picture as quality characteristics have effects on incomes of the same magnitude as in table 5. We conclude that in the 1960s and early 1970s, black faculty earned as much as, or more than, comparable whites. All of the computations show the absence of traditional enormous income differentials.

3. *ACADEMIC QUALITY AND INCOME*

The apparently greater impact of increases in academic qualifications, defined in terms of number of publications and, to a lesser extent, educational quality, on black than on white male faculty is pursued further in tables 7 and 8 and figure 1. Table 7 compares the mean income of black and white male faculty by number of publications in 1973 and 1969, overall and in the science and social science fields where publications are especially important. The table shows a dramatically different impact of scholarly productivity on black as compared to white incomes in 1973 and a markedly different pattern in 1969. In 1973, blacks with many publications appear to have been much more heavily rewarded than their white compatriots while less productive scholars did a bit worse. Taking all disciplines together, blacks with five or more articles earned $1,673 more than whites in 1973 compared to a $254 advantage for those with one to four articles and a $695 deficit for persons with no articles. In the sciences the pattern is more striking, in the social sciences less so, but in both, the marginal impact of articles appears greater for blacks than for whites, at least from below to above five articles. By contrast, exactly the opposite pattern is found in 1969, with the most able blacks earning less than comparable whites by greater amounts than the least productive. While there are difficulties in before/after attribution of causality, the fact that federal affirmative action pressures were exceptionally severe in the 1969-73 period covered suggests that they had a major effect on the return to qualifications. This is not unreasonable since affirmative action was concentrated in the top universities where scholarly production is the major criterion for employment.

More refined estimates of the greater rewards to black than to white scholarly productivity are given in table 8, which uses the regression results of table 5 to estimate the income differential

Table 7

BLACK-WHITE MALE FACULTY INCOMES AND INCOME DIFFERENCES,
BY NUMBERS OF ARTICLES AND FIELD, 1969-73

	Total^a			Science			Social Science		
	Black	White	Difference	Black	White	Difference	Black	White	Difference
Income: 1973									
Number of Articles									
5 or more	$22,071	$20,398	$1,673	$21,497	$19,623	$1,874	$23,081	$20,291	$2,790
1-4	16,348	16,094	254	14,301	15,653	−1,352	16,301	16,216	85
0	14,320	15,015	−695	12,229	14,371	−2,142	17,002	15,663	1,339
Income: 1969^b									
5 or more	$15,777	$16,908	−$1,131	$13,881	$16,444	−$2,563	$14,174	$16,343	−$2,169
1-4	12,692	12,676	16	11,839	13,549	−710	12,675	12,800	−125
0	10,503	10,554	−51	10,562	10,605	−43	10,559	10,787	−228

a. Total data relate to teaching personnel only. Field figures include some administrators.
b. 1969 figures, based on means calculated without taking account of supply weights. Comparisons of 1973 weighted and unweighted means showed little difference in the results, which makes the comparison in the table valid.

SOURCE: Calculated from ACE tapes.

Table 8

REGRESSION ESTIMATES OF THE PREMIUM
FOR BLACK MALE ACADEMIC STARS

	Impact on Log Incomes, and Log Incomes	
	Whites	Blacks
Measures of Academic Quality		
Doctorate vs Master's Degree	.12	.16
5 or More Publications vs 0 Publications	.08	.24
High Quality Ph.D.	.02	.05
Total Impact	.22	.45
Log of Income for Persons with Average Age, Experience, Master's Degree, 0 Publications and Average Other Qualifications	2.57	2.55
Log of Incomes of Academic Stars	2.79	3.00

SOURCE: Calculated, as described in the text, from table 5.

between black and white faculty with specified characteristics, other income determining variables held fixed. The table considers persons of high academic qualifications: having a Ph.D., five or more publications, graduate training at a top school, and with average age (44 years), experience (13 years), and allocation of time, compared to those with a master's degree, no publications, and average other qualifications. It uses the black equation to evaluate the impact of high academic productivity for blacks and the white equation for whites. The results corroborate the sample mean comparisons in table 7. A black income disadvantage of about 2 percent among those with only limited quality, as defined, is turned into an advantage of 21 percent among the highly productive.

Finally, additional evidence that there was a substantial change in the gradient of the publication-income locus for blacks in the 1969-73 period encompassing "affirmative action" pressure is given in figure 1, which contrasts the regression coefficients for the black articles-income schedule with that of whites in 1969 and 1973 using income determining equations like those in table 5. Since the 1969 data do not contain information on hours worked, the hours variables have been omitted to preserve comparability. The figure shows clearly that articles had a greater marginal effect on black than white incomes in 1973 but that articles had a roughly similar marginal effect on the salaries of the two groups in 1969.

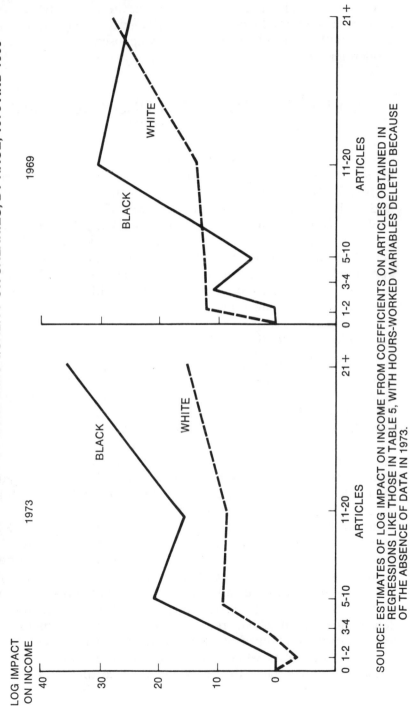

FIGURE 1

CURVATURE OF THE IMPACT OF ACADEMIC QUALITY ON SALARIES, BY RACE, 1973 AND 1969

SOURCE: ESTIMATES OF LOG IMPACT ON INCOME FROM COEFFICIENTS ON ARTICLES OBTAINED IN REGRESSIONS LIKE THOSE IN TABLE 5, WITH HOURS-WORKED VARIABLES DELETED BECAUSE OF THE ABSENCE OF DATA IN 1973.

In sum, equal employment pressures in the early seventies appear to have produced an especially strong market for black faculty with top academic qualities as opposed to more marginal academicians.

III. EMPLOYMENT PATTERNS AND HIRING STANDARDS

The next issue to consider is the way in which employment of black faculty and the hiring standards applied to appointments in specific types of institutions were affected by the late sixties and early seventies increase in demand. This section presents evidence from the ACE surveys that shows a substantial movement of black faculty into primarily white institutions in the period of intense federal affirmative action pressures, and the apparent application of somewhat lower hiring standards to black faculty in institutions of similar quality, with blacks typically reporting fewer publications than whites.

1. *EMPLOYMENT BY INSTITUTION*

The pattern of black and white faculty employment by type of institution is examined in table 9, which records the proportion employed in various categories of colleges and universities in the 1969-73 period under study. Two important aspects of the differential patterns of black and white faculty employment stand out in the table. First is the extraordinary difference in the proportion of blacks and whites employed in the various institutions. In both 1969 and 1973 black faculty tend to be concentrated in the predominantly Negro colleges of the South and are much less likely to be employed in universities, private nonsectarian and sectarian colleges, and junior colleges (except women in 1973) than whites—a pattern which reflects the historic virtual exclusion of black scholars from primarily white institutions. Second, however, is the marked change in the black distribution in the 1969-73 period of affirmative action pressures. In a brief span of four years, the proportion of black faculty in the predominantly Negro schools fell from nearly three-fourths to about one-half; the fraction of black men in universities increased by 8 percentage points while, as a result of the slowdown in the academic marketplace, the fraction of white men so employed

Table 9

PERCENT DISTRIBUTION OF BLACK AND WHITE FACULTY, BY TYPE OF INSTITUTION, 1969-73

Type of institution	Male				Female			
	Black		White		Black		White	
	1969	1973	1969	1973	1969	1973	1969	1973
Universities	10	18	51	44	10	10	41	37
high quality	5	9	13	17	3	6	8	12
medium quality	4	5	16	18	3	2	14	14
low quality	1	4	22	9	4	2	19	11
Public Colleges	12	17	17	20	10	5	17	15
high quality	2	8	6	8	2	5	5	5
other	10	9	11	12	8	0	12	10
Private Colleges (Nonsectarian)	2	4	10	8	3	6	10	9
high quality	0	0	1	1	0	1	1	2
medium quality	1	3	3	2	0	1	2	2
other	1	1	6	5	3	4	7	5
Religious	1	3	9	8	2	3	13	13
Two-year	4	7	12	19	5	25	18	25
Predominantly Negro	71	51	1	1	70	51	1	1

SOURCE: Calculated from ACE tapes for 1968-1969 and 1972-1973.

dropped by 7 percentage points. While the direction of change was clearly toward greater similarity in the distributions, sizable differences still remained in 1973.

The impact of differences in scholarly qualifications on the distributions is examined in table 10, which records the probability of being employed in various institutions by number of articles: data in lines 1 and 2 show that the concentration of blacks in southern black colleges is not associated with number of articles; blacks with 0, 1-4, and 5 or more articles are about as likely to work in the southern black colleges as not. Once the basic concentration of blacks in the southern colleges is given, however, the evidence in the remainder of the table—probabilities of being employed in prestigious or high quality colleges and universities, given that one is not employed in the southern black schools—reveals only modest and uneven differences in the distributions for persons with the same number of articles. Black faculty working outside of southern black colleges with five or more articles have, for example, about the same chance of being in high or medium quality universities as whites, while those with 0 or 1-4 articles have a better chance of such employment than comparable whites (.37 vs. .23 and .46 vs. .35). The critical difference in the distributions, then, relates to the continued though declining concentration of black faculty in southern black colleges and the relative paucity of black scholars in primarily white colleges and universities.

2. HIRING STANDARDS

Analysis of the relations between number of articles and institutions of employment is pursued further in table 11, which rearranges the basic data in table 10 to show the number of articles published by black and white male faculty in various types of academic institutions in 1973. Taking number of articles as the measure of academic standards, larger numbers of articles by black faculty would indicate that higher standards were being applied to their appointments; fewer articles would indicate the opposite. The data reveal sizable differences in scholarly productivity between black and white male faculty in the institutional categories considered, with blacks reporting fewer published articles than whites. In high quality universities, for example, blacks averaged roughly half as many articles as whites, with just 29 percent of blacks having five or more articles compared to 67 percent for whites. In other institutions, except the pre-

Table 10

PROBABILITY OF EMPLOYMENT IN VARIOUS TYPES OF ACADEMIC INSTITUTIONS
BY NUMBERS OF ARTICLES, 1973

	Black Men			White Men		
			Number	of Articles		
	0	1-4	5+	0	1-4	5+
Probability of Employment in Southern Black Colleges	.55	.50	.56	.01	.01	.01
Probability of Being Employed in Other Institutions	.45	.50	.44	.99	.99	.99
Conditional Probability of Employment if outside Southern Black College, in:						
University						
high quality	.08	.23	.31	.06	.12	.33
medium quality	.02	.06	.25	.05	.10	.19
Private 4-year Nonsectarian college with 500+ Student Scores	.02	.13	0	.05	.05	.04
Public 4-year college with 500+ Student Scores	.25	.04	.09	.07	.08	.08
Total, High and Medium Quality	.37	.46	.65	.23	.35	.64
All Other	.63	.54	.35	.77	.65	.36

SOURCE: Calculated from ACE Survey, 1972-73.

dominantly black colleges, the pattern is similar. Correcting for the broad field of employment, or age, moreover, does not greatly affect these differences as the relatively small supply of black men in sciences (where many publications are common) is balanced by relative underrepresentation in humanities (where publications are less frequent) and mean ages of the two groups of academicians are the same (see table 4). While more detailed analysis of faculty employed in particular types of institutions based on a larger data set and a more comprehensive measure of academic quality is needed, the crude data on articles suggest that somewhat lower standards were applied to black appointments. This does not mean, however, that overall academic quality was being diluted by equal employment pressures, for institutions could be selecting black faculty with about the same number of publications or overall qualifications as would be held by marginal white appointments. That is, differences in mean numbers of publications between the groups cannot be used to infer the effect of demand on the average number of publications of all faculty in the relevant institutional group. Given the choice of similarly productive or qualified black and white faculty, colleges and universities may tilt in favor of the black candidate. If the average black faculty had fewer articles than the average white because of, say, lower educational position (Master's rather than Ph.D. degrees), this will result in a lower mean number of publications for black faculty and a higher mean for white faculty while the institution average remains unchanged. Whether this process or some other reason explains the observed difference in articles published remains to be seen.

IV. CHANGING STATUS OF OTHER MINORITY FACULTY

How have other minority groups, including those who were well-represented in academia prior to the initiation of affirmative action, fared in the period under study? How do their income and employment differ from those of majority whites?

This section analyzes these two questions using the ACE survey data. The analysis is less detailed and more tentative than that given for blacks because it focuses on only one, albeit very important, indicator of academic quality—number of articles—

Table 11

NUMBERS OF ARTICLES PUBLISHED BY BLACK AND
WHITE MALE FACULTY IN ACADEMIC
INSTITUTIONS, 1973[a]

	Percentage Distribution of Male Faculty, by Number of Articles						
	0	1-2	3-4	5-10	11-20	21+	Mean Number
High Quality University							
black	25	16	30	6	8	15	8.2
white	13	11	10	17	18	32	15.9
Medium Quality University							
black	15	19	11	47	3	5	6.4
white	17	15	12	19	16	22	12.4
Other University							
black	30	27	27	7	5	4	4.1
white	23	14	13	18	14	17	10.0
Private 4-year (nonsectarian) College							
black	24	58	13	5	0	0	1.7
white	42	21	12	11	7	6	4.3
Public 4-year College							
black	52	23	13	11	1	—	1.8
white	37	21	12	13	9	8	5.9
Predominantly Black College							
black	54	16	12	6	4	7	4.2
white	48	16	6	9	10	11	6.6

a. Quality of universities defined: high quality—average college board scores, 600+; medium quality—board scores, 550-599.

SOURCE: Calculated from ACE Survey, 1972-1973.

rather than the full spectrum of factors which enter the quality-adjustment calculations.

Table 12 presents the basic ACE evidence on the employment of nonblack minorities in academic years 1968-69 and 1972-73. With respect to persons of Oriental descent, the table reveals a moderate gain in the share of academic jobs, apparently concentrated in 2-year institutions. Measured as percentage changes in relative numbers, the gains for Orientals are significantly below those shown for blacks in table 4, which is to be expected given the differences in initial positions. The figures for other nonblack minorities, which show an enormous increase in their relative employment, are unfortunately less satisfactory due to changes in the specific questions relating to minority status. In 1969 these persons were given the option of identifying themselves as being in an "other" category; in 1973, they could choose the specific ethnic groups given in the table. Presumably, the latter format would engender more responses. However, even if, as seems likely, Mexican and Puerto Rican Americans did not classify themselves as being in the "other" category in 1969, making Indians the major group, the data suggest a sizable increase in nonblack, non-Oriental faculty employment in the 1969-73 period.

Table 12

PERCENT OF NONBLACK MINORITY
FACULTY IN AMERICAN COLLEGES AND UNIVERSITIES,
1968-69 TO 1972-73

Group	Total		Two-year Colleges		Universities	
	1968-9	1972-3	1968-9	1972-3	1968-9	1972-3
Oriental	1.3	1.5	0.5	1.3	1.6	1.6
Mexican American	⎫	0.3	⎫	0.6	⎫	0.2
Puerto Rican American	⎬ 0.3	0.3	⎬ 0.3	0.1	⎬ 0.3	0.1
American Indian	⎭	0.8	⎭	0.9	⎭	0.7

SOURCE: American Council on Education, *College and University Faculty: A Statistical Description* (1970), p. 12; American Council on Education, *Teaching Faculty in Academia: 1972-73* (1973), p. 31.

The income of Orientals and other nonblack minority male faculty with different numbers of articles published is examined in table 13. Column 1 records the mean income of the total number of Oriental and other minority faculty (including persons not responding to the articles question) and of those with different numbers of articles published. Columns 2 and 3 contrast the incomes of these persons with incomes of comparable white male faculty in 1973 and 1969, respectively. The final set of figures in the table shows the percentage of the groups with different numbers of articles and, in parentheses, the analogous distribution for whites. There are three findings. First, in both 1973 and 1969, Orientals and other minority faculty had, in general, somewhat lower incomes than white faculty with the same number of publications. While the lower incomes of "other" minorities might be attributed to their trailing whites in other qualifications that raise income (such as level of education), this is not true for the Orientals who tend to be better educated and more qualified than whites in general. The data thus suggest that Oriental faculty suffer from some market discrimination, defined in terms of quality-adjusted incomes. Second, the table shows little consistent change in the relative incomes of the Oriental faculty in the 1969-73 period, which contrasts sharply with the marked increase in relative income of the most productive black scholars documented earlier. There is an apparent improvement in the income position of "other minority" faculty but this must be treated cautiously due to the problem of coverage. Third, the percentage distribution data in the last column reveal that Oriental faculty have greater productivity, in terms of published articles, than whites, while the other minority group reports slightly fewer publications. Because Orientals are concentrated in natural sciences, where publication of numerous short articles is frequent, it might be thought that the Oriental-white differential in articles is due to field differences. Even in the natural sciences, however, it turns out that Oriental faculty publish more than white faculty, according to the ACE data, and have lower incomes on average. While these differences could be due to other factors—such as concentration in high-quality universities where money income is traded off for other types of rewards—the presumption is of some market discrimination.

As a final step in analysis of the market status of nonblack minority faculty, table 14 presents evidence relating to possible hiring standards applied to these workers. It compares, along the lines set out in table 11, the number of articles published by faculty in different types of academic institutions. Because Orientals and other minority faculty were grouped together in the calculations, the evidence is only suggestive with respect to the standards applied to them separately. What stands out in the table is the general pattern for nonblack minority male faculty to publish more articles than white faculty in several types of institutions, notably medium quality and "other" universities, while having about the same articles distributions in the remaining groups. If, as seems reasonable, the Orientals publish more than other nonblack minorities within the groups, there would be further evidence of discrimination in the form of tougher hiring standards against them.

Because this chapter has concentrated on the black minority,

Table 13

INCOMES AND NUMBERS OF ARTICLES PUBLISHED BY ORIENTAL AND OTHER MINORITY MALE FACULTY, 1969-73

	Income	Income as Percent of White Income		Distribution by Articles (White Distribution in Parentheses)
	1973	1973	1969[a]	1973
Orientals				
total	$16,188	94.6	98.3	—
5+ articles	17,660	87.4	92.4	52.4 (35.6)
1-4 articles	15,979	100.3	93.6	22.9 (27.6)
0 articles	13,209	88.7	92.4	24.1 (35.5)
Other Minority				
total	15,339	89.7	84.9	—
5+ articles	18,075	89.4	81.5	30.5 (35.6)
1-4 articles	14,445	90.6	89.7	26.8 (27.6)
0 articles	16,673	111.9	91.0	42.3 (35.5)

a. 1969 figures based on mean incomes not weighted by sample weights. Experiments with weighted and unweighted means in 1973 revealed little difference, so the comparison in the table is valid.

SOURCE: Calculated from ACE tapes.

the results pertaining to discrimination against faculty of Oriental descent should be treated cautiously. A more detailed analysis of their economic status is needed to firm up the tentative findings.

Table 14

ARTICLES PUBLISHED BY NONBLACK MINORITY AND WHITE FACULTY, BY TYPE OF ACADEMIC INSTITUTION, 1973[a]

| Type of Institution | Number of Articles | | | |
	0	1-4	5-10	11+
High Quality University				
nonblack minority	.10	.21	.15	.54
white	.13	.21	.17	.50
Medium Quality University				
nonblack minority	13.	.18	.15	.54
white	.17	.27	.19	.38
Other University				
nonblack minority	.19	.26	.18	.37
white	.23	.27	.15	.14
Private 4-year (nonsectarian) college				
nonblack minority	.51	.23	.06	.20
white	.42	.33	.11	.14
Public 4-year college				
nonblack minority	.42	.33	.11	.14
white	.37	.33	.13	.17

a. Quality of universities as defined in table 11. Approximately one-third of the nonblack minority are orientals.

SOURCE: Calculated from ACE Survey, 1972-73.

V. CONCLUSION

This chapter has shown that demand for black faculty has increased greatly in recent years, presumably as a result of governmental and other pressures—with substantial consequences for the academic market:

1. Black faculty received more job offers than whites in the period and obtained earnings that were as high as or higher than those of white faculty with similar qualifications. Within similar institutions, black male faculty appear to have obtained 7-8 per-

cent ($1,200) income advantage over whites with what appear to be the same academic skills.

2. A sizable premium was accorded to black scholars with many publications in 1973 as a result of a substantial increase in the marginal value of an article for black faculty between 1969-73, which suggests that the pressures of that period raised the reward to quality.

3. The distribution of black faculty employment changed markedly, as the number of blacks in primarily white institutions grew substantially in the period studied. Even so, however, blacks continued to be concentrated in the primarily black colleges of the South in 1973.

4. Because the number of publications by black faculty is markedly below that of whites in similar institutions, hiring standards appear to be lower for black appointments, though this does not, it must be stressed, imply that the new minority appointments fell below the previous minimum standards.

5. There is evidence which suggests that faculty of Oriental descent suffer from some discrimination in the marketplace which has not been reduced by the various minority-hiring pressures. Oriental academicians publish more articles but are paid less than majority whites, possibly even within similar higher educational institutions.

All told, this chapter presents an interesting picture of a market in which blacks, particularly the more productive scholars, are in especially great demand, earning more and receiving more job offers than comparable whites, and in which the Oriental minority, who are well-represented in universities, may have faced continued lower quality-adjusted incomes. While firm conclusion about causality cannot be readily made, this favorable market position of blacks would appear to be traceable to federal affirmative action and other pressures for increased black academic employment, which supports the broad argument that governmental policy, rather than changes in private attitudes, is the critical element in black economic advance in the late sixties and early seventies.

NOTES

1. There is, of course, some problem with level of degree as a measure of quality since persons with limited education who are faculty members may have special talents or skills. The main difference is, however, between the Ph.D. and the Master's, which generally reflects a difference in quality of training.

2. There are two major areas of noncomparability between the surveys: first, the 1969 and 1973 surveys are based on different sample and weighting procedures (see ACR, 1973); second, the 1969 survey did not distinguish administrators from faculty, while the 1973 survey, nominally sent only to faculty, turned up large numbers of administrators who have been deleted from most of our calculations.

3. See Zvi Griliches, *Price Indexes and Quality Change* (Harvard University Press, 1971), for a discussion of hedonic price caculations.

4. Calculated from the ACE survey.

5. At Harvard, for example, the black share of deans far exceeds the black share of faculty.

6. K. Roose and C. J. Anderson, *A Rating of Graduate Programs* (American Council on Education, 1961).

References

Bayer, A. E. *College and University Faculty: A Statistical Description.* American Council on Education, 1970.

Freeman, R. "Changes in the Labor Market for Black Americans." Brookings Papers. Summar 1973.

Greene, H. W. *Holders of Doctorates among American Negroes.* Meador Publishing Co., 1946.

Griliches, Zvi. *Price Indexes and Quality Change.* Harvard University Press, 1971.

Lester, R. A. *Antibias Regulation of Universities.* Carnegie Commission on Higher Education. McGraw-Hill Book Co., 1974.

Mommsen, K. G. "Black Doctorates in American Higher Education: The Case for Institutional Racism." Paper presented at the Southwestern Sociological Association, San Antonio, Texas, 1973.

———. "Black Ph.D.'s in the Academic Marketplace: Supply, Demand and Price." Paper presented at the 68th Annual Meeting of the American Sociological Association, 1973.

National Academy of Sciences. *Minority Groups among United States Doctorate Level Scientists, Engineers and Scholars.* 1973.

Roose, K. and Anderson, C. J., American Council on Education, 1961.

U.S. Bureau of the Census. *Census of Population: Characteristics of Professional Workers,* 1960; *Nonwhite Population by Race,* 1960; *Occupational Characteristics,* 1950, 1960, 1970. Government Printing Office.

U.S. Department of Health, Education, and Welfare. *Higher Education Guidelines.* Executive Order 11246.

Race
and I.Q.
Reconsidered

THOMAS SOWELL

Much controversy has surrounded the question of the relationship between intelligence and heredity, and particularly the question of a relationship between race and intelligence. Yet, despite the emotionally-charged philosophical and political issues involved, this is ultimately an empirical question—independent of anyone's beliefs, hopes, or fears. Whether we currently have the technical expertise to answer it is another matter. Yet even in the physical sciences, it is seldom that a definitive answer to any question springs forth, full-blown, from a chaos of controversy and surmise. More usually, a succession of painstaking studies and a series of theoretical analyses tend ultimately toward some resolution which reasonable men find acceptable, and eventually compelling. This present study hopes to contribute towards such an eventual outcome as regards race and intelligence.

A research project directed by the author at The Urban Institute collected more than 70,000 I.Q. records from schools across the country, covering a dozen ethnic groups,[1] and extending back over a period of up to 50 years, depending upon the record-keeping practices of the individual schools and boards of education. Together with existing mental test score data collected during the period from about 1915 to 1925, these data permit an analysis of the general historical pattern of mental test results for American ethnic groups from differing racial backgrounds. Some of the questions that can be asked in the light of these data include:

1. *Is there anything to explain* as regards racial differences? That is, do the mental test scores of American Negroes (or other racially distinct ethnic minorities) today differ in either level or pattern from those of European immigrant groups at a similar stage of their socioeconomic development?

2. Have the I.Q.'s of European ethnic minorities *changed* substantially over the decades as their socioeconomic position has altered?

3. Have mental test score changes over the years been less for highly endogamous groups, such as the Jews or Orientals, than for various northern and western European groups who have intermarried more freely with members of the general population and thereby altered the minority's gene pool?

Note that the focus of this study is not the very general question of the relative influence of "heredity" and "environment" on "intelligence," but the more specific and policy-relevant question, whether *large intergroup differences* in standard mental test scores are more a function of genetic or of environmental differences between the particular groups considered. It is entirely possible that there are very different answers to these two questions. That is, the variations in mental test scores among individuals in the general population may be more related to differences in their genes than in their rather similar environments, while differences between whole groups facing markedly different environmental conditions may be due to those environmental differences. It is of course also possible that the environmental differences between groups are a function of genetic differences between them, as well as of history and social conditions, and there is no a priori reason to rule out a greater influence for heredity. What is important for this study is to recognize that two very different questions exist. Much of the evidence brought forth thus far, such as I.Q. correlations between twins reared in separate homes, relates only to the general question, though the results are often extended to I.Q. differences between groups living under environmental influences which appear much greater than the differences between the homes in which separated twins are reared.

The validity of mental tests—in various senses of the word "validity"—is a large and complex area which is important in itself but peripheral to the specific issues involved in this study. Environmentalists have frequently pointed out the "cultural bias" of I.Q. tests, College Board examinations, etc., especially when arguing against the genetic determinism of Professor Arthur R. Jensen of Berkeley. It is easy enough to show that some questions on some tests ("Who wrote *Faust*?" for example) presuppose a kind of cultural information which is much more likely to be known to a middle class white child than to children of other races and social classes. However, it cannot be automatically assumed that such questions or tests are the explanation of intergroup differences in test scores, or that these differences are greatest on tests which depend upon such information. On the contrary, it is precisely on those tests which do *not* require such information—abstract tests—that black-white differences in results are greatest.[2]

Jensen cites this as the basis for his contention that black-white differences in I.Q. are innate, for his theory is not one of general mental "inferiority" of Negroes, but specifically that there are different kinds of intellectual ability and that *abstract reasoning* is the specific ability genetically lacking among blacks.[3] It is not simply the *level* of mental test performance but also the *pattern* of mental test performance which Jensen depicts as peculiar to blacks. It is this pattern rather than "test validity" in general which is relevant to the present study.

From an environmentalist viewpoint, the abstract material can be regarded as *more* culturally biased—though less *obviously* so —than material dealing with particular cultural information, because interest in and practice with abstract concepts is a peculiarity of better educated nations and social classes. This alternative hypothesis implicitly concedes that there is a real difference in mental capability which the tests measure, though that difference is regarded as environmentally determined. And in a technologically complex society, the ability to handle abstractions cannot be regarded as an unimportant cultural attribute, or one whose importance is due merely to arbitrary social conventions. Again, what is crucial to the present study is whether (1) this pattern of doing worse on abstract questions is peculiar to blacks, or (2) whether it was common to low-I.Q. immigrant groups from a Caucasian racial background, and in particular whether it was once common to Caucasian groups whose I.Q.'s subsequently rose by large amounts.

Another pattern emphasized by some is the tendency of black children's test scores to be closer to those of white children at earlier ages, and to fall progressively further behind as the years pass.[4] A genetic interpretation of this phenomenon is that black children approach the limits of their capacity sooner—one implication of this being that "early childhood" educational efforts may simply bring black youngsters to their genetic plateau earlier, with no long-run educational results. An alternative hypothesis is that intellectual development builds on past intellectual mastery of more fundamental material, so that any group (of whatever race) whose scores were below average (for whatever reason) at the beginning would tend to fall progressively further behind the norm as intellectual development proceeded. An interesting implication of this latter hypothesis is that while maturational increments of raw test scores are below normal, *other* kinds of incremental gains (*not* dependent upon mastery of previous material) need not be below normal for low I.Q. groups with "normal" genetic endowments—these other increments being from such things as greater test familiarity, a better psychological environment for test-taking, or better teaching. This implication will be examined empirically for black children and for children of European immigrant groups.

It should be noted that a study of black and white Americans is not a study of Negro and Caucasian races in any global sense. There is no reason to believe that either American group is a representative sample of its race, and some historical reasons for believing that there is a definite bias in both samples.[5] Moreover, the subsequent genetic history of the American samples did not correspond to that of the contemporary populations from which they derived—especially as regards intermarriage among constituent groups within each broad racial category, not to mention interbreeding across racial lines. But this limitation for purposes of global or definitive racial comparisons or for the more general question of "heredity versus environment" is not a limitation for the purpose of analyzing American social questions in an American context.

The present study will consider not only the levels of mental test performance, but also the patterns of mental test performance. For an explanation of test score levels to be acceptable, it must also be consistent with the test score patterns. These patterns include not only intergroup differences in performance on abstractions and differences in maturational patterns, but also *intragroup* differences (by sex, geographic location, etc.) which will be explored in section II of this chapter. Both levels and patterns of ethnic group test scores will be considered historically; and, within the broad categories of levels and patterns, groups with European, African, and Oriental ancestry will be considered, as well as groups of Latin American origin (Mexican Americans and Puerto Ricans living on the U.S. mainland).

I. LEVELS OF MENTAL TEST PERFORMANCE

The average I.Q. of American Negroes has generally been around 85, using a wide variety of tests and research methods.[6] How does this compare with the I.Q.'s of European immigrant groups during their periods of similar poverty and social pathology? A survey of Italian American mental test scores research, summarized in 1921, found their I.Q.'s to be 85 in one study, 84 in two studies, 83 in another study, and 77.5 in still another study.[7] Another survey of American ethnic I.Q. studies in 1926 found median I.Q.'s of 85.6 for Slovaks,[8] 83 for Greeks,[9] 85 for Poles,[10] 78 for Spanish,[11] 84 for Portuguese,[12] and 85.5 for southern Europeans as a group.[13] Still another study of I.Q.'s in three Youngstown, Ohio, schools in 1919-20 showed an average I.Q. of 88 for children classified as "American (colored)," while among European immigrant children in the same schools there were lower average I.Q. scores among Italians, Slavs, Greeks, Poles, Lithuanians, Croatians, Syrians, and Gypsies.[14] Similarly, a 1924-25 study of Massachusetts school children from many ethnic backgrounds found blacks with higher I.Q.'s than the Portuguese, and with a higher percentage scoring over 120 on the I.Q. test than among Portuguese, Italian, Polish, or French Canadian youngsters in the same schools.[15]

Data on Jewish I.Q.'s during this period are more difficult to obtain, since Jews are an ethnic-religious group, while nationality groups were the major research category at that time. However, it is known that one-half or more of the Polish and Russian immigrants were Jews. The early mental test averages typically put immigrants from Poland and Russia at or near the bottom of

the list of European immigrants.[16] One study which specifically
identified Jews was conducted among 60,000 school children of
various ethnic backgrounds in twelve American cities in 1910.
This study showed that Polish Jews were more often below the
normal grade in their age than any of the other European ethnic
groups studied; 67 percent of these Jewish children were scholas-
tically retarded in this sense.[17]

The most massive mental testing during the European immigrant period was conducted by the U.S. Army among soldiers in
World War I. While the principal test used, Army Alpha, was
technically not an I.Q. test, since its mean score was not given as
100, its various sections were virtually identical in concept and
execution to the sections of a typical I.Q. test.[18] Indeed, the Army
Alpha was subsequently made the basis of a conventional I.Q.
test, the Otis-Alpha. The results of the Army Alpha followed very
much the same ethnic pattern as did the results of civilian I.Q.
tests of that period. The Italians, Poles, and Russians scored
consistently at or near the bottom of the list of European immigrants on the various army tests.[19] Since at least half the Poles
and Russians were Jews, a leading contemporary psychologist,
Carl Brigham (originator of the College Board S.A.T.), declared
that the army test results tended to "disprove the popular belief
that the Jew is highly intelligent."[20] Tests at Ellis Island in 1912
had shown the Jews to have one of the highest proportions of
people rated "feeble minded" of any immigrant group: 83 percent
of the Jewish immigrants scored in that category.[21] In 1921,
Jews led all immigrants in "number of certificates for mental
defect" at Ellis Island.[22]

The army tests showed the American Negro at the bottom of
all the lists of American ethnic groups' scores, though often with
virtually the same scores as soldiers of Italian, Polish, or Russian
national origin.[23] This was in contrast to contemporary civilian
studies in which blacks outscored some European immigrant
groups. The difference between the army studies and the various
civilian studies of American ethnic groups was that the latter
were typically conducted where such groups were concentrated—
i.e., in northern urban communities. The Negroes included in
civilian samples were therefore typically northern Negroes, while
the Negroes in the army were representative of the existing
distribution of the black population in the country at large—i.e.,
overwhelmingly southern. Over the years, northern blacks have

consistently scored about 10 points higher than southern blacks[24] —roughly 90 versus 80.

The "older" European ethnic groups—the Germans, Irish, English, and other northern and western European groups who had immigrated generations earlier—had I.Q. scores around the American national average, in contrast to the low scores among southern and eastern European immigrants. These intra-European differences in mental test scores were widely noted at the time, as were differences in crime, disease, and other indices of social pathology, as part of the bitter controversies leading up to the restrictive immigration laws of the 1920's.[25] The overwhelming weight of contemporary professional opinion among psychologists was behind a racial or genetic explanation of these differences among European immigrant groups.[26]

If the racial or genetic explanations of large intergroup I.Q. differences are correct, then the relative standing of the various European ethnic groups should remain stable over time, with particularly little change occurring among highly endogamous groups such as the Jews or, to a lesser extent, the Italians.[27] The non-Jewish Poles have also been relatively endogamous, at least to the extent of choosing marriage partners among Slavic groups,[28] who had similarly low I.Q.'s during the immigrant period. An environmental explanation of large intergroup I.Q. differences would lead to opposite empirical results—i.e., a reshuffling of the relative positions of ethnic groups, or at least a progressive narrowing of initial I.Q. differences between those groups already assimilated and those more recently arrived.

While the mental test data as of World War I showed a clear superiority of northern and western European ethnic groups over their southern and eastern European contemporaries, by the 1920s this superiority had disappeared as regards Jewish immigrants. Jewish I.Q.'s were at or above the national average by the mid 1920s,[29] and scattered studies since then have consistently found Jewish I.Q.'s to be above the national average.[30] The mental test performances of other southern and eastern European ethnic groups, such as Italian Americans or Polish Americans, are more difficult to trace in the literature, for data on European immigrant groups largely dried up after the exclusionary immigration laws of the 1920s mooted the controversies over "new" versus "old" immigrants. However, the Urban Institute survey permits Italian and Polish I.Q.'s to be traced from

decade to decade (table 1), along with the I.Q.'s of older immigrant groups such as the Germans and the Irish. It must be emphasized that *historical trends* only can be compared among
these groups—not absolute I.Q. levels—for the samples were
not drawn from identical schools, nor were they identical with
respect to geographical distribution or age distribution.

It is clear that Italian and Polish I.Q.'s have risen significantly
over time, to a level at or above the national average. That rise
is somewhat *understated* by the data shown, because our 1920s
data are biased toward the end of that decade, and is consequently
higher than I.Q. scores in contemporary studies of Italian and
Polish immigrant groups in the 1920s. Using the contemporary
1920s data as a base, for both groups the I.Q. increase has been
from the mid-80s to 100 or more. By contrast, the older European immigrant groups—the Germans and the Irish in our
sample—have I.Q.'s that fluctuated within a few points of the
1920s level, as reported both in this survey and in the literature
of the 1920s. Broadly speaking, those groups who were here
earlier had a decided advantage in mental test scores (and other
socioeconomic indicators) as of about World War I, but this
superiority on mental test scores was lost as the later arriving
groups rose by other socioeconomic indicators. This evidence
clearly supports the environmental explanation of large intergroup I.Q. differences.

American ethnic groups are not the only peoples of European
ancestry to have had I.Q.'s in the same bracket as American
Negroes. Similar average I.Q. levels have been found among the

Table 1

EUROPEAN IMMIGRANT GROUP MEDIAN I.Q.'S

Decades	German I.Q.	Sample Size	Irish I.Q.	Sample Size	Italian I.Q.	Sample Size	Jewish I.Q.	Sample Size	Polish I.Q.	Sample Size
1920s	101	341	102	81	92	153	112	104	91	1,019
1930s	101	1,428	102	1,847	93	3,735	104	1,651	95	5,958
1940s	103	1,235	104	2,066	95	5,093	104	1,278	99	2,267
1950s	102	1,338	105	2,311	99	4,466	102	192	104	1,610
1960s	106	704	107	1,454	103	2,526	*	*	107	2,505
1970s	105	116	105	151	100	228	*	*	109	184

*Sample size less than fifty.

Source: Ethnic Minorities Research Project, The Urban Institute.

Table 2

ITALIAN AMERICAN MEAN I.Q.'S

Decades	Otis Alpha		Otis Beta		California Test of Mental Maturity		Henmon-Nelson		Otis Quick-Scoring	
	I.Q.	Sample Size	I.Q.	Sample Size	I.Q.	Sample Size	I.Q.	Sample Size	I.Q.	Sample Size
1920s	*	*	*	*	*	*	*	*	*	*
1930s	93	517	98	204	*	*	*	*	*	*
1940s	95	281	98	160	*	*	102	132	*	*
1950s	99	235	99	254	101	504	104	96	108	54
1960s	102	269	107	221	104	225	107	259	108	342
1970s	*	*	*	*	*	*	*	*	*	*

*Sample size less than fifty.
Source: Ethnic Minorities Research Project, The Urban Institute.

indigenous population of Ireland,[31] among people in sociocultural isolation in the Hebrides Islands off Scotland,[32] or in white mountain communities in the United States,[33] and among children raised in isolated canal boat communities.[34] The I.Q. levels of all these people have been in the 80s. Their *patterns* will be considered in section 2.

Unfortunately, the I.Q.'s presented in table 1 are a peculiar kind of average—medians of heterogenous test scores—which leaves much to be desired statistically. They are presented at all only because of the unavailability of sufficient numbers of scores from a single test type for all ethnic groups. However, portions of these results can be checked against results from particular, identifiable, I.Q. tests for particular time periods. For example, table 2 shows our I.Q. test results for Italian Americans on the tests most frequently found in our Italian samples. With all the variations of results from test to test, and with all the sampling variations known to be present in this study, it is nevertheless quite clear from table 2 that Italian American I.Q.'s generally rose continuously, decade by decade, until they now equal or exceed the national average.

Table 3 shows the most frequently found test scores among Polish American school children in our sample. Again, the general pattern of rising I.Q.'s is apparent.

The Jewish data in our survey sample did not contain a large enough sample size for any given test to permit a time series

Table 3

POLISH AMERICAN I.Q.'S

Decades	Kuhlman-Anderson		Henmon-Nelson	
	Mean I.Q.	Sample Size	Mean I.Q.	Sample Size
1920s	*	*	*	*
1930s	*	*	*	*
1940s	105	64	104	80
1950s	108	55	102	88
1960s	108	1,529	105	161
1970s	110	119	*	*

*Sample size less than fifty.

Source: Ethnic Minorities Research Project, The Urban Institute.

to be constructed. For one decade—the 1940s—there was a sufficient sample size (141) on one test (the California Test of Mental Maturity) to permit one observation (average I.Q. of 109). The general time pattern of Jewish I.Q.'s in table 1 shows essentially a stability at a little above the national average, with one unusually high observation in the 1920s. This may reflect sampling peculiarities: the Jewish I.Q.'s of the 1920s are drawn predominantly from the midwest, while later Jewish samples are predominantly from the northeast. The differences may be either regional or due to socioeconomic differences between our particular midwestern Jewish sample and our northeast sample.

Among the earlier arriving immigrant groups—the Germans and the Irish—only the Irish sample permits even a two decade time series for a specific I.Q. test. The I.Q.'s of the Irish Americans by specific test are shown in table 4. It so happens that the particular test score found most frequently in the Irish sample— the California Test of Mental Maturity—permits a comparison of results for two immigrant groups (Irish and Italian) on the same test for the same decades (the 1950s and 1960s). From tables 2 and 4, it can be seen that (1) neither group was any longer below the national average by these decades, and that (2) the I.Q. difference between them was narrowing historically.

The I.Q. patterns of Chinese Americans and Japanese Americans are perhaps more complex or more difficult to characterize than those of the European ethnic minorities. While the general historical pattern of Oriental I.Q. scores is a relatively simple one of lower-than-average I.Q.'s in early years[35] and higher than

Table 4

IRISH AMERICAN I.Q.'S

Decades	California Test of Mental Maturity		Otis Quick-Scoring	
	Mean I.Q.	Sample Size	Mean I.Q.	Sample Size
1950s	110	454	*	*
1960s	109	517	110	80

*Sample size less than fifty.

Source: Ethnic Minorities Research Project, The Urban Institute.

average in later years (see below), even in the early, below-average years, Oriental American children out-performed native white children on particular subtests,[36] leading to speculation that language problems had differential impact on particular kinds of questions. A 1931 survey of earlier studies of Chinese and Japanese I.Q.'s showed that average Chinese I.Q.'s ranged from 87 to 107, and the average Japanese I.Q.'s ranged from 85 to 114.[37] The findings of an Urban Institute historical survey of Chinese and Japanese I.Q.'s are shown in table 5.

In short, this survey, like the general literature, finds Oriental Americans' I.Q.'s to equal or exceed the national average, just as Oriental Americans equal or exceed the national average in income and other socioeconomic indicators.[38] For neither the Chinese nor the Japanese was there a large enough sample for individual test type results to be presented with a significant sample size.

Table 5

ORIENTAL AMERICAN I.Q.'S

Decades	Chinese		Japanese	
	Median I.Q.	Sample Size	Median I.Q.	Sample Size
1920s	*	*	*	*
1930s	103	107	*	*
1940s	101	277	*	*
1950s	102	1,015	101	124
1960s	107	765	*	*
1970s	108	105	*	*

*Sample size less than fifty.

Source: Ethnic Minorities Research Project, The Urban Institute.

Table 6

HISPANIC AMERICAN I.Q.'S

Decades	Mexican		Puerto Rican	
	Median I.Q.	Sample Size	Median I.Q.	Sample Size
1920s	*	*	*	*
1930s	*	*	85	81
1940s	83	724	82	202
1950s	83	2,666	79	478
1960s	82	2,916	84	274
1970s	87	193	80	418

*Sample size less than fifty.

Source: Ethnic Minorities Research Project, The Urban Institute.

The mental test literature on Mexican American immigrants and Puerto Rican migrants to the United States is not nearly as vast as that on black Americans or on European immigrants. A 1924 survey of studies of Mexican American I.Q.'s found their average to be 85[39]—the same as that found for a variety of disadvantaged minorities in the United States and abroad. A 1931 survey of previous studies of Mexican American children showed average I.Q.'s ranging from 68 through 97, with a central tendency in the 80's.[40] The Urban Institute survey (table 6) found a similar range of scores for both Mexican Americans and Puerto Ricans living on the U.S. mainland.

Table 7

HISPANIC AMERICAN I.Q.'S BY TEST TYPE

Decades	Mexican Americans		Puerto Ricans	
	California Test of Mental Maturity		Lorge-Thorndike	
	Mean I.Q.	Sample Size	Mean I.Q.	Sample Size
1920s	*	*	*	*
1930s	*	*	*	*
1940s	*	*	*	*
1950s	85	483	*	*
1960s	95	315	80	146
1970s	*	*	80	362

*Sample size less than fifty.

Source: Ethnic Minorities Research Project, The Urban Institute.

The I.Q. results by specific tests (table 7) from this survey do not show any very different pattern from the results derived from heterogenous I.Q. scores. The only striking exception is the 10-point rise of Mexican Americans on the California Test of Mental Maturity from the 1950s to the 1960s.

The absence of any clear trend in I.Q. over time among these two Latin groups might conceivably reflect (1) genetic differences from other groups with upward trends over time, (2) the relatively static socioeconomic position of these two groups, (3) the enduring prevalence of Spanish as the language which is spoken in the home in both groups,[41] or (4) the high incidence of return-migration in both groups,[42] which inhibits acculturation to American norms. The genetic explanation is relatively easily disposed of, however. A special study of Puerto Rican children by the New York City Board of Education in 1958 shows the following relationships (tables 8 and 9) between I.Q. and the number of years in school on the U.S. mainland:

Table 8

PUERTO RICANS' SCHOOLING AND I.Q.

Number of Years in Mainland Schools	Average I.Q.	Number of Pupils Tested
1-2	72	29
3-4	73	33
5-6	82	28
7-8	87	16
9-10	93	10

Source: New York City Board of Education, *The Puerto Rican Study*, p. 74.

The same study found a similarly clear relationship between reading ability and mainland (versus Puerto Rico) schooling:

Table 9

PUERTO RICANS' SCHOOLING AND READING

Group	Average Lag in Grade Score
Island-born, Island Schooled	5.7
Island-born, Mainland Schooled	3.5
Mainland-born of Puerto Rican Parents	2.6

Source: New York City Board of Education, *The Puerto Rican Study*, p. 74.

The I.Q.'s of American Negroes in this survey are similar to those found in other surveys and in the same range as the I.Q.'s of European immigrant groups at a similar stage of their socioeconomic development (table 10). A breakdown of results on particular I.Q. tests (table 11) shows a great diversity—this diversity reflecting the variety of school results (different schools using particular tests) in the very large black samples, rather than simply a tendency of blacks to do well on particular types of tests.

A regional breakdown (table 10) shows an I.Q. difference of at least 10 points in each decade between the South and the other regions as a group. The apparent decline in black I.Q.'s over time reflects the growing proportion of southern I.Q.'s in this sample, while black I.Q.'s within regions were generally rising, though for the 1970s there was an apparent decline within the South. This latter may be a statistical artifact reflecting the recent progress of school integration in the South and its effect on racial research. The identification of individual black school children from record cards is unusually difficult (or impossible), compared to the identification of ethnic groups having distinctive names, religions, or foreign birthplaces, and samples tend therefore to be biased toward all-black schools where blanket identification of all students is possible. Such schools in the center of ghettoes would tend to provide downwardly biased samples of black I.Q.'s, given the long-standing tendency of the higher socioeconomic classes of Negroes to be on the expanding periphery of the ghetto or in integrated or predominantly white neighborhoods.[43] The South's racial segregation policies in the schools have exempted it from this statistical bias until very recently, but southern school integration in the 1970s may now mean that identifiable all-black schools constitute a downwardly biased sample of black children's I.Q.'s there as well, for the first time. Since the problem of identifying black students from school records is not peculiar to this survey, the possible statistical biases of previous I.Q. studies should also be considered.

All in all, the I.Q. levels of blacks in this survey are no different from those of other disadvantaged minorities, past or present. Their relatively static historical pattern is similar to that of Mexican Americans and Puerto Ricans, and parallels a relatively static socioeconomic position of blacks which did not begin to converge toward that of whites until the mid-1960s. By that time, our northeastern sample of all-black schools had disappeared,

Table 10

BLACK AMERICANS' I.Q. BY REGION

Decades	Total		South		Midwest		Northeast		West	
	Median I.Q.	Sample Size	Median I.Q.	Sample Size	Median I.Q.	Sample Size	Median I.Q.	Sample Size	Median I.Q.	Sample Size
1920s	*	*	*	*	*	*	*	*	*	*
1930s	91	178	*	*	*	*	91	135	*	*
1940s	92	2,133	82	470	96	1,521	91	139	*	*
1950s	92	5,193	84	1,194	94	3,962	*	*	*	*
1960s	88	3,743	87	3,389	98	339	*	*	*	*
1970s	82	3,264	82	3,254	*	*	*	*	*	*

*Sample size less than fifty.

Source: Ethnic Minorities Research Project, The Urban Institute.

Table 11

BLACK AMERICANS' I.Q.'S BY TEST TYPE

Decades	California Test of Mental Maturity		Henmon-Nelson Tests of Mental Ability		Kuhlmann-Anderson Intelligence		Otis-Lennon Mental Ability Tests		Otis Quick-Scoring Mental Ability Test		Pinter General Ability Tests	
	Mean I.Q.	Sample Size	Mean I.Q.	Sample Size	Mean I.Q.	Sample Size	Mean I.Q.	Sample Size	Mean I.Q.	Sample Size	Mean I.Q.	Sample Size
1920s	*	*	*	*	*	*	*	*	*	*	*	*
1930s	*	*	*	*	*	*	*	*	*	*	*	*
1940s	*	*	*	*	*	*	*	*	*	*	83	447
1950s	84	1,005	97	131	*	*	*	*	84	515	85	227
1960s	85	2,823	*	*	102	412	*	*	91	263	*	*
1970s	79	1,443	*	*	105	115	82	1,693	*	*	*	*

*Sample size less than fifty.

Source: Ethnic Minorities Research Project, The Urban Institute.

the midwest sample had shrunk to a tenth of its size the previous decade, and the southern sample had become suspect, for reasons noted above. If the integration and individual identification problem can be overcome somehow, new surveys would be very much in order to measure the I.Q. effect of recently rising socioeconomic status on succeeding generations of black school-children.

II. PATTERNS OF MENTAL TEST PERFORMANCE

Several kinds of mental test score patterns will be considered:

1. Variations in an ethnic group's performance from one kind of question to another—abstract versus concrete, for example—either on a given test or on different tests.

2. Variations between a given ethnic group's male and female scores on the same mental tests.

3. Variations in the mental test performance of a given ethnic group under different testing conditions—such as with greater test familiarity, test coaching, or a better psychological environment.

4. Variations in an ethnic group's incremental gain in raw scores with age and/or more teacher input.

5. Variations between the mental test scores of different segments of the same ethnic group located in different geographic regions of the country.

TYPES OF QUESTIONS

Recent studies have demonstrated that different racial or ethnic groups have characteristic patterns of relative success on different kinds of mental test questions—and that the higher socio-economic classes from these respective groups simply repeat the same pattern on a higher *level*.[44] For example, Jewish school children did their best on verbal portions of mental tests and their worst on spatial conceptions, while Chinese children had just the reverse pattern, and Negro and Puerto Rican schoolchildren had still other patterns. The same ethnic patterns were found in different social classes and in different cities. While this clearly suggests a genetic trait, *an intertemporal* comparison would be necessary to see whether these patterns are sufficiently stable through periods of social change to indicate a genetic characteristic. International comparisons of the same racial group in different cultural settings would also be relevant. Little has been done to tie all these patterns together in this way, and the scarcity of intertemporal data makes this especially difficult.

Such scattered data as exist on low-scoring European immigrant groups (as of the World War I era) indicates that they, like American Negroes today, scored lowest on *abstract* questions. A 1917 study of various immigrant groups at Ellis Island showed them to be particularly deficient on abstractions,[45] confirming an impression published in 1913 by the noted psychologist H. H. Goddard, who had tested children there, that "These people cannot deal with abstractions. . . ."[46] L. M. Terman, author of the Stanford-Binet test, likewise concluded from his studies of racial minorities in the southwest that children from such groups "cannot master abstractions."[47] A 1932 study of white children in isolated mountain communities also showed that, in addition to having low I.Q.'s, their deficiencies were "most evident on items involving abstract comprehension."[48] A recent study in England showed that rural working class boys differed from their London and small town counterparts more on abstractions than on any other aspect of the various mental tests which they all took.[49] Orientals, during their era of lower than average test scores, did particularly poorly on tests and subtests requiring abstract reasoning ability.[50] The later concentration (and success) of Orientals in mathematics and the natural sciences[51] suggests that this was an environmental rather than a genetic phenomenon.

Scattered comments by testers support the hypothesis that interest in, and orientation toward, abstraction is an exceptional and acquired taste or facility. White mountaineer children showed difficulty in orienting themselves toward such questions,[52] Indian children in South Africa had a "lack of interest in non-verbal materials,"[53] West African school boys "obviously became bored" with such items, and examiners administering the Army Beta test during World War I reported "a decided disposition" for black soldiers "to lapse into inattention and almost into sleep"[54] during such tests.

SEX DIFFERENCES

A substantial volume of research indicates that females are less affected by environment—good or bad—than are males.[55]

This generalization embraces both physical and mental phenomena. It offers a way of circumventing some of the problems of culturally biased tests and of separating genetic from environmental factors. A low-I.Q. group whose females had higher scores than its males could be regarded as suffering environmental deprivation, whereas the reverse might suggest genetic deficiencies, since females tend to be less affected by environment than males. Moreover, the cultural bias of tests is less a factor in *intragroup* comparisons, especially of children who have not yet reached the age of sharp sex differentiation in exposure to the dominant culture.

Small average male-female differences may be difficult to detect in empirical research, but there are exaggerations of these small differences at some points on the I.Q. distribution, and these exaggerations are more likely to be observable. If both male and female I.Q.'s are normally distributed with identical variance about their respective means, then a relatively small difference in those means will tend to lead to larger and larger overrepresentation of one sex above selected, and progressively higher points on the I.Q. scale. In figure 1, the distribution of I.Q.'s of one sex (S_1) has a somewhat lower mean than the distribution of I.Q.'s of the other sex (S_2). At point M, representing a somewhat higher I.Q. than the mean of either group, the number of members of sex S_2 is greater than the number of members of sex S_1, but not by as much as two-to-one. At some higher I.Q., such as at point N, the number of members of sex S_2 exceeds the number of members of sex S_1 by *more* than two-to-one. It is easy to visualize how this ratio of S_2 to S_1 continually increases as the cut-off level rises. Therefore, by selecting some arbitrarily high level of intellectual performance (an I.Q. of 110 or 120, for example) intragroup male-female differences in representation above that level should be readily apparent statistically.

In principle, either sex could be S_1 or S_2. A complicating factor in reality is that the *variance* of male I.Q.'s has been found to be slightly wider than the variance of female I.Q.'s.[56] For the general population, where the mean I.Q.'s of the sexes are equal, this means a slight over-representation of males at both high and low extremes. For a low-I.Q. group, this difference in variance makes it theoretically possible to have either a male or a female overrepresentation at high-I.Q. levels, even if the mean female I.Q. within the group is higher (S_2) than the group's

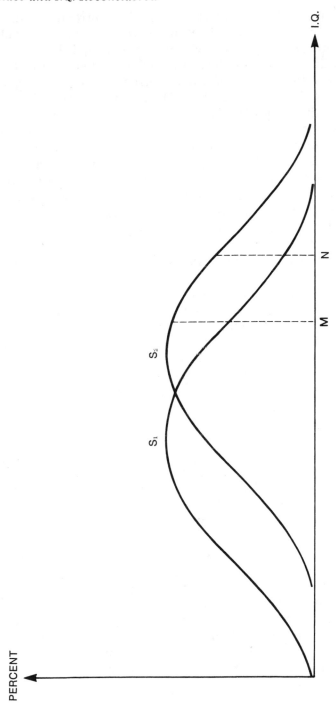

FIGURE 1

mean male I.Q. (S_1). However, a female overrepresentation means that the female I.Q. advantage within the group is sufficient to overcome the greater male variance at high I.Q. levels.

What are the facts? A massive study of individuals with I.Q.'s at or above 140 found males slightly overrepresented in the general population,[57] as they are at low I.Q. extremes as well,[58] in conformity with the principle of greater male variance. For the black population of the United States, however, a number of studies have consistently shown the *females* to be *very substantially overrepresented* among high I.Q. individuals. A 1934 study among black schoolchildren with an average I.Q. of 149 found that there were nearly three times as many girls as boys;[59] a later (1943) study of black schoolchildren found exactly three times as many girls as boys with I.Q.'s at or above 120,[60] and a later doctoral dissertation (1956) found more than five times as many females as males among black people with I.Q.'s of 130 and above.[61]

Some social theorists have attributed such phenomena to peculiar cultural characteristics of the black American population[62] —a "matriarchal" syndrome of some sort. However, before "explaining" the black pattern, it is necessary to see if it is in fact peculiar to blacks. Again, for the earlier or immigrant period, data are scattered and fragmentary, but such information as there is suggests that females did better than males among low I.Q. groups of European ancestry as well. The Ellis Island studies during the period of low Jewish performance on mental tests showed that Jewish *girls* exceeded the national norms "at most ages" at a time when Jewish boys were below those norms "up to the age of 16."[63] Similarly, in England, working class girls scored higher on mental tests than working class boys, though there was no such sex difference in the middle classes.[64] The Urban Institute data do not go far enough back in time to determine the sex breakdown of European minorities when their I.Q.'s were comparable to black I.Q.'s today. For Latin groups, however, there are some data indicating that females maintain a small but consistent I.Q. advantage, despite a culturally male-centered society (table 12).

Only the Mexican Americans had sample sizes large enough for a statistical breakdown of males and females with high I.Q.'s (over 110 in this case). The results are shown in table 13. Again, the females are clearly overrepresented among high I.Q. members of a low I.Q. group, though apparently not as extremely

Table 12

SEX DIFFERENCES IN LATIN I.Q.'S

Decades	Mexican Americans		Puerto Ricans	
	Male	Female	Male	Female
1920s	*	*	*	*
1930s	*	*	*	*
1940s	82	85	81	83
1950s	82	85	78	79
1960s	80	85	82	85
1970s	87	88	80	81

*Sample size less than fifty.
Source: Ethnic Minorities Research Project, The Urban Institute.

so as among black Americans. However, direct comparisons between blacks and Mexican Americans are not possible from these data, which dictate a high-I.Q. cut-off score of 110 for Mexican-Americans, because sample size was below 50 for Mexican American I.Q.'s of 120 and above for each decade of this particular survey. It is striking that the female superiority pattern in I.Q.'s is found in male-dominant Latin groups, suggesting that a similar pattern among blacks is not necessarily a sign of a "matriarchal" culture.

The Orientals were an average or above average I.Q. group for the period covered by the Urban Institute survey, and so should not be expected to have a female superiority pattern. Table 14 shows that they do not.

Table 13

SEX DIFFERENCES AMONG
HIGH-I.Q. MEXICAN AMERICANS

Decades	Mexican Americans: Percent With I.Q.'s Over 110			
	Males	Sample Size	Females	Sample Size
1920s	*	*	*	*
1930s	*	*	*	*
1940s	*	*	*	*
1950s	4.3	60	6.9	87
1960s	6.2	107	9.2	110
1970s	*	*	*	*

*Sample size less than fifty.
Source: Ethnic Minorities Research Project, The Urban Institute.

Table 14

SEX DIFFERENCES IN CHINESE I.Q.'S

Decades	Percent With I.Q.'s Above 110		Percent With I.Q.'s Above 120	
	Males	Females	Males	Females
1920s	*	*	*	*
1930s	*	*	*	*
1940s	20.3	26.7	*	*
1950s	32.8	32.6	12.9	12.9
1960s	44.8	47.5	21.5	17.1
1970s	*	*	*	*

*Sample size less than fifty.
Source: Ethnic Minorities Research Project, The Urban Institute.

The sex-breakdown data showed no general superiority of either sex during the period of average to above-average I.Q.'s of Chinese Americans as a group. The five sets of observations show each sex ahead twice and one tie. It could hardly be more even. This is consistent with the environmental explanation of intergroup I.Q. differences. Japanese sample sizes above an I.Q. of 110 were insufficient to be included with the breakdown of Oriental sex differences.

For American ethnic groups as a whole, the sex proportions among high-I.Q. individuals fit the environmental explanation of large intergroup I.Q. differences. Females are over-represented among high-I.Q. members of low-I.Q. racial or ethnic groups, as would be expected if negative environmental factors are responsible for the groups' low I.Q.'s; and if females are generally less affected than males by environmental factors. Apparently this female trait is sufficient to overcome the normal statistical expectation of male overrepresentation at both I.Q. extremes, due to greater male variance.

TESTING CONDITIONS

Ironically, Arthur R. Jensen provides one of the most revealing insights into the effect of test conditions on disadvantaged chidren:

> When I worked in a psychological clinic, I had to give individual intelligence tests to a variety of children, a good many of whom came from an impoverished background. Usually I felt these children were really brighter than their I.Q. would indicate. They often appeared inhibited in their responsiveness in the testing situation

on their first visit to my office, and when this was the case I usually had them come on two to four different days for half-hour sessions with me in a "play therapy" room, in which we did nothing more than get better acquainted by playing ball, using finger paints, drawing on the blackboard, making things out of clay, and so forth. As soon as the child seemed to be completely at home in this setting, I would re-test him on a parallel form of the Stanford-Binet. A boost in I.Q. of 8 to 10 points or so was the rule; it rarely failed, but neither was the gain very often much above this.[65]

It should be noted that this 8 to 10 point rise in I.Q. represents the disappearance of from one-half to two-thirds of the total I.Q. difference between black and white Americans through purely psychological means. It also has serious implications for the "success" of various "innovative" educational programs run by enthusiasts who create a very positive environment for test-taking—especially in cases where the experimental "success" is not repeated when the same teaching methods are applied on a mass basis by an ordinary sample of public school teachers. The "before" and "after" method of measuring the educational gains from such programs overlooks the fact that the "before" score is not only before the program, but may also be before the child became comfortable with mental tests and middle class examiners. Multiple tests "before" might be one way of reducing the effect of test familiarity; Jensen expresses "very little confidence in a single test score, especially if it is the child's first test and more especially if the child is from a poor background and of a different race from the examiner."[66] Unfortunately, much of the data on which Jensen bases his general conclusions of innate racial differences in intelligence are data generated by others, often under the crude testing conditions which he criticized, rather than on more carefully derived data under the testing conditions which he personally supervised.

What matters most from the standpoint of measuring inter-group mental test differences is not whether testing conditions are "good" or "bad" but whether test conditions have *differential* impacts on different groups. If there are innate differences in mental capacity between high-scoring and low-scoring groups, the better the test conditions and consequently the more accurate the reading of underlying capabilities, the more certain, (and perhaps larger) the differences in test score results. But if the two groups are basically similar, and the test scores are artifacts reflecting differences in attitudes and orientation, then improving the test conditions should narrow the differences in scores by reducing factors with a differential inhibition on the low-scoring group's performance. Again, the evidence is scattered and fragmentary, but it all points in the same direction—toward a narrowing of scores after high-scoring and low-scoring groups are both exposed to the same improvement in test conditions.

In the old Ellis Island studies, during the era when Jewish children ranked at or near the bottom on mental tests, the "greatest improvement" after training in abstract thinking was "among the Hebrew children."[67] A 1961 study found black South Africans gaining more than twice as much from test coaching as white South Africans.[68] Among black Americans, the low scoring southerners gain more from retesting than do the higher scoring northern blacks.[69] Somewhat similar results are found in the case of early childhood, preschool programs such as "Head Start," which produce gains for disadvantaged youngsters but not for others.[70] Unusually good teachers also tend to improve the performance of black schoolchildren more than they improve the performance of white schoolchildren.[71]

The pattern of incremental gains at a moment of time or over a short span of time is in sharp contrast with the pattern of maturational changes in a given cohort over the years. It has been pointed out that black American youngsters typically fall further and further behind their respective age norms as they get older.[72] But far from being a racial peculiarity, this pattern was common among low I.Q. European immigrant groups studied in 1916 to 1920. It was also common among white American children in isolated mountain communities studied in 1930 and in 1940.[73] It is possible to speculate about this pattern—and about whether it is a social phenomenon or a statistical artifact[74]—but, in any event, it is a pattern found among low I.Q. groups of European as well as African ancestry.

One of the test conditions that needs highlighting is that test instructions are often among the most difficult parts of a test. In many parts of the Army Alpha examination, used in the massive testing program in World War I, the modal number of correct answers was *zero*,[75] despite the modest intellectual demands of the questions themselves[76]—indicating that many of those tested did not know what they were supposed to be doing. For example, on Test 4 of the Army Alpha, more than four times as many soldiers received a score of zero than received any other specific score.[77] Yet the actual intellectual *substance* of the test involved only knowing that "yes" and "no" were opposites, as were "day and "night" or "bitter" and "sweet."[78] Even in the Army Beta examination, where more attention was paid to making instructions intelligible for illiterates,[79] repeatedly the number of tests with zero correct answers exceeded those with one correct answer[80]—in defiance of statistical expectations for a random, bell-shaped distribution of correct answers.

For disadvantaged ethnic groups the disproportion was so lopsided as to cast doubt on the validity of any of the results. More than half of all black soldiers tested on Army Alpha—3,721 out of 6,566—received a score of zero on Test 4 of the Army Alpha,[81] whose questions were too simple ("yes" and "no" are opposites, etc.) to have been completely missed by anyone who understood the instructions. In Test 4 of the Army Beta, which required only copying simple symbols from the blackboard onto the examination under numbers from 1 to 9,[82] more than 5,000 black soldiers received a score of zero, while less than 1,000 received each of the other possible scores.[83] The same was true of Test 5 of the Army Beta,[84] which required only making an X between identical numbers lined up in columns of numbers side by side.[85] Significantly, results were far better on more complicated questions whose *instructions* were more obvious. For example, less than half as many black soldiers received scores of zero on Beta Test 2, which involved determining the number of cubes in various pictured piles; approximately 6,000 black soldiers answered four or more correctly, which involved counting hidden cubes whose existence had to be inferred from the shapes of the piles.[86] Before doing that test, they were shown a pile of actual cubes to get the idea.[87] Unless one is prepared to believe that thousands of black soldiers who could count unseen cubes could not tell that "yes" meant the opposite of "no," the conclusion is inescapable that *instructions* can be a major factor in determining test results. The Army tests have been gone into in detail here only because, as published government documents, they are not protected from scrutiny by copyright laws, which make such public scrutiny impossible for most "intelligence" tests. Anyone with access to such tests can verify that they suffer from similar problems.

SELECTIVE MIGRATION

It has long been known that black Americans living in the South have scored lower on mental tests than black Americans living outside the South. The environmental explanation has been that poorer schooling and other social constraints on blacks in the South have led to poorer intellectual performances. The genetic explanation has been that a "selective migration" of the more able Negroes to the north, in search of opportunities, has led to genetically different black populations in different geographic regions of the United States.[88] There is some evidence for the selective migration hypotheses. Southern blacks who migrated north had higher test scores than other southern blacks, even before migration.[89] However, there is also evidence that the I.Q.'s of southerners rose in the North.[90]

The data generated by The Urban Institute surveys permit a somewhat different approach. Northern and southern blacks may be treated as any two other groups with an I.Q. differential whose environmental and hereditary differences are to be judged. Regional and sex differences (table 15) show that (1) black females score consistently above black males in the South as well as in other regions, and (2) I.Q. differences between the southern and other blacks are no greater among females than among males. Neither of these patterns is consistent with a genetic explanation of the differences between the two black populations in different regions. For the southern black population, which is particularly far below the national I.Q. norm, a genetic deficiency would tend to reduce female I.Q.'s more than male I.Q.'s, but in fact female I.Q.'s are consistently higher than male I.Q.'s among southern blacks—in keeping with the theory

Table 15

REGIONAL AND SEX DIFFERENCES IN I.Q.'S
AMONG NEGROES

Decades	South		Midwest		Northeast		West	
	Male I.Q.	Female I.Q.	Male I.Q.	Female I.Q.	Male I.Q.	Female I.Q.	Male I.Q.	Female I.Q.
1920s	*	*	*	*	*	*	*	*
1930s	*	*	*	*	94	95	*	*
1940s	78	84	95	96	92	90	*	*
1950s	83	85	94	95	*	*	*	*
1960s	86	88	99	97	*	*	*	*
1970s	80	83	*	*	*	*	*	*

*Sample size less than fifty.

Source: Ethnic Minorities Research Project, The Urban Institute.

of environmental deprivation and greater female resistance to environmental influences.

III. SUMMARY AND CONCLUSIONS

With all the bitter controversies which have raged over the explanation of black I.Q. levels and patterns, little attention has been paid to the more basic question, whether either the level or the pattern of American Negro test scores were unique—i.e., whether there was anything to explain in the first place. Similar (and lower) I.Q. scores among a variety of European ethnic groups in similar social circumstances in the past undermine the implicit assumption of uniqueness in general, as well as the specific hypothesis that there is a unique racial difference in innate mental ability. The large rises in I.Q. scores (20 points or more) over the decades as the past disadvantaged groups rose socioeconomically, supply an answer to the question which Arthur Jensen asked in the title of his celebrated article "How Much Can We Boost I.Q. and Scholastic Achievement?"

The *patterns* of black mental test scores have been no more unique than the levels of those scores. Scores have been lowest on abstractions, have trended downward for a given age cohort, but have risen by larger increments than have scores in the general population in response to such environmental improvements as better teaching or better test familiarity and test environment. This whole pattern has been common to American Negroes and to European immigrant groups in the past, and elements of this pattern have also appeared in Oriental and other racial groups in the United States and abroad.

While from an historical and international prospective, there is nothing unique about the test scores of black Americans, this in no way denies the validity, relevance, or importance of those scores for current social policy. These issues must be separated and fought out on their own respective merits. For example, a test may be valid for one purpose but not for another; it may accurately predict future performance in an academic setting, though it fails to measure innate potential. There is some evidence that achievement scores actually err slightly on the favorable side in predicting the academic record of low socioeconomic status individuals,[91] even though there is other evidence (from Arthur Jensen) that they err unfavorably in measuring their mental capability.[92] There is no inconsistency here. All that this means is that academic performance over a four-year period in college depends upon many variables besides mental capacity tested on a given day.

Among the tragic consequences of the bitter I.Q. controversy has been a hostility to mental tests which has in many cases made it politically impossible to use them and thereby extract important clues which these tests provide as to the sources of many educational and social problems. For example, recent tests show that among black males who failed the army mental standards for military service, *three-quarters* were from families of four or more children and one-half were from families of six or more children.[93] There is other evidence, from the general American population, on the negative effects of large family size on mental test scores,[94] and in particular the negative effect on the later children. Among National Merit Scholarship finalists from five-child families, 52 percent were the first born and only 6 percent were the fifth born.[95] This has obvious and weighty implications for birth control, which has been denounced as "genocide" by some, when in fact the absence of birth control may be socially suicidal, in a complex and competitive society. The point here is not to attempt a definitive answer to the complex question of family size, but to point out that some of the evidence that has to be taken into account for an intelligent decision consists of mental test scores. These scores cannot be waved aside with such phrases as "irrelevant" or "cultural bias," for the cultural bias applies equally to the black child in a three-child family and to the black child from a six-child family, and the fact that it is the latter who are failing the mental tests indicates that there is something very real involved, even though not something peculiar to black children, as such. No one believes that the first child is genetically superior to the fifth child born to the same parents, but it is clear that he gets something— probably a higher level of parental input—that the later children do not. Mental tests are also a measure of the job that school systems do. Every educational program will always be a "success" as judged by those who run it. A concern for children's mental development requires that there be independent tests as well. It is not mental testing that needs to be stopped, but the blind worship or blind hostility with which different people react to it.

Mental tests can be, and have been, misused. So have fire, the automobile, sex, and money. Yet no one considers banning any of these things, because of the lack of a viable alternative. Binet used I.Q. tests to rescue people who had been declared mentally incompetent by other criteria. Top colleges were opened to youths from unknown and nondescript high schools when these students' performances could be directly compared with national norms through the College Board SATs. Racial and social bigots have of course used mental tests for opposite purposes, but to allow such people to make subjective evaluations instead is to go from the frying pan into the fire. Belief in innate mental inferiority of black children was reported as pervasive among school officials by Dr. James B. Conant in 1961[96]—before Jensen had been heard of. Anyone familiar with history knows that this belief was pervasive even before I.Q. tests were invented.

Mental tests are even more urgently needed by disadvantaged minorities than by members of the general population. Unusual intellectual ability among minority schoolchildren is less likely to be recognized by subjective methods. Dr. Martin D. Jenkins, who pioneered the study of high-I.Q. black children in the 1930's repeatedly found black youngsters with I.Q.'s of 150 and above whose teachers were wholly unaware of their ability.[97] The correct placement of disadvantaged youngsters in colleges appropriate to their educational levels is even more difficult than with youngsters from families which have been going to college for generations, and the failure to match minority students with the right college is often catastrophic for them and for the institution.[98] More generally, revealing patterns *within* an ethnic group —the relationship between family size and test failure, for example—provide valuable insights into specific factors behind low scores, even if comparisons *between* ethnic groups are of little value. Fear of such interethnic comparisons have led many to oppose testing in general or I.Q. testing in particular, or to propose alternative tests on which all groups would score the same. But if test scores are a tool of anlysis rather than a status symbol, no purpose is served by covering up facts that need to be changed by concerted efforts, whose results are continuously monitored.

The intelligent use of I.Q. tests in a calm atmosphere requires a muting of the grossly exaggerated claims which have become the norm among both environmentalists and supporters of hereditary theories of I.Q. determination. For years, environmentalists boldly proclaimed that "science" had "proved" the equality of the races. The research of Professor Arthur R. Jensen has demolished this pious pretense and many of the specific arguments behind it—without establishing the opposite. At the same time sweeping social predictions and prescriptions have been proclaimed by hereditarians on the basis of such evidence as "separated twin" studies in which the twins were "separated" by a few yards, or lived in the same village, went to school together, etc.[99] While science finds no subject taboo, it does impose its intellectual standards, and responsible discussion of the fate of millions of human beings cannot leap in one bound from isolated facts— even where they *are* facts—to conclusions requiring an intimate knowledge of complex social processes which are as yet barely defined, much less understood.

The present study makes no pretense to being definitive, even on the narrow range of issues raised here. A much more comprehensive and controlled sample is needed than could be obtained with heterogeneous testing and record keeping practices and the even more heterogeneous responses of education officials to requests for politically explosive data. Perhaps a national mental test study, along the lines of some European countries, would be useful. While the present study offers no definitive explanation of mental test phenomena involving American ethnic groups, its findings do raise the question whether there is really much to explain.

APPENDIX: RESEARCH METHODS

I.Q. scores were collected primarily from individual student records in schools and boards of education in communities across the country. In a few cases preexisting compilations of individual students records were used. Rigorous methods of producing a random or a stratified sample were not attempted, since official permission to gain access to this sensitive information was a major uncontrollable variable. However, all of these schools came by referrals from such a wide variety of sources as to constitute a crude approximation of a random sample. The path from the initial contact to the particular school was usually circuitous and unpredictable; typically one person referred us to another person, who referred us to a third, fourth, or fifth person, who actually suggested a particular school to include in the study—a school often hundreds of miles from the first person in the sequence.

The standards used for determining what kind of school we wanted were general and changed somewhat over time as our existing stock of data grew. Initially we sought schools with concentrations of the 12 ethnic groups under study, and preferred those schools with I.Q. records reaching furthest back in time. This led us to the usual metropolitan centers, with an under-representation of smaller cities and towns, and of southern data. A conscious effort was then made to seek data from these other categories, and at any given point in time to prefer those ethnic groups whose data were currently in short supply, but the actual availability of schools continued to be a major determinant of where we conducted research—and when or whether permission would be granted remained unpredictable. The research pattern that emerged was one in which general goals determined our initial contacts, and where the week-to-week decisions were determined by the changing size of our staff, the state of our negotiations with education officials, and the condition of the records in the schools we were canvassing before beginning actual collecting. School vacations, our staff vacations, and the availability of short-term additions to our research team added further elements of a randomness. During slack periods we sent researchers wherever we had permission to go, and during periods where permissions exceeded our capabilities, we selected among alternatives—and also cut short some research either because of our exigencies or those of the schools. The specific research procedures used at each school surveyed are written up on "anonymous description forms" for each school. These are available from The National Technical Information Service, U.S. Department of Commerce, Springfield, Virginia 22161 (Accession No. PB265 8.13), together with the computer tapes, so that the sample may be reconstituted and re-analyzed by others, according to their own preferred procedures or purposes. A number of variables not discussed here are included in the tapes and accompanying documents.

Among the general research problems were: (1) determining the ethniciy of the students whose I.Q.'s were compiled, and (2) selecting among I.Q. scores where several were available.

Ethnicity was determined in a variety of ways, some being used as checks against the others when needed. The simplest case was where the individual's school record specified his ethnicity, but this was the exception rather than the rule. Two broad ways of determining ethnicity were by school and by individual. Some schools were known to have been 99 percent or more Negro or Indian or Chinese, and all the individuals in such schools were therefore assigned to those ethnic categories. For other schools and other ethnic groups, individual determinations of ethnicity were more common. Individuals with ethnically distinctive names were identified by name (with the aid of a dictionary of names, or—in the case of Poles—with the help of consultants), but this required some prior assurance that the school population included no black children who would have similar names. Germans and Jews share some names so further information was needed for a determination there. In all cases of individual ethnic determination the policy was to resolve doubts by classifying individual ethnicity as "unknown"—i.e. to maintain the purity of the sample rather than maximize its size.

The nationwide I.Q. averages are based on selecting one I.Q. score per person even though many individuals had multiple I.Q.'s listed on their school records and/or recorded on our computer tape. For elementary school students the I.Q. score nearest the fifth grade was selected. Only for the later phases of the research study were multiple I.Q. scores recorded on our records. Similarly, only for the later phases of the research were specific names of I.Q. tests recorded along with the scores.

NOTES

1. Americans of Chinese, German, Indian, Irish, Italian, Japanese, Jewish, Mexican, Negro, Polish, Puerto Rican, and West Indian ancestry. The data for native American Indians were from only one tribe at one location, and so were considered too inadequate to be used in this study. Similarly, a sample of West Indian I.Q. scores from only one atypical location was not used. These data and computer descriptions are available from The National Technical Information Service, U.S. Department of Commerce, Springfield, Virginia 22161 (Accession No. PB 265 8.13). I am indebted to many individuals for their help and criticism at many stages of this work. An especial appreciation is due to Professor Arthur Goldberger of the University of Wisconsin and Professor Sandra Scarr-Salapatek of the University of Minnesota for their careful and cogent criticisms and suggestions—some of which I followed. Conclusions and errors are of course my sole responsibility.

2. Arthur R. Jensen, "How Much Can We Boost I.Q. and Scholastic Achievement?" *Harvard Educational Review,* vol. 39, no. 1 (Winter 1969), p. 81.

3. Ibid.

4. Ada Hart Arlitt, "The Relationship of Intelligence to Age in Negro Children," *Journal of Applied Psychology,* vol. 6, pp. 380-82.

5. The white population of colonial America has been called a "decapitated" society, since the European aristocracy seldom migrated, and convicts and other social "undesirables" were over-represented. Among Africans, the weaker, less culturally advanced tribes tended to be captured—often by the stronger or more advanced African tribes—and sold into slavery.

6. Audrey M. Shuey, *The Testing of Negro Intelligence,* 2nd ed. (New York: Social Science Press, 1966), p. 493; Jensen, op. cit., p. 81.

7 Rudolf Pintner, *Intelligence Testing: Methods and Results* (New York: Henry Holt and Co., 1923), pp. 351-52.

8. Clifford Kirkpatrick, *Intelligence and Immigration* (Baltimore: The Williams and Wilkins Co., 1926), p. 24.

9. Loc. cit.

10. Loc. cit.

11. Loc. cit.

12. Loc. cit.

13. Loc. cit.

14. Rudolf Pintner and Ruth Keller, "Intelligence Tests of Foreign Children," *Journal of Educational Psychology*, vol. 13, p. 215.

15. Nathaniel D. Mittron Hirsch, "A Study of Natio-Racial Mental Differences," *Genetic Psychology Monographs*, vol. 1, nos. 3 and 4 (May and July, 1926), pp. 287, 320.

16. Carl Brigham, *A Study of American Intelligence* (Princeton: Princeton University Press, 1923), pp. 120-21, 189-90.

17. Clifford Kirkpatrick, op. cit., p. 40.

18. The Army Alpha examination is reproduced in Robert M. Yerkes, *Psychological Examining in the United States Army*, Memoirs of the National Academy of Sciences, volume 15 (Washington: Government Printing Office, 1921), pp. 123-292.

19. Ibid., p. 697.

20. Carl Brigham, op. cit., p. 190.

21. Leon J. Kamin, *The Science and Politics of I.Q.* (New York: John Wiley and Sons, 1974), p. 16.

22. Bertha Boody, *A Psychological Study of Immigrant Children at Ellis Island* (Baltimore: The Williams and Wilkins Co., 1926), p. 86.

23. Cf. Brigham, op. cit., pp. 80, 121.

24. J. J. Eysenck, *The I.Q. Argument* (New York: The Library Press, 1971), p. 23.

25. Kamin, op. cit., chap. 2.

26. Ibid., chap. 1.

27. Thomas Sowell, *Race and Economics* (New York: David McKay Co., 1975), p. 126.

28. U.S. Bureau of the Census, "Characteristics of the Population by Ethnic Origin, November 1969," *Current Population Reports*, Series P-20, N. 221 (Washington: U.S. Government Printing Office, 1971), p. 7.

29. Rudolph Pintner, *Intelligence Testing: Methods and Results*, rev. (New York: Henry Holt and Co., 1931), p. 453.

30. Ernest van den Haag, *The Jewish Mystique* (New York: Stein and Day, 1964), pp. 19-20.

31. Eysenck, op. cit., p. 123.

32. Phillip E. Vernon, *Intelligence and Cultural Environment* (London: Methuen and Co., Ltd., 1970), p. 155.

33. Lester R. Wheeler, "A Comparative Study of the Intelligence of East Tennessee Mountain Children," *Journal of Educational Psychology*, vol. 33, no. 5 (May 1942), pp. 322, 324.

34. H. Gordon, *Mental and Scholastic Tests Among Retarded Children* (London: Board of Education pamphlet no. 44), p. 38.

35. Kwok Tsuen Yeung, "The Intelligence of Chinese Children in San Francisco and Vicinity," *Journal of Applied Psychology*, vol. 5, pp. 267-74; Marvin L. Darsie, "The Mental Capacity of American-Born Japanese

Children," *Comparative Psychology Monographs*, vol. 3, no. 15 (1925), pp. 18-19.

36. Peter Sandiford and Ruby Kerr, "Intelligence of Chinese and Japanese Children," *Journal of Educational Psychology*, September 1926, pp. 361-63; Rudolph Pintner, op cit., 1931 edition, p. 358; Virginia Taylor Graham, "The Intelligence of Chinese Children in San Francisco." *Journal of Comparative Psychology*, vol. 6, pp. 43-71; Marvin L. Darsie, "The Mental Capacity of American-Born Japanese Children," *Comparative Psychology Monographs*, vol. 3, no. 15, (1925); Percival M. Symonds, "The Intelligence of Chinese in Hawaii," *School and Society*, vol. 19, p. 442.

37. Pintner, op. cit., 1931 edition, p. 455.

38. U.S. Bureau of the Census, "Japanese, Chinese, and Filipinos in the United States," *Census of Population, 1970, Subject Reports,* Final Report PC(2)—1G (Washington: U.S. Government Printing Office, 1973), p. 13.

39. William H. Sheldon, "The Intelligence of Mexican Children," *School and Society*, February 24, 1924, p. 141.

40. Pintner, op. cit., 1931 edition, p. 454.

41. Thomas Sowell, *Race and Economics*, p. 110.

42. Ibid., pp. 103, 110.

43. E. Franklin Frazier, *The Negro in the United States* (Chicago: University of Chicago Press, 1969), pp. 258-66.

44. Susan S. Stodolsky and Gerald Lesser, "Learning Patterns in the Disadvantaged," *Harvard Educational Review*, vol. 37, no. 4 (Fall 1967), pp. 567-73.

45. Boody, op. cit., p. 67.

46. H. H. Goddard, "The Binet Tests in Relation to Immigration," *Journal of Psycho-Asthenics*, vol. 18, no. 2 (December 1913), p. 110.

47. Kamin, op. cit., p. 6.

48. Mandel Sherman and Cora B. Key, "The Intelligence of Isolated Mountain Children," *Child Development*, vol. 3, no. 4 (1932), p. 284.

49. Philip E. Vernon, op. cit., p. 145.

50. Sandiford and Kerr, op. cit., p. 362.

51. Thomas Sowell, *Affirmative Action Reconsidered* (Washington: American Enterprise Institute, 1976).

52. Sherman and Key, op. cit., pp. 283-85.

53. Vernon, op. cit., p. 104.

54. Yerkes, op. cit., p. 705.

55. Arthur R. Jensen, "The Race X Sex X Ability Interaction," *Intelligence: Genetic and Environmental Factors*, ed. Robert Cancro (New York: Grune and Stratton, 1971), pp. 116-18; Idem, "How Much Can We Boost I.Q. and Scholastic Achievement?" op. cit., pp. 32, 67.

56. Arthur R. Jensen, "Selection of Minority Students in Higher Education," *University of Toledo Law Review*, Spring-Summer 1970, p. 424.

57. Lewis M. Terman and Melita H. Oden, *The Gifted Child Grows Up* (Stanford: Stanford University Press, 1947), p. 7.

58. Jensen, "Selection of Minority Students in Higher Education," op. cit., p. 424.

59. P. A. Witty and M. D. Jenkins, "The Educational Achievement of a Group of Gifted Negro Children," *Journal of Educational Psychology*, vol. 25 (1934), p. 593.

60. P. A. Witty and V. A. Theman, "A Follow-up Study of the Educational Achievement of Gifted Negroes," *Journal of Educational Psychology*, vol. 34 (1943), p. 43.

61. E. G. Rodgers, *The Relationship of Certain Measurable Factors in the Personal and Educational Background of Two Groups of Baltimore Negroes, Identified as Superior and Average in Intelligence as Fourth Grade Children, to their Educational, Social, and Economic Achievement in Adulthood* (Unpublished Doctoral Dissertation, New York University, 1956), University Microfilms, unpaged Introduction and pp. 75-94.

62. U.S. Department of Labor, *The Negro Family: The Case for National Action*, March 1965 ["The Moynihan Report"], pp. 31-34.

63. Kirkpatrick, op. cit., pp. 26-27.

64. Vernon, op. cit., pp. 66-67.

65. Jensen, "How Much Can We Boost I.Q. and Scholastic Achievement?" op. cit., p. 100.

66. Loc. cit.

67. Boody, op. cit., p. 67.

68. Vernon, op. cit., p. 104.

69. Shuey, op. cit., p. 499.

70. Jensen, "How Much Can We Boost I.Q. and Scholastic Achievement?" op. cit., p. 98.

71. James S. Coleman, et al., *Equality of Educational Opportunity* (Washington, D.C.: U.S. Department of Health, Education and Welfare, 1966), pp. 516, 517; Samuel Bowles, "Toward Equality of Educational Opportunity?" *Harvard Educational Review*, Winter 1966, p. 93.

72. Ada Hart Arlitt, op. cit., pp. 380-82.

73. Kirkpatrick, op. cit., p. 31; Wheeler, op. cit., pp. 326-27.

74. Arthur R. Jensen, "Cumulative Deficit: A Testable Hypothesis," *Developmental Psychology*, vol. 10, no. 6 (1974), pp. 996-1019.

75. Brigham, op. cit., pp. 14, 17, 20, 23, 25, 27.

76. Ibid., pp. 3-31, passim.

77. Yerkes, op. cit., p. 874.

78. Brigham, op. cit., p. 18.

79. Ibid., pp. 32-33.

80. Ibid., pp. 37, 40, 43, 46, 49, 52.

81. Yerkes, op. cit., p. 874.

82. Brigham, op. cit., p. 42.

83. Yerkes, op. cit., p. 875.

84. Loc. cit.

85. Brigham, op. cit., p. 45.

86. Ibid., p. 38. Only three questions could be answered by counting visible cubes.

87. Ibid., pp. 36-37.

88. Shuey, op. cit., chap. 10.

89. Butcher, op. cit., p. 252.

90. Loc. cit.

91. Arthur R. Jensen, "Selection of Minority Students in Higher Education," *University of Toledo Law Review,* Spring-Summer 1970, pp. 440, 443; Donald A. Rock, "Motivation, Moderators, and Test Bias," ibid., pp. 536, 537; E. G. Rodgers, op. cit., p. 22; Ronald L. Flaugher, *Testing Practices, Minority Groups and Higher Education: A Review and Discussion of the Research* (Princeton: Educational Testing Service, 1970), p. 11.

92. Arthur R. Jensen, *Genetics and Education* (New York: Harper and Row, 1972), pp. 5-6; Arthur R. Jensen, "Patterns of Mental Ability and Socioeconomic Status," *Proceedings of the National Academy of Sciences,* August 1968, p. 1332.

93. Jensen, "How Much Can We Boost I.Q. and Scholastic Achievement?" op. cit., p. 95.

94. Lillian Belmont and Francis A. Marolla, "Birth Order, Family Size, and Intelligence," *Science,* vol. 182 (December 14, 1973), p. 1096.

95. Robert C. Nichols, "Heredity, Environment, and School Achievement," *Measurement and Evaluation in Guidance,* vol. 1, no. 2 (Summer 1968), p. 126.

96. James B. Conant, *Slums and Suburbs* (New York: McGraw-Hill Co., Inc., 1961), p. 12.

97. Martin D. Jenkins, "Intellectually Superior Negro Youth: Problems and Needs," Journal of *Negro Education,* Summer 1950, pp. 324-25.

98. Thomas Sowell, *Black Education: Myths and Tragedies* (New York: David McKay Company, 1972), passim.

99. Kamin, op. cit., pp. 50-51.

Sibling I.Q. Correlations among Ethnic Groups

LEON J. KAMIN

The school I.Q. data collected by the Ethnic Minorities Research Project at the Urban Institute contain intelligence test scores for a large number of siblings, classified by ethnic group membership. There is very little empirical information available concerning sibling (or other kinship) I.Q. score correlations as a function of ethnic group. These scores thus seem to merit some separate analysis. They can be approached in two fundamentally distinct ways.

The traditional approach has been to compare kinship correlations, or "heritability" across groups. For blacks and whites, the few relevant existing studies (Osborne and Gregor, 1968; Vandenberg, 1970; Scarr-Salapatek, 1971; Jensen, 1973) have used this method, with inconclusive results. The question whether family resemblances in I.Q. are of similar magnitude for all ethnic groups is, in principle, empirically straightforward. The discovery of differences across various ethnic groups, however, would pose very grave, if not insuperable, problems of interpretation. Though such differences, if discovered, might provide clues relevant to the nature-nurture controversy, it must be stressed that most of the ambiguities and complexities which beset the study of within-group heritability are also present in the comparison of heritabilities or kinship correlations across groups. For

239

example, although ethnicity is certainly a major environmental determinant of influences to which a child growing up in American society is exposed, it is also clear that, since ethnic groups tend to be endogamous, they tend to differ as well in their genetic constitutions. The confounding of genetic and environmental variables which afflicts the study of family resemblances within an ethnic group is thus also present when one compares ethnic groups. Further, estimates of heritability—whether based upon correlations or upon raw variances and covariances—in themselves tell us literally nothing about between-group differences in *mean* I.Q. scores.

The interpretation of a heritability estimate, or of a set of kinship correlations, is in any event inherently ambiguous. Those who favor a genetic interpretation will stress that the data "make genetic sense." That is, kinfolk who share common genes tend to resemble one another in I.Q. Those who favor an environmental interpretation will stress the inevitable confounding of genetic and environmental variables. The nature of the family is such that the more similar individuals are genetically, the more similar are the environments to which they have been exposed. The traditional quantitative estimates of "heritability" may thus reflect nothing more than environmental effects (Kamin, 1974). Finally, there are no obvious a priori predictions, from either a genetic or an environmental viewpoint, as to how "heritabilities" or sibling correlations across different ethnic groups *should* compare. These statistics depend upon the relative magnitudes of both between-family and within-family sources of variance; and in theory each of these sources of variance might contain both genetic and environmental components. We know nothing about the magnitudes of between- and within-family environmental variances as a function of ethnic group. Further, from a genetic standpoint, possible differences among ethnic groups in degree of assortative mating—about which we again know nothing—should also affect kinship correlations. The likelihood that one would be able to unravel environmental and/or genetic causes of ethnic differences in kinship correlations, if such were observed, seems small indeed. The existence of such differences might have some descriptive interest, however, and these differences might at least suggest some hypotheses. The first part of this chapter examines sibling I.Q. resemblance in five separate ethnic groups, with subjects selected from the main body of the Ethnic Minorities Research Project data.

There is an alternative strategy possible with this or similar data. There are some effects in I.Q. data which *cannot* be attributed to genetic causes. The examination of such effects in different ethnic groups may be an especially worthwhile endeavor. We assume that ethnicity accounts for a significant proportion of the environmental variance to which individuals are exposed. Thus, it seems reasonable to suppose that the magnitude of particular environmental effects on I.Q. might vary across ethnic groups. If such differences are in fact found, it is possible that our knowledge and intuitions about the environmental differences among ethnic groups could suggest possible causes. These suggestions could then be empirically tested. We have very little detailed understanding of what environmental experiences are critical in determining I.Q. scores. We thus do not know what aspects of environment to measure in our efforts to relate I.Q. scores to environmental determinants. The existence of ethnic groups provides an anarchic kind of real-life "laboratory" in which large clumps of environmental influences are systematically varied for different groups of "subjects." We can thus expect environmental effects on I.Q. to vary (in unpredictable ways) across ethnic groups.

With sibling I.Q. data, an obvious effect to examine is that of birth order on I.Q. There have been numerous observations that first-born children tend to have a slight, but statistically significant, I.Q. advantage over later-born children (Altus, 1966). This cannot be a genetic effect; genetically, we can rarely distinguish first-born from later-born children. The effect thus must be attributed to environmental experiences. The second part of this paper examines the differences in I.Q. between the elder and younger members of a sib pair. The basic question asked is whether any such difference varies across ethnic groups.

The basic data with which we have to work are far from ideal, so the present analysis should be viewed as little more than an exploratory exercise. The procedure adopted was as follows. From the schools which made I.Q. records available to The Urban Institute, six were arbitrarily selected with the expectation that a reasonable number of sibling pairs from several ethnic groups would be included. There was no attempt, it must be noted, to secure samples which would be nationally representative of the ethnic group as a whole. Within these six schools, enumerators identified as "siblings" all individuals with the same last name and the same street address. The ethnic membership of indi-

viduals was determined in the manner described by Thomas
Sowell in the Appendix to the previous essay. The enumerators
recorded the sex, birth date, test score, name of test, and date of
test for all siblings. When sibships were more than two, information for all sibs was recorded by the enumerators. To simplify
analysis, however, the only data analyzed were those for two sibs
in each family. In all cases, the two *eldest* sibs for whom data
were available were included in the analysis. When a child had
been given more than one I.Q. test, the first test administered was
used in the analysis.

There was, both between and within schools, a considerable
variety of I.Q. tests employed (cf. Sowell). The vast majority
were well-known standardized group tests, though occasional individual tests were encountered. There was variation from school
to school in the age at which I.Q. tests were typically given, but
much less variation within schools. The data, in these respects,
are reminiscent of the thousands of school I.Q.'s analyzed by
Reed and Reed (1965). We can only hope, like they, that a
multitude of random fluctuations will tend to cancel each other
out; and that significant patterns which emerge out of such
"noisy" data are in a sense even more impressive than if the data
had been gathered under carefully controlled and standardized
conditions.

The procedure employed yielded the following numbers of
sibling pairs for analysis. There were 169 pairs of Polish American sibs, 164 pairs of blacks, 117 pairs of Italian Americans, 51
pairs of German Americans, and 24 pairs of Mexican Americans.
These 525 sib pairs (1,050 individuals) provided data which, in
many respects, seem typical of I.Q. data. The mean I.Q. was
100.05, with a standard deviation of 15.85. These values are
astonishingly close to those for which I.Q. tests are theoretically
standardized—despite the fact that our sample is in no sense
representative of any population on which any I.Q. test has been
standardized. Further, the intraclass correlation between siblings,
for the entire group of 525 pairs, was .505. This again is astonishingly close to the modal value reported for the I.Q. correlation
between siblings (Erlenmeyer-Kimling and Jarvik, 1963). Thus,
at least so far as the total sample is concerned, the sample size
seems sufficiently large to compensate for any local irregularities
in the data.

The mean I.Q.'s for the various ethnic groups in our sample
differ considerably; but inasmuch as the samples are in no sense

representative of the ethnic groups as a whole, little interest attaches to such differences. The mean I.Q. for Polish Americans was 107, for German Americans 106, for Italian Americans 103, for Mexican Americans 92, and for blacks 91.

The comparison of sibling resemblance across ethnic groups is potentially of more interest. We shall make such a comparison in two ways. The first, and doubtless less satisfactory, is to calculate separately the intraclass correlation between sibs for each ethnic group. The difficulty here is that intraclass correlation is simultaneously sensitive both to variation between sib pairs and to variation within sib pairs. There are in the present data considerable differences among ethnic groups in the amount of *between*-sib-pair variation. This difference could arise from many different causes; one is the fact that our nonrepresentative ethnic samples differ considerably in the variances of their socioeconomic and demographic characteristics (and of variables confounded with such characteristics). Whatever the cause, such differences influence the magnitude of the intraclass correlation; and since our ethnic samples are not representative, the intraclass correlations in our data are not even of much descriptive interest.

We can, however, also compare the *within*-sib-pair variances of the different ethnic groups. These variances are statistically independent of between-pair variances. They are presumably rarely confounded with differences in group means. The familiar *F*-test is appropriate for assessing the statistical significance of differences among within-pair variances. From the viewpoint of a genetic model, the within-sub-pair variance consists of two additive components: within-family genetic variance, and within-family environmental variance. Thus, if one assumed equal within-family genetic variance for all ethnic groups, a significant *F*-test would indicate different within-family environmental variances across ethnic groups. Whatever interpretation is placed upon the within-sib-pair variance, it has at least the virtue of not being influenced by many of the peculiar sampling biases of the present procedure.

Table 1 presents, for the five ethnic groups, both the intraclass sib correlations and the within-sib-pair variances. Turning first to the correlations, it is apparent that for both Polish Americans and Italian Americans, with reasonably large samples, the correlation is quite close to the traditionally reported .50. For blacks, again with a large sample, the correlation seems low. For much

Table 1

INTRACLASS CORRELATIONS AND WITHIN-PAIR
VARIANCES AS A FUNCTION OF ETHNIC GROUP

Group	Number of Pairs	Correlation	Variance
Polish Americans	169	.545	104.22
German Americans	51	.264	120.19
Italian Americans	117	.472	100.67
Mexican Americans	24	.317	224.65
Blacks	164	.389	148.91

smaller samples of German Americans and Mexican Americans, the correlation also seems low. We cannot, however, place any confidence in these apparent differences. When tested for homogeneity, there are no significant differences among these five correlations (Chi square, 4 d.f., $= 6.93, p > .10$). The weighted average value of the five correlations, using Fisher's z' transformation, is .45.

The within-pair variances present a very different picture. There is significant heterogeneity among the five variances (Bartlett's test, Chi square, 4 d.f., $= 12.76, p < .02$). The within-pair variances for Mexican Americans and blacks seem high relative to those of Polish Americans and Italian Americans, with German Americans appearing to occupy an intermediate position. When individual F-tests were applied, both Mexican Americans and blacks displayed significantly greater variances than either Polish Americans or Italian Americans, though not greater than German Americans. There was no significant difference between Mexican Americans and blacks, nor were there any significant differences among German Americans, Polish Americans, or Italian Americans. The finding that, at least in our samples, within-sib-pair variances were significantly larger for Mexican Americans and for blacks means that whatever within-family factors produce I.Q. differences between sibs, those factors make Mexican American and black sibs *less* similar to one another than are Polish American or Italian American sibs.

This *might* mean that environmental differences within black and Mexican American families are larger, and it would be of some interest to see whether similar effects could be detected in new and independent ethnic samples. There are, however, other possible interpretations, even under the assumption that within-family genetic variances are equal for all groups. To a genetically oriented theorist, for example, an immediate question is whether our method of ascertaining presumptive sib pairs might produce a large proportion of half-sibs, cousins, etc., in some ethnic groups rather than others. We selected as "sibs," it will be recalled, children with the same last name living at the same street address. The black and Mexican American families are presumably the most environmentally "disadvantaged" of our five ethnic groups, and that distinction could well be responsible for any differences of their I.Q. data from those of other ethnic groups. That same environmental disadvantage, however, could conceivably be correlated with a greater frequency of extended families living under a single roof, with different frequencies of divorce and remarriage, and so forth. Thus, if the pairs of Mexican Americans and black children included in our samples contain a significantly larger proportion of pairs of individuals less closely related genetically than full sibs, such a fact alone could in theory attenuate the observed within-sib-pair variances. We are forced to conclude that our examination of sibling resemblance as a function of ethnic group has produced wholly ambiguous results. Though we can detect statistically significant differences, their meaning cannot be much elucidated.

Perhaps it is worth pointing out that if one assumes a null hypothesis of zero heritability of I.Q. scores (Kamin, 1974), then, of course, all differences in the within-sib-pair variances must be attributed to within-family environmental differences between ethnic groups. But even here interpretation would be ambiguous. Perhaps, for example, black and Mexican American siblings growing up together are less closely confined to the common family environment than are siblings in the other ethnic groups. But if it is more common for half-sibs, cousins, and other extended-family members to be living at a single address among these groups, it is conceivable that the duration of time our "sib pairs" had actually lived together in the family might have been lower among blacks and Mexican Americans than among other groups.

We turn now to a consideration of the differences in mean I.Q. as a function of birth order. We would have preferred to have had available the I.Q. scores of siblings identified as the first- and second-born children in their families. We do not in fact have such scores. The pairs selected for analysis, it will be recalled, consisted of the two eldest tested sibs in each family. The ascertainment procedure was such that it seems likely that, in many families, these in fact are the first- and second-born children. That would be the case for any family in which the first- and second-born children attended the same school, and were both tested. However, in families with more than two children, it is possible that one or both of the two eldest children did not attend the school selected for analysis, or for some reason were not tested. If *any* two sibs from such a family were tested in the same school, they would be included in our sample. Thus it would be incorrect to refer to our sib pairs as consisting of first-born and second-born offspring. We shall refer instead to "elder sib" and "younger sib." We shall now examine differences in mean I.Q. between elder and younger sibs as a function of ethnic group. To the degree that our elder sibs are in fact first-born, we would expect on the basis of previous findings that their mean I.Q. would be higher than that of the younger sibs. However, any such difference would clearly be attenuated by the fact that our samples contain some considerable proportion of elder sibs who are doubtless not first-born children.

Table 2 presents, for each ethnic group, the mean I.Q.'s for elder sibs and for younger sibs. The table also indicates the mean I.Q. advantage of the elder sibs. For all groups but blacks, it will be observed, the mean I.Q. of elder sibs is very slightly higher than that of younger sibs. For blacks, the mean I.Q. of the elder sibs is actually lower than that of younger sibs. Further, blacks are the only group within which the difference between the two means is statistically significant ($p \cong .025$).

The effect involved here is in part obscured by the fact that different I.Q. tests were used with different sib pairs (and sometimes for the two members of a single pair). Perhaps a more

Table 2

MEAN I.Q. AS A FUNCTION OF BIRTH ORDER AND
OF ETHNIC GROUP

Group	Number of Pairs	Mean I.Q. of Elder Sib	Mean I.Q. of Younger Sib	Advantage of Elder Sib
Polish Americans	169	106.61	106.42	+ .19
German Americans	51	107.10	105.78	+1.32
Italian Americans	117	102.92	102.18	+ .74
Mexican Americans	24	92.25	90.26	+1.99
Blacks	164	89.32	92.42	−3.10

sensitive procedure would be to ask, for each sib pair, the simple question, "Which sib—the elder or the younger—has the higher I.Q.?" This question, it should be noted, ignores the magnitude of the I.Q. difference, paying attention only to its direction. For the Polish Americans, the elder sib had the higher I.Q. in 56 percent of all cases; for the German Americans, in 56 percent of all cases; for the Italian Americans, in 59 percent of all cases; for the Mexican Americans, in 58 percent of all cases. The common pattern was entirely reversed among blacks, for whom the *younger* sib had the higher I.Q. in 62 percent of all cases. These proportions differ significantly across the five ethnic groups (Chi square, 4 d.f., $= 15.55$, $p < .01$). Within the black sample, the tendency for the younger sib to have the higher I.Q. is statistically significant ($p < .01$). For the four remaining samples, there is of course no suggestion of any difference in the tendency for the elder sib to have the higher I.Q. Pooling the four remaining samples, the tendency for the elder sib to have the higher I.Q. is significant ($p < .05$). This presumably is a reflection, somewhat attenuated, of the tendency for first-born children in most groups to have somewhat higher I.Q.'s. The striking fact, however, is the uniqueness of the black group which significantly reverses a tendency seen in other groups.

There is always the possibility, of course, that this effect represents nothing more than an improbable sampling fluctuation, and an analysis of new and independent data is obviously suggested. There does not, in any event, seem to be much likelihood that the significant differences we have observed between elder and younger sibs are artifacts related to the age of the children when tested. Within each school, there was an obvious tendency to test all children at the same age.

Presuming that the tendency for elder black sibs to have lower I.Q.'s is a genuine effect, it is clearly not of genetic origin. The same is true, of course, of the reverse tendency observed among the other ethnic groups in this study, and of the commonly reported tendency for first-born children to have higher I.Q.'s. These are all clearly environmental effects, though we remain ignorant of the precise environmental causes. The observation that such effects differ significantly across ethnic groups indicates (not surprisingly) that ethnic groups differ significantly in environmental experiences; these differences significantly affect I.Q. The challenge is to identify those aspects of the environment which produce the I.Q. differences.

Without detailed data on possibly relevant environmental causes, plausible interpretations are embarrassingly numerous. We shall cite only two, from opposite ends of the environmental spectrum. Thus, a clearly social interpretation is to suggest the possibility that, in black families, the eldest child is given more household and familial responsibilities—helping to care for younger sibs, and so on. This could lead to less stress on school-work, more frequent absence from school, etc., and thus to poorer performance on I.Q. tests. We might, on the other hand, speculate on the possibility that the mothers of first-born black children are significantly younger than those in other ethnic groups. This could conceivably affect the child's I.Q. through either biological or social mechanisms. It is clear that all such suggestions are at present wildly speculative. Without replication of the present findings, they are also pointless.

We could, in future studies, ask such questions as whether the effect varies, within the black group, as a function of social class. For that matter, within white ethnic groups, is the I.Q. superiority of the first-born children attenuated, or even reversed, at the lower socioeconomic level? Does the relation between I.Q.'s of first-born and younger sibs depend upon whether or not the mother works? These and similar questions suggest forcefully the necessity of a much more detailed examination of environmental influences on I.Q. than has hitherto been attempted. The study of ethnic samples, and the examination of differences of patterns of I.Q. relations across such samples, might play an especially critical role in such environmentally oriented studies. There seems little point in attempting to unravel the nature-nurture confusion by repeated studies of familial resemblance within ethnic groups, or by comparing "heritabilities," or mean differences, across ethnic groups. For 70 years, such studies have produced inconclusive outcomes. The strategy of taking I.Q. effects which must be of environmental origin, and of isolating their precise environmental determinants, seems more promising. There is a real possibility that such studies could refine our measurements of relevant environmental factors to the point where they could account for so much of I.Q. variance that there would be no necessity to postulate any genetic determinants of I.Q. variation.

REFERENCES

Altus, W. D. "Birth Order and Its Sequelae." *Science* 151 (1966): pp. 44-49.

Erlenmeyer-Kimling, L., and Jarvik, L. F. "Genetics and Intelligence: A Review." *Science* 142 (1963): pp. 1477-79.

Jensen, A. R. *Educability and Group Differences.* Harper and Row, 1973.

Kamin, L. J. *The Science and Politics of I.Q.* Erlbaum Associates, 1974.

Osborne, R. T., and Gregor, A. J. "Racial Differences in Heritability Estimates for Tests of Spatial Ability." *Perceptual and Motor Skills* 27 (1968): pp. 753-59.

Reed, E. W., and Reed, S. C. *Mental Retardation: A Family Study.* Saunders, 1965.

Scarr-Salapatek, S. "Race, Social Class, and I.Q." *Science* 174 (1971): pp. 1223-28.

Vandenberg, S. G. "A Comparison of Heritability Estimates of U.S. Negro and White High School Students." *Acta Geneticae Medicae et Gemellologiae* 19 (1970): pp. 280-84.

Part Two
Statistical Data
On American
Ethnic Groups

Introduction

Part Two presents statistical data on the incomes, occupations, education, fertility, and other characteristics of thirteen American ethnic groups. Wherever possible, these data are so cross-tabulated as to permit ready analysis of various factors behind a particular result. For example, an income difference between two ethnic groups might be due to differences in the median age or in the education of these respective groups. The cross-tabulations permit comparisons of the incomes of members of both groups with the *same* age and/or education, so that the ethnic differences, as such, may be compared without the effect of other demographic or socioeconomic differences which may also exist among the various groups. Where family incomes are compared, this can be done with or without taking account of differences in the number of family members earning incomes. Where fertility rates are compared, these can be seen with or without taking account of differences in the respective ethnic groups' women's age distributions across the child-bearing years, their respective educational levels and/or their respective family incomes—all of which may affect fertility as much as, or more than, ethnic differences as such.

The sources of the data are various, so comparisons must be made with caution. Data for those groups with the most detailed cross-tabulation—American Indians, Black Americans, Chinese Americans, Filipino Americans, Japanese Americans, Puerto Ricans, and West Indian immigrants (whether American citizens or not)—were tabulated by the Ethnic Minorities Research Project from computer tapes for the 1970 U.S. Census (Public Use Sample). These groups were directly identifiable from the Decennial Census categories, and the data on their socioeconomic characteristics are directly comparable among these groups.

Data for other groups had to be assembled from other sources. *The Current Population Reports* of the U.S. Census Bureau were the source of data for German Americans, Irish Americans, Italian Americans, Mexican Americans, and Polish Americans. These data were generated by much smaller survey samples, collected at different times and by different procedures from those of the Decennial Census. Therefore, while the data for these five groups are comparable with one another, they can be compared with the data for the seven groups from the 1970 Census only with caution in general, and with particular attention to the different years from which their respective sets of data were taken. Finally, because of Constitutional restrictions on government collection of religious data, statistics on Jewish Americans were obtained from a private research project, the National Jewish Population Study. The tabulations from these three data sources were made to conform as closely to one another as possible, given their disparate sources and sampling procedures. Whether the degree of similarity is great enough will depend upon the particular groups, the particular variables considered, and the particular needs of each research user.

The first table presents a wholesale comparison of selected statistical data for each of the thirteen ethnic groups. The median income of 30-year-old males is the only entry in this tabulation which does not appear in the individual tables under the various ethnic groups. Because American ethnic groups differ substantially in their age distributions — sometimes by one or two decades in median age — a comparison of 30-year-old males across ethnic lines seems useful as a means of eliminating the effect of age and sex of income earners when looking at ethnic differences by education and other variables. While comparisons by age brackets — as in some individual ethnic tables — are also useful for this purpose, the distributions within these brackets may be skewed in different directions for ethnic groups with widely differing median ages, so that narrowing the age range to one year provides a better comparison. With all the caveats about differing data sources, this general statistical overview of American ethnic groups shows many important patterns and contrasts, and raises many questions which need to be answered.

Our occupational categories are identical with those of the Census Bureau, with the notable exception of "Professional, Technical and Kindred" workers. Our "Learned Professions" — lawyers, doctors, scientists, etc. — are separated from professions that are generally much lower paid, such as nursing and teaching school. This is not only because the pay differentials are very substantial between these two sets of professionals, but also because ethnic groups differ significantly in the proportion of their professionals who fall in these different sub-categories. As a result, what might appear to be an ethnic differential in the same occupation may instead be an ethnic difference in occupational distribution and/or in the proportions of females working, which would tend to mean that their "professionals" include relatively more nurses and schoolteachers and relatively few lawyers, doctors, or scientists. Similar considerations may apply to other occupational categories as well, but it is particularly glaring in the case of the omnibus category, "professionals." Moreover, this high-level, highly paid category is often a special focus of concern about minority "representation" and about the question of the extent to which education affects interethnic income differentials. Therefore some attempt at comparability seems especially important in this occupational category.

Our two categories, "Learned Professions" and "Other Professional, Technical, and Kindred" together add up to the category defined by the Census as "Professional, Technical, and Kindred." The specific occupations selected for "Learned Professions" are those designated by Census codes 002, 004, 006, 010-015, 020, 021, 030, 031, 035, 036, 042-045, 051-055, 062, 065, 091-094, 102-105, 110-112, 114, 116, 120, 121, 126, 130, 132, and 133.

Our ethnic categories likewise follow those of the U.S. Census Bureau, with one notable exception. The Census category, "Negro," is separated into two categories: (1) "West Indians" for those persons of Negro ancestry whose parent(s) or themselves were born in the Census categories Jamaica, British West Indies and Associated States, other West Indies, or Trinidad and Tobago; and (2) "Black Americans" for persons of Negro ancestry, including "West Indians," born in the United States. Persons of Negro ancestry not born in the United States and not meeting the definition of "West Indian" are not included in either tabulation, nor are those West Indians of Caucasian or other non-Negro ancestry (these latter are very small groups).

The sample sizes for the tables from the Public Use Sample are one-fiftieth of the population figures shown. Each individual user can decide for himself when the sample size is too small to make the accompanying data usable for his purposes, but all are hereby put on notice that this problem exists, especially in data for the smaller ethnic groups.

Table 1

Income, Median Age, Occupation, and Fertility, by Ethnic Group

	Total U.S. Population	American Indians	Black Americans	Chinese Americans	Filipino Americans	German Americans	Irish Americans
Personal Income (see Sources)*	$5,817	$3,715	$3,680	$5,955	$5,149	$7,467	$6,881
Family Earnings (see Sources)	10,678	6,621	6,812	12,176	10,395	10,402	9,964
Personal Income of 30-year-old Males	—	5,324	5,838	7,638	5,795	—	—
Median Age	28.1	20.4	22.3	26.8	26.2	35.5	36.7
Occupational Distribution							
Prof., tech., and kindred	14.0%	9.6%	7.6%	25.3%	23.1%	14.8%	14.1%
Mgrs. and administra. (non-farm)	8.1	3.1	2.1	8.6	2.8	15.4	15.5
Sales	6.9	2.9	2.2	4.8	3.1	6.1	6.3
Clerical	17.3	12.5	12.6	18.2	15.9	5.8	8.5
Craftsmen and kindred	13.4	12.6	8.4	4.6	8.2	21.7	20.8
Laborers (non-farm)	4.3	7.3	8.9	2.2	4.3	4.9	6.1
Farmers and farm mgrs	1.8	1.3	0.6	0.3	0.5	6.7	3.6
Farm laborers	1.2	3.4	2.3	0.4	5.3	1.6	1.0
Service workers (except private household	10.7	15.2	18.7	17.7	18.5	4.7	6.0
Private household workers	1.5	2.5	8.0	0.9	1.2	0.0	0.0
Operatives	17.0	19.5	22.4	14.4	12.8	18.2	17.9
Unemployed	3.9	10.0	6.3	2.7	4.4	1.6	2.3
Fertility Rates:							
Children per woman, age 15 and over	2.1	2.8	2.4	1.9	1.9	—	—
Children per married woman, age 15 and over	2.5	3.5	3.0	2.6	2.7	—	—

(Table 1 continued on page 258)

TABLE 1 (Continued)

	Total U.S. Population	Italian Americans	Japanese Americans	Jewish Americans	Mexican Americans	Polish Americans	Puerto Ricans	West Indians
Personal Income	$5,817	$7,883	$6,330	—	—	$8,154	$4,417	$5,057
Family Income	10,678	11,089	13,377	19,259	$5,488	11,619	6,728	9,821
Personal Income of 30-year-old Males	—	—	9,528	—	—	—	6,175	6,561
Median Age	28.1	36.1	32.3	—	17.8	39.8	20.3	—
Occupational Distribution								
Prof., tech., and kindred	14.0%	13.5%	18.2%	—	—	14.5%	5.0%	15.2%
Mgrs. and administra. (non-farm)	8.1	14.9	7.9	—	—	15.2	2.8	3.1
Sales	6.9	5.2	6.2	—	—	6.2	3.8	2.8
Clerical	17.3	9.1	18.9	—	—	8.8	15.3	23.3
Craftsmen and kindred	13.4	22.7	12.1	—	—	24.4	10.9	9.2
Laborers (non-farm)	4.3	6.4	6.0	—	—	6.1	5.3	2.6
Farmers and farm mgrs	1.8	0.4	1.9	—	—	1.6	0.1	0.1
Farm laborers	1.2	0.2	1.9	—	—	0.6	0.9	0.5
Service workers (except private household)	10.7	7.5	11.3	—	—	3.0	14.7	19.1
Private household workers	1.5	0.0	1.7	—	—	0.1	0.4	7.7
Operatives	17.0	20.0	11.9	—	—	19.6	34.4	12.7
Unemployed	3.9	2.3	2.1	—	6.2%	1.7	6.3	3.7
Fertility Rates:								
Children per woman, age 15 and over	2.1	—	2.0	—	—	—	2.4	1.8
Children per married woman, age 15 and over	2.5	—	2.5	—	—	—	2.9	2.3

*Mean personal income is calculated only for persons who reported positive or negative income, excluding those with zero income.

TABLE 1 (Continued)

SOURCES: Personal Income and Family Earnings data for American Indians, Black Americans, Chinese Americans, Filipino Americans, Japanese Americans, Puerto Ricans, and West Indians are 1969 mean figures from the 1970 Census Public Use Sample, and the Occupational Distribution is their 1969 occupational distribution from the same source. Personal Income and Family Income data for German Americans, Irish Americans, Italian Americans, and Polish Americans are 1970 median incomes from the *Current Population Reports*, Series P-20, No. 249. The source of the Occupational Distribution for 1969 — which for these four groups represent *male* occupational distribution only — is the *Current Population Reports*, Series P-20, No. 221. Family Income data for Mexican Americans is 1968 median income from the *Current Population Reports*, Series P-20, No. 213, and the unemployment rate is the 1969 unemployment rate from *Current Population Reports*, Series P-20, No. 213. The Jewish Family Income data were 1969 mean income figures, compiled for this study from data supplied by the National Jewish Population Study. Median ages in 1969 for Indian, Black, Chinese, Filipino, and Japanese Americans, and Puerto Ricans, are from the *1970 Census of Population*, Subject Reports PC(2)-1B, PC(2)-1E, PC(2)-1F and PC(2)-1G. Median ages in 1968 for German, Irish, Italian, and Polish Americans are from *Current Population Reports*, Series P-20, No. 221, and for Mexican Americans, Series P-20, No. 213. The median age of the total U.S. population is from the *1970 Census of Population*, Volume I, Part 1.

NOTE: Dashes refer to unavailable information; 0.0 refers to numbers which round off to zero.

AMERICAN INDIANS

Table 2
Personal Income by Age, Education, and Sex (1969)

| | | ALL PERSONS | | | PRECOLLEGE | | | | | |
| | | | | | 0-8 Years | | | 9-12 Years | | |
AGE AND SEX	Median Yrs. of Educ.	Mean Income*	Number of Individuals*	Per-cent	Mean Income*	Number of Individuals*	Per-cent	Mean Income*	Number of Individuals*	Per-cent
ALL INDIVIDUALS:										
18-24		$2,500	80,100	20 8	$2,612	10,400	7.3	$2,358	58,200	29.7
25-34		4,450	91,900	23.8	3,075	22,700	16.0	4,400	55,550	28.4
35-44		4,745	74,050	19.2	3,718	28,850	20.4	4,552	35,200	18.0
45-54		4 324	55,800	14.5	3,222	25,100	17.7	4,589	24,100	12.3
55-64		3,516	40,850	10.6	2,685	23,950	16.9	3,953	13,550	6.9
65 and older		2,078	43,050	11.2	1,601	30,700	21.7	2,619	9,200	4.7
TOTAL	10.0	3,715	385,750	100.0	2,754	141,700	100.0	3,766	195,800	100.0
MALES:										
18-24		3,082	36,150	20.2	3,621	4,550	6.8	2,882	25,950	29.6
25-34		5,524	43,900	24.6	3,837	10,550	15.7	5,587	26,000	29.7
35-44		5,959	33,700	18.9	4,533	14,000	20.9	6,037	14,750	16.8
45-54		5,479	25,250	14.1	4,311	11,350	16.9	5,947	10,800	12.3
55-64		4,449	19,300	10.8	3,644	11,700	17.4	4,796	6,050	6.9
65 and older		2,408	20,400	11.4	1,932	14,900	22.2	3,335	4,050	4.6
TOTAL	10.0	4,702	178,700	100.0	3,594	67,050	100.0	4,872	87,600	100.0
FEMALES:										
18-24		1,926	43,950	21.2	1,222	5,850	7.8	1,875	32,250	29.8
25-34		2,925	48,000	23.2	1,923	12,150	16.3	2,766	29,550	27.3
35-44		3,159	40,350	19.5	2,309	14,850	19.9	2,978	20,450	18.9
45-54		2,947	30,550	14.8	1,812	13,750	18.4	3,062	13,300	12.3
55-64		2,374	21,550	10.4	1,422	12,250	16.4	2,987	7,500	6.9
65 and older		1,758	22,650	10.9	1,267	15,800	21.2	1,977	5,150	4.8
TOTAL	10.1	2,538	207,050	100.0	1,846	74,650	100.0	2,546	108,200	100.0

AGE AND SEX	ALL PERSONS				COLLEGE				
					1-3 Years			4 Years		
	Median Yrs. of Educ.	Mean Income*	Number of Indi- viduals*	Per- cent	Mean Income*	Number of Indi- viduals*	Per- cent	Mean Income*	Number of Indi- viduals*	Per- cent
ALL INDIVIDUALS:										
18-24		$2,500	80,100	20.8	$2,937	10,600	30.8	$3,966	700	9.2
25-34		4,450	91,900	23.8	6,216	9,300	27.0	6,416	2,350	30.7
35-44		4,745	74,050	19.2	6,526	6,300	18.3	10,227	1,800	23.5
45-54		4,324	55,800	14.5	6,234	4,450	12.9	7,865	1,150	15.0
55-64		3,516	40,850	10.6	6,440	2,100	6.1	8,650	750	9.8
65 and older		2,078	43,050	11.2	3,648	1,650	4.8	6,600	900	11.8
TOTAL	10.0	3,715	385,750	100.0	5,216	34,400	100.0	7,503	7,650	100.0
MALES:										
18-24		3,082	36,150	20.2	3,460	5,200	31.4	4,433	350	10.1
25-34		5,524	43,900	24.6	7,052	4,950	29.9	7,392	1,000	29.0
35-44		5,959	33,700	18.9	8,078	2,650	16.0	11,591	1,000	29.0
45-54		5,479	25,250	14.1	7,266	2,050	12.4	9,771	400	11.6
55-64		4,449	19,300	10.8	9,730	950	5.7	8,468	400	11.6
65 and older		2,408	20,400	11.4	4,685	750	4.5	3,683	300	8.7
TOTAL	10.0	4,702	178,700	100.0	6,324	16,550	100.0	8,319	3,450	100.0
FEMALES:										
18-24		1,926	43,950	21.2	2,379	5,400	30.3	3,500	350	8.3
25-34		2,925	48,000	23.2	4,846	4,350	24.4	5,389	1,350	32.1
35-44		3,159	40,350	19.5	4,974	3,650	20.4	7,995	800	19.0
45-54		2,947	30,550	14.8	5,054	2,400	13.4	6,838	750	17.9
55-64		2,374	21,550	10.4	3,480	1,150	6.4	8,940	350	8.3
65 and older		1,758	22,650	10.9	2,740	900	5.0	8,108	600	14.3
TOTAL	10.1	2,538	207,050	100.0	3,923	17,850	100.0	6,700	4,200	100.0

(Table 2 continued on page 262)

AGE AND SEX	Median Yrs. of Educ.	ALL PERSONS			POSTGRADUATE					
					1 Year			2 or More Years		
		Mean Income*	Number of Individuals*	Per-cent	Mean Income*	Number of Individuals*	Per-cent	Mean Income*	Number of Individuals*	Per-cent
ALL INDIVIDUALS:										
18-24		$2,500	80,100	20.8	$4,433	150	6.1	$10,000	50	1.3
25-34		4,450	91,900	23.8	8,205	950	38.8	8,577	1,050	28.0
35-44		4,745	74,050	19.2	9,890	550	22.4	9,919	1,350	38.0
45-54		4,324	55,800	14.5	10,306	450	18.4	8,959	550	14.7
55-64		3,516	40,850	10.6	11,262	200	8.2	6,300	300	6.0
65 and older		2,078	43,050	11.2	5,633	150	6.1	6,237	450	12.0
TOTAL	10.0	3,715	385,750	100.0	8,800	2,450	100.0	8,690	3,750	100.0
MALES:										
18-24		3,082	36,150	20.2	2,690	100	6.1	—	—	—
25-34		5,524	43,900	24.6	8,558	750	45.5	11,345	650	27.1
35-44		5,959	33,700	18.9	12,314	350	21.2	11,013	950	39.6
45-54		5,479	25,250	14.1	10,550	300	18.2	8,528	350	14.6
55-64		4,449	19,300	10.8	—	—	—	6,800	200	8.3
65 and older		2,408	20,400	11.4	5,633	150	9.1	4,875	250	10.4
TOTAL	10.0	4,702	178,700	100.0	9,092	1,650	100.0	9,821	2,400	100.0
FEMALES:										
18-24		1,926	43,950	21.2	8,000	50	6.3	10,000	50	3.7
25-34		2,925	48,000	23.2	6,887	200	25.0	4,425	400	29.6
35-44		3,159	40,350	19.5	5,650	200	25.0	6,950	400	29.8
45-54		2,947	30,550	14.8	9,575	150	18.8	9,712	200	14.8
55-64		2,374	21,550	10.4	11,262	200	25.0	5,300	100	7.4
65 and older		1,758	22,650	10.9	—	—	—	7,600	200	14.8
TOTAL	10.1	2,538	207,050	100.0	8,156	800	100.0	6,688	1,350	100.0

SOURCE: Compiled from 1970 U.S. Census Public Use Sample.

*Number of individuals includes persons who reported zero income. Mean income is calculated only for persons who reported positive or negative income, excluding those with zero income.

Median age of all Americans Indians: 20.4.

Median age of all Indian income earners: 37.8.

AMERICAN INDIANS

Table 3
Personal Earnings by Occupation, Education, and Sex (1969)

OCCUPATIONS	ALL PERSONS			PRECOLLEGE					
				0-8 Years			9-12 Years		
	Mean Earnings	Number of Individuals	Per-cent	Mean Earnings	Number of Individuals	Per-cent	Mean Earnings	Number of Individuals	Per-cent
ALL INDIVIDUALS:									
Learned Professions	$10,552	2,650	1.3	—	—	—	$13,833	450	0.4
Other Prof., Tech., etc.	6,221	17,050	8.3	3,142	1,050	1.9	5,702	5,100	4.4
Mgrs., Offs., & Proprietors	8,192	6,450	3.1	6,180	1,050	1.9	7,983	3,500	3.0
Clerical	4,013	25,550	12.5	5,228	1,650	3.0	3,679	17,700	15.2
Craftsmen	6,338	25,900	12.6	5,535	7,450	13.6	6,142	15,650	13.5
Operatives	4,329	40,000	19.5	4,233	12,850	23.4	4,345	25,000	21.5
Service Workers	3,165	31,150	15.2	3,136	8,400	15.3	2,981	19,900	17.1
Private Household	1,146	5,150	2.5	1,022	2,450	4.5	1,194	2,600	2.2
Laborers	4,146	15,000	7.3	4,472	7,000	12.8	3,730	7,200	6.2
Sales	4,151	5,900	2.9	3,417	850	1.5	3,702	3,450	3.0
Farmers, Farm Managers	2,031	2,750	1.3	1,211	1,500	2.7	2,685	1,000	0.9
Farm Laborers	2,071	7,000	3.4	2,160	4,000	7.7	1,818	2,650	2.3
Unemployed	2,236	20,400	10.0	2,342	6,400	11.7	2,104	12,150	10.4
TOTAL	4,311	204,950	100.0	3,701	54,850	100.0	4,024	116,350	100.0
MALES:									
Learned Professions	11,390	2,200	1.7	—	—	—	13,833	450	0.7
Other Prof., Tech., etc.	6,623	9,150	7.2	3,515	650	1.7	6,251	2,850	4.2
Mgrs., Offs., & Proprietors	8,505	5,000	4.0	7,062	800	2.0	8,382	2,550	3.8
Clerical	5,307	6,900	5.5	4,796	700	1.8	5,141	4,150	6.1
Craftsmen	6,458	24,100	19.1	5,549	7,100	18.2	6,360	14,400	21.3
Operatives	5,078	28,350	22.4	4,832	9,550	24.4	5,196	17,150	25.4
Service Workers	4,235	12,200	9.7	4,206	3,900	10.0	4,035	7,100	10.5
Private Household	5,466	150	0.1	—	—	—	7,600	100	0.1
Laborers	4,287	14,250	11.3	4,634	6,700	17.1	3,812	6,850	10.1
Sales	5,809	2,850	2.3	4,187	400	1.0	5,348	1,400	2.1
Farmers, Farm Managers	2,282	2,400	1.9	1,368	1,350	3.5	3,181	800	1.2
Farm Laborers	2,199	5,850	4.6	2,323	3,750	9.6	2,025	2,000	3.0
Unemployed	2,754	13,000	10.3	2,848	4,200	10.7	2,558	7,750	11.5
TOTAL	5,132	126,400	100.0	4,309	39,100	100.0	4,987	67,550	100.0
FEMALES:									
Learned Professions	6,455	450	0.6	—	—	—	—	—	—
Other Prof., Tech., etc.	5,756	7,900	10.1	2,537	400	2.5	5,006	2,250	4.6
Mgrs., Offs., & Proprietors	7,115	1,450	1.8	3,360	250	1.6	6,913	950	1.9
Clerical	3,534	18,650	23.7	5,547	950	6.0	3,231	13,550	27.8
Craftsmen	4,744	1,800	2.3	5,242	350	2.2	3,640	1,250	2.6
Operatives	2,508	11,650	14.8	2,500	3,300	21.0	2,486	7,850	16.1
Service Workers	2,475	18,950	24.1	2,209	4,500	28.6	2,397	12,800	26.2
Private Household	1,017	5,000	6.4	1,022	2,450	15.6	938	2,500	5.1
Laborers	1,470	750	1.0	850	300	1.9	2,114	350	0.7
Sales	2,602	3,050	3.9	2,733	450	2.9	2,579	2,050	4.2
Farmers, Farm Managers	314	350	0.4	–200	150	1.0	700	200	0.4
Farm Laborers	1,419	1,150	1.5	805	450	2.9	1,184	650	1.3
Unemployed	1,326	7,400	9.4	1,376	2,200	14.0	1,303	4,400	9.0
TOTAL	2,991	78,550	100.0	2,190	15,750	100.0	2,692	48,800	100.0

263

(Table 3 continued on page 264)

| | ALL PERSONS | | | COLLEGE | | | | | |
| | | | | 1-3 Years | | | 4 Years | | |
OCCUPATIONS	Mean Earnings	Number of Indi- viduals	Per- cent	Mean Earnings	Number of Indi- viduals	Per- cent	Mean Earnings	Number of Indi- viduals	Per- cent
ALL INDIVIDUALS:									
Learned Professions	$10,552	2,650	1.3	$8,087	400	1.8	$11,260	500	8.9
Other Prof., Tech., etc.	6,221	17,050	8.3	5,888	4,700	20.8	7,113	3,050	54.5
Mgrs., Offs., & Proprietors	8,192	6,450	3.1	7,771	1,050	4.6	12,890	500	8.9
Clerical	4,013	25,550	12.5	4,468	5,600	24.8	6,162	400	7.1
Craftsmen	6,338	25,900	12.6	9,665	2,300	10.2	9,475	400	7.1
Operatives	4,329	40,000	19.5	4,720	2,150	9.5	—	—	—
Service Workers	3,165	31,150	15.2	4,406	2,550	11.3	5,275	200	3.6
Private Household	1,146	5,150	2.5	4,700	50	0.2	1,200	50	0.9
Laborers	4,146	15,000	7.3	5,103	700	3.1	1,600	50	0.9
Sales	4,151	5,900	2.9	4,853	1,300	5.6	7,250	100	1.8
Farmers, Farm Managers	2,031	2,750	1.3	3,925	200	0.9	6,000	50	0.9
Farm Laborers	2,071	7,000	3.4	—	50	0.2	2,100	50	0.9
Unemployed	2,236	20,400	10.0	2,759	1,550	6.9	2,040	250	4.5
TOTAL	4,311	204,550	100.0	5,437	22,600	100.0	7,653	5,600	100.0
MALES:									
Learned Professions	11,390	2,200	1.7	8,214	350	2.7	12,114	350	11.9
Other Prof., Tech., etc.	6,623	9,150	7.2	6,370	2,500	19.2	7,752	1,250	42.4
Mgrs., Offs., & Proprietors	8,505	5,000	4.0	8,529	850	6.5	9,877	450	15.3
Clerical	5,307	6,900	5.5	5,357	1,750	13.4	8,000	200	6.8
Craftsmen	6,458	24,100	19.1	9,860	2,250	17.2	6,720	250	8.5
Operatives	5,078	28,350	22.4	5,272	1,650	12.6	—	—	—
Service Workers	4,235	12,200	9.7	5,145	1,100	8.4	9,550	100	3.4
Private Household	5,466	150	0.1	—	—	—	1,200	50	1.7
Laborers	4,287	14,250	11.3	5,775	600	4.6	1,600	50	1.7
Sales	5,809	2,850	2.3	6,520	750	5.7	7,250	100	3.4
Farmers, Farm Managers	2,282	2,400	1.9	3,925	200	1.5	6,000	50	1.7
Farm Laborers	2,199	5,850	4.6	—	50	0.4	2,100	50	1.7
Unemployed	2,754	13,000	10.3	3,565	1,000	7.7	9,000	50	1.7
TOTAL	5,132	126,400	100.0	6,488	13,050	100.0	8,247	2,950	100.0
FEMALES:									
Learned Professions	6,455	450	0.6	7,200	50	0.5	9,266	150	5.7
Other Prof., Tech., etc.	5,756	7,900	10.1	5,340	2,200	23.0	6,669	1,800	67.9
Mgrs., Offs., & Proprietors	7,115	1,450	1.8	4,550	200	2.1	40,000	50	1.9
Clerical	3,534	18,650	23.7	4,064	3,850	40.3	4,325	200	7.5
Craftsmen	4,744	1,800	2.3	900	50	0.5	14,066	-150	5.7
Operatives	2,508	11,650	14.8	2,900	500	5.2	—	—	—
Service Workers	2,475	18,950	24.1	3,846	1,450	15.2	1,000	100	3.8
Private Household	1,017	5,000	6.4	4,700	50	0.5	—	—	—
Laborers	1,470	750	1.0	1,075	100	1.0	—	—	—
Sales	2,602	3,050	3.9	2,581	550	5.8	—	—	—
Farmers, Farm Managers	314	350	0.4	—	—	—	—	—	—
Farm Laborers	1,419	1,150	1.5	—	—	—	—	—	—
Unemployed	1,326	7,400	9.4	1,295	550	5.8	300	200	7.5
TOTAL	2,991	78,550	100.0	4,001	9,550	100.0	6,992	2,650	100.0

OCCUPATIONS	ALL PERSONS			POSTGRADUATE					
				1 Year			2 or More Years		
	Mean Earnings	Number of Individuals	Percent	Mean Earnings	Number of Individuals	Percent	Mean Earnings	Number of Individuals	Percent
ALL INDIVIDUALS:									
Learned Professions	$10,552	2,650	1.3	$10,100	350	15.9	$9,831	950	28.4
Other Prof., Tech., etc.	6,221	17,050	8.3	7,945	1,550	70.5	7,509	1,600	47.6
Mgrs., Offs., & Proprietors	8,192	6,450	3.1	9,333	150	6.8	12,025	200	6.0
Clerical	4,013	25,550	12.5	5,400	50	2.3	6,900	150	4.5
Craftsmen	6,338	25,900	12.6	11,600	50	2.3	4,100	50	1.3
Operatives	4,329	40,000	19.5	—	—	—	—	—	—
Service Workers	3,165	31,150	15.2	—	—	—	6,150	100	3.0
Private Household	1,146	5,150	2.5	—	—	—	—	—	—
Laborers	4,146	15,000	7.3	—	—	—	7,700	50	1.5
Sales	4,151	5,900	2.9	5,800	50	2.3	9,933	150	4.5
Farmers, Farm Managers	2,031	2,750	1.3	—	—	—	—	—	—
Farm Laborers	2,071	7,000	3.4	—	—	—	10,000	50	1.5
Unemployed	2,236	20,400	10.0	—	—	—	5,600	50	1.5
TOTAL	4,311	204,550	100.0	8,359	2,200	100.0	8,436	3,350	100.0
MALES:									
Learned Professions	11,390	2,200	1.7	10,100	350	23.3	11,692	700	31.1
Other Prof., Tech., etc.	6,623	9,150	7.2	7,700	900	60.0	7,955	1,000	44.4
Mgrs., Offs., & Proprietors	8,505	5,000	4.0	9,333	150	10.0	12,025	200	8.9
Clerical	5,307	6,900	5.5	—	—	—	9,550	100	4.4
Craftsmen	6,458	24,100	19.1	11,600	50	3.3	4,100	50	2.2
Operatives	5,078	28,350	22.4	—	—	—	—	—	—
Service Workers	4,235	12,200	9.7	—	—	—	—	—	—
Private Household	5,466	150	0.1	—	—	—	—	—	—
Laborers	4,287	14,250	11.3	—	—	—	7,700	50	2.2
Sales	5,809	2,850	2.3	5,800	50	3.3	9,933	150	6.7
Farmers, Farm Managers	2,282	2,400	1.9	—	—	—	—	—	—
Farm Laborers	2,199	5,850	4.6	—	—	—	—	—	—
Unemployed	2,754	13,000	10.3	—	—	—	—	—	—
TOTAL	5,132	126,400	100.0	8,490	1,500	100.0	9,591	2,250	100.0
FEMALES:									
Learned Professions	6,455	450	0.6	—	—	—	4,620	250	22.7
Other Prof., Tech., etc.	5,756	7,900	10.1	8,284	650	92.9	6,766	600	54.5
Mgrs., Offs., & Proprietors	7,115	1,450	1.8	—	—	—	—	—	—
Clerical	3,534	18,650	23.7	5,400	50	7.1	1,600	50	4.5
Craftsmen	4,744	1,800	2.3	—	—	—	—	—	—
Operatives	2,508	11,650	14.8	—	—	—	—	—	—
Service Workers	2,475	18,950	24.1	—	—	—	6,150	100	9.1
Private Household	1,017	5,000	6.4	—	—	—	—	—	—
Laborers	1,470	750	1.0	—	—	—	—	—	—
Sales	2,602	3,050	3.9	—	—	—	—	—	—
Farmers, Farm Managers	314	350	0.4	—	—	—	—	—	—
Farm Laborers	1,419	1,150	1.5	—	—	—	10,000	50	4.5
Unemployed	1,326	7,400	9.4	—	—	—	5,600	50	4.5
TOTAL	2,991	78,550	100.0	8,078	700	100.0	6,081	1,100	100.0

SOURCE: Compiled from 1970 U.S. Census Public Use Sample.

NOTE: Median years of education: 10.6.

AMERICAN INDIANS

Table 4
Family Income Distribution by Number of Income Earners per Family (1969)

INCOME	ALL FAMILIES		NO-EARNER FAMILIES		ONE-EARNER FAMILIES		TWO-EARNER FAMILIES		THREE OR MORE EARNER FAMILIES	
	Number of Families	Percent	Number of Families	Percent	Number of Families	Percent	Number of Families	Percent	Number of Families	Percent
UNDER $ 1,000	12,850	8.7	7,700	35.2	4,300	7.4	850	1.6	—	—
$ 1,000 - $ 1,999	12,850	8.7	5,450	24.9	5,450	9.4	1,750	3.4	200	1.3
$ 2,000 - $ 2,999	13,000	8.8	4,550	20.8	5,800	10.0	2,350	4.5	300	2.0
$ 3,000 - $ 3,999	14,000	9.5	2,050	9.4	7,850	13.5	3,300	6.4	800	5.2
$ 4,000 - $ 4,999	11,200	7.6	600	2.7	6,050	10.4	3,800	7.3	750	4.9
$ 5,000 - $5,999	13,350	9.1	850	3.9	6,500	11.2	4,950	9.5	1,050	6.8
$ 6,000 - $ 6,999	11,550	7.8	250	1.1	5,850	10.0	4,650	9.0	800	5.2
$ 7,000 - $ 7,999	9,150	6.2	200	0.9	3,650	6.3	4,400	8.5	900	5.9
$ 8,000 - $ 9,999	16,650	11.3	100	0.5	6,200	10.6	7,800	15.0	2,550	16.6
$10,000 - $12,999	17,100	11.6	100	0.5	4,400	7.6	9,000	17.3	3,600	23.5
$13,000 - $14,999	6,500	4.4	—	—	1,000	1.7	4,250	8.2	1,250	8.1
$15,000 - $19,999	6,150	4.2	—	—	800	1.4	3,400	6.6	1,950	12.7
$20,000 - $24,999	2,000	1.4	—	—	100	0.2	1,150	2.2	750	4.9
$25,000 OR MORE	1,050	0.7	50	0.2	300	0.5	250	0.5	450	2.9
TOTAL	147,400	100.0	21,900	100.0	58,250	100.0	51,900	100.0	15,350	100.0
MEAN EARNINGS	$6,621		$1,939		$5,440		$8,568		$11,199	
MEDIAN INCOME	5,734		1,596		4,942		7,977		10,250	

SOURCE: Compiled from 1970 U.S. Census Public Use Sample.

AMERICAN INDIANS

Table 5

Family Income by Age, Education, and Sex of Family Head (1969)

AGE AND SEX OF FAMILY HEAD	ALL PERSONS				PRECOLLEGE						
					0-8 Years			9-12 Years			
	Median Yrs. of Educ.	Mean Income	Number of Individuals	Per-cent	Mean Income	Number of Individuals	Per-cent	Mean Income	Number of Individuals	Per-cent
ALL INDIVIDUALS:										
18-24		$4,573	14,150	9.6	$4,384	2,150	3.5	$4,477	9,650	14.4
25-34		6,542	36,900	25.0	4,226	9,000	14.7	6,611	22,250	33.2
35-44		6,931	33,400	22.7	5,202	13,300	21.7	7,145	15,300	22.8
45-54		6,640	25,900	17.6	4,888	12,150	19.8	7,430	10,650	15.9
55-64		5,598	18,350	12.4	4,233	11,100	18.1	6,934	5,600	8.4
65 and older		2,519	18,700	12.7	1,791	13,650	22.2	3,948	3,550	5.3
TOTAL	9.7	5,831	147,400	100.0	4,034	61,350	100.0	6,442	67,000	100.0
MALES:										
18-24		5,113	11,500	9.6	4,812	1,800	3.7	5,180	7,600	13.9
25-34		7,321	31,450	26.3	5,025	7,100	14.6	7,324	19,050	34.7
35-44		7,902	27,150	22.7	5,874	11,100	22.9	8,421	11,950	21.8
45-54		7,581	20,200	16.9	5,985	9,100	18.7	8,219	8,550	15.6
55-64		6,132	15,000	12.5	4,855	9,000	18.5	7,158	4,750	8.7
65 and older		2,564	14,500	12.1	1,878	10,450	21.5	3,785	2,950	5.4
TOTAL	9.8	6,560	119,800	100.0	4,679	48,550	100.0	7,199	54,850	100.0
FEMALES:										
18-24		2,230	2,650	9.6	2,185	350	2.7	1,873	2,050	16.9
25-34		2,047	5,450	19.7	1,242	1,900	14.8	2,367	3,200	26.3
35-44		2,714	6,250	22.6	1,807	2,200	17.2	2,596	3,350	27.6
45-54		3,306	5,700	20.7	1,674	3,050	23.8	4,219	2,100	17.3
55-64		3,208	3,350	12.1	1,566	2,100	16.4	5,685	850	7.0
65 and older		2,365	4,200	15.2	1,506	3,200	25.0	4,850	600	4.9
TOTAL	9.3	2,665	27,600	100.0	1,587	12,800	100.0	3,022	12,150	100.0

(Table 5 continued on page 268)

AMERICAN INDIANS—Table 5 (Continued)

| AGE AND SEX OF FAMILY HEAD | ALL PERSONS | | | | COLLEGE | | | | | |
| | | | | | 1-3 Years | | | 4 Years | | |
	Median Yrs. of Educ.	Mean Income	Number of Individuals	Per-cent	Mean Income	Number of Individuals	Per-cent	Mean Income	Number of Individuals	Per-cent
ALL INDIVIDUALS:										
18-24		$4,573	14,150	9.6	4,978	1,950	15.6	$5,666	300	9.8
25-34		6,542	36,900	25.0	9,727	3,900	31.2	10,256	800	26.2
35-44		6,931	33,400	22.7	9,437	2,650	21.2	13,322	900	29.5
45-54		6,640	25,900	17.6	9,921	2,100	16.8	14,450	400	13.1
55-64		5,598	18,350	12.4	10,632	1,000	8.0	9,500	400	13.1
65 and older		2,519	18,700	12.7	4,561	900	7.2	9,320	250	8.2
TOTAL	9.7	5,831	147,400	100.0	8,658	12,500	100.0	11,083	3,050	100.0
MALES:										
18-24		5,113	11,500	9.6	5,118	1,800	17.2	5,560	250	9.3
25-34		7,321	31,450	26.3	10,158	3,650	34.9	10,533	750	27.8
35-44		7,902	27,150	22.7	10,578	2,000	19.1	13,322	900	33.3
45-54		7,581	20,200	16.9	10,310	1,650	15.8	15,750	300	11.1
55-64		6,132	15,000	12.5	12,550	750	7.2	9,142	350	13.0
65 and older		2,564	14,500	12.1	5,158	600	5.7	7,566	150	5.6
TOTAL	9.8	6,560	119,800	100.0	9,279	10,450	100.0	11,237	2,700	100.0
FEMALES:										
18-24		2,230	2,650	9.6	3,300	150	7.3	6,200	50	14.3
25-34		2,047	5,450	19.7	3,440	250	12.2	6,100	50	14.3
35-44		2,714	6,250	22.6	5,926	650	31.7	–	–	–
45-54		3,306	5,700	20.7	8,494	450	22.0	10,550	100	28.6
55-64		3,208	3,350	12.1	4,880	250	12.2	12,000	50	14.3
65 and older		2,365	4,200	15.2	3,366	300	14.6	11,950	100	28.6
TOTAL	9.3	2,665	27,600	100.0	5,492	2,050	100.0	9,900	350	100.0

AMERICAN INDIANS—Table 5 (Continued)

AGE AND SEX OF FAMILY HEAD	ALL PERSONS				POSTGRADUATE					
					1 Year			2 or more years		
	Median Yrs. of Educ.	Mean Income	Number of Individuals	Per-cent	Mean Income	Number of Individuals	Per-cent	Mean Income	Number of Individuals	Per-cent
ALL INDIVIDUALS:										
18-24		$4,573	14,150	9.6	$3,300	50	3.8	$10,000	50	2.3
25-34		6,542	36,900	25.0	11,425	400	30.8	10,118	550	25.0
35-44		6,931	33,400	22.7	15,057	350	26.9	11,925	900	40.9
45-54		6,640	25,900	17.6	12,950	300	23.1	9,900	300	13.6
55-64		5,598	18,350	12.4	9,100	50	3.8	10,100	200	9.1
65 and older		2,519	18,700	12.7	8,366	150	11.5	4,800	200	9.1
TOTAL	9.7	5,831	147,400	100.0	12,000	1,300	100.0	10,339	2,200	100.0
MALES:										
18-24		5,113	11,500	9.6	3,300	50	4.0	—	—	—
25-34		7,321	31,450	26.3	11,425	400	32.0	11,020	500	25.0
35-44		7,902	27,150	22.7	15,057	350	28.0	12,114	850	42.5
45-54		7,581	20,200	16.9	12,950	300	24.0	9,900	350	15.0
55-64		6,132	15,000	12.5	—	—	—	11,133	150	7.5
65 and older		2,564	14,500	12.1	8,365	150	12.0	4,800	200	10.0
TOTAL	9.8	6,560	119,800	100.0	12,116	1,250	100.0	10,703	2,000	100.0
FEMALES:										
18-24		2,230	2,650	9.6	—	—	—	10,000	50	25.0
25-34		2,047	5,450	19.7	—	—	—	1,100	50	25.0
35-44		2,714	6,250	22.6	—	—	—	8,700	50	25.0
45-54		3,306	5,700	20.7	—	—	—	—	—	—
55-64		3,208	3,350	12.1	9,100	50	100.0	7,000	50	25.0
65 and older		2,365	4,200	15.2	—	—	—	—	—	—
TOTAL	9.3	2,665	27,600	100.0	9,100	50	100.0	6,700	200	100.0

SOURCE: Compiled from 1970 U.S. Census Public Use Sample.

NOTE: Median age of all family heads: 41.8

AMERICAN INDIANS

Table 6
Family Earnings by Number of Income Earners, Education, and Sex of Family Head (1969)

	NUMBER OF INCOME EARNERS			PRECOLLEGE					
				0-8 Years			9-12 Years		
	Mean Family Earnings	Number of Families	Percent of all Families	Mean Family Earnings	Number of Families	Percent of all Families	Mean Family Earnings	Number of Families	Percent of all Families
ALL FAMILIES:									
No Income-Earners	$ 0	21,900	14.9	$ 0	14,650	23.9	$ 0	6,400	9.6
One Income-Earner	4,715	58,250	39.5	3,520	24,100	39.3	4,998	27,150	40.5
Two Income-Earners	8,164	51,900	35.2	6,561	15,850	25.8	8,364	27,050	40.4
Three or More Earners	10,495	15,350	10.4	8,688	6,750	11.0	10,885	6,400	9.6
TOTAL	5,831	147,400	100.0	4,034	61,350	100.0	6,442	67,000	100.0
MALE-HEADED FAMILIES:									
No Income-Earners	0	12,900	10.8	0	9,150	18.8	0	3,200	5.8
One Income-Earner	5,125	46,550	38.9	3,827	19,650	40.5	5,550	21,400	39.0
Two Income-Earners	8,509	47,000	39.2	7,083	13,850	28.5	8,609	24,800	45.2
Three or More Earners	11,039	13,350	11.1	9,127	5,900	12.2	11,488	5,450	9.9
TOTAL	6,560	119,800	100.0	4,679	48,550	100.0	7,199	54,850	100.0
FEMALE-HEADED FAMILIES:									
No Income-Earners	0	9,000	32.6	0	5,500	43.0	0	3,200	26.3
One Income-Earner	3,082	11,700	42.4	2,166	4,450	34.8	2,944	5,750	47.3
Two Income-Earners	4,850	4,900	17.8	2,941	2,000	15.6	5,656	2,250	18.5
Three or More Earners	6,860	2,000	7.2	5,644	850	6.6	7,431	950	7.8
TOTAL	2,665	27,600	100.0	1,587	12,800	100.0	3,022	12,150	100.0

AMERICAN INDIANS—Table 6 (Continued)

	NUMBER OF INCOME EARNERS			COLLEGE					
				1-3 Years			4 Years		
	Mean Family Earnings	Number of Families	Percent of all Families	Mean Family Earnings	Number of Families	Percent of all Families	Mean Family Earnings	Number of Families	Percent of all Families
ALL FAMILIES:									
No Income-Earners	$ 0	21,900	14.9	$ 0	750	6.0	$ —	—	—
One Income-Earner	4,715	58,250	39.5	6,767	4,450	35.6	9,413	1,150	37.7
Two Income-Earners	8,164	51,900	35.2	9,422	5,700	45.6	11,618	1,650	54.1
Three or More Earners	10,495	15,350	10.4	15,251	1,600	12.8	15,240	250	8.2
TOTAL	5,831	147,400	100.0	8,658	12,500	100.0	11,083	3,050	100.0
MALE-HEADED FAMILIES:									
No Income-Earners	0	12,900	10.8	0	450	4.3	—	—	—
One Income-Earner	5,125	46,550	38.9	7,030	3,300	31.6	9,580	1,000	37.0
Two Income-Earners	8,509	47,000	39.2	9,665	5,300	50.7	11,689	1,450	53.7
Three or More Earners	11,039	13,350	11.1	16,100	1,400	13.4	15,240	250	9.3
TOTAL	6,560	119,800	100.0	9,270	10,450	100.0	11,237	2,700	100.0
FEMALE-HEADED FAMILIES:									
No Income-Earners	0	9,000	32.6	0	300	14.6	—	—	—
One Income-Earner	3,082	11,700	42.4	6,013	1,150	56.1	8,300	150	42.9
Two Income-Earners	4,850	4,900	17.8	6,206	400	19.5	11,100	200	57.1
Three or More Earners	6,860	2,000	7.2	9,312	200	9.8	—	—	—
TOTAL	2,665	27,600	100.0	5,492	2,050	100.0	9,900	350	100.0

(Table 6 continued on page 272)

271

	NUMBER OF INCOME EARNERS			POSTGRADUATE					
				1 Year			2 or More Years		
	Mean Family Earnings	Number of Families	Percent of all Families	Mean Family Earnings	Number of Families	Percent of all Families	Mean Family Earnings	Number of Families	Percent of all Families
ALL FAMILIES:									
No Income-Earners	$ 0	21,900	14.9	$ —	—	—	$ 0	100	4.5
One Income-Earner	4,715	58,250	39.5	9,733	450	34.6	9,252	950	43.2
Two Income-Earners	8,164	51,900	35.2	13,075	800	61.5	11,935	850	38.6
Three or More Earners	10,495	15,350	10.4	15,200	50	3.8	12,708	300	13.6
TOTAL	5,831	147,400	100.0	12,000	1,300	100.0	10,339	2,200	100.0
MALE-HEADED FAMILIES:									
No Income-Earners	0	12,900	10.8	—	—	—	0	100	5.0
One Income-Earner	5,125	46,550	38.9	9,733	450	36.0	9,933	750	37.5
Two Income-Earners	8,509	47,000	39.2	13,340	750	60.0	11,935	850	42.5
Three or More Earners	11,039	13,350	11.1	15,200	50	4.0	12,708	300	15.0
TOTAL	6,560	119,800	100.0	12,116	1,250	100.0	10,703	2,000	100.0
FEMALE-HEADED FAMILIES:									
No Income-Earners	0	9,000	32.6	—	—	—	—	—	—
One Income-Earner	3,082	11,700	42.4	—	—	—	6,700	200	100.0
Two Income-Earners	4,850	4,900	17.8	9,100	50	100.0	—	—	—
Three or More Earners	6,860	2,000	7.2	—	—	—	—	—	—
TOTAL	2,665	27,600	100.0	9,100	50	100.0	6,700	200	100.0

SOURCE: Compiled from 1970 U.S. Census Public Use Sample.

NOTE: Median years of education of family heads: 9.7.

AMERICAN INDIANS

Table 7

Fertility Rates by Woman's Education and Family Income (1969)

7a. EDUCATION

| | TOTAL | | PRECOLLEGE | | | | COLLEGE | | | | POSTGRADUATE | | | |
| | | | 0-8 Years | | 9-12 Years | | 1-3 Years | | 4 Years | | 1 Year | | 2 or More Years | |
	Number	Percent	Number	Percent	Number	Percent	Number	Percent	Number	Percent	Number	Percent	Number	Percent
All Women, 15 and older:														
Childless	67,650	29.3	17,400	21.2	40,900	32.7	7,100	39.8	1,250	29.8	400	50.0	600	44.4
1 Child	31,650	13.7	8,500	10.4	19,350	15.5	2,600	14.6	800	19.0	100	12.5	300	22.2
2 Children	30,300	13.1	9,550	11.6	16,700	13.4	3,050	17.1	700	16.7	100	12.5	200	14.8
3 Children	24,600	10.6	8,200	10.0	13,150	10.5	2,200	12.3	750	17.9	100	12.5	200	14.8
4 Children	20,250	8.8	7,900	9.6	10,700	8.6	1,350	7.6	250	6.0	50	6.3	–	–
5 Children	16,150	7.0	6,600	8.0	8,700	7.0	650	3.6	150	3.6	–	–	50	3.7
6 or More	40,600	17.6	23,950	29.2	15,400	12.3	900	5.0	300	7.1	50	6.3	–	–
TOTAL	231,200	100.0	82,100	100.0	124,900	100.0	17,850	100.0	4,200	100.0	800	100.0	1,350	100.0
Mean No. of Children	2.8		3.8		2.4		1.7		2.0		1.4		1.1	
Women, 15-24:														
Childless	44,000	64.6	9,200	69.2	30,600	62.5	3,800	70.4	350	100.0	50	100.0	–	–
1 Child	13,050	19.2	1,800	13.5	10,500	21.5	750	13.9	–	–	–	–	–	–
2 Children	7,150	10.5	1,050	7.9	5,300	10.8	800	14.8	–	–	–	–	–	–
3 Children	2,400	3.5	550	4.1	1,750	3.6	50	0.9	–	–	–	–	50	100.0
4 Children	850	1.2	400	3.0	450	0.9	–	–	–	–	–	–	–	–
5 Children	450	0.7	150	1.1	300	0.6	–	–	–	–	–	–	–	–
6 or More	200	0.3	150	1.1	50	0.1	–	–	–	–	–	–	–	–
TOTAL	68,100	100.0	13,300	100.0	48,950	100.0	5,400	100.0	350	100.0	50	100.0	50	100.0
Mean No. of Children	0.6		0.7		0.6		C.5		0.0		0.0		3.0	

(Table 7 continued on page 274)

AMERICAN INDIANS—Table 7: Education (Continued)

| | TOTAL | | PRECOLLEGE | | | | COLLEGE | | | | POSTGRADUATE | | | |
| | | | 0-8 Years | | 9-12 Years | | 1-3 Years | | 4 Years | | 1 Year | | 2 or More Years | |
	Number	Percent	Number	Percent	Number	Percent	Number	Percent	Number	Percent	Number	Percent	Number	Percent
Women, 25-34:														
Childless	6,850	14.3	1,200	9.9	3,500	11.8	1,400	32.2	400	29.6	200	100.0	150	37.5
1 Child	5,900	12.3	1,800	14.8	2,950	10.0	600	13.8	400	29.6	—	—	150	37.5
2 Children	8,400	17.5	1,650	13.6	5,550	18.8	950	21.8	200	14.8	—	—	50	12.5
3 Children	8,300	17.3	1,650	13.6	5,750	19.5	600	13.8	250	18.5	—	—	50	12.5
4 Children	7,650	15.9	1,850	15.2	5,250	17.8	500	11.5	50	3.7	—	—	—	—
5 Children	5,450	11.4	1,600	13.2	3,650	12.4	200	4.6	—	—	—	—	—	—
6 or More	5,450	11.4	2,400	19.8	2,900	9.8	100	2.3	50	3.7	—	—	—	—
TOTAL	48,000	100.0	12,150	100.0	29,550	100.0	4,350	100.0	1,350	100.0	200	100.0	400	100.0
Mean No. of Children	3.0		3.5		3.1		1.8		1.5		0.0		1.0	
Women, 35-44:														
Childless	4,100	10.2	1,150	7.7	2,000	9.8	650	17.8	100	12.5	50	25.0	150	37.5
1 Child	4,150	10.3	1,150	7.7	2,300	11.2	450	12.3	150	18.8	—	—	100	25.0
2 Children	4,200	10.4	1,450	9.8	2,150	10.5	400	11.0	50	6.3	50	25.0	100	25.0
3 Children	5,250	13.0	1,600	10.8	2,400	11.7	850	23.3	300	37.5	50	25.0	50	12.5
4 Children	4,950	12.3	1,800	12.1	2,450	12.0	550	15.1	100	12.5	50	25.0	—	—
5 Children	4,300	10.7	1,350	9.1	2,600	12.7	300	8.2	50	6.3	—	—	—	—
6 or More	13,400	33.2	6,350	42.8	6,550	32.0	450	12.3	50	6.3	—	—	—	—
TOTAL	40,350	100.0	14,850	100.0	20,450	100.0	3,650	100.0	800	100.0	200	100.0	400	100.0
Mean No. of Children	4.4		5.0		4.3		3.0		2.6		2.3		1.1	

274

AMERICAN INDIANS—Table 7: Education (Continued)

Women, 45 and older:

| | TOTAL | | PRECOLLEGE | | | | COLLEGE | | | | POSTGRADUATE | | | |
| | | | 0-8 Years | | 9-12 Years | | 1-3 Years | | 4 Years | | 1 Year | | 2 or More Years | |
	Number	Percent	Number	Percent	Number	Percent	Number	Percent	Number	Percent	Number	Percent	Number	Percent
Childless	12,700	17.0	5,850	14.0	4,800	18.5	1,250	28.1	400	23.5	100	28.6	300	60.0
1 Child	8,550	11.4	3,750	9.0	3,600	13.9	800	18.0	250	14.7	100	28.6	50	10.0
2 Children	10,550	14.1	5,400	12.9	3,700	14.3	900	20.2	450	26.5	50	14.3	50	10.0
3 Children	8,650	11.6	4,400	10.5	3,250	12.5	700	15.7	200	11.8	50	14.3	50	10.0
4 Children	6,800	9.1	3,850	9.2	2,550	9.8	300	6.7	100	5.9	—	—	—	—
5 Children	5,950	8.0	3,500	8.4	2,150	8.3	150	3.4	100	5.9	—	—	50	10.0
6 or More	21,550	28.8	15,050	36.0	5,900	22.7	350	7.9	200	11.8	50	14.3	—	—
TOTAL	74,750	100.0	41,800	100.0	25,950	100.0	4,450	100.0	1,700	100.0	350	100.0	500	100.0
Mean No. of Children	3.9		4.5		3.4		2.1		2.4		2.0		1.1	

7b. FAMILY INCOME

All Women, 15 and older:

| | TOTAL | | Less Than $5,000 | | $5,000 - 9,999 | | $10,000 - 14,999 | | $15,000 - 19,999 | | $20,000 - 24,999 | | $25,000 and Over | |
	Number	Percent	Number	Percent	Number	Percent	Number	Percent	Number	Percent	Number	Percent	Number	Percent
Childless	67,650	29.3	33,350	30.7	19,750	27.7	9,800	27.2	2,950	30.3	950	28.4	1,050	36.6
1 Child	31,650	13.7	15,050	13.9	9,900	13.9	4,750	13.5	1,800	13.3	400	11.9	250	8.8
2 Children	30,300	13.1	12,600	11.6	9,950	13.9	4,900	13.9	1,700	17.4	550	16.4	600	21.1
3 Children	24,600	10.6	9,250	8.5	7,950	11.1	5,250	14.9	1,300	13.3	650	19.4	200	7.0
4 Children	20,250	8.8	8,450	7.8	7,400	10.4	3,000	9.1	600	6.2	300	9.0	300	10.5
5 Children	16,150	7.0	7,450	6.9	4,550	6.4	3,000	8.5	750	7.7	300	9.0	100	3.5
6 or More	40,600	17.6	22,500	20.7	11,850	16.6	4,550	12.9	1,150	11.8	200	6.0	350	12.3
TOTAL	231,200	100.0	108,650	100.0	71,350	100.0	32,250	100.0	9,750	100.0	3,350	100.0	2,850	100.0
Mean No. of Children	2.8		3.0		2.8		2.7		2.4		2.2		2.4	

(Table 7 continued on page 276)

AMERICAN INDIANS—Table 7: Family Income (Continued)

	TOTAL		Less Than $5,000		$5,000 - 9,999		$10,000 - 14,999		$15,000 - 19,999		$20,000 - 24,999		$25,000 and Over	
	Number	Percent	Number	Percent	Number	Percent	Number	Percent	Number	Percent	Number	Percent	Number	Percent
Women, 15-24:														
Childless	44,000	64.6	19,950	64.6	14,100	61.4	6,900	67.0	1,700	73.9	600	80.0	750	83.3
1 Child	13,050	19.2	5,600	18.1	4,600	20.0	2,200	21.4	450	19.6	100	13.3	100	11.1
2 Children	7,150	10.5	3,250	10.5	2,900	12.6	750	7.3	150	6.5	50	6.7	50	5.6
3 Children	2,400	3.5	1,000	3.2	1,000	4.4	400	3.9	–	–	–	–	–	–
4 Children	850	1.2	600	1.9	250	1.1	–	–	–	–	–	–	–	–
5 Children	450	0.7	350	1.1	50	0.2	50	0.5	–	–	–	–	–	–
6 or More	200	0.3	150	0.5	50	0.2	–	–	–	–	–	–	–	–
TOTAL	68,100	100.0	30,900	100.0	22,950	100.0	10,300	100.0	2,300	100.0	750	100.0	900	100.0
Mean No. of Children	0.6		0.7		0.7		0.5		0.3		0.3		0.2	
Women, 25-34:														
Childless	6,850	14.3	3,100	17.1	1,950	11.1	1,350	14.7	350	17.5	50	6.7	50	12.5
1 Child	5,900	12.3	2,500	13.8	1,850	10.6	1,200	13.0	200	10.0	100	13.3	50	12.5
2 Children	8,400	17.5	2,400	13.2	3,450	19.7	1,700	18.5	600	30.0	100	13.3	150	37.5
3 Children	8,300	17.3	2,400	13.2	3,100	17.7	2,050	22.3	450	22.5	250	33.3	50	12.5
4 Children	7,650	15.9	2,750	15.2	3,200	18.3	1,400	15.2	100	5.0	150	20.0	50	12.5
5 Children	5,450	11.4	2,200	12.1	2,200	12.6	850	9.2	200	10.0	–	–	–	–
6 or More	5,450	11.4	2,800	15.4	1,750	10.0	650	7.1	100	5.0	100	13.3	50	12.5
TOTAL	48,000	100.0	18,150	100.0	17,500	100.0	9,200	100.0	2,000	100.0	750	100.0	400	100.0
Mean No. of Children	3.0		3.1		3.1		2.7		2.4		3.1		2.9	

276

AMERICAN INDIANS—Table 7: Family Income (Continued)

	TOTAL		Less Than $5,000		$5,000 - 9,999		$10,000 - 14,999		$15,000 - 19,999		$20,000 - 24,999		$25,000 and Over	
	Number	Percent	Number	Percent	Number	Percent	Number	Percent	Number	Percent	Number	Percent	Number	Percent
Women, 35-44:														
Childless	4,100	10.2	2,250	14.0	1,150	8.7	400	5.6	100	4.3	150	15.0	50	7.1
1 Child	4,150	10.3	1,600	10.0	1,550	11.7	550	7.7	250	10.0	100	10.0	100	14.3
2 Children	4,200	10.4	1,400	8.7	1,250	9.5	950	13.4	300	13.0	200	20.0	100	14.3
3 Children	5,250	13.0	1,450	9.0	1,650	12.5	1,200	16.9	600	26.1	250	25.0	100	14.3
4 Children	4,950	12.3	1,500	9.3	1,850	14.0	1,000	14.1	250	10.9	100	10.0	250	35.7
5 Children	4,300	10.7	1,550	9.7	1,150	8.7	1,100	15.5	350	15.2	100	10.0	50	7.1
6 or More	13,400	33.2	6,300	39.3	4,600	34.8	1,900	26.8	450	19.6	100	10.0	50	7.1
TOTAL	40,350	100.0	16,050	100.0	13,200	100.0	7,100	100.0	2,300	100.0	1,000	100.0	700	100.0
Mean No. of Children	4.4		4.5		4.5		4.3		3.8		2.8		3.1	
Women, 45 and older:														
Childless	12,700	17.0	8,050	18.5	2,550	14.4	950	11.0	800	25.4	150	17.6	200	23.5
1 Child	8,550	11.4	5,350	12.3	1,900	10.7	800	9.2	400	12.7	100	11.8	—	—
2 Children	10,550	14.1	5,550	12.7	2,350	13.3	1,500	17.3	650	20.6	200	23.5	300	35.3
3 Children	8,650	11.6	4,400	10.1	2,200	12.4	1,600	18.5	250	7.9	150	17.6	50	5.9
4 Children	6,800	9.1	3,600	8.3	2,100	11.9	800	9.2	250	7.9	50	5.9	—	—
5 Children	5,950	8.0	3,350	7.7	1,150	6.5	1,000	11.6	200	6.3	200	23.5	50	5.9
6 or More	21,550	28.8	13,250	30.4	5,450	30.8	2,000	23.1	600	19.0	—	—	250	29.4
TOTAL	74,750	100.0	43,550	100.0	17,700	100.0	8,650	100.0	3,150	100.0	850	100.0	850	100.0
Mean No. of Children	3.9		4.0		4.0		3.9		3.0		2.5		3.9	

SOURCE: Compiled from 1970 U.S. Census Public Use Sample.

BLACK AMERICANS

Table 8
Personal Income by Age, Education, and Sex (1969)

AGE AND SEX	ALL PERSONS				PRECOLLEGE					
					0-8 Years			9-12 Years		
	Median Yrs. of Educ.	Mean Income*	Number of Individuals*	Per-cent	Mean Income*	Number of Individuals*	Per-cent	Mean Income*	Number of Individuals*	Per-cent
ALL INDIVIDUALS:										
18-24		$2,697	2,282,700	19.1	$2,109	257,000	5.7	$2,692	1,720,150	27.8
25-34		4,494	2,441,550	20.4	3,225	407,000	9.0	4,361	1,667,250	27.0
35-44		4,687	2,238,850	18.7	3,589	701,250	15.5	4,636	1,264,200	20.5
45-54		4,301	1,979,600	16.5	3,414	950,700	21.1	4,556	851,750	13.8
55-64		3,409	1,538,550	12.8	2,868	1,010,450	22.4	3,890	430,600	7.0
65 and older		1,727	1,499,500	12.5	1,533	1,189,000	26.3	2,190	242,850	3.9
TOTAL	10.0	3,680	11,980,750	100.0	2,711	4,515,400	100.0	3,902	6,176,800	100.0
MALES:										
18-24		3,114	1,003,500	18.9	2,500	132,650	6.1	3,157	747,700	29.1
25-34		5,710	1,058,750	20.0	4,117	196,700	9.0	5,718	697,500	27.1
35-44		6,044	979,600	18.5	4,645	351,400	16.1	6,255	505,900	19.7
45-54		5,533	910,250	17.2	4,500	470,150	21.6	6,098	360,450	14.0
55-64		4,471	699,450	13.2	3,846	486,450	22.3	5,380	173,650	6.7
65 and older		2,225	654,750	12.3	1,979	539,550	24.8	3,041	88,250	3.4
TOTAL	9.7	4,717	5,306,300	100.0	3,612	2,176,900	100.0	5,125	2,573,450	100.0
FEMALES:										
18-24		2,318	1,279,200	19.2	1,559	124,350	5.3	2,278	972,450	27.0
25-34		3,318	1,382,800	20.7	2,098	210,300	9.0	3,110	969,750	26.9
35-44		3,329	1,259,250	18.9	2,152	349,850	15.0	3,237	758,300	21.0
45-54		2,941	1,069,350	16.0	1,989	480,550	20.5	3,091	491,300	13.6
55-64		2,264	839,100	12.6	1,676	524,000	22.4	2,588	256,950	7.1
65 and older		1,307	844,750	12.7	1,128	649,450	27.8	1,662	154,600	4.3
TOTAL	10.1	2,662	6,674,450	100.0	1,659	2,338,500	100.0	2,817	3,603,350	100.0

| AGE AND SEX | ALL PERSONS | | | | COLLEGE | | | | | |
| | | | | | 1-3 Years | | | 4 Years | | |
	Median Yrs. of Educ.	Mean Income*	Number of Indi- viduals*	Per- cent	Mean Income*	Number of Indi- viduals*	Per- cent	Mean Income*	Number of Indi- viduals*	Per- cent
ALL INDIVIDUALS:										
18-24		$2,697	2,282,700	19.1	$2,936	261,000	31.7	$4,261	39,000	13.4
25-34		4,494	2,441,550	20.4	5,742	228,800	27.8	6,734	97,050	33.3
35-44		4,687	2,238,850	18.7	6,213	150,850	18.3	7,780	66,500	22.8
45-54		4,301	1,979,600	16.5	6,068	98,350	11.9	7,869	40,700	14.0
55-64		3,409	1,538,550	12.8	5,116	48,400	5.9	6,690	27,550	9.5
65 and older		1,727	1,499,500	12.5	2,557	37,100	4.5	3,316	20,250	7.0
TOTAL	10.0	3,680	11,980,750	100.0	4,877	824,500	100.0	6,573	291,050	100.0
MALES:										
18-24		3,114	1,003,500	18.9	3,338	108,550	29.7	4,564	12,500	11.6
25-34		5,710	1,058,750	20.0	7,036	106,100	29.0	7,900	36,150	33.6
35-44		6,044	979,600	18.5	7,729	70,100	19.2	9,691	25,450	23.7
45-54		5,533	910,250	17.2	7,641	44,450	12.2	8,986	17,650	16.4
55-64		4,471	699,450	13.2	6,649	20,800	5.7	7,689	9,500	8.8
65 and older		2,225	654,750	12.3	3,330	15,450	4.2	3,650	6,300	5.9
TOTAL	9.7	4,717	5,306,300	100.0	6,100	365,450	100.0	7,895	107,550	100.0
FEMALES:										
18-24		2,318	1,279,200	19.2	2,624	152,450	33.2	4,118	26,500	14.4
25-34		3,318	1,382,800	20.7	4,436	122,700	26.7	5,987	60,900	33.2
35-44		3,329	1,259,250	18.9	4,665	80,750	17.6	6,488	41,050	22.4
45-54		2,941	1,069,350	16.0	4,504	53,900	11.7	6,906	23,050	12.6
55-64		2,264	839,100	12.6	3,682	27,600	6.0	6,098	18,050	9.8
65 and older		1,307	844,750	12.7	1,952	21,650	4.7	3,161	13,950	7.6
TOTAL	10.1	2,662	6,674,450	100.0	3,750	459,050	100.0	5,734	183,500	100.0

(Table 8 continued on page 280)

BLACK AMERICANS—Table 8 (Continued)

AGE AND SEX	Median Yrs. of Edc.	ALL PERSONS			POSTGRADUATE					
					1 Year			2 or More Years		
		Mean Income*	Number of Individuals*	Per-cent	Mean Income*	Number of Individuals*	Per-cent	Mean Income*	Number of Individuals*	Per-cent
ALL INDIVIDUALS:										
18-24		$2,697	2,282,700	19.1	$4,360	4,900	6.1	$3,744	650	0.7
25-34		4,494	2,441,550	20.4	7,457	25,200	31.3	9,231	16,250	17.6
35-44		4,687	2,238,850	18.7	8,911	24,350	31.5	11,297	30,700	33.2
45-54		4,301	1,979,600	16.5	8,845	13,500	16.8	11,437	24,600	26.6
55-64		3,409	1,538,550	12.8	8,242	7,900	9.8	10,457	13,650	14.8
65 and older		1,727	1,499,500	12.5	5,215	3,650	4.5	7,860	6,650	7.2
TOTAL	10.0	3,680	11,980,750	100.0	7,944	80,500	100.0	10,565	92,500	100.0
MALES:										
18-24		3,114	1,003,500	18.9	4,669	1,900	5.3	4,000	200	0.4
25-34		5,710	1,058,750	20.0	8,290	13,300	37.3	10,386	9,000	19.0
35-44		6,044	979,600	18.5	10,224	10,900	30.6	13,364	15,850	33.5
45-54		5,533	910,250	17.2	9,870	5,450	15.3	13,137	12,100	25.6
55-64		4,471	699,450	13.2	9,350	2,700	7.6	12,465	6,350	13.4
65 and older		2,225	654,750	12.3	6,711	1,400	3.9	9,879	3,800	8.0
TOTAL	9.7	4,717	5,306,300	100.0	8,979	35,650	100.0	12,346	47,300	100.0
FEMALES:										
18-24		2,318	1,279,200	19.2	4,173	3,000	6.7	3,712	450	1.0
25-34		3,318	1,382,800	20.7	6,493	11,900	26.5	7,795	7,250	16.0
35-44		3,329	1,259,250	18.9	7,861	14,450	32.2	8,913	14,850	32.9
45-54		2,941	1,069,350	16.0	8,138	8,050	17.9	9,738	12,500	27.7
55-64		2,264	839,100	12.6	7,613	5,200	11.6	8,638	7,300	16.2
65 and older		1,307	844,750	12.7	4,318	2,250	5.0	5,206	2,850	6.3
TOTAL	10.1	2,662	6,674,450	100.0	7,092	44,850	100.0	8,632	45,200	100.0

SOURCE: Compiled from 1970 U.S. Census Public Use Sample.

*Number of individuals includes persons who reported zero income. Mean income is calculated only for persons who reported positive or negative income, excluding those with zero income.

Median age of all Black Americans: 22.3.

Median of all Black American income earners: 40.7.

Table 9
Personal Earnings by Occupation, Education, and Sex (1969)

| | ALL PERSONS | | | PRECOLLEGE | | | | | |
| | | | | 0-8 Years | | | 9-12 Years | | |
OCCUPATIONS	Mean Earnings	Number of Individuals	Per-cent	Mean Earnings	Number of Individuals	Per-cent	Mean Earnings	Number of Individuals	Per-cent
ALL INDIVIDUALS:									
Learned Professions	$11,661	38,900	0.5	$7,314	1,050	0.0	$7,492	6,100	0.1
Other Prof., Tech., etc.	6,378	523,250	7.1	4,099	19,500	0.9	5,000	149,450	3.6
Mgrs., Offs., & Proprietors	7,174	159,250	2.1	5,123	28,200	1.2	6,359	74,750	1.8
Clerical	4,445	930,450	12.6	4,613	57,450	2.5	4,267	659,600	15.8
Craftsmen	5,655	623,850	8.4	5,091	210,700	9.3	5,802	362,900	8.7
Operatives	4,725	1,660,800	22.4	4,520	521,000	23.0	4,750	1,060,450	25.5
Service Workers	3,381	1,388,600	18.7	3,174	453,250	20.0	3,375	845,150	20.3
Private Household	1,284	591,800	8.0	1,183	343,000	15.1	1,421	237,700	5.7
Laborers	4,085	656,300	8.9	3,918	328,850	14.5	4,214	307,500	7.4
Sales	4,046	159,550	2.2	3,448	21,200	0.9	3,753	108,100	2.6
Farmers, Farm Managers	2,074	41,150	0.6	1,840	30,150	1.3	2,659	10,000	0.2
Farm Laborers	1,837	171,250	2.3	1,765	126,150	5.6	1,974	43,150	1.0
Unemployed	2,362	464,250	6.3	2,280	129,000	5.7	2,328	301,400	7.2
TOTAL	4,146	7,409,450	100.0	3,394	2,269,500	100.0	4,064	4,166,250	100.0
MALES:									
Learned Professions	12,326	32,000	0.8	7,380	1,000	0.1	8,277	4,350	0.2
Other Prof., Tech., etc.	7,377	186,200	4.6	4,821	8,500	0.6	6,104	54,300	2.5
Mgrs., Offs., & Proprietors	7,828	114,300	2.8	5,617	21,800	1.5	7,082	51,850	2.4
Clerical	5,805	293,500	7.2	5,284	35,750	2.5	5,627	191,550	8.9
Craftsmen	5,783	579,800	14.3	5,160	200,200	14.0	5,973	333,000	15.4
Operatives	5,443	1,142,750	28.2	5,032	395,250	27.5	5,589	689,950	32.0
Service Workers	4,316	587,150	14.5	3,962	226,150	15.8	4,406	319,450	14.8
Private Household	2,248	17,600	0.4	2,178	10,850	0.8	2,329	6,350	0.3
Laborers	4,181	608,300	15.0	3,974	312,450	21.8	4,361	277,300	12.8
Sales	5,478	79,100	2.0	4,157	12,950	0.9	5,222	46,900	2.2
Farmers, Farm Managers	2,000	35,300	0.9	1,844	27,300	1.9	2,537	7,300	0.3
Farm Laborers	2,021	137,250	3.4	1,912	106,750	7.4	2,314	30,250	1.4
Unemployed	3,115	239,550	5.9	2,973	76,900	5.4	3,097	146,600	6.8
TOTAL	5,079	4,052,600	100.0	4,236	1,434,850	100.0	5,130	2,159,150	100.0
FEMALES:									
Learned Professions	8,579	6,900	0.2	6,000	50	0.0	5,541	1,750	0.1
Other Prof., Tech., etc.	5,826	337,050	10.0	3,541	11,000	1.3	4,370	95,150	4.7
Mgrs., Offs., & Proprietors	5,511	44,950	1.3	3,438	6,400	0.8	4,721	22,900	1.1
Clerical	3,818	636,950	19.0	3,508	21,700	2.6	3,710	468,050	23.3
Craftsmen	3,976	44,250	1.3	3,776	10,500	1.3	3,901	29,900	1.5
Operatives	3,142	518,050	15.4	2,911	125,750	15.1	3,186	370,500	18.5
Service Workers	2,696	801,450	23.9	2,389	227,100	27.2	2,748	525,700	26.2
Private Household	1,254	574,200	17.1	1,150	332,150	39.8	1,396	231,350	11.5
Laborers	2,875	48,050	1.4	2,851	16,400	2.0	2,861	30,200	1.5
Sales	2,639	80,450	2.4	2,336	8,250	1.0	2,627	61,200	3.0
Farmers, Farm Managers	2,521	5,850	0.2	1,804	2,850	0.3	2,987	2,700	0.1
Farm Laborers	1,093	34,000	1.0	1,001	20,400	2.4	1,176	12,900	0.6
Unemployed	1,560	224,700	6.7	1,257	52,100	6.2	1,599	154,800	7.7
TOTAL	3,021	3,356,850	100.0	1,947	834,650	100.0	2,916	2,007,100	100.0

(Table 9 continued on page 282)

BLACK AMERICANS—Table 9 (Continued)

| | ALL PERSONS | | | COLLEGE | | | | | |
| | | | | 1-3 Years | | | 4 Years | | |
OCCUPATIONS	Mean Earnings	Number of Individuals	Per-cent	Mean Earnings	Number of Individuals	Per-cent	Mean Earnings	Number of Individuals	Per-cent
ALL INDIVIDUALS:									
Learned Professions	$11,661	38,900	0.5	$8,737	6,800	1.2	$10,061	7,500	3.2
Other Prof., Tech., etc.	6,378	523,250	7.1	5,879	101,300	17.3	6,870	155,000	65.9
Mgrs., Offs., & Proprietors	7,174	159,250	2.1	7,820	26,800	4.6	9,241	12,600	5.4
Clerical	4,445	930,450	12.6	4,700	180,050	30.7	5,816	25,000	10.6
Craftsmen	5,655	623,850	8.4	6,770	42,550	7.3	7,966	6,350	2.7
Operatives	4,725	1,660,800	22.4	5,751	71,050	12.1	5,679	6,300	2.7
Service Workers	3,381	1,388,600	18.7	4,344	77,800	13.3	5,408	9,200	3.9
Private Household	1,284	591,800	8.0	1,366	9,750	1.7	1,947	1,050	0.4
Laborers	4,085	656,350	8.9	4,749	17,350	3.0	5,851	2,050	0.9
Sales	4,046	159,550	2.2	4,972	23,600	4.0	6,875	4,700	2.0
Farmers, Farm Managers	2,074	41,150	0.6	3,120	750	0.1	3,780	250	0.1
Farm Laborers	1,837	171,250	2.3	2,988	1,350	0.2	4,000	500	0.2
Unemployed	2,362	464,250	6.3	2,816	27,400	4.7	3,607	4,800	2.0
TOTAL	4,146	7,409,450	100.0	5,186	586,550	100.0	6,820	235,300	100.0
MALES:									
Learned Professions	12,326	32,000	0.8	8,987	5,700	2.0	10,447	6,200	6.6
Other Prof., Tech., etc.	7,377	186,200	4.6	7,018	41,600	14.4	8,033	45,500	48.5
Mgrs., Offs., & Proprietors	7,828	114,300	2.8	8,775	18,550	6.4	9,728	9,300	9.9
Clerical	5,805	293,500	7.2	6,217	52,300	18.1	7,416	9,650	10.3
Craftsmen	5,783	579,600	14.3	6,904	39,350	13.6	8,236	5,850	6.2
Operatives	5,443	1,142,750	28.2	6,545	51,250	17.7	6,232	4,900	5.2
Service Workers	4,316	587,150	14.5	5,415	34,300	11.9	6,422	5,150	5.5
Private Household	2,248	17,600	0.4	2,850	400	0.1	—	—	—
Laborers	4,181	608,300	15.0	4,854	16,000	5.5	6,017	1,950	2.1
Sales	5,478	79,100	2.0	6,443	14,500	5.0	8,601	3,200	3.4
Farmers, Farm Managers	2,000	35,300	0.9	2,345	550	0.2	3,000	150	0.2
Farm Laborers	2,021	137,250	3.4	3,988	900	0.3	5,100	300	0.3
Unemployed	3,115	239,550	5.9	3,820	13,750	4.8	4,631	1,750	1.9
TOTAL	5,079	4,052,600	100.0	6,411	289,150	100.0	8,024	93,900	100.0
FEMALES:									
Learned Professions	8,579	6,900	0.2	7,440	1,100	0.4	8,219	1,300	0.9
Other Prof., Tech., etc.	5,826	337,050	10.0	5,086	59,700	20.1	6,387	109,500	77.4
Mgrs., Offs., & Proprietors	5,511	44,950	1.3	5,672	8,250	2.8	7,869	3,300	2.3
Clerical	3,818	636,950	19.0	4,079	127,750	43.0	4,810	15,350	10.9
Craftsmen	3,976	44,250	1.3	5,121	3,200	1.1	4,810	500	0.4
Operatives	3,142	518,050	15.4	3,694	19,800	6.7	3,742	1,400	1.0
Service Workers	2,696	801,450	23.9	3,500	43,500	14.6	4,119	4,050	2.9
Private Household	1,254	574,200	17.1	1,303	9,350	3.1	1,947	1,050	0.7
Laborers	2,875	48,050	1.4	3,500	1,350	0.5	2,600	100	0.1
Sales	2,639	80,450	2.4	2,622	9,100	3.1	3,195	1,500	1.1
Farmers, Farm Managers	2,521	5,850	0.2	5,250	200	0.1	4,950	100	0.1
Farm Laborers	1,093	34,000	1.0	988	450	0.2	2,350	200	0.1
Unemployed	1,560	224,700	6.7	1,805	13,650	4.6	3,020	3,050	2.2
TOTAL	3,021	3,356,850	100.0	3,996	297,400	100.0	6,021	141,400	100.0

| | ALL PERSONS | | | POSTGRADUATE | | | | | |
| | | | | 1 Year | | | 2 or More Years | | |
OCCUPATIONS	Mean Earnings	Number of Indi- viduals	Per- cent	Mean Earnings	Number of Indi- viduals	Per- cent	Mean Earnings	Number of Indi- viduals	Per- cent
ALL INDIVIDUALS:									
Learned Professions	$11,661	38,900	0.5	$10,386	4,300	6.2	$16,784	13,150	15.9
Other Prof., Tech., etc.	6,378	523,250	7.1	8,038	48,050	69.3	9,276	49,950	60.5
Mgrs., Offs., & Proprietors	7,174	159,250	2.1	10,650	6,400	9.2	12,242	10,500	12.7
Clerical	4,445	930,450	12.6	6,752	4,400	6.3	8,865	3,950	4.8
Craftsmen	5,655	623,850	8.4	8,407	650	0.9	8,135	700	0.8
Operatives	4,725	1,660,800	22.4	6,179	1,200	1.7	5,556	800	1.0
Service Workers	3,381	1,388,600	18.7	5,027	1,850	2.7	5,470	1,350	1.6
Private Household	1,284	591,800	8.0	400	150	0.2	5,500	150	0.2
Laborers	4,085	656,350	8.9	5,022	450	0.6	2,366	150	0.2
Sales	4,046	159,550	2.2	6,972	900	1.3	10,328	1,050	1.3
Farmers, Farm Managers	2,074	41,150	0.6	–	–	–	–	–	–
Farm Laborers	1,837	171,250	2.3	12,900	50	0.1	700	50	0.1
Unemployed	2,362	464,250	6.3	3,644	900	1.3	4,320	750	0.9
TOTAL	4,146	7,409,450	100.0	8,131	69,300	100.0	10,666	82,550	100.0
MALES:									
Learned Professions	12,326	32,000	0.8	10,726	3,700	11.7	17,679	11,050	25.2
Other Prof., Tech., etc.	7,377	186,200	4.6	8,782	17,000	53.5	10,076	19,300	44.1
Mgrs., Offs., & Proprietors	7,828	114,300	2.8	11,021	4,950	15.6	12,396	7,850	17.9
Clerical	5,805	293,500	7.2	7,591	2,250	7.1	11,660	2,000	4.6
Craftsmen	5,783	579,600	14.3	8,618	550	1.7	8,530	650	1.5
Operatives	5,443	1,142,760	20.2	7,243	800	2.5	5,808	600	1.4
Service Workers	4,316	587,150	14.5	5,872	1,100	3.5	5,570	1,000	2.3
Private Household	2,248	17,600	0.4	–	–	–	–	–	–
Laborers	4,181	608,300	15.0	5,022	450	1.4	2,366	150	0.3
Sales	5,478	79,100	2.0	6,669	650	2.0	10,216	900	2.1
Farmers, Farm Managers	2,000	35,300	0.9	–	–	–	–	–	–
Farm Laborers	2,021	137,250	3.4	–	–	–	700	50	0.1
Unemployed	3,115	239,550	5.9	6,166	300	0.9	4,280	250	0.6
TOTAL	5,079	4,052,600	100.0	9,009	31,750	100.0	12,231	43,800	100.0
FEMALES:									
Learned Professions	8,579	6,900	0.2	8,291	600	1.6	12,073	2,100	5.4
Other Prof., Tech., etc.	5,826	337,050	10.0	7,631	31,050	82.7	8,772	30,650	79.1
Mgrs., Offs., & Proprietors	5,511	44,950	1.3	9,386	1,450	3.9	11,788	2,650	6.8
Clerical	3,818	636,950	19.0	5,874	2,150	5.7	6,000	1,950	5.0
Craftsmen	3,976	44,250	1.3	7,250	100	0.3	3,000	50	0.1
Operatives	3,142	518,050	15.4	4,050	400	1.1	4,800	200	0.5
Service Workers	2,696	801,450	23.9	3,786	750	2.0	5,185	350	0.9
Private Household	1,254	574,200	17.1	400	150	0.4	5,500	150	0.4
Laborers	2,875	48,050	1.4	–	–	–	–	–	–
Sales	2,639	80,450	2.4	7,760	250	0.7	11,000	150	0.4
Farmers, Farm Managers	2,521	5,850	0.2	–	–	–	–	–	–
Farm Laborers	1,093	34,000	1.0	12,900	50	0.1	–	–	–
Unemployed	1,560	224,700	6.7	2,383	600	1.6	4,340	500	1.3
TOTAL	3,021	3,356,850	100.0	7,388	37,550	100.0	8,896	38,750	100.0

SOURCE: Compiled from 1970 U.S. Census Public Use Sample.

NOTE: Median years of education: 10.4.

BLACK AMERICANS

Table 10
Family Income Distribution by Number of
Income Earners per Family (1969)

INCOME	ALL FAMILIES		NO-EARNER FAMILIES		ONE-EARNER FAMILIES		TWO-EARNER FAMILIES		THREE OR MORE EARNER FAMILIES	
	Number of Families	Percent	Number of Families	Percent	Number of Families	Percent	Number of Families	Percent	Number of Families	Percent
UNDER $ 1,000	336,750	7.2	195,600	31.9	114,500	6.8	23,200	1.3	3,450	0.6
$ 1,000 - $ 1,999	406,150	8.7	163,300	26.7	177,300	10.5	56,750	3.1	8,800	1.5
$ 2,000 - $ 2,999	433,000	9.2	127,950	20.9	203,800	12.1	85,350	4.7	15,900	2.7
$ 3,000 - $ 3,999	429,300	9.2	71,250	11.6	224,100	13.3	111,650	6.2	22,300	3.8
$ 4,000 - $ 4,999	395,450	8.4	29,800	4.9	203,200	12.0	134,400	7.5	28,050	4.8
$ 5,000 - $ 5,999	386,800	8.3	12,300	2.0	187,650	11.1	153,850	8.5	33,000	5.7
$ 6,000 - $ 6,999	361,400	7.7	5,150	0.8	162,000	9.6	157,000	8.7	37,250	6.4
$ 7,000 - $ 7,999	331,750	7.1	3,300	0.5	133,900	7.9	156,150	8.7	38,400	6.6
$ 8,000 - $ 9,999	530,300	11.3	2,450	0.4	160,150	9.5	286,950	15.9	80,750	13.9
$10,000 - $12,999	528,050	11.3	1,050	0.2	85,000	5.0	329,550	18.3	112,450	19.3
$13,000 - $14,999	210,050	4.5	300	0.0	16,000	0.9	137,350	7.6	56,400	9.7
$15,000 - $19,999	230,400	4.9	100	0.0	13,800	0.8	125,500	7.0	91,000	15.6
$20,000 - $24,999	69,500	1.5	–		4,350	0.3	30,050	1.7	35,100	6.0
$25,000 OR MORE	39,250	0.8	100	0.0	4,650	0.3	15,650	0.9	18,850	3.2
TOTAL	4,688,150	100.0	612,650	100.0	1,690,400	100.0	1,803,400	100.0	581,700	100.0
MEAN EARNINGS	$6,812		$1,830		$4,993		$8,703		$11,481	
MEDIAN INCOME	5,888		1,678		4,618		8,163		10,612	

SOURCE: Compiled from 1970 U.S. Census, Public Use Sample.

284

BLACK AMERICANS

Table 11
Family Income by Age, Education, and Sex of Family Head (1969)

AGE AND SEX OF FAMILY HEAD	ALL PERSONS				PRECOLLEGE					
					0-8 Years			9-12 Years		
	Median Yrs. of Educ.	Mean Income	Number of Indi-viduals	Per-cent	Mean Income	Number of Indi-viduals	Per-cent	Mean Income	Number of Indi-viduals	Per-cent
ALL INDIVIDUALS:										
18-24		$4,629	390,750	8.3	$3,219	54,050	2.8	$4,639	297,550	13.1
25-34		6,451	1,072,450	22.9	4,359	183,350	9.3	6,252	740,600	32.7
35-44		7,161	1,073,750	22.9	5,548	356,100	18.1	7,175	589,900	26.1
45-54		7,473	918,500	19.6	6,049	462,400	23.5	8,137	376,800	16.6
55-64		6,099	669,050	14.3	5,189	452,450	23.0	7,290	176,000	7.8
65 and older		2,696	563,650	12.0	2,376	456,750	23.2	3,666	82,800	3.7
TOTAL	9.7	6,160	4,688,150	100.0	4,671	1,965,100	100.0	6,580	2,263,650	100.0
MALES:										
18-24		5,928	262,250	7.8	4,440	33,900	2.3	5,994	197,150	12.7
25-34		8,208	742,100	22.0	5,748	123,800	8.5	8,107	499,350	32.3
35-44		8,804	747,500	22.2	6,790	256,700	17.6	9,047	391,200	25.3
45-54		8,566	691,300	20.5	6,938	353,150	24.2	9,452	274,350	17.7
55-64		6,778	516,600	15.3	5,761	355,300	24.3	8,221	129,100	8.3
65 and older		2,693	411,850	12.2	2,364	337,900	23.1	3,660	56,000	3.6
TOTAL	9.6	7,343	3,371,600	100.0	5,409	1,460,750	100.0	8,162	1,547,150	100.0
FEMALES:										
18-24		1,977	128,500	9.8	1,166	20,150	4.0	1,977	100,400	14.0
25-34		2,503	330,350	25.1	1,471	59,550	11.8	2,413	241,250	33.7
35-44		3,397	326,250	24.8	2,341	99,400	19.7	3,489	198,700	27.7
45-54		4,146	227,200	17.3	3,176	109,250	21.7	4,617	102,450	14.3
55-64		3,801	152,450	11.6	3,098	97,150	19.3	4,728	46,900	6.5
65 and older		2,707	151,800	11.5	2,410	118,890	23.6	3,679	26,800	3.7
TOTAL	9.9	3,131	1,316,550	100.0	2,534	504,350	100.0	3,165	716,500	100.0

(Table 11 continued on page 286)

285

BLACK AMERICANS—Table 11 (Continued)

AGE AND SEX OF FAMILY HEAD	ALL PERSONS				COLLEGE					
					1-3 Years			4 Years		
	Median Yrs. of Educ.	Mean Income	Number of Individuals	Per-cent	Mean Income	Number of Individuals	Per-cent	Mean Income	Number of Individuals	Per-cent
ALL INDIVIDUALS:										
18-24		$4,629	390,750	8.3	$6,171	32,650	11.6	$7,931	5,400	5.5
25-34		6,451	1,072,450	22.9	9,167	97,350	34.6	11,270	32,000	32.7
35-44		7,161	1,073,750	22.9	9,791	73,730	26.2	12,407	26,550	27.1
45-54		7,473	918,500	19.6	10,662	44,050	15.7	13,253	17,100	17.5
55-64		6,099	669,050	14.3	9,131	20,700	7.4	10,988	10,200	10.4
65 and older		2,696	563,650	12.0	4,161	12,700	4.5	4,895	6,700	6.8
TOTAL	9.7	6,160	4,688,150	100.0	8,988	281,200	100.0	11,275	97,950	100.0
MALES:										
18-24		5,928	262,250	7.8	6,820	25,650	11.7	8,305	4,600	5.9
25-34		8,208	742,100	22.0	10,485	75,950	34.8	12,167	26,450	33.9
35-44		8,804	747,500	22.2	11,151	55,950	25.6	13,921	20,750	26.6
45-54		8,566	691,300	20.5	11,724	35,000	16.0	14,227	13,900	17.8
55-64		6,778	516,600	15.3	10,262	16,350	7.5	11,808	7,800	10.0
65 and older		2,693	411,850	12.2	4,531	9,650	4.4	4,880	4,450	5.7
TOTAL	9.6	7,343	3,371,600	100.0	10,144	218,550	100.0	12,321	77,950	100.0
FEMALES:										
18-24		1,977	128,500	9.8	3,795	7,000	11.2	5,778	800	4.0
25-34		2,503	330,350	25.1	4,491	21,400	34.2	6,995	5,550	27.7
35-44		3,397	326,250	24.8	5,515	17,800	28.4	6,991	5,800	29.0
45-54		4,146	227,200	17.3	6,557	9,050	14.4	9,024	3,200	16.0
55-64		3,801	152,450	11.6	4,883	4,350	6.9	8,322	2,400	12.0
65 and older		2,707	151,800	11.5	2,990	3,050	4.9	4,925	2,250	11.2
TOTAL	9.9	3,131	1,316,550	100.0	4,957	62,650	100.0	7,196	20,000	100.0

BLACK AMERICANS—Table 11 (Continued)

AGE AND SEX OF FAMILY HEAD	ALL PERSONS				POSTGRADUATE					
					1 Year			2 or More Years		
	Median Yrs. of Educ.	Mean Income	Number of Individuals	Per-cent	Mean Income	Number of Individuals	Per-cent	Mean Income	Number of Individuals	Per-cent
ALL INDIVIDUALS:										
18-24		$4,629	390,750	8.3	$9,185	1,050	3.0	$6,800	50	0.1
25-34		6,451	1,072,450	22.9	11,331	11,450	33.2	13,749	7,700	16.8
35-44		7,161	1,073,750	22.9	14,217	11,250	32.6	16,663	16,200	35.4
45-54		7,473	918,500	19.6	14,225	6,300	18.3	18,079	11,850	25.9
55-64		6,099	669,050	14.3	13,142	2,850	8.3	16,243	6,850	15.0
65 and older		2,696	563,650	12.0	7,493	1,600	4.6	10,754	3,100	6.8
TOTAL	9.7	6,160	4,688,150	100.0	12,707	34,500	100.0	16,065	45,750	100.0
MALES:										
18-24		5,928	262,250	7.8	9,761	900	3.2	6,800	50	0.1
25-34		8,208	742,100	22.0	12,088	9,600	34.3	14,019	6,950	17.7
35-44		8,804	747,500	22.2	15,510	9,150	32.7	17,771	13,750	35.1
45-54		8,566	691,300	20.5	15,678	4,850	17.3	19,308	10,050	25.6
55-64		6,778	516,600	15.3	13,777	2,400	8.6	17,719	5,650	14.4
65 and older		2,693	411,850	12.2	8,259	1,100	3.9	11,106	2,750	7.0
TOTAL	9.6	7,343	3,371,600	100.0	13,748	28,000	100.0	17,011	39,200	100.0
FEMALES:										
18-24		1,977	128,500	9.8	5,733	150	2.3	—	—	—
25-34		2,503	330,350	25.1	7,400	1,850	28.5	11,243	750	11.5
35-44		3,397	326,250	24.8	8,580	2,100	32.3	10,441	2,450	37.4
45-54		4,146	227,200	17.3	9,365	1,450	22.3	11,215	1,800	27.5
55-64		3,801	152,450	11.6	9,755	450	6.9	9,295	1,200	18.3
65 and older		2,707	151,800	11.5	5,810	500	7.7	7,985	350	5.3
TOTAL	9.9	3,131	1,316,550	100.0	8,222	6,500	100.0	10,404	6,550	100.0

SOURCE: Compiled from 1970 U.S. Census Public Use Sample.

NOTE: Median age of all family heads: 43.2.

287

BLACK AMERICANS

Table 12
Family Earnings by Number of Income Earners,
Education, and Sex of Family Head (1969)

	NUMBER OF INCOME EARNERS			PRECOLLEGE					
				0-8 Years			9-12 Years		
	Mean Family Earnings	Number of Families	Percent of all Families	Mean Family Earnings	Number of Families	Percent of all Families	Mean Family Earnings	Number of Families	Percent of all Families
ALL FAMILIES:									
No Income-Earners	$ 0	612,650	13.1	$ 0	347,500	17.7	$ 0	246,250	10.9
One Income-Earner	4,377	1,690,400	36.1	3,437	697,700	35.5	4,661	843,350	37.3
Two Income-Earners	8,369	1,803,400	38.5	6,411	633,750	32.3	8,692	927,450	41.0
Three or More Earners	10,983	581,700	12.4	9,501	286,150	14.6	11,776	246,600	10.9
TOTAL	6,160	4,688,150	100.0	4,671	1,965,100	100.0	6,580	2,263,650	100.0
MALE-HEADED FAMILIES:									
No Income-Earners	0	258,650	7.7	0	195,950	13.4	0	54,350	3.5
One Income-Earner	5,149	1,094,000	32.4	3,949	498,650	34.1	5,769	502,800	32.5
Two Income-Earners	8,824	1,554,000	46.1	6,775	532,650	36.5	9,149	800,150	51.7
Three or More Earners	11,642	464,950	13.8	9,951	233,500	16.0	12,679	189,850	12.3
TOTAL	7,343	3,371,600	100.0	5,409	1,460,750	100.0	8,162	1,547,150	100.0
FEMALE-HEADED FAMILIES:									
No Income-Earners	0	354,000	26.9	0	151,550	30.0	0	191,900	26.8
One Income-Earner	2,961	596,400	45.3	2,152	199,050	39.5	3,024	340,550	47.5
Two Income-Earners	5,532	249,400	18.9	4,497	101,100	20.0	5,819	127,300	17.8
Three or More Earners	8,363	116,750	8.9	7,506	52,650	10.4	8,756	56,750	7.9
TOTAL	3,131	1,316,550	100.0	2,534	504,350	100.0	3,165	716,500	100.0

	NUMBER OF INCOME EARNERS			COLLEGE					
				1-3 Years			4 Years		
	Mean Family Earnings	Number of Families	Percent of all Families	Mean Family Earnings	Number of Families	Percent of all Families	Mean Family Earnings	Number of Families	Percent of all Families
ALL FAMILIES:									
No Income-Earners	$ 0	612,650	13.1	$ 0	13,950	5.0	$ 0	3,300	3.4
One Income-Earner	4,377	1,690,400	36.1	6,129	96,100	34.2	7,732	29,800	30.4
Two Income-Earners	8,369	1,803,400	38.5	10,765	141,750	50.4	12,933	54,450	55.6
Three or More Earners	10,983	581,700	12.4	14,032	29,400	10.5	16,324	10,400	10.6
TOTAL	6,160	4,688,150	100.0	8,988	281,200	100.0	11,275	97,950	100.0
MALE-HEADED FAMILIES:									
No Income-Earners	0	258,650	7.7	0	5,450	2.5	0	1,800	2.3
One Income-Earner	5,149	1,094,000	32.4	7,120	59,150	27.1	8,734	18,150	23.3
Two Income-Earners	8,824	1,554,000	46.1	11,087	128,950	59.0	13,245	49,600	63.6
Three or More Earners	11,642	464,950	13.8	14,648	25,000	11.4	17,259	8,400	10.8
TOTAL	7,343	3,371,600	100.0	10,144	218,550	100.0	12,321	77,950	100.0
FEMALE-HEADED FAMILIES:									
No Income-Earners	0	354,000	26.9	0	8,500	13.6	0	1,500	7.5
One Income-Earner	2,961	596,400	45.3	4,543	36,950	59.0	6,171	11,650	58.2
Two Income-Earners	5,532	249,400	18.9	7,527	12,800	20.4	9,740	4,850	24.2
Three or More Earners	8,363	116,750	8.9	10,533	4,400	7.0	12,400	2,000	10.0
TOTAL	3,131	1,316,550	100.0	4,957	62,650	100.0	7,196	20,000	100.0

(Table 12 continued on page 290)

NUMBER OF INCOME EARNERS			POSTGRADUATE					
			1 Year			2 or More Years		
	Mean Family Earnings	Number of Families	Percent of all Families	Mean Family Earnings	Number of Families	Percent of all Families	Mean Family Earnings	Number of Families	Percent of all Families
ALL FAMILIES:								
No Income-Earners	$ 0	612,650	13.1	$ 0	700	2.0	$ 0	950	2.1
One Income-Earner	4,377	1,690,400	36.1	8,416	9,500	27.5	12,282	13,950	30.5
Two Income-Earners	8,369	1,803,400	38.5	14,265	20,800	60.3	17,510	25,200	55.1
Three or More Earners	10,983	581,700	12.4	17,630	3,500	10.1	21,663	5,650	12.3
TOTAL	6,160	4,688,150	100.0	12,707	34,500	100.0	16,065	45,750	100.0
MALE-HEADED FAMILIES:								
No Income-Earners	0	258,650	7.7	0	400	1.4	0	700	1.8
One Income-Earner	5,149	1,094,000	32.4	9,443	5,300	18.9	13,427	9,950	25.4
Two Income-Earners	8,824	1,554,000	46.1	14,501	19,300	68.9	17,871	23,350	59.6
Three or More Earners	11,642	464,950	13.8	18,338	3,000	10.7	22,296	5,200	13.3
TOTAL	7,343	3,371,600	100.0	13,748	28,000	100.0	17,011	39,200	100.0
FEMALE-HEADED FAMILIES:								
No Income-Earners	0	354,000	26.9	0	300	4.6	0	250	3.8
One Income-Earner	2,961	596,400	45.3	7,121	4,200	64.6	9,433	4,000	61.1
Two Income-Earners	5,532	249,400	18.9	11,230	1,500	23.1	12,954	1,850	28.2
Three or More Earners	8,363	116,750	8.9	13,380	500	7.7	14,344	450	6.9
TOTAL	3,131	1,316,550	100.0	8,222	6,500	100.0	10,404	6,550	100.0

SOURCE: Compiled from 1970 U.S. Census Public Use Sample.

NOTE: Median years of education of family heads: 9.7

Table 13
Fertility Rates by Woman's Education and Family Income (1969)

13a. EDUCATION

	TOTAL		PRECOLLEGE				COLLEGE				POSTGRADUATE			
			0-8 Years		9-12 Years		1-3 Years		4 Years		1 Year		2 or More Years	
	Number	Percent	Number	Percent	Number	Percent	Number	Percent	Number	Percent	Number	Percent	Number	Percent
All Women, 15 and older:														
Childless	2,359,900	31.9	708,950	27.9	1,368,150	33.1	176,600	38.4	71,450	38.9	16,650	37.1	18,100	40.0
1 Child	1,302,650	17.6	401,100	15.8	736,500	17.8	102,750	22.4	41,450	22.6	9,850	22.0	10,400	23.0
2 Children	1,029,550	13.9	302,550	11.9	606,400	14.7	69,700	15.2	33,000	18.0	9,000	20.1	8,900	19.7
3 Children	755,350	10.2	239,350	9.4	444,650	10.8	43,700	9.5	18,550	10.1	5,050	11.3	4,050	9.0
4 Children	560,400	7.6	198,700	7.8	321,850	7.8	26,200	5.7	9,350	5.1	2,350	5.2	1,950	4.3
5 Children	404,350	5.5	154,300	6.1	224,900	5.4	18,150	3.9	5,150	2.8	1,100	2.5	850	1.9
6 or More	992,600	13.4	536,950	21.1	426,700	10.3	22,600	4.9	4,550	2.5	850	1.9	950	2.1
TOTAL	7,404,800	100.0	2,542,400	100.0	4,129,150	100.0	459,700	100.0	183,500	100.0	44,850	100.0	45,200	100.0
Mean No. of Children	2.4		3.1		2.2		1.6		1.4		1.4		1.3	
Women, 15-24:														
Childless	1,242,800	61.8	219,100	66.7	901,250	60.2	1C1,300	66.2	18,700	70.6	2,200	73.3	250	55.6
1 Child	408,700	20.3	47,000	14.3	316,250	21.1	39,350	25.7	5,450	20.6	450	15.0	200	44.4
2 Children	208,900	10.4	27,950	8.5	169,450	11.3	9,450	6.2	1,850	7.0	200	6.7	—	—
3 Children	91,650	4.6	17,000	5.2	71,850	4.8	2,300	1.5	350	1.3	150	5.0	—	—
4 Children	35,300	1.8	9,600	2.9	25,250	1.7	400	0.3	50	0.2	—	—	—	—
5 Children	14,050	0.7	3,850	1.2	10,000	0.7	200	0.1	—	—	—	—	—	—
6 or More	8,150	0.4	3,750	1.1	4,200	0.3	100	0.1	100	0.4	—	—	—	—
TOTAL	2,009,550	100.0	328,250	100.0	1,498,250	100.0	153,100	100.0	26,500	100.0	3,000	100.0	450	100.0
Mean No. of Children	0.7		0.7		0.7		0.4		0.4		0.4		0.4	

(Table 13 continued on page 292)

291

BLACK AMERICANS—Table 13: Education (Continued)

| | TOTAL | | PRECOLLEGE | | | | COLLEGE | | | | POSTGRADUATE | | | |
| | | | 0-8 Years | | 9-12 Years | | 1-3 Years | | 4 Years | | 1 Year | | 2 or More Years | |
	Number	Percent	Number	Percent	Number	Percent	Number	Percent	Number	Percent	Number	Percent	Number	Percent
Women, 25-34:														
Childless	220,150	15.9	31,300	14.9	130,300	13.4	28,550	23.3	21,850	35.9	4,900	41.2	3,250	44.8
1 Child	239,350	17.3	28,150	13.4	156,550	16.1	31,700	25.8	17,800	29.2	3,600	30.3	1,550	21.4
2 Children	267,700	19.4	28,100	13.4	195,300	20.1	28,500	23.2	12,250	20.1	2,050	17.2	1,500	20.7
3 Children	217,550	15.7	27,900	13.3	166,050	17.1	16,200	13.2	5,850	9.6	900	7.6	650	9.0
4 Children	164,400	11.9	25,500	12.1	128,400	13.2	8,200	6.7	1,850	3.0	200	1.7	250	3.4
5 Children	114,250	8.3	22,450	10.7	85,300	8.8	5,400	4.4	950	1.6	100	0.8	50	0.7
6 or More	159,400	11.5	46,900	22.3	107,850	11.1	4,150	3.4	350	0.6	150	1.3	–	–
TOTAL	1,382,800	100.0	210,300	100.0	969,750	100.0	122,700	100.0	60,900	100.0	11,900	100.0	7,250	100.0
Mean No. of Children	2.7		3.5		2.8		1.8		1.2		1.1		1.1	
Women, 35-44:														
Childless	177,650	14.1	50,400	14.4	98,350	13.0	13,100	16.2	8,300	20.2	3,250	22.5	4,250	28.6
1 Child	168,450	13.4	41,700	11.9	99,150	13.1	12,850	15.9	8,150	19.9	3,050	21.1	3,550	23.9
2 Children	180,000	14.3	37,650	10.8	109,150	14.4	16,250	20.1	9,700	23.6	3,650	25.3	3,600	24.2
3 Children	165,500	13.1	33,050	9.4	108,300	14.3	13,100	16.2	7,000	17.1	2,200	15.2	1,850	12.5
4 Children	140,850	11.2	32,550	9.3	92,150	12.2	9,650	12.0	4,300	10.5	1,300	9.0	900	6.1
5 Children	116,300	9.2	29,500	8.4	76,750	10.1	6,800	8.4	2,200	5.4	700	4.8	350	2.4
6 or More	310,500	24.7	125,000	35.7	174,450	23.0	9,000	11.1	1,400	3.4	300	2.1	350	2.4
TOTAL	1,259,250	100.0	349,850	100.0	758,300	100.0	80,750	100.0	41,050	100.0	14,450	100.0	14,850	100.0
Mean No. of Children	3.7		4.5		3.6		2.7		2.1		1.9		1.6	

BLACK AMERICANS—Table 13: Education (Continued)

| | TOTAL | | PRECOLLEGE | | | | COLLEGE | | | | POSTGRADUATE | | | |
| | | | 0-8 Years | | 9-12 Years | | 1-3 Years | | 4 Years | | 1 Year | | 2 or More Years | |
	Number	Percent	Number	Percent	Number	Percent	Number	Percent	Number	Percent	Number	Percent	Number	Percent
Women, 45 and older:														
Childless	719,300	26.1	408,150	24.7	238,250	26.4	33,650	32.6	22,600	41.1	6,300	40.6	10,350	45.7
1 Child	486,150	17.7	284,850	17.2	164,550	18.2	18,850	18.3	10,050	18.3	2,750	17.7	5,100	22.5
2 Children	372,950	13.5	208,850	12.6	132,500	14.7	15,500	15.0	9,200	16.7	3,100	20.0	3,800	16.8
3 Children	280,650	10.2	161,400	9.8	98,450	10.9	12,100	11.7	5,350	9.7	1,800	11.6	1,550	6.8
4 Children	219,850	8.0	131,050	7.9	76,050	8.4	7,950	7.7	3,150	5.7	850	5.5	800	3.5
5 Children	159,750	5.8	98,400	5.9	52,850	5.9	5,750	5.6	2,000	3.6	300	1.9	450	2.0
6 or More	514,550	18.7	361,300	21.8	140,200	15.5	9,350	9.1	2,700	4.9	400	2.6	600	2.6
TOTAL	2,753,200	100.0	1,654,000	100.0	902,850	100.0	103,150	100.0	55,050	100.0	15,500	100.0	22,650	100.0
Mean No. of Children	2.9		3.2		2.7		2.1		1.6		1.4		1.2	

13b. FAMILY INCOME

| | TOTAL | | Less Than $5,000 | | $5,000 - 9,999 | | $10,000 - 14,999 | | $15,000 - 19,999 | | $20,000 - 24,999 | | $25,000 and Over | |
	Number	Percent	Number	Percent	Number	Percent	Number	Percent	Number	Percent	Number	Percent	Number	Percent
All Women, 15 and older:														
Childless	2,359,900	31.9	1,131,450	32.1	673,500	30.1	350,650	32.6	132,350	35.4	44,100	36.8	27,850	35.7
1 Child	1,302,650	17.6	610,600	17.3	393,850	17.6	192,200	17.9	68,550	18.4	22,900	19.1	14,550	18.7
2 Children	1,029,550	13.9	459,600	13.0	322,550	14.4	162,850	15.2	54,150	14.5	17,150	14.3	13,250	17.0
3 Children	755,350	10.2	339,300	9.6	238,050	10.6	118,250	11.0	40,400	10.8	12,150	10.1	7,200	9.2
4 Children	560,400	7.6	260,050	7.4	178,450	8.0	82,050	7.6	27,100	7.3	8,000	6.7	4,750	6.1
5 Children	404,350	5.5	192,950	5.5	130,550	5.8	56,350	5.2	15,550	4.2	5,050	4.2	3,900	5.0
6 or More	992,600	13.4	529,700	15.0	298,700	13.4	112,050	10.4	35,250	9.4	10,400	8.7	6,500	8.3
TOTAL	7,404,800	100.0	3,523,650	100.0	2,235,650	100.0	1,074,400	100.0	373,350	100.0	119,750	100.0	78,000	100.0
Mean No. of Children	2.4		2.5		2.5		2.2		2.0		1.9		2.0	

(Table 13 continued on page 294)

293

BLACK AMERICANS—Table 13: Family Income (Continued)

	TOTAL		Less Than $5,000		$5,000 - 9,999		$10,000 - 14,999		$15,000 - 19,999		$20,000 - 24,999		$25,000 and Over	
	Number	Percent	Number	Percent	Number	Percent	Number	Percent	Number	Percent	Number	Percent	Number	Percent
Women, 15-24:														
Childless	1,242,800	61.8	482,850	58.1	418,450	60.5	217,700	68.0	82,250	74.9	26,400	73.7	15,150	72.7
1 Child	408,700	20.3	170,150	20.5	146,900	21.2	62,900	19.6	18,400	16.8	6,700	18.7	3,650	17.5
2 Children	208,900	10.4	96,200	11.6	76,950	11.1	26,250	8.2	5,950	5.4	1,950	5.4	1,600	7.7
3 Children	91,650	4.6	47,450	5.7	31,600	4.6	9,200	2.9	2,650	2.4	500	1.4	250	1.2
4 Children	35,300	1.8	20,200	2.4	11,900	1.7	2,450	0.8	300	0.3	250	0.7	200	1.0
5 Children	14,050	0.7	8,650	1.0	4,250	0.6	950	0.3	200	0.2	–	–	–	–
6 or More	8,150	0.4	5,350	0.6	2,000	0.3	750	0.2	50	0	–	–	–	–
TOTAL	2,009,550	100.0	830,850	100.0	692,050	100.0	320,200	100.0	109,800	100.0	35,800	100.0	20,850	100.0
Mean No. of Children	0.7		0.8		0.7		0.5		0.4		0.4		0.4	
Women, 25-34:														
Childless	220,150	15.9	84,400	15.5	63,050	13.2	46,100	18.3	17,450	23.1	5,600	28.7	3,550	30.0
1 Child	239,350	17.3	76,750	14.1	82,150	17.2	52,800	20.9	20,150	26.6	4,700	24.1	2,800	23.6
2 Children	267,700	19.4	89,350	16.4	98,600	20.6	56,200	22.3	17,200	22.7	3,950	20.3	2,400	20.3
3 Children	217,550	15.7	82,150	15.1	80,150	16.8	40,150	15.9	10,700	14.1	2,950	15.1	1,450	12.2
4 Children	164,400	11.9	70,650	13.0	61,100	12.8	25,650	10.2	5,300	7.0	1,100	5.6	600	5.1
5 Children	114,250	8.3	53,850	9.9	40,500	8.5	16,250	6.4	2,200	2.9	750	3.8	700	5.9
6 or More	159,400	11.5	87,950	16.1	52,800	11.0	15,150	6.0	2,700	3.6	450	2.3	350	3.0
TOTAL	1,382,800	100.0	545,100	100.0	478,350	100.0	252,300	100.0	75,700	100.0	19,500	100.0	11,850	100.0
Mean No. of Children	2.7		3.1		2.8		2.3		1.8		1.7		1.7	

BLACK AMERICANS—Table 13: Family Income (Continued)

	TOTAL		Less Than $5,000		$5,000 - 9,999		$10,000 - 14,999		$15,000 - 19,999		$20,000 - 24,999		$25,000 and Over	
	Number	Percent	Number	Percent	Number	Percent	Number	Percent	Number	Percent	Number	Percent	Number	Percent
Women, 35-44:														
Childless	177,650	14.1	81,250	16.1	49,200	11.9	28,850	13.5	11,550	14.1	4,000	15.3	2,800	15.9
1 Child	168,450	13.4	66,050	13.1	53,300	12.9	29,200	13.6	12,250	14.9	4,500	17.2	3,150	17.9
2 Children	180,000	14.3	61,800	12.2	58,450	14.1	36,100	16.8	14,700	17.9	5,150	19.7	3,800	21.6
3 Children	165,500	13.1	57,200	11.3	54,450	13.2	33,200	15.5	13,800	16.8	4,500	17.2	2,350	13.4
4 Children	140,850	11.2	49,450	9.8	48,750	11.8	26,600	12.4	10,350	12.6	3,400	13.0	2,300	13.1
5 Children	116,300	9.2	45,600	9.0	41,850	10.1	19,350	9.0	6,450	7.8	1,700	6.5	1,350	7.7
6 or More	310,500	24.7	143,700	28.5	107,950	26.1	41,000	19.1	13,100	15.9	2,900	11.1	1,850	10.5
TOTAL	1,259,250	100.0	505,050	100.0	413,950	100.0	214,300	100.0	82,200	100.0	26,150	100.0	17,600	100.0
Mean No. of Children	3.7		3.9		3.9		3.4		3.1		2.8		2.8	
Women, 45 and older:														
Childless	719,300	26.1	482,950	29.4	142,800	21.9	58,000	20.2	21,100	20.0	8,100	21.1	6,350	22.9
1 Child	486,150	17.7	297,650	18.1	111,500	17.1	47,300	16.4	17,750	16.8	7,000	18.3	4,950	17.9
2 Children	372,950	13.5	212,250	12.9	88,550	13.6	44,300	15.4	16,300	15.4	6,100	15.9	5,450	19.7
3 Children	280,650	10.2	152,500	9.3	71,850	11.0	35,700	12.4	13,250	12.5	4,200	11.0	3,150	11.4
4 Children	219,850	8.0	119,750	7.3	56,700	8.7	27,350	9.5	11,150	10.6	3,250	8.5	1,650	6.0
5 Children	159,750	5.8	84,850	5.2	43,950	6.7	19,800	6.9	6,700	6.3	2,600	6.8	1,850	6.7
6 or More	514,550	18.7	292,700	17.8	135,950	20.9	55,150	19.2	19,400	18.4	7,050	18.4	4,300	15.5
TOTAL	2,753,200	100.0	1,642,650	100.0	651,300	100.0	287,600	100.0	105,650	100.0	38,300	100.0	27,700	100.0
Mean No. of Children	2.9		2.8		3.2		3.1		3.1		3.0		2.7	

SOURCE: Compiled from 1970 U.S. Census Public Use Sample.

295

CHINESE AMERICANS

Table 14

Personal Income by Age, Education, and Sex (1969)

| AGE AND SEX | Median Yrs. of Educ. | ALL PERSONS | | | PRECOLLEGE | | | | | |
| | | Mean Income* | Number of Indi- viduals* | Per- cent | 0-8 Years | | | 9-12 Years | | |
					Mean Income*	Number of Indi- viduals*	Per- cent	Mean Income*	Number of Indi- viduals*	Per- cent
ALL INDIVIDUALS:										
18-24		$2,499	54,400	18.9	$1,991	2,700	3.6	$2,601	23,600	24.0
25-34		6,506	66,900	23.3	3,820	5,850	7.7	5,470	19,400	19.7
35-44		7,931	61,150	21.3	4,138	14,700	19.4	6,770	23,400	23.8
45-54		8,274	44,400	15.4	4,897	15,200	20.1	7,543	17,200	17.5
55-64		6,351	31,450	10.9	4,183	16,900	22.3	6,512	8,900	9.0
65 and older		2,646	29,200	10.2	2,080	20,450	27.0	3,448	5,850	5.9
TOTAL	11.8	5,955	287,500	100.0	3,570	75,800	100.0	5,544	98,350	100.0
MALES:										
18-24		2,487	26,700	17.8	2,212	1,250	3.5	2,800	11,150	22.5
25-34		7,764	33,300	22.2	3,832	1,950	5.5	6,539	8,450	17.0
35-44		9,953	31,450	21.0	5,435	5,600	15.8	8,257	11,550	23.3
45-54		10,315	24,850	16.6	6,113	6,900	19.5	9,150	9,700	19.6
55-64		7,819	17,750	11.9	5,218	8,900	25.2	7,690	5,250	10.6
65 and older		2,961	15,700	10.5	2,410	10,750	30.4	3,697	3,500	7.1
TOTAL	12.2	7,403	149,750	100.0	4,417	35,350	100.0	6,770	49,600	100.0
FEMALES:										
18-24		2,511	27,700	20.1	1,675	1,450	3.6	2,418	12,450	25.5
25-34		4,464	33,600	24.4	3,809	3,900	9.6	3,963	10,950	22.5
35-44		4,522	29,700	21.6	2,851	9,100	22.5	4,531	11,850	24.3
45-54		4,694	19,550	14.2	2,837	8,300	20.5	4,825	7,500	15.4
55-64		3,580	13,700	9.9	2,495	8,000	19.8	3,900	3,650	7.5
65 and older		2,183	13,500	9.8	1,620	9,700	24.0	2,927	2,350	4.8
TOTAL	11.3	3,737	137,750	100.0	2,468	40,450	100.0	3,772	48,750	100.0

AGE AND SEX	ALL PERSONS				COLLEGE					
					1-3 Years			4 Years		
	Median Yrs. of Educ.	Mean Income*	Number of Individuals*	Percent	Mean Income*	Number of Individuals*	Percent	Mean Income*	Number of Individuals*	Percent
ALL INDIVIDUALS:										
18-24		$2,499	54,400	18.9	$2,139	21,750	45.2	$3,308	4,150	16.1
25-34		6,506	66,900	23.3	5,756	12,500	26.0	7,443	10,200	39.5
35-44		7,931	61,150	21.3	7,372	8,050	16.7	10,416	5,550	21.5
45-54		8,274	44,400	15.4	9,221	3,350	7.0	12,397	3,100	12.0
55-64		6,351	31,450	10.9	7,985	1,550	3.2	10,720	2,000	7.7
65 and older		2,646	29,200	10.2	2,084	950	2.0	3,502	850	3.3
TOTAL	11.8	5,955	287,500	100.0	4,705	48,150	100.0	8,089	25,850	100.0
MALES:										
18-24		2,487	26,700	17.8	1,954	11,500	46.7	3,291	1,850	14.4
25-34		7,764	33,300	22.2	7,150	6,000	24.4	9,567	4,300	33.5
35-44		9,963	31,450	21.0	9,294	3,650	14.8	12,288	3,150	24.5
45-54		10,315	24,850	16.6	10,756	2,100	8.5	15,278	1,850	14.4
55-64		7,819	17,750	11.9	9,528	950	3.9	11,692	1,350	10.5
65 and older		2,961	15,700	10.5	1,964	400	1.6	1,864	350	2.7
TOTAL	12.2	7,403	149,750	100.0	5,652	24,600	100.0	10,324	12,850	100.0
FEMALES:										
18-24		2,511	27,700	20.1	2,358	10,250	43.5	3,320	2,300	17.7
25-34		4,464	33,600	24.4	3,433	6,500	27.6	5,086	5,900	45.4
35-44		4,522	29,700	21.6	4,978	4,400	18.7	4,707	2,400	18.5
45-54		4,694	19,550	14.2	6,486	1,250	5.3	6,786	1,250	9.6
55-64		3,580	13,700	9.9	5,318	600	2.5	7,911	650	5.0
65 and older		2,183	13,500	9.8	2,177	550	2.3	4,650	500	3.8
TOTAL	11.3	3,737	137,750	100.0	3,430	23,550	100.0	4,931	13,000	100.0

(Table 14 continued on page 298)

| AGE AND SEX | ALL PERSONS | | | | POSTGRADUATE | | | | | | |
| | Median Yrs. of Educ. | Mean Income* | Number of Indi- viduals* | Per- cent | 1 Year | | | 2 or More Years | | | |
					Mean Income*	Number of Indi- viduals*	Per- cent	Mean Income*	Number of Indi- viduals*	Per- cent
ALL INDIVIDUALS:										
18-24		$2,499	54,400	18.9	$3,143	1,800	10.9	$6,421	400	1.7
25-34		6,506	66,900	23.3	6,203	9,550	58.1	9,621	9,400	41.0
35-44		7,931	61,150	21.3	10,618	2,800	17.0	16,066	6,650	29.0
45-54		8,274	44,400	15.4	13,952	1,250	7.6	15,827	4,300	18.8
55-64		6,351	31,450	10.9	9,140	600	3.6	17,977	1,500	6.6
65 and older		2,646	29,200	10.2	7,788	450	2.7	8,935	650	2.8
TOTAL	11.8	5,955	287,500	100.0	7,415	16,450	100.0	13,207	22,900	100.0
MALES:										
18-24		2,487	26,700	17.8	2,913	750	6.7	8,475	200	1.2
25-34		7,764	33,300	22.2	6,836	7,000	62.2	11,290	5,600	34.8
35-44		9,953	31,450	21.0	11,113	2,200	19.6	16,999	5,300	32.9
45-54		10,315	24,850	16.6	15,889	950	8.4	17,360	3,350	20.8
55-64		7,819	17,750	11.9	15,566	150	1.3	20,021	1,150	7.1
65 and older		2,961	15,700	10.5	8,725	200	1.8	8,772	500	3.1
TOTAL	12.2	7,403	149,750	100.0	8,361	11,250	100.0	14,979	16,100	100.0
FEMALES:										
18-24		2,511	27,700	20.1	3,336	1,050	20.2	3,683	200	2.9
25-34		4,464	33,600	24.4	3,865	2,550	49.0	6,611	3,800	55.9
35-44		4,522	29,700	21.6	7,571	600	11.5	11,170	1,350	19.9
45-54		4,694	19,550	14.2	7,816	300	5.8	9,436	950	14.0
55-64		3,580	13,700	9.9	6,731	450	8.7	6,225	350	5.1
65 and older		2,183	13,500	9.8	7,040	250	4.8	10,400	150	2.2
TOTAL	11.3	3,737	137,750	100.0	4,851	5,200	100.0	7,843	6,800	100.0

SOURCE: Compiled from 1970 U.S. Census Public Use Sample.

*Number of individuals includes persons who reported zero income. Mean income is calculated only for persons who reported positive or negative income, excluding those with zero income.

Median age of all Chinese Americans: 26.8.

Median age of all Chinese American income earners: 38.7.

Table 15
Personal Earnings by Occupation, Education, and Sex (1969)

OCCUPATIONS	ALL PERSONS			PRECOLLEGE					
				0-8 Years			9-12 Years		
	Mean Earnings	Number of Indi-viduals	Per-cent	Mean Earnings	Number of Indi-viduals	Per-cent	Mean Earnings	Number of Indi-viduals	Per-cent
ALL INDIVIDUALS:									
Learned Professions	$13,838	19,200	10.1	$16,000	50	0.1	$15,166	450	0.7
Other Prof., Tech., etc.	7,615	28,900	15.2	3,733	300	0.7	7,507	3,200	4.7
Mgrs., Offs., & Proprietors	9,441	16,350	8.6	6,941	3,650	8.8	8,977	6,500	9.5
Clerical	4,563	34,750	18.2	4,392	2,100	5.0	4,677	17,900	26.2
Craftsmen	8,103	8,750	4.6	6,916	1,500	3.6	8,769	5,250	7.7
Operatives	3,944	27,450	14.4	3,371	15,000	36.1	4,963	10,300	15.1
Service Workers	4,082	33,750	17.7	3,896	13,300	32.0	4,289	15,750	23.1
Private Household	2,302	1,700	0.9	2,404	1,050	2.5	2,275	600	0.9
Laborers	3,719	4,250	2.2	4,186	950	2.3	3,763	2,450	3.6
Sales	6,157	9,150	4.8	3,289	1,400	3.4	5,036	3,600	5.3
Farmers, Farm Managers	7,600	550	0.3	7,316	300	0.7	7,000	150	0.2
Farm Laborers	3,382	850	0.4	2,233	300	0.7	3,660	250	0.4
Unemployed	3,499	5,100	2.7	2,417	1,700	4.1	3,519	1,900	2.8
TOTAL	6,378	190,750	100.0	4,022	41,600	100.0	5,490	68,300	100.0
MALES:									
Learned Professions	14,138	17,300	14.7	16,000	50	0.2	15,166	450	1.1
Other Prof., Tech., etc.	9,385	16,100	13.7	4,600	100	0.4	9,731	1,750	4.2
Mgrs., Offs., & Proprietors	10,142	13,850	11.8	7,628	3,150	13.5	9,754	5,300	12.8
Clerical	5,742	11,100	9.5	4,990	1,000	4.3	6,072	5,450	13.1
Craftsmen	8,432	8,200	7.0	7,355	1,350	5.8	9,057	4,950	11.9
Operatives	5,395	11,900	10.1	4,878	4,500	19.3	6,177	6,050	14.6
Service Workers	4,588	25,300	21.6	4,371	10,250	44.0	4,830	11,800	28.4
Private Household	3,850	600	0.5	3,711	450	1.9	4,266	150	0.4
Laborers	3,965	3,750	3.2	4,913	750	3.2	3,811	2,250	5.4
Sales	8,810	5,400	4.6	4,662	400	1.7	7,663	1,850	4.5
Farmers, Farm Managers	9,800	350	0.3	8,900	200	0.9	10,500	100	0.2
Farm Laborers	3,792	650	0.6	2,250	200	0.9	3,625	200	0.5
Unemployed	4,887	2,850	2.4	3,050	900	3.9	4,075	1,200	2.9
TOTAL	7,958	117,350	100.0	5,114	23,300	100.0	6,696	41,500	100.0
FEMALES:									
Learned Professions	11,107	1,900	2.6	—	—	—	—	—	—
Other Prof., Tech., etc.	5,388	12,800	17.4	3,300	200	1.1	4,824	1,450	5.4
Mgrs., Offs., & Proprietors	5,556	2,500	3.4	2,610	500	2.7	5,545	1,200	4.5
Clerical	4,010	23,650	32.2	3,850	1,100	6.0	4,066	12,450	46.5
Craftsmen	3,186	550	0.7	2,966	150	0.8	4,016	300	1.1
Operatives	2,833	15,550	21.2	2,725	10,500	57.4	3,234	4,250	15.9
Service Workers	2,568	8,450	11.5	2,298	3,050	16.7	2,672	3,950	14.7
Private Household	1,459	1,100	1.5	1,425	600	3.3	1,611	450	1.7
Laborers	1,875	500	0.7	1,462	200	1.1	3,225	200	0.7
Sales	2,836	3,750	5.1	2,740	1,000	5.5	2,260	1,750	6.5
Farmers, Farm Managers	3,700	200	0.3	4,190	100	0.5	0	50	0.2
Farm Laborers	2,050	200	0.3	2,200	100	0.5	3,800	50	0.2
Unemployed	1,741	2,250	3.1	1,706	800	4.4	2,567	700	2.6
TOTAL	3,651	73,400	100.0	2,631	18,300	100.0	3,623	26,800	100.0

(Table 15 continued on page 300)

OCCUPATIONS	ALL PERSONS			COLLEGE					
				1-3 Years			4 Years		
	Mean Earnings	Number of Individuals	Per-cent	Mean Earnings	Number of Individuals	Per-cent	Mean Earnings	Number of Individuals	Per-cent
ALL INDIVIDUALS:									
Learned Professions	$13,838	19,200	10.1	$9,753	750	2.5	$11,901	4,000	22.3
Other Prof., Tech., etc.	7,615	28,900	15.2	6,426	5,850	19.4	7,475	6,650	37.0
Mgrs., Offs., & Proprietors	9,441	16,350	8.6	10,349	2,750	9.1	12,110	1,450	8.1
Clerical	4,563	34,750	18.2	4,168	10,650	35.3	5,080	2,500	13.9
Craftsmen	8,103	8,750	4.6	7,214	1,400	4.6	9,420	250	1.4
Operatives	3,944	27,450	14.4	2,877	1,550	5.1	3,625	400	2.2
Service Workers	4,082	33,750	17.7	3,820	3,400	11.3	3,852	1,050	5.8
Private Household	2,302	1,700	0.9	500	50	0.2	—	—	—
Laborers	3,719	4,250	2.2	3,371	700	2.3	2,300	50	0.3
Sales	6,157	9,150	4.8	4,691	2,100	7.0	11,492	1,250	7.0
Farmers, Farm Managers	7,600	550	0.3	—	—	—	12,000	50	0.3
Farm Laborers	3,382	850	0.4	4,680	250	0.8	—	—	—
Unemployed	3,499	5,100	2.7	2,657	700	2.3	11,650	300	1.7
TOTAL	6,378	190,750	100.0	5,326	30,150	100.0	8,579	17,950	100.0
MALES:									
Learned Professions	14,138	17,300	14.7	9,753	750	4.5	12,441	3,650	33.0
Other Prof., Tech., etc.	9,385	16,100	13.7	7,310	3,400	20.2	9,987	2,750	24.9
Mgrs., Offs., & Proprietors	10,142	13,850	11.8	11,134	2,350	14.0	12,188	1,250	11.3
Clerical	5,742	11,100	9.5	5,242	3,250	19.3	6,362	800	7.2
Craftsmen	8,432	8,200	7.0	7,407	1,350	8.0	9,420	250	2.3
Operatives	5,395	11,900	10.1	3,402	950	5.7	4,000	250	2.3
Service Workers	4,588	25,300	21.6	4,142	2,350	14.0	4,869	650	5.9
Private Household	3,850	600	0.5	—	—	—	—	—	—
Laborers	3,965	3,750	3.2	3,933	600	3.6	2,300	50	0.5
Sales	8,810	5,400	4.6	6,820	1,200	7.1	12,352	1,150	10.4
Farmers, Farm Managers	9,800	350	0.3	—	—	—	12,000	50	0.5
Farm Laborers	3,792	650	0.6	5,850	200	1.2	—	—	—
Unemployed	4,887	2,850	2.4	3,025	400	2.4	16,875	200	1.8
TOTAL	7,958	117,350	100.0	6,630	16,800	100.0	10,680	11,050	100.0
FEMALES:									
Learned Professions	11,107	1,900	2.6	—	—	—	6,271	350	5.1
Other Prof., Tech., etc.	5,388	12,800	17.4	5,200	2,450	18.4	5,705	3,900	56.5
Mgrs., Offs., & Proprietors	5,556	2,500	3.4	5,737	400	3.0	11,625	200	2.9
Clerical	4,010	23,650	32.2	3,696	7,400	55.4	4,476	1,700	24.6
Craftsmen	3,186	550	0.7	2,000	50	0.4	—	—	—
Operatives	2,833	15,550	21.2	2,045	600	4.5	3,000	150	2.2
Service Workers	2,568	8,450	11.5	3,100	1,050	7.9	2,200	400	5.8
Private Household	1,459	1,100	1.5	500	50	0.4	—	—	—
Laborers	1,875	500	0.7	—	100	0.7	—	—	—
Sales	2,836	3,750	5.1	2,119	900	6.7	1,600	100	1.4
Farmers, Farm Managers	3,700	200	0.3	—	—	—	—	—	—
Farm Laborers	2,050	200	0.3	—	50	0.4	—	—	—
Unemployed	1,741	2,250	3.1	966	300	2.2	1,200	100	1.4
TOTAL	3,651	73,400	100.0	3,685	13,350	100.0	5,215	6,900	100.0

| OCCUPATIONS | ALL PERSONS | | | POSTGRADUATE | | | | | |
| | | | | 1 Year | | | 2 or More Years | | |
	Mean Earnings	Number of Individuals	Percent	Mean Earnings	Number of Individuals	Percent	Mean Earnings	Number of Individuals	Percent
ALL INDIVIDUALS:									
Learned Professions	$13,838	19,200	10.1	$9,915	4,150	32.4	$16,531	9,800	49.1
Other Prof., Tech., etc.	7,615	28,900	15.2	6,835	6,050	47.3	9,675	6,850	34.3
Mgrs., Offs., & Proprietors	9,441	16,350	8.6	9,633	750	5.9	13,948	1,250	6.3
Clerical	4,563	34,750	18.2	4,396	800	6.3	6,287	800	4.0
Craftsmen	8,103	8,750	4.6	6,910	250	2.0	3,050	100	0.5
Operatives	3,944	27,450	14.4	3,400	50	0.4	3,266	150	0.8
Service Workers	4,082	33,750	17.7	4,950	200	1.6	7,600	50	0.3
Private Household	2,302	1,700	0.9	—	—	—	—	—	—
Laborers	3,719	4,250	2.2	—	50	0.4	2,700	50	0.3
Sales	6,157	9,150	4.8	12,566	300	2.3	11,230	500	2.5
Farmers, Farm Managers	7,600	550	0.3	6,700	50	0.4	—	—	—
Farm Laborers	3,382	850	0.4	—	—	—	2,400	50	0.3
Unemployed	3,499	5,100	2.7	4,400	150	1.2	2,957	350	1.8
TOTAL	6,378	190,750	100.0	7,882	12,800	100.0	12,973	19,950	100.0
MALES:									
Learned Professions	14,138	17,300	14.7	10,485	3,800	40.9	16,791	8,600	55.8
Other Prof., Tech., etc.	9,385	16,100	13.7	7,804	3,600	38.7	11,822	4,500	29.2
Mgrs., Offs., & Proprietors	10,142	13,850	11.8	9,633	750	8.1	15,357	1,050	6.8
Clerical	5,742	11,100	9.5	6,000	300	3.2	5,750	300	1.9
Craftsmen	8,432	8,200	7.0	8,625	200	2.2	3,050	100	0.6
Operatives	5,395	11,900	10.1	3,400	50	0.5	4,800	100	0.6
Service Workers	4,588	25,300	21.6	4,950	200	2.2	7,600	50	0.3
Private Household	3,850	600	0.5	—	—	—	—	—	—
Laborers	3,965	3,750	3.2	—	50	0.5	2,700	50	0.3
Sales	8,810	5,400	4.6	12,566	300	3.2	11,230	500	3.2
Farmers, Farm Managers	9,800	350	0.3	—	—	—	—	—	—
Farm Laborers	3,792	650	0.6	—	—	—	2,400	50	0.3
Unemployed	4,887	2,850	2.4	12,000	50	0.5	7,500	100	0.6
TOTAL	7,958	117,350	100.0	9,055	9,300	100.0	14,496	15,400	100.0
FEMALES:									
Learned Professions	11,107	1,900	2.6	3,728	350	10.0	14,670	1,200	26.4
Other Prof., Tech., etc.	5,388	12,800	17.4	5,411	2,450	70.0	5,563	2,350	51.6
Mgrs., Offs., & Proprietors	5,556	2,500	3.4	—	—	—	6,550	200	4.4
Clerical	4,010	23,650	32.2	3,435	500	14.3	6,610	500	11.0
Craftsmen	3,186	550	0.7	50	50	1.4	—	—	—
Operatives	2,833	15,550	21.2	—	—	—	200	50	1.1
Service Workers	2,568	8,450	11.5	—	—	—	—	—	—
Private Household	1,459	1,100	1.5	—	—	—	—	—	—
Laborers	1,875	500	0.7	—	—	—	—	—	—
Sales	2,836	3,750	5.1	—	—	—	—	—	—
Farmers, Farm Managers	3,700	200	0.3	6,700	50	1.4	—	—	—
Farm Laborers	2,050	200	0.3	—	—	—	—	—	—
Unemployed	1,741	2,250	3.1	600	100	2.9	1,140	250	5.5
TOTAL	3,651	73,400	100.0	4,765	3,500	100.0	7,821	4,550	100.0

SOURCE: Compiled from 1970 U.S. Census Public Use Sample.

NOTE: Median years of education: 12.1.

CHINESE AMERICANS

Table 16
Family Income Distribution by Number of
Income Earners per Family (1969)

INCOME	ALL FAMILIES		NO-EARNER FAMILIES		ONE-EARNER FAMILIES		TWO-EARNER FAMILIES		THREE OR MORE EARNER FAMILIES	
	Number of Families	Percent	Number of Families	Percent	Number of Families	Percent	Number of Families	Percent	Number of Families	Percent
UNDER $ 1,000	3,000	3.0	1,850	35.6	950	2.6	150	0.4	50	0.3
$ 1,000 - $ 1,999	2,500	2.5	1,100	21.2	800	2.2	550	1.4	50	0.3
$ 2,000 - $ 2,999	3,150	3.2	1,000	19.2	1,350	3.8	650	1.7	150	0.8
$ 3,000 - $ 3,999	4,650	4.7	750	14.4	2,300	6.4	1,450	3.7	150	0.8
$ 4,000 - $ 4,999	4,900	5.0	—	—	2,850	7.9	1,550	4.0	500	2.7
$ 5,000 - $ 5,999	4,750	4.8	100	1.9	2,150	6.0	2,150	5.5	350	1.9
$ 6,000 - $ 6,999	5,950	6.0	250	4.8	2,700	7.5	2,400	6.1	600	3.2
$ 7,000 - $ 7,999	5,700	5.8	—	—	2,200	6.1	2,600	6.6	900	4.8
$ 8,000 - $ 9,999	11,600	11.7	50	1.0	4,350	12.1	5,400	13.8	1,800	9.6
$10,000 - $12,999	16,500	16.7	50	1.0	6,600	18.4	6,650	17.0	3,200	17.1
$13,000 - $14,999	7,600	7.7	—	—	2,500	7.0	3,100	7.9	2,000	10.7
$15,000 - $19,999	14,400	14.6	—	—	3,650	10.2	6,850	17.5	3,900	20.9
$20,000 - $24,999	7,200	7.3	50	1.0	1,750	4.9	3,150	8.1	2,250	12.0
$25,000 OR MORE	7,050	7.1	—	—	1,800	5.0	2,450	6.3	2,800	15.0
TOTAL	98,950	100.0	5,200	100.0	35,950	100.0	39,100	100.0	18,700	100.0
MEAN EARNINGS	$12,176		$2,140		$10,607		$12,912		$16,448	
MEDIAN INCOME	10,591		1,682		9,218		11,195		14,600	

SOURCE: Compiled from 1970 U.S. Census Public Use Sample.

CHINESE AMERICANS

Table 17

Family Income by Age, Education, and Sex of Family Head (1969)

AGE AND SEX OF FAMILY HEAD	ALL PERSONS				PRECOLLEGE					
					0-8 Years			9-12 Years		
	Median Yrs. of Educ.	Mean Income	Number of Individuals	Per-cent	Mean Income	Number of Individuals	Per-cent	Mean Income	Number of Individuals	Per-cent
ALL INDIVIDUALS:										
18-24		$ 7,137	2,950	3.0	$ 3,520	250	1.0	$ 7,948	1,350	4.3
25-34		10,088	21,800	22.0	5,208	1,200	4.6	8,714	5,550	17.6
35-44		12,472	26,450	26.7	7,832	4,600	17.5	10,844	9,400	29.8
45-54		13,840	22,900	23.1	9,720	6,450	24.6	12,730	8,500	26.9
55-64		11,039	15,450	15.6	8,110	7,700	29.3	10,970	4,500	14.3
65 and older		6,954	9,400	9.5	5,471	6,050	23.0	8,257	2,250	7.1
TOTAL	11.9	11,356	98,950	100.0	7,672	26,250	100.0	10,687	31,550	100.0
MALES:										
18-24		7,455	2,650	2.8	4,400	200	0.8	8,582	1,250	4.2
25-34		10,282	21,000	22.6	5,369	1,150	4.8	9,086	5,250	17.7
35-44		12,756	25,300	27.2	8,061	4,250	17.7	11,019	9,050	30.5
45-54		14,411	21,250	22.8	10,309	5,800	24.2	13,101	7,950	26.8
55-64		11,431	14,300	15.4	8,551	7,050	29.4	11,207	4,150	14.0
65 and older		6,570	8,500	9.1	5,059	5,500	23.0	7,745	2,000	6.7
TOTAL	12.0	11,655	93,000	100.0	7,900	23,950	100.0	10,938	29,650	100.0
FEMALES:										
18-24		4,325	300	5.0	0	50	2.2	25	100	5.3
25-34		4,993	800	13.4	1,500	50	2.2	2,216	300	15.8
35-44		6,223	1,150	19.3	5,050	350	15.2	6,314	350	18.4
45-54		6,481	1,650	27.7	4,469	650	28.3	7,363	550	28.9
55-64		6,187	1,150	19.3	3,330	650	28.3	8,164	350	18.4
65 and older		10,583	900	15.1	9,590	550	23.9	12,360	250	13.2
TOTAL	10.4	6,682	5,950	100.0	5,298	2,300	100.0	6,776	1,900	100.0

(Table 17 continued on page 304)

AGE AND SEX OF FAMILY HEAD	ALL PERSONS				COLLEGE						
					1-3 Years			4 Years			
	Median Yrs. of Educ.	Mean Income	Number of Indi- viduals	Per- cent	Mean Income	Number of Indi- viduals	Per- cent	Mean Income	Number of Indi- viduals	Per- cent
ALL INDIVIDUALS:										
18-24		$ 7,137	2,950	3.0	$ 5,973	950	8.8	$10,416	300	3.4
25-34		10,088	21,800	22.0	8,881	3,600	33.3	12,201	2,500	28.6
35-44		12,472	26,450	26.7	11,907	3,200	29.6	13,742	2,750	31.4
45-54		13,840	22,900	23.1	15,942	1,950	18.1	16,943	1,900	21.7
55-64		11,039	15,450	15.6	13,568	800	7.4	15,800	1,200	13.7
65 and older		6,954	9,400	9.5	2,566	300	2.8	8,900	100	1.1
TOTAL	11.9	11,356	98,950	100.0	10,968	10,800	100.0	14,110	8,750	100.0
MALES:										
18-24		7,455	2,650	2.8	5,976	850	8.4	9,700	250	3.0
25-34		10,282	21,000	22.6	9,040	3,500	34.7	12,319	2,450	29.3
35-44		12,756	25,300	27.2	12,565	2,800	27.7	13,742	2,750	32.9
45-54		14,411	21,250	22.8	16,177	1,900	18.8	18,222	1,650	19.8
55-64		11,431	14,300	15.4	13,486	750	7.4	16,391	1,150	13.8
65 and older		6,570	8,500	9.1	2,566	300	3.0	8,900	100	1.2
TOTAL	12.0	11,655	93,000	100.0	11,240	10,100	100.0	14,396	8,350	100.0
FEMALES:										
18-24		4,325	300	5.0	5,950	100	14.3	14,000	50	12.5
25-34		4,993	800	13.4	3,300	100	14.3	6,400	50	12.5
35-44		6,223	1,150	19.3	7,300	400	57.1	—	—	—
45-54		6,481	1,650	27.7	7,000	50	7.1	8,500	250	62.5
55-64		6,187	1,150	19.3	14,800	50	7.1	2,200	50	12.5
65 and older		10,583	900	15.1	—	—	—	—	—	—
TOTAL	10.4	6,682	5,950	100.0	7,050	700	100.0	8,137	400	100.0

| AGE AND SEX OF FAMILY HEAD | ALL PERSONS | | | | POSTGRADUATE | | | | | |
| | | | | | 1 Year | | | 2 or More Years | | |
	Median Yrs. of Educ.	Mean Income	Number of Indi-viduals	Per-cent	Mean Income	Number of Indi-viduals	Per-cent	Mean Income	Number of Indi-viduals	Per-cent
ALL INDIVIDUALS:										
18-24		$ 7,137	2,950	3.0	$ 6,450	100	1.3	$ —	—	—
25-34		10,088	21,800	22.0	9,456	4,800	61.5	13,842	4,150	30.1
35-44		12,472	26,450	26.7	12,934	1,600	20.5	19,458	4,900	35.5
45-54		13,840	22,900	23.1	19,768	950	12.2	20,310	3,150	22.8
55-64		11,039	15,450	15.6	22,866	150	1.9	23,177	1,100	8.0
65 and older		6,954	9,400	9.5	25,975	200	2.6	13,670	500	3.6
TOTAL	11.9	11,356	98,950	100.0	12,068	7,800	100.0	18,050	13,800	100.0
MALES:										
18-24		7,455	2,650	2.8	6,450	100	1.3	—	—	—
25-34		10,282	21,000	22.6	9,452	4,750	62.5	14,188	3,900	29.2
35-44		12,756	25,300	27.2	12,934	1,600	21.1	19,605	4,850	36.3
45-54		14,411	21,250	22.8	20,494	900	11.8	20,671	3,050	22.8
55-64		11,431	14,300	15.4	22,100	100	1.3	23,177	1,100	8.2
65 and older		6,570	8,500	9.1	30,566	150	2.0	13,966	450	3.4
TOTAL	12.0	11,655	93,000	100.0	12,036	7,600	100.0	18,370	13,350	100.0
FEMALES:										
18-24		4,325	300	5.0	—	—	—	—	—	—
25-34		4,993	800	13.4	9,900	50	25.0	8,440	250	55.6
35-44		6,223	1,150	19.3	—	—	—	5,200	50	11.1
45-54		6,481	1,650	27.7	6,700	50	25.0	9,300	100	22.2
55-64		6,187	1,150	19.3	24,400	50	25.0	—	—	—
65 and older		10,583	900	15.1	12,200	50	25.0	11,000	50	11.1
TOTAL	10.4	6,682	5,950	100.0	13,300	200	100.0	8,555	450	100.0

SOURCE: Compiled from 1970 U.S. Census Public Use Sample.
NOTE: Median age of all family heads: 44.3.

CHINESE AMERICANS

Table 18
Family Earnings by Number of Income Earners, Education, and Sex of Family Head (1969)

| | NUMBER OF INCOME EARNERS | | | PRECOLLEGE | | | | | |
| | | | | 0-8 Years | | | 9-12 Years | | |
	Mean Family Earnings	Number of Families	Percent of all Families	Mean Family Earnings	Number of Families	Percent of all Families	Mean Family Earnings	Number of Families	Percent of all Families
ALL FAMILIES:									
No Income-Earners	$ 0	5,200	5.3	$ 0	2,550	9.7	$ 0	1,500	4.8
One Income-Earner	9,750	35,950	36.3	5,385	8,350	31.8	7,880	9,850	31.2
Two Income-Earners	12,329	39,100	39.5	8,728	8,950	34.1	11,563	12,450	39.5
Three or More Earners	15,570	18,700	18.9	12,236	6,400	24.4	14,917	7,750	24.6
TOTAL	11,356	98,950	100.0	7,672	26,250	100.0	10,687	31,550	100.0
MALE-HEADED FAMILIES:									
No Income-Earners	0	4,500	4.8	0	2,300	9.6	0	1,100	3.7
One Income-Earner	10,048	33,550	36.1	5,544	7,300	30.5	7,947	9,400	31.7
Two Income-Earners	12,530	37,400	40.2	8,975	8,400	35.1	11,681	11,800	39.8
Three or More Earners	15,851	17,550	18.9	12,327	5,950	24.8	15,206	7,350	24.8
TOTAL	11,655	93,000	100.0	7,900	23,950	100.0	10,938	29,650	100.0
FEMALE-HEADED FAMILIES:									
No Income-Earners	0	700	11.8	0	250	10.9	0	400	21.1
One Income-Earner	5,576	2,400	40.3	4,285	1,050	45.7	6,483	450	23.7
Two Income-Earners	7,894	1,700	28.6	4,954	550	23.9	9,415	650	34.2
Three or More Earners	11,269	1,150	19.3	11,027	450	19.6	9,593	400	21.1
TOTAL	6,682	5,950	100.0	5,298	2,300	100.0	6,776	1,900	100.0

	NUMBER OF INCOME EARNERS			COLLEGE					
				1-3 Years			4 Years		
	Mean Family Earnings	Number of Families	Percent of all Families	Mean Family Earnings	Number of Families	Percent of all Families	Mean Family Earnings	Number of Families	Percent of all Families
LL FAMILIES:									
No Income-Earners	$ 0	5,200	5.3	$ 0	350	3.2	$ 0	250	2.9
One Income-Earner	9,750	35,950	36.3	8,440	4,100	38.0	11,552	3,400	38.9
Two Income-Earners	12,329	39,100	39.5	11,497	4,550	42.1	15,151	3,800	43.4
Three or More Earners	15,570	18,700	18.9	17,522	1,800	16.7	20,647	1,300	14.9
TOTAL	11,356	98,950	100.0	10,968	10,800	100.0	14,110	8,750	100.0
MALE-HEADED FAMILIES:									
No Income-Earners	0	4,500	4.8	0	350	3.5	0	250	3.0
One Income-Earner	10,048	33,550	36.1	8,771	3,650	36.1	11,870	3,200	38.3
Two Income-Earners	12,530	37,400	40.2	11,617	4,450	44.1	15,428	3,650	43.7
Three or More Earners	15,851	17,550	18.9	18,066	1,650	16.3	20,726	1,250	15.0
TOTAL	11,655	93,000	100.0	11,240	10,100	100.0	14,396	8,350	100.0
MALE-HEADED FAMILIES:									
No Income-Earners	0	700	11.8	—	—	—	—	—	—
One Income-Earner	5,576	2,400	40.3	5,755	450	64.3	6,475	200	50.0
Two Income-Earners	7,894	1,700	28.6	6,150	100	14.3	8,400	150	37.5
Three or More Earners	11,269	1,150	19.3	11,533	150	21.4	14,000	50	12.5
TOTAL	6,682	5,950	100.0	7,050	700	100.0	8,137	400	100.0

(Table 18 continued on page 308)

307

NUMBER OF INCOME EARNERS			POSTGRADUATE					
			1 Year			2 or More Years		
	Mean Family Earnings	Number of Families	Percent of all Families	Mean Family Earnings	Number of Families	Percent of all Families	Mean Family Earnings	Number of Families	Percent of all Families
ALL FAMILIES:									
No Income-Earners	$ 0	5,200	5.3	$ 0	300	3.8	$ 0	250	1.8
One Income-Earner	9,750	35,950	36.3	10,240	3,200	41.0	17,201	7,050	51.1
Two Income-Earners	12,329	39,100	39.5	12,457	3,850	49.4	18,570	5,500	39.9
Three or More Earners	15,570	18,700	18.9	29,788	450	5.8	25,890	1,000	7.2
TOTAL	11,356	98,950	100.0	12,068	7,800	100.0	18,050	13,800	100.0
MALE-HEADED FAMILIES:									
No Income-Earners	0	4,500	4.8	0	300	3.9	0	200	1.5
One Income-Earner	10,048	33,550	36.1	10,296	3,150	41.4	17,448	6,850	51.3
Two Income-Earners	12,530	37,400	40.2	12,495	3,750	49.3	18,792	5,350	40.1
Three or More Earners	15,851	17,550	18.9	30,462	400	5.3	26,505	950	7.1
TOTAL	11,655	93,000	100.0	12,036	7,600	100.0	18,370	13,350	100.0
FEMALE-HEADED FAMILIES:									
No Income-Earners	0	700	11.8	—	—	—	0	50	11.1
One Income-Earner	5,576	2,400	40.3	6,700	50	25.0	8,725	200	44.4
Two Income-Earners	7,894	1,700	28.6	11,050	100	50.0	10,633	150	33.3
Three or More Earners	11,269	1,150	19.3	24,400	50	25.0	10,200	50	11.1
TOTAL	6,682	5,950	100.0	13,300	200	100.0	8,555	450	100.0

SOURCE: Compiled from 1970 U.S. Census Public Use Sample.
NOTE: Median years of education of family heads: 11.9.

CHINESE AMERICANS

Table 19
Fertility Rates by Woman's Education and Family Income (1969)

19a. EDUCATION

| | TOTAL | | PRECOLLEGE | | | | COLLEGE | | | | POSTGRADUATE | | | |
| | | | 0-8 Years | | 9-12 Years | | 1-3 Years | | 4 Years | | 1 Year | | 2 or More Years | |
	Number	Percent	Number	Percent	Number	Percent	Number	Percent	Number	Percent	Number	Percent	Number	Percent
All Women, 15 and older:														
Childless	53,150	35.6	5,050	12.1	25,200	42.6	11,950	50.6	5,300	40.8	2,950	56.7	2,700	39.7
1 Child	19,600	13.1	5,500	13.2	7,150	12.1	2,950	12.5	2,200	16.9	600	11.5	1,200	17.6
2 Children	25,350	17.0	7,750	18.6	9,450	16.0	3,200	13.6	2,600	20.0	600	11.5	1,750	25.7
3 Children	20,650	13.8	7,150	17.2	7,400	12.5	3,500	14.8	1,450	11.2	650	12.5	500	7.4
4 Children	14,450	9.7	6,450	15.5	5,350	9.1	1,200	5.1	850	6.5	200	3.8	400	5.9
5 Children	7,500	5.0	4,350	10.5	2,150	3.6	400	1.7	300	2.3	50	1.0	250	3.7
6 or More	8,600	5.8	5,350	12.9	2,400	4.1	400	1.7	300	2.3	150	2.9	–	–
TOTAL	149,300	100.0	41,600	100.0	59,100	100.0	23,600	100.0	13,000	100.0	5,200	100.0	6,800	100.0
Mean No. of Children	1.9		3.1		1.6		1.2		1.4		1.1		1.3	
Women, 15-24:														
Childless	34,350	87.5	2,000	76.9	19,450	85.3	9,550	92.7	2,150	93.5	1,000	95.2	200	100.0
1 Child	3,500	8.9	450	17.3	2,250	9.9	650	6.3	100	4.3	50	4.8	–	–
2 Children	1,200	3.1	150	5.8	900	3.9	100	1.0	50	2.2	–	–	–	–
3 Children	200	0.5	–	–	200	0.9	–	–	–	–	–	–	–	–
4 Children	–	–	–	–	–	–	–	–	–	–	–	–	–	–
5 Children	–	–	–	–	–	–	–	–	–	–	–	–	–	–
6 or More	–	–	–	–	–	–	–	–	–	–	–	–	–	–
TOTAL	39,250	100.0	2,600	100.0	22,800	100.0	10,300	100.0	2,300	100.0	1,050	100.0	200	100.0
Mean No. of Children	0.2		0.3		0.2		0.1		0.1		0.0		0.0	

(Table 19 continued on page 310)

CHINESE AMERICANS—Table 19: Education (Continued)

	TOTAL		PRECOLLEGE				COLLEGE				POSTGRADUATE			
			0-8 Years		9-12 Years		1-3 Years		4 Years		1 Year		2 or More Years	
	Number	Percent	Number	Percent	Number	Percent	Number	Percent	Number	Percent	Number	Percent	Number	Percent
Women, 25-34:														
Childless	9,850	29.3	300	7.7	1,950	17.8	1,550	23.8	2,450	41.5	1,550	60.8	2,050	53.9
1 Child	7,000	20.8	500	12.8	2,200	20.1	1,550	23.8	1,500	25.4	450	17.6	800	21.1
2 Children	8,650	25.7	1,150	29.5	3,050	27.9	1,800	27.7	1,450	24.6	300	11.8	900	23.7
3 Children	5,250	15.6	1,100	28.2	2,150	19.6	1,350	20.8	400	6.8	200	7.8	50	1.3
4 Children	1,850	5.5	600	15.4	1,000	9.1	100	1.5	100	1.7	50	2.0	—	—
5 Children	550	1.6	200	5.1	350	3.2	—	—	—	—	—	—	—	—
6 or More	450	1.3	50	1.3	250	2.3	150	2.3	—	—	—	—	—	—
TOTAL	33,600	100.0	3,900	100.0	10,950	100.0	6,500	100.0	5,900	100.0	2,550	100.0	3,800	100.0
Mean No. of Children	1.6		2.5		2.0		1.6		1.0		0.7		0.7	
Women, 35-44:														
Childless	3,400	11.4	550	6.0	1,750	14.6	400	9.1	300	12.5	150	25.0	250	18.5
1 Child	2,750	9.3	550	6.0	1,200	10.1	500	11.4	200	8.3	50	8.3	250	18.5
2 Children	6,000	20.2	1,300	14.3	2,700	22.8	850	19.3	550	22.9	150	25.0	450	33.3
3 Children	7,050	23.7	1,900	20.9	2,650	22.4	1,450	33.0	600	25.0	200	33.3	250	18.5
4 Children	5,850	19.7	2,400	26.4	2,050	17.3	800	18.2	500	20.8	—	—	100	7.4
5 Children	2,750	9.3	1,450	15.9	850	7.2	250	5.7	150	6.3	—	—	50	3.7
6 or More	1,900	6.4	950	10.4	650	5.5	150	3.4	100	4.2	50	8.3	—	—
TOTAL	29,700	100.0	9,100	100.0	11,850	100.0	4,400	100.0	2,400	100.0	600	100.0	1,350	100.0
Mean No. of Children	2.9		3.5		2.6		2.7		2.7		2.1		1.9	

Women, 45 and older:

| | TOTAL | | PRECOLLEGE | | | | COLLEGE | | | | POSTGRADUATE | | | |
| | | | 0-8 Years | | 9-12 Years | | 1-3 Years | | 4 Years | | 1 Year | | 2 or More Years | |
	Number	Percent	Number	Percent	Number	Percent	Number	Percent	Number	Percent	Number	Percent	Number	Percent
Childless	5,550	11.9	2,200	8.5	2,050	15.2	450	18.8	400	16.7	250	25.0	200	13.8
1 Child	6,350	13.6	4,000	15.4	1,500	11.1	250	10.4	400	16.7	50	5.0	150	10.3
2 Children	9,500	20.3	5,150	19.8	2,800	20.7	450	18.8	550	22.9	150	15.0	400	27.6
3 Children	8,150	17.4	4,150	16.0	2,400	17.8	700	29.2	450	18.8	250	25.0	200	13.8
4 Children	6,750	14.4	3,450	13.3	2,300	17.0	300	12.5	250	10.4	150	15.0	300	20.7
5 Children	4,200	9.0	2,700	10.4	950	7.0	150	6.3	150	6.3	50	5.0	200	13.8
6 or More	6,250	13.4	4,350	16.7	1,500	11.1	100	4.2	200	8.3	100	10.0	—	—
TOTAL	46,750	100.0	26,000	100.0	13,500	100.0	2,400	100.0	2,400	100.0	1,000	100.0	1,450	100.0
Mean No. of Children	3.0		3.3		2.8		2.4		2.4		2.6		2.6	

19b. FAMILY INCOME

All Women, 15 and older:

| | TOTAL | | Less Than $5,000 | | $5,000 - 9,999 | | $10,000 - 14,999 | | $15,000 - 19,999 | | $20,000 - 24,999 | | $25,000 and Over | |
	Number	Percent	Number	Percent	Number	Percent	Number	Percent	Number	Percent	Number	Percent	Number	Percent
Childless	53,150	35.6	13,800	41.6	12,350	32.4	11,000	33.1	7,600	35.8	3,900	34.1	4,500	37.0
1 Child	19,600	13.1	4,650	14.0	6,150	16.1	4,450	13.4	2,450	11.6	900	7.9	1,000	8.2
2 Children	25,350	17.0	4,750	14.3	5,550	14.6	6,650	20.0	3,850	18.2	2,450	21.4	2,100	17.3
3 Children	20,650	13.8	4,050	12.2	6,000	15.7	4,250	12.8	2,750	13.0	1,750	15.3	1,850	15.2
4 Children	14,450	9.7	2,550	7.7	3,850	10.1	3,900	11.7	2,050	9.7	1,200	10.5	900	7.4
5 Children	7,500	5.0	1,650	5.0	1,900	5.0	1,500	4.5	1,100	5.2	450	3.9	900	7.4
6 or More	8,600	5.8	1,700	5.1	2,300	6.0	1,500	4.5	1,400	6.6	800	7.0	900	7.4
TOTAL	149,300	100.0	33,150	100.0	38,100	100.0	33,250	100.0	21,200	100.0	11,450	100.0	12,150	100.0
Mean No. of Children	1.9		1.7		2.0		1.9		2.0		2.0		2.1	

(Table 19 continued on page 312)

311

CHINESE AMERICANS—Table 19: Family Income (Continued)

	TOTAL		Less Than $5,000		$5,000 - 9,999		$10,000 - 14,999		$15,000 - 19,999		$20,000 - 24,999		$25,000 and Over	
	Number	Percent	Number	Percent	Number	Percent	Number	Percent	Number	Percent	Number	Percent	Number	Percent
Women, 15-24:														
Childless	34,350	87.5	7,100	87.7	8,250	80.5	7,800	89.1	4,900	89.9	3,050	93.8	3,250	94.2
1 Child	3,500	8.9	750	9.3	1,350	13.2	750	8.6	450	8.3	100	3.1	100	2.9
2 Children	1,200	3.1	150	1.9	600	5.9	150	1.7	100	1.8	100	3.1	100	2.9
3 Children	200	0.5	100	1.2	50	0.5	50	0.6	—	—	—	—	—	—
4 Children	—	—	—	—	—	—	—	—	—	—	—	—	—	—
5 Children	—	—	—	—	—	—	—	—	—	—	—	—	—	—
6 or More	—	—	—	—	—	—	—	—	—	—	—	—	—	—
TOTAL	39,250	100.0	8,100	100.0	10,250	100.0	8,750	100.0	5,450	100.0	3,250	100.0	3,450	100.0
Mean No. of Children	0.2		0.2		0.3		0.1		0.1		0.1		0.1	
Women, 25-34:														
Childless	9,850	29.3	3,350	47.5	2,050	24.4	2,150	23.4	1,400	29.2	350	15.9	550	28.2
1 Child	7,000	20.8	1,300	18.4	2,100	25.0	1,750	19.0	1,100	22.9	400	18.2	350	17.9
2 Children	8,650	25.7	1,200	17.0	1,850	22.0	2,900	31.5	1,200	25.0	800	36.4	700	35.9
3 Children	5,250	15.6	650	9.2	1,700	20.2	1,500	16.3	600	12.5	550	25.0	250	12.8
4 Children	1,850	5.5	350	5.0	450	5.4	650	7.1	300	6.3	50	2.3	50	2.6
5 Children	550	1.6	150	2.1	100	1.2	100	1.1	150	3.1	—	—	50	2.6
6 or More	450	1.3	50	0.7	150	1.8	150	1.6	50	1.0	50	2.3	—	—
TOTAL	33,600	100.0	7,050	100.0	8,400	100.0	9,200	100.0	4,800	100.0	2,200	100.0	1,950	100.0
Mean No. of Children	1.6		1.2		1.7		1.8		1.6		1.9		1.5	

312

CHINESE AMERICANS—Table 19: Family Income (Continued)

	TOTAL		Less Than $5,000		$5,000 - 9,999		$10,000 - 14,999		$15,000 - 19,999		$20,000 - 24,999		$25,000 and Over	
	Number	Percent	Number	Percent	Number	Percent	Number	Percent	Number	Percent	Number	Percent	Number	Percent
Women, 35-44:														
Childless	3,400	11.4	1,000	19.8	1,000	11.8	500	7.5	450	9.7	250	9.6	200	9.1
1 Child	2,750	9.3	500	9.9	950	11.2	550	8.2	400	8.6	250	9.6	100	4.5
2 Children	6,000	20.2	900	17.8	1,000	11.8	1,800	26.9	1,100	23.7	800	30.8	400	18.2
3 Children	7,050	23.7	1,050	20.8	2,100	24.7	1,500	22.4	1,150	24.7	550	21.2	700	31.8
4 Children	5,850	19.7	850	16.8	1,950	22.9	1,550	23.1	750	16.1	350	13.5	400	18.2
5 Children	2,750	9.3	550	10.9	850	10.0	550	8.2	400	8.6	150	5.8	250	11.4
6 or More	1,900	6.4	200	4.0	650	7.6	250	3.7	400	8.6	250	9.6	150	6.8
TOTAL	29,700	100.0	5,050	100.0	8,500	100.0	6,700	100.0	4,650	100.0	2,600	100.0	2,200	100.0
Mean No. of Children	2.9		2.5		3.0		2.9		3.0		2.8		3.1	
Women, 45 and older:														
Childless	5,550	11.9	2,350	18.1	1,050	9.6	550	6.4	850	13.5	250	7.4	500	11.0
1 Child	6,350	13.6	2,100	16.2	1,750	16.0	1,400	16.3	500	7.9	150	4.4	450	9.9
2 Children	9,500	20.3	2,500	19.3	2,100	19.2	1,800	20.9	1,450	23.0	750	22.1	900	19.8
3 Children	8,150	17.4	2,250	17.4	2,150	19.6	1,200	14.0	1,000	15.9	650	19.1	900	19.8
4 Children	6,750	14.4	1,350	10.4	1,450	13.2	1,700	19.8	1,000	15.9	800	23.5	450	9.9
5 Children	4,200	9.0	950	7.3	950	8.7	850	9.9	550	8.7	300	8.8	600	13.2
6 or More	6,250	13.4	1,450	11.2	1,500	13.7	1,100	12.8	950	15.1	500	14.7	750	16.5
TOTAL	46,750	100.0	12,950	100.0	10,950	100.0	8,600	100.0	6,300	100.0	3,400	100.0	4,550	100.0
Mean No. of Children	3.0		2.6		3.1		3.2		3.2		3.4		3.3	

SOURCE: Compiled from 1970 U.S. Census Public Use Sample.

313

FILIPINO AMERICANS

Table 20
Personal Income by Age, Education, and Sex (1969)

| AGE AND SEX | Median Yrs. of Educ. | ALL PERSONS | | | PRECOLLEGE | | | | | |
| | | | | | 0-8 Years | | | 9-12 Years | | |
		Mean Income*	Number of Indi-viduals*	Per-cent	Mean Income*	Number of Indi-viduals*	Per-cent	Mean Income*	Number of Indi-viduals*	Per-cent
ALL INDIVIDUALS:										
18-24		$3,059	31,600	16.2	$3,038	2,550	4.7	$2,715	17,100	24.6
25-34		5,609	59,700	30.5	3,763	4,500	8.2	5,032	21,550	31.1
35-44		6,566	35,600	18.2	5,079	6,150	11.2	5,549	13,800	19.9
45-54		6,003	21,850	11.2	5,048	9,300	17.0	5,441	6,900	9.9
55-64		5,505	27,200	13.9	4,959	17,600	32.2	5,823	6,600	9.5
65 and older		3,142	19,550	10.0	2,623	14,600	26.7	3,867	3,450	5.0
TOTAL	11.5	5,149	195,500	100.0	4,147	54,700	100.0	4,641	69,400	100.0
MALES:										
18-24		3 422	12,400	12.1	4,650	850	2.4	3,129	8,100	22.7
25-34		6,561	25,650	25.1	5,008	1,350	3.7	6,228	10,100	28.3
35-44		8,250	16,550	16.2	6,458	2,700	7.5	7,113	6,150	17.2
45-54		7,082	10,550	10.3	6,189	4,750	13.2	6,988	3,350	9.4
55-64		5,761	21,500	21.0	5,259	14,500	40.3	6,258	5,250	14.7
65 and older		3,350	15,650	15.3	2,874	11,850	32.9	4,148	2,800	7.8
TOTAL		5,880	102,300	100.0	4,654	36,000	100.0	5,650	35,750	100.0
FEMALES:										
18-24		2,769	19,200	20.6	1,516	1,700	9.1	2,234	9,000	26.7
25-34		4,590	34,050	36.5	2,518	3,150	16.8	3,224	11,450	34.0
35-44		4,443	19,050	20.4	3,286	3,450	18.4	3,652	7,650	22.7
45-54		4,620	11,300	12.1	3,208	4,550	24.3	3,336	3,550	10.5
55-64		3,839	5,700	6.1	2,332	3,100	16.6	2,840	1,350	4.0
65 and older		2,048	3,900	4.2	1,203	2,750	14.7	2,463	650	1.9
TOTAL	12.3	4,023	93,200	100.0	2,481	18,700	100.0	3,020	33,650	100.0

FILIPINO AMERICANS—Table 20 (Continued)

AGE AND SEX	Median Yrs. of Educ.	ALL PERSONS			COLLEGE					
					1-3 Years			4 Years		
		Mean Income*	Number of Indi- viduals*	Per- cent	Mean Income*	Number of Indi- viduals*	Per- cent	Mean Income*	Number of Indi- viduals*	Per- cent
ALL INDIVIDUALS:										
18-24		$3,059	31,600	16.2	$3,046	8,050	26.9	$3,823	2,750	12.9
25-34		5,609	59,700	30.5	5,094	10,800	36.1	5,628	10,750	50.4
35-44		6,566	35,600	18.2	6,004	5,750	19.2	7,502	5,350	25.1
45-54		6,003	21,850	11.2	6,084	2,850	9.5	7,489	1,300	6.1
55-64		5,505	27,200	13.9	7,092	1,800	6.0	7,186	750	3.5
65 and older		3,142	19,550	10.0	3,750	650	2.2	7,657	450	2.1
TOTAL	11.5	5,149	195,500	100.0	4,934	29,900	100.0	6,085	21,350	100.0
MALES:										
18-24		3,422	12,400	12.1	3,529	2,750	19.9	4,666	500	6.8
25-34		6,561	25,650	25.1	5,738	5,750	41.5	6,286	2,950	40.1
35-44		8,250	16,550	16.2	7,812	2,700	19.5	9,444	2,600	35.4
45-54		7,082	10,550	10.3	6,804	1,100	7.9	9,179	600	8.2
55-64		5,701	21,500	21.0	8,592	1,000	7.2	7,511	450	6.1
65 and older		3,350	15,650	15.3	3,750	550	4.0	5,080	250	3.4
TOTAL	10.7	5,880	102,300	100.0	5,974	13,850	100.0	7,592	7,350	100.0
FEMALES:										
18-24		2,769	19,200	20.6	2,760	5,300	33.0	3,618	2,250	16.1
25-34		4,590	34,050	36.5	4,054	5,050	31.5	5,385	7,800	55.7
35-44		4,443	19,050	20.4	3,653	3,050	19.0	5,097	2,750	19.6
45-54		4,620	11,300	12.1	5,537	1,750	10.9	5,800	700	5.0
55-64		3,839	5,700	6.1	4,591	800	5.0	5,725	300	2.1
65 and older		2,048	3,900	4.2	0	100	0.6	14,100	200	1.4
TOTAL	12.3	4,023	93,200	100.0	3,746	16,050	100.0	5,115	14,000	100.0

(Table 20 continued on page 316)

FILIPINO AMERICANS—Table 20 (Continued)

| AGE AND SEX | Median Yrs. of Educ. | ALL PERSONS | | | POSTGRADUATE | | | | | |
| | | | | | 1 Year | | | 2 or More Years | | |
		Mean Income*	Number of Individuals*	Percent	Mean Income*	Number of Individuals*	Percent	Mean Income*	Number of Individuals*	Percent
ALL INDIVIDUALS:										
18-24		$3,059	31,600	16.2	$6,428	1,000	12.3	$6,400	150	1.2
25-34		5,609	59,700	30.5	6,247	5,350	65.6	8,169	6,750	56.3
35-44		6,566	35,600	18.2	7,389	1,100	13.5	11,303	3,450	28.7
45-54		6,003	21,850	11.2	8,291	300	3.7	12,289	1,200	10.0
55-64		5,505	27,200	13.9	8,175	250	3.1	18,737	200	1.7
65 and older		3,142	19,550	10.0	4,016	150	1.8	16,500	250	2.1
TOTAL	11.5	5,149	195,500	100.0	6,508	8,150	100.0	9,896	12,000	100.0
MALES:										
18-24		3,422	12,400	12.1	5,500	150	4.8	0	50	0.8
25-34		6,561	25,650	25.1	7,233	2,100	66.7	9,368	3,400	54.8
35-44		8,250	16,550	16.2	8,472	550	17.5	13,331	1,850	29.8
45-54		7,082	10,550	10.3	8,283	150	4.8	12,545	600	9.7
55-64		5,761	21,500	21.0	10,066	200	6.3	7,750	100	1.6
65 and older		3,350	15,650	15.3	–	–	–	21,300	200	3.2
TOTAL	10.7	5,880	102,300	100.0	7,603	3,150	100.0	11,179	6,200	100.0
FEMALES:										
18-24		2,769	19,200	20.6	6,560	850	17.0	6,400	100	1.7
25-34		4,590	34,050	36.5	5,555	3,250	65.0	6,704	3,350	57.8
35-44		4,443	19,050	20.4	5,900	550	11.0	8,623	1,600	27.6
45-54		4,620	11,300	12.1	8,300	150	3.0	12,033	600	10.3
55-64		3,839	5,700	6.1	2,500	50	1.0	29,725	100	1.7
65 and older		2,048	3,900	4.2	4,016	150	3.0	2,100	50	0.9
TOTAL	12.3	4,023	93,200	100.0	5,757	5,000	100.0	8,325	5,800	100.0

SOURCE: Compiled from 1970 U.S. Census Public Use Sample.

*Number of individuals includes persons who reported zero income.
Mean income is calculated only for persons who reported positive or negative income, excluding those with zero income.

Median age of all Filipinos: 26.2.

Median age of all Filipino income earners: 36.8.

Table 21
Personal Earnings by Occupation, Education, and Sex (1969)

| | ALL PERSONS | | | PRECOLLEGE | | | | | |
| | | | | 0-8 Years | | | 9-12 Years | | |
OCCUPATIONS	Mean Earnings	Number of Indi- viduals	Per- cent	Mean Earnings	Number of Indi- viduals	Per- cent	Mean Earnings	Number of Indi- viduals	Per- cent
ALL INDIVIDUALS:									
Learned Professions	$11,081	8,500	6.6	$7,750	100	0.3	$8,060	500	1.1
Other Prof., Tech., etc.	6,789	21,300	16.5	6,833	600	2.0	5,957	2,850	6.4
Mgrs., Offs., & Proprietors	7,397	3,600	2.8	4,957	350	1.2	6,981	1,600	3.6
Clerical	4,544	20,500	15.9	3,646	750	2.5	4,783	7,650	17.1
Craftsmen	6,750	10,550	8.2	6,753	3,400	11.3	6,577	4,850	10.8
Operatives	4,966	16,550	12.8	4,973	5,600	18.6	5,211	7,950	17.8
Service Workers	3,975	23,900	18.5	4,538	8,500	28.2	3,652	10,350	23.1
Private Household	1,737	1,600	1.2	1,866	600	2.0	914	700	1.6
Laborers	5,727	5,550	4.3	5,976	2,950	9.8	5,363	1,900	4.2
Sales	4,291	4,050	3.1	4,281	550	1.8	3,297	1,850	4.1
Farmers, Farm Managers	3,785	700	0.5	3,812	400	1.3	3,050	200	0.4
Farm Laborers	3,694	6,800	5.3	3,852	5,050	16.7	3,383	1,550	3.5
Unemployed	3,606	5,650	4.4	3,596	1,300	4.3	2,915	2,800	6.3
TOTAL	5,470	129,250	100.0	4,825	30,150	100.0	4,711	44,750	100.0
MALES:									
Learned Professions	11,222	6,000	7.9	5,700	50	0.2	8,914	350	1.3
Other Prof., Tech., etc.	7,738	7,650	10.0	7,628	350	1.5	6,756	1,500	5.5
Mgrs., Offs., & Proprietors	8,653	2,350	3.1	7,475	200	0.9	7,714	1,050	3.8
Clerical	6,920	6,950	9.1	3,316	300	1.3	6,865	2,450	8.9
Craftsmen	6,829	10,200	13.4	6,791	3,300	14.1	6,687	4,700	17.1
Operatives	5,983	10,950	14.4	6,089	3,800	16.2	6,106	5,550	20.2
Service Workers	4,874	14,450	19.0	5,067	6,200	26.4	4,489	6,150	22.4
Private Household	3,116	300	0.4	3,725	200	0.9	—	—	—
Laborers	5,730	5,200	6.8	6,071	2,850	12.2	5,402	1,800	6.5
Sales	6,228	1,900	2.5	5,180	250	1.1	5,200	700	2.5
Farmers, Farm Managers	5,362	400	0.5	4,550	300	1.3	6,900	50	0.2
Farm Laborers	3,742	6,350	8.3	3,871	4,700	20.0	3,456	1,600	5.5
Unemployed	4,612	3,550	4.7	3,794	950	4.1	3,750	1,700	6.2
TOTAL	6,279	76,250	100.0	5,327	23,450	100.0	5,686	27,500	100.0
FEMALES:									
Learned Professions	10,742	2,500	4.7	9,800	50	0.7	6,066	150	0.9
Other Prof., Tech., etc.	6,257	13,650	25.8	5,720	250	3.7	5,070	1,350	7.8
Mgrs., Offs., & Proprietors	5,036	1,250	2.4	1,600	150	2.2	5,581	550	3.2
Clerical	3,838	13,550	25.6	3,866	450	6.7	3,803	5,200	30.1
Craftsmen	4,428	350	0.7	5,500	100	1.5	3,133	150	0.9
Operatives	2,977	5,600	10.6	2,615	1,800	26.9	3,140	2,400	13.9
Service Workers	2,599	9,450	17.8	3,110	2,300	34.3	2,426	4,200	24.3
Private Household	1,419	1,300	2.5	937	400	6.0	914	700	4.1
Laborers	4,714	350	0.7	3,250	100	1.5	4,650	100	0.6
Sales	2,579	2,150	4.1	3,533	300	4.5	2,139	1,150	6.7
Farmers, Farm Managers	1,683	300	0.6	1,600	100	1.5	1,766	150	0.9
Farm Laborers	3,022	450	0.8	3,600	350	5.2	1,200	50	0.3
Unemployed	1,905	2,100	4.0	3,057	350	5.2	1,625	1,100	6.4
TOTAL	4,306	53,000	100.0	3,069	6,700	100.0	3,158	17,250	100.0

(Table 21 continued on page 318)

OCCUPATIONS	ALL PERSONS			COLLEGE 1-3 Years			COLLEGE 4 Years		
	Mean Earnings	Number of Individuals	Per-cent	Mean Earnings	Number of Individuals	Per-cent	Mean Earnings	Number of Individuals	Per-cent
ALL INDIVIDUALS:									
Learned Professions	$11,081	8,500	6.6	$8,900	50	0.2	$8,992	1,300	7.6
Other Prof., Tech., etc.	6,789	21,300	16.5	5,756	3,650	18.1	7,267	7,300	42.9
Mgrs., Offs., & Proprietors	7,397	3,600	2.8	8,022	450	2.2	7,641	600	3.5
Clerical	4,544	20,500	15.9	4,410	6,400	31.7	4,485	4,200	24.7
Craftsmen	6,750	10,550	8.2	7,545	1,550	7.7	5,827	550	3.2
Operatives	4,966	16,550	12.8	4,440	2,100	10.4	4,790	550	3.2
Service Workers	3,975	23,900	18.5	4,024	3,100	15.3	2,816	1,250	7.4
Private Household	1,737	1,600	1.2	3,400	300	1.5	—	—	—
Laborers	5,727	5,550	4.3	5,363	550	2.7	7,200	100	0.6
Sales	4,291	4,050	3.1	5,581	1,100	5.4	6,011	450	2.6
Farmers, Farm Managers	3,785	700	0.5	1,600	50	0.2	—	—	—
Farm Laborers	3,694	6,800	5.3	1,850	100	0.5	2,400	100	0.6
Unemployed	3,606	5,650	4.4	3,962	800	4.0	7,033	600	3.5
TOTAL	5,470	129,250	100.0	4,967	20,200	100.0	6,200	17,000	100.0
MALES:									
Learned Professions	11,222	6,000	7.9	8,900	50	0.5	9,290	1,000	15.4
Other Prof., Tech., etc.	7,738	7,650	10.0	6,712	1,450	14.2	9,769	1,800	27.7
Mgrs., Offs., & Proprietors	8,653	2,350	3.1	7,400	400	3.9	9,228	350	5.4
Clerical	5,920	6,950	9.1	5,215	2,300	22.5	5,842	1,300	20.0
Craftsmen	6,829	10,200	13.4	7,706	1,500	14.7	5,620	500	7.7
Operatives	5,983	10,950	14.4	5,400	1,200	11.8	6,160	250	3.8
Service Workers	4,874	14,450	19.0	5,679	1,450	14.2	4,690	550	8.5
Private Household	3,116	300	0.4	1,900	100	1.0	—	—	—
Laborers	5,730	5,200	6.8	5,311	450	4.4	7,200	100	1.5
Sales	6,228	1,900	2.5	7,000	750	7.4	8,250	200	3.1
Farmers, Farm Managers	5,362	400	0.5	—	—	—	—	—	—
Farm Laborers	3,742	6,350	8.3	1,850	100	1.0	4,000	50	0.8
Unemployed	4,612	3,550	4.7	5,555	450	4.4	9,612	400	6.2
TOTAL	6,279	76,250	100.0	6,099	10,200	100.0	7,853	6,500	100.0
FEMALES:									
Learned Professions	10,742	2,500	4.7	—	—	—	8,000	300	2.9
Other Prof., Tech., etc.	6,257	13,650	25.8	4,995	2,200	22.0	6,449	5,500	52.4
Mgrs., Offs., & Proprietors	5,036	1,250	2.4	13,000	50	0.5	5,420	250	2.4
Clerical	3,838	13,550	25.6	3,959	4,100	41.0	3,877	2,900	27.6
Craftsmen	4,428	350	0.7	2,700	50	0.5	7,900	50	0.5
Operatives	2,977	5,600	10.6	3,161	900	9.0	3,650	300	2.9
Service Workers	2,599	9,450	17.8	2,569	1,650	16.5	1,342	700	6.7
Private Household	1,419	1,300	2.5	4,150	200	2.0	—	—	—
Laborers	4,714	350	0.7	5,600	100	1.0	—	—	—
Sales	2,579	2,150	4.1	2,542	350	3.5	4,220	250	2.4
Farmers, Farm Managers	1,683	300	0.6	1,600	50	0.5	—	—	—
Farm Laborers	3,022	450	0.8	—	—	—	800	50	0.5
Unemployed	1,905	2,100	4.0	1,914	350	3.5	1,875	200	1.9
TOTAL	4,306	53,000	100.0	3,812	10,000	100.0	5,178	10,500	100.0

OCCUPATIONS	ALL PERSONS			POSTGRADUATE					
				1 Year			2 or More Years		
	Mean Earnings	Number of Individuals	Percent	Mean Earnings	Number of Individuals	Percent	Mean Earnings	Number of Individuals	Percent
ALL INDIVIDUALS:									
Learned Professions	$11,081	8,500	6.6	$8,115	1,300	18.7	$12,704	5,250	51.5
Other Prof., Tech., etc.	6,789	21,300	16.5	7,160	3,750	54.0	7,177	3,150	30.9
Mgrs., Offs., & Proprietors	7,397	3,600	2.8	6,875	200	2.9	10,387	400	3.9
Clerical	4,544	20,500	15.9	3,938	900	12.9	5,350	600	5.9
Craftsmen	6,750	10,550	8.2	2,000	100	1.4	12,500	100	1.0
Operatives	4,966	16,550	12.8	2,100	150	2.2	3,175	200	2.0
Service Workers	3,975	23,900	18.5	3,962	400	5.8	3,483	300	2.9
Private Household	1,737	1,600	1.2	—	—	—	—	—	—
Laborers	5,727	5,550	4.3	—	—	—	6,000	50	0.5
Sales	4,291	4,050	3.1	1,500	50	0.7	100	50	0.5
Farmers, Farm Managers	3,785	700	0.5	—	—	—	8,700	50	0.5
Farm Laborers	3,694	6,800	5.3	—	—	—	—	—	—
Unemployed	3,606	5,650	4.4	1,500	100	1.4	—	50	0.5
TOTAL	5,470	129,250	100.0	6,423	6,950	100.0	9,837	10,200	100.0
MALES:									
Learned Professions	11,222	6,000	7.9	8,677	900	31.0	12,708	3,650	64.0
Other Prof., Tech., etc.	7,738	7,650	10.0	7,882	1,150	39.7	6,942	1,400	24.6
Mgrs., Offs., & Proprietors	8,653	2,350	3.1	8,666	150	5.2	16,250	200	3.5
Clerical	5,920	6,950	9.1	5,400	350	12.1	7,420	250	4.4
Craftsmen	6,829	10,200	13.4	2,000	100	3.4	12,500	100	1.8
Operatives	5,983	10,950	14.4	3,150	100	3.4	3,000	50	0.9
Service Workers	4,074	14,450	19.0	5,900	100	3.4	—	—	—
Private Household	3,116	300	0.4	—	—	—	—	—	—
Laborers	5,730	5,200	6.8	—	—	—	—	—	—
Sales	6,228	1,900	2.5	—	—	—	—	—	—
Farmers, Farm Managers	5,362	400	0.5	—	—	—	8,700	50	0.9
Farm Laborers	3,742	6,350	8.3	—	—	—	—	—	—
Unemployed	4,612	3,550	4.7	1,000	50	1.7	—	—	—
TOTAL	6,279	76,250	100.0	7,317	2,900	100.0	11,060	5,700	100.0
FEMALES:									
Learned Professions	10,742	2,500	4.7	6,850	400	9.9	12,696	1,600	35.6
Other Prof., Tech., etc.	6,257	13,650	25.8	6,840	2,600	64.2	7,365	1,750	38.9
Mgrs., Offs., & Proprietors	5,036	1,250	2.4	1,500	50	1.2	4,525	200	4.4
Clerical	3,838	13,550	25.6	3,009	550	13.6	3,871	350	7.8
Craftsmen	4,428	350	0.7	—	—	—	—	—	—
Operatives	2,977	5,600	10.6	—	50	1.2	3,233	150	3.3
Service Workers	2,599	9,450	17.8	3,316	300	7.4	3,483	300	6.7
Private Household	1,419	1,300	2.5	—	—	—	—	—	—
Laborers	4,714	350	0.7	—	—	—	6,000	50	1.1
Sales	2,579	2,150	4.1	1,900	50	1.2	100	50	1.1
Farmers, Farm Managers	1,683	300	0.6	—	—	—	—	—	—
Farm Laborers	3,022	450	0.8	—	—	—	—	—	—
Unemployed	1,905	2,100	4.0	2,000	50	1.2	0	50	1.1
TOTAL	4,306	53,000	100.0	5,783	4,050	100.0	8,288	4,500	100.0

SOURCE: Compiled from 1970 U.S. Census Public Use Sample.

NOTE: Median years of education: 12.1.

319

FILIPINO AMERICANS

Table 22
Family Income Distribution by Number of Income Earners per Family (1969)

INCOME	ALL FAMILIES		NO-EARNER FAMILIES		ONE-EARNER FAMILIES		TWO-EARNER FAMILIES		THREE OR MORE EARNER FAMILIES	
	Number of Families	Percent	Number of Families	Percent	Number of Families	Percent	Number of Families	Percent	Number of Families	Percent
UNDER $ 1,000	2,050	2.9	1,700	37.4	350	1.6	—	—	—	—
$ 1,000 - $ 1,999	1,950	2.8	900	19.8	700	3.2	300	1.0	50	0.4
$ 2,000 - $ 2,999	2,450	3.5	700	15.4	1,250	5.6	500	1.7	—	—
$ 3,000 - $ 3,999	3,250	4.6	450	9.9	1,750	7.9	900	3.0	150	1.1
$ 4,000 - $ 4,999	3,750	5.3	250	5.5	2,500	11.3	950	3.2	50	0.4
$ 5,000 - $ 5,999	4,800	6.8	150	3.3	3,000	13.5	1,350	4.5	300	2.2
$ 6,000 - $ 6,999	5,300	7.5	150	3.3	2,700	12.2	2,050	6.8	400	2.9
$ 7,000 - $ 7,999	5,800	8.2	100	2.2	2,550	11.5	2,500	8.3	650	4.7
$ 8,000 - $ 9,999	8,250	11.7	—	—	2,750	12.4	4,750	15.9	750	5.5
$10,000 - $12,999	13,200	18.8	100	2.2	2,850	12.9	7,100	23.7	3,150	23.0
$13,000 - $14,999	5,300	7.5	—	—	450	2.0	3,600	12.0	1,250	9.1
$15,000 - $19,999	8,500	12.1	—	—	800	3.6	4,100	13.7	3,600	26.3
$20,000 - $24,999	3,550	5.0	—	—	200	0.9	1,300	4.3	2,050	15.0
$25,000 OR MORE	2,200	3.1	50	1.1	300	1.4	550	1.8	1,300	9.5
TOTAL	70,350	100.0	4,550	100.0	22,150	100.0	29,950	100.0	13,700	100.0
MEAN EARNINGS	$10,395		$2,690		$7,241		$11,362		$15,940	
MEDIAN INCOME	9,406		1,611		6,556		10,697		15,139	

SOURCE: Compiled from 1970 U.S. Census Public Use Sample.

FILIPINO AMERICANS

Table 23
Family Income by Age, Education, and Sex of Family Head (1969)

AGE AND SEX OF FAMILY HEAD	ALL PERSONS				PRECOLLEGE						
					0-8 Years			9-12 Years			
	Median Yrs. of Educ.	Mean Income	Number of Individuals	Percent	Mean Income	Number of Individuals	Percent	Mean Income	Number of Individuals	Percent	
ALL INDIVIDUALS:											
18-24		$ 6,153	3,600	5.1	$ 4,262	400	1.8	$ 5,306	2,150	8.9	
25-34		9,331	20,150	28.6	6,230	1,050	4.8	7,757	7,600	31.3	
35-44		10,913	15,100	21.5	8,560	2,400	10.9	9,190	5,600	23.1	
45-54		11,944	8,500	12.1	11,675	3,850	17.5	10,897	2,450	10.1	
55-64		10,046	15,000	21.3	9,438	9,250	42.0	10,066	4,300	17.7	
65 and older		6,514	8,000	11.4	4,995	5,100	23.1	7,222	2,150	8.9	
TOTAL	11.2	9,656	70,350	100.0	8,459	22,050	100.0	8,550	24,250	100.0	
MALES:											
18-24		6,795	2,950	4.6	7,650	200	1.0	5,713	1,900	8.6	
25-34		9,994	17,850	27.7	8,390	750	3.6	8,795	6,500	29.5	
35-44		11,594	13,650	21.2	9,130	2,150	10.4	9,764	5,050	22.9	
45-54		12,412	7,750	12.0	12,334	3,550	17.2	11,140	2,350	10.7	
55-64		10,099	14,550	22.6	9,451	9,050	43.8	10,245	4,150	18.8	
65 and older		6,258	7,750	12.0	5,051	4,950	24.0	6,894	2,100	9.5	
TOTAL	11.1	10,052	64,500	100.0	8,803	20,650	100.0	9,093	22,050	100.0	
FEMALES:											
18-24		3,238	650	11.1	875	200	14.3	2,220	250	11.4	
25-34		4,181	2,300	39.3	833	300	21.4	1,629	1,100	50.0	
35-44		4,506	1,450	24.8	3,660	250	17.9	3,918	550	25.0	
45-54		7,113	750	12.8	3,883	300	21.4	5,200	100	4.5	
55-64		8,305	450	7.7	8,850	200	14.3	5,116	150	6.8	
65 and older		14,440	250	4.3	3,166	150	10.7	21,000	50	2.3	
TOTAL	11.7	5,288	5,850	100.0	3,392	1,400	100.0	3,109	2,200	100.0	

(Table 23 continued on page 322)

FILIPINO AMERICANS—Table 23 (Continued)

AGE AND SEX OF FAMILY HEAD	Median Yrs. of Educ.	ALL PERSONS			COLLEGE					
					1-3 Years			4 Years		
		Mean Income	Number of Indi-viduals	Per-cent	Mean Income	Number of Indi-viduals	Per-cent	Mean Income	Number of Indi-viduals	Per-cent
ALL INDIVIDUALS:										
18-24		$ 6,153	3,600	5.1	$ 8,767	700	6.8	$ 9,100	200	3.4
25-34		9,331	20,150	28.6	8,889	4,650	44.9	10,370	2,400	41.4
35-44		10,913	15,100	21.5	10,194	2,800	27.1	13,145	2,150	37.1
45-54		11,944	8,500	12.1	10,392	1,000	9.7	14,390	500	8.6
55-64		10,046	15,000	21.3	13,937	800	7.7	14,285	350	6.0
65 and older		6,514	8,000	11.4	6,412	400	3.9	18,675	200	3.4
TOTAL	11.2	9,656	70,350	100.0	9,674	10,350	100.0	12,224	5,800	100.0
MALES:										
18-24		6,795	2,950	4.6	9,042	650	6.9	9,300	150	3.0
25-34		9,994	17,850	27.7	9,107	4,450	47.3	10,868	1,900	37.6
35-44		11,594	13,650	21.2	11,027	2,350	25.0	13,888	2,000	39.6
45-54		12,412	7,750	12.0	11,453	800	8.5	14,390	500	9.9
55-64		10,099	14,550	22.6	14,406	750	8.0	14,285	350	6.9
65 and older		6,258	7,750	12.0	6,412	400	4.3	11,000	150	3.0
TOTAL	11.1	10,052	64,500	100.0	10,090	9,400	100.0	12,607	5,050	100.0
FEMALES:										
18-24		3,238	650	11.1	5,200	50	5.3	8,500	50	6.7
25-34		4,181	2,300	39.3	4,050	200	21.1	8,480	500	66.7
35-44		4,506	1,450	24.8	5,844	450	47.4	3,233	150	20.0
45-54		7,113	750	12.8	6,150	200	21.1	—	—	—
55-64		8,305	450	7.7	6,900	50	5.3	—	—	—
65 and older		14,440	250	4.3	—	—	—	41,700	50	6.7
TOTAL	11.7	5,288	5,850	100.0	5,552	950	100.0	9,646	750	100.0

FILIPINO AMERICANS—Table 23 (Continued)

AGE AND SEX OF FAMILY HEAD	ALL PERSONS				POSTGRADUATE					
					1 Year			2 or More Years		
	Median Yrs. of Educ.	Mean Income	Number of Indi- viduals	Per- cent	Mean Income	Number of Indi- viduals	Per- cent	Mean Income	Number of Indi- viduals	Per- cent
ALL INDIVIDUALS:										
18-24		$ 6,153	3,600	5.1	$ 5,000	100	4.1	$11,600	50	0.9
25-34		9,331	20,150	28.6	11,074	1,550	63.3	13,491	2,900	53.2
35-44		10,913	15,100	21.5	11,894	450	18.4	18,016	1,700	31.2
45-54		11,944	8,500	12.1	16,500	100	4.1	17,733	600	11.0
55-64		10,046	15,000	21.3	11,860	250	10.2	19,600	50	0.9
65 and older		6,514	8,000	11.4	—	—	—	32,066	150	2.8
TOTAL	11.2	9,656	70,350	100.0	11,278	2,450	100.0	15,919	5,450	100.0
MALES:										
18-24		6,795	2,950	4.6	7,800	50	2.2	—	—	—
25-34		9,994	17,850	27.7	11,579	1,450	64.4	13,205	2,800	54.9
35-44		11,594	13,650	21.2	11,804	450	20.0	18,350	1,650	32.4
45-54		12,412	7,750	12.0	16,500	100	4.4	18,266	450	8.8
55-64		10,099	14,550	22.6	10,550	200	8.9	19,600	50	1.0
65 and older		6,258	7,750	12.0	—	—	—	32,066	150	2.9
TOTAL	11.1	10,052	64,500	100.0	11,685	2,250	100.0	15,933	5,100	100.0
FEMALES:										
18-24		3,238	650	11.1	2,200	50	25.0	11,600	50	14.3
25-34		4,181	2,300	39.3	3,750	100	50.0	21,500	100	28.6
35-44		4,506	1,450	24.8	—	—	—	7,000	50	14.3
45-54		7,113	750	12.8	—	—	—	16,133	150	42.9
55-64		8,305	450	7.7	17,100	50	25.0	—	—	—
65 and older		14,440	250	4.3	—	—	—	—	—	—
TOTAL	11.7	5,288	5,850	100.0	6,700	200	100.0	15,714	350	100.0

SOURCE: Compiled from 1970 U.S. Census Public Use Sample.

NOTE: Median age of all family heads: 42.5.

FILIPINO AMERICANS

Table 24
Family Earnings by Number of Income Earners,
Education, and Sex of Family Head (1969)

	NUMBER OF INCOME EARNERS			PRECOLLEGE					
				0-8 Years			9-12 Years		
	Mean Family Earnings	Number of Families	Percent of all Families	Mean Family Earnings	Number of Families	Percent of all Families	Mean Family Earnings	Number of Families	Percent of all Families
ALL FAMILIES:									
No Income-Earners	$ 0	4,550	6.5	$ 0	2,250	10.2	$ 0	1,450	6.0
One Income-Earner	6,606	22,150	31.5	4,965	6,350	28.8	5,789	8,250	34.0
Two Income-Earners	10,880	29,950	42.6	9,140	7,300	33.1	9,758	10,650	43.9
Three or More Earners	15,117	13,700	19.5	14,353	6,150	27.9	14,271	3,900	16.1
TOTAL	9,656	70,350	100.0	8,459	22,050	100.0	8,550	24,250	100.0
MALE-HEADED FAMILIES:									
No Income-Earners	0	2,800	4.3	0	1,650	8.0	0	750	3.4
One Income-Earner	6,906	20,000	31.0	5,121	5,900	28.6	6,081	7,350	33.3
Two Income-Earners	10,926	28,500	44.3	9,138	7,000	33.9	9,865	10,250	46.5
Three or More Earners	15,078	13,150	20.4	14,360	6,100	29.5	14,781	3,700	16.8
TOTAL	10,052	64,500	100.0	8,803	20,650	100.0	9,093	22,050	100.0
FEMALE-HEADED FAMILIES:									
No Income-Earners	0	1,750	29.9	0	600	42.9	0	700	31.8
One Income-Earner	3,816	2,150	36.8	2,922	450	32.1	3,400	900	40.9
Two Income-Earners	9,939	1,400	23.9	9,200	300	21.4	7,037	400	18.2
Three or More Earners	16,036	550	9.4	13,500	50	3.6	4,825	200	9.1
TOTAL	5,288	5,850	100.0	3,392	1,400	100.0	3,109	2,200	100.0

	NUMBER OF INCOME EARNERS			COLLEGE					
				1-3 Years			4 Years		
	Mean Family Earnings	Number of Families	Percent of all Families	Mean Family Earnings	Number of Families	Percent of all Families	Mean Family Earnings	Number of Families	Percent of all Families
ALL FAMILIES:									
No Income-Earners	$ 0	4,550	6.5	$ 0	500	4.8	$ 0	200	3.4
One Income-Earner	6,606	22,150	31.5	6,033	3,100	30.0	9,710	1,450	25.0
Two Income-Earners	10,880	29,950	42.6	10,940	5,150	49.8	12,277	2,950	50.9
Three or More Earners	15,117	13,700	19.5	15,673	1,600	15.5	17,170	1,200	20.7
TOTAL	9,656	70,350	100.0	9,674	10,350	100.0	12,224	5,800	100.0
MALE-HEADED FAMILIES:									
No Income-Earners	0	2,800	4.3	0	250	2.7	—	—	—
One Income-Earner	6,906	20,000	31.0	6,201	2,800	29.8	10,479	1,200	23.8
Two Income-Earners	10,926	28,500	44.3	11,033	4,750	50.5	12,238	2,800	55.4
Three or More Earners	15,078	13,150	20.4	15,673	1,600	17.0	16,023	1,050	20.8
TOTAL	10,052	64,500	100.0	10,090	9,400	100.0	12,607	5,050	100.0
FEMALE-HEADED FAMILIES:									
No Income-Earners	0	1,750	29.9	0	250	26.3	0	200	26.7
One Income-Earner	3,816	2,150	36.8	4,466	300	31.6	6,020	250	33.3
Two Income-Earners	9,939	1,400	23.9	9,837	400	42.1	13,000	150	20.0
Three or More Earners	16,036	550	9.4	—	—	—	25,200	150	20.0
TOTAL	5,288	5,850	100.0	5,552	950	100.0	9,646	750	100.0

(Table 24 continued on page 326)

325

| | NUMBER OF INCOME EARNERS | | | POSTGRADUATE | | | | | |
| | | | | 1 Year | | | 2 or More Years | | |
	Mean Family Earnings	Number of Families	Percent of all Families	Mean Family Earnings	Number of Families	Percent of all Families	Mean Family Earnings	Number of Families	Percent of all Families
ALL FAMILIES:									
No Income-Earners	$ 0	4,550	6.5	$ 0	50	2.0	$ 0	100	1.8
One Income-Earner	6,606	22,150	31.5	7,600	1,050	42.9	13,474	1,950	35.8
Two Income-Earners	10,880	29,950	42.6	13,830	1,150	46.9	16,997	2,750	50.5
Three or More Earners	15,117	13,700	19.5	18,737	200	8.2	21,146	650	11.9
TOTAL	9,656	70,350	100.0	11,278	2,450	100.0	15,919	5,450	100.0
MALE-HEADED FAMILIES:									
No Income-Earners	0	2,800	4.3	0	50	2.2	0	100	2.0
One Income-Earner	6,906	20,000	31.0	8,327	900	40.0	13,474	1,850	36.3
Two Income-Earners	10,926	28,500	44.3	13,830	1,150	51.1	17,033	2,600	51.0
Three or More Earners	15,078	13,150	20.4	19,283	150	6.7	20,363	550	10.8
TOTAL	10,052	64,500	100.0	11,685	2,250	100.0	15,933	5,100	100.0
FEMALE-HEADED FAMILIES:									
No Income-Earners	0	1,750	29.9	—	—	—	—	—	—
One Income-Earner	3,816	2,150	36.8	3,233	150	75.0	5,000	100	28.6
Two Income-Earners	9,939	1,400	23.9	—	—	—	16,366	150	42.9
Three or More Earners	16,036	550	9.4	17,100	50	25.0	25,450	100	28.6
TOTAL	5,288	5,850	100.0	6,700	200	100.0	15,714	350	100.0

SOURCE: Compiled from 1970 U.S. Census Public Use Sample.

NOTE: Median years of education of family heads: 11.2.

FILIPINO AMERICANS

Table 25
Fertility Rates by Woman's Education and Family Income (1969)

25a. EDUCATION

	TOTAL		PRECOLLEGE 0-8 Years		PRECOLLEGE 9-12 Years		COLLEGE 1-3 Years		COLLEGE 4 Years		POSTGRADUATE 1 Year		POSTGRADUATE 2 or More Years	
	Number	Percent	Number	Percent	Number	Percent	Number	Percent	Number	Percent	Number	Percent	Number	Percent
All Women, 15 and older:														
Childless	41,200	40.5	5,200	25.9	17,300	42.4	6,850	42.7	6,600	47.1	3,100	62.0	2,150	37.1
1 Child	14,400	14.2	2,150	10.7	4,900	12.0	2,900	18.1	2,500	17.9	850	17.0	1,100	19.0
2 Children	13,100	12.9	2,800	14.0	4,750	11.6	2,200	13.7	1,650	11.8	650	13.0	1,050	18.1
3 Children	11,400	11.2	2,100	10.5	5,300	13.0	1,700	10.6	1,450	10.4	250	5.0	600	10.3
4 Children	8,350	8.2	2,200	11.0	3,700	9.1	950	5.9	800	5.7	50	1.0	650	11.2
5 Children	5,300	5.2	1,900	9.5	1,900	4.7	650	4.0	650	4.6	50	1.0	150	2.6
6 or More	7,950	7.8	3,700	18.5	2,950	7.2	800	5.0	350	2.5	50	1.0	100	1.7
TOTAL	101,700	100.0	20,050	100.0	40,800	100.0	16,050	100.0	14,000	100.0	5,000	100.0	5,800	100.0
Mean No. of Children	1.9		3.1		1.9		1.5		1.4		0.7		1.6	
Women, 15-24:														
Childless	20,950	75.6	2,000	65.6	12,200	75.5	4,000	75.5	1,900	84.4	750	88.2	100	100.0
1 Child	4,250	15.3	500	16.4	2,100	13.0	1,200	22.6	350	15.6	100	11.8	—	—
2 Children	1,500	5.4	400	13.1	1,000	6.2	100	1.9	—	—	—	—	—	—
3 Children	600	2.2	50	1.6	550	3.4	—	—	—	—	—	—	—	—
4 Children	350	1.3	100	3.3	250	1.5	—	—	—	—	—	—	—	—
5 Children	50	0.2	—	—	50	0.3	—	—	—	—	—	—	—	—
6 or More	—	—	—	—	—	—	—	—	—	—	—	—	—	—
TOTAL	27,700	100.0	3,050	100.0	16,150	100.0	5,300	100.0	2,250	100.0	850	100.0	100	100.0
Mean No. of Children	0.4		0.6		0.4		0.3		0.2		0.1		0.0	

(Table 25 continued on page 328)

FILIPINO AMERICANS—Table 25: Education (Continued)

| | TOTAL | | PRECOLLEGE | | | | COLLEGE | | | | POSTGRADUATE | | | |
| | | | 0-8 Years | | 9-12 Years | | 1-3 Years | | 4 Years | | 1 Year | | 2 or More Years | |
	Number	Percent	Number	Percent	Number	Percent	Number	Percent	Number	Percent	Number	Percent	Number	Percent
Women, 25-34:														
Childless	13,000	38.2	950	30.2	3,400	29.7	1,750	34.7	3,600	46.2	2,000	61.5	1,300	38.8
1 Child	6,000	17.6	250	7.9	1,550	13.5	900	17.8	1,850	23.7	700	21.5	750	22.4
2 Children	6,300	18.5	750	23.8	2,200	19.2	1,100	21.8	1,050	13.5	400	12.3	800	23.9
3 Children	4,500	13.2	450	14.3	2,000	17.5	800	15.8	900	11.5	100	3.1	250	7.5
4 Children	2,600	7.6	400	12.7	1,450	12.7	200	4.0	250	3.2	50	1.5	250	7.5
5 Children	900	2.6	150	4.8	500	4.4	150	3.0	100	1.3	—	—	—	—
6 or More	750	2.2	200	6.3	350	3.1	150	3.0	50	0.6	—	—	—	—
TOTAL	34,050	100.0	3,150	100.0	11,450	100.0	5,050	100.0	7,800	100.0	3,250	100.0	3,350	100.0
Mean No. of Children	1.5		2.2		2.0		1.6		1.1		0.6		1.2	
Women, 35-44:														
Childless	3,300	17.3	600	17.4	800	10.5	550	18.0	750	27.3	150	27.3	450	28.1
1 Child	2,000	10.5	400	11.6	700	9.2	350	11.5	250	9.1	50	9.1	250	15.6
2 Children	2,600	13.6	500	14.5	750	9.8	700	23.0	350	12.7	250	45.5	50	3.1
3 Children	3,750	19.7	650	18.8	1,800	23.5	500	16.4	500	18.2	—	—	300	18.8
4 Children	2,850	15.0	300	8.7	1,350	17.6	400	13.1	450	16.4	—	—	350	21.9
5 Children	2,050	10.8	400	11.6	900	11.8	300	9.8	300	10.9	50	9.1	100	6.3
6 or More	2,500	13.1	600	17.4	1,350	17.6	250	8.2	150	5.5	50	9.1	100	6.3
TOTAL	19,050	100.0	3,450	100.0	7,650	100.0	3,050	100.0	2,750	100.0	550	100.0	1,600	100.0
Mean No. of Children	3.0		3.1		3.6		2.6		2.4		2.1		2.4	

328

FILIPINO AMERICANS—Table 25: Education (Continued)

| | TOTAL | | PRECOLLEGE | | | | COLLEGE | | | | POSTGRADUATE | | | |
| | | | 0-8 Years | | 9-12 Years | | 1-3 Years | | 4 Years | | 1 Year | | 2 or More Years | |
	Number	Percent	Number	Percent	Number	Percent	Number	Percent	Number	Percent	Number	Percent	Number	Percent
Women, 45 and older:														
Childless	3,950	18.9	1,650	15.9	900	16.2	550	20.8	350	29.2	200	57.1	300	40.0
1 Child	2,150	10.3	1,000	9.6	550	9.9	450	17.0	50	4.2	–	–	100	13.3
2 Children	2,700	12.9	1,150	11.1	800	14.4	300	11.3	250	20.8	–	–	200	26.7
3 Children	2,550	12.2	950	9.1	950	17.1	400	15.1	50	4.2	150	42.9	50	6.7
4 Children	2,550	12.2	1,400	13.5	650	11.7	350	13.2	100	8.3	–	–	50	6.7
5 Children	2,300	11.0	1,350	13.0	450	8.1	200	7.5	250	20.8	–	–	50	6.7
6 or More	4,700	22.5	2,900	27.9	1,250	22.5	400	15.1	150	12.5	–	–	–	–
TOTAL	20,900	100.0	10,400	100.0	5,550	100.0	2,650	100.0	1,200	100.0	350	100.0	750	100.0
Mean No. of Children	3.6		4.1		3.5		2.8		3.1		1.3		1.5	

25b. FAMILY INCOME

| | TOTAL | | Less Than $5,000 | | $5,000 - 9,999 | | $10,000 - 14,999 | | $15,000 - 19,999 | | $20,000 - 24,999 | | $25,000 and Over | |
	Number	Percent	Number	Percent	Number	Percent	Number	Percent	Number	Percent	Number	Percent	Number	Percent
All Women, 15 and older:														
Childless	41,200	40.5	12,950	51.2	8,750	32.3	9,500	38.5	5,450	39.9	2,500	39.7	2,050	43.6
1 Child	14,400	14.2	3,000	11.9	5,250	19.4	3,300	13.4	1,700	12.5	550	8.7	600	12.8
2 Children	13,100	12.9	3,250	12.8	3,350	12.4	3,300	13.4	1,950	14.3	800	12.7	450	9.6
3 Children	11,400	11.2	2,250	8.9	2,950	10.9	2,750	11.1	1,800	13.2	900	14.3	750	16.0
4 Children	8,350	8.2	1,550	6.1	2,800	10.4	2,500	10.1	600	4.4	750	11.9	150	3.2
5 Children	5,300	5.2	600	2.4	1,750	6.5	1,150	4.7	1,000	7.3	400	6.3	400	8.5
6 or More	7,950	7.8	1,700	6.7	2,200	8.1	2,200	8.9	1,150	8.4	400	6.3	300	6.4
TOTAL	101,700	100.0	25,300	100.0	27,050	100.0	24,700	100.0	13,650	100.0	6,300	100.0	4,700	100.0
Mean No. of Children	1.9		1.5		2.1		2.0		2.0		2.0		1.9	

(Table 25 continued on page 330)

329

FILIPINO AMERICANS—Table 25: Family Income (Continued)

	TOTAL		Less Than $5,000		$5,000 - 9,999		$10,000 - 14,999		$15,000 - 19,999		$20,000 - 24,999		$25,000 and Over	
	Number	Percent	Number	Percent	Number	Percent	Number	Percent	Number	Percent	Number	Percent	Number	Percent
Women, 15-24:														
Childless	20,950	75.6	5,050	73.2	5,550	68.9	5,550	78.7	2,850	86.4	1,150	82.1	800	80.0
1 Child	4,250	15.3	1,150	16.7	1,550	19.3	900	12.8	400	12.1	150	10.7	100	10.0
2 Children	1,500	5.4	450	6.5	500	6.2	450	8.4	50	1.5	50	3.6	–	–
3 Children	600	2.2	150	2.2	250	3.1	100	1.4	–	–	50	3.6	50	5.0
4 Children	350	1.3	100	1.4	150	1.9	50	0.7	–	–	–	–	50	5.0
5 Children	50	0.2	–	–	50	0.6	–	–	–	–	–	–	–	–
6 or More	–	–	–	–	–	–	–	–	–	–	–	–	–	–
TOTAL	27,700	100.0	6,900	100.0	8,050	100.0	7,050	100.0	3,300	100.0	1,400	100.0	1,000	100.0
Mean No. of Children	0.4		0.4		0.5		0.3		0.2		0.3		0.4	
Women, 25-34:														
Childless	13,000	38.2	5,450	55.6	1,950	21.4	2,450	33.6	1,800	37.1	650	38.2	700	53.8
1 Child	6,000	17.6	800	8.2	2,400	26.4	1,550	21.2	900	18.6	250	14.7	100	7.7
2 Children	6,300	18.5	1,750	17.9	1,900	20.9	1,150	15.8	1,000	20.6	350	20.6	150	11.5
3 Children	4,500	13.2	950	9.7	1,200	13.2	1,050	14.4	800	16.5	200	11.8	300	23.1
4 Children	2,600	7.6	450	4.6	1,000	11.0	850	11.6	100	2.1	200	11.8	–	–
5 Children	900	2.6	150	1.5	250	2.7	150	2.1	250	5.2	50	2.9	50	3.8
6 or More	750	2.2	250	2.6	400	4.4	100	1.4	–	–	–	–	–	–
TOTAL	34,050	100.0	9,800	100.0	9,100	100.0	7,300	100.0	4,850	100.0	1,700	100.0	1,300	100.0
Mean No. of Children	1.5		1.2		2.0		1.7		1.4		1.5		1.2	

330

FILIPINO AMERICANS—Table 25: Family Income (Continued)

	TOTAL		Less Than $5,000		$5,000 - 9,999		$10,000 - 14,999		$15,000 - 19,999		$20,000 - 24,999		$25,000 and Over	
	Number	Percent	Number	Percent	Number	Percent	Number	Percent	Number	Percent	Number	Percent	Number	Percent
Women, 35-44:														
Childless	3,300	17.3	1,200	30.0	550	11.1	650	12.0	300	12.0	350	25.0	250	31.3
1 Child	2,000	10.5	500	12.5	550	11.1	600	11.1	150	6.0	100	7.1	100	12.5
2 Children	2,600	13.6	450	11.2	600	12.1	850	15.7	550	22.0	150	10.7	—	—
3 Children	3,750	19.7	700	17.5	850	17.2	1,150	21.3	600	24.0	250	17.9	200	25.0
4 Children	2,850	15.0	600	15.0	850	17.2	900	16.7	200	8.0	300	21.4	—	—
5 Children	2,050	10.8	150	3.7	800	16.2	450	8.3	350	14.0	100	7.1	200	25.0
6 or More	2,500	13.1	400	10.0	750	15.2	800	14.8	350	14.0	150	10.7	50	6.3
TOTAL	19,050	100.0	4,000	100.0	4,950	100.0	5,400	100.0	2,500	100.0	1,400	100.0	800	100.0
Mean No. of Children	3.0		2.5		3.4		3.1		3.3		2.8		2.6	
Women, 45 and older:														
Childless	3,950	18.9	1,250	27.2	700	14.1	850	17.2	500	16.7	350	19.4	300	18.8
1 Child	2,150	10.3	550	12.0	750	15.2	250	5.1	250	8.3	50	2.8	300	18.8
2 Children	2,700	12.9	600	13.0	350	7.1	850	17.2	350	11.7	250	13.9	300	18.8
3 Children	2,550	12.2	450	9.8	650	13.1	450	9.1	400	13.3	400	22.2	200	12.5
4 Children	2,550	12.2	400	8.7	800	16.2	700	14.1	300	10.0	250	13.9	100	6.3
5 Children	2,300	11.0	300	6.5	650	13.1	550	11.1	400	13.3	250	13.9	150	9.4
6 or More	4,700	22.5	1,050	22.8	1,050	21.2	1,300	26.3	800	26.7	250	13.9	250	15.6
TOTAL	20,900	100.0	4,600	100.0	4,950	100.0	4,950	100.0	3,000	100.0	1,800	100.0	1,600	100.0
Mean No. of Children	3.6		3.1		3.8		3.7		3.9		3.2		3.1	

SOURCE: Compiled from 1970 U.S. Census Public Use Sample.

331

GERMAN AMERICANS

Table 26

Personal Income Distribution by Sex (1970, 1971)

Income and Sex	Percentage Distribution	
	1970	1971
MALE		
Under $1,000	8.2	7.7
$1,000 to $1,999	6.4	5.9
$2,000 to $2,999	6.9	6.7
$3,000 to $3,999	6.2	6.4
$4,000 to $4,999	5.4	5.7
$5,000 to $6,999	12.9	12.5
$7,000 to $9,999	23.6	21.5
$10,000 to $14,999	20.1	21.3
$15,000 to $24,999	8.0	9.4
$25,000 and over	2.3	2.9
Total Percent	100.0	100.0
MEDIAN MALE INCOME	$7,467	$7,693
FEMALE		
Under $1,000	26.3	24.1
$1,000 to $1,999	19.7	19.7
$2,000 to $2,999	12.8	12.2
$3,000 to $3,999	9.7	10.5
$4,000 to $4,999	8.5	8.5
$5,000 to $6,999	12.0	11.9
$7,000 to $9,999	8.2	9.2
$10,000 to $14,999	2.1	3.1
$15,000 to $24,999	0.5	0.5
$25,000 and over	0.3	0.3
Total Percent	100.0	100.0
MEDIAN FEMALE INCOME	$2,316	$2,510

SOURCE: U.S. Bureau of the Census, *Current Population Reports,* Series P-20, No. 249.

GERMAN AMERICANS

Table 27
Family Income Distribution (1970)

Income	Percentage Distribution		
	1968	1970	1971
Under $1,000	1.5	1.4	1.0
$1,000 to $1,999	2.5	1.8	1.7
$2,000 to $2,999	2.8	3.1	3.1
$3,000 to $3,999	5.1	4.7	4.2
$4,000 to $4,999	13.9	4.9	4.8
$5,000 to $5,999		4.8	5.0
$6,000 to $6,999	14.2	5.8	5.7
$7,000 to $7,499			
$7,500 to $7,999		6.7	6.0
$8,000 to $8,999	22.5	7.6	5.8
$9,000 to $9,999		7.0	7.1
$10,000 to $14,999	25.2	27.9	28.5
$15,000 to $24,999	9.7	19.5	21.5
$25,000 and over	2.5	4.7	5.6
Total Percent	100.0	100.0	100.0
MEDIAN FAMILY INCOME	$8,607	$10,402	$10,977

SOURCE: U.S. Bureau of the Census, *Current Population Reports,* Series P-20, No. 221; Series P-20, No. 249.

NOTE: The percentages for 1970 and 1971 apply to single thousands up to $10,000. For 1968, however, 13.9 percent applies to the income range $4,000 to $5,999; 14.2 percent applies to the range $6,000 to $7,499; and 22.5 percent applies to the range $7,500 to $9,999.

GERMAN AMERICANS

Table 28

Occupational Distribution by Sex (1969, 1971, 1972)

Occupation and Sex	Percentage Distribution		
	1969	1971	1972
MALE			
Professional, technical, and kindred workers	14.8	15.9	15.0
Managers and administrators, except farm		15.5	13.9
Managers, officers, and proprietors, except farm	15.4		
Sales workers	6.1	6.8	7.0
Clerical and kindred workers	5.8	6.3	6.0
Craftsmen and kindred workers		19.9	21.7
Craftsmen, foremen, and kindred workers	21.7		
Operatives and kindred workers	18.2		
Operatives, including transport		16.0	16.5
Laborers, except farm		4.5	5.2
Laborers, except farm and mine	4.9		
Farmers and farm managers	6.7	6.0	5.9
Farm laborers and farm foremen	1.6	2.3	2.0
Service workers, except private household	4.7	6.9	6.7
Private household workers	0.0	0.0	0.1
Total percent*	100.0	100.0	100.0
FEMALE			
Professional, technical, and kindred workers	16.6	16.4	17.6
Managers and administrators, except farm		5.0	4.6
Managers, officers, and proprietors, except farm	4.1		
Sales workers	7.6	7.1	5.9
Clerical and kindred workers	33.6	35.1	34.6
Craftsmen and kindred workers		1.6	1.2
Craftsmen, foremen, and kindred workers	0.9		
Operatives and kindred workers	13.0		
Operatives, including transport		10.0	9.8
Laborers, except farm		1.1	0.8
Laborers, except farm and mine	0.3		
Farmers and farm managers	0.4	0.5	0.6
Farm laborers and farm foremen	2.9	2.1	2.8
Service workers, except private household	15.9	14.8	16.6
Private household workers	4.5	6.1	5.4
Total percent*	100.0	100.0	100.0

*The various occupational percentages add up to a total of 100.0 percent because unemployed workers are not counted in this tabulation. Gaps in the Percentage Distribution columns are the result of changes in reporting terminology after 1969.

SOURCE: U.S. Bureau of the Census, *Current Population Reports,* Series P-20, No. 221; Series P-20, No. 249.

334

GERMAN AMERICANS

Table 29

Education, by Age (1969, 1972)

AGE	Percent Distribution							
	Median School Years Completed	Elementary		High School		College		Total
		0 to 7 Years	8 Years	1 to 3 Years	4 Years	1 to 3 Years	4 Years or more	
1969: Education Levels								
25 to 34 years old	12.6	1.6	4.1	14.8	47.4	14.6	17.5	100.0
35 years and over	12.0	10.6	22.0	16.1	34.2	8.6	8.5	100.0
1972: Education Levels								
25 to 34 years old	12.7	1.1	2.3	10.6	51.1	15.6	19.2	100.0
35 years and over	12.2	9.4	18.9	16.1	36.1	9.3	10.2	100.0

SOURCE: U.S. Bureau of the Census, *Current Population Report,* Series P-20, No. 221; Series P-20, No. 249.

IRISH AMERICANS

Table 30

Personal Income Distribution by Sex (1970, 1971)

Income and Sex	Percentage Distribution 1970	1971
MALE		
Under $1,000	8.8	7.7
$1,000 to $1,999	8.3	7.6
$2,000 to $2,999	6.6	6.9
$3,000 to $3,999	6.2	5.8
$4,000 to $4,999	6.3	5.3
$5,000 to $6,999	14.6	12.7
$7,000 to $9,999	21.7	20.0
$10,000 to $14,999	18.3	22.4
$15,000 to $24,999	7.2	8.9
$25,000 and over	1.9	2.6
Total Percent	100.0	100.0
MEDIAN MALE INCOME	$6,881	$7,530
FEMALE		
Under $1,000	25.3	23.4
$1,000 to $1,999	19.5	19.1
$2,000 to $2,999	12.2	12.3
$3,000 to $3,999	10.6	11.0
$4,000 to $4,999	8.3	9.6
$5,000 to $6,999	12.9	12.9
$7,000 to $9,999	8.0	7.9
$10,000 to $14,999	2.4	3.2
$15,000 to $24,999	0.6	0.4
$25,000 and over	0.1	0.2
Total Percent	100.0	100.0
MEDIAN FEMALE INCOME	$2,422	$2,612

SOURCE: U.S. Bureau of the Census, *Current Population Reports,* Series P-20, No. 249.

IRISH AMERICANS

Table 31

Family Income Distribution (1968, 1970, 1971)

Income	Percentage Distribution		
	1968	1970	1971
Under $1,000	2.3	2.0	1.1
$1,000 to $1,999	3.3	2.6	2.3
$2,000 to $2,999	4.9	4.0	3.7
$3,000 to $3,999	5.6	4.6	4.1
$4,000 to $4,999	15.0	5.2	4.8
$5,000 to $5,999		6.2	5.7
$6,000 to $6,999	13.4	5.8	5.7
$7,000 to $7,499			
$7,500 to $7,999		5.7	5.2
$8,000 to $8,999	21.8	7.9	5.7
$9,000 to $9,999		6.5	5.6
$10,000 to $14,999	23.2	28.2	29.4
$15,000 to $24,999	8.3	17.4	20.9
$25,000 and over	2.1	4.0	5.9
Total Percent	100.0	100.0	100.0
MEDIAN FAMILY INCOME	$8,127	$9,964	$11,060

SOURCE: U.S. Bureau of the Census, *Current Population Reports,* Series P-20, No. 221; Series P-20, No. 249.

NOTE: The percentages shown for 1970 and 1971 apply to single thousands up to $10,000. For 1968, however, 15.0 percent applies to the income range $4,000 to $5,999; 13.4 percent applies to the range $6,000 to $7,499; and 21.8 percent applies to the range $7,500 to $9,999.

IRISH AMERICANS

Table 32

Occupational Distribution by Sex (1969, 1971, 1972)

Occupation and Sex	Percentage Distribution		
	1969	1971	1972
MALE			
Professional, technical, and kindred workers	14.1	12.1	11.2
Managers and administrators; except farm		16.3	14.4
Managers, officers, and proprietors, except farm	15.5		
Sales workers	6.3	7.2	7.1
Clerical and kindred workers	8.5	7.1	7.6
Craftsmen and kindred workers		20.5	23.8
Craftsmen, foremen, and kindred workers	20.8		
Operatives and kindred workers	17.9		
Operatives, including transport		17.1	18.5
Laborers, except farm		5.1	5.7
Laborers, except farm and mine	6.1		
Farmers and farm managers	3.6	3.4	2.8
Farm laborers and farm foremen	1.0	1.6	1.1
Service workers, except private household	6.0	9.4	7.8
Private household workers	0.0	0.1	0.2
Total percent*	100.0	100.0	100.0
FEMALE			
Professional, technical, and kindred workers	14.9	15.5	12.9
Managers and administrators, except farm		4.5	5.0
Managers, officers, and proprietors, except farm	6.0		
Sales workers	7.0	7.2	7.5
Clerical and kindred workers	35.6	38.4	38.7
Craftsmen and kindred workers		1.1	1.3
Craftsmen, foremen, and kindred workers	0.9		
Operatives and kindred workers	13.1		
Operatives, including transport		10.3	11.2
Laborers, except farm		0.6	0.7
Laborers, except farm and mine	0.6		
Farmers and farm managers	0.2	0.2	0.3
Farm laborers and farm foremen	1.2	1.0	0.9
Service workers, except private household	16.9	17.4	17.1
Private household workers	3.6	3.9	4.3
Total percent*	100.0	100.0	100.0

*The various occupational percentages add up to a total of 100.0 percent because unemployed workers are not counted in this tabulation. Gaps in the Percentage Distribution columns are the result of changes in reporting terminology after 1969.

SOURCE: U.S. Bureau of the Census, *Current Population Reports,* Series P-20, No. 221; Series P-20, No. 249.

338

IRISH AMERICANS

Table 33

Education, by Age (1969, 1972)

AGE	Median School Years Completed	Percent Distribution						Total
		Elementary		High School		College		
		0 to 7 Years	8 Years	1 to 3 Years	4 Years	1 to 3 Years	4 Years or more	
1969: Education Levels								
25 to 34 years old	12.6	2.6	3.7	18.8	45.1	15.9	13.9	100.0
35 years and over	12.0	14.3	16.3	18.8	32.9	8.4	9.3	100.0
1972: Education Levels								
25 to 34 years old	12.6	3.0	3.4	15.0	46.2	16.1	16.3	100,0
35 years and over	12.1	13.0	14.9	18.5	35.2	8.8	9.5	100.0

SOURCE: U.S. Bureau of the Census, *Current Population Report,* Series P-20, No. 221; Series P-20, No. 249.

ITALIAN AMERICANS
Table 34
Personal Income Distribution by Sex (1970, 1971)

Income and Sex	Percentage Distribution	
	1970	1971
MALE		
Under $1,000	6.1	7.2
$1,000 to $1,999	7.2	5.2
$2,000 to $2,999	5.4	6.8
$3,000 to $3,999	5.4	5.8
$4,000 to $4,999	5.4	5.3
$5,000 to $6,999	12.8	11.4
$7,000 to $9,999	24.9	22.8
$10,000 to $14,999	22.3	24.4
$15,000 to $24,999	8.3	9.2
$25,000 and over	2.1	1.8
Total Percent	100.0	100.0
MEDIAN MALE INCOME	$7,883	$8,072
FEMALE		
Under $1,000	23.4	21.2
$1,000 to $1,999	18.0	19.1
$2,000 to $2,999	12.9	12.0
$3,000 to $3,999	10.4	10.0
$4,000 to $4,999	10.1	9.7
$5,000 to $6,999	15.4	16.8
$7,000 to $9,999	7.3	8.7
$10,000 to $14,999	1.8	2.0
$15,000 to $24,999	0.5	0.5
$25,000 and over	0.1	0.0
Total Percent	100.0	100.0
MEDIAN FEMALE INCOME	$2,667	$2,813

SOURCE: U.S. Bureau of the Census, *Current Population Reports,* Series P-20, No. 249.

ITALIAN AMERICANS

Table 35

Family Income Distribution (1968, 1970, 1971)

Income	Percentage Distribution		
	1968	1970	1971
Under $1,000	0.9	0.6	1.0
$1,000 to $1,999	1.7	2.3	1.1
$2,000 to $2,999	2.4	2.5	2.7
$3,000 to $3,999	3.4	3.2	3.6
$4,000 to $4,999	14.9	4.5	3.8
$5,000 to $5,999		4.4	5.0
$6,000 to $6,999	13.3	4.9	4.1
$7,000 to $7,499		5.9	5.5
$7,500 to $7,999			
$8,000 to $8,999	25.8	7.4	5.9
$9,000 to $9,999		8.0	7.2
$10,000 to $14,999	27.1	29.8	31.1
$15,000 to $24,999	8.9	22.1	23.7
$25,000 and over	1.6	4.4	5.3
Total Percent	100.0	100.0	100.0
MEDIAN FAMILY INCOME	$8,808	$11,089	$11,646

SOURCE: U.S. Bureau of the Census, *Current Population Reports,* Series P-20, No. 221; Series P-20, No. 249.

NOTE: The percentages shown for 1970 and 1971 apply to single thousands up to $10,000. For 1968, however 14.9 percent applies to the income range $4,000 to $5,999; 13.3 percent applies to the range $6,000 to $7,499; and 25.8 percent applies to the range $7,500 to $9,999.

ITALIAN AMERICANS

Table 36

Occupational Distribution by Sex (1969, 1971, 1972)

Occupation and Sex	Percentage Distribution		
	1969	1971	1972
MALE			
Professional, technical, and kindred workers	13.5	14.3	12.7
Managers and administrators, except farm		16.7	14.5
Managers, officers, and proprietors, except farm	14.9		
Sales workers	5.2	7.4	6.4
Clerical and kindred workers	9.1	8.2	8.8
Craftsmen and kindred workers		21.4	22.3
Craftsmen, foremen, and kindred workers	22.7		
Operatives and kindred workers	20.0		
Operatives, including transport		16.3	15.8
Laborers, except farm		6.1	8.6
Laborers, except farm and mine	6.4		
Farmers and farm managers	0.4	0.5	0.5
Farm laborers and farm foremen	0.2	0.0	0.4
Service workers, except private household	7.5	7.1	9.8
Private household workers	0.0	0.0	0.1
Total percent*	100.0	100.0	100.0
FEMALE			
Professional, technical, and kindred workers	9.7	12.2	11.6
Managers and administrators, except farm		6.0	5.7
Managers, officers, and proprietors, except farm	4.5		
Sales workers	7.4	7.6	7.4
Clerical and kindred workers	39.4	37.6	38.6
Craftsmen and kindred workers		1.3	1.0
Craftsmen, foremen, and kindred workers	2.2		
Operatives and kindred workers	25.3		
Operatives, including transport		17.7	18.0
Laborers, except farm		0.9	0.7
Laborers, except farm and mine	0.2		
Farmers and farm managers	0.0	0.0	0.0
Farm laborers and farm foremen	0.2	0.1	0.1
Service workers, except private household	10.4	15.3	15.4
Private household workers	0.9	1.2	1.6
Total percent*	100.0	100.0	100.0

*The various occupational percentages add up to a total of 100.0 percent because unemployed workers are not counted in this tabulation. Gaps in the Percentage Distribution columns are the result of changes in reporting terminology after 1969.

SOURCE: U.S. Bureau of the Census, *Current Population Reports,* Series P-20, No. 221; Series P-20, No. 249.

ITALIAN AMERICANS

Table 37

Education, by Age (1969, 1972)

AGE	Percent Distribution							
	Median School Years Completed	Elementary		High School		College		Total
		0 to 7 Years	8 Years	1 to 3 Years	4 Years	1 to 3 Years	4 Years or more	
1969: Education Levels								
25 to 34 years old	12.5	5.3	3.3	16.3	50.4	12.7	11.9	100.0
35 years and over	10.3	23.5	17.7	20.0	27.6	5.2	5.9	100.0
1972: Education Levels								
25 to 34 years old	12.6	3.3	3.3	13.0	51.1	12.8	16.5	100.0
35 years and over	11.1	19.2	17.0	19.7	31.9	6.1	6.0	100.0

SOURCE: U.S. Bureau of the Census, *Current Population Report,* Series P-20, No. 221; Series P-20, No. 249.

343

JAPANESE AMERICANS

Table 38
Personal Income by Age, Education, and Sex (1969)

AGE AND SEX	Median Yrs. of Educ.	ALL PERSONS			PRECOLLEGE					
					0-8 Years			9-12 Years		
		Mean Income*	Number of Indi-viduals*	Per-cent	Mean Income*	Number of Indi-viduals*	Per-cent	Mean Income*	Number of Indi-viduals*	Per-cent
ALL INDIVIDUALS:										
18-24		$2,840	54,350	13.6	$2,780	700	1.1	$2,819	25,050	12.2
25-34		6,633	80,700	20.2	3,398	3,050	4.9	5,901	35,100	17.1
35-44		7,873	102,400	25.7	4,301	6,400	10.3	6,503	63,200	30.8
45-54		8,227	83,400	20.9	5,340	12,900	20.7	7,718	52,050	25.4
55-64		7,056	33,850	8.5	5,508	13,450	21.6	7,013	15,250	7.4
65 and older		2,874	43,900	11.0	2,368	25,800	41.4	3,320	14,600	7.1
TOTAL	11.7	6,330	398,600	100.0	3,852	62,300	100.0	6,086	205,250	100.0
MALES:										
18-24		3,123	25,300	14.7	3,420	400	1.7	3,142	11,850	14.5
25-34		8,195	34,850	20.2	3,742	900	3.7	7,786	13,450	16.4
35-44		11,166	37,500	21.8	7,073	1,750	7.3	9,501	18,300	22.3
45-54		11,041	39,600	23.0	7,802	4,800	20.0	10,312	24,300	29.6
55-64		9,261	17,300	10.0	7,358	5,950	24.7	9,120	7,950	9.7
65 and older		3,947	17,850	10.4	3,240	10,250	42.6	4,544	6,150	7.5
TOTAL	12.0	8,542	172,400	100.0	5,495	24,050	100.0	8,259	82,000	100.0
FEMALES:										
18-24		2,574	29,050	12.8	2,140	300	0.8	2,483	13,200	10.7
25-34		4,758	45,850	20.3	3,169	2,150	5.6	3,861	21,650	17.6
35-44		4,608	64,900	28.7	2,338	4,650	12.2	4,376	44,900	36.4
45-54		4,831	43,800	19.4	3,345	8,100	21.2	4,691	27,750	22.5
55-64		4,082	16,550	7.3	3,410	7,500	19.6	4,208	7,300	5.9
65 and older		2,022	26,050	11.5	1,698	15,550	40.7	2,291	8,450	6.0
TOTAL	11.4	3,968	226,200	100.0	2,475	38,250	100.0	3,961	123,250	100.0

344

| AGE AND SEX | ALL PERSONS | | | | COLLEGE | | | | | | |
| | | | | | 1-3 Years | | | 4 Years | | | |
	Median Yrs. of Educ.	Mean Income*	Number of Indi-viduals*	Per-cent	Mean Income*	Number of Indi-viduals*	Per-cent	Mean Income*	Number of Indi-viduals*	Per-cent
ALL INDIVIDUALS:										
18-24		$2,840	54,350	13.6	$2,544	21,450	31.7	$3,603	5,650	15.4
25-34		6,633	80,700	20.2	6,288	17,200	25.4	8,346	14,750	40.2
35-44		7,873	102,400	25.7	6,179	14,450	21.4	11,179	9,950	27.1
45-54		8,227	83,400	20.9	8,920	10,100	14.9	12,041	3,950	10.8
55-64		7,056	33,850	8.5	10,217	2,450	3.6	10,555	1,350	3.7
65 and older		2,874	43,900	11.0	2,841	1,950	2.9	7,323	1,050	2.9
TOTAL	11.7	6,330	398,600	100.0	5,887	67,600	100.0	8,833	36,700	100.0
MALES:										
18-24		3,123	25,300	14.7	2,773	9,850	32.9	3,818	2,350	11.9
25-34		8,195	34,850	20.2	7,277	7,500	25.0	10,313	6,900	35.0
35-44		11,166	37,500	21.8	11,146	5,350	17.9	12,969	6,300	32.0
45-54		11,041	39,600	23.0	11,041	5,100	17.0	14,418	2,600	13.2
55-64		9,261	17,300	10.0	13,375	1,500	5.0	11,569	1,050	5.3
65 and older		3,947	17,850	10.4	3,265	650	2.2	9,655	500	2.5
TOTAL	12.0	8,542	172,400	100.0	7,519	29,950	100.0	11,099	19,700	100.0
FEMALES:										
18-24		2,574	29,050	12.8	2,342	11,600	30.8	3,459	3,300	19.4
25-34		4,758	45,850	20.3	5,129	9,700	25.8	5,448	7,850	46.2
35-44		4,608	64,900	28.7	5,445	9,100	24.2	5,541	3,650	21.5
45-54		4,831	43,800	19.4	5,915	5,000	13.3	6,425	1,350	7.9
55-64		4,082	16,550	7.3	4,887	950	2.5	6,300	300	1.8
65 and older		2,022	26,050	11.5	2,602	1,300	3.5	4,733	550	3.2
TOTAL	11.4	3,968	226,200	100.0	4,195	37,650	100.0	5,017	17,000	100.0

(Table 38 continued on page 346)

345

JAPANESE AMERICANS—Table 38 (Continued)

AGE AND SEX	ALL PERSONS				POSTGRADUATE					
					1 Year			2 or More Years		
	Median Yrs. of Educ.	Mean Income*	Number of Individuals*	Per-cent	Mean Income*	Number of Individuals*	Per-cent	Mean Income*	Number of Individuals*	Per-cent
ALL INDIVIDUALS:										
18-24		$2,840	54,350	13.6	$3,984	1,350	10.0	$6,866	150	1.1
25-34		6,633	80,700	20.2	6,785	6,600	48.9	9,027	4,000	30.2
35-44		7,873	102,400	25.7	9,926	2,850	21.1	15,141	5,550	41.9
45-54		8,227	83,400	20.9	13,482	1,650	12.2	17,616	2,750	20.8
55-64		7,056	33,850	8.5	9,755	750	5.6	14,658	600	4.5
65 and older		2,874	43,900	11.0	6,033	300	2.2	6,425	200	1.5
TOTAL	11.7	6,330	398,600	100.0	8,187	13,500	100.0	13,600	13,250	100.0
MALES:										
18-24		3,123	25,300	14.7	4,426	800	11.9	10,000	50	0.5
25-34		8,195	34,850	20.2	6,750	3,250	48.5	10,063	2,850	28.5
35-44		11,166	37,500	21.8	13,553	1,300	19.4	16,424	4,500	45.0
45-54		11,041	39,600	23.0	17,519	900	13.4	20,634	1,900	19.0
55-64		9,261	17,300	10.0	11,800	350	5.2	16,190	500	5.0
65 and older		3,947	17,850	10.4	9,800	100	1.5	6,425	200	2.0
TOTAL	12.0	8,542	172,400	100.0	9,698	6,700	100.0	15,188	10,000	100.0
FEMALES:										
18-24		2,574	29,050	12.8	3,156	550	8.1	5,300	100	3.1
25-34		4,758	45,850	20.3	6,701	3,350	49.3	5,786	1,150	35.4
35-44		4,608	64,900	28.7	6,154	1,550	22.8	8,006	1,050	32.3
45-54		4,831	43,800	19.4	7,392	750	11.0	9,973	850	26.2
55-64		4,082	16,550	7.3	7,671	400	5.9	7,000	100	3.1
65 and older		2,022	26,050	11.5	4,150	200	2.9	—	—	—
TOTAL	11.4	3,968	226,200	100.0	6,475	6,800	100.0	7,689	3,250	100.0

SOURCE: Compiled from 1970 U.S. Census Public Use Sample.

*Number of individuals includes persons who reported zero income. Mean income is calculated only for persons who reported positive or negative income, excluding those with zero income.

Median age of all Japanese Americans: 32.3.

Median age of all Japanese American income earners: 41.3.

Table 39
Personal Earnings by Occupation, Education, and Sex (1969)

OCCUPATIONS	ALL PERSONS			PRECOLLEGE					
				0-8 Years			9-12 Years		
	Mean Earnings	Number of Individuals	Per-cent	Mean Earnings	Number of Individuals	Per-cent	Mean Earnings	Number of Individuals	Per-cent
ALL INDIVIDUALS:									
Learned Professions	$13,960	12,600	4.8	$ —	—	—	$10,770	850	0.6
Other Prof., Tech., etc.	8,454	35,100	13.4	5,000	100	0.4	7,633	7,150	5.0
Mgrs., Offs., & Proprietors	11,235	20,600	7.9	8,332	1,250	4.6	10,643	9,700	6.8
Clerical	5,507	49,600	18.9	5,045	1,550	5.7	5,614	28,950	20.4
Craftsmen	8,710	31,850	12.1	9,026	4,100	15.0	8,827	22,200	15.7
Operatives	5,051	31,200	11.9	4,840	4,900	17.9	5,113	22,950	16.2
Service Workers	3,742	29,600	11.3	3,207	6,350	23.2	3,893	18,500	13.1
Private Household	1,739	4,350	1.7	1,675	1,450	5.3	1,958	2,500	1.8
Laborers	5,710	15,600	6.0	4,811	3,000	11.0	6,038	10,250	7.2
Sales	6,422	16,250	6.2	6,195	1,200	4.4	5,873	9,350	6.6
Farmers, Farm Managers	7,880	4,850	1.9	7,200	1,350	4.9	7,330	2,650	1.9
Farm Laborers	3,747	4,950	1.9	2,746	1,500	5.5	4,404	3,100	2.2
Unemployed	3,548	5,600	2.1	3,216	600	2.2	3,244	3,500	2.5
TOTAL	6,868	262,150	100.0	5,115	27,350	100.0	6,219	141,650	100.0
MALES:									
Learned Professions	14,284	11,650	8.1	—	—	—	11,493	750	1.0
Other Prof., Tech., etc.	10,369	18,150	12.6	5,000	100	0.7	10,105	3,400	4.6
Mgrs., Offs., & Proprietors	12,273	16,050	11.1	8,888	900	6.2	11,866	7,250	9.9
Clerical	7,579	11,800	8.2	6,300	550	3.8	7,549	5,900	8.0
Craftsmen	9,058	29,600	20.5	9,257	3,900	26.8	9,177	20,600	28.0
Operatives	6,531	14,850	10.3	6,930	1,800	12.4	6,798	10,550	14.3
Service Workers	4,840	9,100	6.3	4,444	1,700	11.7	5,013	5,450	7.4
Private Household	3,020	250	0.2	1,750	100	0.7	5,800	100	0.1
Laborers	5,899	14,650	10.1	4,743	2,900	19.9	6,339	9,450	12.8
Sales	9,753	8,600	5.9	9,636	550	3.8	9,719	4,150	5.6
Farmers, Farm Managers	8,187	4,500	3.1	7,256	1,150	7.9	7,770	2,500	3.4
Farm Laborers	4,861	3,050	2.1	3,584	650	4.5	5,556	2,150	2.9
Unemployed	4,797	2,300	1.6	3,260	250	1.7	4,423	1,300	1.8
TOTAL	8,382	144,550	100.0	6,791	14,550	100.0	8,152	73,550	100.0
FEMALES:									
Learned Professions	9,978	950	0.8	—	—	—	5,350	100	0.1
Other Prof., Tech., etc.	6,403	16,950	14.4	—	—	—	5,392	3,750	5.5
Mgrs., Offs., & Proprietors	7,570	4,550	3.9	6,900	350	2.7	7,024	2,450	3.6
Clerical	4,860	37,800	32.1	4,355	1,000	7.8	5,119	23,050	33.8
Craftsmen	4,131	2,250	1.9	4,525	200	1.6	4,321	1,600	2.3
Operatives	3,706	16,350	13.9	3,627	3,100	24.2	3,680	12,400	18.2
Service Workers	3,254	20,500	17.4	2,754	4,650	36.3	3,425	13,050	19.2
Private Household	1,660	4,100	3.5	1,670	1,350	10.5	1,797	2,400	3.5
Laborers	2,805	950	0.8	6,300	100	0.8	2,481	800	1.2
Sales	2,677	7,650	6.5	3,284	650	5.1	2,803	5,200	7.6
Farmers, Farm Managers	3,928	350	0.3	6,875	200	1.6	0	150	0.2
Farm Laborers	1,960	1,900	1.6	2,105	850	6.6	1,794	950	1.4
Unemployed	2,677	3,300	2.8	3,185	350	2.7	2,547	2,200	3.2
TOTAL	4,393	117,600	100.0	3,209	12,800	100.0	4,132	68,100	100.0

(Table 39 continued on page 348)

	ALL PERSONS			COLLEGE					
				1-3 Years			4 Years		
OCCUPATIONS	Mean Earnings	Number of Indi- viduals	Per- cent	Mean Earnings	Number of Indi- viduals	Per- cent	Mean Earnings	Number of Indi- viduals	Per- cent
ALL INDIVIDUALS:									
Learned Professions	$13,960	12,600	4.8	$11,491	1,150	2.5	$12,917	4,400	16.7
Other Prof., Tech., etc.	8,454	35,100	13.4	7,649	7,700	16.9	8,919	9,650	36.7
Mgrs., Offs., & Proprietors	11,235	20,600	7.9	11,230	4,450	9.7	12,358	3,350	12.7
Clerical	5,507	49,600	18.9	4,931	14,350	31.4	6,378	3,650	13.9
Craftsmen	8,710	31,850	12.1	8,295	4,300	9.4	6,977	900	3.4
Operatives	5,051	31,200	11.9	4,891	2,850	6.2	4,100	250	1.0
Service Workers	3,742	29,600	11.3	3,606	3,600	7.9	3,264	850	3.2
Private Household	1,739	4,350	1.7	620	250	0.5	750	100	0.4
Laborers	5,710	15,600	6.0	5,216	2,150	4.7	7,725	200	0.8
Sales	6,422	16,250	6.2	5,633	3,300	7.2	9,978	2,050	7.8
Farmers, Farm Managers	7,880	4,850	1.9	10,042	350	0.8	11,120	500	1.9
Farm Laborers	3,747	4,950	1.9	2,900	250	0.5	0	50	0.2
Unemployed	3,548	5,600	2.1	3,521	950	2.1	6,142	350	1.3
TOTAL	6,868	262,150	100.0	6,418	45,650	100.0	9,409	26,300	100.0
MALES:									
Learned Professions	14,284	11,650	8.1	11,504	1,100	4.6	13,016	4,050	22.6
Other Prof., Tech., etc.	10,369	18,150	12.6	9,174	4,100	17.1	11,113	4,900	27.4
Mgrs., Offs., & Proprietors	12,273	16,050	11.1	12,426	3,200	13.3	12,803	3,050	17.0
Clerical	7,579	11,800	8.2	6,493	3,100	12.9	9,280	1,750	9.8
Craftsmen	9,058	29,600	20.5	8,706	3,950	16.5	7,606	800	4.5
Operatives	6,531	14,850	10.3	5,109	2,050	8.5	3,875	200	1.1
Service Workers	4,840	9,100	6.3	4,055	1,450	6.0	3,328	350	2.0
Private Household	3,020	250	0.2	0	50	0.2	–	–	–
Laborers	5,899	14,650	10.1	5,340	2,100	8.7	7,725	200	1.1
Sales	9,753	8,600	5.9	8,632	1,850	7.7	11,119	1,800	10.1
Farmers, Farm Managers	8,187	4,500	3.1	10,042	350	1.5	11,120	500	2.8
Farm Laborers	4,861	3,050	2.1	2,750	200	0.8	0	50	0.3
Unemployed	4,797	2,300	1.6	5,120	500	2.1	7,640	250	1.4
TOTAL	8,382	144,550	100.0	8,113	24,000	100.0	11,146	17,900	100.0
FEMALES:									
Learned Professions	9,978	950	0.8	11,200	50	0.2	11,771	350	4.2
Other Prof., Tech., etc.	6,403	16,950	14.4	5,912	3,600	16.6	6,656	4,750	56.5
Mgrs., Offs., & Proprietors	7,570	4,550	3.9	8,170	1,250	5.8	7,833	300	3.6
Clerical	4,860	37,800	32.1	4,500	11,250	52.0	3,705	1,900	22.6
Craftsmen	4,131	2,250	1.9	3,657	350	1.6	1,950	100	1.2
Operatives	3,706	16,350	13.9	4,331	800	3.7	5,000	50	0.6
Service Workers	3,254	20,500	17.4	3,304	2,150	9.9	3,220	500	6.0
Private Household	1,660	4,100	3.5	775	200	0.9	750	100	1.2
Laborers	2,805	950	0.8	0	50	0.2	–	–	–
Sales	2,677	7,650	6.5	1,806	1,450	6.7	1,760	250	3.0
Farmers, Farm Managers	3,928	350	0.3	–	–	–	–	–	–
Farm Laborers	1,960	1,900	1.6	3,500	50	0.2	–	–	–
Unemployed	2,677	3,300	2.8	1,744	450	2.1	2,400	100	1.2
TOTAL	4,393	117,600	100.0	4,539	21,650	100.0	5,707	8,400	100.0

OCCUPATIONS	ALL PERSONS			POSTGRADUATE					
				1 Year			2 or More Years		
	Mean Earnings	Number of Indi- viduals	Per- cent	Mean Earnings	Number of Indi- viduals	Per- cent	Mean Earnings	Number of Indi- viduals	Per- cent
ALL INDIVIDUALS:									
Learned Professions	$13,960	12,600	4.8	$10,663	1,500	15.5	$17,169	4,700	40.7
Other Prof., Tech., etc.	8,454	35,100	13.4	7,812	5,550	57.5	10,775	4,950	42.9
Mgrs., Offs., & Proprietors	11,235	20,600	7.9	14,066	900	9.3	14,476	950	8.2
Clerical	5,507	49,600	18.9	6,671	700	7.3	10,175	400	3.5
Craftsmen	8,710	31,850	12.1	3,525	200	2.1	12,033	150	1.3
Operatives	5,051	31,200	11.9	5,933	150	1.6	6,600	100	0.9
Service Workers	3,742	29,600	11.3	5,300	150	1.6	12,133	150	1.3
Private Household	1,739	4,350	1.7	200	50	0.5	—	—	—
Laborers	5,710	15,600	6.0	—	—	—	—	—	—
Sales	6,422	16,250	6.2	7,233	300	3.1	16,000	50	0.4
Farmers, Farm Managers	7,880	4,850	1.9	—	—	—	—	—	—
Farm Laborers	3,747	4,950	1.9	—	—	—	1,100	50	0.4
Unemployed	3,548	5,600	2.1	3,433	150	1.6	11,500	50	0.4
TOTAL	6,868	262,150	100.0	8,473	9,650	100.0	13,642	11,550	100.0
MALES:									
Learned Professions	14,284	11,650	8.1	10,720	1,450	28.4	17,879	4,300	45.5
Other Prof., Tech., etc.	10,369	18,150	12.6	9,392	2,000	39.2	11,641	3,650	38.6
Mgrs., Offs., & Proprietors	12,273	16,050	11.1	14,620	750	14.7	14,652	900	9.5
Clerical	7,579	11,800	8.2	7,633	300	5.9	13,850	200	2.1
Craftsmen	9,058	29,600	20.5	3,525	200	3.9	12,033	150	1.6
Operatives	6,531	14,850	10.3	5,933	150	2.9	6,600	100	1.1
Service Workers	4,840	9,100	6.3	6,200	50	1.0	18,200	100	1.1
Private Household	3,020	250	0.2	—	—	—	—	—	—
Laborers	5,899	14,650	10.1	—	—	—	—	—	—
Sales	9,753	8,600	5.9	7,300	200	3.9	16,000	50	0.5
Farmers, Farm Managers	8,187	4,500	3.1	—	—	—	—	—	—
Farm Laborers	4,861	3,050	2.1	—	—	—	—	—	—
Unemployed	4,797	2,300	1.6	—	—	—	—	—	—
TOTAL	8,382	144,550	100.0	9,990	5,100	100.0	14,858	9,450	100.0
FEMALES:									
Learned Professions	9,978	950	0.8	9,000	50	1.1	9,537	400	19.0
Other Prof., Tech., etc.	6,403	16,950	14.4	6,921	3,550	78.0	8,344	1,300	61.9
Mgrs., Offs., & Proprietors	7,570	4,550	3.9	11,300	150	3.3	11,300	50	2.4
Clerical	4,860	37,800	32.1	5,950	400	8.8	6,500	200	9.5
Craftsmen	4,131	2,250	1.9	—	—	—	—	—	—
Operatives	3,706	16,350	13.9	—	—	—	—	—	—
Service Workers	3,254	20,500	17.4	4,850	100	2.2	0	50	2.4
Private Household	1,660	4,100	3.5	200	50	1.1	—	—	—
Laborers	2,805	950	0.8	—	—	—	—	—	—
Sales	2,677	7,650	6.5	7,100	100	2.2	—	—	—
Farmers, Farm Managers	3,928	350	0.3	—	—	—	—	—	—
Farm Laborers	1,960	1,900	1.6	—	—	—	1,100	50	2.4
Unemployed	2,677	3,300	2.8	3,433	150	3.3	11,500	50	2.4
TOTAL	4,393	117,600	100.0	6,773	4,550	100.0	8,170	2,100	100.0

SOURCE: Compiled from 1970 U.S. Census Public Use Sample.

NOTE: Median years of education: 11.9.

JAPANESE AMERICANS

Table 40
Family Income Distribution by Number of
Income Earners per Family (1969)

INCOME	ALL FAMILIES		NO-EARNER FAMILIES		ONE-EARNER FAMILIES		TWO-EARNER FAMILIES		THREE OR MORE EARNER FAMILIES	
	Number of Families	Percent	Number of Families	Percent	Number of Families	Percent	Number of Families	Percent	Number of Families	Percent
UNDER $ 1,000	2,850	2.1	2,000	26.3	700	1.6	150	0.3	—	—
$ 1,000 - $ 1,999	2,900	2.2	1,550	20.4	1,150	2.6	200	0.4	—	—
$ 2,000 - $ 2,999	3,450	2.6	1,350	17.8	1,450	3.2	650	1.2	—	—
$ 3,000 - $ 3,999	3,600	2.7	1,000	13.2	1,750	3.9	850	1.5	—	—
$ 4,000 - $ 4,999	4,450	3.4	600	7.9	2,700	6.0	1,150	2.0	—	—
$ 5,000 - $ 5,999	5,100	3.8	350	4.6	3,000	6.7	1,550	2.7	200	0.8
$ 6,000 - $ 6,999	5,000	3.8	200	2.6	2,850	6.4	1,850	3.3	100	0.4
$ 7,000 - $ 7,999	6,050	4.6	150	2.0	3,550	7.9	1,900	3.4	450	1.9
$ 8,000 - $ 9,999	12,400	9.3	100	1.3	6,000	13.4	5,600	9.9	700	2.9
$10,000 - $12,999	24,700	18.6	150	2.0	9,150	20.4	11,450	20.3	3,950	16.5
$13,000 - $14,999	15,300	11.5	50	0.7	3,900	8.7	8,450	15.0	2,900	12.1
$15,000 - $19,999	25,900	19.5	—	—	5,300	11.8	13,850	24.6	6,750	28.2
$20,000 - $24,999	11,750	8.8	50	0.7	1,400	3.1	5,550	9.8	4,750	19.8
$25,000 OR MORE	9,350	7.0	50	0.7	1,950	4.3	3,200	5.7	4,150	17.3
TOTAL	132,800	100.0	7,600	100.0	44,850	100.0	56,400	100.0	23,950	100.0
MEAN EARNINGS	$13,377		$2,930		$10,700		$14,392		$19,312	
MEDIAN INCOME	12,502		2,185		9,750		13,675		17,704	

SOURCE: Compiled from 1970 U.S. Census Public Use Sample.

350

JAPANESE AMERICANS

Table 41

Family Income by Age, Education, and Sex of Family Head (1969)

AGE AND SEX OF FAMILY HEAD	ALL PERSONS				PRECOLLEGE						
					0-8 Years			9-12 Years			
	Median Yrs. of Educ.	Mean Income	Number of Indi-viduals	Per-cent	Mean Income	Number of Indi-viduals	Per-cent	Mean Income	Number of Indi-viduals	Per-cent	
ALL INDIVIDUALS:											
18-24		$ 7,561	3,500	2.6	$ 5,000	100	0.5	$ 7,769	1,550	2.3	
25-34		11,400	23,800	17.9	3,010	700	3.6	10,586	9,450	14.3	
35-44		12,707	37,150	28.0	6,602	2,100	10.7	11,227	18,600	28.2	
45-54		14,729	37,800	28.5	12,400	3,750	19.0	14,277	23,700	35.9	
55-64		13,871	16,850	12.7	12,486	5,450	27.7	13,568	8,050	12.2	
65 and older		6,320	13,700	10.3	6,059	7,600	38.6	6,273	4,650	7.0	
TOTAL	11.8	12,401	132,800	100.0	8,988	19,700	100.0	12,086	66,000	100.0	
MALES:											
18-24		8,100	3,150	2.6	5,000	100	0.6	8,713	1,300	2.2	
25-34		11,958	21,450	18.0	3,522	450	2.6	11,674	8,300	14.3	
35-44		13,929	32,350	27.2	9,027	1,450	8.5	12,727	15,350	26.5	
45-54		15,293	34,950	29.4	13,089	3,500	20.6	14,844	21,850	37.7	
55-64		14,330	15,100	12.7	13,121	4,750	27.9	13,902	7,250	12.5	
65 and older		6,223	11,950	10.0	5,765	6,750	39.7	6,329	3,950	6.8	
TOTAL	11.9	13,097	118,950	100.0	9,543	17,000	100.0	12,995	58,000	100.0	
FEMALES:											
18-24		2,714	350	2.5	—	—	—	2,860	250	3.1	
25-34		6,305	2,350	17.0	2,090	250	9.3	2,739	1,150	14.4	
35-44		4,469	4,800	34.7	1,192	650	24.1	4,139	3,250	40.6	
45-54		7,815	2,850	20.6	2,760	250	9.3	7,586	1,850	23.1	
55-64		9,905	1,750	12.6	8,178	700	25.9	10,550	800	10.0	
65 and older		6,981	1,750	12.6	8,394	850	31.5	5,953	700	8.7	
TOTAL	11.1	6,429	13,850	100.0	5,499	2,700	100.0	5,495	8,000	100.0	

(Table 41 continued on page 352)

AGE AND SEX OF FAMILY HEAD	ALL PERSONS				COLLEGE					
					4 Years			1-3 Years		
	Median Yrs. of Educ.	Mean Income	Number of Indi-viduals	Per-cent	Mean Income	Number of Indi-viduals	Per-cent	Mean Income	Number of Indi-viduals	Per-cent
ALL INDIVIDUALS:										
18-24		$ 7,561	3,500	2.6	$ 7,681	1,200	6.6	$ 7,077	450	3.0
25-34		11,400	23,800	17.9	11,389	4,300	23.7	13,788	5,400	35.5
35-44		12,707	37,150	28.0	13,829	5,100	28.1	14,485	5,700	37.5
45-54		14,729	37,800	28.5	14,275	5,300	29.2	17,206	2,150	14.1
55-64		13,871	16,850	12.7	15,303	1,550	8.5	16,590	1,000	6.6
65 and older		6,320	13,700	10.3	3,414	700	3.9	13,750	500	3.3
TOTAL	11.8	12,401	132,800	100.0	12,699	18,150	100.0	14,517	15,200	100.0
MALES:										
18-24		8,100	3,150	2.6	8,165	1,100	6.8	7,077	450	3.1
25-34		11,958	21,450	18.0	11,747	3,800	23.5	13,653	5,050	34.7
35-44		13,929	32,350	27.2	14,406	4,700	29.1	14,742	5,450	37.5
45-54		15,293	34,950	29.4	15,032	4,700	29.1	17,206	2,150	14.8
55-64		14,330	15,100	12.7	15,807	1,300	8.0	16,590	1,000	6.9
65 and older		6,223	11,950	10.0	3,581	550	3.4	14,177	450	3.1
TOTAL	11.9	13,097	118,950	100.0	13,262	16,150	100.0	14,601	14,550	100.0
FEMALES:										
18-24		2,714	350	2.5	2,350	100	5.0	—	—	—
25-34		6,305	2,350	17.0	8,670	500	25.0	15,742	350	53.8
35-44		4,469	4,800	34.7	7,050	400	20.0	8,880	250	38.5
45-54		7,815	2,850	20.6	8,341	600	30.0	—	—	—
55-64		9,905	1,750	12.6	12,680	250	12.5	—	—	—
65 and older		6,981	1,750	12.6	2,800	150	7.5	9,900	50	7.7
TOTAL	11.1	6,429	13,850	100.0	7,992	2,000	100.0	12,653	650	100.0

JAPANESE AMERICANS—Table 41 (Continued)

AGE AND SEX OF FAMILY HEAD	ALL PERSONS				POSTGRADUATE					
					1 Year			2 or More Years		
	Median Yrs. of Educ.	Mean Income	Number of Individuals	Per-cent	Mean Income	Number of Individuals	Per-cent	Mean Income	Number of Individuals	Per-cent
ALL INDIVIDUALS:										
18-24		$ 7,561	3,500	2.6	$ 7,600	200	4.3	$ —	—	—
25-34		11,400	23,800	17.9	10,958	1,800	38.7	12,100	2,150	23.6
35-44		12,707	37,150	28.0	14,785	1,350	29.0	17,751	4,300	47.3
45-54		14,729	37,800	28.5	18,538	850	18.3	21,209	2,050	22.5
55-64		13,871	16,850	12.7	15,785	350	7.5	23,588	450	4.9
65 and older		6,320	13,700	10.3	12,850	100	2.2	5,433	150	1.6
TOTAL	11.8	12,401	132,800	100.0	13,714	4,650	100.0	17,281	9,100	100.0
MALES:										
18-24		8,100	3,150	2.6	7,600	200	4.5	—	—	—
25-34		11,958	21,450	18.0	10,985	1,750	39.3	12,007	2,100	23.9
35-44		13,929	32,350	27.2	15,616	1,200	27.0	17,944	4,200	47.7
45-54		15,293	34,950	29.4	18,538	850	19.1	21,544	1,900	21.6
55-64		14,330	15,100	12.7	15,785	350	7.9	23,588	450	5.1
65 and older		6,223	11,950	10.0	12,850	100	2.2	5,433	150	1.7
TOTAL	11.9	13,097	118,950	100.0	13,944	4,450	100.0	17,380	8,800	100.0
FEMALES:										
18-24		2,714	350	2.5	—	—	—	—	—	—
25-34		6,305	2,350	17.0	10,000	50	25.0	16,000	50	16.7
35-44		4,469	4,800	34.7	8,133	150	75.0	9,650	100	33.3
45-54		7,815	2,850	20.6	—	—	—	16,966	150	50.0
55-64		9,905	1,750	12.6	—	—	—	—	—	—
65 and older		6,981	1,750	12.6	—	—	—	—	—	—
TOTAL	11.1	6,429	13,850	100.0	8,600	200	100.0	14,366	300	100.0

SOURCE: Compiled from 1970 U.S. Census Public Use Sample.

NOTE: Median age of all family heads: 45.5.

JAPANESE AMERICANS

Table 42

Family Earnings by Number of Income Earners,
Education, and Sex of Family Head (1969)

	NUMBER OF INCOME EARNERS			PRECOLLEGE					
				0-8 Years			9-12 Years		
	Mean Family Earnings	Number of Families	Percent of all Families	Mean Family Earnings	Number of Families	Percent of all Families	Mean Family Earnings	Number of Families	Percent of all Families
ALL FAMILIES:									
No Income-Earners	$ 0	7,600	5.7	$ 0	3,450	17.5	$ 0	3,000	4.5
One Income-Earner	9,775	44,850	33.8	5,647	5,450	27.7	8,187	19,100	28.9
Two Income-Earners	13,668	56,400	42.5	10,764	6,300	32.0	13,027	29,350	44.5
Three or More Earners	18,271	23,950	18.0	17,441	4,500	22.8	17,798	14,550	22.0
TOTAL	12,401	132,800	100.0	8,988	19,700	100.0	12,086	66,000	100.0
MALE-HEADED FAMILIES:									
No Income-Earners	0	5,150	4.3	0	2,650	15.6	0	1,650	2.8
One Income-Earner	10,544	38,850	32.7	6,048	4,550	26.8	9,091	15,450	26.6
Two Income-Earners	13,976	52,500	44.1	10,994	5,800	34.1	13,456	26,950	46.5
Three or More Earners	18,463	22,450	18.9	17,735	4,000	23.5	17,965	13,950	24.1
TOTAL	13,097	118,950	100.0	9,543	17,000	100.0	12,995	58,000	100.0
FEMALE-HEADED FAMILIES:									
No Income-Earners	0	2,450	17.7	0	800	29.6	0	1,350	16.9
One Income-Earner	4,798	6,000	43.3	3,619	900	33.3	4,360	3,650	45.6
Two Income-Earners	9,526	3,900	28.2	8,090	500	18.5	8,211	2,400	30.0
Three or More Earners	15,401	1,500	10.8	15,090	500	18.5	13,895	600	7.5
TOTAL	6,429	13,850	100.0	5,499	2,700	100.0	5,495	8,000	100.0

	NUMBER OF INCOME EARNERS			COLLEGE					
				1-3 Years			4 Years		
	Mean Family Earnings	Number of Families	Percent of all Families	Mean Family Earnings	Number of Families	Percent of all Families	Mean Family Earnings	Number of Families	Percent of all Families
ALL FAMILIES:									
No Income-Earners	$ 0	7,600	5.7	$ 0	500	2.8	$ 0	350	2.3
One Income-Earner	9,775	44,850	33.8	10,050	5,550	30.6	12,123	7,500	49.3
Two Income-Earners	13,668	56,400	42.5	13,483	9,500	52.3	16,412	6,000	39.5
Three or More Earners	18,271	23,950	18.0	17,932	2,600	14.3	23,166	1,350	8.9
TOTAL	12,401	132,800	100.0	12,699	18,150	100.0	14,517	15,200	100.0
MALE-HEADED FAMILIES:									
No Income-Earners	0	5,150	4.3	0	300	1.9	0	250	1.7
One Income-Earner	10,544	38,850	32.7	11,026	4,750	29.4	12,212	7,250	49.8
Two Income-Earners	13,976	52,500	44.1	13,779	8,750	54.2	16,203	5,850	40.2
Three or More Earners	18,463	22,450	18.9	17,685	2,350	14.6	24,266	1,200	8.2
TOTAL	13,097	118,950	100.0	13,202	16,150	100.0	14,601	14,550	100.0
FEMALE-HEADED FAMILIES:									
No Income-Earners	0	2,450	17.7	0	200	10.0	0	100	15.4
One Income-Earner	4,798	6,000	43.3	4,253	800	40.0	9,540	250	38.5
Two Income-Earners	9,526	3,900	28.2	10,023	750	37.5	24,566	150	23.1
Three or More Earners	15,401	1,500	10.8	20,260	250	12.5	14,366	150	23.1
TOTAL	6,429	13,850	100.0	7,992	2,000	100.0	12,653	650	100.0

(Table 42 continued on page 356)

| | NUMBER OF INCOME EARNERS | | | POSTGRADUATE | | | | | |
| | | | | 1 Year | | | 2 or More Years | | |
	Mean Family Earnings	Number of Families	Percent of all Families	Mean Family Earnings	Number of Families	Percent of all Families	Mean Family Earnings	Number of Families	Percent of all Families
ALL FAMILIES:									
No Income-Earners	$ 0	7,600	5.7	$ 0	200	4.3	$ 0	100	1.1
One Income-Earner	9,775	44,850	33.8	12,015	2,000	43.0	15,342	5,250	57.7
Two Income-Earners	13,668	56,400	42.5	15,585	2,200	47.3	19,641	3,050	33.5
Three or More Earners	18,271	23,950	18.0	21,820	250	5.4	24,003	700	7.7
TOTAL	12,401	132,800	100.0	13,714	4,650	100.0	17,281	9,100	100.0
MALE-HEADED FAMILIES:									
No Income-Earners	0	5,150	4.3	0	200	4.5	0	100	1.1
One Income-Earner	10,544	38,850	32.7	12,394	1,800	40.4	15,532	5,050	57.4
Two Income-Earners	13,976	52,500	44.1	15,585	2,200	49.4	19,561	2,950	33.5
Three or More Earners	18,463	22,450	18.9	21,820	250	5.6	24,003	700	8.0
TOTAL	13,097	118,950	100.0	13,944	4,450	100.0	17,380	8,800	100.0
FEMALE-HEADED FAMILIES:									
No Income-Earners	0	2,450	17.7	—	—	—	—	—	—
One Income-Earner	4,798	6,000	43.3	8,600	200	100.0	10,550	200	66.7
Two Income-Earners	9,526	3,900	28.2	—	—	—	22,000	100	33.3
Three or More Earners	15,401	1,500	10.8	—	—	—	—	—	—
TOTAL	6,429	13,850	100.0	8,600	200	100.0	14,366	300	100.0

SOURCE: Compiled from 1970 U.S. Census Public Use Sample.

NOTE: Median years of education of family heads: 11.8.

JAPANESE AMERICANS

Table 43

Fertility Rates by Woman's Education and Family Income (1969)

43a. EDUCATION

| | TOTAL | | PRECOLLEGE | | | | COLLEGE | | | | POSTGRADUATE | | | |
| | | | 0-8 Years | | 9-12 Years | | 1-3 Years | | 4 Years | | 1 Year | | 2 or More Years | |
	Number	Percent	Number	Percent	Number	Percent	Number	Percent	Number	Percent	Number	Percent	Number	Percent
All Women, 15 and older:														
Childless	78,500	32.6	6,500	16.2	43,550	32.0	17,600	46.7	6,750	39.7	2,800	41.2	1,300	40.0
1 Child	31,950	13.3	3,650	9.1	17,600	13.0	5,350	14.2	3,350	19.7	1,350	19.9	650	20.0
2 Children	49,250	20.5	5,850	14.6	29,850	22.0	7,050	18.7	4,000	23.5	1,700	25.0	800	24.6
3 Children	34,750	14.4	6,350	15.9	22,300	16.4	3,300	8.8	1,750	10.3	700	10.3	350	10.8
4 Children	21,350	8.9	5,400	13.5	12,450	9.2	2,600	6.9	750	4.4	100	1.5	50	1.5
5 Children	10,750	4.5	3,950	9.9	5,350	3.9	1,050	2.8	300	1.8	–	–	100	3.1
6 or More	14,050	5.8	8,300	20.7	4,800	3.5	700	1.9	100	0.6	150	2.2	–	–
TOTAL	240,600	100.0	40,000	100.0	135,900	100.0	37,650	100.0	17,000	100.0	6,800	100.0	3,250	100.0
Mean No. of Children	2.0		3.5		1.9		1.3		1.3		1.2		1.2	
Women, 15-24:														
Childless	38,200	87.9	1,900	92.7	22,800	88.2	9,950	85.8	2,950	89.4	500	90.9	100	100.0
1 Child	3,600	8.3	100	4.9	1,750	6.8	1,400	12.1	300	9.1	50	9.1	–	–
2 Children	1,250	2.9	50	2.4	950	3.7	200	1.7	50	1.5	–	–	–	–
3 Children	250	0.6	–	–	250	1.0	–	–	–	–	–	–	–	–
4 Children	50	0.1	–	–	50	0.2	–	–	–	–	–	–	–	–
5 Children	–	–	–	–	–	–	–	–	–	–	–	–	–	–
6 or More	100	0.2	–	–	50	0.2	50	0.4	–	–	–	–	–	–
TOTAL	43,450	100.0	2,050	100.0	25,850	100.0	11,600	100.0	3,300	100.0	550	100.0	100	100.0
Mean No. of Children	0.2		0.1		0.2		0.2		0.1		0.1		0.0	

(Table 43 continued on page 358)

357

JAPANESE AMERICANS—Table 43: Education (Continued)

| | TOTAL | | PRECOLLEGE | | | | COLLEGE | | | | POSTGRADUATE | | | |
| | | | 0-8 Years | | 9-12 Years | | 1-3 Years | | 4 Years | | 1 Year | | 2 or More Years | |
	Number	Percent	Number	Percent	Number	Percent	Number	Percent	Number	Percent	Number	Percent	Number	Percent
Women, 25-34:														
Childless	14,200	31.0	450	20.9	5,100	23.6	4,000	41.2	2,650	33.8	1,550	46.3	450	39.1
1 Child	10,350	22.6	300	14.0	4,800	22.2	1,850	19.1	2,050	26.1	950	28.4	400	34.8
2 Children	12,350	26.9	450	20.9	6,400	29.6	2,600	26.8	2,100	26.8	550	16.4	250	21.7
3 Children	5,500	12.0	400	18.6	3,200	14.8	750	7.7	850	10.8	250	7.5	50	4.3
4 Children	2,150	4.7	400	18.6	1,300	6.0	350	3.6	50	0.6	50	1.5	—	—
5 Children	850	1.9	50	2.3	600	2.8	100	1.0	100	1.3	—	—	—	—
6 or More	450	1.0	100	4.7	250	1.2	50	0.5	50	0.6	—	—	—	—
TOTAL	45,850	100.0	2,150	100.0	21,650	100.0	9,700	100.0	7,850	100.0	3,350	100.0	1,150	100.0
Mean No. of Children	1.5		2.3		1.7		1.2		1.2		0.9		0.9	
Women, 35-44:														
Childless	12,350	19.0	900	19.4	7,850	17.5	2,250	24.7	650	17.8	300	19.4	400	38.1
1 Child	8,250	12.7	800	17.2	5,800	12.9	850	9.3	450	12.3	200	12.9	150	14.3
2 Children	17,600	27.1	1,000	21.5	12,100	26.9	2,100	23.1	1,400	38.4	650	41.9	350	33.3
3 Children	14,050	21.6	900	19.4	10,400	23.2	1,650	18.1	700	19.2	250	16.1	150	14.3
4 Children	7,800	12.0	450	9.7	5,500	12.2	1,450	15.9	350	9.6	50	3.2	—	—
5 Children	2,850	4.4	250	5.4	2,000	4.5	550	6.0	50	1.4	—	—	—	—
6 or More	2,000	3.1	350	7.5	1,250	2.8	250	2.7	50	1.4	100	6.5	—	—
TOTAL	64,900	100.0	4,650	100.0	44,900	100.0	9,100	100.0	3,650	100.0	1,550	100.0	1,050	100.0
Mean No. of Children	2.2		2.3		2.3		2.2		2.0		2.0		1.2	

JAPANESE AMERICANS—Table 43: Education (Continued)

| | TOTAL | | PRECOLLEGE | | | | COLLEGE | | | | POSTGRADUATE | | | |
| | | | 0-8 Years | | 9-12 Years | | 1-3 Years | | 4 Years | | 1 Year | | 2 or More Years | |
	Number	Percent	Number	Percent	Number	Percent	Number	Percent	Number	Percent	Number	Percent	Number	Percent
Women, 45 and older:														
Childless	13,750	15.9	3,250	10.4	7,800	17.9	1,400	19.3	500	22.7	450	33.3	350	36.8
1 Child	9,750	11.3	2,450	7.9	5,250	12.1	1,250	17.2	550	25.0	150	11.1	100	10.5
2 Children	18,050	20.9	4,350	14.0	10,400	23.9	2,150	29.7	450	20.5	500	37.0	200	21.1
3 Children	14,950	17.3	5,050	16.2	8,450	19.4	900	12.4	200	9.1	200	14.8	150	15.8
4 Children	11,350	13.1	4,550	14.6	5,600	12.9	800	11.0	350	15.9	—	—	50	5.3
5 Children	7,050	8.2	3,650	11.7	2,750	6.3	400	5.5	150	6.8	—	—	100	10.5
6 or More	11,500	13.3	7,850	25.2	3,250	7.5	350	4.8	—	—	50	3.7	—	—
TOTAL	86,400	100.0	31,150	100.0	43,500	100.0	7,250	100.0	2,200	100.0	1,350	100.0	950	100.0
Mean No. of Children	3.0		3.9		2.6		2.2		1.9		1.5		1.7	

43b. FAMILY INCOME

| | TOTAL | | Less Than $5,000 | | $5,000 - 9,999 | | $10,000 - 14,999 | | $15,000 - 19,999 | | $20,000 - 24,999 | | $25,000 and Over | |
	Number	Percent	Number	Percent	Number	Percent	Number	Percent	Number	Percent	Number	Percent	Number	Percent
All Women, 15 and older:														
Childless	78,500	32.6	18,850	42.6	13,500	26.2	19,500	29.8	13,200	32.4	7,250	35.1	6,200	34.4
1 Child	31,950	13.3	5,650	12.8	9,100	17.7	8,900	13.6	4,350	10.7	2,350	11.4	1,600	8.9
2 Children	49,250	20.5	7,100	16.0	11,450	22.2	14,950	22.8	8,600	21.1	3,200	15.5	3,950	21.9
3 Children	34,750	14.4	4,650	10.5	8,000	15.5	10,250	15.7	6,550	16.1	3,250	15.7	2,050	11.4
4 Children	21,350	8.9	2,950	6.7	4,400	8.5	6,100	9.3	4,000	9.8	1,950	9.4	1,950	10.8
5 Children	10,750	4.5	2,400	5.4	2,050	4.0	2,800	4.3	1,450	3.6	1,050	5.1	1,000	5.6
6 or More	14,050	5.8	2,700	6.1	3,000	5.8	2,950	4.5	2,550	6.3	1,600	7.7	1,250	6.9
TOTAL	240,600	100.0	44,800	100.0	51,500	100.0	65,450	100.0	40,700	100.0	20,650	100.0	18,000	100.0
Mean No. of Children	2.0		1.8		2.1		2.0		2.0		2.1		2.1	

(Table 43 continued on page 360)

JAPANESE AMERICANS—Table 43: Family Income (Continued)

	TOTAL		Less Than $5,000		$5,000 - 9,999		$10,000 - 14,999		$15,000 - 19,999		$20,000 - 24,999		$25,000 and Over	
	Number	Percent	Number	Percent	Number	Percent	Number	Percent	Number	Percent	Number	Percent	Number	Percent
Women, 15-24:														
Childless	38,200	87.9	6,750	83.3	5,950	78.8	10,750	90.0	6,650	93.0	4,800	94.1	3,300	91.7
1 Child	3,600	8.3	1,050	13.0	1,050	13.9	800	6.7	300	4.2	200	3.9	200	5.6
2 Children	1,250	2.9	250	3.1	450	6.0	400	3.3	50	0.7	50	1.0	50	1.4
3 Children	250	0.6	–	–	100	1.3	–	–	50	0.7	50	1.0	50	1.4
4 Children	50	0.1	–	–	–	–	–	–	50	0.7	–	–	–	–
5 Children	–	–	–	–	–	–	–	–	–	–	–	–	–	–
6 or More	100	0.2	50	0.6	–	–	–	–	50	0.7	–	–	–	–
TOTAL	43,450	100.0	8,100	100.0	7,550	100.0	11,950	100.0	7,150	100.0	5,100	100.0	3,600	100.0
Mean No. of Children	0.2		0.2		0.3		0.1		0.2		0.1		0.1	
Women, 25-34:														
Childless	14,200	31.0	3,550	48.3	2,600	22.4	3,050	22.3	2,550	37.5	1,250	36.8	1,200	39.3
1 Child	10,350	22.6	1,100	15.0	3,000	25.9	3,300	24.2	1,600	23.5	850	25.0	500	16.4
2 Children	12,350	26.9	1,600	21.8	3,150	27.2	4,450	32.6	1,600	23.5	650	19.1	900	29.5
3 Children	5,500	12.0	750	10.2	1,450	12.5	1,750	12.8	850	12.5	450	13.2	250	8.2
4 Children	2,150	4.7	300	4.1	650	5.6	900	6.6	150	2.2	50	1.5	100	3.3
5 Children	850	1.9	50	0.7	400	3.4	150	1.1	50	0.7	100	2.9	100	3.3
6 or More	450	1.0	–	–	350	3.0	50	0.4	–	–	50	1.5	–	–
TOTAL	45,850	100.0	7,350	100.0	11,600	100.0	13,650	100.0	6,800	100.0	3,400	100.0	3,050	100.0
Mean No. of Children	1.5		1.1		1.8		1.6		1.2		1.3		1.3	

360

JAPANESE AMERICANS—Table 43: Family Income (Continued)

	TOTAL		Less Than $5,000		$5,000 - 9,999		$10,000 - 14,999		$15,000 - 19,999		$20,000 - 24,999		$25,000 and Over	
	Number	Percent	Number	Percent	Number	Percent	Number	Percent	Number	Percent	Number	Percent	Number	Percent
Women, 35-44:														
Childless	12,350	19.0	2,900	36.5	2,500	15.0	3,300	17.1	2,350	19.0	650	13.3	650	17.6
1 Child	8,250	12.7	900	11.3	2,750	16.5	2,400	12.4	1,450	11.7	450	9.2	300	8.1
2 Children	17,600	27.1	1,650	20.8	5,350	32.1	4,650	24.1	3,550	28.6	1,250	25.5	1,150	31.1
3 Children	14,050	21.6	950	11.9	3,500	21.0	4,800	24.9	2,550	20.6	1,450	29.6	800	21.6
4 Children	7,800	12.0	850	10.7	1,750	10.5	2,600	13.5	1,500	12.1	700	14.3	400	10.8
5 Children	2,850	4.4	450	5.7	400	2.4	1,050	5.4	500	4.0	200	4.1	250	6.8
6 or More	2,000	3.1	250	3.1	400	2.4	500	2.6	500	4.0	200	4.1	150	4.1
TOTAL	64,900	100.0	7,950	100.0	16,650	100.0	19,300	100.0	12,400	100.0	4,900	100.0	3,700	100.0
Mean No. of Children	2.2		1.8		2.1		2.3		2.3		2.5		2.4	
Women, 45 and older:														
Childless	13,750	15.9	5,650	27.0	2,450	15.6	2,400	11.7	1,650	11.5	550	7.6	1,050	13.7
1 Child	9,750	11.3	2,600	12.4	2,300	14.6	2,400	11.7	1,000	7.0	850	11.7	600	7.8
2 Children	18,050	20.9	3,600	17.2	2,500	15.9	5,450	26.5	3,400	23.7	1,250	17.2	1,850	24.2
3 Children	14,950	17.3	2,950	14.1	2,950	18.8	3,700	18.0	3,100	21.6	1,300	17.9	950	12.4
4 Children	11,350	13.1	1,800	8.6	2,000	12.7	2,600	12.7	2,300	16.0	1,200	16.6	1,450	19.0
5 Children	7,050	8.2	1,900	9.1	1,250	8.0	1,600	7.8	900	6.3	750	10.3	650	8.5
6 or More	11,500	13.3	2,400	11.5	2,250	14.3	2,400	11.7	2,000	13.9	1,350	18.6	1,100	14.4
TOTAL	86,400	100.0	20,900	100.0	15,700	100.0	20,550	100.0	14,350	100.0	7,250	100.0	7,650	100.0
Mean No. of Children	3.0		2.6		3.0		2.9		3.2		3.6		3.1	

SOURCE: Compiled from 1970 U.S. Census Public Use Sample.

361

JEWISH AMERICANS

Table 44
Family Income Distribution by Number of Income Earners per Family (1969)

INCOME	ALL FAMILIES		NO-EARNER FAMILIES		ONE-EARNER FAMILIES		TWO-EARNER FAMILIES		THREE OR MORE EARNER FAMILIES	
	Number of Families	Percent	Number of Families	Percent	Number of Families	Percent	Number of Families	Percent	Number of Families	Percent
NO RESPONSE	99,447	32.6	17,693	34.6	48,190	33.5	25,889	30.1	7,675	31.9
UNDER $ 4,000	16,106	5.3	10,231	20.0	4,600	3.2	1,145	1.3	130	0.5
$ 4,000 - 5,999	9,345	3.1	5,182	10.1	3,318	2.3	721	0.8	124	0.5
6,000 - 7,999	10,978	3.6	4,169	8.1	4,371	3.0	2,122	2.5	316	1.3
8,000 - 9,999	15,549	5.1	3,486	6.8	7,751	5.4	3,774	4.4	538	2.2
10,000 - 13,999	34,233	11.2	3,538	6.9	16,671	11.6	11,546	13.4	2,478	10.3
14,000 - 19,999	42,051	13.8	2,930	5.7	19,633	13.7	14,791	17.2	4,697	19.5
20,000 - 24,999	23,727	7.8	1,019	2.0	10,733	7.5	8,778	10.2	3,197	13.3
25,000 - 29,999	16,410	5.4	815	1.6	7,596	5.3	6,031	7.0	1,968	8.2
30,000 - 34,999	9,864	3.2	470	0.9	5,068	3.5	3,674	4.3	652	2.7
35,000 - 39,999	6,874	2.3	581	1.1	3,191	2.2	2,699	3.1	403	1.7
40,000 - 44,999	5,137	1.7	406	0.8	3,078	2.1	1,520	1.8	133	0.6
45,000 - 49,999	2,857	0.9	209	0.4	1,974	1.4	274	0.3	400	1.7
50,000 & OVER	12,529	4.1	465	0.9	7,557	5.3	3,172	3.7	1,335	5.6
TOTAL	305,107	100.0	51,194	100.0	143,731	100.0	86,136	100.0	24,046	100.0
MEAN EARNINGS	$19,259		$9,875		$20,840		$21,045		$22,666	
MEDIAN INCOME	16,371		6,641		17,380		18,387		19,875	

SOURCE: Compiled from National Jewish Population Study, 1969.

362

JEWISH AMERICANS

Table 45
Family Income by Age, Education and Sex of Family Head (1969)

AGE AND SEX OF FAMILY HEAD	ALL PERSONS				PRECOLLEGE					
					0-8 Years			9-12 Years		
	Median Yrs. of Educ.	Mean Income	Number of Indi-viduals	Per-cent	Mean Income	Number of Indi-viduals	Per-cent	Mean Income	Number of Indi-viduals	Per-cent
ALL INDIVIDUALS:										
18-24		$ 9,412	5,740	2.9	$ 5,000	67	0.3	$ 5,601	560	1.0
25-34		17,758	28,245	14.3	4,337	86	0.4	12,457	4,538	7.8
35-44		24,318	39,817	20.1	12,136	576	3.0	16,849	8,145	14.0
45-54		23,312	49,817	25.2	13,388	1,669	8.7	16,879	15,990	27.4
55-64		19,847	38,311	19.3	13,443	3,606	18.7	16,460	16,554	28.4
65 and older		11,597	36,129	18.2	6,880	13,280	68.9	10,860	12,533	21.5
TOTAL	14.7	19,512	198,059	100.0	8,810	19,284	100.0	15,010	58,320	100.0
MALES:										
18-24		9,526	5,446	2.9	5,000	67	0.4	5,256	535	1.0
25-34		18,029	26,667	14.4	4,337	86	0.5	12,895	4,165	7.9
35-44		25,156	37,505	20.3	12,928	499	2.9	17,512	7,258	13.8
45-54		24,266	46,529	25.1	14,978	1,365	7.8	18,086	14,164	26.9
55-64		20,641	35,761	19.3	13,915	3,446	19.8	17,235	15,243	28.9
65 and older		11,788	33,225	17.9	7,040	11,981	68.7	10,916	11,380	21.6
TOTAL	15.0	20,175	185,133	100.0	9,166	17,444	100.0	15,674	52,745	100.0
FEMALES:										
18-24		7,302	294	2.3	—	—	—	13,000	25	0.4
25-34		13,177	1,578	12.2	—	—	—	7,572	373	6.7
35-44		10,728	2,312	17.9	7,000	77	4.2	11,424	887	15.9
45-54		9,798	3,288	25.4	6,253	304	16.5	7,511	1,826	32.8
55-64		8,707	2,550	19.7	3,256	160	8.7	7,454	1,311	23.5
65 and older		9,403	2,904	22.5	5,407	1,299	70.6	10,303	1,153	20.7
TOTAL	12.3	10,016	12,926	100.0	5,426	1,840	100.0	8,726	5,575	100.0

(Table 45 continued on page 364)

AGE AND SEX OF FAMILY HEAD	ALL PERSONS				COLLEGE						
					1-3 Years			4 Years			
	Median Yrs. of Educ.	Mean Income	Number of Indi-viduals	Per-cent	Mean Income	Number of Indi-viduals	Per-cent	Mean Income	Number of Indi-viduals	Per-cent	
ALL INDIVIDUALS:											
18-24		$ 9,412	5,740	2.9	$ 8,204	1,699	4.6	$ 9,350	930	3.5	
25-34		17,758	28,245	14.3	16,463	6,619	17.9	19,941	4,138	15.6	
35-44		24,318	39,817	20.1	21,504	7,607	20.5	26,633	7,503	28.3	
45-54		23,312	49,817	25.2	22,912	11,480	31.0	28,510	6,307	23.8	
55-64		19,847	38,311	19.3	21,047	6,829	18.4	24,806	4,566	17.2	
65 and older		11,597	36,129	18.2	13,792	2,840	7.7	18,247	3,051	11.5	
TOTAL	14.7	19,512	198,059	100.0	19,755	37,074	100.0	24,147	26,495	100.0	
MALES:											
18-24		9,526	5,446	2.9	8,518	1,604	4.7	9,066	863	3.4	
25-34		18,029	26,667	14.4	16,954	5,918	17.3	20,015	4,109	16.1	
35-44		25,156	37,505	20.3	22,927	6,812	19.9	27,124	7,265	28.4	
45-54		24,266	46,529	25.1	23,326	10,973	32.1	28,776	6,213	24.3	
55-64		20,641	35,761	19.3	21,934	6,278	18.3	25,681	4,304	16.8	
65 and older		11,788	33,225	17.9	14,148	2,645	7.7	17,501	2,809	11.0	
TOTAL	15.0	20,175	185,133	100.0	20,487	34,230	100.0	24,473	25,563	100.0	
FEMALES:											
18-24		7,302	294	2.3	2,915	95	3.3	13,000	67	7.2	
25-34		13,177	1,578	12.2	12,318	701	24.6	9,500	29	3.1	
35-44		10,728	2,312	17.9	9,305	795	28.0	11,644	238	25.5	
45-54		9,798	3,288	25.4	13,954	507	17.8	10,952	94	10.I	
55-64		8,707	2,550	19.7	10,940	551	19.4	10,423	262	28.1	
65 and older		9,403	2,904	22.5	8,961	195	6.9	26,909	242	26.0	
TOTAL	12.3	10,016	12,926	100.0	10,956	2,844	100.0	15,225	932	100.0	

AGE AND SEX OF FAMILY HEAD	ALL PERSONS				POSTGRADUATE					
					1 Year			2 or More Years		
	Median Yrs. of Educ.	Mean Income	Number of Indi-viduals	Per-cent	Mean Income	Number of Indi-viduals	Per-cent	Mean Income	Number of Indi-viduals	Per-cent
ALL INDIVIDUALS										
18-24		$ 9,412	5,740	2.9	$11,289	1,204	9.7	$11,194	1,280	2.9
25-34		17,758	28,245	14.3	19,543	2,449	19.7	19,713	10,415	23.4
35-44		24,318	39,817	20.1	26,834	3,621	29.1	29,395	12,365	27.8
45-54		23,312	49,817	25.2	23,123	3,162	25.4	31,504	11,209	25.2
55-64		19,847	38,311	19.3	23,680	1,602	12.9	28,030	5,154	11.6
65 and older		11,597	36,129	18.2	11,938	416	3.3	22,872	4,009	9.0
TOTAL	14.7	19,512	198,059	100.0	22,052	12,454	100.0	26,386	44,432	100.0
MALES:										
18-24		9,526	5,446	2.9	11,644	1,112	9.6	11,303	1,265	2.9
25-34		18,029	26,667	14.4	18,983	2,280	19.6	19,867	10,109	23.2
35-44		25,156	37,505	20.3	27,279	3,501	30.1	29,677	12,170	28.0
45-54		24,266	46,529	25.1	24,137	2,877	24.8	31,846	10,937	25.1
55-64		20,641	35,761	19.3	24,569	1,436	12.4	28,487	5,054	11.6
65 and older		11,788	33,225	17.9	11,938	416	3.6	22,922	3,994	9.2
TOTAL	15.0	20,175	185,133	100.0	22,494	11,622	100.0	26,652	43,529	100.0
FEMALES:										
18-24		7,302	294	2.3	7,000	92	11.1	2,000	15	1.7
25-34		13,177	1,578	12.2	27,094	169	20.3	14,638	306	33.9
35-44		10,728	2,312	17.9	13,854	120	14.4	11,789	195	21.6
45-54		9,798	3,288	25.4	12,885	285	34.3	17,738	272	30.1
55-64		8,707	2,550	19.7	15,984	166	20.0	4,970	100	11.1
65 and older		9,403	2,904	22.5	—	—	—	9,500	15	1.7
TOTAL	12.3	10,016	12,926	100.0	15,879	832	100.0	13,591	903	100.0

SOURCE: Compiled from National Jewish Population Study, 1969.

NOTE· Median age of all family heads: 50.1.

JEWISH AMERICANS

Table 46
Family Income by Number of Income Earners,
Education, and Sex of Family Head (1969)

| | NUMBER OF INCOME EARNERS | | | PRECOLLEGE | | | | | |
| | | | | 0-8 Years | | | 9-12 Years | | |
	Mean Family Income	Number of Families	Percent of all Families	Mean Family Income	Number of Families	Percent of all Families	Mean Family Income	Number of Families	Percent of all Families
ALL FAMILIES:									
No Income-Earners	$10,214	30,577	15.3	$ 5,607	10,061	51.9	$ 8,241	9,865	16.8
One Income-Earner	20,961	93,381	46.9	10,666	5,600	28.9	15,598	25,198	43.0
Two Income-Earners	21,119	59,276	29.8	15,060	3,081	15.9	16,861	17,162	29.3
Three or More Earners	22,713	15,970	8.0	13,048	662	3.4	18,168	6,372	10.9
TOTAL	19,499	199,204	100.0	8,822	19,404	100.0	15,009	58,597	100.0
MALE-HEADED FAMILIES:									
No Income-Earners	10,451	27,143	14.6	5,690	9,195	52.4	8,363	8,629	16.3
One Income-Earner	21,769	87,128	46.8	11,328	4,866	27.7	16,443	22,387	42.3
Two Income-Earners	21,661	56,206	30.2	15,879	2,841	16.2	17,578	15,621	29.5
Three or More Earners	22,723	15,612	8.4	13,048	662	3.8	18,177	6,263	11.8
TOTAL	20,166	186,089	100.0	9,177	17,564	100.0	15,665	52,900	100.0
FEMALE-HEADED FAMILIES:									
No Income-Earners	8,345	3,434	26.2	4,722	866	47.1	7,388	1,236	21.7
One Income-Earner	9,705	6,253	47.7	6,279	734	39.9	8,864	2,811	49.3
Two Income-Earners	11,202	3,070	23.4	5,362	240	13.0	9,593	1,541	27.0
Three or More Earners	22,289	358	2.7	—	--	—	17,674	109	1.9
TOTAL	10,043	13,115	100.0	5,426	1,840	100.0	8,909	5,697	100.0

	NUMBER OF INCOME EARNERS			COLLEGE					
				1-3 Years			4 Years		
	Mean Family Income	Number of Families	Percent of all Families	Mean Family Income	Number of Families	Percent of all Families	Mean Family Income	Number of Families	Percent of all Families
ALL FAMILIES:									
No Income-Earners	$10,214	30,577	15.3	$15,191	3,874	10.4	$14,225	2,411	9.0
One Income-Earner	20,961	93,381	46.9	19,861	17,901	48.0	25,184	13,605	51.0
Two Income-Earners	21,119	59,276	29.8	19,486	12,604	33.8	24,596	8,178	30.6
Three or More Earners	22,713	15,970	8.0	26,058	2,903	7.8	26,562	2,490	9.3
TOTAL	19,499	199,204	100.0	19,732	37,282	100.0	24,142	26,684	100.0
MALE-HEADED FAMILIES:									
No Income-Earners	10,451	27,143	14.6	16,371	3,130	9.1	14,319	2,029	7.9
One Income-Earner	21,769	87,128	46.8	20,624	16,470	47.9	25,502	13,344	51.8
Two Income-Earners	21,661	56,206	30.2	20,004	11,897	34.6	24,717	8,053	31.3
Three or More Earners	22,723	15,612	8.4	26,250	2,874	8.4	26,496	2,326	9.0
TOTAL	20,166	186,089	100.0	20,492	34,371	100.0	24,405	25,752	100.0
FEMALE-HEADED FAMILIES:									
No Income-Earners	8,345	3,434	26.2	10,227	744	25.6	13,727	382	41.0
One Income-Earner	9,705	6,253	47.7	11,082	1,431	49.2	8,940	261	28.0
Two Income-Earners	11,202	3,070	23.4	10,782	707	24.3	16,828	125	13.4
Three or More Earners	22,289	358	2.7	7,000	29	1.0	27,496	164	17.6
TOTAL	10,043	13,115	100.0	10,750	2,911	100.0	15,225	932	100.0

(Table 46 continued on page 368)

	NUMBER OF INCOME EARNERS			POSTGRADUATE					
				1 Year			2 or More Years		
	Mean Family Income	Number of Families	Percent of all Families	Mean Family Income	Number of Families	Percent of all Families	Mean Family Income	Number of Families	Percent of all Families
ALL FAMILIES:									
No Income-Earners	$10,214	30,577	15.3	$20,726	778	6.2	$18,213	3,588	8.0
One Income-Earner	20,961	93,381	46.9	22,727	6,268	50.1	26,764	24,809	55.5
Two Income-Earners	21,119	59,276	29.8	21,029	4,661	37.2	27,325	13,590	30.4
Three or More Earners	22,713	15,970	8.0	24,835	814	6.5	27,968	2,729	6.1
TOTAL	19,499	199,204	100.0	22,108	12,521	100.0	26,322	44,716	100.0
MALE-HEADED FAMILIES:									
No Income-Earners	10,451	27,143	14.6	22,101	631	5.4	18,403	3,529	8.1
One Income-Earner	21,769	87,128	46.8	23,533	5,811	49.7	27,082	24,250	55.3
Two Income-Earners	21,661	56,206	30.2	21,001	4,458	38.1	27,530	13,336	30.4
Three or More Earners	22,723	15,612	8.4	24,434	789	6.7	28,140	2,698	6.2
TOTAL	20,166	186,089	100.0	22,551	11,689	100.0	26,584	43,813	100.0
FEMALE-HEADED FAMILIES:									
No Income-Earners	8,345	3,434	26.2	14,823	147	17.7	6,847	59	6.5
One Income-Earner	9,705	6,253	47.7	12,478	457	54.9	12,997	559	61.9
Two Income-Earners	11,202	3,070	23.4	21,637	203	24.4	16,537	254	28.1
Three or More Earners	22,289	358	2.7	37,500	25	3.0	13,000	31	3.4
TOTAL	10,043	13,115	100.0	15,879	832	100.0	13,591	903	100.0

SOURCE: Compiled from National Jewish Population Study, 1969.
NOTE: Median years of education of family heads: 14.7.

Table 47
Number of Children in Household by Woman's Education and Family Income:* 1969

47a. EDUCATION

| | TOTAL | | PRECOLLEGE | | | | COLLEGE | | | | POSTGRADUATE | | | |
| | | | 0-8 Years | | 9-12 Years | | 1-3 Years | | 4 Years | | 1 Year | | 2 or More Years | |
	Number	Percent	Number	Percent	Number	Percent	Number	Percent	Number	Percent	Number	Percent	Number	Percent
All Women, 15 and older:														
Childless	126,087	44.3	23,493	77.8	55,524	44.6	21,160	31.8	10,936	39.0	6,149	42.2	8,825	42.6
1 Child	47,695	16.8	1,818	6.0	21,218	17.0	14,672	22.1	4,512	16.1	2,444	16.8	3,031	14.6
2 Children	64,960	22.8	2,820	9.3	27,501	22.1	18,234	27.4	7,402	26.4	3,242	22.2	5,761	27.8
3 Children	35,472	12.5	1,290	4.3	15,660	12.6	10,074	15.1	3,924	14.0	2,126	14.6	2,398	11.6
4 Children	8,121	2.9	515	1.7	3,467	2.8	1,891	2.8	1,058	3.8	532	3.7	658	3.2
5 Children	1,184	0.4	169	0.6	669	0.5	248	0.4	67	0.2	–	–	31	0.1
6 or More	1,031	0.4	111	0.4	483	0.4	249	0.4	109	0.4	79	0.5	–	–
TOTAL	284,550	100.0	30,216	100.0	124,522	100.0	66,528	100.0	28,008	100.0	14,572	100.0	20,704	100.0
Mean No. of Children	1.2		0.5		1.2		1.4		1.3		1.3		1.2	
Women, 15-24:														
Childless	13,334	22.4	116	5.8	2,713	9.0	6,180	30.1	1,629	49.4	1,804	73.0	892	71.2
1 Child	15,583	26.2	180	9.0	6,852	22.8	6,846	33.3	1,101	33.4	453	18.3	151	12.1
2 Children	17,168	28.8	945	47.4	10,447	34.8	4,883	23.8	537	16.3	147	5.9	209	16.7
3 Children	10,452	17.5	519	26.0	7,716	25.7	2,121	10.3	29	0.9	67	2.7	–	–
4 Children	2,456	4.1	206	10.3	1,895	6.3	355	1.7	–	–	–	–	–	–
5 Children	320	0.5	29	1.5	209	0.7	82	0.4	–	–	–	–	–	–
6 or More	249	0.4	–	–	180	0.6	69	0.3	–	–	–	–	–	–
TOTAL	59,562	100.0	1,995	100.0	30,012	100.0	20,536	100.0	3,296	100.0	2,471	100.0	1,252	100.0
Mean No. of Children	1.6		2.3		2.0		1.3		0.7		0.4		0.5	

*See note at end of table 47 (p. 373).

(Table 47 continued on page 370)

369

JEWISH AMERICANS—Table 47: Education (Continued)

| | TOTAL | | PRECOLLEGE | | | | COLLEGE | | | | POSTGRADUATE | | | |
| | | | 0-8 Years | | 9-12 Years | | 1-3 Years | | 4 Years | | 1 Year | | 2 or More Years | |
	Number	Percent	Number	Percent	Number	Percent	Number	Percent	Number	Percent	Number	Percent	Number	Percent
Women, 25-34:														
Childless	10,283	26.0	116	38.2	2,321	21.6	2,088	18.0	2,130	27.6	1,720	42.9	1,908	36.7
1 Child	5,624	14.2	–	–	1,340	12.5	1,385	12.0	1,337	17.3	636	15.9	926	17.8
2 Children	16,649	42.1	163	53.6	5,087	47.4	5,335	46.1	3,085	40.0	1,150	28.7	1,829	35.2
3 Children	5,737	14.5	–	–	1,606	15.0	2,226	19.2	1,074	13.9	399	10.0	432	8.3
4 Children	1,049	2.7	25	8.2	300	2.8	464	4.0	92	1.2	101	2.5	67	1.3
5 Children	196	0.5	–	–	81	0.8	84	0.7	–	–	–	–	31	0.6
6 or More	–	–	–	–	–	–	–	–	–	–	–	–	–	–
TOTAL	39,538	100.0	304	100.0	10,735	100..0	11,582	100.0	7,718	100.0	4,006	100.0	5,193	100.0
Mean No. of Children	1.6		1.4		1.7		1.8		1.4		1.1		1.2	
Women, 35-44:														
Childless	4,635	9.8	67	5.6	1,736	11.0	560	4.3	1,141	14.7	199	5.1	932	17.0
1 Child	6,102	12.9	285	23.8	2,241	14.2	1,966	15.1	723	9.3	295	7.5	592	10.8
2 Children	17,383	36.9	387	32.4	5,734	36.2	5,085	39.2	2,477	31.9	1,397	35.7	2,303	42.0
3 Children	14,508	30.8	245	20.5	4,569	28.9	4,447	34.2	2,422	31.2	1,561	39.9	1,264	23.0
4 Children	3,732	7.9	144	12.1	1,082	6.8	863	6.6	818	10.5	431	11.0	394	7.2
5 Children	500	1.2	67	5.6	379	2.4	67	0.5	67	0.9	–	–	–	–
6 or More	226	0.5	–	–	90	0.6	–	–	109	1.4	27	0.7	–	–
TOTAL	47,166	100.0	1,195	100.0	15,831	100.0	12,988	100.0	7,757	100.0	3,910	100.0	5,485	100.0
Mean No. of Children	2.2		2.3		2.2		2.3		2.3		2.6		1.9	

JEWISH AMERICANS—Table 47: Education (Continued)

| | TOTAL | | PRECOLLEGE | | | | COLLEGE | | | | POSTGRADUATE | | | |
| | | | 0-8 Years | | 9-12 Years | | 1-3 Years | | 4 Years | | 1 Year | | 2 or More Years | |
	Number	Percent	Number	Percent	Number	Percent	Number	Percent	Number	Percent	Number	Percent	Number	Percent
Women, 45 and older:														
Childless	97,835	70.7	23,194	86.8	48,754	71.8	12,332	57.6	6,036	65.3	2,426	58.0	5,093	58.0
1 Child	20,386	14.7	1,353	5.1	10,785	15.9	4,475	20.9	1,351	14.6	1,060	25.3	1,362	15.5
2 Children	13,760	10.0	1,325	5.0	6,233	9.2	2,931	13.7	1,303	14.1	548	13.1	1,420	16.2
3 Children	4,775	3.5	526	2.0	1,769	2.6	1,280	6.0	399	4.3	99	2.4	702	8.0
4 Children	884	0.6	140	0.5	190	0.3	209	1.0	148	1.6	—	—	197	2.2
5 Children	88	0.1	73	0.3	—	—	15	0.1	—	—	—	—	—	—
6 or More	556	0.4	111	0.4	213	0.3	180	0.8	—	—	52	1.2	—	—
TOTAL	138,284	100.0	26,722	100.0	67,944	100.0	21,422	100.0	9,237	100.0	4,185	100.0	8,774	100.0
Mean No. of Children	0.5		0.3		0.5		0.9		0.6		0.7		0.8	

47b. FAMILY INCOME

| | TOTAL | | Less Than $4,000 | | $4,000 - 9,999 | | $10,000 - 15,999 | | $16,000 - 19,999 | | $20,000 - 24,999 | | $25,000 and Over | |
	Number	Percent	Number	Percent	Number	Percent	Number	Percent	Number	Percent	Number	Percent	Number	Percent
All Women, 15 and older:														
Childless	126,087	44.3	24,861	88.4	34,365	66.2	26,387	40.6	11,228	33.0	9,347	30.2	19,899	26.7
1 Child	47,695	16.8	1,302	4.6	6,994	13.5	13,939	21.5	7,048	20.7	5,571	18.0	12,841	17.2
2 Children	64,960	22.8	1,098	3.9	6,853	13.2	15,188	23.4	10,573	31.1	8,524	27.5	22,724	30.5
3 Children	35,472	12.5	614	2.2	3,016	5.8	7,327	11.3	3,911	11.5	6,678	21.6	13,926	18.7
4 Children	8,121	2.9	153	0.5	415	0.8	1,614	2.5	938	2.8	541	1.7	4,460	6.0
5 Children	1,184	0.4	—	—	104	0.2	286	0.4	291	0.9	100	0.3	403	0.5
6 or More	1,031	0.4	82	0.3	169	0.3	234	0.4	—	—	182	0.6	364	0.5
TOTAL	284,550	100.0	28,110	100.0	51,916	100.0	64,975	100.0	33,989	100.0	30,943	100.0	74,617	100.0
Mean No. of Children	1.2		0.2		0.6		1.2		1.3		1.5		1.7	

(Table 47 continued on page 372)

JEWISH AMERICANS—Table 47: Family Income (Continued)

	TOTAL		Less Than $4,000		$4,000 - 9,999		$10,000 - 14,999		$15,000 - 19,999		$20,000 - 24,999		$25,000 and Over	
	Number	Percent	Number	Percent	Number	Percent	Number	Percent	Number	Percent	Number	Percent	Number	Percent
Women, 15-24:														
Childless	13,334	22.4	1,365	56.4	4,206	45.8	3,080	21.8	1,801	22.7	890	13.3	1,992	10.4
1 Child	15,583	26.2	350	14.5	2,259	24.6	4,745	33.6	2,012	25.3	1,732	25.8	4,485	23.4
2 Children	17,168	28.8	245	10.1	1,744	19.0	3,902	27.6	2,715	34.2	1,805	26.9	6,757	35.2
3 Children	10,452	17.5	402	16.6	781	8.5	1,836	13.0	1,076	13.5	1,959	29.2	4,398	22.9
4 Children	2,456	4.1	58	2.4	73	0.8	397	2.8	207	2.6	294	4.4	1,427	7.4
5 Children	320	0.5	—	—	58	0.6	67	0.5	134	1.7	30	0.4	31	0.2
6 or More	249	0.4	—	—	67	0.7	96	0.7	—	—	—	—	86	0.4
TOTAL	59,562	100.0	2,420	100.0	9,188	100.0	14,123	100.0	7,945	100.0	6,710	100.0	19,176	100.0
Mean No. of Children	1.6		0.9		1.0		1.5		1.5		1.9		2.0	
Women, 25-34:														
Childless	10,283	26.0	219	32.8	1,965	34.7	3,254	28.5	1,082	17.2	1,368	27.2	2,395	22.9
1 Child	5,624	14.2	42	6.3	541	9.5	2,225	19.5	1,208	19.2	435	8.6	1,173	11.2
2 Children	16,649	42.1	353	52.8	2,219	39.2	4,166	36.4	2,921	46.4	2,580	51.3	4,410	42.2
3 Children	5,737	14.5	49	7.3	772	13.6	1,494	13.1	782	12.4	591	11.8	2,049	19.6
4 Children	1,049	2.7	5	0.7	169	3.0	291	2.5	301	4.8	—	—	283	2.7
5 Children	196	0.5	—	—	—	—	—	—	—	—	55	1.1	141	1.3
6 or More	—	—	—	—	—	—	—	—	—	—	—	—	—	—
TOTAL	39,538	100.0	668	100.0	5,666	100.0	11,430	100.0	6,294	100.0	5,029	100.0	10,451	100.0
Mean No. of Children	1.6		1.4		1.4		1.4		1.7		1.5		1.7	

JEWISH AMERICANS—Table 47: Family Income (Continued)

	TOTAL		Less Than $4,000		$4,000 - 9,999		$10,000 - 15,999		$16,000 - 19,999		$20,000 - 24,999		$25,000 and Over	
	Number	Percent	Number	Percent	Number	Percent	Number	Percent	Number	Percent	Number	Percent	Number	Percent
Women, 35-44:														
Childless	4,635	9.8	111	17.9	903	20.0	1,135	10.9	599	9.2	610	8.4	1,277	7.2
1 Child	6,102	12.9	77	12.4	1,032	22.8	1,690	16.2	799	12.3	812	11.1	1,692	9.5
2 Children	17,383	36.9	209	33.7	1,393	30.8	3,716	35.6	3,146	48.4	2,305	31.6	6,614	37.2
3 Children	14,508	30.8	163	26.2	1,011	22.4	2,879	27.6	1,441	22.2	3,341	45.8	5,673	31.9
4 Children	3,732	7.9	61	9.8	133	2.9	763	7.3	357	5.5	197	2.7	2,221	12.5
5 Children	500	1.2	—	—	46	1.0	219	2.1	157	2.4	—	—	158	0.9
6 or More	226	0.5	—	—	—	—	42	0.4	—	—	29	0.4	155	0.9
TOTAL	47,166	100.0	621	100.0	4,518	100.0	10,444	100.0	6,499	100.0	7,294	100.0	17,790	100.0
Mean No. of Children	2.2		2.0		1.7		2.2		2.1		2.2		2.4	
Women, 45 and older:														
Childless	97,835	70.7	23,166	94.9	27,291	83.9	18,918	65.3	7,746	58.5	6,479	54.4	14,235	52.3
1 Child	20,386	14.7	833	3.4	3,162	9.7	5,279	18.2	3,029	22.9	2,592	21.8	5,491	20.2
2 Children	13,760	10.0	291	1.2	1,497	4.6	3,404	11.7	1,791	13.5	1,834	15.4	4,943	18.2
3 Children	4,775	3.5	—	—	452	1.4	1,118	3.9	612	4.6	787	6.6	1,806	6.6
4 Children	884	0.6	29	0.1	40	0.1	163	0.6	73	0.6	50	0.4	529	1.9
5 Children	88	0.1	—	—	—	—	—	—	—	—	15	0.1	73	0.3
6 or More	556	0.4	82	0.3	102	0.3	96	0.3	—	—	153	1.3	123	0.5
TOTAL	138,284	100.0	24,401	100.0	32,544	100.0	28,978	100.0	13,251	100.0	11,910	100.0	27,200	100.0
Mean No. of Children	0.5		0.1		0.3		0.6		0.7		0.8		0.9	

SOURCE: Compiled from National Jewish Population Study, 1969.

*Note that number of children "in household" at time of survey differs substantially from fertility rate, which includes all children — those now grown, those in colleges, the military boarding schools, and all other places other than at home. Therefore the numbers in this table are not conceptually comparable to those in other tables for other ethnic groups.

MEXICAN AMERICANS

Table 48
Family Income Distribution (1968)

Income	Percentage Distribution
Under $1,000	3.3
$1,000 to $1,999	5.4
$2,000 to $2,999	9.8
$3,000 to $3,999	12.7
$4,000 to $5,999	25.3
$6,000 to $7,499	16.6
$7,500 to $9,999	15.0
$10,000 to $14,999	9.9
$15,000 to $24,999	1.6
$25,000 and over	0.4
Total Percent	100.0
MEDIAN FAMILY INCOME	$5,488

SOURCE: U.S. Bureau of the Census, *Current Population Reports,* Series P-20, No. 213.

MEXICAN AMERICANS

Table 49
Family Income Distribution by Age of Family Head (1970)

Age	Income Distribution
14 to 24 years old	$5,534
25 to 34 years old	7,567
35 to 44 years old	8,058
45 to 54 years old	7,491
55 to 64 years old	7,997
65 years old and over	*
MEDIAN FAMILY INCOME	8,946

*Insufficient sample size

SOURCE: Bureau of the Census, *Current Population Reports,* Series P-20, No. 224.

MEXICAN AMERICANS

Table 50
Occupational Distribution (1971)

Occupation	Percentage Distribution
Professional and technical	4.5
Managers, administrators, except farm	5.4
Sales workers	2.2
Clerical workers	6.2
Craftsmen and kindred	19.7
Operatives, including transport	27.7
Laborers, except farm	15.0
Farmers and farm managers	0.1
Farm laborers and farm foremen	8.2
Service workers	11.1
Total Percent	100.0

SOURCE: U.S. Bureau of the Census, *Current Population Reports*, Series P-20, No. 224.

MEXICAN AMERICANS

Table 51
Education, by Age (1969)

AGE	Percent Distribution						
	Median School Years Completed	Elementary		High School		College	Total
		0 to 7 Years	8 Years	1 to 3 Years	4 Years	1 or more Years	
1969 Education Levels 25 to 34 years old	10.8	23.2	12.1	24.4	32.2	8.4	100.0
35 years and over	7.3	54.8	13.6	13.9	12.0	5.7	100.0

SOURCE: Percentages derived from numerical totals in U.S. Bureau of the Census, *Current Population Reports,* Series P-20, No. 213.

POLISH AMERICANS
Table 52
Personal Income Distribution by Sex (1970, 1971)

Income and Sex	Percentage Distribution 1970	1971
MALE		
Under $1,000	6.6	7.0
$1,000 to $1,999	6.0	5.1
$2,000 to $2,999	4.4	5.0
$3,000 to $3,999	5.0	5.7
$4,000 to $4,999	4.4	5.0
$5,000 to $6,999	12.9	12.6
$7,000 to $9,999	27.9	22.1
$10,000 to $14,999	23.4	23.6
$15,000 to $24,999	7.4	11.7
$25,000 and over	1.9	2.3
Total Percent	100.0	100.0
MEDIAN MALE INCOME	$8,154	$8,366
FEMALE		
Under $1,000	22.4	19.4
$1,000 to $1,999	16.9	19.3
$2,000 to $2,999	10.2	12.6
$3,000 to $3,999	10.0	8.7
$4,000 to $4,999	11.3	9.8
$5,000 to $6,999	15.4	15.2
$7,000 to $9,999	10.4	10.8
$10,000 to $14,999	2.6	3.5
$15,000 to $24,999	0.6	0.5
$25,000 and over	0.2	0.0
Total Percent	100.0	100.0
MEDIAN FEMALE INCOME	$3,052	$2,891

SOURCE: U.S. Bureau of the Census, *Current Population Reports,* Series P-20, No. 249.

POLISH AMERICANS

Table 53

Family Income Distribution (1968, 1970, 1971)

Income	Percentage Distribution		
	1968	1970	1971
Under $1,000	0.9	0.7	0.9
$1,000 to $1,999	2.3	1.6	1.6
$2,000 to $2,999	2.7	2.0	2.2
$3,000 to $3,999	3.7	2.9	3.4
$4,000 to $4,999	13.4	3.6	4.2
$5,000 to $5,999		3.6	3.3
$6,000 to $6,999	13.4	5.0	4.5
$7,000 to $7,499		5.7	5.8
$7,500 to $7,999			
$8,000 to $8,999	25.2	7.0	5.0
$9,000 to $9,999		7.5	6.0
$10,000 to $14,999	28.1	32.4	30.3
$15,000 to $24,999	8.9	22.5	27.1
$25,000 and over	1.3	5.5	5.6
Total Percent	100.0	100.0	100.0
MEDIAN FAMILY INCOME	$8,849	$11,619	$12,182

SOURCE: U.S. Bureau of the Census, *Current Population Reports,* Series P-20, No. 221; Series P-20, No. 249.

NOTE: The percentages shown for 1970 and 1971 apply to single thousands up to $10,000. For 1968, however 13.4 percent applies to the income range $4,000 to $5,999; 13.4 percent applies to the range $6,000 to $7,499; and 25.2 percent applies to the range $7,500 to $9,999.

POLISH AMERICANS

Table 54

Occupational Distribution by Sex (1969, 1971, 1972)

Occupation and Sex	Percentage Distribution		
	1969	1971	1972
MALE			
Professional, technical, and kindred workers	14.5	15.8	18.1
Managers and administrators, except farm		12.3	12.9
Managers, officers, and proprietors, except farm	15.2		
Sales workers	6.2	5.5	6.3
Clerical and kindred workers	8.8	8.6	7.9
Craftsmen and kindred workers		21.3	23.3
Craftsmen, foremen, and kindred workers	24.4		
Operatives and kindred workers	19.6		
Operatives, including transport		21.4	18.3
Laborers, except farm		5.6	4.3
Laborers, except farm and mine	6.1		
Farmers and farm managers	1.6	1.1	0.9
Farm laborers and farm foremen	0.6	0.4	0.4
Service workers, except private household	3.0	8.1	7.7
Private household workers	0.1	0.0	0.0
Total percent*	100.0	100.0	100.0
FEMALE			
Professional, technical, and kindred workers	13.1	13.0	14.1
Managers and administrators, except farm		2.9	4.9
Managers, officers, and proprietors, except farm	3.4		
Sales workers	8.5	8.4	8.0
Clerical and kindred workers	35.6	37.2	36.0
Craftsmen and kindred workers		0.9	1.2
Craftsmen, foremen, and kindred workers	1.1		
Operatives and kindred workers	19.2		
Operatives, including transport		18.1	16.8
Laborers, except farm		1.3	0.9
Laborers, except farm and mine	0.3		
Farmers and farm managers	0.0	1.0	0.1
Farm laborers and farm foremen	1.3	0.8	1.3
Service workers, except private household	15.5	13.7	15.1
Private household workers	2.1	2.9	1.7
Total percent*	100.0	100.0	100.0

*The various occupational percentages add up to a total of 100.0 percent because unemployed workers are not counted in this tabulation. Gaps in the Percentage Distribution columns are the result of changes in reporting terminology after 1969.

SOURCE: U.S. Bureau of the Census, *Current Population Reports,* Series P-20, No. 221; Series P20, No. 249.

POLISH AMERICANS

Table 55

Education, by Age (1969, 1972)

AGE	Median School Years Completed	Elementary		High School		College		Total
		0 to 7 Years	8 Years	1 to 3 Years	4 Years	1 to 3 Years	4 Years or more	
1969: Education Levels								
25 to 34 years old	12.7	1.3	3.0	10.6	53.8	15.1	16.2	100.0
35 years and over	10.9	18.5	19.0	19.2	30.9	5.2	7.2	100.0
1972: Education Levels								
25 to 34 years old	12.8	0.6	1.2	9.5	47.5	17.1	24.1	100.0
35 years and over	11.2	16.5	19.5	19.0	30.8	7.1	7.0	100.0

SOURCE: U.S. Bureau of the Census, *Current Population Report,* Series P-20, No. 221; Series P-20, No. 249.

379

PUERTO RICANS

Table 56
Personal Income by Age, Education, and Sex (1969)

AGE AND SEX	ALL PERSONS				PRECOLLEGE					
					0-8 Years			9-12 Years		
	Median Yrs. of Educ.	Mean Income*	Number of Indi-viduals*	Per-cent	Mean Income*	Number of Indi-viduals*	Per-cent	Mean Income*	Number of Indi-viduals*	Per-cent
ALL INDIVIDUALS:										
18-24		$3,286	166,500	23.4	$3,168	45,400	13.1	$3,370	107,950	33.8
25-34		4,850	215,950	30.4	4,086	92,300	26.6	5,168	110,150	34.5
35-44		5,102	155,500	21.9	4,427	83,700	24.1	5,313	62,350	19.5
45-54		5,213	88,300	12.4	4,308	59,150	17.1	5,865	24,350	7.6
55-64		4,220	50,050	7.0	3,621	38,400	11.1	5,147	9,300	2.9
65 and older		2,095	33,850	4.8	1,915	27,950	8.1	2,684	4,900	1.5
TOTAL	9.1	4,417	710,150	100.0	3,849	346,900	100.0	4,648	319,000	100.0
MALES:										
18-24		3,806	74,350	23.0	3,806	19,550	12.9	3,845	48,450	32.4
25-34		5,876	97,750	30.2	5,006	39,450	26.1	6,195	51,200	34.3
35-44		6,108	73,700	22.8	5,283	38,500	25.5	6,319	30,100	20.1
45-54		6,337	42,100	13.0	5,277	26,300	17.4	6,931	12,750	8.5
55-64		5,235	22,950	7.1	4,409	17,250	11.4	6,416	4,650	3.1
65 and older		2,759	12,850	4.0	2,540	10,150	6.7	3,221	2,250	1.5
TOTAL	9.3	5,418	323,700	100.0	4,756	151,200	100.0	5,612	149,400	100.0
FEMALES:										
18-24		2,744	92,150	23.8	2,364	25,850	13.2	2,902	59,500	35.1
25-34		3,343	118,200	30.6	2,822	52,850	27.0	3,594	58,950	34.8
35-44		3,563	81,800	21.2	3,185	45,200	23.1	3,708	32,250	19.0
45-54		3,527	46,200	12.0	2,955	32,850	16.8	4,161	11,600	6.8
55-64		2,861	27,100	7.0	2,582	21,150	10.8	3,338	4,650	2.7
65 and older		1,626	21,000	5.4	1,494	17,800	9.1	2,196	2,650	1.6
TOTAL	8.9	3,102	386,450	100.0	2,680	195,700	100.0	3,365	169,600	100.0

PUERTO RICANS—Table 56 (Continued)

AGE AND SEX	ALL PERSONS				COLLEGE					
					1-3 Years			4 Years		
	Median Yrs. of Educ.	Mean Income*	Number of Indi- viduals*	Per- cent	Mean Income*	Number of Indi- viduals*	Per- cent	Mean Income*	Number of Indi- viduals*	Per- cent
ALL INDIVIDUALS:										
18-24		$3,286	166,500	23.4	$2,977	11,200	37.8	$3,428	1,750	21.2
25-34		4,850	215,950	30.4	6,230	8,500	28.7	7,612	2,450	29.7
35-44		5,102	155,500	21.9	7,926	5,550	18.8	9,566	2,100	25.5
45-54		5,213	88,300	12.4	8,184	2,850	9.6	16,742	850	10.3
55-64		4,220	50,050	7.0	8,360	1,150	3.9	12,286	700	8.5
65 and older		2,095	33,850	4.8	2,500	350	1.2	1,606	400	4.8
TOTAL	9.1	4,417	710,150	100.0	5,545	29,600	100.0	8,128	8,250	100.0
MALES:										
18-24		3,806	74,350	23.0	3,397	5,500	35.7	4,457	700	17.3
25-34		5,876	97,750	30.2	7,598	4,700	30.5	8,818	1,100	27.2
35-44		6,108	73,700	22.8	9,702	2,900	18.8	10,570	1,150	28.4
45-54		6,337	42,100	13.0	9,094	1,750	11.4	17,966	600	14.8
55-64		5,235	22,950	7.1	11,750	450	2.9	17,841	300	7.4
65 and older		2,759	12,850	4.0	1,600	100	0.6	2,062	200	4.9
TOTAL	9.3	5,418	323,700	100.0	6,993	15,400	100.0	10,321	4,050	100.0
FEMALES:										
18-24		2,744	92,150	23.8	2,604	5,700	40.1	2,641	1,050	25.0
25-34		3,343	118,200	30.6	3,582	3,800	26.8	6,138	1,350	32.1
35-44		3,563	81,800	21.2	5,084	2,650	18.7	7,559	950	22.6
45-54		3,527	46,200	12.0	6,416	1,100	7.7	9,400	250	6.0
55-64		2,861	27,100	7.0	4,485	700	4.9	5,620	400	9.5
65 and older		1,626	21,000	5.4	2,680	250	1.8	1,150	200	4.8
TOTAL	8.9	3,102	386,450	100.0	3,628	14,200	100.0	5,088	4,200	100.0

(Table 56 continued on page 382)

PUERTO RICANS—Table 56 (Continued)

| AGE AND SEX | Median Yrs. of Educ. | ALL PERSONS | | | POSTGRADUATE | | | | | |
| | | | | | 1 Year | | | 2 or More Years | | |
		Mean Income*	Number of Individuals*	Percent	Mean Income*	Number of Individuals*	Percent	Mean Income*	Number of Individuals*	Percent
ALL INDIVIDUALS:										
18-24		$3,286	166,500	23.4	$2,762	200	7.5	$ —	—	—
25-34		4,850	215,950	30.4	7,342	1,450	54.7	9,195	1,100	29.3
35-44		5,102	155,500	21.9	11,428	450	17.0	13,482	1,350	36.0
45-54		5,213	88,300	12.4	11,483	350	13.2	16,564	750	20.0
55-64		4,220	50,050	7.0	9,000	150	5.7	10,914	350	9.3
65 and older		2,095	33,850	4.8	1,700	50	1.9	10,775	200	5.3
TOTAL	9.1	4,417	710,150	100.0	8,071	2,650	100.0	12,385	3,750	100.0
MALES:										
18-24		3,806	74,350	23.0	3,383	150	13.6	—	—	—
25-34		5,876	97,750	30.2	9,472	550	50.0	10,740	750	29.4
35-44		6,108	73,700	22.8	16,800	150	13.6	14,758	900	35.3
45-54		6,337	42,100	13.0	13,733	150	13.6	17,718	550	21.6
55-64		5,235	22,950	7.1	11,500	50	4.5	11,860	250	9.8
65 and older		2,759	12,850	4.0	1,700	50	4.5	16,200	100	3.9
TOTAL	9.3	5,418	323,700	100.0	10,010	1,100	100.0	13,987	2,550	100.0
FEMALES:										
18-24		2,744	92,150	23.8	900	50	3.2	—	—	—
25-34		3,343	118,200	30.6	6,143	900	58.1	5,333	350	29.2
35-44		3,563	81,800	21.2	7,400	300	19.4	8,890	450	37.5
45-54		3,527	46,200	12.0	9,233	200	12.9	12,333	200	16.7
55-64		2,861	27,100	7.0	6,500	100	6.5	8,550	100	8.3
65 and older		1,626	21,000	5.4	—	—	—	5,350	100	8.3
TOTAL	8.9	3,102	386,450	100.0	6,520	1,550	100.0	7,847	1,200	100.0

SOURCE: Compiled from 1970 U.S. Census Public Use Sample.

Median age of all Puerto Ricans from Current Population Reports, Series P-20, Nos. 213 and 224.

*Number of individuals includes persons who reported zero income. Mean income is calculated only for persons who reported positive or negative income, excluding those with zero income.

Median age of all Puerto Ricans: 18.3 in 1969; 19.0 in 1971.

Median age of all Puerto Ricans income earners: 33.7.

Table 57
Personal Earnings by Occupation, Education, and Sex (1969)

OCCUPATIONS	ALL PERSONS			PRECOLLEGE					
				0-8 Years			9-12 Years		
	Mean Earnings	Number of Individuals	Per-cent	Mean Earnings	Number of Individuals	Per-cent	Mean Earnings	Number of Individuals	Per-cent
ALL INDIVIDUALS:									
Learned Professions	$12,361	3,150	0.8	$ —	—	—	$8,430	500	0.3
Other Prof., Tech., etc.	7,166	16,200	4.2	5,173	1,500	0.9	6,309	6,750	3.5
Mgrs., Offs., & Proprietors	7,784	10,950	2.8	6,015	2,200	1.3	6,957	6,300	3.2
Clerical	4,499	59,200	15.3	4,818	8,600	5.3	4,396	43,900	22.6
Craftsmen	6,249	42,100	10.9	5,798	17,000	10.4	6,434	23,200	11.9
Operatives	4,519	132,950	34.4	4,420	74,050	45.3	4,591	57,250	29.4
Service Workers	4,527	57,000	14.7	4,382	30,050	18.4	4,621	25,050	12.9
Private Household	1,691	1,550	0.4	1,755	950	0.6	1,727	550	0.3
Laborers	4,796	20,500	5.3	4,802	10,350	6.3	4,880	9,550	4.9
Sales	5,011	14,800	3.8	4,900	4,500	2.8	4,710	8,350	4.3
Farmers, Farm Managers	4,116	300	0.1	5,166	150	0.1	3,066	150	0.1
Farm Laborers	3,144	3,500	0.9	3,094	2,850	1.7	3,361	650	0.3
Unemployed	2,915	24,500	6.3	2,769	11,250	6.9	2,996	12,450	6.4
TOTAL	4,880	386,700	100.0	4,492	163,450	100.0	4,821	194,650	100.0
MALES:									
Learned Professions	12,908	2,650	1.0	—	—	—	9,871	350	0.3
Other Prof., Tech., etc.	8,995	8,400	3.2	6,538	900	0.8	8,235	3,400	2.7
Mgrs., Offs., & Proprietors	8,332	9,000	3.4	6,557	1,900	1.6	7,281	5,200	4.1
Clerical	5,298	20,000	9.9	5,309	6,400	5.4	5,195	16,850	13.4
Craftsmen	6,426	39,300	15.0	6,005	15,600	13.2	6,590	21,900	17.4
Operatives	5,188	85,200	32.6	5,014	46,550	39.4	5,326	37,600	29.9
Service Workers	4,908	43,850	16.8	4,632	24,750	21.0	5,188	17,950	14.3
Private Household	3,650	200	0.1	3,500	100	0.1	3,800	100	0.1
Laborers	4,838	19,400	7.4	4,815	9,800	8.3	4,960	9,000	7.1
Sales	6,076	9,850	3.8	5,457	3,350	2.8	5,927	5,100	4.0
Farmers, Farm Managers	4,116	300	0.1	5,166	150	0.1	3,066	150	0.1
Farm Laborers	3,310	3,050	1.2	3,296	2,400	2.0	3,361	650	0.5
Unemployed	3,474	14,350	5.5	3,352	6,100	5.2	3,510	7,700	6.1
TOTAL	5,536	261,550	100.0	4,992	118,000	100.0	5,554	125,950	100.0
FEMALES:									
Learned Professions	9,460	500	0.4	—	—	—	5,066	150	0.2
Other Prof., Tech., etc.	5,195	7,800	6.2	3,125	600	1.3	4,355	3,350	4.9
Mgrs., Offs., & Proprietors	5,253	1,950	1.6	2,583	300	0.7	5,422	1,100	1.6
Clerical	3,874	33,200	26.5	3,390	2,200	4.8	3,898	27,050	39.4
Craftsmen	3,758	2,800	2.2	3,485	1,400	3.1	3,801	1,300	1.9
Operatives	3,325	47,750	38.2	3,415	27,500	60.5	3,186	19,650	28.6
Service Workers	3,258	13,150	10.5	3,217	5,300	11.7	3,188	7,100	10.3
Private Household	1,401	1,350	1.1	1,550	850	1.9	1,266	450	0.7
Laborers	4,068	1,100	0.9	4,563	550	1.2	3,572	550	0.8
Sales	2,891	4,950	4.0	3,278	1,150	2.5	2,800	3,250	4.7
Farmers, Farm Managers	—	—	—	—	—	—	—	—	—
Farm Laborers	2,016	450	0.4	2,016	450	1.0	—	—	—
Unemployed	2,125	10,150	8.1	2,078	5,150	11.3	2,164	4,750	6.9
TOTAL	3,511	125,150	100.0	3,193	45,450	100.0	3,477	68,700	100.0

(Table 57 continued on page 384)

PUERTO RICANS—Table 57 (Continued)

OCCUPATIONS	ALL PERSONS			COLLEGE					
				1-3 Years			4 Years		
	Mean Earnings	Number of Individuals	Per-cent	Mean Earnings	Number of Individuals	Per-cent	Mean Earnings	Number of Individuals	Per-cent
ALL INDIVIDUALS:									
Learned Professions	$12,361	3,150	0.8	$10,700	500	2.6	$13,453	650	12.4
Other Prof., Tech., etc.	7,166	16,200	4.2	6,957	3,500	18.4	7,987	2,450	46.7
Mgrs., Offs., & Proprietors	7,784	10,950	2.8	9,875	1,600	8.4	14,750	500	9.5
Clerical	4,499	59,200	15.3	4,681	5,750	30.3	4,453	650	12.4
Craftsmen	6,249	42,100	10.9	7,930	1,700	8.9	8,750	200	3.8
Operatives	4,519	132,950	34.4	6,406	1,650	8.7	—	—	—
Service Workers	4,527	57,000	14.7	5,441	1,550	8.2	6,600	200	3.8
Private Household	1,691	1,550	0.4	100	50	0.3	—	—	—
Laborers	4,796	20,500	5.3	3,366	600	3.2	—	—	—
Sales	5,011	14,800	3.8	5,411	1,500	7.9	11,475	400	7.6
Farmers, Farm Managers	4,116	300	0.1	—	—	—	—	—	—
Farm Laborers	3,144	3,500	0.9	—	—	—		—	—
Unemployed	2,915	24,500	6.3	2,208	600	3.2	8,225	200	3.8
TOTAL	4,880	386,700	100.0	6,124	19,000	100.0	9,121	5,250	100.0
MALES:									
Learned Professions	12,908	2,650	1.0	11,644	450	3.9	12,075	600	18.5
Other Prof., Tech., etc.	8,995	8,400	3.2	7,961	2,100	18.3	10,538	1,050	32.3
Mgrs., Offs., & Proprietors	8,332	9,000	3.4	11,950	1,100	9.6	14,750	500	15.4
Clerical	5,298	26,000	9.9	6,043	2,250	19.6	4,800	350	10.8
Craftsmen	6,426	39,300	15.0	7,987	1,600	13.9	8,750	200	6.2
Operatives	5,188	85,200	32.6	7,923	1,050	9.1	—	—	—
Service Workers	4,908	43,850	16.8	6,172	900	7.8	10,500	100	3.1
Private Household	3,650	200	0.1	—	—	—	—	—	—
Laborers	4,838	19,400	7.4	3,366	600	5.2	—	—	—
Sales	6,076	9,850	3.8	6,540	1,050	9.1	14,666	300	9.2
Farmers, Farm Managers	4,116	300	0.1	—	—	—	—	—	—
Farm Laborers	3,310	3,050	1.2	—	—	—	—	—	—
Unemployed	3,474	14,350	5.5	2,937	400	3.5	8,000	150	4.6
TOTAL	5,536	261,550	100.0	7,427	11,500	100.0	11,004	3,250	100.0
FEMALES:									
Learned Professions	9,460	500	0.4	2,200	50	0.7	30,000	50	2.5
Other Prof., Tech., etc.	5,195	7,800	6.2	5,450	1,400	18.7	6,075	1,400	70.0
Mgrs., Offs., & Proprietors	5,253	1,950	1.6	5,310	500	6.7	—	—	—
Clerical	3,874	33,200	26.5	3,805	3,500	46.7	4,050	300	15.0
Craftsmen	3,758	2,800	2.2	7,025	100	1.3	—	—	—
Operatives	3,325	47,750	38.2	3,750	600	8.0	—	—	—
Service Workers	3,258	13,150	10.5	4,430	650	8.7	2,700	100	5.0
Private Household	1,401	1,350	1.1	100	50	0.7	—	—	—
Laborers	4,068	1,100	0.9	—	—	—	—	—	—
Sales	2,891	4,950	4.0	2,777	450	6.0	1,900	100	5.0
Farmers, Farm Managers	—	—	—	—	—	—	—	—	—
Farm Laborers	2,016	450	0.4	—	—	—	—	—	—
Unemployed	2,125	10,150	8.1	750	200	2.7	8,900	50	2.5
TOTAL	3,511	125,150	100.0	4,127	7,500	100.0	6,062	2,000	100.0

OCCUPATIONS	ALL PERSONS			POSTGRADUATE					
				1 Year			2 or More Years		
	Mean Earnings	Number of Individuals	Per-cent	Mean Earnings	Number of Individuals	Per-cent	Mean Earnings	Number of Individuals	Per-cent
ALL INDIVIDUALS:									
Learned Professions	$12,361	3,150	0.8	$8,440	250	16.1	$14,814	1,250	44.6
Other Prof., Tech., etc.	7,166	16,200	4.2	9,895	1,000	64.5	11,925	1,000	35.7
Mgrs., Offs., & Proprietors	7,784	10,950	2.8	15,900	150	9.7	13,075	200	7.1
Clerical	4,499	59,200	15.3	9,950	100	6.5	5,675	200	7.1
Craftsmen	6,249	42,100	10.9	—	—	—	—	—	—
Operatives	4,519	132,950	34.4	—	—	—	—	—	—
Service Workers	4,527	57,000	14.7	4,100	50	3.2	6,650	100	3.6
Private Household	1,691	1,550	0.4	—	—	—	—	—	—
Laborers	4,796	20,500	5.3	—	—	—	—	—	—
Sales	5,011	14,800	3.8	—	—	—	1,500	50	1.8
Farmers, Farm Managers	4,116	300	0.1	—	—	—	—	—	—
Farm Laborers	3,144	3,500	0.9	—	—	—	—	—	—
Unemployed	2,915	24,500	6.3	—	—	—	—	—	—
TOTAL	4,880	386,700	100.0	10,058	1,550	100.0	12,475	2,800	100.0
MALES:									
Learned Professions	12,908	2,650	1.0	9,166	150	21.4	15,356	1,100	51.2
Other Prof., Tech., etc.	8,995	8,400	3.2	14,066	300	42.9	14,884	650	30.2
Mgrs., Offs., & Proprietors	8,332	9,000	3.4	15,900	150	21.4	11,766	150	7.0
Clerical	5,298	26,000	9.9	13,400	50	7.1	2,850	100	4.7
Craftsmen	6,426	39,300	15.0	—	—	—	—	—	—
Operatives	5,188	85,200	32.6	—	—	—	—	—	—
Service Workers	4,908	43,850	16.8	4,100	50	7.1	6,650	100	4.7
Private Household	3,650	200	0.1	—	—	—	—	—	—
Laborers	4,838	19,400	7.4	—	—	—	—	—	—
Sales	6,076	9,850	3.8	—	—	—	1,500	50	2.3
Farmers, Farm Managers	4,116	300	0.1	—	—	—	—	—	—
Farm Laborers	3,310	3,050	1.2	—	—	—	—	—	—
Unemployed	3,474	14,350	5.5	—	—	—	—	—	—
TOTAL	5,536	261,550	100.0	12,650	700	100.0	13,654	2,150	100.0
FEMALES:									
Learned Professions	9,460	500	0.4	7,350	100	11.8	10,833	150	23.1
Other Prof., Tech., etc.	5,195	7,800	6.2	8,107	700	82.4	6,428	350	53.8
Mgrs., Offs., & Proprietors	5,253	1,950	1.6	—	—	—	17,000	50	7.7
Clerical	3,874	33,200	26.5	6,500	50	5.9	8,500	100	15.4
Craftsmen	3,758	2,800	2.2	—	—	—	—	—	—
Operatives	3,325	47,750	38.2	—	—	—	—	—	—
Service Workers	3,258	13,150	10.5	—	—	—	—	—	—
Private Household	1,401	1,350	1.1	—	—	—	—	—	—
Laborers	4,068	1,100	0.9	—	—	—	—	—	—
Sales	2,891	4,950	4.0	—	—	—	—	—	—
Farmers, Farm Managers	—	—	—	—	—	—	—	—	—
Farm Laborers	2,016	450	0.4	—	—	—	—	—	—
Unemployed	2,125	10,150	8.1	—	—	—	—	—	—
TOTAL	3,511	125,150	100.0	7,923	850	100.0	8,576	650	100.0

SOURCE: Compiled from 1970 U.S. Census Public Use Sample.

NOTE: Median years of education: 9.6.

PUERTO RICANS

Table 58
Family Income Distribution by Number of
Income Earners per Family (1969)

INCOME	ALL FAMILIES		NO EARNER FAMILIES		ONE EARNER FAMILIES		TWO EARNER FAMILIES		THREE OR MORE EARNER FAMILIES	
	Number of Families	Percent	Number of Families	Percent	Number of Families	Percent	Number of Families	Percent	Number of Families	Percent
UNDER $ 1,000	23,900	7.6	18,750	27.5	4,400	3.2	700	0.8	50	0.2
$ 1,000 - $ 1,999	14,550	4.6	8,500	12.4	5,050	3.7	950	1.1	50	0.2
$ 2,000 - $ 2,999	24,600	7.8	15,800	23.1	7,100	5.1	1,450	1.7	250	1.0
$ 3,000 - $ 3,999	32,750	10.4	15,500	22.7	13,950	10.1	3,000	3.5	300	1.2
$ 4,000 - $ 4,999	30,050	9.5	5,800	8.5	19,900	14.4	4,000	4.7	350	1.5
$ 5,000 - $ 5,999	32,350	10.3	2,400	3.5	24,150	17.5	5,600	6.6	200	0.8
$ 6,000 - $ 6,999	30,300	9.6	900	1.3	20,250	14.6	8,350	9.9	800	3.3
$ 7,000 - $ 7,999	23,800	7.5	300	0.4	13,500	9.8	8,900	10.5	1,100	4.6
$ 8,000 - $ 9,999	38,150	12.1	250	0.4	16,300	11.8	18,850	22.3	2,750	11.4
$10,000 - $12,999	34,700	11.0	—	—	8,850	6.4	20,300	24.0	5,550	23.1
$13,000 - $14,999	11,100	3.5	—	—	1,750	1.3	5,600	6.6	3,750	15.6
$15,000 - $19,999	13,150	4.2	50	0.1	1,700	1.2	5,550	6.6	5,850	24.3
$20,000 - $24,999	3,600	1.1	50	0.1	500	0.4	1,000	1.2	2,050	8.5
$25,000 OR MORE	2,300	0.7	—	—	900	0.7	400	0.5	1,000	4.2
TOTAL	315,300	100.0	68,300	100.0	138,300	100.0	84,650	100.0	24,050	100.0
MEAN EARNINGS	$6,728		$2,257		$6,136		$9,244		$13,969	
MEDIAN INCOME	5,983		2,437		5,776		8,992		13,320	

SOURCE: Compiled from 1970 U.S. Census, Public Use Sample.

PUERTO RICANS

Table 59
Family Income by Age, Education, and Sex of Family Head (1969)

AGE AND SEX OF FAMILY HEAD	ALL PERSONS				PRECOLLEGE						
					0-8 Years			9-12 Years			
	Median Yrs. of Educ.	Mean Income	Number of Individuals	Per-cent	Mean Income	Number of Individuals	Per-cent	Mean Income	Number of Individuals	Per-cent	
ALL INDIVIDUALS:											
18-24		$4,460	41,450	13.1	$3,358	15,150	9.1	$5,003	24,050	18.3	
25-34		5,440	109,350	34.7	4,113	49,100	29.5	6,206	54,850	41.6	
35-44		6,331	83,050	26.3	5,236	45,350	27.2	7,031	32,650	24.8	
45-54		7,578	47,000	14.9	6,239	30,350	18.2	9,114	13,750	10.4	
55-64		6,593	23,500	7.5	5,747	17,650	10.6	8,204	4,700	3.6	
65 and older		3,816	10,950	3.5	3,420	8,900	5.3	4,564	1,700	1.3	
TOTAL	8.5	5,894	315,300	100.0	4,874	166,500	100.0	6,544	131,700	100.0	
MALES:											
18-24		5,761	30,050	12.7	4,860	9,850	8.4	6,141	18,300	17.7	
25-34		6,956	80,300	34.0	5,835	32,900	28.0	7,479	42,500	41.1	
35-44		7,745	63,100	26.7	6,675	32,500	27.6	8,228	26,050	25.2	
45-54		8,946	35,850	15.2	7,671	22,150	18.8	10,075	11,150	10.8	
55-64		7,367	18,350	7.8	6,465	13,550	11.5	8,658	3,900	3.8	
65 and older		3,852	8,400	3.6	3,368	6,650	5.7	4,393	1,450	1.4	
TOTAL	9.0	7,237	236,050	100.0	6,265	117,600	100.0	7,712	103,350	100.0	
FEMALES:											
18-24		1,028	11,400	14.4	566	5,300	10.8	1,381	5,750	20.3	
25-34		1,249	29,050	36.7	615	16,200	33.1	1,826	12,350	43.6	
35-44		1,860	19,950	25.2	1,596	12,850	26.3	2,309	6,600	23.3	
45-54		3,182	11,150	14.1	2,370	8,200	16.8	4,996	2,600	9.2	
55-64		3,834	5,150	6.5	3,374	4,100	8.4	5,987	800	2.8	
65 and older		3,698	2,550	3.2	3,573	2,250	4.6	5,560	250	0.9	
TOTAL	7.3	1,890	79,250	100.0	1,529	48,900	100.0	2,289	28,350	100.0	

(Table 59 continued on page 388)

387

| AGE AND SEX OF FAMILY HEAD | ALL PERSONS | | | | COLLEGE | | | | | |
| | | | | | 1-3 Years | | | 4 Years | | |
	Median Yrs. of Educ.	Mean Income	Number of Individuals	Per-cent	Mean Income	Number of Individuals	Per-cent	Mean Income	Number of Individuals	Per-cent
ALL INDIVIDUALS										
18-24		$ 4,460	41,450	13.1	$ 5,984	1,600	15.4	$ 6,636	550	15.9
25-34		5,440	109,350	34.7	9,225	3,600	34.6	12,276	650	18.8
35-44		6,331	83,050	26.3	10,420	3,050	29.3	10,922	1,100	31.9
45-54		7,578	47,000	14.9	11,429	1,600	15.4	19,854	550	15.9
55-64		6,593	23,500	7.5	10,430	500	4.8	12,675	400	11.6
65 and older		3,816	10,950	3.5	0	50	0.5	10,075	200	5.8
TOTAL	8.5	5,894	315,300	100.0	9,430	10,400	100.0	12,072	3,450	100.0
MALES:										
18-24		5,761	30,050	12.7	7,188	1,300	14.4	6,200	500	16.7
25-34		6,956	80,300	34.0	9,747	3,300	36.5	11,645	550	18.3
35-44		7,745	63,100	26.7	11,749	2,600	28.7	11,328	1,050	35.0
45-54		8,946	35,850	15.2	11,833	1,400	15.5	20,540	500	16.7
55-64		7,367	18,350	7.8	11,850	400	4.4	18,320	250	8.3
65 and older		3,852	8,400	3.6	0	50	0.6	13,433	150	5.0
TOTAL	9.0	7,237	236,050	100.0	10,299	9,050	100.0	12,755	3,000	100.0
FEMALES:										
18-24		1,028	11,400	14.4	766	300	22.2	11,000	50	11.1
25-34		1,249	29,050	36.7	3,483	300	22.2	15,750	100	22.2
35-44		1,860	19,950	25.2	2,744	450	33.3	2,400	50	11.1
45-54		3,182	11,150	14.1	8,600	200	14.8	13,000	50	11.1
55-64		3,834	5,150	6.5	6,350	100	7.4	3,266	150	33.3
65 and older		3,698	2,550	3.2	—	—	—	0	50	11.1
TOTAL	7.3	1,890	79,250	100.0	3,603	1,350	100.0	7,522	450	100.0

| AGE AND SEX OF FAMILY HEAD | ALL PERSONS | | | | POSTGRADUATE | | | | | |
| | | | | | 1 Year | | | 2 or More Years | | |
	Median Yrs. of Educ.	Mean Income	Number of Indi- viduals	Per- cent	Mean Income	Number of Indi- viduals	Per- cent	Mean Income	Number of Indi- viduals	Per cent
ALL INDIVIDUALS:										
18-24		$4,460	41,450	13.1	$ 4,375	100	8.7	—	—	—
25-34		5,440	109,350	34.7	9,607	650	56.5	$10,265	500	23.8
35-44		6,331	83,050	26.3	21,266	150	13.0	15,740	750	35.7
45-54		7,578	47,000	14.9	12,200	200	17.4	17,950	550	26.2
55-64		6,593	23,500	7.5	11,500	50	4.3	20,412	200	9.5
65 and older		3,816	10,950	3.5	—	—	—	15,750	100	4.8
TOTAL	8.5	5,894	315,300	100.0	11,206	1,150	100.0	15,460	2,100	100.0
MALES:										
18-24		5,761	30,050	12.7	4,375	100	10.0	—	—	—
25-34		6,956	80,300	34.0	9,254	550	55.0	10,266	600	24.4
35-44		7,745	63,100	26.7	21,266	150	15.0	15,740	750	36.6
45-54		8,946	35,850	15.2	14,966	150	15.0	18,765	500	24.4
55-64		7,367	18,350	7.8	11,500	50	5.0	20,412	200	9.8
65 and older		3,852	8,400	3.6	—	—	—	15,750	100	4.9
TOTAL	9.0	7,237	236,050	100.0	11,537	1,000	100.0	15,598	2,050	100.0
FEMALES:										
18-24		1,028	11,400	14.4	—	—	—	—	—	—
25-34		1,249	29,050	36.7	11,550	100	66.7	—	—	—
35-44		1,860	19,950	25.2	—	—	—	—	—	—
45-54		3,182	11,150	14.1	3,900	50	33.3	9,800	50	100.0
55-64		3,834	5,150	6.5	—	—	—	—	—	—
65 and older		3,698	2,550	3.2	—	—	—	—	—	—
TOTAL	7.3	1,890	79,250	100.0	9,000	150	100.0	9,800	50	100.0

SOURCE: Compiled from 1970 U.S. Census Public Use Sample.

NOTE: Median age of all family heads: 35.8.

PUERTO RICANS

Table 60
Family Earnings by Number of Income Earners,
Education, and Sex of Family Head (1969)

	NUMBER OF INCOME EARNERS			PRECOLLEGE					
				0-8 Years			9-12 Years		
	Mean Family Earnings	Number of Families	Percent of all Families	Mean Family Earnings	Number of Families	Percent of all Families	Mean Family Earnings	Number of Families	Percent of all Families
ALL FAMILIES:									
No Income-Earners	$ 0	68,300	21.7	$ 0	46,250	27.8	$ 0	21,050	16.0
One Income-Earner	5,621	138,300	43.9	4,809	68,950	41.4	5,864	60,850	46.2
Two Income-Earners	8,942	84,650	26.8	8,185	37,500	22.5	9,169	41,000	31.1
Three or More Earners	13,481	24,050	7.6	12,536	13,800	8.3	14,678	8,800	6.7
TOTAL	5,894	315,300	100.0	4,874	166,500	100.0	6,544	131,700	100.0
MALE-HEADED FAMILIES:									
No Income-Earners	0	19,050	8.1	0	13,150	11.2	0	5,350	5.2
One Income-Earner	5,968	117,650	49.8	5,090	58,300	49.6	6,203	51,950	50.3
Two Income-Earners	9,093	77,350	32.8	8,320	33,600	28.6	9,307	38,050	36.8
Three or More Earners	13,780	22,000	9.3	12,784	12,550	10.7	15,081	8,000	7.7
TOTAL	7,239	236,050	100.0	6,265	117,600	100.0	7,712	103,350	100.0
FEMALE-HEADED FAMILIES:									
No Income-Earners	0	49,250	62.1	0	33,100	67.7	0	15,700	55.4
One Income-Earner	3,638	20,650	26.1	3,270	10,650	21.8	3,859	8,900	31.4
Two Income-Earners	7,341	7,300	9.2	7,026	3,900	8.0	7,385	2,950	10.4
Three or More Earners	10,275	2,050	2.6	10,052	1,250	2.6	10,625	800	2.8
TOTAL	1,890	79,250	100.0	1,529	48,900	100.0	2,289	28,350	100.0

	NUMBER OF INCOME EARNERS			COLLEGE					
				1-3 Years			4 Years		
	Mean Family Earnings	Number of Families	Percent of all Families	Mean Family Earnings	Number of Families	Percent of all Families	Mean Family Earnings	Number of Families	Percent of all Families
ALL FAMILIES:									
No Income-Earners	$ 0	68,300	21.7	$ 0	750	7.2	$ 0	150	4.3
One Income-Earner	5,621	138,300	43.9	8,098	4,850	46.6	13,443	1,850	53.6
Two Income-Earners	8,942	84,650	26.8	11,654	3,900	37.5	11,376	1,300	37.7
Three or More Earners	13,481	24,050	7.6	14,822	900	8.7	13,266	150	4.3
TOTAL	5,894	315,300	100.0	9,430	10,400	100.0	12,072	3,450	100.0
MALE-HEADED FAMILIES:									
No Income-Earners	0	19,050	8.1	0	400	4.4	0	50	1.7
One Income-Earner	5,968	117,650	49.8	8,892	4,100	45.3	13,960	1,650	55.0
Two Income-Earners	9,093	77,360	32.8	11,892	3,650	40.3	11,513	1,150	38.3
Three or More Earners	13,780	22,000	9.3	14,822	900	9.9	13,266	150	5.0
TOTAL	7,239	236,050	100.0	10,299	9,050	100.0	12,755	3,000	100.0
FEMALE-HEADED FAMILIES:									
No Income-Earners	0	49,250	62.1	0	350	25.9	0	100	22.2
One Income-Earner	3,638	20,650	26.1	3,760	750	55.6	9,175	200	44.4
Two Income-Earners	7,341	7,300	9.2	8,180	250	18.5	10,333	150	33.3
Three or More Earners	10,275	2,050	2.6	—	—	—	—	—	—
TOTAL	1,890	79,250	100.0	3,603	1,350	100.0	7,522	450	100.0

(Table 60 continued on page 392)

	NUMBER OF INCOME EARNERS			POSTGRADUATE					
				1 Year			2 or More Years		
	Mean Family Earnings	Number of Families	Percent of all Families	Mean Family Earnings	Number of Families	Percent of all Families	Mean Family Earnings	Number of Families	Percent of all Families
ALL FAMILIES:									
No Income-Earners	$ 0	68,300	21.7	$ 0	50	4.3	$ 0	50	2.4
One Income-Earner	5,621	138,300	43.9	10,575	600	52.2	15,352	1,200	57.1
Two Income-Earners	8,942	84,650	26.8	13,085	500	43.5	16,205	450	21.4
Three or More Earners	13,481	24,050	7.6	—	—	—	16,881	400	19.0
TOTAL	5,894	315,300	100.0	11,206	1,150	100.0	15,460	2,100	100.0
MALE-HEADED FAMILIES:									
No Income-Earners	0	19,050	8.1	0	50	5.0	0	50	2.4
One Income-Earner	5,968	117,650	49.8	11,600	500	50.0	15,593	1,150	56.1
Two Income-Earners	9,093	77,350	32.8	12,750	450	45.0	16,205	450	22.0
Three or More Earners	13,780	22,000	9.3	—	—	—	16,881	400	19.5
TOTAL	7,239	236,050	100.0	11,537	1,000	100.0	15,598	2,050	100.0
FEMALE-HEADED FAMILIES:									
No Income-Earners	0	49,250	62.1	—	—	—	—	—	—
One Income-Earner	3,638	20,650	26.1	5,450	100	66.7	9,800	50	100.0
Two Income-Earners	7,341	7,300	9.2	16,100	50	33.3	—	—	—
Three or More Earners	10,275	2,050	2.6	—	—	—	—	—	—
TOTAL	1,890	79,250	100.0	9,000	150	100.0	9,800	50	100.0

SOURCE: Compiled from 1970 U.S. Census Public Use Sample.

NOTE: Median years of education of family heads: 8.5.

PUERTO RICANS

Table 61
Fertility Rates by Woman's Education and Family Income (1969)

61a. EDUCATION

	TOTAL		PRECOLLEGE				COLLEGE				POSTGRADUATE			
			0-8 Years		9-12 Years		1-3 Years		4 Years		1 Year		2 or More Years	
	Number	Percent	Number	Percent	Number	Percent	Number	Percent	Number	Percent	Number	Percent	Number	Percent
All Women, 15 and older:														
Childless	116,200	27.1	37,600	17.8	68,950	35.1	6,500	45.6	1,700	40.5	800	51.6	650	54.2
1 Child	63,000	14.7	26,150	12.4	33,200	16.9	2,550	17.9	700	16.7	300	19.4	100	8.3
2 Children	81,550	19.0	39,300	18.6	38,500	19.6	2,450	17.2	900	21.4	250	16.1	150	12.5
3 Children	62,600	14.6	33,150	15.7	27,150	13.8	1,550	10.9	450	10.7	100	6.5	200	16.7
4 Children	40,750	9.5	25,200	11.9	14,450	7.4	750	5.3	150	3.6	100	6.5	100	8.3
5 Children	23,450	5.5	16,000	7.6	7,150	3.6	150	1.1	150	3.6	–	–	–	–
6 or More	41,300	9.6	33,750	16.0	7,100	3.6	300	2.1	150	3.6	–	–	–	–
TOTAL	428,850	100.0	211,150	100.0	196,500	100.0	14,250	100.0	4,200	100.0	1,550	100.0	1,200	100.0
Mean No. of Children	2.4		3.1		1.7		1.3		1.5		1.0		1.2	
Women, 15-24:														
Childless	81,550	60.6	20,400	49.4	55,550	64.3	4,800	83.5	750	71.4	50	100.0	–	–
1 Child	24,950	18.5	7,300	17.7	16,800	19.4	600	10.4	250	23.8	–	–	–	–
2 Children	16,800	12.5	7,500	18.2	9,100	10.5	200	3.5	–	–	–	–	–	–
3 Children	6,800	5.1	3,400	8.2	3,300	3.8	50	0.9	50	4.8	–	–	–	–
4 Children	3,250	2.4	1,950	4.7	1,200	1.4	100	1.7	–	–	–	–	–	–
5 Children	800	0.6	450	1.1	350	0.4	–	–	–	–	–	–	–	–
6 or More	400	0.3	300	0.7	100	0.1	–	–	–	–	–	–	–	–
TOTAL	134,550	100.0	41,300	100.0	86,400	100.0	5,750	100.0	1,050	100.0	50	100.0	–	–
Mean No. of Children	0.7		1.1		0.6		0.3		0.4		0.0		0.0	

(Table 61 continued on page 394)

PUERTO RICANS—Table 61: Education (Continued)

| | TOTAL | | PRECOLLEGE | | | | COLLEGE | | | | POSTGRADUATE | | | |
| | | | 0-8 Years | | 9-12 Years | | 1-3 Years | | 4 Years | | 1 Year | | 2 or More Years | |
	Number	Percent	Number	Percent	Number	Percent	Number	Percent	Number	Percent	Number	Percent	Number	Percent
Women, 25-34:														
Childless	14,450	12.2	4,650	8.8	7,450	12.6	1,000	26.3	450	33.3	650	72.2	250	71.4
1 Child	17,600	14.9	5,600	10.6	10,050	17.0	1,350	35.5	450	33.3	100	11.1	50	14.3
2 Children	30,100	25.5	12,100	22.9	16,750	28.4	800	21.1	350	25.9	50	5.6	50	14.3
3 Children	25,950	22.0	12,050	22.8	13,150	22.3	600	15.8	50	3.7	100	11.1	–	–
4 Children	14,300	12.1	8,200	15.5	6,100	10.3	–	–	–	–	–	–	–	–
5 Children	7,950	6.7	4,950	9.4	3,000	5.1	–	–	–	–	–	–	–	–
6 or More	7,850	6.6	5,300	10.0	2,450	4.2	50	1.3	50	3.7	–	–	–	–
TOTAL	118,200	100.0	52,850	100.0	58,950	100.0	3,800	100.0	1,350	100.0	900	100.0	350	100.0
Mean No. of Children	2.6		3.1		2.4		1.3		1.3		0.6		0.4	
Women, 35-44:														
Childless	6,700	8.2	3,100	6.9	2,800	8.7	300	11.3	250	26.3	50	16.7	200	44.4
1 Child	7,850	9.6	4,300	9.5	3,350	10.4	150	5.7	–	–	50	16.7	–	–
2 Children	17,800	21.8	8,250	18.3	8,300	25.7	800	30.2	300	31.6	100	33.3	50	11.1
3 Children	16,500	20.2	8,150	18.0	7,500	23.3	650	24.5	50	5.3	–	–	150	33.3
4 Children	11,800	14.4	6,250	13.8	4,800	14.9	450	17.0	150	15.8	100	33.3	50	11.1
5 Children	7,300	8.9	4,700	10.4	2,400	7.4	100	3.8	100	10.5	–	–	–	–
6 or More	13,850	16.9	10,450	23.1	3,100	9.6	200	7.5	100	10.5	–	–	–	–
TOTAL	81,800	100.0	45,200	100.0	32,250	100.0	2,650	100.0	950	100.0	300	100.0	450	100.0
Mean No. of Children	3.5		3.9		3.0		2.8		2.7		2.2		1.7	

394

PUERTO AMERICANS—Table 61: Education (Continued)

	TOTAL		PRECOLLEGE				COLLEGE				POSTGRADUATE			
			0-8 Years		9-12 Years		1-3 Years		4 Years		1 Year		2 or More Years	
	Number	Percent	Number	Percent	Number	Percent	Number	Percent	Number	Percent	Number	Percent	Number	Percent
Women, 45 and older:														
Childless	13,500	14.3	9,450	13.2	3,150	16.7	400	19.5	250	29.4	50	16.7	200	50.0
1 Child	12,600	13.4	8,950	12.5	3,000	15.9	450	22.0	–	–	150	50.0	50	12.5
2 Children	16,850	17.9	11,450	15.9	4,350	23.0	650	31.7	250	29.4	100	33.3	50	12.5
3 Children	13,350	14.2	9,550	13.3	3,200	16.9	250	12.2	300	35.3	–	–	50	12.5
4 Children	11,400	12.1	8,800	12.3	2,350	12.4	200	9.8	–	–	–	–	50	12.5
5 Children	7,400	7.8	5,900	8.2	1,400	7.4	50	2.4	50	5.9	–	–	–	–
6 or More	19,200	20.4	17,700	24.7	1,450	7.7	50	2.4	–	–	–	–	–	–
TOTAL	94,300	100.0	71,800	100.0	18,900	100.0	2,050	100.0	850	100.0	300	100.0	400	100.0
Mean No. of Children	3.5		3.8		2.6		1.9		1.9		1.2		1.3	

61b. FAMILY INCOME

	TOTAL		Less Than $5,000		$5,000 - 9,999		$10,000 - 14,999		$15,000 - 19,999		$20,000 - 24,999		$25,000 and Over	
	Number	Percent	Number	Percent	Number	Percent	Number	Percent	Number	Percent	Number	Percent	Number	Percent
All Women, 15 and older:														
Childless	116,200	27.1	40,200	23.6	40,900	26.1	20,950	31.6	9,450	40.6	2,700	37.5	2,000	39.6
1 Child	63,000	14.7	25,350	14.9	23,650	15.1	9,550	14.4	3,100	13.3	550	7.6	800	15.8
2 Children	81,550	19.0	32,100	18.9	30,950	19.7	12,250	18.4	4,150	17.8	1,500	20.8	600	11.9
3 Children	62,600	14.6	25,900	15.2	22,750	14.5	9,550	14.4	2,550	11.0	1,050	14.6	800	15.8
4 Children	40,750	9.5	16,800	9.9	15,650	10.0	6,050	9.1	1,450	6.2	550	7.6	250	5.0
5 Children	23,450	5.5	10,950	6.4	8,100	5.2	2,900	4.4	700	3.0	450	6.3	350	6.9
6 or More	41,300	9.6	18,750	11.0	14,900	9.5	5,150	7.8	1,850	8.0	400	5.6	250	5.0
TOTAL	428,850	100.0	170,050	100.0	156,900	100.0	66,400	100.0	23,250	100.0	7,200	100.0	5,050	100.0
Mean No. of Children	2.4		2.6		2.4		2.1		1.8		2.0		1.9	

(Table 61 continued on page 396)

PUERTO RICANS—Table 61: Family Income (Continued)

	TOTAL		Less Than $5,000		$5,000 - 9,999		$10,000 - 14,999		$15,000 - 19,999		$20,000 - 24,999		$25,000 and Over	
	Number	Percent	Number	Percent	Number	Percent	Number	Percent	Number	Percent	Number	Percent	Number	Percent
Women, 15-24:														
Childless	81,550	60.6	25,050	48.8	30,600	60.1	15,800	76.3	6,750	86.5	2,000	87.0	1,350	90.0
1 Child	24,950	18.5	10,850	21.2	9,900	19.4	3,150	15.2	700	9.0	250	10.9	100	6.7
2 Children	16,800	12.5	9,150	17.8	6,250	12.3	1,050	5.1	250	3.2	50	2.2	50	3.3
3 Children	6,800	5.1	3,850	7.5	2,450	4.8	450	2.2	50	0.6	—	—	—	—
4 Children	3,250	2.4	1,800	3.5	1,150	2.3	250	1.2	50	0.6	—	—	—	—
5 Children	800	0.6	400	0.8	400	0.8	—	—	—	—	—	—	—	—
6 or More	400	0.3	200	0.4	200	0.4	—	—	—	—	—	—	—	—
TOTAL	134,550	100.0	51,300	100.0	50,950	100.0	20,700	100.0	7,800	100.0	2,300	100.0	1,500	100.0
Mean No. of Children	0.7		1.0		0.7		0.4		0.2		0.2		0.1	
Women, 25-34:														
Childless	14,450	12.2	5,050	10.5	4,550	9.7	2,750	16.6	1,500	33.0	250	20.8	350	38.9
1 Child	17,600	14.9	5,850	12.2	7,050	15.0	3,450	20.8	900	19.8	100	8.3	250	27.8
2 Children	30,100	25.5	10,600	22.1	12,950	27.5	4,850	29.3	1,050	23.1	550	45.8	100	11.1
3 Children	25,950	22.0	12,250	25.5	9,900	21.0	2,850	17.2	600	13.2	250	20.8	100	11.1
4 Children	14,300	12.1	6,550	13.7	6,150	13.1	1,300	7.9	250	5.5	—	—	50	5.6
5 Children	7,950	6.7	4,050	8.4	3,050	6.5	650	3.9	150	3.3	50	4.2	—	—
6 or More	7,850	6.6	3,600	7.5	3,400	7.2	700	4.2	100	2.2	—	—	50	5.6
TOTAL	118,200	100.0	47,950	100.0	47,050	100.0	16,550	100.0	4,550	100.0	1,200	100.0	900	100.0
Mean No. of Children	2.6		2.8		2.7		2.1		1.6		1.8		1.5	

PUERTO RICANS—Table 61: Family Income (Continued)

	TOTAL		Less Than $5,000		$5,000 - 9,999		$10,000 - 14,999		$15,000 - 19,999		$20,000 - 24,999		$25,000 and Over	
	Number	Percent	Number	Percent	Number	Percent	Number	Percent	Number	Percent	Number	Percent	Number	Percent
Women, 35-44:														
Childless	6,700	8.2	2,450	8.6	2,300	7.3	1,100	7.7	550	10.9	200	14.3	100	9.5
1 Child	7,850	9.6	2,550	8.9	3,050	9.7	1,350	9.5	600	11.9	100	7.1	200	19.0
2 Children	17,800	21.8	6,100	21.4	6,500	20.6	3,300	23.2	1,450	28.7	300	21.4	150	14.3
3 Children	16,500	20.2	4,750	16.7	6,500	20.6	3,500	24.6	1,050	20.8	300	21.4	400	38.1
4 Children	11,800	14.4	3,700	13.0	5,000	15.8	2,350	16.5	500	9.9	200	14.3	50	4.8
5 Children	7,300	8.9	3,200	11.2	2,550	8.1	1,050	7.4	150	3.0	250	17.9	100	9.5
6 or More	13,850	16.9	5,750	20.2	5,650	17.9	1,600	11.2	750	14.9	50	3.6	50	4.8
TOTAL	81,800	100.0	28,500	100.0	31,550	100.0	14,250	100.0	5,050	100.0	1,400	100.0	1,050	100.0
Mean No. of Children	3.5		3.6		3.6		3.2		2.9		2.9		2.9	
Women, 45 and older:														
Childless	13,500	14.3	7,650	18.1	3,450	12.6	1,300	8.7	650	11.1	250	10.9	200	12.5
1 Child	12,600	13.4	6,100	14.4	3,650	13.3	1,600	10.7	900	15.4	100	4.3	250	15.6
2 Children	16,850	17.9	6,250	14.8	5,250	19.2	3,050	20.5	1,400	23.9	600	26.1	300	18.8
3 Children	13,350	14.2	5,050	11.9	3,900	14.3	2,750	18.5	850	14.5	500	21.7	300	18.8
4 Children	11,400	12.1	4,750	11.2	3,350	12.2	2,150	14.4	650	11.1	350	15.2	150	9.4
5 Children	7,400	7.8	3,300	7.8	2,100	7.7	1,200	8.1	400	6.8	150	6.5	250	15.6
6 or More	19,200	20.4	9,200	21.7	5,650	20.7	2,850	19.1	1,000	17.1	350	15.2	150	9.4
TOTAL	94,300	100.0	42,300	100.0	27,350	100.0	14,900	100.0	5,850	100.0	2,300	100.0	1,600	100.0
Mean No. of Children	3.5		3.5		3.6		3.6		3.3		3.5		3.1	

SOURCE: Compiled from 1970 U.S. Census Public Use Sample.

WEST INDIANS

Table 62
Personal Income by Age, Education, and Sex (1969)

AGE AND SEX	ALL PERSONS				PRECOLLEGE						
					0-8 Years			9-12 Years			
	Median Yrs. of Educ.	Mean Income*	Number of Indi-viduals*	Per-cent	Mean Income*	Number of Indi-viduals*	Per-cent	Mean Income*	Number of Indi-viduals*	Per-cent	
ALL INVIDUALS:											
18-24		$3,217	19,500	12.3	$2,560	2,150	4.9	$3,143	12,350	15.0	
25-34		5,076	32,250	20.3	3,710	5,800	13.1	4,802	17,600	21.4	
35-44		6,043	35,350	22.2	4,426	7,900	17.8	5,296	18,700	22.7	
45-54		6,114	34,350	21.6	4,479	10,200	23.0	5,937	18,800	22.9	
55-64		5,630	16,600	10.4	4,249	6,450	14.6	5,929	7,600	9.2	
65 and older		2,558	20,900	13.1	2,083	11,800	26.6	2,908	7,150	8.7	
TOTAL	10.7	5,057	158,950	100.0	3,624	44,300	100.0	4,904	82,200	100.0	
MALES:											
18-24		3,616	7,500	10.8	2,847	1,050	5.6	3,109	4,600	13.7	
25-34		6,134	13,400	19.3	4,662	2,150	11.4	6,007	6,550	19.6	
35-44		7,474	16,150	23.3	5,821	3,650	19.3	6,592	7,300	21.8	
45-54		7,601	14,850	21.4	5,779	4,200	22.2	7,314	8,200	24.5	
55-64		6,746	8,000	11.5	4,741	2,800	14.8	7,042	3,900	11.6	
65 and older		3,363	9,450	13.6	2,764	5,050	26.7	3,863	2,950	8.8	
TOTAL	10.9	6,275	69,350	100.0	4,574	18,900	100.0	6,107	33,500	100.0	
FEMALES:											
18-24		2,990	12,000	13.4	2,184	1,100	4.3	3,162	7,750	15.9	
25-34		4,250	18,850	21.0	3,114	3,650	14.4	3,977	11,050	22.7	
35-44		4,634	19,200	21.4	3,012	4,250	16.7	4,324	11,400	23.4	
45-54		4,812	19,500	21.8	3,411	6,000	23.6	4,711	10,600	21.8	
55-64		4,285	8,600	9.6	3,775	3,650	14.4	4,301	3,700	7.6	
65 and older		1,805	11,450	12.8	1,505	6,750	26.6	2,117	4,200	8.6	
TOTAL	10.6	3,990	89,600	100.0	2,800	25,400	100.0	3,959	48,700	100.0	

WEST INDIANS—Table 62 (Continued)

AGE AND SEX	ALL PERSONS				COLLEGE					
					1-3 Years			4 Years		
	Median Yrs. of Educ.	Mean Income*	Number of Indi-viduals*	Per-cent	Mean Income*	Number of Indi-viduals*	Per-cent	Mean Income*	Number of Indi-viduals*	Per-cent
ALL INDIVIDUALS										
18-24		$3,217	19,500	12.3	$3,395	4,350	21.7	$1,814	350	5.5
25-34		5,076	32,250	20.3	5,635	5,450	27.2	7,551	1,550	24.2
35-44		6,043	35,350	22.2	7,328	5,050	25.2	8,705	1,900	29.7
45-54		6,114	34,350	21.6	7,882	2,600	13.0	8,560	1,300	20.3
55-64		5,630	16,600	10.4	6,817	1,600	8.0	10,116	600	9.4
65 and older		2,558	20,900	13.1	3,312	950	4.7	4,269	700	10.9
TOTAL	10.7	5,057	158,950	100.0	5,930	20,000	100.0	7,662	6,400	100.0
MALES:										
18-24		3,610	7,500	10.8	4,833	1,400	14.1	1,900	200	6.7
25-34		6,134	13,400	19.3	6,342	2,650	26.8	7,957	700	23.3
35-44		7,474	16,150	23.3	7,977	3,100	31.3	9,075	900	30.0
45-54		7,601	14,850	21.4	9,147	1,150	11.6	11,960	500	16.7
55-64		6,746	8,000	11.5	9,275	800	8.1	10,050	300	10.0
65 and older		3,363	9,450	13.6	3,435	800	8.1	4,852	400	13.3
TOTAL	10.9	6,275	69,350	100.0	7,101	9,900	100.0	8,415	3,000	100.0
FEMALES:										
18-24		2,990	12,000	13.4	2,803	2,950	29.2	1,700	150	4.4
25-34		4,250	18,850	21.0	4,993	2,800	27.7	7,196	850	25.0
35-44		4,634	19,200	21.4	6,070	1,950	19.3	8,314	1,000	29.4
45-54		4,812	19,500	21.8	6,803	1,450	14.4	6,293	800	23.5
55-64		4,285	8,600	9.6	3,792	800	7.9	10,183	300	8.8
65 and older		1,805	11,450	12.8	2,450	150	1.5	3,541	300	8.8
TOTAL	10.6	3,990	89,600	100.0	4,719	10,100	100.0	6,957	3,400	100.0

(Table 62 continued on page 400)

WEST INDIANS—Table 62 (Continued)

AGE AND SEX	ALL PERSONS				POSTGRADUATE					
					1 Year			2 or More Years		
	Median Yrs. of Educ.	Mean Income*	Number of Individuals*	Per-cent	Mean Income*	Number of Individuals*	Per-cent	Mean Income*	Number of Individuals*	Per-cent
ALL INDIVIDUALS:										
18-24		$3,217	19,500	12.3	$10,925	250	9.1	$ 0.0	50	1.5
25-34		5,076	32,250	20.3	7,450	1,050	38.2	8,131	800	24.2
35-44		6,043	35,350	22.2	9,883	650	23.6	15,560	1,150	34.8
45-54		6,114	34,350	21.6	10,725	500	18.2	15,352	950	28.8
55-64		5,630	16,600	10.4	4,933	200	7.3	16,666	150	4.5
65 and older		2,558	20,900	13.1	1,100	100	3.6	9,500	200	6.1
TOTAL	10.7	5,057	158,950	100.0	8,628	2,750	100.0	13,409	3,300	100.0
MALES:										
18-24		3,616	7,500	10.8	12,733	200	11.1	0.0	50	2.2
25-34		6,134	13,400	19.3	7,088	700	38.9	8,176	650	28.9
35-44		7,474	16,150	23.3	10,700	550	30.6	19,188	650	28.9
45-54		7,601	14,850	21.4	13,500	200	11.1	15,550	600	26.7
55-64		6,746	8,000	11.5	6,500	50	2.8	16,666	150	6.7
65 and older		3,363	9,450	13.6	1,100	100	5.6	9,500	150	6.7
TOTAL	10.9	6,275	69,350	100.0	9,342	1,800	100.0	14,110	2,250	100.0
FEMALES:										
18-24		2,990	12,000	13.4	5,500	50	5.3	—	—	—
25-34		4,250	18,850	21.0	8,233	350	36.8	7,933	150	14.3
35-44		4,634	19,200	21.4	5,800	100	10.5	10,845	500	47.6
45-54		4,812	19,500	21.8	7,950	300	31.6	15,014	350	33.3
55-64		4,285	8,600	9.6	4,150	150	15.8	—	—	—
65 and older		1,805	11,450	12.8	—	—	—	0.0	50	4.8
TOTAL	10.6	3,990	89,600	100.0	7,106	950	100.0	11,867	1,050	100.0

SOURCE: Compiled from 1970 U.S. Census Public Use Sample.

*Number of individuals includes persons who reported zero income.
Mean income is calculated only for persons who reported positive or
negative income, excluding those with zero income.

Median age of all West Indian income earners: 42.8.

400

Table 63
Personal Earnings by Occupation, Education, and Sex (1969)

	ALL PERSONS			PRECOLLEGE					
				0-8 Years			9-12 Years		
OCCUPATIONS	Mean Earnings	Number of Individuals	Per-cent	Mean Earnings	Number of Individuals	Per-cent	Mean Earnings	Number of Individuals	Per-cent
ALL INDIVIDUALS:									
Learned Professions	$14,820	2,250	1.9	$11,550	100	0.4	$12,000	150	0.2
Other Prof., Tech., etc.	7,101	15,350	13.3	4,586	1,150	4.1	6,223	5,550	9.1
Mgrs., Offs., & Proprietors	8,727	3,600	3.1	10,087	400	1.4	7,703	1,350	2.2
Clerical	5,156	26,900	23.3	4,757	2,950	10.4	4,849	17,900	29.3
Craftsmen	6,735	10,600	9.2	5,613	2,500	8.8	7,020	6,100	10.0
Operatives	5,388	14,650	12.7	4,653	5,200	18.4	5,577	8,450	13.8
Service Workers	4,416	22,100	19.1	3,739	8,300	29.4	4,606	11,350	18.6
Private Household	2,448	8,900	7.7	2,392	4,850	17.2	2,480	3,850	6.3
Laborers	5,416	2,950	2.6	5,281	1,100	3.9	5,551	1,550	2.5
Sales	6,064	3,250	2.8	9,128	350	1.2	5,430	1,950	3.2
Farmers, Farm Managers	2,500	100	0.1	5,000	50	0.2	—	50	0.1
Farm Laborers	1,683	600	0.5	3,350	100	0.4	• 1,350	500	0.8
Unemployed	3,040	4,250	3.7	2,762	1,200	4.2	2,452	2,350	3.8
TOTAL	5,472	115,500	100.0	4,186	28,250	100.0	5,089	61,100	100.0
MALES:									
Learned Professions	15,455	1,900	3.3	16,000	50	0.4	12,000	150	0.5
Other Prof., Tech., etc.	7,769	5,400	9.4	4,222	450	3.2	7,281	1,350	4.7
Mgrs., Offs., & Proprietors	9,566	2,700	4.7	10,957	350	2.5	8,390	1,000	3.5
Clerical	6,017	9,850	17.2	5,547	1,700	12.1	5,502	5,650	19.7
Craftsmen	6,801	10,050	17.6	5,785	2,300	16.4	7,122	5,800	20.2
Operatives	6,248	9,750	17.1	5,603	3,300	23.5	6,357	5,550	19.4
Service Workers	5,226	9,600	16.8	3,952	3,700	26.3	5,563	4,600	16.1
Private Household	2,333	300	0.5	1,700	150	1.1	3,066	150	0.5
Laborers	5,927	2,750	4.8	5,415	1,000	7.1	5,626	1,500	5.2
Sales	6,733	1,950	3.4	4,250	200	1.4	6,626	1,150	4.0
Farmers, Farm Managers	2,500	100	0.2	5,000	50	0.4	—	50	0.2
Farm Laborers	2,020	500	0.9	3,350	100	0.7	1,687	400	1.4
Unemployed	3,484	2,300	4.0	3,221	700	5.0	3,123	1,300	4.5
TOTAL	6,550	57,150	100.0	5,106	14,050	100.0	6,092	28,650	100.0
FEMALES:									
Learned Professions	11,371	350	0.6	7,100	50	0.4	—	—	—
Other Prof., Tech., etc.	6,738	9,950	17.1	4,821	700	4.9	5,883	4,200	12.9
Mgrs., Offs., & Proprietors	6,211	900	1.5	4,000	50	0.4	5,742	350	1.1
Clerical	4,659	17,050	29.2	3,684	1,250	8.8	4,548	12,250	37.8
Craftsmen	5,527	550	0.9	3,625	200	1.4	5,050	300	0.9
Operatives	3,679	4,900	8.4	3,003	1,900	13.4	4,086	2,900	8.9
Service Workers	3,795	12,500	21.4	3,567	4,600	32.4	3,953	6,750	20.8
Private Household	2,450	8,600	14.7	2,414	4,700	33.1	2,456	3,700	11.4
Laborers	3,075	200	0.3	3,950	100	0.7	3,300	50	0.2
Sales	5,061	1,300	2.2	15,633	150	1.1	3,712	800	2.5
Farmers, Farm Managers	—	—	—	—	—	—	—	—	—
Farm Laborers	—	100	0.2	—	—	—	—	100	0.3
Unemployed	2,516	1,950	3.3	2,120	500	3.5	1,621	1,050	3.2
TOTAL	4,417	58,350	100.0	3,276	14,200	100.0	4,204	32,450	100.0

(Table 63 continued on page 402)

| OCCUPATIONS | ALL PERSONS | | | COLLEGE | | | | | |
| | | | | 1-3 Years | | | 4 Years | | |
	Mean Earnings	Number of Individuals	Percent	Mean Earnings	Number of Individuals	Percent	Mean Earnings	Number of Individuals	Percent
ALL INDIVIDUALS:									
Learned Professions	$14,820	2,250	1.9	$10,942	350	2.2	$15,625	200	3.8
Other Prof., Tech., etc.	7,101	15,350	13.3	6,926	3,750	24.0	7,792	2,750	51.9
Mgrs., Offs., & Proprietors	8,727	3,600	3.1	7,766	750	4.8	7,950	400	7.5
Clerical	5,156	26,900	23.3	5,798	4,950	31.6	7,905	890	16.0
Craftsmen	6,735	10,600	9.2	6,948	1,550	9.9	11,240	250	4.7
Operatives	5,388	14,650	12.7	7,823	650	4.2	8,025	200	3.8
Service Workers	4,416	22,100	19.1	5,573	2,100	13.4	6,150	300	5.7
Private Household	2,448	8,900	7.7	3,300	150	1.0	2,800	50	0.9
Laborers	5,416	2,950	2.6	4,566	150	1.0	500	50	0.9
Sales	6,064	3,250	2.8	6,058	850	5.4	7,750	100	1.9
Farmers, Farm Managers	2,500	100	0.1	—	—	—	—	—	—
Farm Laborers	1,683	600	0.5	—	—	—	—	—	—
Unemployed	3,040	4,250	3.7	4,725	400	2.6	12,333	150	2.8
TOTAL	5,472	115,500	100.0	6,397	15,650	100.0	8,208	5,300	100.0
MALES:									
Learned Professions	15,455	1,900	3.3	11,600	300	3.6	15,625	200	7.5
Other Prof., Tech., etc.	7,769	5,400	9.4	7,425	1,550	18.6	7,845	1,000	37.7
Mgrs., Offs., & Proprietors	9,566	2,700	4.7	8,472	550	6.6	9,433	300	11.3
Clerical	6,017	9,850	17.2	7,047	1,900	22.8	8,525	400	15.1
Craftsmen	6,801	10,050	17.6	6,948	1,550	18.6	10,050	200	7.5
Operatives	6,248	9,750	17.1	8,275	600	7.2	8,025	200	7.5
Service Workers	5,226	9,600	16.8	7,245	1,100	13.2	8,266	150	5.7
Private Household	2,333	300	0.5	—	—	—	—	—	—
Laborers	5,927	2,750	4.8	6,300	100	1.2	500	50	1.9
Sales	6,733	1,950	3.4	7,770	500	6.0	7,750	100	3.8
Farmers, Farm Managers	2,500	100	0.2	—	—	—	—	—	—
Farm Laborers	2,020	500	0.9	—	—	—	—	—	—
Unemployed	3,484	2,300	4.0	5,000	200	2.4	14,000	50	1.9
TOTAL	6,550	57,150	100.0	7,456	8,350	100.0	8,892	2,650	100.0
FEMALES:									
Learned Professions	11,371	350	0.6	7,000	50	0.7	—	—	—
Other Prof., Tech., etc.	6,738	9,950	17.1	6,575	2,200	30.1	7,762	1,750	66.0
Mgrs., Offs., & Proprietors	6,211	900	1.5	5,825	200	2.7	3,500	100	3.8
Clerical	4,659	17,050	29.2	5,021	3,050	41.8	7,355	450	17.0
Craftsmen	5,527	550	0.9	—	—	—	16,000	50	1.9
Operatives	3,679	4,900	8.4	2,400	50	0.7	—	—	—
Service Workers	3,795	12,500	21.4	3,735	1,000	13.7	4,033	150	5.7
Private Household	2,450	8,600	14.7	3,300	150	2.1	2,800	50	1.9
Laborers	3,075	200	0.3	1,100	50	0.7	—	—	—
Sales	5,061	1,300	2.2	3,614	350	4.8	—	—	—
Farmers, Farm Managers	—	—	—	—	—	—	—	—	—
Farm Laborers	—	100	0.2	—	—	—	—	—	—
Unemployed	2,516	1,950	3.3	4,450	200	2.7	11,500	100	3.8
TOTAL	4,417	58,350	100.0	5,185	7,300	100.0	7,524	2,650	100.0

| OCCUPATIONS | ALL PERSONS | | | POSTGRADUATE | | | | | |
| | | | | 1 Year | | | 2 or More Years | | |
	Mean Earnings	Number of Individuals	Per-cent	Mean Earnings	Number of Individuals	Per-cent	Mean Earnings	Number of Individuals	Per-cent
ALL INDIVIDUALS:									
Learned Professions	$14,820	2,250	1.9	$9,525	400	18.6	$18,690	1,050	34.4
Other Prof., Tech., etc.	7,101	15,350	13.3	10,388	900	41.9	9,944	1,250	41.0
Mgrs., Offs., & Proprietors	8,727	3,600	3.1	13,475	200	9.3	10,570	500	16.4
Clerical	5,156	26,900	23.3	8,250	200	9.3	16,000	50	1.6
Craftsmen	6,735	10,600	9.2	5,250	100	4.7	4,300	100	3.3
Operatives	5,388	14,650	12.7	6,166	150	7.0	—	—	—
Service Workers	4,416	22,100	19.1	—	—	—	15,000	50	1.6
Private Household	2,448	8,900	7.7	—	—	—	—	—	—
Laborers	5,416	2,950	2.6	4,100	50	2.3	13,000	50	1.6
Sales	6,064	3,250	2.8	—	—	—	—	—	—
Farmers, Farm Managers	2,500	100	0.1	—	—	—	—	—	—
Farm Laborers	1,683	600	0.5	—	—	—	—	—	—
Unemployed	3,040	4,250	3.7	700	150	7.0	—	—	—
TOTAL	5,472	115,500	100.0	8,960	2,150	100.0	13,104	3,050	100.0
MALES:									
Learned Professions	15,455	1,900	3.3	10,200	250	17.9	18,536	950	46.3
Other Prof., Tech., etc.	7,769	5,400	9.4	11,518	550	39.3	9,070	500	24.4
Mgrs., Offs., & Proprietors	9,566	2,700	4.7	17,633	150	10.7	9,914	350	17.1
Clerical	6,017	9,850	17.2	7,666	150	10.7	16,000	50	2.4
Craftsmen	6,801	10,050	17.6	5,250	100	7.1	4,800	100	4.9
Operatives	6,248	9,750	17.1	5,750	100	7.1	—	—	—
Service Workers	5,226	9,600	16.8	—	—	—	15,000	50	2.4
Private Household	2,333	300	0.5	—	—	—	—	—	—
Laborers	5,927	2,750	4.8	4,100	50	3.6	13,000	50	2.4
Sales	6,733	1,950	3.4	—	—	—	—	—	—
Farmers, Farm Managers	2,500	100	0.2	—	—	—	—	—	—
Farm Laborers	2,020	500	0.9	—	—	—	—	—	—
Unemployed	3,484	2,300	4.0	—	50	3.6	—	—	—
TOTAL	6,550	57,150	100.0	9,989	1,400	100.0	13,778	2,050	100.0
FEMALES:									
Learned Professions	11,371	350	0.6	8,400	150	20.0	20,150	100	10.0
Other Prof., Tech., etc.	6,738	9,950	17.1	8,614	350	46.7	10,526	750	75.0
Mgrs., Offs., & Proprietors	6,211	900	1.5	1,000	50	6.7	12,100	150	15.0
Clerical	4,659	17,050	29.2	10,000	50	6.7	—	—	—
Craftsmen	5,527	550	0.9	—	—	—	—	—	—
Operatives	3,679	4,900	8.4	7,000	50	6.7	—	—	—
Service Workers	3,795	12,500	21.4	—	—	—	—	—	—
Private Household	2,450	8,600	14.7	—	—	—	—	—	—
Laborers	3,075	200	0.3	—	—	—	—	—	—
Sales	5,061	1,300	2.2	—	—	—	—	—	—
Farmers, Farm Managers	—	—	—	—	—	—	—	—	—
Farm Laborers	—	100	0.2	—	—	—	—	—	—
Unemployed	2,516	1,950	3.3	1,050	100	13.3	—	—	—
TOTAL	4,417	58,350	100.0	7,040	750	100.0	11,725	1,000	100.0

SOURCE: Compiled from 1970 U.S. Census Public Use Sample.

NOTE: Median years of education: 10.9.

403

WEST INDIANS

Table 64
Family Income Distribution by Number of
Income Earners per Family (1969)

INCOME	ALL FAMILIES		NO-EARNER FAMILIES		ONE-EARNER FAMILIES		TWO-EARNER FAMILIES		THREE OR MORE EARNER FAMILIES	
	Number of Families	Percent	Number of Families	Percent	Number of Families	Percent	Number of Families	Percent	Number of Families	Percent
UNDER $ 1,000	1,800	2.8	950	24.1	600	2.9	200	0.7	50	0.5
$ 1,000 - $ 1,999	1,450	2.3	550	13.9	750	3.6	100	0.3	50	0.5
$ 2,000 - $ 2,999	2,950	4.6	1,000	25.3	1,250	6.1	650	2.2	50	0.5
$ 3,000 - $ 3,999	3,150	4.9	400	10.1	1,600	7.8	1,000	3.3	150	1.5
$ 4,000 - $ 4,999	3,750	5.8	750	19.0	2,000	9.7	1,000	3.3	—	—
$ 5,000 - $ 5,999	5,400	8.4	250	6.3	3,250	15.8	1,700	5.7	200	2.0
$ 6,000 - $ 6,999	3,900	6.1	—	—	2,300	11.2	1,400	4.7	200	2.0
$ 7,000 - $ 7,999	5,600	8.7	—	—	2,450	11.9	2,600	8.7	550	5.6
$ 8,000 - $ 9,999	8,650	13.4	—	—	2,850	13.8	4,600	15.4	1,200	12.1
$10,000 - $12,999	11,400	17.7	50	1.3	1,950	9.5	7,450	24.9	1,950	19.7
$13,000 - $14,999	5,200	8.1	—	—	600	2.9	3,300	11.0	1,300	13.1
$15,000 - $19,999	7,350	11.4	—	—	700	3.4	4,500	15.0	2,150	21.7
$20,000 - $24,999	2,300	3.6	—	—	50	0.2	1,000	3.3	1,250	12.6
$25,000 OR MORE	1,500	2.3	—	—	250	1.2	450	1.5	800	8.1
TOTAL	64,400	100.0	3,950	100.0	20,600	100.0	29,950	100.0	9,900	100.0
MEAN EARNINGS	$9,821		$2,529		$7,007		$11,053		$14,859	
MEDIAN INCOME	8,971		2,450		6,370		10,685		13,846	

SOURCE: Compiled from 1970 U.S. Census Public Use Sample.

404

WEST INDIANS

Table 65
Family Income by Age, Education, and Sex of Family Head (1969)

AGE AND SEX OF FAMILY HEAD	ALL PERSONS				PRECOLLEGE					
					0-8 Years			9-12 Years		
	Median Yrs. of Educ.	Mean Income	Number of Individuals	Percent	Mean Income	Number of Individuals	Percent	Mean Income	Number of Individuals	Percent
ALL INDIVIDUALS:										
18-24		$5,546	2,300	3.6	$4,480	250	1.5	$5,501	1,650	5.0
25-34		8,248	11,500	17.9	6,454	1,600	9.3	7,750	6,100	18.6
35-44		10,144	18,200	28.3	7,398	3,900	22.7	9,472	9,100	27.7
45-54		10,726	16,650	25.9	8,617	4,800	28.0	10,498	8,950	27.3
55-64		10,745	7,850	12.2	9,425	2,450	14.3	10,419	4,150	12.7
65 and older		5,115	7,900	12.3	4,123	4,150	24.2	6,073	2,850	8.7
TOTAL	10.8	9,248	64,400	100.0	7,105	17,150	100.0	9,057	32,800	100.0
MALES:										
18-24		6,433	1,550	3.2	7,200	100	0.8	6,311	1,100	4.6
25-34		9,260	8,900	18.2	6,494	1,350	10.3	9,113	4,600	18.8
35-44		11,631	13,350	27.3	9,043	2,850	21.8	11,011	6,050	25.3
45-54		11,719	12,400	25.4	8,784	3,600	27.5	11,727	6,750	28.2
55-64		11,070	6,600	13.5	8,877	2,100	16.0	11,025	3,400	14.2
65 and older		4,966	6,100	12.5	3,902	3,100	23.7	5,839	2,150	9.0
TOTAL	10.9	10,150	48,900	100.0	7,452	13,100	100.0	10,178	23,950	100.0
FEMALES:										
18-24		3,713	750	4.8	2,666	150	3.7	3,881	550	6.2
25-34		4,780	2,600	16.8	6,240	250	6.2	3,918	1,600	18.1
35-44		6,052	4,850	31.3	2,930	1,050	25.9	6,421	3,050	34.5
45-54		7,827	4,250	27.4	8,116	1,200	29.6	6,725	2,200	24.9
55-64		9,032	1,250	8.1	12,714	350	8.6	7,673	750	8.5
65 and older		5,619	1,800	11.6	4,776	1,050	25.9	6,792	700	7.9
TOTAL	10.7	6,402	15,500	100.0	5,985	4,050	100.0	6,022	8,850	100.0

(Table 65 continued on page 406)

AGE AND SEX OF FAMILY HEAD	ALL PERSONS				COLLEGE						
					1-3 Years			4 Years			
	Median Yrs. of Educ.	Mean Income	Number of Indi- viduals	Per- cent	Mean Income	Number of Indi- viduals	Per- cent	Mean Income	Number of Indi- viduals	Per- cent	
ALL INDIVIDUALS:											
18-24		$5,546	2,300	3.6	$7,366	300	3.6	$5,000	50	1.9	
25-34		8,248	11,500	17.9	9,383	2,150	25.4	10,771	700	26.9	
35-44		10,144	18,200	28.3	11,144	3,200	37.9	11,994	850	32.7	
45-54		10,726	16,650	25.9	12,548	1,500	17.8	15,972	450	17.3	
55-64		10,745	7,850	12.2	13,450	800	9.5	13,800	300	11.5	
65 and older		5,115	7,900	12.3	5,230	500	5.9	9,500	250	9.6	
TOTAL	10.8	9,248	64,400	100.0	10,679	8,450	100.0	12,187	2,600	100.0	
MALES:											
18-24		6,433	1,550	3.2	7,840	250	3.8	5,000	50	2.3	
25-34		9,260	8,900	18.2	10,818	1,600	24.2	11,610	500	23.3	
35-44		11,631	13,350	27.3	12,127	2,650	40.2	12,400	750	34.9	
45-54		11,719	12,400	25.4	14,202	900	13.6	16,993	400	18.6	
55-64		11,070	6,600	13.5	14,000	750	11.4	16,575	200	9.3	
65 and older		4,966	6,100	12.5	5,044	450	6.8	9,500	250	11.6	
TOTAL	10.9	10,150	48,900	100.0	11,660	6,600	100.0	12,950	2,150	100.0	
FEMALES:											
18-24		3,713	750	4.8	5,000	50	2.7	—	—	—	
25-34		4,780	2,600	16.8	5,209	550	29.7	8,675	200	44.4	
35-44		6,052	4,850	31.3	6,409	550	29.7	8,950	100	22.2	
45-54		7,827	4,250	27.4	10,066	600	32.4	7,800	50	11.1	
55-64		9,032	1,250	8.1	5,200	50	2.7	8,250	100	22.2	
65 and older		5,619	1,800	11.6	6,900	50	2.7	—	—	—	
TOTAL	10.7	6,402	15,500	100.0	7,181	1,850	100.0	8,544	450	100.0	

AGE AND SEX OF FAMILY HEAD	ALL PERSONS				POSTGRADUATE					
					1 Year			2 or More Years		
	Median Yrs. of Educ.	Mean Income	Number of Indi- viduals	Per- cent	Mean Income	Number of Indi- viduals	Per- cent	Mean Income	Number of Indi- viduals	Per- cent
ALL INDIVIDUALS:										
18-24		$5,546	2,300	3.6	$2,000	50	3.4	—	—	—
25-34		8,248	11,500	17.9	9,287	400	27.6	10,572	550	28.2
35-44		10,144	18,200	28.3	14,340	500	34.5	25,453	650	33.3
45-54		10,726	16,650	25.9	13,092	350	24.1	21,129	600	30.8
55-64		10,745	7,850	12.2	23,400	50	3.4	19,500	100	5.1
65 and older		5,115	7,900	12.3	4,500	100	6.9	11,000	50	2.6
TOTAL	10.8	9,248	64,400	100.0	11,853	1,450	100.0	19,250	1,950	100.0
MALES:										
18-24		6,433	1,550	3.2	2,000	50	3.8	—	—	—
25-34		9,260	8,900	18.2	9,287	400	30.8	10,572	550	30.6
35-44		11,631	13,350	27.3	14,340	500	38.5	25,954	550	30.6
45-54		11,719	12,400	25.4	15,125	200	15.4	21,695	550	30.6
55-64		11,070	6,600	13.5	23,400	50	3.8	19,500	100	5.6
65 and older		4,966	6,100	12.5	4,900	100	7.7	11,000	50	2.8
TOTAL	10.9	10,150	48,900	100.0	12,023	1,300	100.0	19,179	1,800	100.0
FEMALES:										
18-24		3,713	750	4.8	—	—	—	—	—	—
25-34		4,780	2,600	16.8	—	—	—	—	—	—
35-44		6,052	4,850	31.3	—	—	—	22,700	100	66.7
45-54		7,827	4,250	27.4	10,383	150	100.0	14,900	50	33.3
55-64		9,032	1,250	8.1	—	—	—	—	—	—
65 and older		5,619	1,800	11.6	—	—	—	—	—	—
TOTAL	10.7	6,402	15,500	100.0	10,383	150	100.0	20,100	150	100.0

SOURCE: Compiled from 1970 U.S. Census Public Use Sample.

NOTE: Median age of all family heads: 45.1.

Table 66
Family Earnings by Number of Income Earners, Education, and Sex of Family Head (1969)

| | NUMBER OF INCOME EARNERS | | | PRECOLLEGE | | | | | |
| | | | | 0-8 Years | | | 9-12 Years | | |
	Mean Family Earnings	Number of Families	Percent of all Families	Mean Family Earnings	Number of Families	Percent of all Families	Mean Family Earnings	Number of Families	Percent of all Families
ALL FAMILIES:									
No Income-Earners	$ 0	3,950	6.1	$ 0	1,600	9.3	$ 0	2,050	6.3
One Income-Earner	6,233	20,600	32.0	5,324	5,850	34.1	5,507	9,950	30.3
Two Income-Earners	10,792	29,950	46.5	8,159	7,000	40.8	10,373	15,150	46.2
Three or More Earners	14,541	9,900	15.4	12,444	2,700	15.7	15,063	5,650	17.2
TOTAL	9,248	64,400	100.0	7,105	17,150	100.0	9,057	32,800	100.0
MALE-HEADED FAMILIES:									
No Income-Earners	0	2,100	4.3	0	1,150	8.8	0	750	3.1
One Income-Earner	6,899	13,550	27.7	5,579	4,000	30.5	6,172	6,300	26.3
Two Income-Earners	11,230	25,500	52.1	8,286	5,900	45.0	10,944	12,350	51.6
Three or More Earners	15,030	7,750	15.8	12,887	2,050	15.6	15,324	4,550	19.0
TOTAL	10,150	48,900	100.0	7,452	13,100	100.0	10,178	23,950	100.0
FEMALE-HEADED FAMILIES:									
No Income-Earners	0	1,850	11.9	0	450	11.1	0	1,300	14.7
One Income-Earner	4,953	7,050	45.5	4,774	1,850	45.7	4,360	3,650	41.2
Two Income-Earners	8,279	4,450	28.7	7,481	1,100	27.2	7,857	2,800	31.6
Three or More Earners	12,777	2,150	13.9	11,046	650	16.0	13,981	1,100	12.4
TOTAL	6,402	15,500	100.0	5,985	4,050	100.0	6,022	8,850	100.0

| | NUMBER OF INCOME EARNERS | | | COLLEGE | | | | | |
| | | | | 1-3 Years | | | 4 Years | | |
	Mean Family Earnings	Number of Families	Percent of all Families	Mean Family Earnings	Number of Families	Percent of all Families	Mean Family Earnings	Number of Families	Percent of all Families
ALL FAMILIES:									
No Income-Earners	$ 0	3,950	6.1	$ 0	250	3.0	$ 0	50	1.9
One Income-Earner	6,233	20,600	32.0	6,625	2,450	29.0	7,935	1,000	38.5
Two Income-Earners	10,792	29,950	46.5	12,787	4,900	58.0	14,875	1,300	50.0
Three or More Earners	14,541	9,900	15.4	13,358	850	10.1	17,660	250	9.6
TOTAL	9,248	64,400	100.0	10,679	8,450	100.0	12,187	2,600	100.0
MALE-HEADED FAMILIES:									
No Income-Earners	0	2,100	4.3	0	150	2.3	0	50	2.3
One Income-Earner	6,899	13,550	27.7	7,328	1,400	21.2	8,469	650	30.2
Two Income-Earners	11,230	25,500	52.1	12,891	4,500	68.2	14,935	1,200	55.8
Three or More Earners	15,030	7,750	15.8	15,795	550	8.3	17,660	250	11.6
TOTAL	10,150	48,900	100.0	11,660	6,600	100.0	12,950	2,150	100.0
FEMALE-HEADED FAMILIES:									
No Income-Earners	0	1,850	11.9	0	100	5.4	–	–	–
One Income-Earner	4,953	7,050	45.5	5,688	1,050	56.8	6,942	350	77.8
Two Income-Earners	8,279	4,450	28.7	11,612	400	21.6	14,150	100	22.2
Three or More Earners	12,777	2,150	13.9	8,891	300	16.2	–	–	–
TOTAL	6,402	15,500	100.0	7,181	1,850	100.0	8,544	450	100.0

(Table 66 continued on page 410)

| | NUMBER OF INCOME EARNERS | | | POSTGRADUATE | | | | | |
| | | | | 1 Year | | | 2 or More Years | | |
	Mean Family Earnings	Number of Families	Percent of all Families	Mean Family Earnings	Number of Families	Percent of all Families	Mean Family Earnings	Number of Families	Percent of all Families
ALL FAMILIES:									
No Income-Earners	$ 0	3,950	6.1	$ —	—	—	$ —	—	—
One Income-Earner	6,233	20,600	32.0	8,600	400	27.6	15,631	950	48.7
Two Income-Earners	10,792	29,950	46.5	12,234	800	55.2	21,456	800	41.0
Three or More Earners	14,541	9,900	15.4	15,840	250	17.2	27,612	200	10.3
TOTAL	9,248	64,400	100.0	11,853	1,450	100.0	19,250	1,950	100.0
MALE-HEADED FAMILIES:									
No Income-Earners	0	2,100	4.3	—	—	—	—	—	—
One Income-Earner	6,899	13,550	27.7	8,600	350	26.9	15,888	850	47.2
Two Income-Earners	11,230	25,500	52.1	12,313	750	57.7	21,456	800	44.4
Three or More Earners	15,030	7,750	15.8	16,925	200	15.4	25,683	150	8.3
TOTAL	10,150	48,900	100.0	12,023	1,300	100.0	19,179	1,800	100.0
FEMALE-HEADED FAMILIES:									
No Income-Earners	0	1,850	11.9	—	—	—	—	—	—
One Income-Earner	4,953	7,050	45.5	8,600	50	33.3	13,450	100	66.7
Two Income-Earners	8,279	4,450	28.7	11,050	50	33.3	—	—	—
Three or More Earners	12,777	2,150	13.9	11,500	50	33.3	33,400	50	33.3
TOTAL	6,402	15,500	100.0	10,383	150	100.0	20,100	150	100.0

SOURCE: Compiled from 1970 U.S. Census Public Use Sample.
NOTE: Median years of education of family heads: 10.8.

WEST INDIANS

Table 67
Fertility Rates by Woman's Education and Family Income (1969)

67a. EDUCATION

| | TOTAL | | PRECOLLEGE | | | | COLLEGE | | | | POSTGRADUATE | | | |
| | | | 0-8 Years | | 9-12 Years | | 1-3 Years | | 4 Years | | 1 Year | | 2 or More Years | |
	Number	Percent	Number	Percent	Number	Percent	Number	Percent	Number	Percent	Number	Percent	Number	Percent
All Women, 15 and older:														
Childless	34,300	36.2	8,450	31.6	18,900	35.9	4,550	45.0	1,350	39.7	450	47.4	600	57.1
1 Child	17,400	18.3	4,750	17.8	9,600	18.3	2,250	22.3	500	14.7	200	21.1	100	9.5
2 Children	16,550	17.4	4,650	17.4	9,350	17.8	1,550	15.3	750	22.1	150	15.8	100	9.5
3 Children	10,100	10.6	2,500	9.3	6,050	11.5	850	8.4	450	13.2	50	5.3	200	19.0
4 Children	7,500	7.9	2,700	10.1	4,100	7.8	500	5.0	150	4.4	50	5.3	–	–
5 Children	3,300	3.5	1,050	3.9	1,900	3.6	150	1.5	150	4.4	50	5.3	–	–
6 or More	5,700	6.0	2,650	9.9	2,700	5.1	250	2.5	50	1.5	–	–	50	4.8
TOTAL	94,850	100.0	26,750	100.0	52,600	100.0	10,100	100.0	3,400	100.0	950	100.0	1,050	100.0
Mean No. of Children	1.8		2.1		1.7		1.2		1.5		1.2		1.1	
Women, 15-24:														
Childless	13,750	79.7	1,950	79.6	9,150	78.5	2,450	83.1	150	100.0	50	100.0	–	–
1 Child	2,150	12.5	350	14.3	1,450	12.4	350	11.9	–	–	–	–	–	–
2 Children	1,000	5.8	100	4.1	750	6.4	150	5.1	–	–	–	–	–	–
3 Children	250	1.4	50	2.0	200	1.7	–	–	–	–	–	–	–	–
4 Children	50	0.3	–	–	50	0.4	–	–	–	–	–	–	–	–
5 Children	50	0.3	–	–	50	0.4	–	–	–	–	–	–	–	–
6 or More	–	–	–	–	–		–		–		–		–	
TOTAL	17,250	100.0	2,450	100.0	11,650	100.0	2,950	100.0	150	100.0	50	100.0		
Mean No. of Children	0.3		0.3		0.3		0.2		0.0		0.0		0.0	

(Table 67 continued on page 412)

WEST INDIANS—Table 67: Education (Continued)

| | TOTAL | | PRECOLLEGE | | | | COLLEGE | | | | POSTGRADUATE | | | |
| | | | 0-8 Years | | 9-12 Years | | 1-3 Years | | 4 Years | | 1 Year | | 2 or More Years | |
	Number	Percent	Number	Percent	Number	Percent	Number	Percent	Number	Percent	Number	Percent	Number	Percent
Women, 25-34:														
Childless	5,950	31.6	1,000	27.4	3,250	29.4	900	32.1	450	52.9	250	71.4	100	66.7
1 Child	4,650	24.7	750	20.5	2,600	23.5	1,100	39.3	150	17.6	50	14.3	–	–
2 Children	3,800	20.2	1,000	27.4	2,200	19.9	450	16.1	150	17.6	–	–	–	–
3 Children	2,500	13.3	400	11.0	1,800	16.3	200	7.1	50	5.9	–	–	50	33.3
4 Children	1,100	5.8	250	6.8	700	6.3	100	3.6	50	5.9	50	14.3	–	–
5 Children	450	2.4	100	2.7	300	2.7	–	–	–	–	–	–	–	–
6 or More	400	2.1	150	4.1	200	1.8	50	1.8	–	–	–	–	–	–
TOTAL	18,850	100.0	3,650	100.0	11,050	100.0	2,800	100.0	850	100.0	350	100.0	150	100.0
Mean No. of Children	1.6		1.8		1.6		1.2		0.9		0.9		1.0	
Women, 35-44:														
Childless	3,850	20.1	1,050	24.7	1,950	17.1	350	17.9	200	20.0	50	50.0	250	50.0
1 Child	3,400	17.7	700	16.5	2,100	18.4	350	17.9	100	10.0	50	50.0	100	20.0
2 Children	4,050	21.1	900	21.2	2,200	19.3	550	28.2	300	30.0	–	–	100	20.0
3 Children	2,650	13.8	200	4.7	1,800	15.8	350	17.9	250	25.0	–	–	50	10.0
4 Children	2,100	10.9	500	11.8	1,550	13.6	50	2.6	–	–	–	–	–	–
5 Children	1,000	5.2	150	3.5	600	5.3	150	7.7	100	10.0	–	–	–	–
6 or More	2,150	11.2	750	17.6	1,200	10.5	150	7.7	50	5.0	–	–	–	–
TOTAL	19,200	100.0	4,250	100.0	11,400	100.0	1,950	100.0	1,000	100.0	100	100.0	500	100.0
Mean No. of Children	2.5		2.6		2.6		2.3		2.3		0.5		0.9	

412

WEST INDIANS—Table 67: Education (Continued)

Women, 45 and older:

| | TOTAL | | PRECOLLEGE | | | | COLLEGE | | | | POSTGRADUATE | | | |
| | | | 0-8 Years | | 9-12 Years | | 1-3 Years | | 4 Years | | 1 Year | | 2 or More Years | |
	Number	Percent	Number	Percent	Number	Percent	Number	Percent	Number	Percent	Number	Percent	Number	Percent
Childless	10,750	27.2	4,450	27.1	4,550	24.6	850	35.4	550	39.3	100	22.2	250	62.5
1 Child	7,200	18.2	2,950	18.0	3,450	18.6	450	18.8	250	17.9	100	22.2	–	–
2 Children	7,700	19.5	2,650	16.2	4,200	22.7	400	16.7	300	21.4	150	33.3	–	–
3 Children	4,700	11.9	1,850	11.3	2,250	12.2	300	12.5	150	10.7	50	11.1	100	25.0
4 Children	4,250	10.7	1,950	11.9	1,800	9.7	350	14.6	100	7.1	50	11.1	–	–
5 Children	1,800	4.6	800	4.9	950	5.1	–	–	50	3.6	–	–	–	–
6 or More	3,150	8.0	1,750	10.7	1,300	7.0	50	2.1	–	–	–	–	50	12.5
TOTAL	39,550	100.0	16,400	100.0	18,500	100.0	2,400	100.0	1,400	100.0	450	100.0	400	100.0
Mean No. of Children	2.2		2.3		2.2		1.6		1.4		1.7		1.5	

67b. FAMILY INCOME

All Women, 15 and older:

| | TOTAL | | Less Than $5,000 | | $5,000 - 9,999 | | $10,000 - 14,999 | | $15,000 - 19,999 | | $20,000 - 24,999 | | $25,000 and Over | |
	Number	Percent	Number	Percent	Number	Percent	Number	Percent	Number	Percent	Number	Percent	Number	Percent
Childless	34,300	36.2	11,950	40.9	8,750	33.6	6,250	30.9	4,050	38.9	1,250	34.7	2,050	38.7
1 Child	17,400	18.3	5,500	18.8	4,600	17.7	4,150	20.5	1,900	18.3	500	13.9	750	14.2
2 Children	16,550	17.4	4,350	14.9	4,900	18.8	4,100	20.2	1,450	13.9	650	18.1	1,100	20.8
3 Children	10,100	10.6	3,250	11.1	2,300	8.8	2,200	10.9	1,400	13.5	500	13.9	450	8.5
4 Children	7,500	7.9	2,200	7.5	2,000	7.7	1,900	9.4	700	6.7	250	6.9	450	8.5
5 Children	3,300	3.5	800	2.7	1,150	4.4	550	2.7	450	4.3	200	5.6	150	2.8
6 or More	5,700	6.0	1,200	4.1	2,350	9.0	1,100	5.4	450	4.3	250	6.9	350	6.6
TOTAL	94,850	100.0	29,250	100.0	26,050	100.0	20,250	100.0	10,400	100.0	3,600	100.0	5,300	100.0
Mean No. of Children	1.8		1.6		2.0		1.8		1.6		2.0		1.7	

(Table 67 continued on page 414)

WEST INDIANS—Table 67: Family Income (Continued)

	TOTAL		Less Than $5,000		$5,000 - 9,999		$10,000 - 14,999		$15,000 - 19,999		$20,000 - 24,999		$25,000 and Over	
	Number	Percent	Number	Percent	Number	Percent	Number	Percent	Number	Percent	Number	Percent	Number	Percent
Women, 15-24:														
Childless	13,750	79.7	3,150	71.6	4,050	79.4	3,100	81.6	2,000	87.0	500	90.9	950	86.4
1 Child	2,150	12.5	700	15.9	550	10.8	600	15.8	100	4.3	50	9.1	150	13.6
2 Children	1,000	5.8	450	10.2	400	7.8	100	2.6	50	2.2	—	—	—	—
3 Children	250	1.4	50	1.1	50	1.0	—	—	150	6.5	—	—	—	—
4 Children	50	0.3	—	—	50	1.0	—	—	—	—	—	—	—	—
5 Children	50	0.3	50	1.1	—	—	—	—	—	—	—	—	—	—
6 or More	—	—	—	—	—	—	—	—	—	—	—	—	—	—
TOTAL	17,250	100.0	4,400	100.0	5,100	100.0	3,800	100.0	2,300	100.0	550	100.0	1,100	100.0
Mean No. of Children	0.3		0.5		0.3		0.2		0.3		0.1		0.1	
Women, 25-34:														
Childless	5,950	31.6	1,800	32.1	1,600	27.8	1,150	26.1	650	39.4	150	42.9	600	54.5
1 Child	4,650	24.7	1,350	24.1	1,550	27.0	950	21.6	500	30.3	100	28.6	200	18.2
2 Children	3,800	20.2	850	15.2	1,250	21.7	1,100	25.0	300	18.2	50	14.3	250	22.7
3 Children	2,500	13.3	950	17.0	550	9.6	800	18.2	150	9.1	50	14.3	—	—
4 Children	1,100	5.8	300	5.4	500	8.7	300	6.8	—	—	—	—	—	—
5 Children	450	2.4	150	2.7	100	1.7	100	2.3	50	3.0	—	—	50	4.5
6 or More	400	2.1	200	3.6	200	3.5	—	—	—	—	—	—	—	—
TOTAL	18,850	100.0	5,600	100.0	5,750	100.0	4,400	100.0	1,650	100.0	350	100.0	1,100	100.0
Mean No. of Children	1.6		1.7		1.7		1.6		1.1		1.0		0.9	

WEST INDIANS—Table 67: Family Income (Continued)

	TOTAL		Less Than $5,000		$5,000 - 9,999		$10,000 - 14,999		$15,000 - 19,999		$20,000 - 24,999		$25,000 and Over	
	Number	Percent	Number	Percent	Number	Percent	Number	Percent	Number	Percent	Number	Percent	Number	Percent
Women, 35-44:														
Childless	3,850	20.1	1,750	33.0	850	14.9	600	13.2	300	17.6	200	16.7	150	20.0
1 Child	3,400	17.7	1,050	19.8	800	14.0	950	20.9	400	23.5	150	12.5	50	6.7
2 Children	4,050	21.1	800	15.1	1,150	20.2	1,050	23.1	300	17.6	400	33.3	350	46.7
3 Children	2,650	13.8	600	11.3	800	14.0	550	12.1	350	20.6	200	16.7	150	20.0
4 Children	2,100	10.9	600	11.3	800	14.0	550	12.1	100	5.9	50	4.2	—	—
5 Children	1,000	5.2	100	1.9	400	7.0	300	6.6	100	5.9	100	8.3	—	—
6 or More	2,150	11.2	400	7.5	900	15.8	550	12.1	150	8.8	100	8.3	50	6.7
TOTAL	19,200	100.0	5,300	100.0	5,700	100.0	4,550	100.0	1,700	100.0	1,200	100.0	750	100.0
Mean No. of Children	2.5		2.0		2.0		2.6		2.3		2.5		2.0	
Women, 45 and older:														
Childless	10,750	27.2	5,250	37.6	2,250	23.7	1,400	18.7	1,100	23.2	400	26.7	350	14.9
1 Child	7,200	18.2	2,400	17.2	1,700	17.9	1,650	22.0	900	18.9	200	13.3	350	14.9
2 Children	7,700	19.5	2,250	16.1	2,100	22.1	1,850	24.7	800	16.8	200	13.3	500	21.3
3 Children	4,700	11.9	1,650	11.8	900	9.5	850	11.3	750	15.8	250	16.7	300	12.8
4 Children	4,250	10.7	1,300	9.3	650	6.8	1,050	14.0	600	12.6	200	13.3	450	19.1
5 Children	1,800	4.6	500	3.6	650	6.8	150	2.0	300	6.3	100	6.7	100	4.3
6 or More	3,150	8.0	600	4.3	1,250	13.2	550	7.3	300	6.3	150	10.0	300	12.8
TOTAL	39,550	100.0	13,950	100.0	9,500	100.0	7,500	100.0	4,750	100.0	1,500	100.0	2,350	100.0
Mean No. of Children	2.2		1.7		2.5		2.3		2.2		2.5		2.7	

SOURCE: Compiled from 1970 U.S. Census Public Use Sample.

415

INDEX